CHRISTIAN FRUIT
JEWISH ROOT

CHRISTIAN FRUIT JEWISH ROOT

THEOLOGY OF HEBRAIC RESTORATION

John D. Garr, Ph.D.

Christian Fruit—Jewish Root: Theology of Hebraic Restoration
© 2015 by John D. Garr

Published by Golden Key Press
P.O. Box 421218, Atlanta, GA 30342
www.hebraiccommunity.org

Design and typeset: Resolute Creative, Inc., Houston, TX
Printed in the United States of America

Unless otherwise indicated, Scripture quotations are from the New American Standard Bible.

ISBN: 978-1-940685-27-4
ePub ISBN: 978-1-940685-28-1
mobi ISBN: 978-1-940685-29-8
Library of Congress Control Number: 2014916098
        BT93-93.6 2014
        Religion, Christianity, Judaism, History, Theology

DEFINITIONS AND ABBREVIATIONS

Word Definitions:

Definitions of English words are from www.Dictionary.com. Definitions of words in other languages are taken from either www.Dictionary.com. or www.WordReference.com.

Hebrew Word Definitions:

Unless otherwise noted, all Hebrew word definitions are from one of the following: Wilhelm Gesenius, *Hebrew and Chaldee Lexicon of the Old Testament* (Andover, MA: Flagg and Gould, 1824); Francis Brown, S.R. Driver, and Charles A. Briggs, *Hebrew and English Lexicon* (Peabody, MA: Hendrickson Publishers, 1996); Ludwig Koehler, Walter Baumgartner, and Johann Jakob Stramm, *Hebrew and Aramaic Lexicon of the Old Testament*, tr. M.E.J. Richardson (Leiden: Brill Academic, 1994); William Lee Holladay, *Hebrew and Aramaic Lexicon of the Old Testament* (Leiden, E.J. Brill, 1988); or R. Laird Harris, Gleason L. Archer, Jr., and Bruce K. Waltke, eds., *Theological Wordbook of the Old Testament* (Chicago: Moody Press, 1980).

Greek Word Definitions:

Unless otherwise noted, all Greek word definitions are from one of the following: Timothy Friberg, Barbara Friberg, and Neva Miller, *Analytical Lexicon of the Greek New Testament* (Grand Rapids, MI: Baker Books, 2000); Barclay M. Newman, *Greek-English Dictionary* (Reading, UK: United Bible Societies, 2006); Walter Bauer and Fredrick William Danker, *Greek-English Lexicon of the New Testament and Other Early Christian Literature* (Chicago: The University of Chicago Press, 2001); H.G. Lidell and Robert Scott, *Abridged Greek-English Lexicon* (New York: Oxford University Press, 1935); Joseph Thayer, *Thayer's Greek-English Lexicon of the New Testament* (Peabody, MA: Hendrickson Publishers, 1996); Johan Lust, Erik Eynikel, and Katrin Hauspie, *A Greek-English Lexicon of the Septuagint* (Pea-body, MA: Hendrickson Publishers, 2008).

Scripture Versions:

Unless otherwise noted, quotations of Scripture are taken from the New American Standard Bible (1995).

Scripture Version Abbreviations:

ABPE: Aramaic Bible in Plain English (2007)
AJWS: American Jewish World Service (2010)
BBE: The Bible in Basic English (1964)
CEV: Contemporary English Version (1991)
CJB: Complete Jewish Bible (1998)
DBT: Darby Bible Translation (1890)
Douay-Rheims Bible (1899)
ERV: English Revised Version (1894)
ESV: English Standard Version (2007)
HCSB: Holman Christian Standard Bible (2004)
ISV: International Standard Version (1998)
KJV: Authorized King James Version (1611)
NIV: New International Version (1984)
NASB: New American Standard Bible (1995)
NAU: New American Standard Version (Updated) (1995)
NJB: New Jerusalem Bible (1985)
NET: NET Bible (2005)
NKJV: New King James Version (1982)
NRSV: New Revised Standard Version (1989)
JPS: Jewish Publication Society Version (1917)
TNK: *Tanakh*, JPS *Tanakh* (1985)
WBT: Webster's Bible Translation (1833)
WEB: World English Bible (1901)
WNT: Weymouth New Testament (1903)

TO

Isaac C. Rottenberg, of blessed memory, a champion of Jewish-Christian dialogue, a stalwart defender of the Jewish people and a great Christian theologian who, as my esteemed friend and colleague, continually inspired me with his godly lifestyle, the richness of his scholarship, and the depth and balance of his understanding of theology and its practical application for those who believe in the God of Scripture.

TABLE OF CONTENTS

INTRODUCTION

This volume represents insights that I have gained from more than fifty years of research, scriptural analysis, and meditation on the Jewish roots of the Christian faith. I never cease to be amazed that the more one digs in the pages of Scripture and the annals of history, the more one discovers and confirms Christianity's inherent Jewish connection. Without a doubt, Christianity was founded on the Hebraic principles that were set forth by Jewish men and women who were so profoundly carried along by the Holy Spirit that what they said and wrote was truly God-breathed revelation.[1] The divine self-disclosure that the Almighty chose to convey to humanity is inherently Jewish. It is the revelation of the God of the Jews that was recorded in the Bible of the Jews and confirmed by the Messiah of the Jews.

For most of Christian history, statements like these would have seemed utterly scandalous for most, if not all, of the church. Virtually all the theologians, leaders, and laypersons in every denomination of the church across the twenty centuries of ecclesiastical history have believed and taught that God destroyed Judaism, the so-called lifeless and failed religion of the Jews, and replaced it with Christianity, the ostensible vibrant and triumphant faith of Jesus and the apostles. Sadly, throughout most of church history, such supersessionist Christian triumphalism has brought great suffering to the Jewish people and great tragedy to the church itself.[2] Over the past two millennia, every attempt that church leaders have made to distance Christianity from its inherent Jewish roots has resulted in a debasement of the Christian faith and, in effect, the distancing of the church from the God of the Jews. Many of the foundational truths of the faith on which Jesus and the apostles established the church have been distorted by efforts to create a *Judenrein* Christian self-identity, one that has been liberated from the taint of the first-century church's Jewish connection. As a result, aberrant doctrines and practices have been introduced into the church that have been hurtful to both Jews

---

[1] 2 Peter 1:21.
[2] John D. Garr, *Life from the Dead: The Dynamic Saga of the Chosen People* (Atlanta, GA: Golden Key Press, 2014).

and Christians and have robbed millions of believers of their biblically Hebraic heritage.

In one of the most profound declarations in Holy Scripture, however, Jesus said, "You shall know the truth, and the truth shall make you free."[3] Before the truth can actually liberate people, it first will usually make them very uncomfortable, and, if they rebel against it, it will even make them furious! Perhaps English novelist and atheist Aldous Huxley was correct when he said with a note of irony, "You shall know the truth, and the truth shall make you mad."[4] And the history of enraged Christians resolutely fighting against historical and theological truth has been legendary and tragic indeed.

The truth, however, is manifest in the declaration of the resurrected Jesus to the Damascus-bound Saul of Tarsus: "It is hard for you to kick against the goads."[5] Rejection of the truth—even fighting against it—is a no-win situation. And the church and millions of Christians have been the clear losers in the historical redefinition of Christianity vis-à-vis the Jews and Judaism. No matter how loudly theologians and clergy have trumpeted their contempt for Judaism and the Jewish people, and no matter how hard they have tried to redefine Christianity as a Judaism-free religion, these facts remain inescapable: Jesus was a Jew, his religion was biblical Judaism, and he never changed either his ethnicity or his religion!

As you read this book, you will learn how many Jewish roots your Christian faith actually has and how reattaching yourself to those Jewish roots can make your Christian experience healthier, richer, and more fulfilling. Reconnecting with these historical and theological roots of the Christian faith, however, is not designed to make you "Jewish," to bring you under bondage to some form of legalism, or to initiate you into Jewish mysticism or esoterica. Its purpose is to make you a better Christian by helping you become more "like Christ," the Son of God, who was,[6] still is,[7] and will continue to be a Jew.[8] It is designed to help you become more biblical in your

---

[3] John 8:32.

[4] Aldous Huxley, quoted in Michael Powell, *The Mammoth Book of Great British Humor* (London, UK: Constable & Robinson, Ltd., 2010), p. 538.

[5] Acts 26:14.

[6] Apostolic Scripture proves conclusively that Jesus was a Jew: "It is evident that our Lord came from Judah," the tribe whose name was contracted to form the word *Jew* (Hebrews 7:14). It also proves that Jesus was an Israelite: "[They] are Jsraelites . . . these are the patriarchs, and from them is traced the human ancestry of the Messiah" (Romans 9:4–5, NIV).

[7] Apostolic Scripture proves that Jesus is now a Jew in the glorified Judean body in which he ascended to heaven to become the High Priest: "[Jesus] became a high priest forever after the order of Melchizedek. . . . He of whom these things are said belonged to a different tribe [Judah]" (Hebrews 6:20; 7:14).

[8] Apostolic Scripture proves that when Jesus returns to earth, he will still be a Jew in his glorified Judean body: "This same Jesus, who has been taken up from you into heaven, will come in just the same way as you have watched him go into heaven" (Acts 1:11).

experience with God and with your fellowman. And, inevitably, as Marvin Wilson has observed, "the more biblical one becomes, the more Semitic one will be."[9]

Appreciation

I wish to express my thanks to a number of friends, colleagues, and advisers who have shared insights with me and have inspired me with their wisdom. Foremost among these are Marvin R. Wilson, Dwight A. Pryor (of blessed memory), Isaac Rottenberg (of blessed memory), Karl D. Coke, and Brad H. Young. I wish to thank my Hebraic Heritage Christian College colleague Robert Bleakney for his careful and constructive critique of the manuscript of this book. I am also grateful for review and feedback from Victoria Sarvadi and Kate Miller, not to speak of a number of other friends and colleagues who have read and commented on the manuscript. I also wish to express my appreciation to Jacob Abshire for his creative genius in developing the cover designs for so many of my book and journal projects.

On We Go: Forward in Faith!

It's time to move forward in faith, unreservedly committing ourselves to the task of digging through the rubble of the past in order to uncover the foundations of our faith, of casting aside the accretions of man-made ideas and opinions that have been layered over those foundations, and of carefully handling the precious truths that continue to emerge in this exercise of spiritual archaeology. This is a faithful and faith-filled enterprise in which we dig as God shines his pristine light upon us and illuminates our search for truth.

The good news is that we are rediscovering the Jewish roots of our Christian faith. We are reattaching ourselves to those roots. And from those roots, we are receiving the rich sap that endlessly flows into every fiber of our being to produce healthy fruit in our lives. We can only exclaim with Paul: "Thanks be to God, who gives us the victory through our Lord Jesus Christ."[10] To the same God and to his Son Jesus, who is the tap root of our faith, be glory and honor, power, might, and dominion forever and ever.

Shalom & Blessings!
John D. Garr, Ph.D.
Tu B'Shvat, 2015

---

[9] Marvin R. Wilson, *Our Father Abraham: Jewish Roots of the Christian Faith* (Grand Rapids, MI: Wm. B. Eerdmans Publishing Co., 1989), p. 20.
[10] 1 Corinthians 15:57.

PROLOGUE

It is an undeniable fact that every authentic Christian practice or experience has a foundation in biblical and Second Temple Judaism. Simply stated, for every Christian fruit, there is a Jewish root! Christianity is—and always has been—a Jewish religion, and it will never cease to be a Jewish religion. Indeed, Christianity can rightly be called "the other Jewish religion."[1]

Jesus never intended to start a "new and vibrant religion" called "Christianity" to replace the "failed and lifeless religion" called "Judaism." Indeed, "Jesus did not intend to found a new religion separate from Judaism."[2] As a matter of fact, even "the earliest followers of Jesus did not intend to create a new religion."[3] The Master gave his word that he had no such intentions, and he emphatically underscored that fact to his disciples: "Don't even begin to think that I have come to destroy the law or the prophets; I have not come to destroy but to fulfill."[4] This declaration was the centerpiece of the Sermon on the Mount, the most important discourse that Jesus ever gave. It unequivocally reflected the posture that he faithfully maintained towards the Torah and the Prophets—and toward the entire corpus of the Hebrew Scriptures, for that matter.

Jesus always supported and promoted the core principles of the Torah. As a matter of fact, "Jesus' Judaism was a conservative reaction against some radical innovations in the Law stemming from the Pharisees and Scribes of Jerusalem."[5] Immediately after he had preempted the charge that he knew some would make that he was "destroying the law" by misinterpreting it,[6]

---

[1] Christianity and Rabbinic Judaism are the only Jewish sects that survived from the first century.

[2] George Shillington, *Jesus and Paul Before Christianity: Their World and Work in Retrospect* (Eugene, OR: Wipf and Stock Publishers, 2011), p. 225.

[3] Robert L. Tignor, *Egypt: A Short History* (Princeton, NJ: The Princeton University Press, 2010), p. 108.

[4] Matthew 5:17, author's translation based on the Common English Bible.

[5] Daniel Boyarin, *The Jewish Gospels: The Story of the Jewish Christ* (New York: The New Press, 2012), p. 104.

[6] In early rabbinic times, the charge that one was "destroying the Law" was often made by some sages against those who they thought were misinterpreting the Law. In reality, it was the Pharisees and other sects of Judaism, not Jesus, which were "destroying the Law" with their innovative interpretations that often circumvented the plain meaning of God's commandments (Matthew 15:6; Mark 7:13). Jesus' statement, however, went beyond matters of interpretation or misinterpretation of the Torah. It settled the issue of whether or not Jesus came to abrogate or abolish the "Law" so that he might establish "Grace" in its place.

Jesus explained, "For truly I say to you, until heaven and earth pass away, not one *yud* or crown[7] shall pass from the Law until all is accomplished."[8] In making this statement, Jesus first affirmed his belief in the inspiration, authority, and perdurability of even the most minute aspect and feature of the Torah text. Then, he became even more specific about his regard for the Law by declaring that "whoever then annuls one of the least of these commandments, and teaches others to do the same, shall be called least in the kingdom of heaven; but whoever keeps and teaches them, he shall be called great in the kingdom of heaven."[9]

Finally, on the foundation of his definitive affirmation of the infallibility and dependability of the Torah, Jesus began to outline details of his intentions to restore God's divine instructions to their original intent. In what have been called the "antitheses," he systematically set about to strengthen Torah precepts that had been eroded over time when he said again and again, "You have heard it said . . . but I say unto you."[10] On each occasion, Jesus dealt with Torah commandments as heart issues, not merely subjects for punctilious external performance or matters that could be circumvented by fanciful exercises in exegetical gymnastics. In so doing, Jesus confirmed that he was, indeed, a reformer, not an innovator. He was, in fact, implementing a ministry that would later be described by the author of the Book of Hebrews as "a time of *reformation*."[11]

Jesus was determined to restore the Jews and the Judaisms of his day to the original intentions of the Torah, to the essence of God's design for the kingdom of God. The new approach that Jesus took to the message of the Torah, however, was not new at all. Instead, it was a renewal of the purposes of God's Word as the Eternal intended them from the beginning. Jesus espoused a *renewal* of God's covenant with Israel, not a *new* (or different) covenant. This was the same covenant of which God had spoken to the prophet Jeremiah, "This is the covenant which I will make with the house of Israel after those days, declares the LORD: I will put my law within them, and I will write it on their hearts."[12]

---

7 This is the proper rendering of what is translated "tittle" (KJV) or "least stroke of a pen" (NIV) or "stroke of a letter" (ISV). The decorative pen strokes that adorned the tops of some of the Hebrew letters in texts of the Torah scrolls were called "crowns." See Abraham Joshua Heschel, Gordon Tucker, ed. and tr., *Heavenly Torah: As Refracted Through the Generations* (New York: Continuum International Publishing Group, 2006), p. 40.

8 Matthew 5:18, author's translation.

9 Matthew 5:18–19.

10 Matthew 5:17–48.

11 Hebrews 9:10, emphasis added.

12 Jeremiah 31:33, ESV. This is the covenant of which the writer of Hebrews spoke in Hebrews 8:10.

Despite the fact that Christian theologians, overseers, pastors, teachers, and laypeople—from the second-century heretic Marcion[13] to today's academicians and pulpiteers—have attempted to contort the clear words that came from Jesus' mouth in order to make it appear that he was saying just the opposite of what he actually said, the infallible words of the Lord have continued to echo through the corridors of time to this day. Jesus said what he meant, and he meant what he said. His faith and the faith that he established were anchored in the authority of the Hebrew Scriptures.

Jesus was not a supersessionist; he was a reformer, one who reformed through restoration, not innovation. He did not believe that he was creating a new religion to replace the faith of his ancestors. Instead, he was intent upon fulfilling Judaism by filling it full—bringing it to completion through his life, death, resurrection, and ascension. Jesus was a Jew, his religion was Judaism, and he never changed either his ethnicity or his religion. During his entire life and ministry on earth, he knew full well that "salvation is from the Jews."[14] He declared that he was "sent only to the lost sheep of the house of Israel,"[15] and he commanded his disciples, "Do not go among the Gentiles."[16]

When Jesus' death on the cross opened the door of salvation to all of the world, he did not then decide to scrap all that God had been doing for four thousand years and start a new religion out of spite for the Jewish leaders who had rejected his Messiahship. Instead, he began to "bring also" the "other sheep" that were not of the fold of Israel.[17] Even then, he did not destroy the ancient house of Israel, the people who were the linear descendants of Abraham, Isaac, and Jacob, and proceed to create a new people of God called "the church." He rather grafted wild Gentile olive branches into God's family tree of salvation and covenant community.[18] He did not terminate God's covenant with the nation of Israel and create a new one for Gentile Christians. He rather made provision for the inclusion of Gentiles in the ancient and honorable commonwealth of Israel through a spiritual naturalization process that took those who had been "without God in the world" and made them "fellow citizens with the saints" and "of the same body."[19]

---

[13] Marcion made no attempt to hide his distortion of the words of Jesus. He argued that the text of Matthew 5:17 actually said, "Think ye, that I came to fulfill the law or the prophets? I am come to destroy, not to fulfill." See Nathaniel Lardner, *The Works of Nathaniel Lardner* (Whitefish, MT: Kessinger Publishing, 2010), vol. 3, p. 463.

[14] John 4:22.

[15] Matthew 15:24.

[16] Matthew 10:5.

[17] John 10:16.

[18] Romans 11:19–24.

[19] Ephesians 2:19; 3:6.

The apostles of Jesus continued the same faithfulness that their Lord had maintained toward biblical Judaism. Kevin Madigan and Jon Levenson rightly argue that "it is not clear that Paul regarded fidelity to his ancestral religion and faith in Christ as incompatible; one may interpret Paul simply to mean that, with Christ, Israel has now expanded as to include the gentiles."[20] The proposition that was set forth by the apostles was an argument for Gentile inclusion in the Abrahamic Covenant, which should have been for every Jew an expected and logical progression in the fulfillment of God's promise to Abraham, for the Lord had declared to the Patriarch, "In you all the nations of the earth will be blessed."[21] This is why "for Paul, gentile Christians had to become sons, not of Adam, nor of Noah (figures associated with the universality of God's care), but of Abraham, 'the father of all of us' (Romans 4:16)—that is, of the children of Israel."[22] The argument for Gentile inclusion, however, was never an apostolic premise for Jewish exclusion. Neither Peter nor John nor Paul was a supersessionist. None of the apostles even hinted that God's covenant with the Jews had been abrogated, that Christianity had superseded Judaism as God's religion, or that Christians had replaced Jews in the economy of God's salvation.

True Christian faith, therefore, is but an expansion of the faith of Abraham and the faith of the Jewish people. It is a further emendation of the original Abrahamic Covenant that had been previously expanded, but not destroyed, at Sinai.[23] Jesus, then, was the reformer who sought to restore Judaism to its original foundations by advocating a radical return to fulfilling the spirit of the Torah, the easy yoke of obedience,[24] through faith rather than in servility to the letter of the Torah through meticulous performance of prescribed ritual.

Those who truly believe in Jesus as Lord and Savior should, therefore, recognize that every Christian fruit has a Jewish root, and they should "search the Scriptures"[25] to see how they should live in faith and obedience to the living God in the context of the matrix of biblical Judaism from which Christianity emerged. The bottom line is this: all the things that Christians believe and experience that are authentic and of eternal value came from the Jewish people. They may be Christian fruit, but they have Jewish roots!

---

[20] Kevin Madigan and Jon D. Levenson, *Resurrection: The Power of God for Christians and Jews* (New Haven, CT: Yale University Press, 2008), p. 31.
[21] Genesis 22:18.
[22] Madigan and Levenson, p. 31.
[23] Galatians 3:17.
[24] Matthew 11:30.
[25] John 5:39.

CHAPTER 1

GOD

The God of the Bible is not a capricious Jovian despot sitting in regal splendor on an Olympian throne hurling thunderbolts earthward in fits of rage against anyone suspected of daring to disrespect him or violate one of his directives. The one true God is not a reclusive, irascible curmudgeon, scowling over a flowing white beard with darting eyes, hoping to catch some poor, hapless soul in violation of one of his many overbearing demands for punctilious performance. He is not a craftsman who impulsively decided to construct a universe that he could observe from a distance to prove to himself his own genius. He is not a spoiled child who is insanely jealous over the toys that he has created to while away his time, nor is he a mad scientist who tinkers with humanity and the rest of creation, ever experimenting to see just what might happen. The God of Scripture is not "a blurry power living somewhere in the sky, not an abstraction like the Greeks proposed, not a sensual super human like the Romans worshiped, and definitely not the absentee Watchmaker of the Deists."[1]

The Hebrew God is not cold, aloof, and utterly and forever hidden. He is not Deism's deus otiosus[2] who was believed to have created the universe only to have retired and remained essentially idle or unemployed thereafter.[3] He is not the deus absconditus[4] of Thomistic theology[5] who has consciously left the universe to hide somewhere "out there." True, God dwells in light to which no human can approach, and he has never been seen, nor can be seen, by human eyes.[6] From a human perspective, he is, indeed, utterly transcendent, unknown, and inscrutable. No one can ever hope to discover God by means of the empirical method.[7] At the same time, however, God has chosen to reveal himself

---

[1] Philip Yancey, *The Bible Jesus Read* (Grand Rapids, MI: Zondervan Publishing, 2002), p. 33.
[2] The Latin term *deus otiosus* means "idle god."
[3] Philip Goff and Paul Harvey, *Themes in Religion and American Culture* (Chapel Hill, NC: University of North Carolina Press, 2004), p. 238.
[4] The Latin term *deus absconditus* means "hidden god."
[5] Donald K. McKim, *Westminster Dictionary of Theological Terms* (Louisville, KY: Westminster John Knox Press, 1996), p. 75.
[6] 1 Timothy 6:16.
[7] Job 11:7.

through his Word[8] and his Spirit so that he may be known by humankind.[9] Abraham Joshua Heschel summed up these truths very succinctly when he said that God "is not the object of a discovery but the subject of revelation."[10]

The very fact that God has elected to disclose himself proves that he is a relational being who manifests true personhood. The God of Scripture is not, therefore, an isolated, static, emotionless tyrant. Rather, he is the engaged, dynamic, sentient epitome of relational love. "To deny that God is also personal and can in some way be existentially experienced is to . . . eviscerate the biblical record of both Judaism and Christianity."[11] Knowledge of these facts about the person of God as one who engages his human creation in relationship is a legacy from the Jews to the rest of the world. "To the Hebrews, God is a person to be experienced, not simply an idea to be thought."[12]

The God of Scripture is unique[13] and wholly other.[14] "Who is like unto you among the gods, glorious in holiness, fearful in praise, doing wonders," exclaimed the Israelites after they had experienced supernatural, divine deliverance[15] and were celebrating the God who had effected the miracle at the Red Sea. No wonder God said of himself, "I am the LORD, and there is no other; apart from me there is no God. . . . Before me there was no god formed nor will there be one after me."[16] The God of the Jews, by his own admission, is the one and only God. The God whom Christians worship, therefore, is the God of the Jews. As a matter of fact, if it were not for the understanding of the one God that Gentiles received through the divine revelation given to the Hebrew prophets, Gentiles today would still be worshipping trees, statues, planets, stars, and—even worse—emperors and kings.[17] Virtually the entire Gentile world in antiquity was dominated by the superstitions,

---

[8] William P. Anderson, *A Journey Through Christian Theology* (Minneapolis, MN: Augsburg Fortress, 2010), p. 20.

[9] Walter A. Elwell, *Evangelical Dictionary of Theology* (Grand Rapids, MI: Baker Publishing Group, 1984), p. 500.

[10] Abraham Joshua Heschel, *Man Is Not Alone: A Philosophy of Religion* (New York: Farrar, Straus and Giroux, 1951), p. 129.

[11] Marvin R. Wilson, *Exploring Our Hebraic Heritage: A Christian Theology of Roots and Renewal* (Grand Rapids, MI: Wm. B. Eerdmans Publishing Co., 2014), p. 14.

[12] Wilson, *Exploring*, p. 24.

[13] Gordon D. Kaufman, *Theological Imagination: Constructing the Concept of God* (Louisville, KY: Westminster John Knox Press, 1981), p. 86.

[14] Robert C. Sproul, *God's Love: How the Infinite God Cares for His Children* (Colorado Springs, CO: David C. Cook Publishing, 2001), p. 28.

[15] Exodus 15:11.

[16] Isaiah 45:5; 43:10, NIV.

[17] Jewish scholar Pinchas Lapide famously said to one skeptical Christian that without the Jews, "You, my dear friend, would today still be offering horse meat to Wotan on the Godesberg." Pinchas Lapide and Jürgen Moltmann, *Jewish Monotheism and Christian Trinitarian Doctrine: A Dialogue by Pinchas Lapide and Jürgen Moltmann* (Philadelphia, PA: Fortress Press, 1981), p. 68.

legends, and myths of polytheism. And the worship of most of the gods and goddesses of the ancient world almost universally included human sacrifices that were designed to appease the gods[18] and orgiastic rituals that were designed to incite the gods to conjugate so that their worshippers would enjoy bountiful harvests.[19]

Monotheism

In distinct contrast to the polytheism of the Gentile world, God called Abraham as a young man and disclosed unto him the understanding of monotheism when he was still living in his birthplace, Ur of the Chaldees. Though he was a Babylonian by birth and later a Syrian by nationality and, therefore, as Gentile as it was possible to be, Abraham came to understand monotheism by recognizing that *Elohim*, the God of creation, was the one and only God, and he embraced the worship of the one God. Then, at God's direction, he left his family home in Haran of Syria and journeyed to the land of Canaan where he became the first Hebrew and the father of faith. Beginning from that time, the Hebrews knew that there was only one God, *Elohim*, whom the three patriarchs, Abraham, Isaac, and Jacob, knew as *El Shaddai*.[20] By the time of the Exodus, this one God came to be known by the covenant name which he revealed to Moses, YHWH (the I AM).

This is the God who thundered Ten Commandments to the Israelites at Mt. Sinai when he joined them to himself in a covenant as the Chosen People.

---

[18] Sabine Baring-Gould, *The Origin and Development of Religious Belief: Polytheism and Monotheism* (London, UK: Rivingtons, 1884), pp. 378-386. Baring-Gould has chronicled the rites of human sacrifice in the ancient world: in Phoenicia, the fairest and even the only children of parents were sacrificed to Saturn; in Byblos, boys were immolated to Adonis; in Carthage, men and children were offered sometimes from dawn till sunset on the altar of Kronos; in Arabia, children were regularly sacrificed to Hobal the Creator on the sacred stone in the Kaaba until Mohammed abolished the practice; in Egypt, a virgin was cast yearly into the Nile as a bride to Hapis (Osiris), the river god; in Samaria, children were burned to Adramelech; in Persia, human beings were sacrificed by being buried alive; in Laodicea, a young maiden was offered once a year to Astarte; in Crete, seven young boys and seven young girls were killed each year on the altar of the Minotaur; in Cyprus, a man was sacrificed yearly to Zeus; in Greece, humans were commonly sacrificed before the city-states went to war in order to ensure Greek victory; in Rome, human sacrifice was common; in Germany, human beings were offered to Woden; in Gaul and Britain, humans were regularly sacrificed to the gods; the Celtic Druids engaged extensively in human sacrifice; in Lithuania, humans were killed in homage to dragons; in Sweden, rulers and their children were often sacrificed to Odin to ensure the bounty of their crops; in Peru, Incan children were sacrificed every month of the year; in Hawaii, a slave class was exploited for human sacrifices; in Mexico, 70,000 men were slaughtered by the Aztecs at the dedication of a temple, and human sacrifice was a regular ritual; in India, humans were sacrificed to Chamunda; in China, young men and women were offered to river deities; in West Africa, human sacrifice continued into the nineteenth century; and the list goes on.

[19] David Biale, *Eros and the Jews: From Biblical Israel to Contemporary America* (Berkeley, CA: University of California Press, 1997), p. 12. An example was in Mylitta, where every woman was required once in her life to prostitute herself in honor of the goddess (Baring-Gould, p. 373).

[20] Exodus 6:3, TNK.

The Decalogue began with its two most important commandments:[21] 1) "I am YHWH your God" and 2) "You shall have no other gods before me. You shall not make unto yourself any idol . . . You shall not bow down to them or worship them."[22] Later, God confirmed and condensed the first two of his Ten Words into one commandment, the *Shema*, that for over three millennia has been the core of Jewish self-identity: "Hear, O Israel, the LORD our God, the LORD is one"[23] or "Hear, O Israel, the LORD our God, is God alone." When the Hebrews came to be known as Israelites and then as Jews, they maintained this unique identity in the ancient world. From the beginning of their corporate identity as "Israel," therefore, the Hebrews were strict monotheists. They believed in "one personal and transcendent God."[24] These were the only people on earth who worshiped only one very personal God, the invisible God of heaven and earth.[25] Indeed, as Grant Allen observed, "The only people who ever invented or evolved a pure monotheism at first hand were the Jews."[26]

As a faithful Jew, Jesus unequivocally declared the *Shema* to be the first and most important of all commandments: "The foremost [commandment] is, Hear, O Israel, the Lord our God is one Lord. And you shall love the Lord your God with all your heart, and with all your soul, and with all your mind, and with all your strength."[27] Jesus knew that the understanding of monotheism is essential to all biblical faith. Without the clear monotheistic understanding of God that Jesus had, the Christian religion would have had no foundation and would have been utterly meaningless. In order to maintain its credibility, therefore, Christianity must always maintain its understanding of and belief in the one God of Scripture, the God of the Jews.

Christian Re-Imaging of God

The problem that so many Christians have with understanding God is that he has been re-imaged through the centuries to such a degree that, for

---

[21] Judaism recognizes the first commandment (the first word) as "I am the LORD your God" and the second as "You shall have no other gods before me [and] you shall not make unto yourself any idol . . . to bow down to them." Christianity recognizes the first commandment as "You shall have no other God's before me" and the second as "You shall not make unto yourself any idol."

[22] Exodus 20:3-5.

[23] Deuteronomy 6:4.

[24] This is the definition of monotheism given by F. L. Cross and E. A. Livingstone, eds., "Monotheism," in *Oxford Dictionary of the Christian Church* (New York: Oxford University Press, 1974).

[25] People in some other cultures who have elevated the worship of one god above all others are called "henotheists," in that they have worshiped one deity without denying the existence of other deities. These were not, however, "monotheists" in the absolute sense of the word.

[26] Grant Allen, *Evolution of the Idea of God* (London, UK: Grant Richards, 1897), p. 68.

[27] Mark 12:29–30.

many Christians, he is no longer the one who revealed himself successively to the prophets of old and finally in the person of Jesus. As the early Christian church became Hellenized and Latinized, perspectives on God came to be influenced more by Greek philosophers and Latin empire builders than by Hebrew prophets, sages, and apostles.[28] The God of Scripture was re-imaged in the likeness of politico-religious potentates who used this view of him to consolidate and validate their power and privilege. In such circumstances, God was even viewed as being capricious and Machiavellian.[29] He was transformed into a model for empire builders and sadistic manipulators, both civil and ecclesiastical. God has, therefore, so often been mischaracterized in Christian churches that great percentages of believers have come to the same conclusion that Thomas Matthews reached when, even in adulthood, he thought that God was "a watchful, vengeful, enormous, omniscient policeman, instantly aware of the slightest tinge of irreverence in my innermost thought, always ready to pounce."[30]

Part of the reason for the historical imagery of God as an ominous judge has been the mischaracterization of the God of the Hebrew Scriptures by Christian thinkers. Despite the fact that the Hebrew people always viewed their God as a father who exercised perfect *chesed* ("tender mercy") toward his creation in general and toward his Chosen People in particular, much of Christianity has failed to grasp that imagery, often preferring to conceive of God as a distant, detached, implacable despot. Unfortunately, this has also contributed to a sad Christian misrepresentation of the Father as an austere judge whose only verdict was always the death penalty (or "ninety-nine years in the electric chair!"). No wonder this God has been viewed very unfavorably by so many people when he has been compared with Jesus, the loving and gracious Savior, who has been thought by so many to interpose himself between an angry, vindictive God and weak, unfortunate human beings.

The first heresy that challenged the earliest Christian church focused on just such a mischaracterization and re-imaging of the God of the Hebrews when a theology adapted from Greek Gnosticism infected a significant part of the second-century church. In this re-imaging of God, Marcion of Sinope (in modern Turkey) asserted that the God of the Hebrews was not the God of Christianity. For him, the God of the Jews was a vicious and rancorous

---

[28] Richard R. Hopkins, *How Greek Philosophy Corrupted the Christian Concept of God* (Springville, UT: Horizon Publishers, 1998), pp. 11–30.
[29] Oluwole J. Odeyemi, *Where God Was on 9/11: The Unravelling of the Many Mysteries of the Bible* (Central Milton Keynes, UK: AuthorHouse UK, 2005.), p. xxiv.
[30] Thomas Matthews, quoted in Terrence Fretheim, *The Suffering God: An Old Testament Perspective* (Philadelphia: Fortress Press, 1984), pp. 4–5.

character whom he identified as the Demiurge of Platonism, the craftsman who had created the universe and in so doing had entrapped higher spiritual realities in evil matter.[31] For Marcion, Jesus was the good God whose task it was to destroy the evil Hebrew God and cast him into Hades.[32] Even though Marcion was branded a heretic for his radical Gnostic ideas and was excommunicated from the church by his own father, his theology, which distorted Christianity in his generation, has continued to influence Christian thought to one degree or another ever since that time. Even in the present day, neo-Marcionism continues to manifest itself in the form of antinomianism,[33] supersessionism,[34] Judaeophobia,[35] anti-Judaism,[36] and Antisemitism,[37] not to speak of various ongoing mischaracterizations of the God of Scripture, both subtle and overt, which make every effort to strip God of his identification as the God of Abraham, the God of Isaac, and the God of Jacob—and, therefore, the God of the Jews.

As a consequence, the God who revealed his ineffable name as YHWH and thereby defined himself as "I will be [there]" has been re-imaged by philosopher-theologians as a withdrawn, distant, or absent emotional iceberg. The Marcionic caricature of God that sets Jesus in opposition to the Hebrew God has made God appear to be schizophrenic at best.[38] The "Old Testament" God has been viewed as a judge: angry, spiteful, and obsessed with obsequious obeisance. It was necessary, therefore, for Jesus to be manifest in order to reveal the other, hidden side of God, the love dimension that had been obscured by the grim, detached, dispassionate divine nature. Then, in spite of the church's continuing creedal statements that emphasized that the absolute humanity of Jesus was consubstantial with his absolute deity, Christianity increasingly detached itself in practice from the humanity of Jesus the Jew and eventually lost sight of the manifestation of God in the human Jesus to the point that the Jewish Jesus himself came to be imaged

---

[31] Sebastian Moll, *The Arch-Heretic Marcion* (Tübingen, Germany: Mohr Siebeck, 2010), p. 60.

[32] Samuel H. Moffett, *A History of Christianity in Asia: Beginnings to 1500* (San Francisco: HarperSanFrancisco, 1992), p. 62.

[33] Antinomianism literally means "against the Law." It describes those who believe that Christianity has no need for any part of God's law, including the moral law, because faith only is required for salvation.

[34] Supersessionism is "replacement theology," the teaching that Christianity has replaced Judaism and that Christians have replaced Jews in the economy of salvation.

[35] Judaeophobia is morbid fear of Jews and things Jewish.

[36] Anti-Judaism is opposition to Judaism by those who consider Judaism to be a dead religion that God has abolished or a religion that is inferior to Christianity.

[37] Antisemitism is prejudice against or hatred of the Jews simply because they are Jews or because of Judaism or their Jewish heritage. At bottom, Antisemitism is a hatred of the God of the Jews.

[38] Mark Mattes, ed., *Twentieth-Century Lutheran Theologians* (Göttingen, Germany: Vandenhoeck & Ruprecht, 2013), p. 128.

as the transcendent—and, therefore, distant—cosmic Christ.[39] This theoretical cosmic Christ was totally "stripped of the inconveniences of his tribal Jewish heritage . . . equipped with the standardized toneless gestures . . . and refined in the astringent essence of rational formalism."[40] In the cosmic Christ, rationalist philosopher-theologians discovered, in effect, a Jesus who was different from the Jesus whom the apostles described and in whom they placed their unreserved faith. In fact, in these philosophies, Jesus is no Jesus at all because every vestige of his Jewish humanity has been wrested from him. Any theology or Christology, however, that does not clearly affirm that Jesus is both God and Messiah—as both the divine *Logos* and the Jewish human—is clearly heretical from all biblical perspectives and must not be entertained by anyone who believes in the authority of Holy Scripture. Paul was very emphatic in his argument that anyone who came preaching "another Jesus" should be rejected.[41]

The God of Covenant and Relationality

Despite Christian theology's dominant tradition that has stressed metaphysical concepts of God—the God of transcendence and independence from the world who is indivisible, incorporeal, incomprehensible, and impassible—some theologians have been working in more recent times to recover biblical emphases about God. In doing so, they have advanced the view that the concept of divine relationality solves many of the problems current in Christian faith and practice by restoring God's self-image, the image that he chose as a means of revealing himself in the Hebrew Scriptures. H. Richard Niebuhr has argued that truth about God is manifest in "certainties about fundamental, indestructible relations between persons."[42] The God of Scripture is Spirit,[43] but he is a real person, not an "it" or a "force." He is not Aristotle's impassive "Unmoved Mover," the God of ultimate, impersonal detachment. He is Abraham's Heschel's "Most Moved

---

[39] The concept of the "cosmic Christ" originated in patristic literature to identify "Christ" as utterly transcending the humanness of Jesus. In more recent times, however, the term has come to identify those who, following the traditions of the Gnostics, consider Jesus to have become the "cosmic energy" that permeates the universe and is thought to unify all religions. This is a syncretism that ultimately views Christ as being the "Christ within," which is nothing more than a postmodernist version of classical monism. See Joerg Rieger, *Christ and Empire: From Paul to Postcolonial Times* (Minneapolis, MN: Fortress Press, 2007), pp. 269–270.

[40] Robert C. Neville, *A Theology Primer* (New York: State University of New York Press, 1991), pp. 148–150.

[41] 2 Corinthians 11:4.

[42] H. Richard Niebuhr, *The Meaning of Revelation* (Louisville, KY: Westminster John Knox Press, 1941), p. 76.

[43] John 4:24.

Mover," the God of personal, responsive pathos.[44] John Oswalt is correct when he says that "the Israelite concept of God is unique, there is nothing like it anywhere else. No place else is God thought to be a transcendent Person, utterly different from his creation."[45] While the personhood of God does not equate with personality as it is understood in today's world, in Hebraic thought, it confirms God's actions in history in the context of relationality both within himself and with his people. The distinct difference between other religions and Judaism—as well as Christianity that emerged from Judaism's matrix—is a clear focus on the personhood of God, a personhood that requires and is worked out in relationship.

God's personhood demands interrelationship and mutuality within his own being. Though the interrelationality of the persons within God's being did not demand or require creation, that interrelationality prompted the creation. It also made the creation an inescapable eventuality for the full manifestation of divine relationality through God's voluntary self-limitation of divine power and prerogatives in order to create relational beings. God formed humanity in his own image and likeness to demonstrate the divine relationality between human beings, as well as the relationship between God and humanity. It is clear that God created humanity for the "I-Thou" relationship that Martin Buber described,[46] a relationship that would be "mutual, reciprocal, symmetrical, and contentless," one in which "both partners retain their own subjectivity in the encounter, in which they become aware of the other person as a subject, rather than an object."[47] By his own initiative, God is the source of the "I-Thou" relationship with humanity. As a personal God, he simply cannot remain detached from humanity in an "I-It" relationship.[48]

Allan Lazaroff described the relational and interpersonal nature of the God of the Hebrew Scriptures: "The concern [of Scripture] is not conceptual knowledge but rather dyadic relations between people and between them and a person-like God, the latter relationships forming a model for the former."[49] It should come as no surprise, therefore, that God, as conceived and represented in Scripture, is preeminently a tender lover, not a despotic judge. This God says,

[44] Fritz Rothschild, "Introduction," in *Between God and Man: An Interpretation of Judaism from the Writings of Abraham J. Heschel*, Fritz A. Rothschild, ed. (New York: The Free Press, 1959), pp. 7–8.

[45] John N. Oswalt, "Abraham's Experience of Yahweh," in *Perspectives on Our Father Abraham*, Steven A. Hunt, ed. (Grand Rapids, MI: Wm. B. Eerdmans Publishing Col., 2010, p. 41.

[46] Martin Buber, *I and Thou*, tr. Ronald Gregor Smith (New York: Charles Scribner's Sons, 1958), pp. 20–30.

[47] Alister E. McGrath, *Christian Theology: An Introduction* (Malden, MA: Wiley-Blackwell Publishing, 1993), p. 208.

[48] Buber, pp. 20–30.

[49] Allan Lazaroff, quoted in Jerald M. Stinson, "A Love Story," *Harvard Divinity Bulletin*, vol. 35–36, p. 107.

"You are precious in my eyes, and I love you."[50] Everything about the divine being exudes love, for love is God's very essence,[51] and it demands expression and action, not static being. This is why "of all the languages, Hebrew conveys most faithfully the dynamism of the word of God, and always shows us an action in it."[52] This is also why "the authority of faith is more dependent upon orthopraxy than upon orthodoxy."[53] Believing is demonstrated by doing. As faith without works is dead, so belief without practice is worthless, and "love" without "loving" is nothing.

As Abraham Joshua Heschel argued, nouns do not adequately describe God: adverbs modify and indicate the verbal nature of God in his relationship with humanity.[54] Gerhard von Rad agreed that Israel's starting point has always been "event over *logos*"[55] that has grounded Hebrew thinking in "historical traditions," a concept that is foreign to the Greek "urge towards a universal understanding of the world" by seeking a "uniform natural principle" of the cosmos.[56] This idea underscores the historical focus of Hebrew thinking, in which function is preferred over form and deed is preferred over creed.[57] Byron Sherwin has argued that a Jew "is not only obligated to *do* what he or she *believes*, but to *believe* what he or she *does*."[58] Henry Jansen concludes, therefore, that the Old Testament does not "speak abstractly about God but only about God in relation."[59] The God of Scripture is not the philosophical, hidden, or unemployed God of creation. In fact, he identified himself as concrete, revealed, and ever-active, the God of Abraham, the God of Isaac, and the God of Jacob.[60] He is, therefore, the God who is because he does and who does in relationship to the creation and his Chosen People.

---

[50] Isaiah 43:4.

[51] 1 John 4:8, 16.

[52] Paul Evdokimov, *Woman and the Salvation of the World,* tr. Anthony P. Gythiel (Crestwood, NY: St. Vladimir's Seminary Press, 1994), p. 140.

[53] Letty M. Russell, *Household of Freedom: Authority in Feminist Theology* (Philadelphia: The Westminster Press, 1987), p. 24.

[54] Heschel, pp. 160–161.

[55] Gerhard von Rad, *Old Testament Theology: The Theology of Israel's Prophetic Traditions,* vol. I (Louisville, KY: Westminster John Knox Press, 1962), p. 116.

[56] von Rad, p. 116.

[57] Denis Prager and Joseph Telushkin, *Nine Questions People Ask About Judaism* (New York: Simon & Schuster, Inc., 1975), p. 18.

[58] Byron Sherwin, "An Incessantly Gushing Fountain: The Nature of Jewish Theology," in *Contemporary Jewish Theology,* Elliot N. Dorff and Louise E. Newman, eds. (New York: Oxford University Press, 1999), p. 8.

[59] Henry Jansen, *Relationality and the Concept of God* (Amsterdam-Atlanta, GA: Rodopi B.V., 1994), p. 86.

[60] Genesis 28:13; Exodus 4:5; Matthew 22:32.

This is why neither the Hebrew Scriptures nor the Jewish people describe God primarily as "the God of creation." As a matter of fact, only a minuscule portion of the Hebrew Scriptures is devoted to creation narratives. The preponderance of information contained therein deals with God in the context of his relationship with humanity. Only three chapters of *B'reshit* (Genesis) deal with the creation. Twelve chapters tell the story of God's covenantal relationship with Abraham, and the remaining 24 chapters rehearse God's faithfulness to maintain that relationship with Abraham's son, grandson, great-grandson, and great-great-grandchildren. This is why God described himself not as "the God of Creation" or "the God of the Universe," but as "the God of Abraham, the God of Isaac, and the God of Jacob."[61] It is clear, therefore, that God is not merely a self-contained, all-pervasive force—the "Unmoved Mover"—but a purely relational being. Even in the most ancient of Hebraic prayer formulae, the *berakhot*, God is consistently approached and addressed with the benediction, "Blessed are you, O LORD our God, sovereign of the universe." Significantly, in this blessing, God is perceived as "our God," before he is then praised as "sovereign of the universe." The particularity of divine relationality is addressed before God is praised for the position that he holds because God's relationship with his Chosen People is more important to him than his sovereignty.

"It is perhaps easy," says Karen Armstrong, "to imagine [a] lofty deity as long as we place him in heaven."[62] In the record of the Hebrew Bible, however, "God does not remain wholly transcendent, locked into the celestial sphere" but "enters human history and becomes inextricably involved with humanity."[63] Hebraic thinking, then, speaks of God not from philosophical categories but from the perspective of relationship. This model, based on the Hebrew Scriptures themselves, reveals a "better way" that Christian theologians should adopt unreservedly—a way in which theological discussions about God have their beginning point in experience, not in theory. This represents what Elizabeth Johnson calls a theology of God "from below" that does not "seek to prove the existence of such a God by reasoning," but instead begins from the point of experience and then engages "in the hermeneutical task of interpreting the meaning . . . that far transcends any esoteric puzzles of one or three in a literal mathematical sense."[64]

---

[61] Exodus 3:6.
[62] Karen Armstrong, *In the Beginning: A New Interpretation of Genesis* (New York: The Ballantine Publishing Group, 1996), p. 13.
[63] Armstrong, p. 13.
[64] Elizabeth Johnson, *She Who Is: The Mystery of God in Feminist Theological Discourse* (New York: Crossroad Publishing Company, 1998), p. 123.

In maintaining continuity with the Hebraic approach to God as being God in relationship with his people, understanding about God is not based on rationalism, philosophical categories, or metaphysics, but on history and experience. And the only history that is meaningful in the Hebraic culture is that of family relationship. This is confirmed by the fact that the only Hebrew word that suggests a concept of history is תּוֹלְדֹת (*toledot*), which means "generations" or "genealogy" and speaks directly to the birth of children and grandchildren.[65]

The Personal God

YHWH, the God of Scripture, was the only God who was personal and relational. Instead of being an abstraction, a power, or "simply an idea to be thought," as God was viewed in other cultures, the God of the Hebrews was a "person to be experienced."[66] As John Zizioulas rightly observes, "God as person . . . makes the one divine substance to be that which it is: the one God."[67] When God introduced himself in Scripture, he did not speak of himself "as the One who is." Instead, he introduced himself as "*Yahweh* in the first person as 'I am—I shall be', and even then not in a static but in a dynamic mode, as 'I am who I am—I shall be who I shall be.'"[68] When the God of the Bible chose not speak of himself in the third person and said, instead, "I AM," he revealed the very essence of his personhood. From eternity past to eternity future, God has always been and will always be "I AM," the personal, relational God.

God "is not a law but a judge, not a power but a father," says Abraham Joshua Heschel.[69] Indeed, the use of the generic personal pronoun *he* in reference to God in Scripture serves the function of connoting personhood, not gender. Since the God of Scripture is genderless, "when Scripture speaks of God as 'he,' the pronoun is primarily personal (generic) rather than masculine (specific); it emphasizes God's personality . . . in contrast to impersonal entities."[70] If God were only a force, a neuter reference ("it") would be proper; however, in Hebrew there is no neuter.

God is also identified as Father only for the purposes of revealing his personhood and of underscoring his relationship to the creation and especially to

65 Genesis 5:1; 6:9; 10:1; 37:2.
66 Wilson, *Exploring*, p. 24.
67 John D. Zizioulas, *Being as Communion* (Crestwood, NY: St. Vladimir's Seminary Press, 1985), p. 17.
68 Thomas F. Torrance, *The Christian Doctrine of God: One Being Three Persons* (New York: T & T Clark, 1996), p. 235.
69 Abraham Joshua Heschel, *God in Search of Man: A Philosophy of Judaism* (New York: Farrar, Straus and Giroux, 1955), p. 68.
70 Carl F. H. Henry, *God, Revelation and Authority* (Wheaton, IL: Crossway Books, 1999), p. 159.

his Chosen People in terms of blessing and keeping, which are the unique roles of fatherhood.[71] The term *Father*, then, is a relational term, not an ontological statement. As J. Philip Newell observes, "Fatherhood imagery [points] to the One from whom we have come, to God as our seed or origin of life."[72] As Gregory Nazianzus said, the word *Father* is not the name of a nature or essence but of a relation.[73] God is not ontologically Father; he is relationally Father.

The "God Who Is" Is "God with Us"

In the Hebrew Scriptures, then, one discovers the God who is engaged with his people. Indeed, the name by which he revealed himself confirms this truth. While the many names that men have given to God underscore their attempts to define him in terms of power, majesty, dominion, judgment, and the like, the sacred name by which God revealed himself is YHWH, the condensate of God's self-revelational disclosure about himself in which he said, "*Eyeh asher ehyeh*," "I am that I am," or "I will be what I will be," or "I will be [there]."[74] This phrase entails "the freedom of God to decide on the manner of God's presence."[75] Implied in the personal name that God chose for himself and in his own definition of his name are 1) an affirmation of his aseity, for "I am because I am" is an indication that God is the source of his own existence; 2) a declaration of his eternity, for "I will be what I will be" is a declaration that God is the one who exists in the eternal present, the one who is both within and outside of time; and 3) a proclamation of his immutability, for "I will be there" indicates that God's covenantal faithfulness never changes. Each of these categories, however, is secondary to the name's declaration of God's constancy, his faithfulness to his relationships. "I am that I am" is not a Greek metaphysical or philosophical statement. It is a declaration of the steadfastness and faithfulness of divine relationality.[76] Martin

---

[71] The blessing and keeping functions of fatherhood are seen in the first of the three blessings included in the Aaronic Benediction: "The LORD bless you and keep you." This blessing is from God as Father.

[72] J. Philip Newell, *Echo of the Soul: The Sacredness of the Human Body* (Norwich, UK: Canterbury Press Norwich, 2000), p. 3.

[73] Gregory Nazianzus, "The Third Theological Oration," *Nicene and Post-Nicene Fathers,* tr. Philip Schaff and Henry Wace (Grand Rapids, MI: Wm. B. Eerdmans Publishing Co., 1974), pp. 301-309.

[74] When Moses inquired about God's personal name, the Almighty replied to him in Exodus 3:14, "אֶהְיֶה אֲשֶׁר אֶהְיֶה" (*"Ehyeh-Asher-Ehyeh,"* "I am that I am"). This is the meaning of the name with which God subsequently commissioned Moses: יהוה (YHWH), which is commonly represented as *Yahweh* and universally translated "LORD." It is clear that this God-revealed name is a statement of God's relationality, not his dominion or dominance over creation. It is a statement that God will always be God in utter faithfulness to his covenantal relationship with all his creation, with humanity, and with his uniquely Chosen People.

[75] Johanna W. H. Van Wijk-Bos, *Making Wise the Simple: The Torah in Christian Faith and Practice* (Grand Rapids, MI: Wm. B. Eerdmans Publishing Co., 2005), p. 245.

[76] See John D. Garr, *Rediscovering the God of Scripture* (Atlanta, GA: Golden Key Press, 2015).

Buber maintains that this verbal description of God does not even connote static existence in a Greek sense. He translates the phrase *ehyeh asher ehyeh* as, "I will be present as I will be present."[77] The "name," therefore, describes "happening," "being there," or "being *present*."[78]

When God is understood in terms of his own self-disclosure, a foundation is established for recognizing that true being is relational. Because of the influence of Greek thought, however, most of the Western world today considers being as abstract, static, and impersonal rather than dynamic, concrete, and personal. All being, however, is relational. In relationship to God, being should be understood not as a substantive but as a verb and as an intransitive verb, connoting continual dynamic action unlimited by any predicate. It is in this context that God's being not only created the universe but also sustains it moment by moment with the same continually spoken word: "Let there be." This is why John Macquarrie has discussed God's being as a "letting-be," a being that enables and empowers his creation.[79]

The God who facilitates relationality between humans does so because he is pure relationality, the God of love and pathos. Relationality was not, therefore, an acquired trait for God; it was an ontological fact of the very essence of divine being. Relationality was not a quality that was manifest in time; it was a characteristic that was present in the very nature of God from before all time. As John Zizioulas has said, "The substance of God, 'God,' has no ontological content, no true being, apart from communion."[80] Without relationality there is no God, for "nothing in existence is conceivable in itself, as an individual, such as the τοδε τι [*tode ti*] of Aristotle, since even God exists thanks to an event of communion." In reality, it was from the revelation of God in Scripture that the "ancient world heard for the first time that it is communion which makes being 'be': nothing exists without it, not even God."[81]

In a similar manner, God's very being could be revealed "only through personal relationships and personal love. Being means life, and life means *communion*."[82] This understanding affects even the very essence of God: "The being of God is a relational being: without the concept of communion it would not be possible to speak of the being of God."[83] In fact, "while the solitary God of classical theism is associated with a bare, static, monolithic

---

[77] Martin Buber, quoted in V. Viron Coppola, *Quest:* (Bloomington, IN: Xlibris Corporation, 2003), p. 399.
[78] Martin Buber, referenced in Wilson, *Exploring*, p. 126.
[79] John Macquarrie, *Principles of Christian Theology* (London: SCM, 1977), p. 179–182.
[80] Zizioulas, p. 16.
[81] Zizioulas, p. 17.
[82] Zizioulas, p. 16.
[83] Zizioulas, p. 16.

kind of unity, a unity of divine nature, the triune symbol calls for a differentiated unity of variety or manifoldness in which there is distinction, inner richness, and complexity."[84] Because the one God who is tripersonal exists eternally as the loving communion of Father, Son, and Holy Spirit, "there is no problem of the lonely God" in the God of Scripture. The triune God did not have to create "in order to experience love,"[85] for that love was and is eternally manifest within the being of God in the mutual interpenetration and the interchange of infinite love within and among the persons of God.[86]

The God of Scripture, then, is Immanuel, "God with us."[87] This was the reason that God chose to make his fullest self-disclosure in the person of his only begotten Son, Jesus.[88] Karl Rahner affirms this truth: "We are dealing with the absolute God as he turned to us in the concrete uniqueness of Jesus Christ, so that this God really becomes the most concrete absolute."[89] God became human in order to participate fully in humanness[90] so that he could profoundly and in all actuality be "God with us." The prophet Isaiah accurately predicted the manner in which God would become truly immanent: "For unto us a child is born, unto us a son is given, and his name shall be called . . . Immanuel."[91]

The Immanuel concept of "God with us" answers the age-old paradox which questions whether God is transcendent or immanent. In classical theism, God is conceived as being utterly transcendent and, therefore, omnipotent, immutable, incorporeal, incomprehensible, and impassible.[92] Greek philosophy espoused an extreme form of transcendence in which they maintained that God could not possibly interact in any way with the creation.[93] The Hebrews, however, knew better: from the time of Abraham, they had

---

[84] Johnson, p. 220.

[85] John Ernest Sanders, *The God Who Risks: A Theology of Divine Providence* (Downers Grove, IL: InterVarsity Press, 2007), p. 184.

[86] The manifestation of divine love within and among the three modes (or persons) of divine being, Father, Son, and Spirit, is set forth in the idea of perichoresis or circumincession, which speaks of the mutually encircling and interpenetration of each of the three of the others. This is the essence of the idea of God as "three in one," one being of spirit substance manifest in three hypostases.

[87] Isaiah 7:14.

[88] Hebrews 1:2.

[89] Karl Rahner, quoted in Paul Lakeland, *Postmodernity: Christian Identity in a Fragmented Age* (Minneapolis, MN: Fortress Press, 1997), p. 108.

[90] Hebrews 2:14.

[91] Isaiah 7:14; Matthew 1:23.

[92] Rob Lister, *God Is Impassible and Impassioned: Toward a Theology of Divine Emotion* (Wheaton, IL: Crossway, 2013), pp. 102–103. Also Charles Taliaferro, Victoria S. Harrison, and Stewart Goetz, eds., *The Routledge Companion to Theism* (New York, Routledge, 2013) and J. K. Mozley, *The Impassibility of God* (Cambridge, UK: Cambridge University Press, 1926).

[93] Joseph M. Hallman, "Impassibility," in *Encyclopedia of Early Christianity, Second Edition*, Everett Ferguson, ed. (New York: Routledge, 1999), p. 566.

been engaged by the God of creation as his agents in the earth. Elias Bickerman observes the difference between Greek and Jewish thought in this succinct statement: "The Jew believes that for God everything is possible, while the Greek philosopher argues that God neither attempts to nor can interfere with the working mechanism He created."[94] The Hebrew Scriptures were clear: God appeared and interacted with human beings as in the classic theophany that occurred at Abraham's tent complex at Mamre when God ate food and communed with the Patriarch.[95] The Jews, therefore, recognized that while divine transcendence and divine immanence were opposites, both represented truth and, therefore, had to be held in dynamic tension.

In Judaism, various approaches were made to accommodating for divine transcendence and divine immanence. The Aramaic *Targumim* substituted the term *Memra* (Word) for "God" and "Lord" in their translations of the Hebrew Scriptures so that the theophanies were to be viewed as appearances of the Word of God, not God himself.[96] Some believed that the "Lord" who appeared to prophets—and, indeed, to the whole company of Israel at Sinai —was the "angel of the Lord" or "Metraton," a divine viceroy or emissary who could deliver divine promises and blessings.[97]

Paul, a Jewish theologian and Christian apostle, answered the question of divine transcendence and immanence by giving a new and revelatory interpretation of the foundational declaration of monotheism, the *Shema*, in which he interpreted the commandment's words *Elohim* (God) and *YHWH* (LORD) in this way: "There is but one God, the Father, from whom are all things and we exist for him; and one Lord, Jesus Christ, by whom are all things, and we exist through him."[98] The apostle further explained divine transcendence, noting that the Father is the "only Sovereign, the King of kings and the Lord of lords, who alone possesses immortality and dwells in unapproachable light, whom no man has seen or can see."[99] The apostle John demonstrated how God could be transcendent and immanent at the same time: "In the beginning was the Word, and the Word was with God, and Word was God. . . . And the Word became flesh and dwelt among us."[100] The apostolic

---

[94] Elias Joseph Bickerman, *The Jews in the Greek Age* (New York: The Jewish Theological Seminary of America Press, 1988), p. 291.

[95] Genesis 18:1-33.

[96] Daniel Boyarin, *Borderlines: The Partition of Judaeo-Christianity* (Philadelphia, PA: University of Pennsylvania Press, 2004), p. 117.

[97] Carey C. Newman, James R. Davila and Gladys S. Lewis, eds., *The Jewish Roots of Christological Monotheism: Papers from the St. Andrews Conference on the Historical Origins of the Worship of Jesus* (Leiden, The Netherlands: Koninklijke Brill, 1999).

[98] 1 Corinthians 8:6.

[99] 1 Timothy 6:15–16.

[100] John 1:1, 14.

teaching of the incarnation of God as Immanuel; therefore, "God with us" was solidly a Jewish idea which preserved the transcendence of the Father while at the same time manifesting the immanence of God in the person of Jesus.

The God of the Jews

While many scholars have argued that Christian theology and Christology are founded on ideas from Eastern mystery religions,[101] the truth is that the triunity of God is based on solid Jewish thought that is documented in the Hebrew Scriptures and in the literature of Second Temple Judaism. It is also confirmed by the thinking of much later Jewish mystics who tried to explain the dynamic tension between divine transcendence and divine immanence by positing *sefirot* (emanations) of God,[102] wherein God was revealed primarily as *Keter* (Crown), *Memra* (Word), and *Shekhinah* (glory or Spirit)[103] and then through seven additional emanations.[104] This understanding was, in effect, a parallel of some aspects of the doctrine of the Trinity.[105] The foundations of these concepts, however, long predated the thinking of the medieval Jewish philosophers and may well have been current in Jewish thought before and during the time of Jesus.[106] The *Logos* (*Memra*) doctrine was certainly present in pre-Christian Judaism as Daniel Boyarin has so thoroughly demonstrated.[107]

The God of the church, then, is the God of the Jews, plain and simple. Jewish monotheism is the cornerstone of all biblical religion. Both Christianity and Judaism, therefore, rest on the same foundation. The only true God is the God of the Jews! The Christian God, therefore, has always been and will always be the God of the Jews.

God: Christian Fruit—Jewish Root!

---

[101] Peter D. Beaulieu, *Beyond Secularism and Jihad? A Triangular Inquiry into the Mosque, the Manger, and Modernity* (Lanham Md: University Press of America, 2012), p. 134.

[102] Howard Schwartz, *Reimagining the Bible: The Storytelling of the Rabbis* (New York: Oxford University Press, 1998), p. 114.

[103] Some in mystical Judaism posit the existence of "three hidden lights which have no beginning . . . [which] constitute one essence." See Gershom Gerhard Scholem, *Origins of the Kabbalah* (Princeton, NJ: The Princeton University Press, 1962), p. 353. The *Keter*, *Memra*, and *Shekhinah* have been called the "trinity" of mystical Judaism. See Tzvi Nassi (Hirsch Prinz), *The Great Mystery or How Can Three Be One?* (London: William Macintosh, 1863), p. 48.

[104] Howard Schwartz, *Tree of Souls: The Mythology of Judaism* (Oxford: Oxford University Press, 2004), pp. 7–19.

[105] Paul Molnar, *Divine Freedom and the Doctrine of the Immanent Trinity* (London, UK: T & T Clark, Ltd., 2002), p. 221. Also Fred Paddock and Mado Spiegler, *Judaism and Anthroposophy* (Great Barrington, MA: SteinerBooks, 2003), p. 73, and Elizabeth Clare Prophet, *Inner Faces of God, Kabalah* (Livingston, MT: Summit University Press, 1992), vol. 1, p. lvi.

[106] Nassi, p. 48.

[107] Daniel Boyarin, pp. 89–127.

CHAPTER 2

SCRIPTURE

A Jewish book is the world's all-time bestseller! The Holy Bible,[1] the book of books, the written record of the Word that God delivered by revelation to humanity, is thoroughly Jewish, both in precept and authorship. In fact, it has even been said that the Bible is a Jewish book from Genesis to maps! And, indeed, the maps that are in the back of many Bibles are maps of the Holy Land, which God unilaterally gave to his Chosen People, the Jews.

The Bible that Christians honor as the one foundation for all doctrine and practice was written entirely by or under the auspices of Jews.[2] As Marvin Wilson notes, "The Bible is the priceless religious treasure God gave to the world through the Jewish people."[3] In fact, as Claude Montefiore rightly declared, "the Bible was written by Jews and for Jews."[4] Samuel Sandmel rightly observed that "the Bible was the adhesive that held the Jews together." Without it, he says, the Jews "would have surely disappeared, and quickly. With it, they preserved their peoplehood and their lifestyle."[5] One rabbi was heard to observe with great irony, "The greatest mistake of history was our failure to copyright this book. Imagine the royalties on history's best seller!" In reality, however, as Bruce Chilton and Jacob Neusner point out, "neither Judaism nor Christianity owns the Bible . . . Scripture is divine property."[6] God gave his Word to the Jewish people, but he intended for them to be channels through which that Word could be disseminated to the entire world for the obedience of faith of all nations. The living Word was carefully delivered to humanity through the words of prophets, sages, and apostles.

---

[1] The word *Bible* is derived from the name of the ancient Phoenician city of Byblos, a exporter of papyrus (paper) to the ancient world.
[2] This is with the possible exception of the Book of Job which recounts the experiences of a non-Jewish patriarch. No one knows for sure when or where Job lived.
[3] Wilson, *Exploring*, p. 39.
[4] Claude G. Montefiore, *The Bible for Home Reading* (Oxford, UK: Horace Hart, 1896), vol. 1, p. 4.
[5] Samuel Sandmel, *Judaism and Christian Beginnings* (New York: Oxford University Press, 1978), p. 17.
[6] Bruce D. Chilton and Jacob Neusner, *Classical Christianity and Rabbinic Judaism: Comparing Theologies* (Grand Rapids, MI: Baker Academic, 2004), p. 265.

If Jews and Judaism had given the world nothing more, they have enriched the world immeasurably by giving humankind the Bible, God's Word. Christians should be eternally grateful to this unique people for giving them the foundation of their faith. Indeed, the very canonization of the various books of the Hebrew Scriptures which Christians recognize as the Word of God and their collation into one Bible of recognized authority was a Jewish idea. As Eliezer Schweid observes, "It may truly be said that the canonization of the Hebrew Bible marks the beginning of Judaism . . . Thanks to the authority of the Great Synagogue, the Jewish people received the gift of the Bible in a single book."[7] And this was a gift that was passed on to Christians by the Jewish people.

This Jewish book is about YHWH, the God of the Jews, about his Chosen People, and about their land, Israel. And, virtually the entire Bible was either written or thought in Hebrew, the ancient language of the Jewish people.[8] Jews from every stratum of Israelite society were the people of this book of books. And, for Christians the focus of the entire book—both the Hebrew Scriptures (commonly called the "Old Testament") and the Apostolic Scriptures (commonly called the "New Testament")—is the one who was, is, and will always be a Jew, *Yeshua HaMashiach*, Jesus the Messiah.

The apostle Paul declared that the primary advantage that the Jewish people had over the rest of the world's populace was the fact that the very words of God had been committed to them.[9] All of the words of the Hebrew Scriptures were delivered to prophets and sages by God himself, and it was God in the person of his Son, Jesus Christ, who made the fullest disclosure of the Word and will of God, delivering the words of life that are reported in and reflected upon in the Apostolic Scriptures. "In the past God

---

[7] Eliezer Schweid, *The Philosophy of the Bible as Foundation of Jewish Culture* (Brighton, MA: Academic Studies Press, 2008), vol. 1, pp. 34–35. Schweid notes that the Jewish canon of the Hebrew Scriptures, which is included in the various canons recognized as authoritative by virtually all Christian denominations, was formed by the "Great Synagogue" which "was founded under the aegis of Ezra the Scribe during the return from the first Babylonian exile."

[8] The Masoretic text of the Book of Daniel and a few other short passages in the Hebrew Scriptures were composed in Aramaic, a Semitic language similar to Hebrew. The extant Apostolic Scriptures are in Greek; however, there is strong evidence that the Gospel of Matthew was written in Hebrew and translated into Greek. In the early second century, Irenaeus reported, "Matthew issued a written Gospel among the Hebrews in their own dialect, while Peter and Paul were preaching at Rome and laying the foundations of the Church" (Irenaeus, *Adversus Haereses* 3.1.1). The assertion of Irenaeus was confirmed by Papias, Origen, Eusebius, Epiphanius, Jerome, and others. It is also very likely that the other Gospels were originally composed in Hebrew. See Johann David Michaelis, *Introduction to the New Testament*, tr. Herbert Marsh (Cambridge, England: Cambridge University Press, 1793), vol. 1, p. 103. The remainder of the Apostolic Scriptures were certainly *thought* in Hebrew and/or Aramaic and then *translated* into Greek.

[9] Romans 3:1-2.

spoke to our forefathers through the prophets at many times and in various ways, but in these last days he has spoken to us by his Son."[10]

Holy Scripture is not merely a compilation of pithy sayings, aphorisms, historical observations, and suggestions for life. It is a record of divine self-disclosure, the revelation of God and his will for humankind. As Martin Buber said, this revelatory action of God occurs when "the human substance is melted by the spiritual fire which visits it, and there now breaks forth from it a Word, a statement which is human in its meaning and form, human conception and human speech, and yet witness to Him who stimulated it and to His will."[11] All of Scripture, then, has one thing in common: "Holy men of God spoke as they were carried along by the Holy Spirit."[12] Because they were so "inspired" by God himself, the human authors of Scripture made no attempt to add to the Word they had received from God, nor did they attempt to redact what God had revealed to them in such a way as to include their own preconceived notions.[13] This is why the Holy Scriptures have continuity of language and precept that makes the collection of books a unified whole.

Unity and Continuity

The Bible contains sixty-six canonical books,[14] written by some forty different Jewish authors from every walk of life who lived over a period of fifteen centuries in widely scattered localities and extraordinarily different cultural milieus. These Jewish authors of Scripture did not attempt to interpret what they had heard in their innermost beings; therefore, "prophecy never had its origin in the will of man, but men spoke from God as they were carried along by the Holy Spirit."[15] Is it any wonder, then, that the authors of Scripture without reservation asserted some four thousand times that

---

[10] Hebrews 1:1, NIV.
[11] Martin Buber, *Eclipse of God: Studies in the Relation Between Religion and Philosophy* (New York: Harper Publishers, 1952), p. 173.
[12] 2 Peter 1:21, author's translation.
[13] 2 Peter 1:20.
[14] The word *canon* comes from the Greek *kanón*, which means "rule" or "measuring rod." When applied to the Scriptures, it is a list of the books that are considered authoritative. While the term is Christian, the idea of having an established canon of Scripture is Jewish. See Eugene Ulrich, "The Notion and Definition of Canon" in Lee Martin McDonald and James A. Sanders, eds., *The Canon Debate* (Grand Rapids, MI: Baker Publishing Group, 2002), pp. 28–34. The canon of Scripture, which varies according to Christian denomination, includes all of the thirty-nine books of the Hebrew Scriptures that the sages concluded were canonical. In the Hebrew Scriptures (*Tanakh*), some of the books that are separate in the Christian canon are combined so that the Hebrew Scriptures total twenty-four books. The Protestant canon includes sixty-six books, including twenty-seven books of the Apostolic Scriptures. The Roman Catholic canon contains seventy-three books, the Eastern Orthodox canon has seventy-five books, while the Ethiopian Orthodox Tewahedo Church canon accepts eighty-one books.
[15] 2 Peter 1:21.

what they wrote was the *ipsissima verba*, the "very words" of God him-self? Clearly, all of Holy Scripture was indeed "God-breathed,"[16] for it is-sued forth from the very *neshamah*[17] of God into the prophets, sages, and apostles who recorded it.

In reality, the Bible is a library, a compilation of many books. It is "a monumental masterpiece, an anthology of gifted human authors."[18] Mar-velously, it is essentially one book, developing one grand theme from begin-ning to end. It is not a mishmash of philosophical ideas and truisms. It is a cohesive, linearly developed anthology of works that maintain the same theme and message. The amazing continuity of thought and the lack of pre-ceptual contradiction in the pages of the Bible attest to its divine origin. The fact that such a rich diversity of Jewish authors could have agreed entirely on every precept serves only to strengthen the authenticity of the Bible's claim to divine inspiration. The fact that they agree on matters relating to the under-standing of God and his relationship with humanity defies the imagination. It also underscores the reliability of the text of Scripture and its dependability as the basis for faith and practice in the believing community. It is for this reason that the Bible can rightly be called "a magnificent mouthpiece of the living God."[19]

The Bible is not a book that was dropped out of heaven, written with angelic ink by the divine hand on some celestial fiber. It is an earthy book, written by real men and, perhaps, women.[20] Far from the musings of enrap-tured philosophers hoping to find satisfaction in rationalism and far from the mindless phantasmagoria of bedeviled monist monks seeking escape from existence into nothingness, this book is about real-life, down-to-earth men

---

[16] 2 Timothy 3:16. This passage is often translated, "All scripture is given by inspiration of God"; however, the Greek word θεόπνευστος (*theópneustos*) literally means "God breathed."

[17] The Hebrew word נְשָׁמָה (*neshamah*) means "breath."

[18] Wilson, *Exploring*, p. 14.

[19] Wilson, *Exploring*, p. 14.

[20] Some scholars suggest that the Song of Songs and the Book of Hebrews may have been written by women. In the case of the Song of Songs, credit is given to the Shulamite bride of Solomon because she carries fully 53% of the dialogue. See Adolph von Harnack, "Probabilia uber die Addresse und den Verfasser des Habraerbriefes," *Zeitschrift fur die Neutestamentiche Wissenschaft und die Kunde der aelteren Kirche [Journal of New Testament Study and Information Concerning the Ancient Church]* (Berlin: Forschungen und Fortschritte, 1900), vol. 1, pp. 16–41. Also Lee Anna Starr, *The Bible Status of Woman* (Zarephath, NJ: Pillar of Fire Press, 1955), pp. 392–415, and Carol Meyers, "An Introduction to the Bible," in Carol L. Meyers, Toni Craven, and Ross S. Kraemer, eds., *Women in Scripture: A Dictionary of Named and Unnamed Women in the Hebrew Bible, the Apocryphal/Deuterocanonical Books, and the New Testament* (Grand Rapids, MI: Wm. B. Eerdmans Publishing, 2001), p. 9. In the case of the Book of Hebrews, it is thought that Priscilla may have written the text, which could account for the fact that its author is not named (because in the Greek world women were generally illiterate and were not well regarded). See Dorothy Irvin, "*Omnis Analogia Claudet*," in *Women Priests: A Catholic Commentary on the Vatican Declaration*, Leonard Swidler and Arlene Swidler, eds. (Mahwah, NJ: Paulist Press, 1977), pp. 271–277.

and women who lived and valued life and who had the expectation that they would live forever in resurrected human bodies on a renewed earth.[21] The Bible never glamorizes superheroes or demigods: it speaks of men and women who failed miserably, who repented in contrition, and who were redeemed gloriously by a God of grace and mercy.[22]

Profound Scientific Facts

This unique Jewish book is not primarily a book of science, yet within its pages, it contains profound scientific truths, many of which have only recently been authenticated by the world's greatest scientific minds.[23] And, the fact that it contains no scientific errors is an obvious confirmation that "the invisible things of [God] from the creation of the world are clearly seen, being understood by the things that are made."[24] While skeptics and atheists have sought for centuries to invalidate the Holy Scriptures by developing "scientific" theories and hypotheses, the truth remains that no scientific *fact* has ever contradicted or will ever contradict the words of the Holy Writ.[25]

Could ancient Jews have set forth scientific axioms of such staggering accuracy as a result of their own calculations completely without the instruments of modern science and technology? The premise of such self-generated accomplishment is preposterous! Their declarations could only have been the result of communication with the omniscient Creator. The Jews who wrote the Bible were channels of divine revelation from the Creator whose knowledge of the material universe infinitely exceeds that of the human scientific community.

A Unified Moral Statement

Is it possible that forty different Jewish writers from different centuries, different educational backgrounds, and different environments could set forth precepts of morality that differ not in the least? It is difficult to get forty people together in one room at one time to agree on anything! Yet, in the Bible there is one standard of absolute ethics that is repeated again and

---

21 Psalm 37:11 says that the "meek will inherit the land"; 2 Peter 3:13 predicts that in the Age to Come, there will be "new heavens and a new earth wherein righteousness dwells." Revelation 21:1 speaks of God's creation of "new heavens and a new earth."

22 The classic example was David who, though he was "a man after God's own heart" (1 Samuel 13:14), sinned heinously and was found to be guilty of both adultery and murder (2 Samuel 11:4, 15). He repented, however, and was restored to the favor and graces of God (2 Samuel 12:13; Psalm 51:10).

23 Gerald L. Schroeder, *The Science of God: The Convergence of Scientific and Biblical Wisdom* (New York: Simon & Schuster, 1997), p. 73. Citing a wide array of evidence from astrophysics and biology, Schroeder concludes, "Science confirms the Bible's wisdom."

24 Romans 1:20, KJV.

25 Wayne Grudem, *Systematic Theology: An Introduction to Biblical Doctrine* (Grand Rapids, MI: Zondervan Publishing, 1994), p. 83.

again.[26] This could only be the product of God's revelation of his character and personality to different men at different times.[27] All the Bible's authors share the same conception of God's eternal requirements upon mankind.

One thing that is certain about God is that he is immutable—never changing his commitment to his people and the conceptual bases of that commitment. In fact, God confirmed his immutability by his own word: "I am YHWH, I change not . . ."[28] Since God is thoroughly consistent and is not subject to change, we might reasonably expect his standards for the conduct of his subjects to remain constant also. And, so they are. Though men have offered many different standards of so-called "ethics"—most of them situational or based in consequentialism—God's code of absolute ethics has remained the same since creation. And his code is not an onerous, restrictive system of bondage. Far from being entirely negative, it is a list of profoundly positive opportunities for service and human fulfillment.[29]

The Bible Is One Book

While many have characterized the Bible as being two books, the Old and New Testaments, the reality is that the Bible is only one book. The one page in most Bibles that is not inspired of God is placed between the Book of Malachi and the Gospel of Matthew and reads, "The New Testament." This device has dichotomized Holy Scripture at best and has left many Christians with a truncated Bible at worst.[30] Millions of Christians have been denied full access to their rightful heritage from God through the Hebrew prophets, kings, and sages because of the bifurcation of Scripture.

Many Christian theologians, however, continue to trumpet the antinomian idea that the Old Testament has passed into obscurity and has no more value for Christians.[31] Some have even suggested that the clergy should teach

---

[26] John N. Oswalt, *The Bible among the Myths: Unique Revelation of Just Ancient Literature* (Grand Rapids, MI: Zondervan Publishing, 2009), p. 89.

[27] Duncan S. Ferguson, *Bible Basics: Mastering the Content of the Bible* (Louisville, KY: Westminster John Knox Press, 1995), p. 13.

[28] Malachi 3:6.

[29] Wayne G. Johnson, *Morality: Does "God" Make a Difference?* (Lanham, MD: University Press of America, 2005), p. 202.

[30] Some Christian denominations so emphasize the "New Testament" over the "Old Testament" that their communicants carry a New Testament rather than a Bible.

[31] Adolph von Harnack declared with emphasis that the Old Testament is of no value to the Christian church. See G. C. Berkouwer, *The Person of Christ* (Grand Rapids, MI: Wm. B. Eerdmans Publishing Co., 1954), p. 113. Harnack said that continued preservation of the Old testament "as a canonical document of Protestantism is the result of religious and churchly paralysis." Adolf von Harnack, *Marcion: Das Evangelium vom Fremden Gott* (Darmstadt, Germany: Wissenschaftliche Buchgesellschaft, 1960, p. 127, cited in Francis Watson, *Text and Truth: Redefining Biblical Theology* (Edinburgh, UK: T. & T. Clark, 1997), p. 143.

exclusively from the New Testament writings. As a proof text for their folly, they have enlisted Paul's declaration that God "has made us able ministers of the new testament"[32] as though the apostle thought that the new testament was a book![33]

This should come as no surprise, however, for, throughout ecclesiastical history, most of the church has sought to devalue the Hebrew Scriptures. Even the commonly used term *Old Testament* is inherently pejorative and disparaging.[34] From the time of Marcion in the second century onward, various church leaders have argued that the "Old Testament" was replaced by the "New Testament."[35] They have maintained that "the Old Testament is subordinated to, if not altogether devalued by, the New Testament within biblical theology and as word of God."[36] The truth is that the "Old Testament" was the Bible of Jesus and the apostles and that everything that they understood about divine truth, the plan of salvation, the person of Messiah, and the mission and work of the church was found in the pages of the Hebrew Scriptures. Listen to Jesus' evaluation of the Old Testament: "You diligently study the Scriptures because you think that by them you possess eternal life. These are the Scriptures that testify about me.[37] Consider Paul's opinion: "All Scripture is God-breathed and is useful for teaching, rebuking, correcting, and training in righteousness, so that the man of God may be thoroughly equipped for every good work."[38] When Jesus and Paul made these statements, the Apostolic Scriptures had not even been written; therefore, when they spoke of the Scriptures, they could only be referring to the Hebrew Scriptures. Philip Yancey's reference to the Hebrew Scriptures as "the Bible Jesus read" is a simple fact that every Christian must acknowledge.[39] The truth is that neither Jesus nor Paul ever quoted from the "New Testament."

---

[32] 2 Corinthians 3:6.

[33] The "new testament" is the new covenant. The Apostolic Scriptures are writings about events that occurred under the new covenant. In reality, however, the "new covenant" is merely a "renewed" covenant as Hebrews 8:10 clearly says, "This is the new covenant that I will make with the house of Israel after those days, declares the LORD: I will put my laws into their minds, and write them on their hearts, and I will be their God, and they shall be my people." The laws of God which were the basis of the "old covenant" were never changed or abrogated. What was changed was the place where they were written —on the minds and hearts of believers, rather than on tablets of stone.

[34] Lee Martin McDonald, *The Origin of the Bible: A Guide for the Perplexed* (New York: T & T Clark, 2011), p. 16.

[35] Tremper Longmann III, *Old Testament Essentials: Creation, Conquest, Exile and Return* (Downers Grove, IL: InterVarsity Press, 2014), p. 11.

[36] Rolf P. Knierim, *The Task of Old Testament Theology: Method and Cases* (Grand Rapids, MI: Wm. B. Eerdmans Publishing Co., 1995), p. 130.

[37] John 5:39.

[38] 2 Timothy 3:16.

[39] Philip Yancey, *The Bible Jesus Read* (Grand Rapids, MI: Zondervan Publishing, 2002).

Jesus understood, as all his Jewish contemporaries did, that the Hebrew Scriptures could be subdivided into three portions: *Torah* (Law), *Nevi'im* (Prophets), and *Ketuvim* (Writings). This subdivision gave rise to the use of the Hebrew acronym *Tanakh* as the term to describe the Hebrew Scriptures.[40] The thrust of Jesus' insistence that every word must be established by two or three witnesses was seen in his own custom of using all three subdivisions of the Hebrew Scriptures to confirm his teaching and practice.[41] It was certainly a part of the instructional methodology he employed as evidenced in his teaching of the disciples on the Emmaus Road: "This is what I told you while I was still with you: Everything must be fulfilled that is written about me in the Law of Moses, the Prophets and the Psalms."[42]

It has been suggested that there is nothing new in Holy Scripture after Deuteronomy[43]—that is, all the principles of God's religion for humankind under both old and new covenants are to be found in the words of the Torah, and all subsequent writings are *midrashim* (interpretations and expansions). While this statement is perhaps an exaggeration, it does, however, underscore a fundamental truth that while the Word of God was, indeed, manifest progressively, the fundamental principles of all divine understanding were established by God in the Torah.[44] Expressions and applications of divine truth may change with time and culture; however, the underlying principles of divine truth are immutable. Since God never changes, his Word always remains the same; therefore, the truth that is contained in the Apocalypse is also found in Genesis and in all the writings between these two books. Perhaps this is why God commanded the Israelites when he gave them the Torah, "Do not add to it or take away from it."[45] And it is surely the reason why John pronounced judgments upon anyone who would add to or to take away from the words of the Apocalypse, saying, "God will add to him the plagues that are written in this book . . . [or] God will take away his part from the tree of life."[46]

---

[40] In Hebrew, the acronym was תנכ (TaNaKh), with the ת (T) standing for תּוֹרָה—"Torah"(Law), the נ (N) standing for נְבִיאִים—*Nevi'im* (Prophets), and the כ (K) standing for כְּתוּבִים—*Ketuvim* (Writings).

[41] Matthew 18:16.

[42] Luke 24:44. The book of Psalms was the first book in the *Ketuvim*. When Jesus listed "Psalms," therefore, he was using that book to represent the entire corpus of the *Ketuvim*.

[43] Daniel O'Neil, *Heaven's Eagle* (Nashville, TN: Thomas Nelson Publishing, 2013), p. 215.

[44] The fact that everything is established in precept in the Torah in no way elevates the five books of Moses to a status of higher inspiration than the portions of Scripture that came after it, including the Apostolic Scriptures. There is no hierarchy of inspiration in Scripture: "All Scripture is God-breathed (inspired of God)." Indeed, the Apostolic Scriptures actually form a lens that brings everything in the Hebrew Scriptures into picture-perfect focus for the believer. The Apostolic Scriptures are, therefore, an integral and essential part of what God would call the Hebrew Scriptures.

[45] Deuteronomy 12:32.

[46] Revelation 22:18–19.

The Apostolic Scriptures were never given to supersede or replace the Hebrew Scriptures. Brevard Childs makes this truth clear: "The New Testament does not replace the Old with a new doctrine." Instead, "the Old Testament trajectory found its complete continuity in the New."[47] The purpose of the Apostolic Scriptures was to reveal the new covenant that was given to perfect the system of praise, worship, and service that had been outlined in the Hebrew Scriptures. "The Old Testament witness was reformulated by the New, not in the sense that Israel's faith was negated, nor even that Israel's testimony was defective. Rather, the Old was encompassed within the New."[48] The apostolic writings are not superior in quality or level of inspiration to those of the Hebrew Scriptures; they merely represent a further unfolding of God's plan for the ages, the completion of the plan of salvation. Indeed, if the abundance of quotations and allusions to the Hebrew Scriptures were to be removed from Apostolic Scripture, it would be virtually nonexistent and would certainly be utterly confusing and incomprehensible.

The term *Old Testament* is at best pejorative, for it indicates that the Holy Scriptures that served as the Bible of Jesus and the apostles have somehow become outmoded or antiquated and need to be replaced. The term *New Testament* is essentially supersessionist, for it can be used to speak of Scripture that has somehow replaced the "Old Testament" that had become deficient and ineffective. In reality, much better terms are available for describing both compilations of Holy Scripture. The "Old Testament" is best described as the "Hebrew Scriptures," for this is specifically what they are, the writings of the Hebrew peoples. The "New Testament" is best termed the "Apostolic Scriptures," the thinking or writing of the apostles.

The Jewish New Testament

The New Testament is as much a Jewish book as the Old Testament. It, too, was written by Jews about the Jewish religion and how it was reformed and perfected by the Jewish Messiah, Jesus Christ. The principal rule on which the canonicity of the New Testament books was established was their "apostolicity," the fact that they were either written by one of the apostles or under the auspices of one of the apostles.[49] The New Testament authors were

---

47 Bernard Childs, *Biblical Theology of the Old and New Testaments* (Minneapolis, MN: Augsburg Fortress Press, 1992), p. 240.
48 Childs, p. 240.
49 Tomas Bokedal, *The Formation and Significance of the Christian Biblical Canon: A Study in Text, Ritual, and Interpretation* (London, UK: Bloomsbury T. & T Clark, 2014), p. 350.

Jews, and their religion was Judaism.[50] They were not trying to break away from their faith community so they could start a new religion called Christianity. They were simply trying to make their understanding that everything which the Hebrew Scriptures had predicted concerning the Messiah had been fully realized in the life, death, and resurrection of Jesus of Nazareth. The apostolic writings, therefore, were anchored in the Hebrew Scriptures.

The theological and Christological ideas espoused in the Apostolic Scriptures were not grounded in pagan mystery religions as some Christian theologians,[51] Jewish scholars,[52] Muslim clerics,[53] and secularists[54] have argued. They were securely established on the rock-solid foundation of concepts that were written or orally transmitted from Jewish prophets and sages who

---

[50] Mark, the author of the second Gospel of the Christian canon, was probably a Jew. His first name, John (*Yochanan*) was Jewish, and his second name, Mark, was Gentile. James MacKnight suggests that Mark "was a Levite because Barnabas, his mother's brother, was of that order." See James MacKnight, *The Harmony of the Four Gospels* (London, UK: Longman, Hurst, Rees, and Orme, 1809), vol. 1, p. 70. Whatever the case, Mark wrote under the auspices of the apostle Peter, so what he wrote was thoroughly Jewish. Luke, the author of the Gospel of Luke and the Book of Acts, was a Gentile but probably a proselyte to Judaism. In *Questiones hebraicae in Genesim*, Jerome argued that he was a proselyte from paganism to Judaism before he became a believer in Jesus. See Richard Watson, *An Exposition of the Gospels of St. Matthew and St. Mark and Some Other Detached Parts of Holy Scripture* (London, UK: John Mason, 1833), p. 532. One of the biblical arguments for Luke's being a proselyte is found in Acts 21:28-31 where Paul was accused of bringing Trophimus of Ephesus, a Greek, into the temple. Since Luke was with him also at the time, if Luke had not been a proselyte, he would have been accused of violating the temple protocol too. Whatever the case, Luke's writings were produced under the auspices of the apostle Paul and were, therefore, as thoroughly Jewish as Paul's writings were.

[51] Tom Harpur, *For Christ's Sake* (New York: Oxford University Press, 1986), pp. 106–108. Bruce Metzger points out that as far back as the early seventeenth century, Isaac Casaubon tried to prove that the sacraments of the early church were products of mystery religions. See Bruce M. Metzger, "Considerations of Methodology in the Study of Mystery Religions," *Harvard Theological Review* 48 (1955), pp. 13ff. Jonas Alexis notes that the early twentieth-century German History of Religions School that was begun by Richard Reitzenstein promoted the idea that Christianity borrowed from pagan religions. See Jonas E. Alexis, *Christianity and Rabbinic Judaism: A History of Conflict Between* (Bloomington, IN: WestBow Press, 2013), p. 553. Rudolph Bultmann contended that John's Gospel could be understood only in context of myths "recorded in the writings of the Mandaean Gnostics." See John Ashton, *The Religion of Paul the Apostle* (New Haven, CT: Yale University Press, 2000), p. 12. Even as late as the mid-twentieth century, French theologian Alfred Loisy was still arguing that "a Mithraic rite called the *taurobolium* was the basis for the Christian belief that people are saved 'through the blood' of Jesus." See Alf H. Walle, *Pagans and Practitioners: Expanding Biblical Scholarship* (New York: Peter Lang Publishing, 2010), p. 41.

[52] Hyam Maccoby, *The Mythmaker: Paul and the Invention of Christianity* (San Francisco, CA: HarperSanFrancisco Publishers, 1986), p. 16. Maccoby argued that Paul's belief in "the atoning death of a divine being" and the "mystical sharing of the death of the deity [as] the only path to salvation" had "Hellenistic sources, chiefly by a fusion of concepts taken from Gnosticism and concepts taken from the mystery religions, particularly from that of Attis."

[53] Payam Nabarz, *The Mysteries of Mithra: The Pagan Belief that Shaped the Christian World* (Rochester, VT: Inner Traditions Publishing, 2005)

[54] Bertrand Russell, *History of Western Philosophy* (London, UK: Routledge Classics, 2004), p. 311. Russell said, "Elements of mystery religions, both Orphic and Asiatic, enter largely into Christian theology; in all of them, the central myth is that of a dying god who rises again." See also Samuel Angus, *The Mystery Religions and Christianity* (New York: Citadel Press, 1989).

long predated the Christian era. What Jesus and the apostles espoused was not so much a *new* covenant as a *renewed* covenant, not so much an innovation as a restoration of the Jewish religious experience to the original intentions of the ancient instructions that God himself gave. The Apostolic Scriptures, therefore, are a continuation of, not a departure from, the Hebrew Scriptures. The writings of the apostles maintained continuity with the prior words of an unchanging God. A clear example of this truth is demonstrated by the fact that 278 of the 404 verses of the Apocalypse are direct references to the Hebrew Scriptures. The rest of the books in Apostolic Scripture are also deeply rooted in the Hebrew Scriptures. The apostolic authors often quoted directly from[55] or alluded to passages of Scripture,[56] and they reiterated Hebraic concepts that were taught in Scripture. Indeed, as Jonathan Kuntaraf has said, "All the apostles believed in and quoted from the only Bible they had,"[57] and that Bible was simply the Hebrew Scriptures.

The maze of confusion that exists in Christian teaching and practice today results from its failure to recognize this simple fact: one cannot hope to understand New Testament religion without understanding Old Testament religion; therefore, one cannot comprehend the Apostolic Scriptures without knowing the Hebrew Scriptures. Without the Hebrew Scriptures, one does not have a passport to be transported through the pages of Apostolic Scripture. The *whole* Bible must be viewed as the Word of God or none at all. Unless Christian doctrines and polity are anchored in the Hebrew Scriptures on which they were established, they cannot be understood or practiced as Jesus and the apostles intended them. One cannot understand Jesus or the apostles unless they are returned to their first-century Jewish milieu.

Another fundamental problem that has produced massive Christian misunderstanding of the Bible—and particularly of the Apostolic Scriptures— has been the fact that those who have attempted to interpret the Bible have not done so with the Hebrew mindset and worldview with which it was written. Christians have been reading a Jewish book with Greek, Latin, German, Spanish, African, Chinese, or American eyes. Therefore, they have had distorted views of biblical reality. In order to be true to the time-honored

---

55 Jesus and the apostolic authors often quoted Scripture virtually verbatim. Jesus: Matthew 4:4 (Deuteronomy 8:3); Mark 9:48 (Isaiah 66:24); Luke 4:18–19 (Isaiah 61:1–2); John 10:34 (Psalm 82:6); Revelation 2:27 (Psalm 2:9). The apostles: Romans 10:13 (Joel 3:1-5); 1 Peter 2:23 (Isaiah 53:9); James 4:67 (Proverbs 3:34); Revelation 145:3–4 (Psalm 111:2). Some 250 passages from the Hebrew Scriptures are quoted in the Apostolic Scriptures.

56 Because of the phenomenal biblical literacy of the first-century Jewish populace, a technique called *remez* (allusion) was often used wherein only a few words of a passage of Hebrew Scripture were mentioned, which prompted the audience to connect with the rest of the passage.

57 Jonathan O. Kuntaraf, Kathleen Kiem Hoa Kuntaraf, *God's Book of Wisdom* (Hagerstown, MD: Review and Herald Publishing Association, 2007), p. 21.

grammatico-historical hermeneutic,[58] theologians and Bible teachers in every nation must begin to view the Scriptures through the same eyes that Jesus and the apostles viewed them, Jewish eyes![59] The Bible must be interpreted in the light of the grammar of the language in which it was written or thought (Hebrew) and in the light of the history and culture in which it was written (the Hebrew/Israelite/Jewish people and Second Temple Judaism).

Though it may offend the sensibilities of some, the Bible was not originally written in Elizabethan English, later to be translated into Hebrew and Greek! Fully 87 percent of the Bible was written in Hebrew, with the remaining parts first thought in Hebrew and then translated into Aramaic or Greek. The Bible, then, is a book written by Jews for Jews in the language of the Jews about the God of the Jews; therefore, it can never be rightly divided[60] and interpreted unless it is returned to the people and the land from which it emerged. Its eternal truths can, indeed, be contextualized for all the cultures of the earth, but only when they are fully understood in the light of the original matrix from which they came.

Going Back to the Book

"The Bible is the Word of God," Harold Ockenga declared. "It is the watershed of modern theological controversy. On the right . . . are all those who believe that the Bible is the revelation of God and is infallibly inspired. . . . On the left are all those who reject the Bible as the primary authority in faith and life."[61] Because the foundations of all biblical faith, Judaism and Christianity, rest on the words of Holy Scripture, it is essential for all those who believe in God to return to the texts of the Bible. The power of the words of Holy Scripture can never be underestimated. As the

---

[58] From the time of the Antiochian School in the third and fourth centuries, the grammatico-historical hermeneutic, which has also been called the "Reformation Hermeneutic," has been the safest method for interpreting Holy Scripture. This method is even more ancient than the Antiochian School, however, because it also rests on the Jewish *peshat* hermeneutic that helps to draw out the plain, straightforward, and simple meaning of the text.

[59] Daniel J. Harrington and Christopher R. Matthews, eds., *Encountering Jesus in the Scriptures* (Mahwah, NJ: Paulist Press, 2012), p. 168. Harrington says, "Jesus cannot be understood fully unless he is understood through first-century Jewish eyes and heard through first-century Jewish ears."

[60] The Greek word translated "rightly divided" in 2 Timothy 2:15 is ὀρθοτομέω (*orthotomeo*), which means "to cut a straight line." Maintaining the integrity of the text of Scripture begins with careful adherence to the grammatico-historical hermeneutic which demands that the interpreter "cut a straight line" in and with the text which does not meander or deviate from the plain and simple truth that the text sets forth and also maintains the integrity of the text so that the interpreter is not guilty of "distorting the word of God" (2 Corinthians 4:2, NIV).

[61] Harold John Ockenga, *The Word of the Lord: The Campbell Morgan Bible Lectureship, July, 1951* (Glasgow, UK: Pickering and Inglis, 1951), p. 3.

author of Hebrews said that "the word of God is alive and powerful."[62] These words become even more powerful demonstrations of divine truth when they are considered in the light of the original language of Holy Scripture: Hebrew. This is why Peter Wortsman says, "It was with Hebrew words that the Judeo-Christian God quite literally *called* the world into being. . . . The Hebrew language as such is a bridge, a lasting link between God and man."[63] If God thought it important enough to transmit the revelation of himself to humanity by means of the Hebrew language, is sit not reasonable to recognize that the best way for coming to an understanding of the divine self-disclosure is through the words of the very same language in which God communicated his revelation in the first place?

One cannot underestimate the importance of a true "back-to-the-Bible" movement that is essential for reconnecting the church with original Christianity by restoring the foundations of the faith of Jesus and the apostles to their inherent roots. This can never be achieved, however, without a reconnection of traditional Christian biblical understanding with the Jews—with the language, culture, history, and traditions of the Chosen People. All of the roots of the Christian faith are inherently Jewish in precept and application, and it is these roots, severed by centuries of Hellenization and Latinization of Christian faith, to which the church must be reattached. As Marvin Wilson wisely observes: "If the withered or rotted roots of today's church are to become revived through a new understanding of the church's Hebrew beginnings, the church must nourish itself from the sources, those central documents vital to Hebraic thought and life."[64] Frank Talmage took this argument further: "Christian biblical scholarship must learn and teach the Jewish line of Hebrew Scripture in midrash, questioning thereby the treatment of Judaism as something fulfilled and made obsolete by Christianity, to which the Hebrew Scriptures are assigned the status of 'Old Testament.'"[65] Deborah Clemens draws a powerful conclusion that "truths learned in the Hebrew communion have spiritual and universal consequences. By analyzing how God has interacted

---

[62] Hebrews 4:12.
[63] Peter Wortsman in Johann Reuchlin, *Recommendation Whether to Confiscate, Destroy, and Burn All Jewish Books* (Mahwah, NJ: Paulist Press, 2000; originally published: Tübingen, Germany: Thomas Anshelm, 1511), p. 4.
[64] Wilson, *Exploring*, p. 38.
[65] Frank Talmage, *Disputation and Dialogue: Readings in the Jewish-Christian Encounter* (Jersey City, NJ: KTAV Publishing House, 1975), p. 327. Talmage said, "The Christian anti-Judaic myth can never be held in check, much less overcome, until Christianity submits itself to that therapy of Jewish consciousness that allows the 'return of the repressed.'"

with the world in the past, predictions are indeed possible about God's next steps. The written words convey life. . . . The Hebrew Bible is by intent a light to all nations."[66]

Without the Bible, No One Would Know

It has been rightly said that without the Bible no one would know anything about God's will for humanity. "Without the Bible, we might believe in the existence of God, but we would not know who He is, what He is like, if He wants or expects anything from us, or how to get to know Him," says Max Anders.[67] And, no one would have any knowledge of the Eternal God if this great document had not been carefully composed by Jewish seers and preserved through fire and sword at the expense of thousands of Jewish and Christian lives. God revealed to the Jews everything that he determined to disclose about himself; therefore, it might also be quite accurately stated that without the Jews no one would know anything about God. Indeed, "humankind owes the idea of the uniqueness of God to the Jewish religion, and with this, the idea of humankind's own unmistakable singularity. And with the idea of messianism, humankind owes to Judaism the category and the judgment of a reality in which the *future* has primacy over the past."[68] Perhaps this is why Jesus himself proclaimed that "salvation is from the Jews."[69] What a debt of gratitude Gentile believers owe to the Jewish people for the Bible, the document of salvation!

But, what does this Jewish book have to do with Christian believers today? Is it not antiquated and outmoded? No, a thousand times no! It is simply the most modern, up-to-date manual on proper human behavior that is available anywhere in the world. Read it, and it will solve emotional problems. Read it, and it will solve financial problems. Read it, and it will solve spiritual problems. Read it, and it will solve societal problems. Read it, and it will solve political problems. Read it, and it will solve religious problems, too! The Bible, a Jewish book, is the foundation of all Christian teaching and practice.

Scripture: Christian Fruit—Jewish Root!

---

[66] Deborah Clemens, "Dialogue between the Testaments," in *Reading the Bible in Faith: Theological Voices from the Pastorate*, William Henry Lazareth, ed. (Grand Rapids, MI: Wm. B. Eerdmans Publishing Co., 2001), p. 74.

[67] Max Anders, *What You Need to Know About the Bible in 12 Lessons* (Nashville, TN: Thomas Nelson, 1995), p. 41.

[68] Reiner Wiehl, "Hermann Cohen's Ethics and Philosophy of Religion," in *Neo-Kantianism in Contemporary Philosophy*, Rudolph A. Makkreel and Sebastian Luft, eds. (Bloomington, IN: Indiana University Press, 2010), p. 288. Wiehl references the philosophy of early twentieth-century German-Jewish philosopher Hermann Cohen.

[69] John 4:22.

CHAPTER 3

MESSIAH

The very idea of Messiah is deeply rooted in the Hebrew Scriptures and in Second Temple Judaism. The first hint that a Messiah-Deliverer was to come was given in the third chapter of Genesis in God's pronouncement to Eve in the Garden of Eden, "Your seed will bruise the head of the serpent."[1] In subsequent times, this initial cryptic declaration was given greater clarity by prophets and sages of Israel. Moses prophesied, "The LORD your God will raise up for you a prophet like me from among you, from your countrymen, you shall listen to him."[2] Even Balaam, the pagan prophet-for-hire, made this prediction, "I see him, but not now . . . a star shall come out of Jacob, and a scepter shall rise out of Israel. . . . A ruler shall have dominion and will destroy the remnant from the city."[3] The expectation of the emergence of a significant leader who would establish justice on the earth was widespread within the ancient Hebrew and Israelite world.

Later, King David prophesied more definitively: "The LORD says to my lord: Sit at my right hand until I make your enemies a footstool for your feet. The LORD will extend your mighty scepter from Zion, saying, Rule in the midst of your enemies! . . .The LORD has sworn and will not change his mind: You are a priest forever, in the order of Melchizedek. The LORD is at your right hand; he will crush kings on the day of his wrath. He will judge the nations."[4] Then the prophet Isaiah gave still more clarity to the Messiah imagery: "For to us a child is born . . . and the government will be on his shoulders. And he will be called Wonderful Counselor, Mighty God, Ever-lasting Father, Prince of Peace. Of the greatness of his government and peace there will be no end. He will reign on David's throne and over his kingdom,

---

[1] Genesis 3:15. In Christian thought, this passage is understood as the *Protoevangelion*, the first proclamation of the good news of the Messiah.
[2] Deuteronomy 18:15. Many suggest that the intention of Moses' prediction was to indicate that he would be succeeded by Joshua; however, the subsequent language transcends anything that Joshua did and must, therefore, refer to a subsequent Messianic figure.
[3] Numbers 24:17, 19.
[4] Psalm 110:1–2, 4–6.

establishing and upholding it with justice and righteousness from that time on and forever."[5]

Daniel expanded on the Messiah theme with increased insight: "As I looked, thrones were set in place, and the Ancient of Days took his seat . . . I looked, and there before me was one like the son of man, coming with the clouds of heaven. He approached the Ancient of Days and was led into his presence. He was given authority, glory, and sovereign power; all nations and peoples of every language worshiped him. His dominion is an everlasting dominion that will not pass away, and his kingdom is one that will never be destroyed."[6] This kingdom was the same that Nebuchadnezzar had seen in his dream. The rock that demolished the image and filled the whole earth was to be the dominion that was to come when "the God of heaven will set up a kingdom that will never be destroyed."[7] The Messianic Son of Man was to effect the handing over of "the power and greatness of all the kingdoms to the holy people of the Most High," resulting in the establishment of the "everlasting kingdom."[8]

Micah received a further illuminating word from God: "In the last days, the mountain of the LORD's temple will be established as the highest of the mountains . . . Many nations will come and say, Come, let us go up to the mountain of the LORD, to the temple of the God of Jacob. He will teach us his ways, so that we may walk in his paths. The law will go out from Zion, the word of the LORD from Jerusalem."[9] Then, he made a very specific prophecy about the matrix from which the Messiah would come: "But you, Bethlehem Ephrathah, though you are small among the clans of Judah, out of you will come for me one who will be ruler over Israel, whose origins are from of old, from ancient times."[10]

It was no wonder then that when Rome annexed Judea and established its domination over all of Israel, the cries throughout the land for a Messianic deliverer that had been heard for centuries were only intensified. Because of Rome's policy of immediate and vicious response to any perceived threat to its authority, the people lived in constant fear for their lives. Additionally, they were oppressed by exorbitant taxation and the confiscation of personal property. "Given the constant friction between Roman rule and Jewish sensibilities, the belief that God would soon send his agent, the Messiah, to

---

[5] Isaiah 9:6-7, NIV.
[6] Daniel 7:9, 13–14, NIV.
[7] Daniel 2:44–45.
[8] Daniel 7:27.
[9] Micah 6:3.
[10] Micah 5:2.

intervene decisively and finally on the Jews' behalf, constantly simmered in the background,"[11] says Alan Levenson. Details of this Messianic expectation varied. Some envisioned a human figure;[12] others expected a divine person.[13] Some looked for a king; others, for a prophet; still others, for a priest. Some expected that the Messiah would usher in an age of universal peace;[14] others believed that the coming of the Messiah would bring about the end of the world.[15] Still others "expected direct divine intervention into history without any Messiah figure at all."[16] In all cases, however, the Jewish Messianic expectation was that the last days "would be a time of vindication for the Jewish people and their beliefs."[17] The Messiah of Israel would be the one who would right the wrongs of a clearly evil world, bring universal peace, and establish righteousness in the earth. Divine justice that had seemingly failed to reach the wicked ones in society would be finally and fully exacted upon them. At the same time, the suffering righteous ones would be completely rewarded for their faithfulness of God and to his Word. The world that had been out of balance since the fall of Adam and Eve and their rebellion against God would be brought into equilibrium by the all-wise Messiah.

A Different Messianic Figure

In the midst of the almost universal first-century expectation that a Davidic Messiah would arise, overthrow the occupying Roman forces, and liberate Judea, a completely different and unexpected Messianic figure emerged. Between 4 and 6 BC, a baby was born in Bethlehem where his parents, Joseph and Miriam,[18] had journeyed from Nazareth in order to fulfill

---

[11] Alan T. Levenson, *The Wiley-Blackwell History of Jews and Judaism* (Chichester, UK: Blackwell Publishing, 2012), p. 143.

[12] Michael S. Kogan, *Opening the Covenant: A Jewish Theology of Christianity* (New York: Oxford University Press, 2007), p. 100.

[13] Boyarin, *Jewish Gospels*, p. 57. Boyarin, Jewish Talmudic scholar, maintains that the expectation that the "Messiah/Christ would be a god-man" was already "part and parcel of Jewish tradition" before the Common Era began. "The belief in Jesus as God is not the departure on which some new religion came into being but simply another variant (and not a deviant one) of Judaism," he says (p. 53). See also Kogan, p. 100.

[14] David Sears, *Compassion for Humanity in the Jewish Tradition* (Northvale, NJ: Jason Aronson, 1998), p. 145.

[15] Richard A. Gabriel, *Gods of Our Fathers: The Memory of Egypt in Judaism and Christianity* (Westport, CT: Greenwood Press, 2002), p. 161.

[16] Kogan, p. 100.

[17] Alan Levenson, p. 143.

[18] The apostles taught that Miriam was a virgin who had conceived by the Holy Spirit to bear her son (Luke 1:28-35). Joseph received an angelic visitation confirming this truth (Matthew 1:20-15) so that he continued his marital agreement with the then pregnant Miriam and became her husband and the "supposed" father of Jesus (Luke 3:23).

the requirements of the Quirinian census and taxation program. The angel of the Lord instructed the infant's parents to name him Yeshua[19] (Jesus) because he would "save his people from their sins."[20] This infant was heralded by shepherds who also experienced an angelic visitation during which they had been assured that the child would be a "Savior, Messiah the Lord."[21] Then they went to Bethlehem where, as the angels had promised, they found the baby wrapped in strips of cloth and lying in an animal feeding trough because, at the frenetic time of the Roman taxation census, there was no room in any inn for him or his parents.[22]

Perhaps as much as two years later,[23] wise men from Babylon came to King Herod's court in Jerusalem seeking the one who they believed had been "born king of the Jews" because they had "seen his star in the East" and had come to worship him. The ever-paranoid Herod was greatly troubled by this news, so he demanded that the Jewish priests and sages tell him where the Messiah was supposed to be born.[24] For these scholars of Holy Scripture, the answer was easy. Quoting from Micah, they answered Herod, "In Bethlehem of Judea."[25] The king inquired further of the wise men pressing them to pinpoint the time at which the star had appeared to them. Then, he instructed them, "Go and search diligently for the child, and when you have found him, bring me word, that I too may come and

---

[19] In Hebrew the name of Jesus, יֵשׁוּעַ (Yeshua), is derived from the verbal root יָשַׁע—yasha' ("to save") and is cognate with יְשׁוּעָה—yeshuah ("salvation" or "health"). יֵשׁוּעַ (Yeshua) is actually an abbreviated, common alternative form of יְהוֹשֻׁעַ (Yehoshua or Joshua). The closest possible transliteration of Yeshua into English through the language stream through which the name came into English (from Hebrew to Aramaic to Greek to Latin to English) is "Jesus." When the Hebrew יֵשׁוּעַ (Yeshua— Ye-shoo'-a) was transliterated into Aramaic (the most common Semitic language in the first-century eastern Mediterranean) the final ayin (ע) was dropped, making the name יֵשׁוּ (Yeshu— Ye-shoo'). Then, when the Aramaic was transliterated into Greek, an iota (pronounced yota) was substituted for the yud and a sigma (pronounced s) was substituted for the shin in יֵשׁוּ (since there is no sh sound in Greek). Then a final sigma was added to indicate the masculine nominative case. The Aramaic Yeshu, then, became the Greek Ιησους (Iesous—Yā-soos'). When the Greek was transliterated into Latin, Ιησους became Iesus—Ye-sus' which was later anglicized as "Jesus." The direct transliteration of יֵשׁוּעַ into English is Yeshua (or Y'shua). The angel instructed Mary to name her son Yeshua "because he will save his people from their sins."

[20] In Luke 1:31, Mary was instructed by Gabriel to name her child Yeshua (Jesus). In Matthew 1:21, Joseph was told to name the child Yeshua (Jesus). The name given the infant was in keeping with the tradition among the ancients of naming children based on expectations or traits.

[21] Luke 2:11, HCSB.

[22] Luke 2:2, 6.

[23] While most "manger" scenes depict the shepherds and the wise men together, the visit of the wise men was in all probability around two years after the birth of Jesus. This is confirmed by the fact that Herod ordered the slaughter of all boys in and around Bethlehem who were two years old or younger and he did so "in accordance with the time he had learned from the wise men" (Matthew 2:16).

[24] Matthew 2:4.

[25] Micah 5:2.

worship him."[26] As they followed the star, they were ushered into Bethlehem to the very house where the "young child" and his mother were living. Then, having been warned in a dream not to return to Herod, the sages retreated to Babylon by another route.[27] After they had departed, Joseph and Miriam were also warned by the angel about Herod's evil intentions, so they fled to Egypt just in time to avoid Herod's campaign to slaughter all the male infants in Bethlehem and vicinity who were two years old or younger.[28] Then, sometime later, after Herod's death, family of Yeshua returned to Israel.[29]

Scripture and history give very few details about Yeshua's early development other than the fact that his parents "did everything according to the Law of Moses,"[30] including initiating him into the Abrahamic covenant through circumcision when he was eight days old. The obvious parental diligence for the Torah was to establish a lifestyle of faith and obedience wherein Yeshua could later say, "I have kept my Father's commandments."[31] From his infancy, then, this son of Abraham, Isaac, and Jacob was dutifully Torah observant and supportive of his Jewish family and community. It was said that the child "increased in wisdom and stature, and in favor with God and men."[32]

The next bit of evidence of this truth is seen during his family's annual visit to Jerusalem for one of the pilgrimage festivals that were incumbent upon all Israelites. The twelve-year-old Yeshua was so precocious that he actively engaged in discussions with the Jerusalem sages in the temple precincts.[33] This pubescent young man intuitively knew the Torah so well that those who observed him there "were amazed at his understanding and his answers."[34] Even then, Yeshua had a high self-awareness and a sense of divine mission on earth, even telling his parents, "Didn't you know that I must be about my Father's business."[35] From this time throughout his life, it was clear that Jesus understood his role to be that of both the Son of Man[36] and the Son of God.[37]

What is clear and consistent about Yeshua from Scripture is that from infancy, through childhood and puberty, and into adulthood, he was intimately connected with his Jewish family, his Jewish community, and with his Jewish

---

[26] Matthew 2:8.
[27] Matthew 2:12.
[28] Matthew 2:13.
[29] Matthew 2:14.
[30] Luke 2:39.
[31] John 15:10.
[32] Luke 2:52.
[33] Luke 2:46.
[34] Luke 2:47.
[35] Luke 2:49.
[36] Matthew 18:11.
[37] John 10:36.

faith. Jesus was a Jew, and his religion was Judaism, and throughout his life, he never changed either his ethnicity or his religious convictions. Jesus was not a cynic philosopher, strolling around the countryside in squalor, spouting pithy and angry sayings.[38] He was what he had always been, what he clearly said he was: a true son of Israel, unabashedly a Jew.[39] "Jesus was born, lived and died a Jew of His times. He, His family and all His original disciples followed the laws, traditions and customs of His people. The key concepts of Jesus' teaching, therefore, cannot be understood apart from the Jewish heritage."[40]

Little is known either from history or Scripture about Yeshua's subsequent life until he reached the age of thirty.[41] The text of Scripture says, "When he began his ministry, Jesus himself was about thirty years of age."[42] The fact that he delayed the start of his ministry until he reached the age of thirty is further proof that Jesus followed both the Torah and Jewish tradition.[43] It was at this time that Jesus went to visit his cousin John the Baptizer who was conducting immersion exercises at the ford of the Jordan River where the Israelites had entered the land of promise centuries before that time. There, he insisted that John supervise his baptism, "for in this way it is fitting for us to fulfill all righteousness."[44] In the thunder that most people heard during this event, some recognized the words of God: "This is my beloved Son in whom I am well pleased."[45]

Immediately after his immersion in the Jordan, Jesus was impelled by the Spirit to go into the Judean desert where he fasted and prayed for forty days. Afterwards, he experienced three major temptations from Satan: "Command these stones to be made bread,"[46] "Worship me and you will receive all the

---

[38] Ben Witherington III, *The Jesus Quest: The Third Search for the Jew of Nazareth* (Carol Steam, IL: InterVarsity Press, 1997), pp. 58–92.

[39] John 4:9.

[40] *Within Context: Guidelines for the Catechetical Presentation of Jews and Judaism in the New Testament* (Secretariat for Catholic-Jewish Relations of the National Conference of Catholic Bishops, the Education Department of the United States Catholic Conference, and Interfaith Affairs Department of the Anti-Defamation League of B'nai B'rith, 1986), p. 59.

[41] There are many infancy, childhood, and young adult narratives that purport to tell the story of Jesus; however, these are generally thought to be spurious.

[42] Luke 3:23.

[43] The Mishnah, in *Pirkei Avot* 5.21, gives this ascending order of responsibilities with age: at five, study of Scripture; at ten, study of Mishnah; at thirteen, subject to the commandments; at fifteen, study of Talmud; at eighteen, the bridal canopy; at twenty, for pursuit of livelihood; at thirty, the peak of strength; at forty, wisdom; at fifty, able to give counsel; at sixty, old age; at seventy, fullness of years; at eighty, the age of strength; at ninety, a bent body; at one hundred, as good as dead.

[44] Matthew 3:15.

[45] Matthew 3:17.

[46] Luke 4:3.

kingdoms of the world,"[47] and "Throw yourself down from the pinnacle of the Temple."[48] He overcame each of these temptations by quoting the Torah: "Man does not live by bread alone, but man lives by everything that proceeds out of the mouth of the LORD,"[49] "You shall not put the LORD your God to the test,"[50] and "You shall fear only the LORD your God; and you shall worship him and swear by his name."[51] Immediately after he overcame each of Satan's temptations, Jesus launched forth into the ministry that God had assigned him.

The Kingdom of God

From the beginning, it was clear that Jesus understood his mission in life. He was certain that he was the principal agent of the Kingdom of God.[52] Everything that Jesus "recognized and desired is fulfilled in the message of the kingdom," said Jewish scholar David Flusser.[53] "There God's unconditional love for all becomes visible, and the barriers between sinner and righteous are shattered. . . . The poor, the hungry, the meek, the mourners, and the persecuted inherit the kingdom of heaven."[54] The hallmark of Jesus' ministry, then, was "the transvaluation of all the usual moral values."[55] Jesus was determined to restore Jews and Judaism to the original designs and intents of the Torah, to the essence of God's design for the kingdom of God, the dominion of the Almighty over all the earth. He taught, therefore, with an air of divine authority that transcended what was usually displayed by sages of his time.[56]

"What enlightens such vision, fires such enthusiasm, encourages such risk?" asks Daniel Moore. "Conviction. Divine election. A heightened self-awareness as favored son. An innovative prowess as teacher, revolutionary, but not in the expected sense. One, bedewed with John's baptism, imbued with the Holy Spirit, and convinced of his unique sonship and mission."[57] Yeshua was clearly a teacher sent from God.[58] And as he taught, many of his

---

[47] Luke 4:5–7.
[48] Luke 4:9–10.
[49] Deuteronomy 8:3; Matthew 4:4.
[50] Deuteronomy 6:13; Matthew 4:10.
[51] Deuteronomy 6:16; Matthew 4:7.
[52] As Jesus employed it, the term *Kingdom of God* denoted a dynamic, active enterprise, the reign of God—not a geographical territory.
[53] David Flusser, *The Sage from Galilee: Rediscovering Jesus' Genius,* Stephen Notley, ed. (Grand Rapids, MI: Wm. B. Eerdmans Publishing Co., 2007), p. 81.
[54] Flusser, p. 81.
[55] Flusser, p. 81.
[56] Matthew 7:29; Mark 1:22.
[57] Daniel F. Moore, *Jesus, an Emerging Jewish Mosaic: Jewish Perspectives, Post-Holocaust* (New York: T. & T. Clark International, 2008), p. 287.
[58] John 3:2.

contemporaries came to view him as a prophet, something that had not been seen in Israel for over four hundred years.[59] Then, it became increasingly clear to his disciples that he was even more than a prophet: he was the Messiah. When, in a moment of divine insight, Peter was prompted to exclaim, "*Attah hu haMashiach ben-Elohim chayim*" ("You are he, the Messiah, son of the living God"),[60] Jesus immediately declared the apostle's revelation to be the foundation of the community of faith that he had come to establish.

As a teacher, prophet, and Messiah, Jesus was ministering in the tradition of the itinerating teachers[61] and the miracle workers[62] who were a fixture of Jewish life in Second-Temple times. He advocated and promoted the core principles of the Torah. While delivering the most important message of his life, the Sermon on the Mount, he unequivocally declared, "Think not that I have come to destroy the law or the prophets. I have not come to destroy but to fulfill."[63] Then, in what has been called "the antitheses," he systematically set about to strengthen Torah precepts that had been eroded over time when he said six times, "You have heard it said . . . but I say unto you."[64] In each case, he dealt with Torah commandments as heart issues, not merely subjects for external performance.

In Jesus' greatest pronouncement regarding the Torah, he affirmed that everything addressed in God's instructions throughout Scripture was contingent upon two commandments: "Love God" and "Love man (neighbor),"[65] and he commanded that both love for God and love for humanity be unconditional. In direct contradiction to those in the Qumran community who had said that it was proper to love one's neighbor while hating one's enemy, Jesus even went so far as to command his disciples to love their enemies.[66] He relentlessly pursued the message that the Kingdom of God was at hand,[67] even instructing his disciples to make that proclamation the hallmark of their own ministries.[68]

---

[59] Matthew 16:14; 21:11, 46; Mark 6:15; Luke 7:16.

[60] Matthew 16:16.

[61] Itinerating Jewish rabbis were common in the first century as they sought to carry out the opening instruction of the Mishnah in *Pirkei Avot*: "Raise up many disciples."

[62] In *Ta'anit* 3:8, the Mishnah spoke of Honi the Circle Maker as one such man of faith who performed miracles in first-century Israel, especially in bringing rain in the time of drought. In *Berakhot* 5:5, the Mishnah also spoke of Hanina ben Dosa whose prayers cured Gamaliel's son. Neither of these men, however, was considered to be a savior. See Sharon Barcan Elswit, *The Jewish Story Finder: A Guide to 668 Tales Listing Subjects and Sources* (Jefferson, NC: McFarland & Company, Inc., Publishers, 2012), p. 14.

[63] Matthew 5:17, KJV.

[64] Matthew 5:21–22, 27–28, 31–32, 33–34, 38–39, 43–44.

[65] Matthew 22:40.

[66] Matthew 5:43–48.

[67] Matthew 10:7; Mark 1:14, 15.

[68] Luke 9:1.

The new approach that Jesus took to the message of the Torah was not new at all. Instead, it was a renewal of the original intents and purposes of God's word. He espoused a *renewal* of God's covenant with Israel, not the creation of a *new* and different covenant. This was the covenant about which Jeremiah had prophesied, "This is the covenant which I will make with the house of Israel after those days, declares the LORD: I will put my law within them, and I will write it on their hearts."[69] This message was refreshing and popular to growing segments of the Jewish community both in Judea and in the Galilee. Jesus was met with crowds numbering in the thousands[70] who were anxious to hear his words and to witness the miraculous events that accompanied them. The more popular he became, the more the people's expectations rose that this, indeed, was the Messiah who would bring universal peace to the earth.

Jesus, however, warned his closest associates that he not only would not overthrow the Romans but that he would suffer at their hands. He even "ordered his disciples not to tell anyone that he was the Messiah,"[71] and he began to explain to them that he had to go to Jerusalem and be killed.[72] Even the hint of such a thing was anathema to the men who had followed him for years: "This shall never happen to you," Peter exclaimed in a rebuke to his Lord, which prompted Jesus to use these shockingly strong words in response to his outspoken disciple: "Get behind me, Satan! You are a stumbling block to me; for you do not have in mind concerns of God, but merely human concerns."[73]

Jesus knew within himself that before he would ever be the Davidic King Messiah, he would first have to fulfill the role of the suffering Messiah that some had come to call *Mashiach ben Yosef* (Messiah, son of Joseph).[74] This was the Messiah of whom the prophet Isaiah had declared, "He was pierced for our rebellion, crushed for our iniquities; the chastening for our well-being fell upon him, and by his scourging we are healed. . . . the LORD has laid on

---

[69] Jeremiah 31:33, ESV. This is the covenant of which the writer of Hebrews spoke in Hebrews 8:10.
[70] John 6:1–15.
[71] Matthew 16:20.
[72] Matthew 16:21.
[73] Matthew 16:23, NIV.
[74] *Mashiach ben Yosef* was likely first mentioned in the Qumran community. The idea appears in the Babylonian Talmud, *Sanhedrin* 98b. In *Sukkah* 52a, the Babylonian Talmud also records a discussion about Messiah ben Joseph and the death and mourning over the Messiah mentioned in Zechariah 12:10. The idea of multiple Messiahs was derived from the prophecy of Zechariah 1:20, which predicts the rise of four "craftsmen" who would overcome those who had brought destruction to Jerusalem and would rebuild the city. The sages believed that these four craftsmen would be *Mashiach ben Yosef*, *Mashiach ben David*, *Mashiach ben Levi*, and Elijah the prophet (*Sukkah* 52a). *Mashiach ben Yosef* would be the suffering servant of Isaiah 53, *Mashiach ben David* would be the king Messiah, and *Mashiach ben Levi* would be the Messiah as priest (the expectation of the Qumran community in particular).

him the iniquity of us all."[75] This was also the one of whom the prophet Zechariah had spoken: "I will pour out on the house of David and on the inhabitants of Jerusalem, the spirit of grace and of supplication, so that they will look on me whom they have pierced; and they will mourn for him, as one mourns for an only son."[76] Both before and after the time of Jesus, Jewish scholars of Scripture understood these prophetic passages to speak of the suffering and death of the Messiah as a vicarious atonement for Israel.[77] The vast majority of the people, however, were so swept up in their desperation for deliverance from Roman occupation that they did not want to hear any message except "King Messiah." Later, the apostles of Jesus understood that all three Messianic expectations—*Mashiach ben Yosef*, *Mashiach Ben Levi*, and *Mashiach ben David*—had been or would be fulfilled in Jesus.[78]

Roman Death

As more and more people came to recognize Jesus as Messiah, he was increasingly confronted with this popular notion that the Messiah could never be anyone who did not overthrow the occupiers of the land of Israel and usher in a time of universal peace. The vast majority of the Jewish people wondered how anyone who refused to fight the Romans could even remotely be considered to the Messiah. Jesus, however, refused to be drawn into this trap. Instead of fomenting rebellion against Rome, he simply answered, "My kingdom is not an earthly kingdom."[79] These were even his final words when he stood in Pilate's judgment hall and answered the procurator's question, "Are you the king of the Jews?"

It was clear that Jesus had been dealing with issues of sin, repentance, and salvation for the masses of people and that he had been exposing spiritual corruption in high places. He had no agenda advocating any sedition or insurrection against Rome. Still the growing numbers of people who recognized him as Messiah were perceived as a threat by the Roman authorities whose reaction was immediate and brutal. With the assistance and collaboration of the leaders of the Sadducean party who controlled the temple complex and the priesthood, they brought Jesus to a mock trial and ordered his

---

[75] Isaiah 53:5–6.

[76] Zechariah 12:10.

[77] Boyarin, *Jewish Gospels,* pp. 132–145.

[78] The apostles understood that Jesus was *Mashiach ben Yosef,* the suffering Messiah, they understood that his ascension into heaven was for the purpose of becoming *Mashiach ben-Levi,* the High Priest (after the order of Melchizedek), and they believed that he would return to earth again to be *Mashiach ben-David,* King Messiah. In that kingdom, he would be both Messiah and Priest according to Zechariah 6:13.

[79] John 18:36.

execution. Then, he was flogged almost beyond recognition by a Roman soldier, nailed to a Roman cross by a Roman executioner, and finally killed when a Roman spear was thrust into his side by another Roman soldier.

Despite the fact that conscious efforts were made for centuries afterward to absolve the Romans of the crime of murdering Jesus and to indict and convict the Jewish people of the crime of deicide as "Christ-killers,"[80] the simple truth was and remains that the Romans, the brutal occupying force that ruled Palestine with an iron hand, killed Jesus. The *titulus crucis* that was placed on the cross over Jesus' head said it all—and in three languages— "This is Jesus, the King of the Jews." Clearly, as Barrie Wilson observes, "the charge was political; the trial was political; and the crucifixion was political. The fear itself was political, that Jesus would lead an insurrection against Roman power."[81] There was nothing religious about the murder of Jesus, nothing that could be blamed on the Jews or their religion.[82] He died a victim of raw political power exercised by Roman hands.

The Romans, no doubt, gloated in the fact that another threat to their dominance had been eliminated efficiently and with finality, as their brutal custom was. One more Messianic pretender was dead, dashing the faith of his followers and the others who had silently hoped this was surely the deliverer. Jesus was dead. Or so they thought. Based on rumors that had circulated about Jesus' claim that he would resurrect from the dead after three days,[83] the Romans sealed the tomb in which his body lay and set a watch to be sure that no one could secret the body away.[84] And they waited.

Life from the Dead

Very early in the morning of the third day, long before sunrise, some of the women who were disciples of Jesus made their way to the tomb in order

---

[80] Hyam Maccoby, *Antisemitism and Modernity: Innovation and Continuity* (Abingdon, UK: Routledge Press, 2006), p. 18.

[81] Barrie Wilson, *How Jesus Became Christian* (New York: Macmillan Publishing, 2008), p. 193.

[82] Pilate was a notoriously vicious and calculating man. Philo described him as being of "inflexible, stubborn, and cruel disposition." See James Charlesworth, *Jesus and Archaeology* (Grand Rapids, MI: Wm. B. Eerdmans Publishing Co., 2006), p. 331. The Roman procurator controlled the chief priests completely because the office of the high priest had been regularly auctioned to the highest bidder by the Roman government. The very involvement of the chief priests and a "mob" of "Jews" was, therefore, part of Pilate's elaborate plan to avoid reprisals from the people if protests against the execution of Jesus were to arise among the general populace. His "hand-washing" exercise was not the result of a smitten conscience; it was high theater to take the blame from Rome and affix it on the Jewish leadership. See Rebekah Simon-Peter, *The Jew Named Jesus: Discover the Man and His Message* (Nashville, TN: Abingdon Press, 2013), p. 68.

[83] Matthew 27:63.

[84] Matthew 27:65–66.

to see that their Master's body was properly interred.[85] Jesus had been entombed immediately after his death because the Sabbath of the Festival of Unleavened Bread was only minutes away. Finally, when the first day of the week arrived, these faithful women were able to discharge one of the highest religious obligations in the Judaism of their day—properly anointing and burying their dead.[86] When they arrived at the tomb and found the stone rolled away and the tomb empty, they were crestfallen because they thought that someone had stolen the body and had deprived them of their right to show their last respects to their Lord. Then, one of the women, Mary Magdalene, was startled when she came face to face with Jesus and with the reality that his body was no longer in the tomb because he had risen from the dead.

Hurriedly, Mary ran to the disciples with her story of life from the dead, which the men dismissed as a grieving woman's hallucination. Finally, she convinced them to go to the tomb to see for themselves, and when they did, they found that Mary's fantastic story was true: Jesus had, indeed, been resurrected from the dead. What the Roman authorities thought they could silence through the death of a leader who had shown no animus toward them backfired in their faces. The tomb and its guards could not hold the Messiah, for "God raised him from the dead."[87] From that moment, the crucifixion of Jesus spelled death, not for the Master, but for the Roman Empire itself.

The resurrection of Jesus met all the criteria for recognition as an established historical fact. It was not a ruse, for the resurrected Jesus was repeatedly seen and in different circumstances—even by total skeptics.[88] After forty days of such appearances, including one in which 500 people saw him,[89] Jesus' ascended into heaven in the presence of 120 believers.[90] The large number of eyewitnesses, coupled with the fact that all of those who bore witness to the resurrection were willing to die as martyrs rather than recant their testimony, offers solid proof that Jesus was, indeed, resurrected from the dead. These truths have prompted Orthodox Jewish scholar Pinchas Lapide to conclude that the resurrection was, in fact, a historical event that God used as a means for opening the door of

---

[85] Mark 16:1.
[86] Markus Bockmuehl, *Jewish Law in Gentile Churches: Halakah and the Beginning of Christian Public Ethics* (Edinburgh, UK: T & T Clark, 2000), pp. 23–48.
[87] Acts 2:24; 13:30, 34.
[88] John 20:24–28. The apostle Thomas had said, "Unless I see in his hands the imprint of the nails, and put my finger into the place of the nails, and put my hand into his side, I will not believe." Upon seeing the resurrected Jesus face to face and being invited by Jesus to stretch forth his finger and see his wounded hands and to reach out his hand and put it into the wound in his side, Thomas exclaimed, "My Lord and my God!"
[89] 1 Corinthians 15:6.
[90] Acts 1:15.

faith to the Gentiles. Lapide said, "I accept the resurrection of Jesus not as an invention of the community of disciples, but as an historical event. . . . I believe that the Christ event leads to a way of salvation which God has opened up in order to bring the Gentile world into the community of God's Israel."[91]

Even after the resurrection, however, the disciples continued to pressure Jesus with the contemporary Jewish Messianic expectation, asking him, "Lord, are you at this time going to restore the kingdom to Israel?"[92] The ingrained popular expectation that this essential qualification for Messiahship had infused into the Jews, including Jesus' disciples, just refused to be silenced, even in the face of the death, burial, and resurrection of Jesus. The Master did not deny his disciples' expectations as false, however. He simply said, "It is not for you to know times or epochs which the Father has fixed by his own authority."[93] What he did do was to commission them to return to Jerusalem and wait until they received the gift of the Holy Spirit that would empower them to witness the good news of the Kingdom of God among all the nations of the world. He reiterated what he had said in his "Great Commission" when he had instructed them to "go and make disciples of all nations . . . teaching them to observe all that I have commanded you."[94]

The disciples fulfilled their commission. At great risk to life and limb, they traversed the land, preaching the good news and bearing witness to the breaking forth of the kingdom with their testimony that God had raised Jesus from the dead as the firstfruits of those who sleep in the dust of the earth.[95] For them, Jesus' resurrection was conclusive, tangible evidence that all the righteous dead would arise in the resurrection at the last day. The nascent movement that began with 120 members[96] continued to gain in strength until tens of thousands of Torah-observant Jews,[97] including "a large number of temple priests,[98] became a part of "The Way," as the community came to be known.[99]

---

[91] Lapide and Moltmann, p. 59. Lapide maintained that Christianity would never have expanded beyond Jerusalem if the resurrection of Jesus had not been a historical fact. See also Michael Shahan, ed., *A Report from the Front Lines: Conversations on Public Theology: A Festschrift in Honor of Robert Benne* (Grand Rapids, MI: Wm. B. Eerdmans Publishing, 2009), p. 33.

[92] Acts 1:6.

[93] Acts 1:7.

[94] Matthew 28:19.

[95] 1 Corinthians 15:20–23.

[96] Acts 1:15.

[97] The text of Acts 21:20 says that "myriads" of Jewish believers were added to the Jesus community. The Greek word *myriad* means "tens of thousands."

[98] Acts 6:7.

[99] Michael Brown, p. 94.

No less than 3,000 believers were added to this community on the day of Pentecost,[100] and another 5,000 believers were added shortly thereafter.[101]

The early Jesus movement was exclusively Jewish.[102] In fact, all of the members of the Jesus community were at first Jews, just like their Jewish Lord, and they remained faithful to the faith of Abraham, Isaac, and Jacob. Because there was no monolithic Judaism, they maintained that their Jewish interpretation of Scripture was as authentic as that of any other sect of the Jews, and because they truly believed that their Master was the Messiah, they accepted his teachings as being as authoritative as those of Moses and the prophets and even more so.

The message of eternal life that had begun in a remote setting in a tiny nation in the Middle East then gained momentum and spread like wildfire through the known world. In effect, through his disciples, Jesus fulfilled the commission that God had given to Israel: "I will also make you a light of the nations so that my salvation may reach to the end of the earth."[103] The words that Simeon had spoken over the infant Jesus had come to pass: "[You are] a light of revelation to the Gentiles, and the glory of your people Israel."[104] Millions of Gentiles came to the faith of Israel in a movement that Rome with all its vicious might could not crush. What would have died on the cross with Jesus was also resurrected with him. A community of faith that believed unequivocally in resurrection power and eternal life arose to become the agents of the erupting Kingdom of God, a kingdom that brought salvation and spiritual renewal to countless men and women of all ethnicities around the world.

Through the faith of Jesus, Gentiles who were "without hope and without God in the world," who were "alienated from the commonwealth of Israel," and who were "strangers to the covenants of promise," were "brought near by the blood of Jesus" so that they were "no longer strangers and aliens," but became "fellow citizens with the saints and members of the household of God."[105] Those who had been "dead in transgressions and sins" were made "alive together with the Messiah"[106] by being saved by grace.[107] They were translated from the kingdoms of death and darkness into

---

[100] Acts 2:41.
[101] Acts 4:4.
[102] Rodney Stark, noted in Michael L. Brown, *Answering Jewish Objections to Jesus: Volume 4: New Testament Objections* (Grand Rapids, MI: Baker Book House, 2007), p. 183.
[103] Isaiah 49:6.
[104] Luke 2:31-32.
[105] Ephesians 2:13–14, 19, composite of NIV, EST, AND NASB.
[106] Ephesians 2:5; Colossians 2:13.
[107] Ephesians 2:1, 5.

the kingdom of God's dear Son.[108] For these Gentiles, life from the dead first took the form of a spiritual resurrection in which those who chose to believe in Jesus were buried with him by being immersed in repentance and then were resurrected with him to a new life through faith in the mighty power of God.[109] Through the Messiahship of Jesus, the same life that had been offered to Israel at Sinai was also offered to the entire world. And this life was truly resurrection life from spiritual death that would eventuate for them in eternal life in the resurrection of the dead at the end of time.

A Book and an Expectation

Martin Buber, the great Jewish philosopher, posed the rhetorical question, "What have you [Christians] and we [Jews] in common?" Then he answered his own question, "A book and an expectation."[110] Christianity not only shares a book and an expectation with the Jews; it literally inherited from the Jews both the book and the expectation. The book is the Hebrew Scriptures, and the expectation is the coming of the Messiah. Without the Jews, Gentiles would have neither a Bible nor a Messianic expectation. The two sibling faiths—Rabbinic Judaism and Christianity—were birthed out of the matrix of biblical and Second Temple Judaism, the womb that produced both the Scriptures and the Messianic expectation, so both Rabbinic Judaism and Christianity owe the core elements of their faith to the heritage of biblical and Second Temple Judaism.

It is for this reason that both Rabbinic Judaism and Christianity have passionate beliefs in the Messiah. For Jews, the core of faith is the expectation that the long-awaited Messiah will *come*.[111] For Christians, the very foundation of faith is the blessed hope of the good news[112] that the Messiah will *return*.[113] In both cases, the coming,—or the returning—Messiah signals the event of the ages: the resurrection of the righteous dead and the time "when the holy ones possess the kingdom."[114] The final denouement of the ages of human existence upon planet earth will emerge when the Messiah

---

[108] Colossians 1:14.

[109] Colossians 2:12, paraphrased.

[110] Martin Buber, *Israel and the World: Essays in a Time of Crisis* (New York: Schocken Books, 1948), p. 39.

[111] Maimonides' twelfth principle of Jewish faith says, "I believe with perfect faith in the coming of the Mashiach, and though he may tarry, still I await him every day." See Marvin Olasky, *The Religions Next Door: What We Need to Know About Judaism* (Nashville, TN: Broadman & Holman Publishers, 2004), p. 20.

[112] Titus 2:13.

[113] John 14:3.

[114] Daniel 7:22.

comes to establish God's everlasting dominion over all the earth and his eternal *shalom* that will reign for ever and ever.

Long before there ever was such a thing as a Christian, Jews expected the coming of the *Tzemakh Tzadik*, the "Righteous Branch," or the "Branch of David." God had made this Messianic promise to Jeremiah: "I will make a righteous Branch sprout from David's line; he will do what is just and right in the land."[115] He had confirmed the promise to Isaiah: "Then a shoot will spring from the stem of Jesse, and a Branch from his roots will bear fruit."[116] He had even expanded upon it to Zechariah: "I am going to bring my servant, the Branch . . . and I will remove the sin of this land in a single day."[117] In the days of the sages, these prophetic pledges were formalized in the *Birkat David* of the *Amidah*: "Speedily cause the offspring of your servant David to flourish, and let him be exalted by your saving power, for we wait all day long for your salvation. Blessed are you, O LORD, who causes salvation to flourish." These words of Messianic expectation were central to the prayer life of first-century Jews, including that of Jesus and the apostles.

When the Jesus movement emerged from Second Temple Judaism, the Jews who founded that movement were also deeply committed to the Pharisean Messianic expectation. They read the same Hebrew Scriptures, and, because there was no authoritative interpretation of those Scriptures, they did their best to deduce from the scrolls their own understanding of divine truth. Apparently the "Branch of David" theme was foremost in their thinking as it was in most of Second Temple Judaism, because the earliest name that these Jews used to identify their own sect of Judaism was the "*Notzrim.*" In this case, they adopted the Hebrew word that Isaiah had used to express the Messianic expectation, "Then a shoot will spring from the stem of Jesse, and a נֵצֶר (*Netzer*—"branch") from his roots will bear fruit."[118] The earliest Jewish community that recognized Yeshua as Messiah drew from the "Branch of David" imagery for the self-identity of their community. From the beginning, therefore, the sect of Judaism that became Christianity associated its very identity with the Messiah expectation. Then, as time continued, this identity became enshrined in the term *Christian* ("like Christ"), which was first imposed in derision by skeptics of the Messianic community at Antioch and only later became a badge of honor for them.[119] The word *Christian* is a translation of the Greek word χριστιανός—*Christianós*, which itself is a calque translation

---

115 Jeremiah 23:5; 33:15, NIV.
116 Isaiah 11:1.
117 Zechariah 3:8–9.
118
119 Acts 11:26; 1 Peter 4:16.

of the Hebrew word מְשִׁיחַ — *Messianic.*[120] The words and their meaning were the same in both languages, based on the same biblical character: Greek: Χριστός — *Christos* (Christ); Hebrew: מָשִׁיחַ — *Mashiach* (Messiah). Both terms identified belief in Jesus' Messiahship as central to community self-identity.

For both Jew and Christian, then, the very word *Messiah* speaks of the *eschaton*, the time of the end of the age when the Branch of David will come and cause God's salvation to flourish by bringing forth life from the dead, thereby keeping faith with those who sleep in the dust of the earth. At that time, God's promise to Isaiah will be fulfilled: "Your dead will live. Their corpses will rise. You who lie in the dust, awake and shout for joy. . . . the earth will give birth to the dead."[121] Thus, God's power over death that was demonstrated in the resurrection of Jesus will consummate the faith of all believers, giving eternal life to those who sleep in the dust of the earth.

Christian Theology and Christology

Even the foundational principles of Christian theology and Christology are established in Jewish thought about God and the Messiah. While Christianity has come to define monotheism as a unity in the diversity of three modes of divine existence called "persons," it has done so on the basis of the interpretation of the Hebrew Scriptures advanced by Jesus and his Jewish apostles. As Boyarin notes, the expectation that the "Messiah/Christ would be a god-man" was already "part and parcel of Jewish tradition" before Christianity emerged.[122] "The belief in Jesus as God is not a departure on which some new religion came into being but simply another variant (and not a deviant one) of Judaism," he says.[123]

Additionally, Boyarin says that despite the fact that both Jewish and Christian scholars in the modern era have advanced arguments that "the theology of the suffering of the Messiah was an after-the-fact apologetic response to explain the suffering and ignominy Jesus suffered," the truth is that "the notion of the humiliated and suffering Messiah was not at all alien within Judaism

---

[120] The Greek word Χριστός (*Christós*) is a calque translation of the Hebrew word מָשִׁיחַ (*Mashiach*). *Mashiach* literally mean "smeared with oil," "anointed with oil," or simply "anointed." In order to preserve the integrity of the Hebrew word *Mashiach*, the Greek believers used the word *christós* that had been applied to the "anointing" of the athletes who participated in the Olympic games, who were said to have been "smeared with oil." See Joel B. Green, Scot McKnight, and Howard Marshall, *Dictionary of Jesus and the Gospels: A Compendium of Contemporary Biblical* (Downers Grove, IL: InterVarsity Press, 1992), pp. 106–107. Also Donald E. Gowan, *The Westminster Theological Wordbook of the Bible* (Louisville, KY: Westminster John Knox Press, 2003), p. 14.

[121] Isaiah 26:19.

[122] Boyarin, *Jewish Gospels*, p. 57.

[123] Boyarin, *Jewish* Gospels, p. 53.

before Jesus' advent, and it remained current among Jews well into the future following that—indeed, well into the early modern period."[124] Further, he says that Jews in and before the first century of the Common Era "had no difficulty whatever with understanding a Messiah who would vicariously suffer to redeem the world."[125]

The Christian Christ Is Still A Jew

The Messiah was, is, and will ever be a Jew: 1) he was born a Jew, 2) he lived a Jew, 3) he died a Jew, 4) he resurrected a Jew, 5) he ascended a Jew, 6) he sits at the Father's right hand a Jew, and 7) he will return to earth a Jew. These facts are confirmed by Scripture in the following manner: 1) The sages from Babylon who followed his star asked, "Where is he that is born the King of the Jews."[126] 2) The woman at the well of Samaria specifically said to Jesus, "Why is it that you, a Jew, asks of me water to drink."[127] 3) At his crucifixion, a Roman *titulus* was placed over Jesus' head, saying in Hebrew, Greek, and Latin, "This is Jesus, the King of the Jews."[128] 4) Peter said of the resurrection of Jesus, "God had sworn with an oath to [David], that of the fruit of his loins, *according to the flesh*, he would raise up Christ to sit on his throne."[129] 5) Peter said concerning Jesus' resurrection and ascension, "He was not abandoned to the realm of the dead, nor did his body see decay. God has raised this Jesus to life . . . exalted to the right hand of God."[130] 6) The writer of Hebrews said that because "it is clear that [Jesus] descended from Judah," God restored the "order of Melchizedek" so that Jesus could be the eternal High Priest.[131] 7) When Jesus ascended into heaven, the angels assured the believers, "This *same* Jesus, who has been taken from you into heaven, will come back in the same way you have seen him go into heaven."[132]

Without a doubt, then, Christianity owes its understanding of the Messiah, its experience of the Messiah, and its expectation of the return of the Messiah to the Jews. The Jewish Messianic expectation has become and will ever remain the blessed hope of Christianity.[133]

Messiah: Christian Fruit—Jewish Root!

---

[124] Boyarin, *Jewish Gospels*, pp. 132–145.
[125] Boyarin, *Jewish Gospels*, pp. 132–133.
[126] Matthew 2:2.
[127] John 4:9.
[128] Matthew 27:37.
[129] Acts 2:30, KJV.
[130] Acts 2:31-33.
[131] Hebrews 7:11–17.
[132] Acts 1:11, NIV, emphasis added.
[133] Titus 2:13.

CHAPTER 4

SALVATION

"Salvation is from the Jews."[1] Without the slightest hesitation or equivocation, Jesus made this utterly simple declaration to the Samaritan woman at the well of Sychar. Simply stated, the Jewish people were the source of the salvation that God extended to all humanity through the life, death, resurrection, and ascension of Jesus. This is why Charles Hodge argued that "the plan of salvation has always been one and the same; having the same promise, the same Saviour, the same condition, and the same salvation."[2] Indeed, "the faith which saved Abraham was, both as to its nature and as to its object, that which is the condition of salvation under the Gospel,"[3] for the Savior of Christians was "the Savior of the saints who lived before his advent in the flesh."[4] It should not come as a surprise, then, that "early Christian understanding of salvation was dependent upon Judaism."[5] In fact, the very idea that salvation was even needed was anchored in God's salvation that was manifest in the Hebrew Scriptures.

Every believer who comes to faith in Jesus as Messiah and Lord and who is consequently "saved"[6] and is forensically declared "righteous" before God[7] has shared precisely the same experience that Abraham had with God. "Abram believed the LORD, and he credited it to him as righteousness."[8] This manifestation of faith by Abraham was the act of believing God's oath that the son of promise would be born to Sarah and himself. While this was not the first time Abraham had believed God, it was "the first time that the Scriptures expressly mention his faith." Walter Kaiser maintains that this passage "connects the Seed (whom we can identify with Christ) as the object

---

[1] John 4:22.
[2] Charles Hodge, *Systematic Theology* (London, UK: Thomas Nelson and Sons, 1872), vol. 2, p. 368.
[3] Hodge, vol. 3, pp. 551–552.
[4] Hodge, vol. 3, pp. 552.
[5] Edward Kessler and Neil Wenborn, eds., *The Dictionary of Jewish-Christian Relations* (Cambridge, UK: Cambridge University Press, 2005), pp. 393–394.
[6] Acts 16:31; Romans 10:9.
[7] Romans 3:22.
[8] Genesis 15:6, NIV.

of Abraham's belief."[9] Harold Stigers pinpoints the reason for Abraham's righteousness: "Paul speaks of Abram's belief, not as an example of saving faith, but as the vehicle through which the grace of God is bestowed . . . God would give Abram a son because he trusted God to do it. He therefore was of *right character*, righteous in the eyes of God."[10] God imputed righteousness to Abraham instead of (or for) his faith.[11]

The specific passage of Scripture that Paul quoted is this: "For what does the Scripture say? Abraham believed God, and it was credited to him as righteousness."[12] Then, the apostle took the argument further, "Understand, then, that those who have faith are children of Abraham. Scripture foresaw that God would justify the Gentiles by faith, and announced the gospel in advance to Abraham: All nations will be blessed through you."[13] In this text, Paul directly connects the salvation of the Christian believer with the experience of Abraham both in method ("grace through faith"[14]) and in substance ("righteousness imputed for faith"[15]). With this Pauline conclusion in mind, is it any wonder that Herbert Leupold answers the question, "Is Abram's faith different from the justifying faith of the New Testament believer?"[16] by saying, "We answer unhesitatingly and emphatically, No."[17]

In light of the specific declarations in Apostolic Scripture that place the beginnings of salvation by grace through faith in the life of Abraham, it is nothing short of amazing that some Christian scholars have argued that there was no salvation in the Old Testament. Franz Hesse said that there is no optimism in the historical literature of the Old Testament related to any kind of salvation history.[18] According to him, the Old Testament "is not concerned with salvation in the true sense of the word."[19] The truth is, however, that the Hebrew Scriptures are full of the idea of salvation. As a matter of fact, the doctrine of salvation in the New Testament "derives its name,"

---

[9] Walter C. Kaiser, *Toward Rediscovering the Old Testament* (Grand Rapids, MI: Zondervan Publishing Co., 1991), p. 126.
[10] Harold G. Stigers, *A Commentary on Genesis* (Grand Rapids, MI: Zondervan Publishing, 1976), p. 154, author's emphasis.
[11] Romans 4:22.
[12] Romans 4:3
[13] Galatians 3:7–8, NIV.
[14] Romans 4:5; Ephesians 2:8–9.
[15] Romans 4:22; James 2:23.
[16] Herbert Karl Leupold, *Exposition of Genesis* (Chillicothe, OH: DeWard Publishing Co., 2010), vol. 1, p. 478.
[17] Leupold, p. 478.
[18] Franz Hesse, noted in Niels Peter Lemche, *The Old Testament Between Theology and History: A Critical Survey* (Louisville, KY: Westminster John Knox Press, 2008), p. 347.
[19] Franz Hesse, noted in John Goldingay, *Approaches to Old Testament Interpretation* (Leicester, UK: Inter-Varsity Press, 1981), p. 83.

says Robert Girdlestone, "from a word which was engrained in the history and language of Israel from the period of the deliverance of the people out of Egypt up to the time of their restoration from captivity."[20] This word, יָשַׁע (yasha‘), which means "to save," was specifically employed when Israel's deliverance from Egyptian slavery was discussed.[21] Likewise, the word יְשׁוּעָה (yeshuah), meaning "salvation"[22] or "health"[23] was also frequently used to describe the same event.[24]

Throughout the Hebrew Scriptures, then, salvation was often connected with the exodus deliverance. The Psalmist made it clear that the Lord "saved them [from Egypt] because of his name, to make his power known."[25] Eugene Merrill maintains that "this puts to rest any idea that Israel, by its own wisdom and strength, was able to bring about its salvation from Egypt." Merrill is entirely correct in saying that "if the LORD does not save at his own initiative and for his own sake alone, then salvation cannot and will not take place."[26] This is true in every instance where salvation occurs.

God initiated and effected the salvation of the Israelites from Egypt, and saved them by grace for the sake of his own name and his promise to Abraham, not because of their merit. The concept of salvation, then, was clearly established in the Hebrew Scriptures. The teachings of Apostolic Scripture about salvation merely built upon the foundational ideas expressed in the Hebrew Scriptures. Indeed, the parallels between the salvation of believers from the bondage to sin and the salvation of the Israelites from bondage in Egypt could not be clearer. As Gerhard von Rad has argued, "the preservation of the people of God is the same thing . . . as the maintenance of salvation history."[27]

Salvation: The Person

Salvation is first a person, and that person is Jesus. In this sense, salvation is from the Jews because it is beyond dispute that the one who is

[20] Robert B. Girdlestone, *Synonyms of the Old Testament* (Peabody, MA: Hendrickson Publishers, 2000), pp. 124–126.
[21] Exodus 14:30; Deuteronomy 33:29.
[22] Genesis 49:18.
[23] Psalm 42:11.
[24] Exodus 14:13.
[25] Psalm 106:8.
[26] Eugene H. Merrill, *Everlasting Dominion: A Theology of the Old Testament* (Nashville, TN: Broadman & Holman Publishing, 2006), p. 120.
[27] Gerhard von Rad, noted in Niels Peter Lemche, *The Old Testament Between Theology and History: A Critical Survey* (Louisville, KY: Westminster John Knox Press, 2008), p. 347. Also Robert Gnuse, *Heilgeschicte as a Model for Biblical Theology: The Debate Concerning the Uniqueness and Significance of Israel's Worldview* (Lanham, MD: University Press of America, 1989).

salvation personified was a Jew. The author of Hebrews specifically declared that even in his heavenly role as high priest Jesus is still the one who "came from the tribe of Judah," the name of which (יְהוּדָה— *Yehudah*) was contracted to form the word יְהוּדִי— *Yehudi* (Jew). The Hebrew name that the angel instructed both Joseph and Mary to give their son was יֵשׁוּעַ (*Yeshua*), and the explicit reason for their being instructed to give the infant this name was "because he will save his people from their sins."[28] This explanation was accurate and was clearly understood by both Joseph and Mary because the name *Yeshua* is derived from the verbal root יָשַׁע (*yasha'*), which means "to save," "to preserve," "to rescue," or "to deliver." It is also directly related to the word יְשׁוּעָה (*yeshuah*), which means "salvation." Similarly, the name *Yeshua* is also very similar to the name *Joshua*—in Hebrew יְהוֹשֻׁעַ (*Yehoshua*) —which means "YHWH is salvation." The name that was given to the Son of God, then, clearly speaks of the personification of the salvation that comes from YHWH.

The Savior's name *Yeshua* is specifically connected with salvation in Apostolic Scripture. Peter declared to the leaders of Israel, "Salvation is found in no one else, for there is no other *name* under heaven given to mankind by which we must be *saved*."[29] Paul specifically identified Jesus as the personification of God's salvation when he said, "God has brought to Israel a Savior, Jesus."[30] Then, he also made this dramatic declaration about Jesus: "At the name of Jesus every knee will bow . . . and every tongue will confess that Jesus Christ is Lord,"[31] specifically identifying Jesus as God manifest in the flesh, for the prophecy to which the apostle alluded says unequivocally that it is at the name of YHWH that every knee will bow: "I am God, and there is no other. I have sworn by myself . . . that to me every knee will bow, and every tongue will swear allegiance."[32]

Ultimately, just as God and his salvation became synonymous so that God was personified as salvation,[33] so Jesus' role as the bringer of salvation and as the personification of God's salvation was well established on the foundation of the Hebrew prophets. Isaiah unmistakably declared that salvation is a person, the Messiah: "Behold . . . your salvation comes . . . his reward is with him, and his recompense before him."[34] This

---

28 Matthew 1:21, NIV.
29 Acts 4:12, NIV, emphasis added.
30 Acts 13:33.
31 Philippians 2:10–11.
32 Isaiah 43:23.
33 Psalm 118:14, 21. The Psalmist said, "The LORD is my strength and song. And he has become my salvation."
34 Isaiah 62:11.

prophet said that the one who would bring salvation would be God himself: "Behold, your God will come with vengeance; the recompense of God will come, but he will save you."[35] Zechariah, however, made it clear that the Messiah was the one who would bring God's salvation to Israel: "Behold, your king is coming to you: he is just, and endowed with salvation."[36] The Messiah, therefore, would be a man but he would be more than a mere man: he would be Immanuel, "God with us," the saving God of Israel manifest in the flesh as the suffering servant of YHWH.[37]

Salvation: The Concept

Salvation as a concept and as an experience is also Jewish. Rabbinic Judaism and Christianity, which was birthed from Judaism's matrix, are the only religions in the world that teach the concept of sin and atonement, which is both the foundation and the process of biblical salvation. The doctrine of sin and atonement is especially important to Christianity, but it was also central to the Jewish experience, as well.[38] It is an undeniable fact that Christianity has received its understanding of both sin and atonement directly from the Hebrew Scriptures and from the thinking and traditions of the Jewish people.

The fact that the concept of sin and atonement is vital to Judaism is readily demonstrated by the fact that *Yom Kippur* (the Day of Atonement), one of the seven festivals outlined in the Torah,[39] is the highest and holiest day of the Jewish liturgical calendar. The Day of Atonement was instituted by God himself in order to provide an annual day on which the Israelites—and later the Jewish people—would make the prescribed sacrifice and be absolved of their corporate and individual sins. Atonement, therefore, was made essential to Jewish faith from the giving of the Torah to Israel. Walter Kaiser points out that "the repeated statement of the law of Moses on the effects of the sacrifices offered for sin in the Levitical law is 'and he shall be forgiven'."[40] Indeed, "so effective and so all-embracing was this forgiveness that it availed for such sins as lying, theft, fraud, perjury, and debauchery[41]. . . . In fact, in

---

[35] Isaiah 35:4.

[36] Zechariah 9:9.

[37] Isaiah 53:11–12.

[38] Robert S. Ellwood, *The Encyclopedia of World Religions* (New York: Infobase Publishing, 2007), p. 425.

[39] *Yom Kippur* is a solemn holy day, the highest and holiest day of the year; however, in Leviticus 23:2, it is included in the list of "God's festivals," with the details of its observance outlined in Leviticus 23:27–33.

[40] Kaiser, *Toward Discovering*, p. 133. See Leviticus 1:4; 4:20, 21, 31, 35; 5:10, 16.

[41] Leviticus 6:1–7.

connection with the Day of Atonement, what is implicit in these other lists is clearly stated: '*all* their sins' were atoned."[42] While it is true that "salvation in the full New Testament sense as a once-for-all forensic transaction is unknown in the Old Testament,"[43] *Yom Kippur* featured a forensic transaction that was real and efficacious even though it was necessary for it to be renewed annually.

As Israel transitioned from the sacrificial system of the temple to the liturgical exercise of the synagogue, the Jewish sages introduced the Days of Awe (*Yamim Noraim*) which originally were just the days of *Rosh Hashanah* and *Yom Kippur* but were expanded first to the Ten Days of Awe, the time between and including *Rosh Hashanah* and *Yom Kippur*, and then to the Forty Days of Awe, the time from the first day of the month of Elul through the Day of Atonement on the tenth day of Tishri. The Days of Awe gave the Jewish people a prescribed period of time in which they were to engage in introspection by evaluating their lives over the previous year to see if they had committed any sin against God or their fellowman. The last ten days of this time period became an intensification of the days-of-awe theme because those Days of Awe began on the day of the Festival of Trumpets (*Yom Teruah*[44]—literally "the day of blowing [of shofars]"), the first day of the month of Tishri. Each year, therefore, extensive preparation has long been made by the Jewish people for the Day of Atonement and for the exercise of repentance for sins against God and man that is expected to take place on that day. The wailing sound of the shofar is a material demonstration of the penitent heart crying out to God with a broken and contrite spirit that God always accepts.[45]

Yom Kippur is a day when fasting is required of every Jewish worshipper[46] and when prayers are made in which the Jewish worshippers confess their sins and ask for divine forgiveness. Since the Temple no longer stands, the two-goat sacrifice that was outlined in the Torah cannot be fulfilled;[47] however, nearly two thousand years ago, the sages decreed that Torah study, prayer, and *tzedakah* (social justice or charity) would substitute for the

---

[42] Kaiser, *Toward Discovering*, p. 133.
[43] Merrill, p. 115.
[44] *Yom Teruah* is generally called *Rosh Hashanah*, which means "the head of the year" and so designates the first day of the Jewish civil New Year.
[45] Psalm 34:18; 51:17.
[46] The requirement of fasting is waived for those who are infirm or in ill health.
[47] Leviticus 16:5–34. This passage describes the elaborate ceremony that God prescribed for the Day of Atonement, which included the slaughter of the YHWH goat and the priest's confession of the sins of Israel upon the head of the scapegoat. The conclusion of this prescription was this: "Now you shall have this as a permanent statute, to make atonement for the children of Israel for all their sins once every year" (vs. 34).

Temple sacrifices. In whatever form it has been observed, the Day of Atonement, therefore, has been God's prescription for dealing with the sins of his Chosen People for 3500 years. It remains the classic example in the Hebrew Scriptures of the concept of human sin and the need for atonement, repentance, and divine forgiveness, which are the very essence of salvation.

Christianity, Sin, and Atonement

Christians would not even have any idea about what is sin if it were not for the Jewish people and their communication of the written record of God's commandments.[48] Here is John's definition of sin in Christian Scripture: "Sin is the transgression of the law."[49] James also said, "To the one who knows the right thing and does not do it, to him it is sin."[50] How, then, can sin be both transgression of the law (lawlessness) and knowing to do the right thing and not doing it? The answer is simple. In the law of God (Torah), there are both 365 negative commandments (the "thou shalt nots") and 248 positive commandments (the "thou shalts"). Either violating the negative commandments or failing to fulfill the positive commandments is equally a transgression of the law and, therefore, is sin. For Christians, therefore, the very definition of sin is dependent upon the Torah. Paul specifically declared, "If it had not been for the Law, I would not have known sin, for I would not have known about coveting if the Law had not said, 'You shall not covet.'"[51] Not only would Christians not be aware of the conduct of which God disapproves without the Torah, they would also not know the good things that they should do to please God if it were not for the Torah. It is vital, therefore, for Christians to be connected with the Hebrew Scriptures and to employ the same worldview and mindset that the Jewish people used in their approach to God and his instructions.

Atonement is also a Jewish idea that was made clear in the Hebrew Scriptures and was demonstrated in the lives of the Hebrew people in biblical history. The very nature of human beings makes atonement necessary, for "all have sinned and come short of God's glory."[52] Sin requires repentance, which in Hebrew is תְּשׁוּבָה (teshuvah—literally "return," from the verb שׁוּב—shuv, meaning "to turn"). In Hebrew thought, therefore, the whole person

---

48 Romans 7:7.
49 1 John 3:4, KJV. Many translations render this statement as, "Sin in lawlessness." The term lawlessness in the Greek text is ἄνομος (ánomos), which means "without law."
50 James 4:17.
51 In Romans 7:7, Paul declares, "If it had not been for the law, I would not have known sin, for I would not have known about coveting if the Law had not said, 'You shall not covet.'"
52 Romans 3:23.

turns from the path of sin and is redirected toward God. In contrast, the Greek word μετάνοια (*metánoia*) which is used for repentance in the Apostolic Scriptures means "a change of mind," and as such is a reflection of the Greek emphasis on the mind almost to the exclusion of the rest of the human person, particularly the body.[53] Repentance is far more than a "change of mind" (*metánoia*); however, it is *teshuvah* ("turning around"), the redirection of the whole person in a 180-degree turn from the path of sin and death to the narrow way of righteousness and life. The fact that the whole person, and not just the mind, is changed is demonstrated by the fact that repentance is confirmed and witnessed in baptism of the body, not the mind.

In the rich tradition of *teshuvah*, John the Baptizer came preaching the baptism of repentance,[54] which is produced by the condition of godly sorrow.[55] This is what King David demonstrated when he prayed his prayer: "Wash me thoroughly from my iniquity and cleanse me from my sin. For I know my transgressions, and my sin is ever before me. . . . Purge me with hyssop, and I shall be clean: Wash me, and I shall be whiter than snow. . . . Create in me a clean heart, O God. And renew a steadfast spirit within me."[56]

The Jewish people's *Yom-Kippur* repentance experience was the basis for the announcement that John and Jesus made of the breaking forth of God's kingdom. This kingdom would be founded upon one thing: repentance and acceptance of the eternal sacrifice for sin and the provision for righteousness that would be fulfilled in the death and resurrection of Jesus, the "Lamb of God who takes away the sin of the world."[57] This is why "God presented Christ as a sacrifice of atonement, through the shedding of his blood—to be received by faith."[58] Jesus summed up this experience in one simple statement:

---

[53] The Septuagint captured the Hebrew idea of *teshuvah* much better than the New Testament text when it used the Greek word στρέφω—*strpého*, which means "to turn" or "to return," to translate the Hebrew word שׁוּב—(*shuv*), meaning "to turn," the root of תְּשׁוּבָה (*teshuvah*). In contrast, the Septuagint generally used the Greek word *metánoia* to translate the Hebrew word נָחַם (*nacham*), which meant "to sigh" as a way of expressing regret or sorrow as in 1 Samuel 15:11 where God is said to have regretted that he anointed Saul king over Israel. In some cases, *nacham* is also translated into English as "repent." Interestingly, the Septuagint used the Greek word μεταμέλω (*metamélo*), which is related to *metánoia*, to express the danger that the Israelites "might *change their minds* and return to Egypt" (Exodus 13:17, emphasis added). Clearly, the Greek word *strepho* is a better translation of Hebrew word *shuv* than *metánoia* is. For some reason, however, the word *metánoia* was preferred in the Koine Greek of the Apostolic Scriptures over the Septuagint's word *strepho*; therefore, the full extent of the meaning of repentance (that of "turning") is not nearly as clear in the Greek New Testament as it was in the Septuagint version of the Old Testament.

[54] Mark 1:4.

[55] 2 Corinthians 7:10.

[56] Psalm 51:2–3, 7, 10.

[57] John 1:29.

[58] Romans 3:25.

"You must be born again [from above]."[59] The process of the rebirth is detailed in this way: "If you confess with your mouth Jesus as Lord, and believe in your heart that God raised him from the dead, you will be saved, for with the heart a person believes, resulting in righteousness, and with the mouth he confesses, resulting in salvation."[60]

Paul spoke of the continuation of atonement in the Christian experience: "For if while we were enemies we were reconciled to God through the death of his Son, much more, having been reconciled, we shall be saved by his life. And not only this, but we also exult in God through our Lord Jesus Christ, through whom we have received the reconciliation [atonement]."[61] The apostle was even more graphic in his expansion of the Jewish theme of sin and atonement: "Giving thanks to the Father, who has qualified us to share in the inheritance of the saints in light. For he rescued us from the domain of darkness, and transferred us to the kingdom of his beloved Son, in whom we have redemption, the forgiveness of sins."[62] And again, he exulted, "Even when we were dead in our transgressions, [he] made us alive together with Christ . . . and raised us up with him . . . for by grace you have been saved through faith; and that not of yourselves, it is the gift of God."[63] Paul fully understood the provision that God had made through the sacrifice of his Son Jesus to reconcile the world to himself. This was the completed work of grace that brought salvation to those who believed in Jesus.

Salvation: The Continuing Process

In addition to being a crisis experience of spiritual rebirth, salvation is also a continuing process. Though salvation is achieved positionally at the moment of faith and the acceptance of God's salvation in Jesus, every believer must continue to "work out his salvation with fear and trembling."[64] This "working out" of salvation is actually an outworking of salvation in which the saving grace of God's gift of salvation that a believer received at the moment of faith empowers the believer to walk with God in continuing faith and grace, fulfilling God's Word and will in his life. This is the process of sanctification, wherein believers set apart their lives to the purposes of God. This work, however, is also a "washing of water

---

[59] John 3:7.
[60] Romans 10:9.
[61] Romans 5:10–11.
[62] Colossians 1:12–14.
[63] Ephesians 2:6-8.
[64] Philippians 2:12.

by the word of God,"[65] and it is a work of grace, accomplished solely through faith and not by mere works of obedience. In answer to the prayer of Jesus, believers are sanctified through the truth, which is the Word of God.[66]

This "washing of water by the word of God" clearly parallels the Israelites' ongoing *mikveh* experience,[67] wherein they periodically immersed and washed themselves in order to remain ceremonially pure. The "various washings" or ablutions that were "imposed upon [the Israelites] until the time of reformation" were fulfilled for Christians in the spiritual exercises of study and prayer.[68] As believers studied the Scriptures, insights of truth led to higher levels of repentance and consecration that helped them to become more "set apart" ("holy"), qualified for the Master's use.[69] What was demonstrated physically in the Israelite *mikveh* tradition came to be an important spiritual exercise in the lives of believers as they were washed by the Word and sanctified by the truth. Interestingly, the Christian immersion experience parallels the Jewish experience wherein they metaphorically immerse themselves in God and are thereby purified.[70] Since Jeremiah points out that God is Israel's "hope" (in Hebrew, "*mikveh*"),[71] Avi Sagi has suggested that "metaphorically, God himself is a "*mikveh*" and that "by 'immersing' itself in God, Israel is purified."[72] This premise was confirmed by Akiva who said, "The *mikveh* of Israel is the Lord; even as a *mikveh* purifies the impure, so does the Holy One, Blessed be

---

[65] Ephesians 5:16.

[66] John 17:17.

[67] In Judaism, a *mikveh* is a ceremonial immersion pool. The Hebrew word מִקְוֵה (*mikveh*) literally means "a gathering," in this case, a "gathering" or "collection" of water. A *mikveh* could, therefore, be any body of "living water." As a matter of fact, the entire earth was immersed in the *mikveh* of waters in the beginning of time (Genesis 1:2). The best *mikveh* is an ocean. A river or a stream of water can also be a *mikveh*, as can any body of water that is fed by a continually flowing stream. Finally, a pool of water collected from a spring or flowing stream can also be a *mikveh*. When the practice of immersion became universal among the Jews, ceremonial pools (*mikva'ot*) were constructed throughout Israel and beyond to collect "living water" and make the *mikveh* experience more readily accessible to the people.

[68] This is why study and prayer, along with fellowship, have always been the three functions of synagogal life. This was demonstrated in the earliest church when the disciples of Jesus "devoted themselves" to 1) the apostles' teaching, 2) the apostles' fellowship, which included breaking of bread, 3) and to the prayers (Acts 2:42).

[69] 2 Timothy 2:21.

[70] This "purification" has been accomplished by immersion in the Torah and by fulfilling the requirements of *Yom Kippur*, the Day of Atonement.

[71] The word *mikveh* can also mean "hope." Jeremiah used the word *mikveh* in this sense to describe God: "Our LORD, the hope [*mikveh*] of Israel, all who forsake you will be put to shame . . . because they have forsaken the LORD, the spring of living water" (Jeremiah 17:13). The sages have taken the term *fountain of living water* as a metaphorical representation for the *mikveh*. It was this prophecy of Jeremiah to which Jesus alluded in John 7:37-39.

[72] Avi Sagi and Zvi Zohar, *Transforming Identity: The Ritual Transition from Gentile to Jew—Structure and Meaning* (New York: Continuum Publishing, 2007), p. 125.

He, purify Israel."[73] Building on this same idea, Lippman Heller has compared immersion in the *mikveh* to entering under the wings of the *Shekhinah*.[74]

The washing of the Word which is part of progressive sanctification and, therefore, of the continuing process of salvation is not complete until the righteous dead are resurrected at the end of time. This is why Jesus said that "he who endures to the end, the same shall be saved."[75] The salvation and rebirth process achieves its ultimate purpose when one's faith is completed and fulfilled in the resurrection. At that time, even the very jaws of the grave cannot prevail against one whose faith has been solidly anchored on the rock of divine revelation that is fundamental to the faith of salvation: "You are the Messiah, the Son of the living God."[76]

Salvation, then, is unfolded in the life of the believer in three stages: 1) Positional Salvation when the believer's faith is credited for righteousness and entrance into the kingdom of God; 2) Progressive Salvation in which the believer "works out his salvation" through the process of sanctification; and 3) Ultimate Salvation when those who have believed unto salvation and who have worked out their salvation through obedience to God's Word endure to the end and experience the resurrection from the dead. Each of these phases of salvation was clearly demonstrated in the experience and faith of the Jewish people even before the time of Jesus.

Hebraic Salvation: The God Who Saves

The idea of a divine savior long predates the Christian era. As a matter of fact, centuries before the advent of Christ, God said of himself, "I, even I, am YHWH. And there is no savior besides me."[77] The God of Scripture was and remains the God of salvation. He alone is the one who redeems human beings from sin. He alone is the one who saves his people from calamity. He alone is the one who brings ultimate salvation in the form of universal *shalom!* And he accomplishes all aspects of salvation through the person of his Son, Jesus Christ, whose name, *Yeshua*, means "God saves."

Salvation is, indeed, redemption from sin, from the fallen state of humanity that began in the Garden of Eden and continues unabated through time. The idea that human beings can be saved from their sins through faith in the atoning blood of Jesus[78] is solidly rooted in the Hebrew Scriptures

---

[73] Mishnah, *Yoma* 8.9.
[74] Lippman Heller, quoted in Avi Sagi, p. 125.
[75] Matthew 10:22.
[76] Matthew 16:16–18.
[77] Isaiah 43:11.
[78] Romans 5:9; Revelation 5:9.

where salvation through the vicarious atonement of a substitutionary sacrifice was established: "For the life of the flesh is in the blood, and I have given it to you on the altar to make atonement for your souls; for it is the blood by reason of the life that makes atonement."[79] No wonder King David prayed, "Deliver me from bloodguiltiness, O God, the God of my salvation."[80] This is why the Psalmist could assure the Israelites that "there is forgiveness with [the LORD], with the LORD there is lovingkindness, and with him is abundant redemption, and he will redeem Israel from all his iniquities."[81] Further, the prophet Ezekiel reiterated this promise from YHWH to Israel: "I will save you from all your uncleanness."[82]

Biblical soteriology, however, also encompasses God's saving his people not only from spiritual ills but also from physical dangers as is demonstrated in the constantly repeated refrain, "The Lord is my deliverer,"[83] and the declaration of faith, "The Lord is my salvation."[84] The prayer of the patriarchs was, "Save me from my enemies, O my God."[85] Ultimately, salvation speaks of "the arrival of a peaceable kingdom."[86] The salvation that is depicted in the Apostolic Scriptures, therefore, is like that of the Hebrew Scriptures in that does not project escape from the physical world. Instead, "it is a picture of a world at peace and at one, a peace in which the rampages of the stuff of the universe are healed."[87]

The Root of Salvation

Clearly, then, the salvation that Christians value so highly has a Jewish foundation! Indeed, salvation, first as a person and then as a concept, comes to Gentiles and all Christians from the matrix of biblical and Second Temple Judaism. Salvation as redemption from sin, deliverance from physical and spiritual dangers, and inheritance of final emancipation in the perfect *shalom* of the *Olam HaBa* (the Age to Come) is established on the solid foundation of the faith established by the patriarchs, prophets, and sages of Israel and made certain by the death and resurrection of *Yeshua HaMashiach*.

Salvation: Christian Fruit—Jewish Root!

---

[79] Leviticus 17:11.
[80] Psalm 51:14.
[81] Psalm 130:4, 7.
[82] Ezekiel 36:29.
[83] Psalm 18:2; 40:17; 70:5; 144:2.
[84] Exodus 15:2; 2 Samuel 22:3, 47; Job 13:16; Psalm 18:46; 27:1; 38:22; 51:14; Isaiah 12:2; Micah 7:7; Habakkuk 3:18.
[85] Psalm 3:7.
[86] Nicola Hoggard Creegan, "The Salvation of Creatures," in *God of Salvation: Soteriology in Theological Perspective*, Ivor J. Davidson and Murray A. Rae, eds. (Burlington, VT: Ashgate Publishing Co., 2011), p. 79.
[87] Creegan, in Davidson, p. 79.

CHAPTER 5

BAPTISM

When Jesus told Nicodemus, "You must be born again,"[1] he was not speaking in a vacuum, nor was he inventing something totally new that had never before been considered in the history of humanity. Instead, he was building on the foundational understanding of what had already been revealed to the Israelites, and he was taking that understanding to a new level which would ultimately be fulfilled in his own death, burial, resurrection, and ascension.

Both the concept and the experience that have become foundational to Christian faith for millions of believers over the past twenty centuries are rooted in the revelation of God's will to his Chosen People from the time of Abraham until the manifestation of the Messiah. Both the new birth and its outward sign—water baptism—were prefaced by the understanding and experience of the Israelite peoples. The foundational event of Christian faith and its material witness have deep roots in the soil of the Hebrew Scriptures and the traditions of Second Temple Judaism.

The Foundations of Baptism

The interconnectivity and the interrelationship between the spiritual and the material was an ongoing part of the Hebrew worldview.[2] There was no dichotomy between the two as there was in Hellenistic dualism. The Jews understood, therefore, that both a spiritual event and a natural demonstration took place with the ceremonial ablutions and immersions in water that they had made significant parts of their lives. There was nothing, however, magical about the water or one's immersion in it. What was important was the attitude of the heart, the spiritual condition that preceded

---

[1] John 3:7.

[2] Naomi Zirkind, *Strength and Dignity: Torah Wisdom for Women on their Multitude of Vital Roles* (Seattle, WA: CreateSpace Publishing, 2013), p. 134. Zirkind reports Menachem Schneerson as saying that the "connection between the spiritual and material matters in a Jew's life is due to the fact that a Jew receives everything that he has—even aspects of material sustenance such as children, health, and income—directly from God."

and accompanied the physical act of immersion. This was called the *kavanah* of the worshipper, the focused intent and concentration on the spiritual relationship with God that was demonstrated in the outward, physical act of worship.[3]

This interrelationship between the spiritual and the natural was clearly manifest in Paul's understanding of baptism. He well knew that the deliverance of Israel from Egyptian bondage was a spiritual act from the hand of God. The Passover lamb had provided the means of deliverance that became the Israelites' salvation from their slavery. Subsequent to their salvation, however, they also experienced a baptism, which Paul described as "unto Moses" in the waters of the Red Sea.[4] Indeed, the Red Sea,[5] as Witness Lee observed, "was created by God as a baptistry for the children of Israel."[6] The passing of each Israelite into the chasm between the walled-up waters of the Sea represented a massive step of faith. They actually experienced a spiritual burial in the watery Red-Sea grave and a resurrection as they emerged on the eastern shores of the sea.[7]

The principle of baptism, therefore, was established even before the giving of the law at Sinai. Passing through and being immersed in water was an outward expression of inward faith. It was also the physical demonstration of deliverance and salvation. Immersion in water would forever define ceremonial purity in Judaism, and out of that matrix, it would come to be confirmation of repentance and justification in Christianity.

The *Mikveh* Tradition

Water baptism had been a prominent practice among the Israelite community long before the time of John the Baptizer and Jesus. The idea of the application of water to one's person for the achievement of ceremonial purity was an ancient one, dating at least to the time of the incorporation of Israel into a nation at Mt. Sinai. Among the many appliances that were employed in the Tabernacle of Witness, one, the Bronze Laver, was specifically connected with water.[8] When the priests were scheduled to appear in the sanctuary to minister before the Lord, they first immersed themselves in

---

[3] Hayim Donin and Hayim Halevy Donin, *To Pray as a Jew: A Guide to the Prayer Book and the Synagogue Service* (New York: Basic Books, 1980), p. 19.
[4] 1 Corinthians 10:2.
[5] The "Red Sea" was actually the "Reed Sea" (סוּף יַם—*Yam Suph*) in Scripture.
[6] Witness Lee, *Life-Study of Exodus* (Anaheim, CA: Living Stream Ministry, 2011), p. 346.
[7] John Phillips, *Exploring the Old Testament Book by Book: An Expository Survey* (Grand Rapids, MI: Kregel Publications, 2009), p. 76.
[8] Exodus 40:30.

water[9] and then as they approached the altar, they washed their hands and feet in water from the laver so that they would be ceremonially clean when they stood in the Holy Place.[10] Additionally, the sacrifices that were to be offered in the tabernacle, especially the internal organs and the legs of the sacrificial animals, were also washed in the water of the laver before they were brought to the altar.[11] These ablutionary elements in the temple cultus continued throughout the time of both the tabernacle and the temple.

In the course of the instructions to Moses regarding the ceremonial washings that would be required of the priesthood, then, God established the unchanging principle of cleansing, not to remove physical contamination, but to establish ritual purity.[12] From the record of Scripture, water always played a key role in the spiritual experiences of the Israelites, especially in the tabernacle and temple ritual. This spiritual principle would be fully manifest, however, when it was applied to the Israelites and later to the Christian community.

After many generations, the purity and separation from idolatry that God demanded of the Israelites had become so neglected that he purposed to bring dramatic correction into their lives. Nebuchadnezzar, the king of Babylon, was summoned as God's servant to effect this correction.[13] Jerusalem and the temple complex were destroyed, and the people were taken captive into Babylon. Initially, the people responded to their captivity with this lament: "How can we sing the songs of Zion in a strange land." So they "hung their harps on the willows of Babylon."[14] After a time, however, the core of this God-intoxicated people[15] could no longer hold their peace, and they began to pour out their hearts in worship to God. They praised and worshiped God first as individuals, then in the context of family, and finally in the extended family and community groups that were to become the foundation of the synagogue movement.

As the Israelites came more and more to think of worship as an act that was to be fulfilled in the context of community gatherings as well as in the

9 Alfred Edersheim, *The Temple: Its Ministry and Services* (Grand Rapids, MI: Kregel Publications, 1997), p. 42. Edersheim points out that the priests immersed themselves and washed in "well-appointed bathrooms" in a subterranean passage that was located under the temple complex.

10 Exodus 30:21.

11 Leviticus 1:9.

12 Lyman Abbott and Thomas Jefferson Conant, *A Dictionary of Religions Knowledge: For Popular and* (New York: Harper & Brothers, Publishers, 1875), p. 965.

13 Jeremiah 27:6.

14 Psalm 137:2.

15 Marvin R. Wilson, *Our Father*, p. 161. Also Albert Vorspan and David Saperstein, *Jewish Dimensions of Social Justice: Tough Moral Choices of Our Time* (New York: UAHC Press, 1998), p. 357.

temple cult, they began to consider the importance of God's demands on the priests of the temple to see if he would be pleased if they took upon themselves some of those priestly requirements.[16] It was in this context that the idea of immersion in water as a means of ceremonial purity and change of status came into common practice among all the Israelites. If God required the priests to be ceremonially clean through ablutions and immersions, the sages reasoned, it would surely be proper for any worshipper to demonstrate the same purity of his heart through the outward sign of immersion before he appeared before the Lord.

This reasoning formed the foundation for the *mikveh* tradition among the Jews after they returned from Babylon to restore Jerusalem and the temple. Eventually, the Jewish people constructed ceremonial pools throughout the land "in essentially every location with any significance to the practice of the Jewish religion."[17] The *mikva'ot* (*pl.* of *mikveh*) were designed to facilitate the *t'vilah* ("ritual purification") by means of the immersion of worshippers in water—not for purposes of personal hygiene,[18] but for ceremonial purity.[19] They patterned the *mikva'ot* after the pools in which the priests had immersed themselves before going into the presence of God in the temple. By the first century, the Jewish people were not even permitted to enter the temple complex unless they had first immersed themselves in one of the *mikva'ot* of the immersion complex that had been constructed at the southern end of the temple.[20] It was these *mikva'ot* that made it possible for 3,000 new believers in Jesus to be baptized on the Day of Pentecost in a city that has no river, lake, or significant stream.[21]

Eventually, detailed requirements for immersion pools were devised, including restrictions on the kind and volume of water that was to be used in them. They had to be of sufficient depth that would permit the average

---

[16] Jacob Neusner, *Judaism: The Evidence of Mishnah* (Chicago, IL: The University of Chicago Press, 1981), p. 70. Also, Jacob Neusner, "Judaism after the Destruction of the Temple" in *Israelite and Judaean History*, John H. Hayes and James M. Miller, eds. (London, UK: SCM Press, 1977), p. 70. Neusner was very specific in saying that the dominant theme for the Pharisees was their "concern for matters of rite . . . as if one were a temple priest."

[17] William M. Harmening, *Mystery at Corinth: Seeking a Jewish Answer to a Christian Mystery* (Lincoln, NE: iUniverse Publishing, 2006), p. 61.

[18] The *mikva'ot* were never considered to be nor were they ever used as public baths. As a matter of fact, before worshippers were allowed to enter the *mikveh*, they were required to wash their bodies thoroughly.

[19] Because the *mikveh* is for ceremonial purity, the water must touch every part of the worshippers' bodies. They are required, therefore, to be completely nude, with no object—including jewelry, makeup, or even nail polish—interposed "between the body and the water of the ritual bath." See Ronald L. Eisenberg, *Jewish Traditions: A JPS Guide* (Philadelphia, PA: Jewish Publication Society, 2004), p. 556.

[20] William James Hamblin and David Roth Seely, *Solomon's Temple: Myth and History* (London, UK: Thames & Hudson, Ltd., 2007), p. 45.

[21] Jerusalem has only one small stream, the Brook Kidron, which is between the city and the Mount of Olives.

person to squat down or bend over and completely immerse himself or herself in the water. The waters of the *mikveh* had to contain "living waters," either from a spring or a moving stream or, in some circumstances, from rainfall.[22] In the *mikveh* experience in ancient times, worshippers often descended seven steps into the pool, completely immersed themselves in the water, and then ascended seven steps out of the pool.[23] Usually three witnesses, but at least one witness, had to observe the self-immersion to be certain that the worshipper had been completed submerged in the water.[24] Witnesses were so important that those who immersed themselves were often said to have been immersed "in the name," or "under the authority of," the witness(es).[25] This tradition was carried forward in John's baptism wherein believers were "baptized unto John,"[26] just as the Israelites had been "baptized unto Moses"[27] at the Red Sea. When this dynamic was applied to the baptism of the earliest Christians, the witness was being baptized in the name (authority) of Jesus,[28] representing the witness of the Father, Son, and Holy Spirit.[29] The universal Christian baptism in the name of Jesus (Father, Son, and Holy Spirit) limited the development of factionalism in the church such as Paul condemned when he said, "Has Christ been divided? Paul was not crucified for you, was he? Or were you baptized in the name of Paul?"[30]

Since immersion in water would inevitably eventuate in death if one were to remain for too long under the surface of the water, those who immersed themselves in the *mikveh* and emerged therefrom came to be viewed as having experienced a "death, burial, and resurrection."[31] Additionally, the immersion experience was understood as a rebirth process.[32] Because the waters of the *mikveh* were believed to symbolize the waters of the womb, it was believed that those who emerged from those waters after

---

22 Osher Chaim Levene, *Set in Stone: The Meaning of Mitzvah Observance* (Jerusalem, Israel: Targum Press, 2004), p. 168.
23 The seven steps represented the six days of creation and the Sabbath. See Ronald Eisenberg, p. 556.
24 This witnessing factor was based on the biblical and Jewish idea that every matter is established in the presence of two or three witnesses (Deuteronomy 17:6; Matthew 18:16).
25 This is seen in Paul's question of the believers at Corinth: "Into what [name] then were you baptized?" They replied, "Into John's baptism." In other words, John (or one of his disciples) was the witness to their immersion. After Paul explained to these believers the work of Jesus, however, "they were baptized in the name of the Lord Jesus" (Acts 19:3–5).
26 Acts 19:3.
27 1 Corinthians 10:2.
28 Acts 2:38.
29 Matthew 28:19.
30 1 Corinthians 1:13.
31 Yitzhak Buxbaum, *Jewish Spiritual Practices* (Northvale, NJ: Jason Aronson, Inc., 1994), p. 569.
32 Thomas Macy Finn, *From Death to Rebirth: Ritual and Conversion in Antiquity* (Mahwah, NJ: Paulist Press, 1997), p. 132.

having immersed themselves therein were considered to have been reborn or born again.[33] This concept was extended to various areas of life, including the monthly renewal that takes place in the bodies of women when they are re-equipped with the potential for generating new life. The immersion of women after menses was a rebirth process, and it was also "part of the *tumah*[34] and *tahara*[35]—death and resurrection process,"[36] a transition from being forbidden to participate in holy things into being completely free to engage in them.

Immersion also produced a change of status, from "forbidden" to "permitted"[37] in the case of the removal of ritual impurity in the lives of the Israelites, especially women. In the case of the transformative rite of proselyte immersion, it also represented a forensic change of status in which a Gentile actually became a Jew.[38] What one was after immersion was different from what he or she had been prior to immersion. For this reason, the practice was also used in the consecration of priests, the coronation of kings, and the elevation of individuals to other offices both civil and religious.

Proselyte Baptism

By the time of Jesus, immersion had become central to one of the major applications of the *mikveh* tradition. In this case, Gentile converts to the nation of Israel and to the religion of the Jewish people were incorporated into the nation and the people by means of immersion in the *mikveh*.[39] This tradition began to develop at the time when the Jewish people responded to God's instruction through Isaiah that they were to be his witnesses to the nations. In

---

[33] Haviva Ner-David, *Life on the Fringes: A Feminist Journey Toward Traditional* (Elmwood Park, NJ: JFL Publishing, 2000), p. 184.

[34] The Hebrew word טֻמְאָה (*tumah*) means "to become impure." When applied to women *tumah* referred to the state of ritual impurity that is associated with menses. It never implied that any physical impurity was associated with menses. *Tumah* is also thought to mean "entombed." The idea of "entombed" means that a person is blocked or unable to participate in holy things.

[35] The Hebrew word טָהֳרָה (*taharah*) means "to be transparent or clean." It is "purification," freedom from ritual impurity. In the *taharah* state, one is said to have the ability to manifest spirituality as defined in the Torah.

[36] Wendy Blumfield, *Life After Birth: Every Woman's Guide to the First Year of Motherhood* (Shaftesbury, UK: Element Books, Ltd., 1992), p. 192.

[37] This was the case with a wife who after menses immersed in the *mikveh*. After being "forbidden" to her husband since the onset of menses, she was thereafter "permitted" to him so that they could engage in ritually pure sexual intercourse.

[38] Ovadiah Bertinoro, *The Mishnah: A New Translation* (Brooklyn, New York: Mesorah Publications, Ltd., 1979), p. 83. Also, Michael Kaufman, *Love, Marriage, and Family in Jewish Law and Tradition* (Northvale, NJ: Jason Aronson, 1996), p. 197.

[39] Larry R. Helyer, *Exploring Jewish Literature of the Second Temple Period: A Guide for New Testament Students* (Downers Grove, IL: InterVarsity Press, 2002), p. 480.

order to fulfill this divine commission, the sages established the first missionary effort that eventually came to be described as *proselytizing*.[40] Through proselytizing,[41] the Jews actively sought to convert Gentiles to the faith of Israel. Four things were required for the conversion of a proselyte: 1) circumcision, 2) the offering of a sacrifice, 3) being taught the Torah, and 4) immersion in the *mikveh*.[42] These converts were called "proselytes of justice" because they embraced the Torah and committed themselves to holy and just lifestyles.[43]

In second-temple times, the act of immersing oneself in the *mikveh* completed the conversion process. The moment that converts broke the plane of the water after they had fully immersed themselves, they experienced a legal change of status. Until that time, they had been Gentiles. At that moment, however, they became Israelites. In the water of the *mikveh,* they had experienced death, burial, and resurrection. They became dead to what they had been, and they were made alive unto a new identity as Israelites. Some sages even taught that a Gentile who was converted by being immersed in the *mikveh* became "like a newborn child,"[44] completely separated from his Gentile past.

Around the time of the first century and beyond, some debate arose among the rabbis as to whether immersion in the *mikveh* could actually serve as a substitute for circumcision in the case of adult male proselytes to Judaism. Even in the late second century, Rabbi Joshua asserted that if a proselyte were immersed but not circumcised, the experience was valid; however, Rabbi Eliezer argued the opposite side of the issue.[45] These positions no doubt reflected what had been an ongoing debate among the sages as to the terms on which Gentiles could become converts to Judaism. It is possible that the views presented in this rabbinic discussion influenced Paul's argument for a waiver of the requirement of circumcision on the Gentiles who were coming to faith in Jesus when he said, "In him you were circumcised with a circumcision not performed by human hands. Your whole self ruled by the flesh was put off when you were circumcised by Christ, having been buried with him in baptism."[46] These views may also have had a major

---

[40] The word *proselytism* comes from the Greek προσήλυτος (*prosélutos*), which is ultimately combination of προς—*pros* ("toward") and ἔρχομαι—*érchomai* ("to come"). In Hebrew, the word for proselytizing, גרות (*gerut*), which means "conversion," is connected with the word גֵּר (*ger*), meaning "stranger," "alien," or "sojourner," which was a clear reference to "Gentiles."

[41] Andreas J. Köstenberger and Peter T. O'Brien, *Salvation to the Ends of the Earth: A Biblical Theology of Mission* (Downers Grove, IL: InterVarsity Press, 2001), p. 254.

[42] Green, *et. al.*, p. 56.

[43] E. House, *Treatise on Infant Church Membership* (Rochester, NY: Wm. Alling & Co: 1835), p. 5.

[44] Babylonian Talmud, *Yeban* 2.

[45] Babylonian Talmud, *Yevamot* 46a.

[46] Colossians 2:11–12. It is clear that Paul equated "circumcision" with "baptism" when he made this declaration.

impact on Peter's declaration to the Jerusalem Council when he argued, "Now therefore why do you put God to the test by placing upon the neck of the disciples a yoke which neither our fathers nor we have been able to bear?"[47] Additionally, they may well have influenced both the statement that James made to the council: "Therefore it is my judgment that we do not trouble those who are turning to God from among the Gentiles,"[48] and the council's decision not to impose circumcision on the Gentiles who were converting to the Christian faith.[49]

John the Baptizer's Immersion

It was into this milieu that John the Baptizer came, preaching the message of repentance and immersing those who did repent in the waters of the Jordan River. John did not somehow dream up the idea of immersion. He was simply following the tradition of his Jewish family and spiritual associates, especially that of the nearby Qumran community which featured continual immersions in the *mikveh* as part of its ceremonial religious exercises. Stephen Wylen is wonderfully accurate when he describes the forerunner of Jesus as "John the Mikvah-man"![50] John purposely positioned himself at the southern end of the Jordan River,[51] just north of Qumran, and began preaching the need for all the people of Israel, not just potential proselytes, to repent and be baptized in order to prepare for the breaking forth of the Kingdom of God.[52]

This location at the ford of the Jordan[53] was the exact place where the Israelites some fifteen centuries earlier had entered the Promised Land.[54] When the newly repentant Jews were led by John into the Jordan River, they were walking back into the river at the same place where their ancestors had come into the land. In this physical demonstration, it was as though they were momentarily abandoning their status as God's Chosen People.

---

[47] Acts 15:10.

[48] Acts 15:20.

[49] Acts 15:28–29.

[50] Stephen M. Wylen, *The Jews in the Time of Jesus* (Mahwah, NJ: Paulist Press, 1996), p. 90.

[51] Scripture describes this location by saying, "These things were done in Bethabara beyond Jordan, where John was baptizing" (John 1:28). The word *Bethabara* means "House of the Ford." This was the village situated near the junction of the Jordan River and Wadi el-Kharrar, just five miles north of the place where the Jordan empties into the Dead Sea. It was the place where the Israelites had passed through the Jordan River centuries before that time.

[52] Matthew 3:2.

[53] John J. Rousseau, *Jesus and His Word: An Archaeological and Cultural Dictionary* (Minneapolis, MN: Augsburg Fortress Press, 1995), p. 183.

[54] Robert Mimpriss, *The Gospel History of Our Lord's Life & Ministry* (London, England: Thomas Varty Educational Depository, 1842), p. 93.

Then, when they turned around, immersed themselves in the waters of the river, and returned to the land, it was as though they had been reborn into the covenant of God. Because the Hebrew word for repentance, *teshuvah*, means "to turn around," the Israelites' physical act demonstrated graphically the repentance that were experiencing spiritually. Clearly, then, "John's baptizing in the Jordan and his ministry in the wilderness evoke the exodus-conquest tradition of Israel's beginnings."[55] It was a demonstration that was pregnant with meaning to all of the Jews who came to be immersed in John's baptism.

In this physical demonstration of the Hebrew concept of repentance, those Israelites who came to John's baptism were reenacting their father Abraham's experience that had been foundational to the Hebrew family from which they were descended. Abraham had been a Babylonian by birth and a Syrian by nationality: he was as Gentile as it was possible to be. However, at the moment when he crossed over the Euphrates River in faithful obedience to God's command for him to leave his own country, Abraham became the first Hebrew.[56] Crossing over (actually through) the waters of the Euphrates was the physical act that demonstrated Abraham's faith, his absolute trust in God's instructions. When he crossed over the Euphrates, Abraham the Gentile became Abraham the Hebrew. In similar fashion, the Jews who experienced John's baptism demonstrated by the physical act of immersing themselves in Jordan and returning to the Promised Land that they were repenting and renewing for themselves the covenant of faith that God had established with Abraham, the foundation of the kingdom.

John, then, took the *mikveh* experience of Israel out of the ceremonial immersion pools and returned it to the Jordan River for the purpose of making a graphic illustration. God wanted repentance, the turning of the hearts of the people back to God. Only those who manifest these spiritual qualities had demonstrated the true fruit of repentance and were worthy of immersion as an outward sign of the inward grace that they had experienced.[57]

You Must Be Born Again

In his immortal encounter with Nicodemus, Jesus said, "Except a man be born again, he cannot see the kingdom of God." The pious Israelite

---

[55] Leland Ryken, James C. Wilhoit, and Trember Longman III, eds., *Dictionary of Biblical Imagery* (Downers Grove, IL: InterVarsity Press, 1998), 73.

[56] The Hebrew word for *Hebrew*, *ivri* (עִבְרִי), comes from two words, 1) *avar* (עָבַר), which means "to cross over" and 2) *eber* (עֵבֶר) which means "beyond," "across," or "from the other side."

[57] Matthew 3:8.

leader and teacher responded with these logical questions: "How can a man be born when he is old? Can he enter the second time into his mother's womb, and be born?" Then, as Jesus continued his discourse, he finally asked Nicodemus incredulously, "Are you a teacher in Israel and do not understand these things?" Since Nicodemus was a rabbi, he was, no doubt, familiar with the *mikveh* tradition. His problem was not one of understanding the symbolism of water of the *mikveh* as being a womb and immersion as being a rebirth to a new status. It was of understanding that one had to be born of both water and the Spirit in order to enter the kingdom of God.[58] Like all the Jewish people of his time, Nicodemus believed that his natural birth to Jewish parents had placed him in the kingdom of God. Jesus, however, said that being born of the Spirit was to become the deciding factor of kingdom identity.

Abraham had been born again as a Hebrew by crossing the Euphrates. All the Israelites had been born again into a new status as God's nation first by being baptized in the waters of the Red Sea and then by passing through the waters of the Jordan River. Countless Gentile proselytes had been born again as Israelites by emerging from the waters of the *mikveh*. The ultimate induction into the kingdom of God that Jesus was announcing, however, was a spiritual rebirth, not merely a change of physical or sociological status. Water immersion would continue to serve as a sacrament, an outward sign or demonstration of the inward grace that had brought salvation through faith; however, the true work was a purely spiritual rebirth by the Spirit.[59] One had to be born of the Spirit in order to be incorporated into the kingdom. In fact, one had to be born "from above" as the Greek text implies.[60] Being born again is being born from above, begotten by the Word of God unto a hope of eternal life.[61] Being begotten by the Word brings about adoption into the family of the Father.[62]

Baptism in the earliest church continued to follow the *mikveh* tradition of the Jews. Just as those who immersed themselves in a *mikveh* were baptized "in the name" of the witness(es) who observed and certified their

---

[58] The change of status for those who would enter the Kingdom of God was effected not by immersion in water (1 Peter 3:21) but by the infusion of the Holy Spirit so that one was "born from above." The immersion was an outward sign of the inward grace (Colossians 2:12) that had been applied to the believer by the divine imputation of righteousness through faith (Romans 4:24).

[59] 1 Peter 3:21.

[60] The Greek phrase translated "born again" is γεννάω ἄνωθεν (*gennáo ánothen*) which primarily means "to be born from a higher place." Secondarily, it means "born anew" or "born over again."

[61] 1 Peter 1:3.

[62] Romans 8:15.

immersion, believers in Jesus were said to be "baptized in the name of Jesus."[63] This baptism was also carried out in the name (or authority of) "the Father, and of the Son, and of the Holy Spirit" as Jesus had commanded in the Great Commission;[64] however, the focus remained on Jesus because he was the one who had died, resurrected, and ascended to bring forgiveness of sins and eternal life to the believer. In reality, believers were baptized into Jesus himself and, in effect, into his death: "Do you not know that all of us who have been baptized into Christ Jesus have been baptized into his death?"[65] In the process, those "who were baptized into Christ have clothed [themselves] with Christ."[66]

Being born again (from above) also represents a crossing over. Just like Abraham became the first Hebrew by crossing over the Euphrates, believers are translated (carried across) out of the kingdoms of darkness into the kingdom of God's dear Son.[67] Just as the Israelites passed through (crossed over) the Red Sea and their descendants later passed through (crossed over) the Jordan River, so believers pass through the waters of baptism, crossing over into life as a "new creation" in Christ Jesus.[68] This is why spiritual rebirth has always been witnessed by water baptism. The Great Commission requires first faith, then baptism.[69] What has taken place in the realm of the Spirit is graphically demonstrated by the physical act of baptism. Death to sin and resurrection to new life is witnessed by immersion in the water of a *mikveh*.[70]

Ancient Antecedents, Present Reality

Both the spiritual rebirth and water baptism are important for believers. Christian understanding of the experiences of rebirth and baptism is expanded exponentially when both experiences are returned to the Hebraic

---

[63] Paul also referred to this tradition when he addressed the division in the Corinthian church by saying, "Were you baptized in the name of Paul?" (1 Corinthians 1:13). For Christian baptism, the only witness who was important was Jesus; therefore, Christian baptism was performed "in the name of the Father, Son, and Holy Spirit" (Matthew 28:19), with the focus on Jesus: "Repent, and each of you be baptized in the name of Jesus Christ for the forgiveness of your sins" (Acts 2:38). Because the Christians understood that the death, burial, and resurrection of Jesus had freed them from sin, they recognized their immersion as having been "in the name of Jesus."

[64] Matthew 28:19.

[65] Romans 6:3.

[66] Galatians 3:27.

[67] Colossians 1:13.

[68] 2 Corinthians 5:17; Galatians 6:15.

[69] Mark 16:16.

[70] Richard Ingham, *A Handbook on Christian Baptism* (London, England: E. Stock Publishers, 1871), p. 104.

matrix from which they emerged in the ministry of John the Baptist, Jesus, and the apostles. Both are established on a solid foundation of faith that was established in God's dealings with his Chosen People in history. Establishing the context of apostolic teaching maintains its continuity with the ongoing dealings of God with his people in history. It confirms the understanding of a God who never changes,[71] of a Jesus who is the "same yesterday, and today, and forever."[72] It also provides a foundation for present experience by helping believers understand today what was actually practiced by Jesus and the apostles in the earliest church.

Christian rebirth and baptism are solidly anchored in the faith traditions of the ancient Israelites. There is continuity between God's dealings with Abraham and his descendants and the completed work that Jesus accomplished through his own death, burial, and resurrection. Christian believers are privileged to share in the experience of Jesus because they are immersed into his death[73] through the baptism of repentance[74] which is then witnessed by baptism in water. Just as their Master was buried and resurrected, so they are buried with him in baptism and are resurrected to eternal life. By his grace, they have passed over from the dominion of darkness into the kingdom of God's dear Son. Baptism, then, "associates the believer with a historical event, the death and burial of Jesus the Christ."[75] The act of baptism is, therefore, a virtual anamnesis of the pivotal events on which all of Christian faith hinges: "Christ has died, Christ has risen, and Christ is coming again."

Baptism, then, is not an innovative practice that was created by John and appropriated by Jesus and his apostles for an initiation rite into the Christian faith. It was, instead, the perpetuation of the long-standing Jewish immersion tradition that had rich symbolism of new life for the Jewish people. As a consequence of this legacy that Christianity inherited from biblical and Second-Temple Judaism, millions of Christians through the centuries have experienced the graphic physical demonstration of the spiritual resurrection that occurred in their lives when, believing upon the Lord Jesus Christ, they were saved from their sins and inherited the promise of eternal life.[76]

Baptism: Christian fruit—Jewish root.

---

[71] Malachi 3:6; James 1:17.
[72] Hebrews 13:8.
[73] Romans 6:3.
[74] Mark 1:14.
[75] Frank J. Matera, *Romans* (Grand Rapids, MI: Baker Academic, 2010), p. 150.
[76] 1 John 2:25.

CHAPTER 6

COMMUNION

Communion, or the Lord's Supper as it is called in many denominations and congregations,[1] has long been one of the most sacred celebrations in the Christian church, a demonstration of the faith of believers in the efficacy of the shed blood of Jesus, their Lord and Savior. In many churches, it is considered to be more than a simple memorial,[2] for it is viewed as a sacrament, an outward sign of inward grace[3] or even a visible means of grace.[4] Throughout Christian history, in one way or another, believers have joined together in groups both small and large to celebrate the communion of the body and blood of Jesus by sharing bread and wine,[5] just as their Lord directed them when he instituted this celebration on the final night of his human life on earth.[6] This memorial that has been central to virtually all Christian communities across the annals of time was not, however, completely original to Jesus or his disciples. Instead, it emerged in complete continuity with the Jewish community and the worship tradition in which Jesus and the apostles lived their lives: biblical and Second-Temple Judaism.

Communion joins baptism as the only liturgical exercises that Jesus specifically instructed his disciples to observe, and Communion was the only recurring memorial ceremony that Jesus enjoined upon his disciples. In fact, Communion was designed from its beginning to celebrate the only event in the life of Christ that he instructed believers to remember. Jesus never directed

---

[1] In 1 Corinthians 11:20, the memorial remembrance of the death of Jesus in the form that he commanded is termed "the Lord's supper." In 1 Corinthians 10:16, it is called "communion," a translation of the Greek word κοινωνία—*koinonía* ("sharing").

[2] Harmon L. Smith, *Where Two or Three Are Gathered: Liturgy and the Moral Life* (Eugene, OR: Wipf & Stock Publishers, 1989), p. 64.

[3] Charles Henry Wright and Charles Neil, eds., *A Protestant Dictionary* (London, England: Hodder and Stoughton, 1904), p. 654.

[4] Ralph L. Underwood, *Pastoral Care and the Means of Grace* (Minneapolis, MN: Augsburg Fortress Press, 1993), p. 128. Also Thomas A. Langford, *Reflections on Grace*, Philip A. Rolnick and Jonathan R. Wilson, eds. (Eugene, OR: Wipf & Stock, 2007), p. 45.

[5] Many Christian congregations have preferred to use grape juice rather than wine in their celebration of Communion. Scripture does not specify or restrict the "cup" as being either wine or grape juice.

[6] 1 Corinthians 10:16: "The cup of blessing that we give thanks for, is it not a sharing in the blood of Christ? The bread that we break, is it not a sharing in the body of Christ?" (HCSB).

his disciples to remember either his birth or his resurrection.[7] He did, how-ever, command them to remember his death by saying, "This do in re-membrance of me."[8] Of course, "in the New Testament situation, it was impossible to commemorate the death of Jesus without commemorating His resurrection also, or without commemorating His death in the light of His res-urrection,"[9] because, without the resurrection of Jesus, his death would have been of no eternal consequence. As Paul said, however, "because Christ our Passover has been sacrificed for us . . . therefore let us observe the festival."[10]

Significantly, then, from the very earliest of church history, Christians have been found faithfully fulfilling their Lord's imperative by sharing bread and wine in remembrance of the death of Jesus. Communion has been the one continuing exercise that has united Christians in a visible and physical act of worship that has had some degree of continuity in virtually every corporate expression of Christian faith. These words of instruction from the apostle Paul concerning the celebration of Communion have echoed to all succeeding Christian generations, underscoring to them the importance of celebrating Communion: "As often as you eat this bread and drink from this cup, you proclaim the Lord's death until he comes."[11] Be-lievers of all nations have been invited to the Lord's Table to share in the Communion of Christ.

The Meaning of Communion

The word *communion* is derived from the Latin word *communio*, which means "sharing in common." *Communio* corresponds to the Greek word κοινωνία (*koinonía*),[12] which means "fellowship" in the context of "sharing." In ancient Greek, *koinonía* meant "the unbroken fellowship between the gods and men." It also meant "a sense of brotherhood."[13] In the context of

---

[7] The celebrations of the birth and resurrection of Jesus in which Christians regularly engage were not enjoined upon the Christian community by either Jesus or the apostles. While such celebrations are commendable when they direct all honor to the incarnate and resurrected Christ, the one practice that Jesus requested of his disciples was that they celebrate Passover in remembrance of his death. This command was echoed specifically by Paul in his instructions to Gentile believers in 1 Corinthians 5:7–8: "Christ, our Passover lamb, has been sacrificed. Let us therefore celebrate the festival . . . with the unleavened bread of sincerity and truth."

[8] Luke 22:19.

[9] Jean-Jacques Von Allmen, *The Lord's Supper* (Cambridge, UK: James Clarke & Co., 2002), p. 25.

[10] 1 Corinthians 5:7.

[11] 1 Corinthians 11:26, ISV.

[12] In ancient Greek society, the word *koinonia* was applied to fellowship among friends and relationship with a deity, as well as to a community.

[13] Colin Brown, ed., *The New International Dictionary of the New Testament* (Exeter, UK: Paternoster Press, 1975), pp. 291–292. Also, Heidi Campbell, *Exploring Religious Community Online: We Are One in the Network* (New York: Peter Lang Publishing, 2005), p. 31.

its Greek antecedent, the word *communion* can be said to be a means of demonstrating the fellowship of Christians with God and with other Christians. The word *communion*, therefore, "expresses one of the deepest truths about the church, namely that it is *koinonía*, a sharing of the common life of the body of Christ, the church. . . . Of this *koinonía* holy communion is the most conspicuous and pregnant sign."[14] As Francis Moloney has defined it, "Communion is a common union, many partaking of one thing wherein they do agree."[15] The ceremony manifests first the "common union"[16] of all believers with and in the Messiah and then the common union of all believers with one another in the one body of the Messiah. Eduardus Van der Borght confirms the priority of communion with Christ by noting that in 1 Corinthians 10:16, the word *koinonía* does not signify "the community of church members among themselves" but "is used only for the communion with Christ."[17] The communion of the body, therefore, is first the unity with Christ. It is manifestly true, therefore, that "Holy Communion—Holy Koinonia—is communion with God in Christ and communion with one another."[18]

The King James Version translates the word *koinonía* in 1 Corinthians 10:16 as "communion" when it relates to the Christian experience of sharing or participating in the "blood of Christ" and of the "body of Christ" by receiving bread and wine in the same manner in which the apostles received them from the hand of Jesus during the Last Supper. This was probably done in order to maintain the old ecclesiastical terms that had been used in previous Bible translations.[19] Despite the fact that most translations now render *koinonía* in this passage as "participation" (NIV, ESV), "sharing" (NASB, HCSB, RSV, NJB, CSB), or "fellowship" (ISV), the term *communion* has continued to be used in the Christian church as a means of describing the ceremony that Jesus himself instituted from the elements of his final

---

[14] James D. Crichton, *Christian Celebration: The Mass* (New York: Cassell Publishers, Ltd., 1971), p. 112.

[15] Francis J. Moloney, *A Body Broken for a Broken People: Eucharist in the New Testament* (Peabody, MA: Hendrickson Publishers, 1997), p. 161. Also Samuel Freeman, *The Case of Mixt Communion* (London, England: T. Basset, 1683), p. 27.

[16] The lexical root of the word *communion* is "common union." Kevin W. Irwin, *Models of the Eucharist* (Mahwah, NJ: Paulist Press, 2005), p. 86.

[17] Eduardus Van der Borght, *The Unity of the Church: A Theological State of the Art and Beyond* (Leiden, The Netherlands: Koninklijke Brill, 2010), p. 257.

[18] Roger Greenacre and Jeremy Haselock, *The Sacrament of Easter* (Leominster, UK: Fowler Wright Books, 1995), p. 110.

[19] When King James I of England ordered a new translation of the Scriptures in the common vernacular of the realm, Richard Bancroft, the Archbishop of Canterbury, objected to such a "modern-language" version and succeeded in establishing his own set of rules for the translation of the "Authorized King James Version." The third of his fifteen rules required that the old ecclesiastical terms used in the Bishops' Bible were to be preferred over any new terminology.

Passover celebration in order to establish a continuing remembrance of his death among all of his disciples.

The Purpose of Communion

The primary reason for Christian celebrations of Communion (or the Lord's Supper) is to remember the death of the Lord Jesus "until he comes."[20] The very fact that this remembrance exercise was enjoined upon Christians by their Lord is based on the time-honored Jewish practice of זִכָּרוֹן—*zikkaron*,[21] which involves the remembrance of God's mighty acts in salvation history. This is manifest in the Hebrew verb זָכַר (*zakar*), which means "to remember" and "to make a memorial." It is not enough merely to recall God's acts in history in a momentary or fleeting way. A memorial must be made to those events so that the believer engages in a virtual anamnesis[22] or reenactment of them.[23] As Jean-Jacques Von Allmen says, "The anamnesis is . . . more than a mnemonic ceremony; it is a re-enactment of the event which the celebration commemorates."[24] When Christians celebrate Communion, therefore, it is as though they are re-enacting the events of the Last Supper, figuratively placing themselves in the Upper Room with Jesus and the apostles.

The Jewish people have always been expected to celebrate Passover in a "we-were-there"[25] perspective in which they have envisioned themselves as having been present for the very first Passover that initiated the Exodus from Egypt. God specifically instructed the Israelites, "You shall say to your son, '*We* were slaves to Pharaoh in Egypt, and the LORD brought *us* from Egypt with a mighty hand.'"[26] Throughout their generations, the Israelites were to consider themselves to have been present when the mighty acts of God were manifest, especially when they joined together in celebrations of those events.

---

[20] 1 Corinthians 11:26.

[21] *Rosh Hashanah, t*he Jewish civil New Year that coincides with the biblical Festival of Trumpets, is also called *Yom Hazikaron*, the "Day of Remembrance." Simon Glustrom, *The Language of Judaism* (Lanham, MD: Rowman & Littlefield Publishing, 2004), p. 147.

[22] The word *anamnesis* comes directly into English from the Attic Greek word ἀνάμνησις (*anámnesis*), which means both "reminiscence" and "memorial sacrifice." This is the word that translated the Hebrew word which Jesus used when he instructed his disciples, "Do this in *remembrance* of me" (Luke 22:19, emphasis added).

[23] The Greek word *anamnesis* can also be translated "reenactment." See Nils Dahl, "Memory and Commemoration in Early Christianity," in *Jesus in the Memory of the Early Church* (Minneapolis, MN: Augsburg Press, 1976), pp. 11–29, and Graydon F. Snyder, *First Corinthians: A Faith Community Commentary* (Macon, GA: Mercer University Press, 1992), pp. 157–159.

[24] Von Allmen, p. 24.

[25] God himself introduced this idea in Deuteronomy 29:14–15 when he said, "I am making this covenant, with its oath, not only with you who are standing here with us today in the presence of the LORD our God but also with those who are not here today."

[26] Deuteronomy 6:21.

"The divine voice calls on us to remember and to celebrate, the forms come about through us and evolve throughout our history," says Arthur Green.[27]

In the same manner in which their Jewish counterparts celebrate Passover, Christians should celebrate Communion not merely as a casual recollection of the death of Jesus and his institution of the memorial of Communion. Whether in sacramental tradition where Communion is thought to reenact the death of Jesus[28] or in various other traditions where it is seen as a reenactment of the Last Supper,[29] the celebration of the sacrifice of Jesus should maintain the Jewish tradition in which it was instituted by being perceived as a memorial of sharing in the death of Christ. A balanced, Hebraic approach to the anamnesis of Communion can avoid the extremes in which, on the one hand, Communion is exalted as a necessary continuing repetition of Calvary or, on the other hand, is downgraded to the status of a purely sentimental "memorial meal."[30] The key is to find the safe middle ground between the polarized extremes.

Harmon Smith made a wise observation about Communion when he said, "We do not celebrate the Holy Communion in order now to remember Jesus in the sense that we think of him, reflect on him, or allow our minds to conjure an image of him. . . . To remember Jesus is not something we do, but something that is done to and for us by the one who is remembered."[31] Ralph McMichael details the nature of such intimate communion with Christ: "This remembrance is not an exercise in keeping a distance from him,

---

[27] Arthur Green, *Radical Judaism: Rethinking God and Tradition* (New Haven, CT: Yale University Press, 2010), p. 26.

[28] Anne-Claire Mulder, *Divine Flesh, Embodied Word: Incarnation as a Hermeneutical Key to a Feminist Theologian's Reading of Luce Irigaray's Work* (Amsterdam, The Netherlands: Amsterdam University Press, 2006), pp. 58–59. Mulder notes that the original conceptualization of Communion as an anamnesis was developed in the sense of an act of remembrance "of Jesus' life, visions and death" which was "oriented towards the future, towards a salvation in the future when the kingdom of God would be realised." She notes the subsequent development in church tradition when the concept of anamnesis came to focus on the event of the past and became "a mimesis or repetition, especially a repetition of the crucifixion." Eventually, the Catholic Eucharist came to be viewed by many as, in effect, a perpetuation of the crucifixion. See Christoph Schönborn, *Living the Catechism of the Catholic Church: The Sacraments* (San Francisco, CA: Ignatius Press, 1996), p. 31. Schönborn says, "Through the Eucharistic sacrifice the sacrifice of the Cross is perpetuated." While in Catholic tradition, the Eucharist was believed to be a "pledge of the glory to come," its focus remained on the crucifixion.

[29] Graydon F. Snyder, "The Architecture of Death and Resurrection," in Warren Lewis and Hans Rollmann, eds., *Restoring the First-Century Church in the Twenty-First Century* (Eugene, OR: Wipf and Stock Publishers, 2005), p. 121. Snyder translates the words of Paul in 1 Corinthians 11:24–26 in this manner: "And when he had given thanks, he broke it (the bread) and said, 'This act (of breaking bread) is [creates] my body for you. Do this (breaking of bread) as a reenactment [of the Last Supper] with me.' In the same way he took the cup also, after supper, saying, '(The act of drinking from) this cup creates the new covenant through my blood. Do this, as often as you drink it, as a reenactment [of the Last Supper] with me.'"[24] This rendering obviously involves a great deal of interpolation.

[30] Von Allmen, p. 24.

[31] Smith, p. 64.

locating him in the alien past. It is the way to be present with him in his history and his presence in ours."[32] Michael Welker observes that "in holy communion the risen and exalted Christ is present! With him, the reconciliation of human beings with God is present, and the reconciliation of humans among themselves becomes effective."[33] In reality, the primary purpose of Communion, therefore, is "intimate communion with Christ"[34] who said to all believers, "He who eats my flesh and drinks my blood abides in me, and I in him."[35]

Anthony C. Thiselton captures the essence of the purpose of the Communion anamnesis of remembrance and reenactment. The remembrance of Christ's death through communion first "retains the biblical aspect of a self-involving remembering in gratitude, worship, trust, acknowledgment, and obedience," he says.[36] Then, it also "carries with it the experience *of* "being 'there' in identification with the crucified Christ who is also 'here' in his raised presence."[37] Then, it embraces "a self-transforming retrieval of the founding event of the personal identity of the believer (as a believer) and the corporate identity of the church (as the Christian church of God)."[38] Finally, Communion features "a looking forward to the new 'possibility' for transformed identity opened up by the eschatological consummation."[39]

Paul specifically noted that the ceremony of Communion enables every believer to remember in the most powerful manner possible: "For whenever you eat this bread and drink this cup, you proclaim the Lord's death until he comes."[40] This reenactment proclamation is what Herman Wegman had in mind when he said, "To remember was 'looking towards the future', towards the time of the Messiah and towards the time of the kingdom of God."[41] Inherent in the Communion exercise, therefore, is the kingdom expectation, the remembrance and expectation of the time when Jesus has promised to celebrate the Passover and Communion with his disciples again in the age

---

[32] Ralph N. McMichael, *Eucharist: A Guide for the Perplexed* (New York: T & T Clark International, 2010), p. 129.
[33] Michael Welker, *What Happens in Holy Communion?* (Grand Rapids, MI: Wm. B. Eerdmans Publishing Co., 2000), p. 87.
[34] Schönborn, p. 34.
[35] John 6:36.
[36] Anthony C. Thiselton, *The First Epistle to the Corinthians: A Commentary on the Greek Text* (Grand Rapids, MI: Wm. B. Eerdmans Publishing Co., 2000), p. 880, author's emphasis.
[37] Thiselton, p. 880, author's emphasis.
[38] Thiselton, p. 880, author's emphasis.
[39] Thiselton, p. 880, author's emphasis.
[40] 1 Corinthians 11:26.
[41] Wegman in Mulder, pp. 58-59.

to come.[42] The Master's promise is clear: "I tell you, I will not drink from this fruit of the vine from now on until that day when I drink it new with you in my Father's kingdom."[43] Interestingly, the declarations Jesus made concerning the kingdom were made in the context of the "Jewish expectation of the *eschaton*, the end of the world, included the hope of a great Messianic Banquet with the Messiah."[44]

Ancient Biblical Antecedents

Though Communion has assumed many forms and has been celebrated in various manners, the core of this ceremony was not entirely original to Jesus or the apostles or the Christian church. It is rooted in aspects of ancient celebrations that were carried out first by the Hebrews, then by the Israelites, and finally by the Jewish people long before the advent of Christ. The sharing of bread and wine in a religious ceremony, both in public collective assemblies and in the privacy and intimacy of the family, predated even the giving of the Torah. In fact, this practice is traceable at least to the time when Abraham brought to Melchizedek, the priest-king of Salem, the tithe of the resources that he had gained during his rescue of Lot. In this spiritual exercise of tithing, Melchizedek, priest of God Most High, "brought out bread and wine"[45] and proceeded to bless Abraham, while also blessing the Lord.[46] Melchizedek's action was more than a mere social convention in which the priest was demonstrating his generosity and hospitality toward Abraham. What he did was clearly a religious exercise that involved worship that was extended to God and blessing that was given to Abraham.

The actions of Melchizedek were a foretaste of what would happen two millennia later when Jesus, a descendant of Abraham, had finished his commission as a prophet and Messiah among the Israelites and was about to assume the role of the High Priest seated at the right hand of God.[47] Jesus was the fulfillment of the promise of Melchizedek, especially when he ascended to heaven and became the "priest forever according to the order of

---

[42] In Luke 22:15, Jesus said of Passover, "I have eagerly desired to eat this Passover with you before I suffer. For I tell you, I will not eat it again until it finds fulfillment in the kingdom of God." Also, in Mark 14:25, Jesus said of Communion, "I will not drink again from the fruit of the vine until that day when I drink it new in the kingdom of God."

[43] Matthew 26:29, NIV.

[44] William M. Ramsay, *The Layman's Guide to the New Testament* (Louisville, KY: John Knox Press, 1981), p. 247.

[45] Genesis 14:18.

[46] Genesis 14:19–20.

[47] Hebrews 8:1; 10:12.

Melchizedek,"[48] the one of whom King David had specifically prophesied.[49] It was only natural, therefore, that Jesus would have used the same elements that Melchizedek used in his blessing of Abraham to institute the remembrance ceremony of Communion that would extend the Abrahamic blessing of faith to millions of believers. When Jesus blessed the heavenly Father for the bread and wine and instituted Communion, he was, therefore, continuing the Hebraic tradition that had been handed down generationally from at least the time of Abraham.

After the giving of the Torah at Mount Sinai, the Israelites also used bread and wine as central elements in their religious celebrations, two of which were to be foundational to the Communion remembrance practice that Jesus initiated. The first of these antecedents to Communion was the Passover (*Pesach*) festival wherein the Israelites celebrated their exodus from Egypt on each anniversary of the first Passover precisely as God had commanded them in Scripture.[50] The celebration was carried out, as it is today, in the context of the Jewish home. This practice continued in the earliest church with the celebration of Passover and the "breaking of bread" from house to house—the exercise of communal meals and the celebration of Communion in that context.

By the time of Christ, all the Jewish people, including Jesus and the apostles, were sharing bread and wine[51] in their Passover Seder.[52] The unleavened bread (*matzah*) was called the "bread of affliction"[53] because it represented the suffering of the Israelites in Egyptian slavery. The wine represented the blood that had been shed in Egypt and the blood of the paschal lamb. Bread and wine became even more central to the Jewish Passover celebration when the destruction of the temple in 70 AD made it impossible for the Israelites to kill and consume the Passover lamb. First Jesus and then his disciples celebrated Passover annually along with the others of their Jewish families and communities during this time. It was at Jesus' final commemoration of Passover that the Master took the "bread of affliction" and the wine and introduced a new memorial that would prompt his disciples to

---

[48] Hebrews 7:17.

[49] Psalm 110:4.

[50] Exodus 12:1–27; Numbers 9:1–6.

[51] Originally, only three elements were required for the celebration of Passover: roasted lamb, unleavened bread, and bitter herbs (Exodus 12:8). By the time of Jesus, however, wine had been added to the ceremony, including the use of four cups of wine to symbolize the four aspects of the deliverance from Egypt. For details on this development, see John D. Garr, *Passover: The Festival of Redemption* (Atlanta, GA: Golden Key Press, 2013).

[52] The Hebrew word *seder* means "order"—in this case, the recognized order or liturgy for celebrating the Passover in each Jewish home.

[53] Deuteronomy 16:3.

remember his death and their deliverance from the bondage of sin. Communion, therefore, is solidly rooted in the Passover remembrance which foreshadowed the sacrifice of the Paschal Lamb for the sins of the whole world.

The second antecedent to Communion was the weekly Sabbath (*Shabbat*) meal which also featured these same time-honored elements in its celebration—bread and the wine. As the *Erev Shabbat* (evening of the Sabbath) unfolded on Friday evening in every observant Jewish household, bread was broken and consumed, and wine was shared by the members of the family. Various blessings of praise were said to God, and blessings were spoken over family members[54] and finally for the meal after it had been eaten.[55] Since Jesus was Lord of the Sabbath, he did precisely as God had commanded and "remembered" the Sabbath, celebrating the holy day every week in remembrance of the fact that God had created the earth in six days and had rested on the seventh day[56] as well as in remembrance of the fact that God had delivered the Israelites, his ancestors, from Egypt.[57] It was not revolutionary, therefore, that Jesus chose to use these same elements that were employed in the family *Shabbat* observance when he instituted the celebration of Communion. In doing so, he transformed both the Passover and *Shabbat* celebrations into remembrances of his death and its atoning efficacy[58] and of the peace and divine rest that come through faith in his name.[59]

Among the earliest Christian believers, therefore, Communion was immediately established as a very central exercise of faith. "This was completely natural, because in the beginning the Church was entirely Jewish, and they saw, in Holy Communion, the completion of the Exodus from Egypt. . . . Thus the reality of the Atonement was celebrated time after time, and through Communion it was placed before the believers in a tangible

---

[54] These blessings included the blessing of the husband for his wife and the blessing of the parents for their children.

[55] The *Birkat ha-Mazon* was the blessing that was carried out at the end of the Sabbath meal in obedience to God's commandment: "When you have eaten and are satisfied, you shall bless the LORD your God for the good land which he has given you" (Deuteronomy 8:10). This contrasts with most Christian meal blessings which take place before the meal is eaten.

[56] The first giving of the Ten Commandments required the Israelites to "remember the Sabbath" because "in six days the LORD made the heavens and the earth . . . but he rested on the seventh day" (Exodus 20:11).

[57] The second giving of the Ten Commandments enjoined remembrance of the Sabbath upon the Israelites because "you were slaves in Egypt and God brought you out" (Deuteronomy 5:15).

[58] When John the Baptizer saw Jesus coming to his immersion ritual at the Jordan River, he said, "Behold the Lamb of God who takes away the sins of the world," making a clear reference to the Passover lamb (John 1:29).

[59] In Matthew 11:28, Jesus said, "Come to me, all who labor and are heavy laden, and I will give you rest." Jesus was the *Sar Shalom* (Prince of Peace) who brought divine rest from human restlessness by destroying the power of sin.

form."[60] At least to some degree, therefore, virtually every Christian congregation or community in the world that celebrates Communion shares in a rich and inspiring legacy which was birthed from the matrix of biblical and Second Temple Judaism and has been passed down to all succeeding generations of faithful Christian believers. Indeed, "the ancient ceremonies which the church observed . . . [were] borrowed from the Jews," for "Jesus Christ and his apostles [never] thought fit to abolish them or substitute new ones in their room."[61]

When Jesus Instituted Communion

When Jesus instituted Communion, it was in the context of his final Passover celebration. He had specifically said to his disciples, "I have earnestly desired to eat this Passover with you before I suffer."[62] When the Passover season approached, Jesus, as a dutiful son of Israel, instructed Peter and John to "go and make preparations for us to eat the Passover." He even described the provision that the Father had made in advance for his final Passover celebration: "Go into the city, and a man carrying a jar of water will meet you. Follow him. Say to the owner of the house he enters, 'The Teacher asks: Where is my guest room, where I may eat the Passover with my disciples?' He will show you a large room upstairs furnished and ready. Make the preparations for us there."[63] Jesus established Communion, therefore, by using elements of the traditional Passover meal that his disciples had prepared. The Last Supper, then, was not just a final—and casual—meal for Jesus or the apostles. It was both an old and a new Passover celebration!

The method of the Passover observance had been given in general terms in the Torah itself;[64] however, Israel's sages had expanded upon this outline to establish a *seder* (order) for celebrating the festival. This was a part of the oral tradition that had been passed down from generation to generation in the Israelite and Jewish communities. By the time of the second temple, most of the celebration that is currently practiced by the Jewish people was already in place, at least in some rudimentary form. A generation before the time of Jesus, Hillel, one of Israel's greatest sages, affirmed the biblical premise that only three things were required for the proper celebration of Passover: the Passover lamb (*pesach*), the bitter herbs (*maror*), and the unleavened bread

---

[60] Ulf Ekman, *Take, Eat: A Book on Holy Communion* (Uppsala, Sweden: Livets Ords Förlag, 2012), p. 3.
[61] House, pp. 6–7.
[62] Luke 22:15.
[63] Luke 22:8, 10–12, NASB, NIV.
[64] Exodus 12:8; Numbers 9:1.

(*matzah*).[65] This teaching was reinforced by Hillel's disciple Gamaliel, a contemporary of Jesus, who was Paul's teacher. By the time of Jesus, other elements of celebration, including the use of wine, had also been added to the traditional order; however, these three elements remained the core of the annual remembrance of Passover.

From the evidence of the Gospel accounts, Jesus and his disciples celebrated the Passover by following the order that was traditional to their time. The Last Supper was not just a casual gathering that Jesus used for the spontaneous introduction of a totally new ceremony that would be called the "Lord's Supper" or "Communion." It was a careful exercise in the fulfillment of the divine commandment to celebrate Passover by remembering the greatest work that had been accomplished until that time in salvation history. Into this remembrance, Jesus injected an outline for celebrating the coming event that would be the greatest divine work in all of human history, the death (and subsequent resurrection) of the Son of God. Because Jesus was a Torah-observant Jew, he celebrated Passover in conformity with the norm for celebrating the festival in that time, the sages' *Seder*.

As they ate the Passover meal, Jesus and his disciples likely reclined around a triclinium, a somewhat u-shaped table or a u-shaped arrangement of couches.[66] This was in keeping with the tradition that Passover celebrants were not slaves, who sat or stood while eating, but freemen, nobles who in that day ate while reclining and leaning on one elbow. To begin the Passover, as was the case with all Jewish celebrations, Jesus would have spoken the *Kiddush Berakhah* (sanctification blessing), thereby sanctifying the occasion.[67] He would have raised the cup of the fruit of the vine, saying, "Blessed are you, O LORD our God, King of the universe, who creates the fruit of the vine."

During the course of the meal, Jesus took the unleavened bread (*matzah*) of the Passover meal and blessed God for the bread by means of the traditional *HaMotzi* blessing,[68] saying: "Blessed are you, O LORD our God, King of the Universe, who brings forth bread from the earth." Then he gave the bread to his disciples, saying, "This is my body which is given [broken] for

---

[65] Based on the Torah description of three elements for Passover observance (*pesach, matzah, and maror*), Hillel even suggested that the three elements should be eaten at the same time "together" (like a sandwich). Lawrence A. Hoffman and David Barrow, eds., *My People's Passover Haggadah: Traditional Texts, Modern Commentaries* (Woodstock, VT: Jewish Lights Publishing, 2008), vol. 2, p. 128.

[66] Green, *et. al.*, p. 799.

[67] Luke 22:17. In this account of the Last Supper, Jesus took the cup and gave thanks to God, saying to his disciples, "Take this and share it among you." This was the *Kiddush Berakhah*. This sharing of the cup was not part of the Communion order which Jesus established during and at the end of the Passover when he took the bread and again took the cup and in them established Communion. This is further evidence of the fact that Jesus followed the order (*seder*) of the sages in celebrating Passover.

[68] *HaMotzi* means "brings forth" as in "brings forth bread from the earth."

you."[69] In effect, by partaking of this bread, the disciples were "eating the flesh" of the Son of God as he had instructed them.[70] It is also very significant that Jesus shared the *matzah* with his disciples *during* the meal, not after it. Finally, Jesus again took the cup "after the supper," and said, "This cup which is poured out for you is the new covenant in my blood." This was the "Cup of Redemption," the third of the four cups of the Passover Seder that had become traditional by that time. In this action, Jesus conformed his celebration of the Passover—including its new covenant application—to the tradition of the Jewish people at that time wherein it was understood that after the Paschal lamb had been eaten, no additional food was to be consumed.

It should also be noted that, in conformity with the tradition that had been established by the prophets and sages of Israel, Jesus blessed (praised) God for the bread and the wine, the elements of the Passover. He did not "bless" the bread or the fruit of the vine as is commonly believed in many Christian circles, for neither the bread nor the wine required blessing in order to be "sanctified" for sacred use. They were already inherently "good" because they were part of God's creation which at the beginning of time he had declared to be "very good."[71] The idea that material things need to be "blessed" or "sanctified" in order to become "holy" for sacred use is a product of the influence of Greek dualistic philosophy, including Neoplatonism and Gnosticism, wherein everything material was considered to be inherently evil. This, of course, does not conform to the biblical concept that everything material is "good" because God created it as such, a fact that Paul confirms: "I know and am convinced in the Lord Jesus that nothing is unclean in itself."[72] In the record of the Gospels, therefore, Jesus simply took bread, blessed God, and gave it to his disciples and then took the cup, blessed God, and gave it to them.[73]

After breaking and distributing the bread, Jesus also shared the second of the three elements essential to the celebration of Passover: the bitter herbs. He did this by dipping bread in the bitter herbs in the company of Judas, demonstrating the bitterness of his betrayal in the house of his friends. The

---

[69] Luke 22:19; 1 Corinthians 11:24.

[70] John 6:53–55.

[71] Genesis 1:31.

[72] Romans 14:14.

[73] Most translations render the text, ". . . [Jesus] took bread and blessed *it.*" The word *it* is interpolated into the text by the translators under the influence of church tradition which asserts that the elements of Communion must be "blessed" by a priest or minister. The word *it*, however, is not in the original text itself. Jesus, therefore, did precisely as his Jewish ancestors and contemporaries did when he blessed God, not the bread or the fruit of the vine.

Master said of his betrayer, "It is the one to whom I will give this piece of bread when I have dipped it in the dish."[74] Even to this day, the Jewish people dip the unleavened bread of Passover first in *maror* (bitter herbs), then in *charoset* (a mixture of nuts, apples, and honey), and finally in a mixture of *maror* and *charoset*.

Next, Jesus and the disciples ate the roasted paschal lamb, the third element essential to the proper celebration of Passover. This was another of the things that his disciples were commissioned to prepare so their Master could eat the Passover that he had so much desired to share with them before his death. Everything was done in conformity with God's Word and with the tradition of the Jewish people.

Finally, after the meal, Jesus took the Cup of Redemption, the third of the four cups that by then had come to be used in the traditional order for Passover by that time, [75] and again blessed God, this time with the traditional *Borei Pri Hagafen* blessing:[76] "Blessed are you, O LORD our God, King of the universe, who creates the fruit of the vine." Then, Jesus enjoined his disciples to drink of the cup. He instructed them to recognize that as they received the fruit of the vine, they were partaking of the cup of the new covenant in his blood—in effect receiving the blood of the Son of God as he had also previously commanded them.[77]

As further proof that Jesus and his disciples were celebrating the Passover when the ordinance of Communion was established, the Gospels note that following their observance, Jesus and the disciples "sang a hymn" before they left the Upper Room."[78] Doubtless, this "hymn" was the second part of the *Hallel*, which was comprised of the Psalms that were sung before the Passover meal (113–114) and the Psalms that were sung after the meal (115–118).[79] Of considerable importance to the disciples was the fact that the *Hallel* included the declaration that "the stone which the builders rejected has become the chief cornerstone."[80] This was a prophecy which Jesus

---

[74] John 13:26.

[75] The four cups correspond to the four declarations of deliverance that God made to the Israelites in Exodus 6:6–7 when he was preparing to free them from Egyptian slavery: 1) the Cup of Sanctification: "I will free you from your oppression"; 2) the Cup of Deliverance (or the Cup of Judgment): "I will delivery you from slavery"; 3) the Cup of Redemption (or the Cup of Blessing): "I will redeem you with an outstretched arm"; and 4) the Cup of Consummation (the Cup of Praise or Redemption): "I will take you as my own people, and I will be your God."

[76] *Pri Hagafen* means "fruit of the vine."

[77] John 6:53–55.

[78] Matthew 26:30.

[79] Craig S. Keener, *The Historical Jesus of the Gospels* (Grand Rapids, MI: Wm. B. Eerdmans Publishing Co., 2009), p. 298. Also, Tosefta, *Sukkah* 3:2.

[80] Psalm 118:22.

confirmed that he had fulfilled in the midst of Israel,[81] and it was one which the apostles used as confirmation of his Messiahship thereafter.[82]

Jesus gave no indication to his disciples that because he would fulfill the Passover on the following day by shedding his blood on the cross of Calvary, there would be no further need for them to continue to observe Passover. Indeed, he gave this injunction: ". . . this do in remembrance of me,"[83] indicating that he was adding to the traditional Passover, not subtracting from it or eliminating all of its prior traditions of observance. Paul further encouraged even Gentile believers with these words, "Therefore, let us observe the festival [Passover] with the unleavened bread of sincerity and truth" because "Christ our Passover has been sacrificed for us."[84]

Jesus expected his disciples to continue the observance of Passover as God had commanded Israel with the provision that as believers in the Messiah, they should thereafter add to it the practice of remembering his death. As further evidence of the importance he attached to the continuing remembrance of Passover, the Master assured his disciples that he himself would one day partake of the elements of Passover "with you in my Father's kingdom."[85]

A New Covenant Liturgy

The order which Jesus established for the celebration of Communion on the night of the Last Supper was apparently passed on to all the believing community by the disciples, for Paul gave specific instructions to the church with the following liturgical formula: "For I received from the Lord that which I also delivered to you: that the Lord Jesus in the night in which he was betrayed took bread; and when he had given thanks, he broke it and said, 'This is my body, which is broken for you; do this in remembrance of me.' In the same way, he also took the cup also after supper, saying, 'This cup is the new covenant in my blood. Do this, as often as you drink it, in remembrance of me.'"[86] Paul's outline for the celebration of Communion was brief and simple. It was intended as a clear order for the celebration that would avoid the introduction of error and even heresy into the practice that was to define Christian community. It did not, however, preclude further liturgical development. Like the Torah commandments for the elements of Passover observance, it outlined the things that were essential to the celebration of the Christian Passover or

---

[81] Matthew 21:42.
[82] Acts 4:11.
[83] Luke 22:15–16, 19.
[84] 1 Corinthians 5:7.
[85] Matthew 26:29; Mark 14:26.
[86] 1 Corinthians 11:23–26.

the Christian family *Shabbat* meal. The entire order was designed to empha-size the Hebraic *zikkaron* dynamic that was to be applied to remembrance of the finished work of Calvary, together with the resurrection and ascension of the Lamb of God and the expectation of the return of the Messiah at the end of the age.[87]

Paul's instructions were given as a corrective to the improper manner in which Communion was then being observed in the Corinthian church. While purporting to celebrate Communion, some of the Corinthian Chris-tians were promoting socio-economic distinctions that were creating class divisions in the community,[88] and some were even drinking wine to excess and becoming drunk![89] In so doing, they were partaking of the Commu-nion "in an unworthy manner," which the apostle said was an act of "sin-ning against the body and blood of the Lord."[90] Paul instructed the Corinthians believers to "examine themselves" before they planned to par-take of the Lord's Supper so that they would be able to discern the body and blood of Jesus in the bread and wine that they consumed. Otherwise, they would bring judgment upon themselves for partaking of the bread and wine in an unworthy manner.[91]

Many subsequent Christian communities have mistakenly extrapolated this text to mean that believers who have imperfections—including sin—in their lives should not celebrate Communion for fear that they might even die if they were to partake of it in an "unworthy" state.[92] This, however, was not the intent of Paul's instructions, which were clearly directed at the "unworthy manner" in which the Corinthians were partaking of Communion and the Passover. This is why he had already argued further that they should "observe the festival [of Passover] with the unleavened bread of sincerity and truth."[93]

Proper order for the celebration of Communion at Passover, the *Shabbat* meal, or any other occasion, therefore, should follow the liturgical outline

---

[87] For a Hebraic Christian liturgy for the celebration of Communion or the Lord's Supper, see John D. Garr, *Passover*, pp. 125–145. The basic elements of this liturgy can be employed in home, prayer and study groups, or Christian assemblies.
[88] 1 Corinthians 11:18–19. By engaging in such divisive actions, the Corinthian Christians were importing the practices of pagan Greek festivals into their own Christian experience.
[89] 1 Corinthians 11:20–21.
[90] 1 Corinthians 11:27.
[91] ! Corinthians 11:27–29.
[92] This inaccurate interpretation of Paul's message has kept untold numbers of Christians from experiencing the blessing of Communion for fear that their faults and failures would bring divine judgment upon them in the form of sickness and even death. The truth is that every human being has sinned and has come short of the glory of God (Romans 3:23) and is, therefore, in need of repentance and renewal. In reality, the open heart of confession and repentance is most easily and securely manifest in the presence of the awesome grace of God through the remembrance practice of Communion.
[93] 1 Corinthians 5:8.

that Paul "received from the Lord" through the witness of the apostles who shared the experience with their Master in his last Passover observance and in their first celebration of Communion in the Lord's Supper. This order is so simple that anyone, including families in their own homes, can follow it. Though this Communion is a divine mystery, there is nothing mysterious about the proper manner and order in which it should be observed in whatever occasion arises where two or more Christians gather for worship.

The Corinthian exercise confirms that Communion was celebrated in communal meals, whether in the context of family or in larger extended-family communities. Just as Jesus had instituted Communion in continuity with the Passover meal, so it continued to be observed in the "table-fellowship" exercises that had been common among the Jewish community from which this practice emerged. Mattias Klinghardt notes that in the earliest development of Christianity, "all Christian communities—in the most diverse areas of mission, with the most diverse theological profiles, from the most diverse backgrounds and traditions, and with a broad spectrum of social backgrounds . . . would gather for a meal."[94] In fact, it was not until the fourth century that "the communion (*koinonia*) of the community no longer consist[ed] of the assembly for a full communal meal."[95] It seems that when the "table fellowship" of the first-century Jewish community was abandoned, Communion became more and more institutionalized.

The Institutionalization of Communion

In the centuries following the death of the apostles, an increasing institutionalization of Christian faith and experience occurred. The biblical holy days and ceremonies that Jesus and the apostles observed were gradually replaced with festivals and practices associated with the Gentile cultures into which Christianity expanded. Simple acts of faith were expanded or replaced and extrapolated into exercises that were (and are) clearly foreign to the faith practices of the first-century Jewish church. Hierarchical episcopacies that were patterned after the leadership dynamics of the Greek and Latin worlds asserted themselves.[96] Even though neither Jesus nor the apostles ever considered themselves to be priests,[97] Christian leaders increasingly arrogated

---

[94] Mattias Klinghardt, quoted in Welker, p. 40.
[95] Klinghardt, in Welker, p. 40.
[96] The appropriation of pagan leadership models into the church included the development of monarchical episcopates in Eastern Christianity (which were patterned after the Greek city-state model of governance) and the papacy in Western Christianity (which was patterned after Rome's emperor system).
[97] As a matter of fact, the apostles continued to recognize the Levitical priesthood until the destruction of the temple rendered it a moot issue.

priestly offices to themselves. Sidlow Baxter was historically and ecclesiologically correct when he argued that "the apostles themselves were *not* priests, but laymen; nor did they ever *become* priests; nor did they ever *appoint* priests to succeed them!"[98] With the emergence of a Christian "priesthood," the ceremonies of earliest Christianity that had been celebrated in the context of family and community were hijacked by and brought under the control of an increasingly powerful clergy. Eventually, Communion itself (the Eucharist) came to be recognized as a means of grace and salvation that could be dispensed only by the clergy. Amazingly, this idea reached such proportions that it came to be enshrined in the concept of sacramentalism,[99] in which the eucharistic action of the priest upon the worshipper was considered to be *ex opere operato*[100] and was, therefore, efficacious regardless as to the attitude, merits, or holiness of either the priest or the communicant![101]

When Communion became the province of the clergy, laypersons participated in the exercise only by being "acted upon," not by acting themselves, as the Israelites had done in both the Sabbath and Passover meals and as earliest Christians had done when they celebrated the expanded fulfillment of their ancestral tradition. As the church became more and more institutionalized, the worship practices of the community were also increasingly institutionalized and ever more tightly controlled. The participative life of earliest Christianity was replaced by performance-based, audience-based liturgical exercises that were eventually restricted exclusively to a professional clergy. The extent of this exclusivity was demonstrated in the fourth-century Christian work, *The Apostolic Constitutions*, which declared with great specificity,

---

[98] J. Sidlow Baxter, *Awake, My Heart: Daily Devotional Studies for the Year* (Grand Rapids, MI: Kregel Publications, 1960), p. 127. Baxter quotes Hebrews 7:24, "But this Priest [Christ], because He continueth ever, hath an unchangeable priesthood," and then he notes that "the Greek word here translated as "unchangeable" ἀπαράβατος (*aparábatos*) really means *intransmissible*, untransferable. That priesthood was never transmitted even to the apostles. It is solitary, inviolable, exclusive, incommunicable" (author's emphasis). The high priestly office of Jesus was never transferred exclusively to the apostles or to other Christian leaders. In fact, all believers—not just leaders but also laity—share equally in the Melchizedek order of priesthood through their direct connection to Jesus, the High Priest. This was the dynamic for the manifestation of priesthood in earliest Christianity. Translocal leaders, congregational leaders, heads of households, and individuals were all considered to be laypersons, and they shared equally in the priesthood of Jesus though the priestly functions that they fulfilled varied according to their role or function.

[99] Sacramentalism is the doctrine which asserts that the sacraments of the church are inherently efficacious and necessary to salvation and that participation in them confers grace. The *Catechism of the Catholic Church* states, "The sacraments are efficacious signs of grace, instituted by Christ and entrusted to the Church, by which divine life is dispensed to us, the visible rites by which the sacraments are celebrated signify and make present the graces proper to each sacrament." See *The Catechism of the Catholic Church*, "Article 2: The Paschal Mystery in the Church's Sacraments," which is posted at the Internet website: http://www.vatican.va/archive/ENG0015/__P35.HTM.

[100] *Ex opere operato* in Latin means "from the work worked."

[101] John F. Nash, *Christianity, the One, the Many: What Christianity Might Have Been and Could Still Become* (Bloomington, IN: Xlibris Corporation, 2007), p. 238.

"Neither do we permit the laity to perform any of the offices belonging to the priesthood; as, for instance, neither the sacrifice [communion], nor baptism, nor the laying on of hands, nor the blessing . . . For such sacred offices are conferred by the laying on of hands of the bishop."[102]

Herman Wegman was right to describe the eventual Catholic expression of Communion thus: "[This] form of anamnesis . . . is in shrill contrast with the memorial/remembrance which the earliest Christian communities experienced together with the Jews from whom they received this."[103] Unfortunately, at least to some degree, the Catholic perspective on Communion also carried over into virtually all other Christian communities. As Hughes Old has noted, "Holy communion is no longer, therefore, *at this point* an act of private devotion; it is the action of the community."[104] And so it is. Virtually every denomination and fellowship within the worldwide Christian community considers Communion to be an act of worship that can be celebrated only in the context of a congregation and under the leadership of a minister or priest. When this perspective is contrasted with the earliest Communion celebration as it was initiated by Jesus and as it continued to be practiced by the apostles, it is clearly in error, for the first-century practice was carried out in the context of family and community and without priestly oversight. After centuries of departure from the way in which it was celebrated in original Christianity, Communion needs to be returned to the matrix from which it emerged. The Hebraic foundations of communion for the design of the anamnesis (*zikkaron*) and its enactment must be restored. This includes both the content of the exercise and the manner in which it is administered.

When to Celebrate Communion

In ecclesiastical history, various perspectives emerged as to when, where, why, and how Communion should be celebrated. In the first-century church, there was no fixed frequency for Communion, though it is said that the believers broke bread from house to house[105] and continued daily in prayers "in the temple" and, as their tradition was, in their own homes.[106] Since the church's Jewish communicants continued to celebrate the Sabbath during the first

---

102 *The Constitutions of the Apostles*, III, X. For the entire text of *The Constitutions of the Apostles*, see R. Wedgwood and William Whiston, *Essay on the Constitutions or Decrees of the Holy Apostles* (London, England: Simpkin, Marshall, and Co., 1851), p. lxvii.
103 Herman Wegman, "De 'komaf' van het liturgisch gedenken. Anamnesegespiegeld aan menselijk ervaren," in *Tijdschrift voor Theologie*, vol. 25, 2 (1985), p. 171, referenced in Mulder, pp. 58–59.
104 Crichton, p. 112.
105 Acts 2:42.
106 Acts 2:46.

decade of the first century, it is possible and perhaps even likely that they engaged in a special weekly corporate celebration of Communion on that day.[107] They would simply have added the exercise which their Lord had commanded them to observe to their daily family meals and family *Shabbat* celebrations.

By the middle of the second century, however, as Sabbath observance was gradually transitioned to Sunday by Gentile Christianity, "the picture is clear: for the community Synaxis, Sunday and Eucharist form a unity as the symbolic celebration of the presence of the Risen Lord amidst his own."[108] Even then, however, the celebration of Communion without priestly oversight continued as laypersons customarily took from the weekly Communion "enough of the blessed gifts for communion during the week."[109] This practice of Communion outside Mass was manifest in "unauthorized" celebrations of communion in prisoners' cells, at funerals, and in private homes that lasted until the seventh century.[110] Despite the proscriptions against private celebrations of Communion that were issued by the Councils of Laodicea (360-390) and Carthage (390), these practices continued at least until 1562 when Session 22 of Trent succeeded in entirely suppressing them in the Western Church.[111]

When the celebration Communion was finally restricted exclusively to the clergy, its timing became an issue. Where there were sufficient numbers of priests, the celebration was often daily and certainly weekly. By the time of the Reformation, the question of the frequency of the celebration of Communion was reconsidered. Some Protestants believed that there should be no celebration of Communion at all. These argued that receiving the preaching of the Word and the operation of the Spirit fulfilled Jesus' instructions that his disciples "eat his flesh and drink his blood"[112] and that any ceremony of Communion was therefore superfluous. In the Reformed tradition of Geneva,

---

[107] It has been suggested that as the earliest church celebrated Communion after midnight on Saturday night when their Sabbath exercise in fellowship, study, and prayer carried over into the evening of the first day of the week. (In biblical times, the evening of the day came before the morning of the day, as in the account of creation in Genesis 1; therefore, the evening of the first day of the week was Saturday night, not Sunday night.) This may have been what was taking place when Paul preached until midnight in Acts 20:8–11 and afterward "broke bread." See Paul F. Bradshaw, *The Search for the Origins of Christian Worship: Sources and Methods for the Study of Early Liturgy* (Charlottesville, VA: The University of Virginia Press, 2002), p. 54. The Quartodecimans, who continued to memorialize Jesus' death on the very day of Passover (Nisan 14), maintained this tradition into the seventh century by celebrating the resurrection by receiving Communion after midnight on the night after Passover. See Robin Knowles Wallace, *The Christian Year: A Guide for Worship and Preaching* (Nashville, TN: Abingdon Press, 2011), p. 48.

[108] Maxwell E. Johnson and John Francis Baldovin, *Between Memory and Hope: Readings on the Liturgical Year* (Collegeville, MN: The Liturgical Press, 2000), p. 78.

[109] Johnson and Baldovin, p. 78.

[110] Johnson and Baldovin, p. 78.

[111] Johnson and Baldovin, p. 79.

[112] John 6:56.

Communion was celebrated only four times a year: Christmas, Easter, Pentecost, and the first Sunday in October. Though John Calvin wanted to have a weekly celebration, it was considered to be too burdensome for those who had become accustomed to celebrating it only once a year.[113] This position may have resulted from the emphasis on preaching over Communion in this tradition in which Calvin said that the celebration of Communion without the preaching of the Word was a "dumb show."[114] Over time, however, many Christian denominations gravitated toward a weekly celebration of Communion.

While various fellowships of Christians have adopted differing approaches to the celebration of Communion, it is clear that the original practice as instituted by Jesus and carried out by the apostles involved "breaking bread from house to house" and doing so whenever the opportunity for praise and worship presented itself. This was done in the context of the family temple (*mikdash me'at*—"miniature temple") either as a part of daily prayers or in the family *Erev Shabbat* celebration. Additionally, Communion was celebrated in the context of the extended family celebrations of the *kahal* (community) that was called in Greek the *ekklesía* (congregation). No priests were present to officiate in the Communion celebration of first-century Christianity because none of the leaders of the church was considered to be a priest. Communion in corporate settings, therefore, was originally a lay exercise in which elders of the community, not priests, served the people.

The bottom line for the frequency and manner of Communion celebration is this: believers may join in remembering the death of Jesus in the way in which he prescribed it at any time and in any family or corporate setting in which they choose to do so. Jesus made it clear that the quorum for Christian worship was "two or three gathered in my name."[115] This makes it possible for families of any size to join in worship in their own family temples (homes) as well as in corporate communities of any size in order to manifest the acts of worship that the Hebrew Scriptures and the Apostolic Writings prescribe, including the celebration of Communion. Christians, therefore, can remember Christ's death by celebrating Communion annually on the day of Passover if they wish, or they may do so quarterly, monthly, weekly, or daily as they see fit. There is simply no biblical requirement for restricting the celebration to any specific time interval. It can be celebrated at

---

[113] Hughes Oliphant Old, *Worship: Reformed According to Scripture* (Louisville, KY: Westminster John Knox Press, 2002), p. 163.

[114] Gordon S. Wakefield, *The Westminster Dictionary of Spirituality* (Louisville, KY: Westminster Press, 1983), p. 65.

[115] Matthew 18:20. The *minyan* (quorum) for Jewish worship was ten people; however, Jesus said the minimum was two.

any time and in any setting where two or more assemble for worship. Whether it be two or three or a million or more, the body of Christ (the church) is fully manifest in each setting where believers join in worship.

Family Communion

The immediate antecedents for Communion in the earliest church were the Passover and *Shabbat* celebrations, both of which were carried out from the beginning primarily, if not exclusively, in the context of family.[116] Sharing bread and wine was always a significant feature in worship in the Jewish home. Because these two elements that were used in Communion were also central to the family *Shabbat* meal that was celebrated in Jewish homes before, during, and after the time of Jesus, it was only natural that the earliest believers shared bread and wine in remembrance of their Lord's death and resurrection. What they were doing was both the Jewish and the Christian thing to do. What they and their ancestors had been doing in the context of their homes was filled with even greater meaning when they recognized in those traditional elements of Hebraic worship the blood and body of Jesus.

Communion can be celebrated daily in the context of family and congregation. No clerical authorization is required, nor is a priest or minister essential for the celebration, for it is not necessary to have someone with the "priestly office" to "bless" and "consecrate" the bread and the fruit of the vine in order for them to be used for sacred purposes. In reality, every believer is a priest, a part of the priesthood of all believers that functions under the authority of the High Priest, Jesus Christ.[117] Parents, therefore, have the liberty to share Communion with their families and friends in the context of their own homes. They have the right to bless the Lord for the provision of bread and wine just as Jewish families have done for centuries and just as Jesus and his apostles did. They are free to engage in formal or informal celebrations of Communion by employing the major principles of the general liturgical order that Paul outlined in 1 Corinthians 11:23–26.

Christians are also free to celebrate Communion in whatever kind of fellowship, congregation, or community in which they have chosen to align themselves and with whatever forms of leadership that they have chosen to

---

[116] When the Passover was initiated, Moses did not command Aaron to sacrifice one lamb for all of Israel or one lamb for each tribe. He instructed each family to encircle the door (thresholds, lintels, and doorposts) of its home with the blood of a lamb and then to eat its own lamb. "Every man shall take a lamb for his family . . . one for each household" (Exodus 12:3, NIV). Only if the family was too small to consume all of the lamb was the lamb to be shared with neighbors. Passover, then, was entirely a family affair.

[117] 1 Peter 2:9.

recognize as being divinely appointed to protect and serve them.[118] Likewise, they are free to use whatever liturgical exercises that they deem to be worthy expressions of worship in the celebration of Communion.[119] Just as there was no monolithic Judaism in the days before, during, and after the time of Jesus, so there is no God-ordained monolithic Christianity. True Christian faith, like Judaism, is founded in the absolute free will of every individual, family, and community to worship God according to the dictates of the conscience within the general parameters that God has established in the Holy Scriptures, and believers can do so with great flexibility as they contextualize those divine principles for their own families, communities, societies, and cultures. This is the amazing pluriformity principle of the Christian faith that Paul advocated and demonstrated in his ministry,[120] and it is the dynamic that liberates believers from legalistic constraints and delivers them into the glorious freedom of the children of God.[121] What is important is not punctilious, legalistic observance, but remembrance of the pivotal events of biblical history, the Exodus from Egypt and the death, burial, resurrection, and ascension of Jesus Christ, *Yeshua HaMashiach*.

The Blessing of Communion

All of God's instructions for remembrance practices are designed to be a blessing to those who celebrate them. This is true of Communion as well. Embedded in Communion are many deep-rooted biblical blessings for those who faithfully and rightfully observe the commandment of Jesus to remember his death until he comes.

First, Communion is one means by which believers can experience the dynamic of incorporating the body and blood of Jesus into the very fiber of their spiritual being.[122] The exercise transcends mere memorialization, for believers are invited by the Lord to discern the body and blood of Jesus in the bread and wine of Communion as they receive those elements. Through personal recognition based on the authority of the Word of God as spoken

---

[118] Leadership is a divinely commissioned dynamic for the Christian church. Leaders are gifted and commissioned by God himself and are then recognized and affirmed by the community in which they are called to serve.

[119] The Communion celebration can range from the most informal to the most formal, from the most spontaneous to the most highly liturgical.

[120] In Romans 14:5, Paul said, "Let everyone be persuaded in his own mind." Respect for the free will of every believer is the antidote to legalism. This is why Paul described his ministry methodology in this way: "I have become all things to all people so that by all possible means I might save some" (1 Corinthians 9:22).

[121] This freedom is a foretaste of the liberty of which Paul spoke in Romans 8:21 that will be fulfilled in the resurrection of the righteous dead.

[122] John 6:54–56.

by Jesus himself, the bread and fruit of the vine become to believers the broken body and the shed blood of Christ.[123]

Second, the celebration of Communion is a perfect time to receive the blessing of divine forgiveness through the confession of sin and the reception of pardon. Those who have sinned should never avoid Communion out of fear that their unworthiness might somehow bring divine judgment upon them. Instead, they should confess their sins to God knowing that "if we confess our sins, he is faithful and righteous to forgive us our sins and to cleanse us from all unrighteousness."[124] Since the wine of Communion demonstrates the blood of Jesus, it is easy to see and understand during Communion that "the blood of Jesus, [God's] Son cleanses us from every sin."[125] It is, therefore, appropriate for believers who are receiving Communion in the context of home, fellowship, or congregation to pray the prayer that Jesus taught his disciples to pray, which in its Lucan version includes the petition, "Forgive us our sins as we forgive those who sin against us."[126]

Third, while Communion focuses so vividly on the broken body and shed blood of Jesus, it is a good exercise for receiving healing for whatever condition, whether mental, emotional, spiritual, or physical, that afflicts the human person. The Psalmist connected the forgiveness of sins with the healing of diseases: "Bless the LORD, O my soul, and forget none of his benefits; who pardons all your iniquities, who heals all your diseases."[127] The benefits (blessings) of God, therefore, specifically include forgiveness and healing. Recognizing and celebrating the divine provision for physical healing was a prominent part of the synagogue liturgy that predated the time of Jesus, for the second benediction of the *Amidah*, the synagogue prayer *par excellence*, declared in praise to God, "You are mighty forever, O LORD. You give life to the dead. You are great to save. . . . You support the falling, and heal the sick." Both Jesus and the apostles spoke this blessing when they worshiped

---

[123] This approach is thoroughly biblical. It avoids the extremes of "transubstantiation" on the one hand (wherein some Christian denominations believe the bread and the wine are actually transubstantiated so that they are no longer bread and wine but are the actual body and blood of Jesus) and the "representation" doctrine on the other hand (wherein other Christian denominations believe the bread and wine merely represent the body and blood of Jesus). The bread and wine are not transubstantiated into the body and blood of Jesus by the act of a priest or celebrant. They remain bread and wine; however, the believer recognizes in these material substances the body and blood of Jesus, and this occurs solely upon the authority of the Word of God in which Jesus said, "This is my body" and "This is my blood." If anything, a *logos*-substantiation occurs so that in the act of eating and drinking, the believer, upon the authority of the Word of God, discerns or recognizes in bread and wine the body and blood of Jesus.
[124] 1 John 1:9.
[125] 1 John 1:7.
[126] Luke 11:4. If one prays the Matthean version, "Forgive us our debts," or "Forgive us our trespasses," the result is the same. "Debts" or "trespasses" in these versions are the same as "sins" in the Lucan version.
[127] Psalm 103:2–3.

in the synagogue. This same language of healing is included in the prophetic ministry of the Messiah: "He was pierced for our transgressions, he was crushed for our iniquities; the chastening of our well-being fell upon him, and by his scourging we are healed."[128] Clearly, Jesus suffered for the healing of every person, body and spirit, so healing is a provision of the atonement. Communion is, therefore, a perfect time to receive both spiritual and physical healing from God.

Time for Restoration

After centuries of raging controversies over the nature, time, and order of Communion, it is surely time for all Christian communities to engage themselves in an effort to recover and restore the original foundations of their faith. Anything that was good enough for Jesus and the apostles is surely good enough for the church today! When Christians begin to understand that their faith is inherently Jewish and that their Lord was and is the Jewish Messiah, they will be convicted of their need for restoration and renewal of the ancient faith once delivered to the saints.[129] They will then discover and renew the Hebraic foundations of their faith—foundations that will empower them with an ever-increasing passion for truth and love for God through his Son Jesus Christ in the power of the Holy Spirit.

Since the death of Jesus, followed by his resurrection, was the pivotal point of salvation history, it, like God's sovereign redemption and deliverance of the Israelites from Egyptian slavery, certainly deserves the continuing "remembrance" of all believers. If God commanded Passover observance under the penalty of excommunication from Israel,[130] he surely expects the remembrance of Passover's fulfillment in Jesus, the Lamb of God, to continue until the Messiah returns to resurrect and clothe all the righteous in immortality. That will be the day when Jesus himself will renew the ceremony that he celebrated with his disciples on the eve of his death by eating the bread and drinking from the cup anew in the Father's kingdom. At that time, everything biblical and Hebraic will be restored, and believers will rejoice in the finished work of Calvary that will be materially demonstrated in the worship experience of Communion. Then, they will celebrate the communion of the body and blood of their Lord with him forevermore.

Communion: Christian fruit—Jewish root.

---

128 Isaiah 53:5.
129 Jude 1:3.
130 Numbers 9:13: "If anyone who is ceremonially clean and not on a journey fails to celebrate the Passover, they must be cut off from their people for not presenting the LORD's offering at the appointed time."

CHAPTER 7

GOSPEL

The Gospel of Jesus Christ has been the signature declaration of Christianity since its inception. "At the heart of the Christian faith stands the gospel of Jesus Christ—the death, burial, and resurrection of Jesus Christ."[1] Indeed, the gospel is summarized succinctly in the liturgical Memorial Acclamation: "Christ has died, Christ is risen, Christ is coming again. Alleluia!"[2] As Emil Brunner has said, "Faith in Jesus Christ constitutes the Christian religion. The entré to and the foundation of the whole Christian faith is 'Christology,' that is, faith in Jesus Christ . . . There has never been any other Christianity than this, in which faith in Jesus the Christ constitutes both its foundation and its central point."[3]

Both Jesus and the apostles declared unequivocally that the Messiah is the foundation on which the community of Christians is built. Jesus established this fact when he began the work of establishing his restored and reformed Jewish community when he said, "It is on this rock[4] that I will build my congregation."[5] Paul repeated and expanded Jesus' declaration, affirming that "the members of God's household" have been "built on the foundation of the apostles and prophets, Christ Jesus himself being the cornerstone,"[6] and declaring that "no man can lay a foundation other than

---

[1] David S. Dockery and Gregory Alan Thornbury, *Shaping A Christian Worldview: The Foundations of Christian* (Nashville, TN: B & H Publishing Group, 2002), p. 68.

[2] To this affirmation might be added the declaration *Christ has come*, for the birth and life of Jesus are as much a part of the gospel as the death, resurrection, and return of the Messiah. Without the virgin birth of Jesus and the sinless life that he lived, his death would have been meaningless, and his resurrection would never have occurred.

[3] Emil Bruner, *The Mediator: A Study of the Central Doctrine of the Christian Faith* (Cambridge, UK: The Lutterworth Press, 1934), p. 232.

[4] The "rock" on which Jesus would build his church was the divine revelation that Peter had received, "You are the Messiah, Son of the living God" (Matthew 16:17). Some have mistakenly thought that the church was built on Peter; however, Jesus said to Peter, "You are *Petros* ("Rock," *m.*), and upon this *petra* ("rock" *f.*), I will build my church." The rock on which the church is built, therefore, is the *petra*, the revelation of Jesus as Messiah and Lord, not *Petros*, Simon Peter.

[5] Matthew 16:18, ISV.

[6] Ephesians 2:20.

the one which is laid, which is Jesus Christ."[7] Larry Hurtado says that it is for this reason that "Jesus' own activity is . . . the *arche*, the origin and foundation of the gospel, and thereby the authoritative pattern for his followers called to proclaim the gospel in his train."[8] If the church does not understand that its one foundation is Jesus, it cannot help but crumble into decay and ruin.

It is entirely interesting that both Jesus and the apostles used the term *gospel* to describe the message about the breaking forth of the kingdom of God in the person and ministry of the Son of God. Since the word *gospel* was used in antiquity to announce conquests of kings[9] and to make imperial proclamations of emperors,[10] their use of the word *gospel* flew in the face of Rome. *Gospel* bespoke the kingship of Jesus and a kingdom that was not of this world. When Jesus used the phrase *gospel of the kingdom* and the apostles used the phrase *gospel of Christ*, they were, in effect, saying that Jesus is Lord and King, and Caesar is neither! Imagine the *chutzpah* that was required to make such a declaration in their day. Needless to say, this was "gutsy vocabulary for Paul to use in the nations, especially Rome."[11]

What Is the Gospel?

The word *gospel* simply means "to bring or announce good news." The English word *gospel* is derived from the Old English *god-spell*, which is a calque translation[12] either of the Aramaic word *ewang'eliyawn* or of the Greek word εὐαγγέλιον—*euangélion*[13] (*eu*—"good" + *angélion*—"message," or simply "good news"). The word *euangélion* appears 76 times in Apostolic Scripture while its verbal form, *euangelizó*, appears 54 times. Interestingly enough, as James R. Edwards points out, when the word *euangélion* was used in the secular Greek world, it always appeared in the plural, meaning one good

---

[7] 1 Corinthians 3:11.

[8] Larry Hurtado, *Lord Jesus Christ: Devotion to Jesus in Earliest Christianity* (Grand Rapids, MI: Wm. B. Eerdmans Publishing Co., 2003), p. 309.

[9] Jerry L. Sumney, *Reading Paul's Letter to the Romans* (Atlanta, GA: Society of Biblical Literature, 2012), p. 52.

[10] F. C. Grant, *Ancient Roman Religion* (Huntsville, AL: Liberal Arts Press, 1957), p. 174. Grant quotes a 9 BC decree by the Provincial Assembly of Asia Minor in honor of Caesar Augustus which said, "Whereas the Providence . . . has brought our life to the peak of perfection in giving to us Augustus Caesar . . . whereas, having become manifest, Caesar has fulfilled all the hopes of earlier times, and finally that the birthday of the god [Augustus] has been for the whole world the beginning of the gospel (*euangélion*) concerning him, therefore, let all reckon a new era beginning from the date of his birth." The term *euangélion*, therefore, was commonly used in the ancient Greco-Roman world.

[11] Victoria Sarvadi, personal communication.

[12] A word-for-word or morpheme translation of a word or phrase from another language.

[13] When the *gamma* is doubled in a Greek word, the first *gamma* is pronounced as an "n"; hence the transliteration of εὐαγγέλιον as *euangélion*.

message among others. When it appears in the Apostolic Scriptures, however, it is always used in the singular, signifying "the good news of God in Jesus Christ, beside which there is no other."[14] Because they are proclamations of the "good news" of Jesus Christ, the first four books of the Apostolic Scriptures are called "Gospels." Since the Greek word *euangélion*, Latinized as *evangelium*, is also the etymological source of the word *evangelist*, the authors of the four Gospels are sometimes called the Four Evangelists.

Michael Horton defines the gospel this way: "The Good News is that God has fulfilled his promise that he made to Israel and to the world by sending his Son for the forgiveness of sins and the inauguration of his new creation."[15] The term *gospel* has, indeed, been connected closely with Christian faith since the time of the ministry of Jesus himself; however, the core of the gospel may better be described by the phrase *Jesus is Lord*. John specifically stated the purpose of the written "gospels" in these terms: "These things were written, that you might believe that Jesus Christ is the Son of God and that believing you might have life through his name."[16]

The Gospel of God: The Everlasting Gospel

Ultimately, the gospel that was proclaimed by Jesus himself and then by his disciples cannot be understood until it is returned to the milieu in which their teaching was set forth. The various interpretations of the Gospel of Jesus Christ must be analyzed in the light of the teachings of the Hebrew Scriptures and the instructions of Apostolic Scripture. When both are used and coordinated, the basis of the Christian faith is established, and the truth of the eternal message of salvation becomes very clear.

The place to begin is in the beginning. If the Gospel of Jesus Christ is the "everlasting gospel" as the apostle John declared it to be,[17] the understanding of this gospel must be established in the context of eternity, "from everlasting to everlasting." The Psalmist defined the phrase from *everlasting to everlasting* as being descriptive of the time "before the mountains were born, or [God] gave birth to the earth and the world."[18] Then, he continued by saying, "The lovingkindness of the LORD is from everlasting to everlasting on those who fear him . . . to those who keep his covenant and remember to do

---

[14] James R. Edwards, *The Gospel According to Mark* (Grand Rapids, MI: Wm. B. Eerdmans Publishing Co., 2002), p. 24.
[15] Michael Horton, *The Gospel-Driven Life: Being Good News People in A Bad News World* (Grand Rapids, MI: Baker Books, 2009), p. 89.
[16] John 20:30–31.
[17] Revelation 14:6.
[18] Psalm 90:2.

his commandments."[19] The Gospel of God, the good news about God, is, therefore, the everlasting truth that "the LORD is gracious and merciful . . . abounding in steadfast love" and that "the LORD is good to all [and] has compassion on all he has made."[20]

God's everlasting love for all of his creation—and especially for the human family that he created in his own image—is the good news that existed within the very essence of Godself even before God initiated creation. In fact, the love of God that is beyond comprehension[21] is precisely what prompted God to create everything that exists. Hendrikus Berkhof was correct when he noted that "the structure of the Trinity describes precisely the fellowship with man, for which God emerges out of himself."[22] John Sanders succinctly observed that it was in loving freedom that the "triune God decide[d] to create creatures with whom to share this agape love."[23] It is profoundly good news that the love which Father, Son, and Spirit manifest toward each other can now live in the hearts of individual believers and in the corporate body of the Messiah.

The foundation of the Gospel of Jesus, then, rests in the "Gospel of God" of which Paul wrote: "The gospel of God which he promised beforehand through his prophets in the holy Scriptures, concerning his Son, who was descended from David according to the flesh and was declared to be the Son of God in power according to the Spirit of holiness by his resurrection from the dead, Jesus Christ our Lord."[24] The Gospel of Jesus is the culmination of the Gospel of God, the good news that God has always had for humanity from the moment of their creation. Unless the gospel is first recognized as the "Gospel of God," therefore, its comprehensive nature and its application "from everlasting to everlasting" cannot be understood. This is what Gustaf Wingren meant when he said, "[T]here is a unity between man's pre-history and the Gospel, and when man accepts the Gospel he always accepts this pre-history. Or, to put in a different way, the assent of faith to the second article is dependent on assent to the first article."[25]

The first "good news" for the human creation was the life that God deposited in them, differentiating them from the rest of creation in that

---

19 Psalm 103:17, ESV.
20 Psalm 145:9, NIV.
21 Ephesians 3:19; Philippians 4:7.
22 Hendrikus Berkhof, *Christian Faith: An Introduction to the Study of Faith* (Grand Rapids, MI: Wm. B. Eerdmans Publishing, 1979), p. 337.
23 Sanders, p. 176.
24 Romans 1:1–5, ESV.
25 Gustaf Wingren, *Creation and Law*, tr. Ross Mackenzie (Philadelphia, PA: Muhlenberg Press, 1961), p. 120.

they were given "living being."[26] He did so by breathing his own breath into the human body that he had formed from the dust of the earth.[27] This was the creation of life that was the foundation for the recreation of spiritual life[28] and the impartation of eternal life[29] that are the foci of the Gospel of Jesus Christ. This eternal life is that which Paul said God "promised before the beginning of time"[30] or "before the ages began."[31] Wingren said it well: "The core of the Gospel is the resurrection of Christ, and this core is Creation, new and victorious Creation that overcomes destruction and death. Creation and Gospel . . . support one another. Indeed, they are one."[32] The divine intentions set forth in the creation of humankind come to fruition through the actions of God to obtain victory over sin and death[33] through the gift of his Son Jesus. Indeed and in truth, the "life" that was in the *Logos* was "the light of men."[34] And for this reason, the Lamb of God was "slain from the creation of the world"[35] so that he might remove the darkness and bring the light of his presence into the lives of those who believe.

The first pronouncement of "good news" that God made directly to humanity also contained the "everlasting good news" for mankind. As a matter of fact, from the moment when God proposed to create human beings by saying, "Let us make humanity in our image, according to our likeness,"[36] he also said, "Let them have dominion . . . over all the earth."[37] The core reason for the human creation as God conceived it was to produce beings that, as his plenipotentiaries, would have authority over everything that he had created in their terrestrial domain. Humanity, therefore, was connected

---

[26] Genesis 2:7.The KJV translates this passage, "man became a living soul." The NIV, ISV, and NASB render it more accurately as "man became a living being."

[27] The vivification of the first human involved more than mere oxygenation of the lungs. The "breath" of God infused the human body with a spark of the divine, the God-breathed Word (2 Timothy 3:16) that has pointed and drawn every human being to the Creator and has generated faith in the heart of every believer (Romans 10:17).

[28] The life that was lost in the fall of humanity into sin in the beginning is recreated and restored in the spiritual rebirth when believers are "born again (from above)" by the Spirit of God (John 3:3, 7). Spiritual rebirth, in turn, makes possible the full realization of the gift of eternal life in the resurrection at the end of the age. Paul confirms this truth: "If the Spirit of him who raised Jesus from the dead dwells in you, he who raised Christ Jesus from the dead will also give life to your mortal bodies" (Romans 8:11).

[29] John 3:16; Romans 5:21; 6:23.

[30] Titus 1:2, NIV.

[31] Titus 1:2, NRSV.

[32] Gustaf Wingren, *Creation and Gospel: The New Situation in European Theology* (New York: Edwin Mellen Publishing, 1979), pp. 158–159.

[33] 1 Corinthians 15:55–56.

[34] John 1:4.

[35] Revelation 13:8.

[36] Genesis 1:26a.

[37] Genesis 1:26b, KJV.

with land, and land was connected with humanity.[38] The earthling who came from the earth was given authority over the earth in a dominion that was to be exercised by serving and guarding the earth.[39] This is why Adam and Eve were assigned the responsibility of "cultivating" the earth from which their substance had been taken.[40] The nature of their task is clear from the fundamental meaning of עָבַד (abad), the Hebrew word that is translated "cultivate" (or "till"). This word fundamentally means "to serve."[41] Humanity and the earth are, therefore, integrally interconnected so that humans have "dominion over the earth" by serving the earth. This dominion and service are significant parts of the "everlasting good news" of God to humankind.

This is why all of God's promises to humanity have had land contracts associated with them. This could not be more clearly demonstrated than in the life of Abraham of whom Scripture said, "On that day the LORD made a covenant with Abram, saying, To your descendants I have given this land, from the river of Egypt as far as the great river, the river Euphrates."[42] The "good-news" land contract that God gave to Abraham was fulfilled centuries later when his descendants finally inherited the real estate that God had prepared for them. The land gave them corporate identity and a measure of shalom and security in a world of conflict.

The "dominion" aspect of God's promises continued into the time of Jesus and were demonstrated when the disciples asked their Master, "What shall we [who have forsaken all to follow you] receive therefore?"[43] Jesus replied with this promise: "In the new world, when the Son of Man will sit on his glorious throne, you who have followed me will also sit on twelve thrones, judging the twelve tribes of Israel."[44] Even in the Age to Come, the good news for the children of God is that they will have dominion over all the earth.[45] The apostle John said, "Blessed and holy is the one who has a part in the first resurrection . . . they will be priests of God and of Christ and will reign with him for a thousand years."[46] Likewise, Jesus said,

---

[38] Genesis 3:19 says, "You were made from dust, and to dust you will return."

[39] Human beings were assigned the responsibility of caring for the earth. In return, the earth would care for them. Human beings were made from the earth, and to the earth they will return when they die.

[40] Genesis 2:15.

[41] The Hebrew word abad is the source of the word eved, which means "servant" or "slave." In the beginning of time, therefore, God himself established the fact that dominion could be properly manifest only through servanthood.

[42] Genesis 15:18.

[43] Matthew 19:27.

[44] Matthew 19:28, ESV.

[45] Zechariah 14:9; Daniel 7:18.

[46] Revelation 20:6.

"Come, you who are blessed of my Father, inherit the kingdom prepared for you from the foundation of the world."[47] Jesus did not promise believers an inheritance in heaven. Instead, he said, "The meek shall inherit the earth"[48] that the Lord "has given to mankind."[49] Even in the Age to Come, there will be "new heavens and a new earth in which righteousness dwells."[50] God's good news for humanity, then, is the inheritance of the earth that God has prepared for the children of men.

The Gospel in the Hebrew Scriptures

Clearly, the gospel was a continuing feature in the Hebrew Scriptures. In fact, Paul specifically declared that Abraham heard the proclamation of precisely the same gospel that he himself was then preaching to the Gentiles: "The Scripture, foreseeing that God would justify the Gentiles by faith, preached the gospel (προευαγγελίζομαι—*proeuangelízomai*[51]) unto Abraham, saying, All the nations will be blessed in you. So then those who are of faith are blessed with Abraham, the believer."[52] The promise of inherited blessing and the land grant that accompanied God's covenant with Abraham was, for Paul, the essence of the gospel, for he made no distinction between the message that was preached to Abraham and the message that was being delivered by the apostles!

The same truth that was manifest in the gospel of Jesus was also proclaimed to the Israelites at Mount Sinai. God set before Israel "life and prosperity, and death and adversity,"[53] and then he encouraged them to "choose life."[54] The good news was that Israel did have a choice. This, too, was a part of God's original good news for humankind when he deposited free will in every person so that each one had the power to decide. For the Israelites, the outcome of life was not determined by blind fate. They were not automatons. Their lives were not predicated on the actions of capricious gods. They had been given the divine gift of free moral agency: they could decide for themselves whether to accept God's instructions or not. When they agreed with God, however, the good news was that their lives were filled with blessing, prosperity, and the security of God's *shalom*.

---

[47] Matthew 25:34.
[48] Psalm 37:11; Matthew 5:5.
[49] Psalm 115:16, NIV.
[50] 2 Peter 3:13.
[51] This is the verbal form of the noun *euangélion*, meaning literally "to announce or promise good tidings beforehand."
[52] Galatians 3:8.
[53] Deuteronomy 30;15.
[54] Deuteronomy 30:19

Amazingly, the ancient Israelites heard the proclamation of the same gospel that the first-century believers received from Jesus and the apostles. The writer of Hebrews confirmed this truth by declaring that "the promise of entering his rest still stands . . . for unto us was the gospel preached (εὐαγγελίζω—*euangelízo*), *as well as unto them*: but the word preached did not profit them, not being mixed with faith. . . . Since therefore it remains for some to enter it, and those who formerly received the gospel (εὐαγγελίζω—*euangelízo*) failed to enter because of disobedience . . . let us therefore strive to enter that rest."[55] God did not, therefore, create a new gospel for the church. It was the same gospel that had been preached for two millennia—first to Abraham and then to his descendants, the Israelites.

This was the good news of which Isaiah spoke: "How beautiful upon the mountains are the feet of him who brings good news, who publishes peace, who brings *good news* of happiness, who publishes salvation, who says to Zion, 'Your God reigns!' . . . Break forth together into singing, you waste places of Jerusalem, for the LORD . . . has redeemed Jerusalem."[56] The Hebrew word translated "good news" in this text is בָּשַׂר (*basar*), which means "to bear news" or "to preach." Interestingly, the "news" here was the publication of "*shalom*" that came with "salvation" when God reigned in Zion. This proclamation of the good news caused the inhabitants of Jerusalem to "break forth together into singing." It was the Hebrew word *basar* that came from the lips of Jesus when he said stood up in the synagogue of Nazareth and said, "The Spirit of the LORD is upon me, because he anointed me to *preach the gospel* to the poor,"[57] for he was reading directly from the Hebrew text of Isaiah 61:1. Then, Jesus also used the same word when he instructed his disciples to "*preach the gospel* to all creation."[58]

Solomon employed another Hebrew term for such a proclamation: "Like cold water to a weary soul, so is *good news* from a distant land."[59] The Hebrew phrase that is translated "good news" is שְׁמוּעָה טוֹבָה (*shemuah tovah*), which means "good news" or "good report." This is probably the word which the Hebrew-speaking Jesus would have used when he said, "This *gospel* of the kingdom shall be preached in the whole world as a testimony to all the nations, and then the end will come." When the Master spoke of the "gospel," he would have communicated that theme in the same terms that Solomon had used to describe the "good news" from a distant land.

---

[55] Hebrews 4:2 (NIV), 6, 11 (ESV), emphasis added.
[56] Isaiah 52:7, 9 (ESV).
[57] Luke 14:18, emphasis added.
[58] Mark 16:15, emphasis added.
[59] Proverbs 25:25.

Using this language would have communicated the truth in biblical terms with which the people would have instantly recognized.

When Paul spoke of the proclamation of the gospel, he also employed the text of Isaiah's prophecy, saying, "How beautiful are the feet of those preach the gospel of peace, and bring glad tidings of good things!"[60] Then, he continued his prophetic analogy by saying, "But not all the Israelites accepted the gospel, For Isaiah says, Lord who has believed our message?"[61] This entire declaration was an answer to the apostle's rhetorical questions, "How then will they call on him in whom they have not believed? How will they believe in him whom they have not heard? And how will they hear without a preacher? and how will they preach unless they are sent?"[62] Again, Paul used a clear premise that was anchored solidly in the Hebrew Scriptures to establish his methodology for proclaiming the "good news" in a manner in which the people could receive salvation by confessing with their mouths the Lord Jesus and believing in their hearts that God had raised him from the dead.[63]

The Good News of Jesus

The Good News that had been a feature of Jewish life and expectation for at least two millennia was exponentially expanded in the life and ministry of Jesus. The gospel that had been preached to Abraham and the Israelites came to its fulfillment and was embodied in one person, the only begotten Son of God. Jesus himself was the personification of the Gospel of God that the Father had "promised beforehand through his prophets in the Holy Scriptures concerning his Son."[64] God's Good News was summarized by John the apostle in just one sentence: "God so loved the world that he gave his only begotten Son that whoever believes in him shall not perish, but have eternal life."[65] This was the glad tidings of Jesus that was heralded to people of all socio-economic classes, with the focus on the most neglected members of society, the poor. "The Spirit of the Lord is upon me, because he has anointed me to preach the gospel to the poor," Jesus confessed.[66] When questioned by John the Baptizer as to whether or not he was the Messiah who was to come, Jesus responded simply, "The poor have the gospel preached to them."[67]

---

60 Romans 10:15, KJV.
61 Romans 10:16, KJV and NIV.
62 Romans 10:14–15.
63 Romans 10:9.
64 Romans 1:1-2, ESV.
65 John 3:16.
66 Luke 4:18, quoting Isaiah 61:1.
67 Luke 7:22.

The good news was that *salvation* had broken forth for Israel in the person of the *Savior*. The people whose ancestors had been saved from Egyptian bondage centuries before through the offering of the Passover lamb were now being offered the good news that God had provided the means by which they could be saved from the bondage of sin by the blood of "the lamb of God who takes away the sin of the world."[68] God's kingdom was breaking forth, and entry to it was no longer solely by physical birth into the lineage of Abraham, Isaac, and Jacob, but by spiritual rebirth into the dominion of God's dear Son.[69] "Unless one is born of water and the Spirit, he cannot enter into the kingdom of God," Jesus said.[70] He assured the Israelites that in order to enter into in God's dominion, everyone had to be "born again" or "born from above."[71] Thereby they acquired dual citizenship when, living in the flesh in an earthly dominion, they also lived contemporaneously in the Spirit as citizens of the kingdom that was from heaven.[72]

Paul made it clear that "the Gospel of Jesus Christ is the power of God for salvation unto everyone who believes, to the Jew first and also to the Greek."[73] Though Paul confessed that the "message of the cross is foolishness to those who are perishing," he also understood that "unto us who are being saved it is the power of God."[74] Paul believed that the gospel was the demarcation between good and evil, the power of God to deliver from sin and empower for service. As Brennan Manning has said, "The gospel of Jesus Christ is no Pollyanna tale for the neutral—it is a cutting knife, rolling thunder, and convulsive earthquake in the human spirit."[75]

The Gospel of Jesus Christ was the same Gospel of God which always put a price on discipleship. The God who made demands upon Israel with the instructions of his kingdom has never changed. While Christianity has often used "love" and "grace" as excuses for accommodating every kind of evil and even abomination, Jesus said, "If you love me, keep my commandments,"[76] and he declared unequivocally, "If you wish to enter into life, keep the commandments."[77] There was no doubt about the gospel that Jesus preached: "If anyone wishes to come after me, he must deny himself, and

---

[68] John 1:29.
[69] Colossians 1:13.
[70] John 3:5.
[71] John 3:3.
[72] Philippians 3:20; Romans 8:1–2.
[73] Romans 1:16.
[74] 1 Corinthians 1:18.
[75] Brennan Manning, *The Signature of Jesus: The Call to a Life Marked by Holy Passion and Relentless Faith* (Colorado Springs, CO: Multnomah Books, 1988), p. 172.
[76] John 14:15.
[77] Matthew 19:17.

take up his cross and follow me."[78] The Gospel of Christ is fulfilled in the discipline of discipleship.

The Good News for Jews and Gentiles

From the beginning, God intended for his gospel to be proclaimed to both Jews and Gentiles. When he gave the good news to Abraham, God declared that "all the nations of the earth will be blessed through him."[79] Then, God also predicted that "through [Abraham's] descendants all the nations of the earth will be blessed."[80] Both Abraham and his progeny after him were to bless the nations by sharing the Gospel of God with them. The gospel was "to the Jew first and also to the Gentile."[81] The good news that Jesus commissioned his disciples to preach was the same gospel that God had proclaimed to Abraham and to his descendants at Sinai and thereafter. The word of faith is this: "Our God reigns, and his kingdom is forever." The entrance into his kingdom has always been by faith—faith to believe the Word of God and the proclamation of the good news. It continues to be by faith—faith in God's provision of salvation through the shed blood of Jesus.

The divine Word of God has always been the basis for proclaiming the gospel. This proclamation was greatly expedited to the Jewish people, who were the first ones to hear the good news about Jesus, because they were already very familiar with the Hebrew Scriptures that were read in their synagogues on every Sabbath day—and, for that matter, on every day at morning, noon, and evening prayers. It was for this reason that the apostle Paul reasoned with his Jewish countrymen from the Scriptures when he shared the gospel with them. At Thessalonica, "Paul, as his custom was, went into [the synagogue of the Jews], and for three Sabbaths reasoned with them from the Scriptures, explaining and demonstrating that the Christ had to suffer and rise again from the dead."[82] In another case, Paul and Silas went to the synagogue in Berea, where they found that the Jews were "more fairminded than those in Thessalonica, in that they received the word with all readiness, and searched the Scriptures daily to find out whether these things were so."[83]

In the *modus operandi* that Paul employed in proclaiming the gospel wherein he "became all things to all people so that by all means he might

---

[78] Matthew 16:24.
[79] Genesis 18:18.
[80] Genesis 22:18, ESV.
[81] Romans 1:16.
[82] Acts 17:2–3.
[83] Acts 17:10–11.

save some,"[84] the apostle took an entirely different approach when sharing the gospel with Gentiles. Because he knew the Gentiles had no direct knowledge of the Hebrew Scriptures, he relied on presenting the good news through the demonstration of the Spirit and power of God.[85] In this case, the word of the gospel that is alive and powerful[86] penetrated into the hearts of the Gentiles who had already had the fundamental principles of the Torah written in their consciences by God himself.[87] A prime example occurred in the Philippian jail from which the apostles were released by a violent earthquake. The jailer "rushed in and fell trembling before Paul and Silas" asking them, "Sirs, what must I do to be saved?" Paul's response was the heart of the gospel: "Believe in the Lord Jesus Christ, and you will be saved, along with everyone in your household."[88]

The Good News, therefore, was—and still is—tailored by divine strategy to be contextualized in terms that all people can receive it. In the case of the Jewish people who knew the Torah, the requirement was that the Word be mixed with faith. Then, their faith grew as they more clearly understood the Word that they already knew. For Gentiles who did not possess a knowledge of the Word, the demonstration of the power that the Word produced opened their hearts to make a leap of faith and believe on Jesus. "It was as though the Gentiles were quickened in their spirits, pained or convicted of their sin by the agency of the Holy Spirit, and on blind faith called on the name of the Lord Yeshua, trusting him for salvation."[89] Then, their understanding grew as they were schooled in the words of Holy Scripture, which confirmed to them again and again the absolute efficacy of their acts of faith.

Avoiding Other Gospels

Paul had constant apprehension that those whom he had led into pure faith in Jesus through the preaching of the Gospel of God would be enticed by "another gospel" into falling away from the faith and embracing error. "I am afraid that, as the serpent deceived Eve by his craftiness," he said, "your minds will be led astray from the simplicity and purity of devotion to Christ. For if one comes and preaches another Jesus whom we have not preached, or you receive a different spirit which you have not received, or a

---

[84] 1 Corinthians 9:22.
[85] 1 Corinthians 2:4–5.
[86] Hebrews 4:12.
[87] Romans 2:15.
[88] Acts 16:3–31.
[89] Victoria Sarvadi, personal conversation.

different gospel which you have not accepted."[90] The good news of Jesus stands in utter simplicity: "Christ has died; Christ is risen; Christ is coming again." Any teaching, therefore, that is not totally and irrevocably Christo-centric represents "a different gospel" and "a different spirit"—and, indeed, "a different Jesus"!

The "different gospel" can take on myriads of forms. For the Corinthians, it was confusion and class conflict.[91] For the Galatians, it was legalism, the works-righteousness replacement for faith in Jesus that prompted Paul to exclaim, "I am amazed that you are so quickly deserting him who called you by the grace of Christ, for a different gospel."[92] For those in Ephesus, it took the form of accommodating Gnostic ideas.[93] For the Laodiceans, it was a prosperity gospel that prompted them to compromise their faith for material gain, all the while mistakenly thinking that their wealth was a sure sign that they had secured God's approval on their lives.[94] For others, it was a gospel of austerity, of celibacy, of self-abnegation, and even self-flagellation that was completely foreign to the teachings of Jesus and the apostles and the Hebraic heritage which fashioned and informed their teaching.[95]

If the church has learned anything from history, it is that the church has learned nothing from history. The same things that Paul excoriated in the first century continue to be manifest in Christianity in the twenty-first century. An astounding array of "gospels," all of which claim Jesus and the gospel as their own, are spread out like a smorgasbord bidding unsuspecting Christians to eat their fill. From unabashed efforts at syncretism designed to accept and recognize all world religions as equal paths to God, to a gospel that makes "gain godliness," to a gospel that endorses violent revolution in the name of "equality," to a Robin-Hood gospel that advocates stealing from achievers and giving to non-achievers all in the name of "social justice," to outright and blatant gospels of legalism and works righteousness—they are all there. Many other gospels also sing their siren song, luring the spiritually naive and the biblically illiterate toward the rocks of spiritual shipwreck and death.

One of these "different gospels" has been what is sometimes called the "Gospel of the Grace of God."[96] Some theologians have even said that

---

[90] 2 Corinthians 11:3-4.

[91] 1 Corinthians 14:40; 11:21.

[92] Galatians 1:6.

[93] 1 Timothy 2:9-15. In this passage, Paul excoriated new believers who attempted to bring ideas from Gnosticism and goddess worship into the Christian assembly.

[94] Revelation 3:17. John said that while the Laodiceans were rich in material goods and social status, they were poor and naked and blind spiritually. They had embraced "another gospel."

[95] Colossians 2:18.

[96] The term *gospel of the grace of God* is never mentioned in Holy Scripture.

the "Gospel of the Kingdom of God" that Jesus preached has been replaced by the "Gospel of the Grace of God" which Paul preached![97] In this formulation, the entire focus is on "faith" and reliance on the "grace" of God so that people virtually "continue in sin that grace may abound," the condition that Paul rebuked in Romans 6:1. In the "Gospel of the Grace of God," there are few of the discipleship requirements that were central to the Gospel of the Kingdom that Jesus and the apostles preached. This is the "other gospel" which prompted Dietrich Bonhoeffer to exclaim that Christians "have gathered like ravens around the carcass of cheap grace and there have drunk the poison which has killed the following of Christ. . . . The word of cheap grace has been the ruin of more Christians than any commandment of works."[98] In the economy of "cheap grace," some people are inoculated with just enough small doses of Christianity to make them immune from ever really knowing or experiencing God in terms of the radical discipleship that Jesus and the apostles advocated.[99]

Bonhoeffer had a clear view of the true gospel, which he called "costly grace," in comparison with the "cheap grace" of the "other gospel" which he described this way: "Cheap grace . . . amounts to a denial of the living Word of God, in fact, a denial of the Incarnation of the Word of God. . . . Grace alone does everything, they say, and so everything can remain as it was before. . . Cheap grace is the preaching of forgiveness without requiring repentance, baptism without church discipline, communion without confession, absolution without personal confession. Cheap grace is grace without discipleship, grace without the cross, grace without Jesus Christ, living and incarnate."[100] The impact of this "other" gospel has produced an ironic and debilitating impact on Christianity which Manning described in this manner: "[T]here has never been

---

[97] Keith Intrater and Dan Juster, *Israel, the Church, and the Last Days* (Shippensburg, PA: Destiny Image Publishers, 2003), p. 14. Intrater and Juster discuss the teaching of Dispensationalism that posits a "church age" or a "Dispensation of Grace" as a great parenthesis between the "Dispensation of Law" and the "Dispensation of the Kingdom of God." They point out that this teaching makes the following arguments: "When Jesus came, He offered the Kingdom to Israel, but Israel rejected the Kingdom. Therefore, the Kingdom was postponed, and God inserted a 'Parenthetical Church Age' that was not foreseen by the prophets. This church age will end when the Rapture takes place. At that time the Kingdom of God will be preached again. The gospel that was preached by Jesus and His disciples, known as 'the Gospel of the Kingdom,' is not the same gospel that believers preach today. We are not to preach the Gospel of the Kingdom. We preach 'the Gospel of the grace of God'. . . . In dispensationalist circles, one never preaches 'the Kingdom of God,' but 'the Gospel of God's grace.'"

[98] Dietrich Bonhoeffer, *Witness to Jesus Christ* John de Gruchy, ed. (Minneapolis, MN: Augsburg Press, 1991), p. 165–166.

[99] Dick Westley, *A Theology of Presence: The Search for Meaning in the American Catholic Experience* (Evanston, IL: Northwestern University Press, 1988), p. 43. Also Jerome Davis, *Christianity and Social Adventuring* (New York: Century Company, 1927), pp. 32, 39, and Everett Leadingham, *I Believe, Now Tell Me Why* (Beacon Hill Press, 1994), p. 143.

[100] Bonhoeffer, p. 158.

a time in Christian history when the name of Jesus Christ so frequently is mentioned and the content of his life and teaching so frequently ignored."[101]

Paul, however, was not preaching "another gospel," the "gospel of the grace of God." Nothing could be further from the truth, for Paul insisted that he was preaching the Gospel of God and the Gospel of Jesus Christ,[102] and those gospels were the everlasting gospel, the Gospel of the Kingdom of God. Far from advocating a lifestyle that exempted believers from obedience to the eternal instructions that God gave in the Hebrew Scriptures, Paul clearly taught the Gospel of the Kingdom: "What matters is the keeping of the commandments of God."[103] The apostle John agreed: "For this is the love of God, that we keep his commandments; and his commandments are not burdensome. . . . Whoever keeps his commandments abides in God, and God in him."[104] James also could not have been more supportive of this argument: "Whoever looks intently into the perfect law that gives freedom . . . they will be blessed in what they do. . . . Speak and act as those who are going to be judged by the law that gives freedom."[105] This was also the basis of Paul's instructions: "Conduct yourselves in a manner worthy of the gospel of Christ."[106] No doubt, this is why Peter warned believers to "be on your guard so that you may not be carried away by the error of the lawless and fall from your secure position."[107]

Restoring the *Good* News

It is time for the true *good* news that Jesus and the apostles preached to be restored to the Christian community. The objective of that good news was to "see the light of the gospel of the glory of Christ, who is the image of God."[108] It was to shine the overpowering radiance of God's Word upon the Messiah himself so that "in all things he might have the preeminence."[109] As Johannes Nissen has said, "All of salvation history is directed toward Christ and is completely "christocentric" in nature. From the creation on, humankind has been called by God to redemption in Jesus Christ."[110] The

---

[101] Manning, p. 172.
[102] Romans 1:1.
[103] 1 Corinthians 7:19.
[104] 1 John 5:3a, NASB; b, ESV.
[105] James 2:12, NIV.
[106] Philippians 1:27.
[107] 2 Peter 3:17, NIV.
[108] 2 Corinthians 4:4.
[109] Colossians 1:18.
[110] Johannes Nissen, *The Gospel of John and the Religious Quest: Historical and Contemporary* (Eugene, OR: Wipf and Stock Publishers, 2013), p. 168.

good news is, indeed, completely Christocentric, focused in the person and work of Jesus Christ to fulfill all things that God had spoken in the Hebrew Scriptures by filling all of those words full of his grace and truth, thereby bringing perfection and completion to the faith of the prophets and sages of Israel—"the glorious gospel of the blessed God."[111]

Just as the word *evangélion* in the Septuagint translation of the Hebrew Scriptures as well as in Greek literature "was commonly used of reports of victory from the battlefield,"[112] so the *evangélion* of God announces and celebrates the victory of the Son of God over sin and death through his resurrection from the dead. It also bespeaks the victory of the returning King of kings in the final battle of the ages at Armageddon when every enemy that has exalted itself against God will be defeated and "every knee will bow and every tongue will confess that Jesus Christ is Lord to the glory of God the Father."[113] This is the profound good news of God's reign over the earth that was announced in the beginning: "Let them have dominion,"[114] and it is the same good news proclaimed victoriously and gloriously at the end: "The holy people of the Most High will receive the kingdom and will possess it forever—yes, for ever and ever."[115]

This ancient *gospel* that had been proclaimed from the foundation of the world was the good news that God himself would intervene in the affairs of human beings and bring salvation to the ends of the earth, thereby restoring his first promise to mankind: "Let them have dominion over all the earth." God in Christ has initiated the restoration of all things spoken by the prophets since the world began,[116] and he will yet fulfill his promise when the righteous Judge of all says, "Come, you blessed of my Father, inherit the kingdom prepared for you from the foundation of the world."[117] The Gospel of God, the good news of the coming kingdom on earth is the fulfillment of the visions, hopes, and aspirations of Hebrew prophets, kings, sages, and apostles. It is God's final word of redemption of the world through his Son Jesus. And it is the continuing hope of all believers.

Gospel: Christian Fruit—Jewish Root!

---

[111] 1 Timothy 1:11.

[112] James R. Edwards, p. 24. Edwards points out that in the Septuagint, even when Israel was defeated, the term *evangélion*. In the case of Saul's defeat at the hands of the Philistines, the victors "sent messengers throughout the land of the Philistines to proclaim the *euangelizesthai*" (1 Samuel 31:9). Similarly, the messenger who reported the death of Saul to David thought he was bringing "*euaggelilómenos* to David" (2 Samuel 4:10; 18:26).

[113] Philippians 2:11.

[114] Genesis 1:26.

[115] Daniel 7:18.

[116] Acts 3:20–21.

[117] Matthew 25:34.

CHAPTER 8

FAITH

Perhaps the single most important foundational principle of both the Hebrew Scriptures and the Apostolic Writings is the following statement that is made in both texts: "The just shall live by faith."[1] This simple declaration —a mere three words in Hebrew[2]—is the foundation of human relationship with God. It is the key to initiating and then to maintaining the status that makes it possible for fellowship and even intimacy to exist between finite human beings and the infinite God of the universe. Faith is the basis, therefore, of both Judaism and Christianity.

God's Search for Humans

Fundamentally, it has always been and will ever be utterly impossible for any human being to employ the empirical method of scientific research and thereby discover God—either proving his existence[3] or understanding his ways.[4] God is unfathomable, inscrutable, and incomprehensible,[5] the God whom no human "has seen or can see" because he dwells "in light that no man can approach unto."[6] The very fact that human-divine communication and relationship are even possible, then, rests on the irrevocable fact that the God of Scripture determined not only to create human beings in his own image and likeness but that he also determined to engage those same human beings and to impart to them a revelation of himself. Without this ongoing act of divine self-disclosure in which "holy men spoke as they were carried along by the Holy Spirit" when God communicated with them,[7] humans of

---

[1] Habakkuk 2:4; Romans 1:17; Galatians 3:11.
[2] The Hebrew of the text in Habakkuk 2:4 is וְצַדִּיק בֶּאֱמוּנָתוֹ יִחְיֶה (v'tzadik be'emunato yichyeh), literally, "And the just one shall live by his faith."
[3] Job 11:7.
[4] In Isaiah 55:9, God says, "As the heavens are higher than the earth, so are my ways higher than your ways and my thoughts than your thoughts" (NIV).
[5] 1 Corinthians 2:14.
[6] 1 Timothy 6:16–17.
[7] 2 Peter 1:21.

even the highest acumen and erudition would never know—and could never know—anything about God.

While most religions view history as man's interminable search for "the beyond," the Hebrew Scriptures reveal another kind of search: God's unrelenting quest to find humans with whom he can have relationship. As Abraham Joshua Heschel said, therefore, the Bible is not a record of man's search for God but rather of God's search for man.[8] God himself confirmed this truth when he said, "I searched for a man among them who would build up the wall and stand in the breach before me for the land."[9] Jesus also said unequivocally that "the Father is seeking such people to worship him."[10] The God of Scripture has not been playing hide-and-seek with humanity; he has been actively engaged in revealing himself to human beings and in actively engaging them in fellowship and intimacy.

There is nothing about human existence or ability, however, that merits communication with the Divine. The wisest thought that a human being can rationalize in his mind is "foolishness to God."[11] God himself declares, "My thoughts are not your thoughts, nor are your ways my ways . . . For as the heavens are higher than the earth, so are my ways higher than your ways and my thoughts than your thoughts."[12] Similarly, there is no activity in which humans can engage that would even catch God's eye, much less merit his favor. Consequently, no one has either gained status before God or has maintained status with God by his knowledge, by his socio-economic status, or by his works. There is only one thing that God has ever accepted or will ever accept from human beings, and that is faith, the act of the human will to "believe God" and to maintain and prove the constancy of that belief by putting the faith into action. [13]Faith—and faith alone—gets and maintains God's attention!

Abraham's Faith

This fundamental premise was established and repeatedly confirmed in the life of Abraham, the father of faith and of the faithful. The Scriptures declare simply, "Abraham believed God."[14] The Patriarch of faith had

---

[8] Heschel, *God in Search,* p. 425.

[9] Ezekiel 22:30.

[10] John 4:23, ESV.

[11] 1 Corinthians 3:19.

[12] Isaiah 55:8–9.

[13] Even the conscious decision of the human will to believe God, however, is the product of divine grace Faith is not self-generated; it "comes by hearing . . . the word of God" (Romans 10:17). Faith is manifest when the human will and the Word of God work in concert.

[14] Romans 4:3; James 2:23.

every confidence that God existed and that only God rewarded those who diligently seek him.[15] For him, faith was the "substance of things hoped for, the evidence of things not seen."[16] How did Abraham have such faith? A Babylonian by birth and a Syrian by nationality, this man came to understand the first and foremost of all divine instructions: "I am the LORD God,"[17] and he recognized this over four centuries before Decalogue was given at Sinai. At the same time, Abraham also understood the premise of the *Shema*, which Jesus said was the first and greatest of all the commandments: "The LORD our God, the LORD is one" or "The LORD our God is God alone."[18]

Abraham first demonstrated what it means to believe God when he responded to God's personal commandment, *"Lech l'chah"* ("Go for yourself"), by leaving his home and most of his family in Haran, Syria, and beginning a walk with God that would continue unabated for the rest of his life. When Abraham crossed over the River Euphrates and entered the land of Canaan, he became the first Hebrew.[19] From that moment, he became a stranger in the land that God had promised him. His faith, however, was not diminished. "No unbelief made him waver concerning the promise of God, but he grew strong in his faith as he gave glory to God."[20]

Later, Abraham demonstrated that same faith and faithfulness to God when he was asked to sacrifice the very son whom God had promised and delivered to him and his wife Sarah in their old age when both of them were "as good as dead." Upon hearing God's command, Abraham did not hesitate or procrastinate. He "arose very early in the morning" on the next day and proceeded to Mount Moriah to fulfill God's instructions.[21] The phrase *very early in the morning* is applied to Abraham three times in Scripture,[22] where it continually underscores his incredible faith to obey God's instructions almost instantly and without hesitation. Repeatedly, therefore, the Patriarch demonstrated the fact that true faith is the unflinching and immediate commitment to the fulfillment of divine imperatives.

In the final analysis, Abraham's faith was vindicated when God "provided himself the lamb"[23] as a substitutionary sacrifice instead of Isaac. If God

---

[15] Hebrews 11:6.

[16] Hebrews 11:1.

[17] Deuteronomy 5:6. This is the first word ("commandment") of the Decalogue.

[18] Deuteronomy 6:4; Mark 12:29. The *Shema* was given to Moses some 500 years after the time of Abraham.

[19] Abraham's identity as a "Hebrew" was established in his crossing over, for the word *Hebrew* comes from the Hebrew word *avar* which means "to cross over."

[20] Romans 4:20, ESV.

[21] Genesis 22:3.

[22] Genesis 19:27; 21:14; 22:3.

[23] Genesis 22:8.

had chosen not to make that provision, however, Abraham still had absolute faith that the same God who had miraculously given Isaac to him could also resurrect him from the dead.[24]

Faith in Action

Abraham demonstrated clearly what true faith is: active belief in God or belief in action. He was justified and declared to be righteous by divine imputation on the grounds of his faith alone.[25] At the same time, Abraham's faith inspired immediate obedience to divine commands; therefore, Abraham's faith produced works so that, in actuality, he was justified before God both by his faith and by the actions that were produced by that faith.[26] Without his acts of obedience, Abraham would have had no proof that he had actually had any faith. Indeed, Abraham's faith was working with and through his actions.[27] Clearly, then, "faith without works is dead."[28]

Faith is not thinking; it is doing. Faith is not a static intellectual exercise; it is a dynamic bodily action. It is "putting legs" on prayers. It is hearing God and unequivocally and unhesitatingly reacting to what has been heard. Of course, in the Hebrew culture, the very act of hearing God implied doing, for the Hebrew word שָׁמַע (shema), meaning "to hear," actually has the deeper meaning of "to hear and obey." This is why Jesus said, "All things for which you pray and ask, believe that you have received them, and they will be granted you,"[29] while John declared, "Whatever we ask we receive from him, because we keep his commandments and do the things that are pleasing in his sight."[30] True believing is acting on faith, standing on promises, obeying divine instructions, and wrestling with God until the blessing comes to fruition.

Faithfulness

Faith in action is faithfulness, the true meaning of the Hebrew word אֱמוּנָה (emunah), which is translated "faith" in only two places in the King James Version[31] but is rendered "faithfulness" in nineteen other instances. The word that is translated "have faith" in Job 39:12 in the New American Standard Bible is אָמַן—aman, the verbal root for emunah, which means "to

---

[24] Hebrews 11:19.
[25] Romans 4:2.
[26] James 2:21.
[27] James 2:22.
[28] James 2:20.
[29] Mark 11:24.
[30] 1 John 3:22.
[31] Deuteronomy 32:20; Habakkuk 2:4.

confirm" or "to support." *Aman* is translated "believe" twenty-two times in the King James Version. Because of the fundamental meaning of *aman*, it is clear from the perspective of the Hebrew Scriptures that "faith" (*emunah*) is "faithfulness," in the sense of "firmness, steadfastness, constancy, stability, reliability, and support."[32] Also derived from the verb *aman* is the word אֱמֶת (*emet*), which means "truth." This etymological fact confirms Paul's statement that "faith comes by hearing . . . the Word of God."[33] Additionally, all Christians readily understand the meaning of *aman* in the context of the word *Amen*, a Hebrew loanword in English which means "truly" or "so be it."

Nuances of Languages

Though the original Apostolic Scriptures were either written or thought in Hebrew, the oldest versions that are extant are in Greek. With the change in languages from Hebrew to Greek, the apostles adopted Greek words that translated as closely as possible the terms used in the Hebrew Scriptures. This, however, often introduced new nuances of thought that are inherent in the Greek language itself which are not nearly as clear as they are in Hebrew and often do not reflect Hebraic thought accurately or fully.

In the case of the Greeks, the dominant philosophical mindset focused on rationalism. They were fascinated with the mind and essentially understood "God" to be "Infinite Mind."[34] The Hebrew word אֱמוּנָה (*emunah*) was translated into Greek with the word πίστις (*pístis*). *Pístis* was nuanced toward the mind so that when employed in a Greek sense rather than in a Hebrew sense it bespoke "faith" as "intellectual assent to a philosophical premise." David Dilling agrees with Martin Buber's view that when *emunah* became *pístis*, the "action of a whole person . . . involving the active aspect of fidelity and the receptive aspect of trust was reduced to an intellectualistic matter of accepting a set of propositions."[35] Even the verbal expression of faith, "to believe," when translated into Greek becomes πιστεύω (*pisteúo*), means "to *think* to be true." Since Hebraic faith is, indeed, a decision of the conscious will to "believe God" and then to act on one's belief, the inclination of Greek faith toward the mind was virtually inescapable: hence the definition

---

[32] Marvin Wilson, *Our Father*, p. 183.

[33] Romans 10:17.

[34] Benjamin Franklin Cocker, *Christianity and Greek Philosophy; or The Relation Between the Spontaneous and Reflective Thought in Greece and the Positive Teaching of Christ and the Apostles* (New York: Harper & Brothers, Publishers, 1872), p. 135.

[35] David R. Dilling, *Martin Buber on Meaning in Education* (Ann Arbor, MI: University Microfilms, 1976), p. 81. Dilling references Martin Buber's ideas in his book, *Two Types of Faith* (London, UK: Routledge & Kegan Paul, 1951).

of *pístis* is "the conviction of truth about anything," "that which evokes trust,"[36] or simply "confidence." While *pístis* can also mean "faithfulness," "reliability," "fidelity," and "commitment," still the Greek mindset is inclined more toward the intellectual component of agreement with what is understood to be truth than toward unequivocal commitment to God that is then manifest in faithfulness and obedience to his instructions.[37] For the Greeks, *pístis* represented the "state of mind" at which one arrives "when the correctly chosen aspects of the subject-matter are placed before him in an effective manner."[38] For the Hebrews, *emunah* was hearing and obeying God in faithfulness of right actions in response to divine truth.

Emunah, then, is first belief in God, then believing God (active belief), and finally faithfulness to act on the belief. Abraham believed *in* God (through his understanding of monotheism), and then he *believed God*, taking belief beyond "believing in" God to the plane of believing specifically what God said. Finally, Abraham acted on his conviction that God existed, that he meant what he said, and that he would do what he said. This is the *emunah* continuum of truly biblical faith: belief in God, believing God, and acting upon belief.

Why Faith?

Why does God place such a high value on faith that Abraham, the one person who met the criteria in the divine search for man, became the Father of Faith, and, indeed, the "father of us all [believers]"?[39] Since faith is never imposed but is the conscious choice of the human will to believe and act, it is something that humans with the inherent free will with which God created them can choose to have or not to have, to do or not to do.[40] Faith, like love, can be expressed only by those who have the power to choose for themselves whether or not to have faith. When faith and love are freely given, they are so pure and genuine that the utterly pure and holy God accepts them.

Since God searches for men and women who desire relationship with him and who will worship him in spiritual truth,[41] those who choose to

---

[36] Bauer-Danker, p. 661.

[37] In *Phaedrus* 70 B, Plato used *pístis* as a means of persuasion, an argument, or a proof. In his *Rhetoric* 1.1.1-4 and 1.2.1, Aristotle used *pístis* as proof or conviction.

[38] William M. A. Grimaldi, "Studies in the Philosophy of Aristotle's *Rhetoric*" in *Landmark Essays on Aristotelian Rhetoric*, Richard Leo Enos and Lois Peters Agnew, eds. (Abingdon, UK: Routledge, 1998), vol. 14, p. 71.

[39] Romans 4:16.

[40] Benedict XVI, Biuliano Vigni, and Vincenzo Santarcangelo *Learning to Believe:* (London, UK: St. Paul's Publishing, 2012).

[41] John 4:23. In this passage, which is usually translated, "in spirit and in truth," a Greek hendiadys is employed so that the translation can be "in spiritual truth" or "in the Spirit which is truth" or "in the truth which is Spirit."

believe his Word and embrace his truth in love are highly favored of God. Mary, the mother of Jesus, experienced this favor when she boldly said to the angel who informed her of her impending virginal conception of God's Son, "Be it unto me according to your word."[42] This is the kind of faith that produces miracles like the birth of Jesus. It is also the kind of faith that produces the miracle of spiritual rebirth for the one who chooses to believe the Word of the gospel and places implicit faith in the completed work of Calvary.

Salvation by Faith

Paul encapsulated the very foundation of Christian faith in this manner: "Therefore, having been justified by faith, we have peace with God through our Lord Jesus Christ through whom also we have obtained our introduction by faith into this grace in which we stand; and we exult in hope of the glory of God."[43] Human beings come to salvation when they determine to place their faith in God and his one atonement for human sin, which is the blood of Jesus Christ. Paul made it crystal clear that "a man is not justified by the works of the law, but through faith in Jesus Christ."[44] This means that justification before God—the status of being declared right or "righteous" before God—rests solely on faith. "Abraham believed God, and it was credited to him for [in the place of] righteousness."[45] Everyone who believes in God and his provision for salvation is saved when, just as God did for Abraham, he accepts the believer's faith and instead credits to him the perfect personal righteousness of Jesus Christ.[46] It is God, not man, who balances the scales of divine justice by accepting faith as equal with righteousness, thereby sovereignly declaring the "all-wrong" sinner to be an "all-right" believer!

Good Works: Faith's Product

As soon as one stands in God's presence *sola fide* (by faith alone), he immediately discovers that faith in God produces good works. As James Jefferies says, "What is true is that faith alone saves, but the faith that saves is never alone."[47] Just as Jesus himself was approved of God as a man who "went about doing good,"[48] so believers who stand in faith are empowered to cause God's light to shine so that others may see their good works and glorify the

---

[42] Luke 1:38.
[43] Romans 5:1–2.
[44] Galatians 2:16.
[45] Genesis 15:6; Galatians 3:6.
[46] Romans 3:25-26; 5:17; 2 Peter 1:1.
[47] James J. Jefferies, *Wake-up Call* (Maitland, FL: Xulon Press, 2005), p. 72.
[48] Acts 10:38.

Father in heaven.[49] There is no bifurcation between faith and works, between grace and law.[50] Good works are the product of faith,[51] and law is fulfilled, not destroyed, by grace through faith.[52] This is *emunah*—faith in action. It is the lifestyle of the believer that rests solely and securely by faith and faith alone in God's grace and consequently transmits that grace in every way as he imitates the life of Jesus in good works that glorify the Father.

No human being can gain or maintain status before God by his own efforts, even if those efforts are honest attempts at keeping God's commandments. Just as it was for Israel of old, salvation is entirely God's gift. It cannot be merited by acquired knowledge, be it ever so esoteric or mystical. It cannot be earned by works, even by efforts to balance the scales of divine justice in a *karma*-like accrual of good works to outweigh the bad. "All have sinned and fall short of God's glory,"[53] and "there is none righteous, no not one."[54] Because of inherent human sin that results from the generationally transmitted evil inclination (*yetzer ha-ra*)[55] and its inevitable consequence of human failure, the only hope of salvation is God's gift of grace which generates in the heart of the believer the faith that God accepts unto salvation.

Restoring the Truth

Faith is not, however, exclusively a Christian idea. The Hebrew Scriptures were filled with faith long before the Christian church came into existence. As a matter of fact, those who would suggest that there was no faith (even "saving faith") in the "Old Testament" should consider this important fact in Christian Scripture: the passage that has been called the "Roll Call of Faith" does not mention a single Christian name![56] Every person listed is a Hebrew, an Israelite, or a Jew. Faith, then, was a Jewish concept before it became a Christian tenet. And this Jewish idea has always been and will continue to be the bedrock foundation of Christianity.

Faith: Christian Fruit—Jewish Root!

---

[49] Matthew 5:16.
[50] James D. G. Dunn, *Jesus, Paul, and the Law: Studies in Mark and Galatians* (Louisville, KY: Westminster John Knox Press, 1990), p. 198.
[51] James 2:22.
[52] Romans 3:31.
[53] Romans 3:23.
[54] Romans 3:10.
[55] Rabbinic thought maintains that God created in Adam and Eve two inclinations, the *yetzer ha-tov* (inclination toward good) and the *yetzer ha-ra* (inclination toward evil) and that these two inclinations war against each other continually. In Romans 7:18–23, Paul expressed these same sentiments. The *yetzer ha-ra* idea contrasts with the Augustinian concept of "original sin" which suggests that the sin of Adam was lust which is passed on generationally through the "concupiscence" of marital intercourse.
[56] Hebrews 11.

CHAPTER 9

GRACE

Both Judaism and Christianity are firmly established on the grace of God. Grace emanates from the core of divine existence, for the God of Scripture, in his very nature, is "compassionate and gracious . . . abounding in kindness and faithfulness . . . forgiving iniquity, transgression, and sin."[1] Indeed, it is grace that distinguishes YHWH from all other gods: he is the faithful, covenant-keeping God who never abandons his steadfast love (grace) for those who serve him.[2] This is what makes God worthy of his people's worship.[3] This is why the Christian understanding of salvation rests entirely on the divine gracious favor that the Almighty freely and unconditionally bestows upon human beings solely on the basis of his unfathomable love without the slightest consideration of human merit.

A Christian Concept?

Jim McClure makes a very accurate declaration when he says that "the theology of grace is at the centre of the core of the Christian faith which is unintelligible apart from it";[4] however, he immediately makes a sweeping statement that is far less accurate when he declares that "the doctrine of grace distinguishes Christianity from all other religions."[5] While it is certainly true that "in the New Testament the concept of grace is taken to a new level . . . personified in the Son of God,"[6] the theology of grace is not exclusively Christian, for it has a solid foundation in both biblical and Second Temple Judaism.

---

[1] Exodus 34:6, TNK.
[2] 2 Chronicles 6:14: "O LORD, the God of Israel, there is no god like thee . . . who keepest covenant and mercy with thy servants" (JPS).
[3] Psalm 18:2–3: "The LORD is my rock and my fortress and my deliverer . . . the horn of my salvation . . . I will call upon the LORD, who is worthy to be praised: so shall I be saved from my enemies" (NASB, KJV).
[4] Jim B. McClure, *Grace Revisited* (Geelong, Australia: Trailblazer Ministries, 2010), p. 53.
[5] McClure, p. 53.
[6] McClure, p. 53.

Most Christians though have thought that grace as a concept is unique to Christianity. The German Protestant theologian Ernst Troeltsch unreservedly declared, "Only in Christian theism does the idea of grace come to its rightful place: anti-eudaemonistic, and tied to the moral value and health of the soul. . . . grace could not arrive until the atoning sacrifice of Christ overcame [the separation between righteousness and love]."[7] Joseph Price and Donald Musser echoed Troeltsch's sentiment, saying that "grace always relates to God's activity in Jesus Christ. . . . Although the Hebrew Scriptures include terms that approach the understanding of grace as it appears in the Christian story, grace as it enters Christian life is chiefly a New Testament term."[8] Such stereotypical Christian perspectives that assume that grace was unknown or at least underdeveloped in the Hebrew Scriptures are, however, either demonstrably untrue, or they are inadequate in their evaluation of the Hebraic view of grace that was espoused by the patriarchs, prophets, and sages of Israel.

What Is Grace?

Eugene Merrill has given this succinct and powerful definition of grace: "God's grace is the gift of persevering, loving, purposeful generosity that becomes visible in a climactic way in the life, teaching, death, and resurrection of Jesus."[9] John Hardon's definition is also revealing when he says that grace is "the condescension or benevolence shown by God toward the human race."[10] Grace has been described as God's sovereign act of giving to human beings gifts and blessings that they do not deserve. Thus, grace is often said to be "the unmerited favor of God."[11] In fact, it is "the unmerited favor whereby God draws human partners into fellowship with Himself through the salvific work of Jesus Christ and the power, presence and action of the Holy Spirit."[12] Grace has sometimes been considered to be distinct from mercy, which has been described as God's act of withholding from human beings judgment that they do deserve. Thus, for the majority of Christians, "mercy is deserved punishment withheld" while "grace is undeserved favor bestowed."[13] Lines of distinction between grace and mercy that

---

[7] Ernst Troeltsch, *The Christian Faith* (Minneapolis, MN: Augsburg Fortress Press, 1991), p. 176.

[8] Joseph Price and Donald W. Musser, eds., *New and Enlarged Handbook of Christian Theology* (Nashville, TN: Abingdon Press, 1993), p. 225.

[9] Thomas O'Meara, "Grace," in *The Encyclopedia of Religion* (New York: Macmillan, 1987), p. 84.

[10] John Hardon, ed., *Modern Catholic Dictionary* (Bardstown, KY: Eternal Life Publications, 2000).

[11] Justin S. Holcomb, *On the Grace of God* (Wheaton, IL: Crossway, 2013), p. 12.

[12] Susan B. Carole, *Called Into Communion: A Paradigm Shift in Holiness Theology* (Eugene, OR: Wipf and Stock Publishers, 2013), p. 54.

[13] Henry Blackaby, *Discovering God's Daily Agenda* (Nashville, TN: Thomas Nelson, Inc., 2007), p. 8. Also Charles Swindoll, *Insights on James, 1 & 2 Peter* (Carol Stream, IL: Tyndale House Publishers, 2010), p. 68.

are stated in Western forensic terms,[14] however, are not nearly as well defined in the Hebrew Scriptures, where both grace and mercy "involve unmerited favor."[15]

Grace in Scripture

In the Apostolic Scriptures, the English word *grace* is used to translate the Greek word χάρις (*cháris*), which literally means "that which affords joy, pleasure, delight, brings delight, sweetness, charm, or loveliness."[16] *Cháris* was generally used in the Septuagint Greek version of the Hebrew Scriptures to translate the Hebrew word חֵן (*chen*), which literally means "to bend" or "to stoop," and figuratively means "grace, favor, acceptance, or elegance." At the same time, the Septuagint often used *cháris* to render the word חֶסֶד (*chesed*),[17] a term that is virtually untranslatable from Hebrew into English because of the sweeping connotations that it contains in Hebrew thought.[18] *Chesed* usually is rendered as "lovingkindness," "tender mercies" or "steadfast love," and it also connotes "compassion" and "grace." In most places, the Septuagint translates *chesed* with the Greek word ἔλεος— *éleos* ("mercy") in order to preserve the meaning of *chesed* as "tender mercies." Because *chen* and *chesed* are "closely related semantically,"[19] however, both speak of the grace of God's love that is extended to humanity. Indeed, God's grace is always manifest through his merciful acts.[20]

The *Bauer-Danker Lexicon* defines *cháris* as "a beneficent disposition toward someone," or "an act which one grants to another that is not otherwise

---

14 Nicholas Adams, George Pattison, and Graham Ward, eds., *The Oxford Handbook of Theology and Modern European Thought* (Oxford, UK: Oxford University Press, 2013), pp. 635–639. Also Bruce L. McCormack and Joseph White, *Thomas Aquinas and Karl Barth: An Unofficial Catholic-Protestant Dialogue* (Grand Rapids, MI: Wm. B. Eerdmans Publishing Co., 2013), p. 227.

15 John S. Feinberg, *No One Like Him: The Doctrine of God* (Wheaton, IL: Crossway Books, 2001), p. 359. Feinberg says that while both grace and mercy involve "unmerited favor," grace can be given to people who are not in need as well as to those who are in need whereas mercy can only be given to those who are "miserable and . . . of great need."

16 In ancient Greek thought, *cháris* was viewed as the authentic power of reciprocity in the giving of gifts. See Jean-Pierre Vernant, *Mythe et pensée chez les Grècs: Études de psychologie historique* (Paris, France: La Découverte, 1966), p. 131, noted in Gadi Algazi, Valentin Groebner, and Bernhard Jussen, *Negotiating the Gift: Pre-modern Figurations of Exchange* (Göttingen, Germany: Vandenhoeck & Ruprecht, 2003), p. 167.

17 The similarities between *chen* and *chesed* prompted Martin Luther to translate both terms with the German word *Gnade* ("grace").

18 W. Gunther Plaut and David E. S. Stein, *The Torah: A Modern Commentary* (New York: UJR Press, 2005), p. 324. Also, David McDonald says, "In English, mercy means *compassion* or *pity*. In Hebrew, *chesed* means *fidelity* and *strength*." See David McDonald, *Lent: Giving Up Guild for Forty Days* (Littleton, CO: Samizdat Creative, 2011), p. 111.

19 Gerhard Ebeling, *The Truth of the Gospel: An Exposition of Galatians*, tr. David Green (Minneapolis, MN: Fortress Press, 1985), p. 27.

20 Ronald Hals, *Grace and Faith in the Old Testament* (Minneapolis: Augsburg Press, 1980), p. 13.

obligatory."[21] Calvin Roetzel defines it simply as "that which brings delight, joy, happiness, or good fortune."[22] David McDonald says that "*chesed* is the power that binds us to God and to one another,"[23] while Nelson Glueck maintains that the word *chesed* is the "essence of the covenant relationship."[24] Joseph Sittler says that while *chen* is "God's initiating grace," *chesed* is God's "faithfulness or loyalty in all covenants and relationships based on *chen*."[25] In whatever case, *chesed* is the gift of God's favor. In many ways, the word *chesed* captures the true essence of divine grace even more clearly than the word *chen*, which can also mean "charm," "elegance," or "adornment." It is certainly connected with the divine acts of deliverance and salvation. Perhaps this is why the word *chesed* is used over three times more often in the Hebrew Scriptures than the word *chen*.

As a matter of fact, the first time the word *chesed* is used in Scripture is when it describes the salvation or deliverance of Lot from Sodom. When Lot and his family dithered in Sodom, not taking seriously the need to evacuate the city immediately, the angels who had been sent to deliver them "seized [Lot] and his wife and his two daughters by the hand for the LORD [was] being merciful to him."[26] When that happened, Lot recognized the mercy of God, saying, "You have shown me great *chesed* in saving my life."[27] The word *chesed*, therefore, has often, if not generally, been associated with salvation in the Hebrew Scriptures, especially as it related to the deliverance of the Chosen People.

Jesus: Full of Grace and Truth

The grace of God took on new dimensions in the life and ministry of Jesus, who elevated the grace of God for salvation that had been manifest in the Israelite nation to a level of perfect fulfillment when he became *Chesed* personified and extended God's salvation to all humanity. The apostle John understood the transition in the grace of God that had been manifest in the coming of Jesus: "For the law was given through Moses; grace and truth

---

[21] Walter Bauer, Frederick W. Danker, William F. Arndt, and Felix W. Gingrich, eds., *Greek-English Lexicon of the New Testament and Other Early Christian Literature* (Chicago: The University of Chicago Press, 1999), p. 1080.

[22] Calvin J. Roetzel, *The HarperCollins Bible Dictionary* (New York: HarperCollins,1996), pp. 386–387.

[23] McDonald, p. 111.

[24] Nelson Glueck, *Hesed in the Bible*, tr. Alfred Gottschalk (Eugene, OR: Wipf & Stock Publishers, 2011), p. 55.

[25] Joseph Sittler, *Evocations of Grace: The Writings of Joseph Sittler on Ecology, Theology, and Ethics*, Steven Bouma-Prediger and Peter W. Bakken, eds. (Grand Rapids, MI: Wm. B. Eerdmans Publishing Co., 2000), p. 93.

[26] Genesis 19:15–17, ESV.

[27] Genesis 19:19.

came through Jesus Christ."[28] This observation, however, was merely a follow-up to his previous declaration: "The Word was made flesh, and tabernacled among us . . . full of grace and truth."[29] The fact that Jesus was "full of grace and truth" was a seal to the prologue of John's Gospel and its teaching that Jesus was God manifest in the flesh. All the grace and all the truth that God had disclosed in the Hebrew Scriptures—in the Torah, in the Prophets, and in the Sacred Writings—had been totally revealed in Jesus, the one who was both fully God and fully human.

John was aware that both grace and truth were found in the Torah, the law of Moses, so he was in no way attempting to minimize or destroy the Torah or to give the indication that the Torah was somehow void of or deficient in grace any more than it was void of or deficient in truth. He was, however, emphasizing the profound manifestation of the grace and truth of God that had been revealed in the person of Jesus. Whereas the law had then been delivered by a *voice*,[30] this time the grace had come through a *person*, Jesus. The grace and truth that were manifest in the Torah had become incarnate in Jesus so that its fullness—its deepest intention and purpose—had then become clear and obvious by being personified in the Son of God. In fact, Jesus put a face on the grace and glory of God.[31] John's observation was in the same context as that of Paul, who had boasted that he was "a Hebrew of the Hebrews, as to the law, a Pharisee . . . as to righteousness under the law, blameless,"[32] but then confessed, "I count all [these] things to be loss in view of the surpassing value of knowing Christ Jesus my Lord . . . and count them but rubbish so that I may gain Christ."[33] Everything that Paul had previously believed and experienced had become as nothing in his eyes compared to his experience of the living Jesus.

In Jesus, the grace of God that was revealed in the Hebrew Scriptures came to full embodiment: he was grace incarnate. For Jesus, however, being the personification of grace did not lead to disavowal of the Torah and God's instructions contained therein. Indeed, he maintained "clear lines of continuity with the law of Moses."[34] In fact, he "gave a stricter interpretation of Moses than the rabbis."[35] The life and teachings of Jesus that were the fullest

---

[28] John 1:17.
[29] John 1:14.
[30] Numbers 7:89. See Chaim Miller, ed., *Sefer Devarim: With Rashi's Commentary* (Brooklyn, NY: Kol Menachem, 2005), p. 65.
[31] 2 Corinthians 4:6 specifically declares, "For God, who said, Light shall shine out of darkness, is the one who has shone in our hearts to give the light of the knowledge of the glory of God in the face of Jesus Christ."
[32] Philippians 3:5, ESV.
[33] Philippians 3:7–8.
[34] VanGemeren, p. 37.
[35] VanGemeren, p. 38.

manifestation of the truth encapsulated in the Torah prompted him to make his self-defining declaration, "I am the truth."[36] At the same time, however, Jesus was the fullest manifestation of the grace of God. This is why John could say, "For from his fullness we have all received grace upon grace."[37] What Jesus brought in infinite love was the incarnation of all the grace and truth of God that had been revealed in the Hebrew Scriptures. Grace and truth were fully demonstrated in his life, death, and resurrection. He could manifest the fullness of grace and truth because he was God himself, love incarnate—the way, the truth, and the life.[38] God's grace in Jesus, therefore, is perfectly demonstrated in what Tullian Tchividjian has called "God's one-way love."[39]

Grace and Salvation

Grace is the very foundation of salvation. Indeed, it is "the *sine qua non* of salvation," which comes "not in response to a man's just desserts but as an expression of God's undeserved love."[40] Merrill says that "Old Testament salvation—even on just the level of deliverance from physical and psychological peril—must be balanced by the equally clear evidence that salvation was (and is) based on grace and grace alone."[41] He also points out that the Psalms of David connect salvation with grace by means of statements like these: "Turn, LORD! Rescue me; save me because of your *chesed*";[42] "Let your face shine upon me; save me for your *chesed's* sake";[43] and "Help me, O LORD my God; save me according to your *chesed*."[44] Merrill maintains that "the grammar in these passages makes it clear that God's gracious interposition of *hesed* is the very basis for any human hope of salvation."[45]

This is why Paul unequivocally declared, "For by grace you have been saved through faith; and that not of yourselves, it is the gift of God."[46] Five things are clear from this one succinct passage of Holy

---

[36] John 14:6.

[37] John 1:16.

[38] John 14:6.

[39] Tullian Tchividjian, *One Way Love: Inexhaustible Grace for an Exhausted World* (Colorado Springs, CO: David C. Cook, 2013), p. 213. Tchividjian argues that "God's one-way love" needs to be brought to bear "on the exhaustion that seems to define so much modern life." He maintains, therefore, that "the Good News of God's inexhaustible grace for an exhausted world has never been more urgent" (pp. 19–20).

[40] Merrill, p. 115. Also Victor P. Hamilton, *The Book of Genesis: Chapters 1-17* (Grand Rapids, MI: William B. Eerdmans Publishing Co., 1990), p. 276.

[41] Merrill, p. 119.

[42] Psalm 6:4.

[43] Psalm 31:16.

[44] Psalm 109:26.

[45] Merrill, p. 119.

[46] Ephesians 2:8.

Scripture: 1) Salvation is solely by grace; it can never be achieved by human efforts or works of righteousness; 2) Salvation is by faith alone, for even though manifest faith will inevitably produce good works, the crisis experience of salvation takes place at the moment that saving faith is released from the heart of the believer to God who accepts that faith and in its stead imputes righteousness to the believer; 3) Salvation can in no way be self-generated, for no one has the capacity to save himself; 4) Salvation is purely a gift of God, not a reward for human behavior; and 5) Salvation is effected solely on the basis of divine initiative which is generated in God's sovereignty.

Salvation history has always been and will always be the product of God's search for man, not of man's search for God,[47] and God's search for man has always been characterized by sovereign grace, acceptance of faith, generation of salvation, and conferral of the gift of salvation solely through divine initiative. For Jews and for people of all other ethnicities who have been grafted into God's family tree of covenant salvation[48] and thereby have become naturalized citizens of the commonwealth of Israel,[49] salvation rests entirely in the beneficence of God's divine grace and in his election and calling of human beings to come into relationship with him through the power of the Holy Spirit. Of a truth, "the LORD seeks all hearts with loving care,"[50] and he has done so faithfully for all of human history. No wonder God's "*chesed* is better than life."[51]

False Caricatures of Jewish Faith

One of the greatest prevarications ever made by Christians against the Jewish people has been the argument that "Jews are saved by works of obedience to the law" while "Christians are saved by grace through faith." Neither the Scriptures nor the Jewish people teach (or have ever taught) that Jews are saved by works. Above all other people on the earth, the Jewish people have understood that their unique status before God as his chosen people is the result of God's limitless *chesed*, not their own works. They did not choose God; God chose them in their father Abraham, and he further chose them as a nation when he summoned them to Mt. Sinai and joined them to himself in a covenant. Jews, therefore, affirm that their salvation is through the sovereign choice of divine *chesed*. "For any good Jew, the law is a

---

[47] Heschel, *God in Search of Man*, p. 136.
[48] Romans 11:17–19.
[49] Ephesians 2:12–14, 19.
[50] 1 Chronicles 28:9, author's translation.
[51] Psalm 63:3.

sign of God's grace and love. It has nothing to do with earning salvation," a rabbi once said.[52]

One of the most preposterous and vicious false dichotomies of all time is the Law vs. Grace controversy wherein Christians have posited a contrast between law and grace of such severity that neither can even exist in the presence of the other,[53] for grace is the antithesis of law,[54] and law is antipodal to grace.[55] Even more seriously, some scholars maintain that law destroys grace, and grace destroys law. The very idea that there is no grace in God's law and that there is no law in God's grace is preposterous and heretical. At the same time, the doctrine is deleterious in its consequences for both Jewish and Christian communities—though for distinctly different reasons.

Replacement Theology

In history, the law-grace dichotomy became one of the dominant themes in the heresy of supersessionism, the idea that Christianity was God's choice to replace Judaism and that Christians had been chosen by God to replace the Jews. Though the church continued to recognize the Hebrew Scriptures as the "Old Testament," in effect, it hijacked the Jewish Scriptures by adopting an almost exclusively allegorical interpretative methodology[56] that made it possible for the church to conscript all the blessings of the *Tanakh* for itself while leaving all the curses for the Jews![57] With this approach to Holy

---

[52] Stephen Smith, *Saving Salvation* (Harrisburg, PA: Morehouse Publishing, 2005), p. 98. Smith was quoting from a lecture given by a rabbi to a seminary class. The same rabbi also said, "Earning salvation through some kind of works of the law has always been a Christian problem, not a Jewish one."

[53] Warren W. Wiersbe, *Wiersbe's Expository Outlines on the New Testament* (Colorado Springs, CO: Cook Communications, 1992), p. 373. Wiersbe says, "The Law completely cancels grace, just as works will cancel faith; the two cannot exist side by side."

[54] Frank Thielman, *Paul & the Law: A Contextual Approach* (Downers Grove, IL: InterVarsity Press, 1994), p. 44.

[55] Theodore Dwight Bozeman, *The Precisianist Strain: Disciplinary Religion and Antinomian Backlash in Puritanism to 1638* (Chapel Hill, NC: The University of North Carolina Press, 2004), p. 204.

[56] Andreas J. Köstenberger and Richard Duane Patterson, eds., *Invitation to Biblical Interpretation: Exploring the Hermeneutical Triad of History, Literature, and Theology* (Grand Rapids, MI: Kregel Academic, 2011), p. 83. Also Richard M. Edwards, *Scriptural Perspicuity in the Early English Reformation* (New York: Peter Lang Publishing, 2009), p. 45, and Christopher A. Hall, *Reading Scripture with the Church Fathers* (Downers Grove, IL: InterVarsity Press, 1998), p. 102.

[57] Richard N. Longenecker, *New Testament Social Ethics for Today* (Grand Rapids, MI: Wm. B. Eerdmans Publishing Co., 1984), p. 41. Longenecker said, "The Church pressed the Old Testament into a defense of its exclusivism, with the result that Christians began claiming for themselves all the heroes, all the promises, and all the blessings of the Old Testament—leaving for the Jews all the sinners, all the curses, and all the judgments. . . . every promise was seen as applicable to the Church, and every judgment read as descriptive of the Jews." Also, Rosemary Radford Ruether, *Faith and Fratricide: The Theological Roots of Anti-Semitism* (New York: Seabury Press, 1974), p. 131. Reuther observed that the church's approach to the Hebrew Scriptures "turns the Jewish Scriptures . . . into a remorseless denunciation of the Jews, while the Church, in turn, is presented as totally perfect and loses the prophetic tradition of self-criticism!"

Scripture, the church was able to pick and choose from a biblical smorgasbord. What it liked—or desperately needed to validate itself or its practices—it moved to its plate. What it did not like, it left for the Jews. Increasingly, what it kept was good, spiritual, liberating, joyous, and full of grace. What it left for the Jews was described as a "curse," "legalism," "bondage," and worse.

Out of this mentality came the idea of some that there was no law in the *New* Testament.[58] If there is no law in the New Testament, why did Jesus instruct his disciples to keep his commandments,[59] why did Paul speak of "the law of Christ,"[60] and why did James insist that Christians should "continue in" the "perfect law of liberty"?[61] The truth is that there not only *is* law in the *New* Testament, it is *full of* law. In fact, there are over 1000 laws in the *New* Testament while there are only 613 laws in the Torah! Likewise, many Christian scholars have argued that there was no grace in the *Old* Testament.[62] If there is no grace in the *Old* Testament, how did Noah find "grace in the eyes of the LORD,"[63] how did Moses and the Israelites "find grace in [God]s sight,"[64] and how could David confidently declare that the Lord would "give grace and glory: no good thing will he withhold from them that walk uprightly"?[65] The truth is that there not only *is* grace in the *Old* Testament, it is *full of* grace, which is proven by the fact that the Hebrew word *chen* ("grace," "favor") appears 67 times and the word *chesed* ("grace," "lovingkindness") is found 239 times in the *Old* Testament! All of this evidence prompts the conclusion that both Old and New Testaments are full of both law and grace.

Grace is not "against the law,"[66] and "law and grace are not antagonists."[67] Law and grace are complementary parts of one continuum. They are not, as Zahl suggests, "opposite forces" that are "separate in experience" so that there is "either grace in love or law in judgment."[68] In truth,

---

[58] Paul F. M. Zahl, *Grace in Practice: A Theology of Everyday Life* (Grand Rapids, MI: Wm. B. Eerdmans Publishing Co., 2007), p. 78. Zahl says, "In human historical experience, there is no such thing as grace in law . . . Neither is there law in grace."

[59] John 14:15.

[60] Galatians 6:2.

[61] James 1:25.

[62] Witness Lee, *Christ in His Excellency* (Goshen, IN: Living Stream Ministry, 2000), p. 63. Lee said, "No wonder the Old Testament rarely uses the word *grace*, and even when it does, the meaning is unclear."

[63] Genesis 6:8.

[64] Exodus 33:16.

[65] Psalm 84:11.

[66] Zahl, p. 92.

[67] Catherine Dorsette, *The Worth of a Man* (Bloomington, IN: AuthorHouse, 2014), p. 109.

[68] Zahl, p. 92.

there is no law without grace, and there is no grace without law. Without law, grace is often exploited as an excuse for libertinism. Without grace, law can become a justification for injustice and abuse. When there is no law, freedom gives way to anarchy.[69] When there is no grace, freedom is destroyed by excessive legalism and rigidity. Law and grace, therefore, are mutually supportive.[70] Both are gifts of an all-wise and all-loving God to his chosen people, both Jews and Christians, and both are designed for the benefits of blessing and peace to those who use them rightly according to God's perfect design. Those who do so come to understand what it means to experience "the law of *chesed*"[71] that enriches both their lives and the lives of others. This "law of grace" is the "law of liberty" that both David and James called "perfect,"[72] and that Paul declared to be "holy and just and good."[73] In reality, therefore, no amount of exegetical gymnastics can ever make the law of God illegal![74] And no legalistic contortionist can ever limit or obviate the immeasurable, inexhaustible, and unfathomable grace of the living God!

The Reformation Dichotomy

The sixteenth-century Reformation produced an even more novel approach to the law-grace dichotomy when Protestant leaders sought a memorable way of invalidating the theology and polity of the Roman Catholic Church while establishing the authenticity of their own concepts and practices. The reformers began to parallel Catholicism with "law" and "legalism" while identifying Protestantism with "grace." This, in effect, initiated an ever-expanding effort to render "the Law" as being entirely a bondage-engendering enemy of Christian faith that had been destroyed by Jesus through the introduction of "grace." "Grace," then, could not stand in the presence of or be influenced by "Law." If anything that portended of "law" was present,

---

69 This is the essence of Solomon's dictum: "Where there is no revelation, people run wild, but blessed is he who keeps the law"(Proverbs 29:18a, HCSB; b, ESV). This passage is often rendered, as in KJV, "Where there is no vision, the people perish." The Hebrew word translated "vision," however, is חָזוֹן (*chazon*), which means "prophetic vision" or "divine oracle." *Chazon* is the essence of the Torah, God's law. The implication is that without Torah, people "cast off restraint" (NIV). This is the specific reason for Solomon's addition of the second part of his dictum, "But, blessed is he who keeps the law."

70 Archibald Hall, *A Treatise on the Faith and Influence of the Gospel* (Glasgow, Scotland: William Collins, 1831), p. 96. Hall accurately declared, "Believers are not without law to God, but under law to Christ" (p. 98).

71 Proverbs 31:26. In this passage, the quintessential Woman of Valor "opens her mouth with wisdom" with a tongue that teaches "the law of kindness (*chesed*)."

72 Psalm 19:7; James 1:25.

73 Romans 7:12, NIV.

74 Robert S. Somerville, personal conversation.

then dreaded legalism or, even worse, "Galatianism," was at work and clearly had to be eliminated.

It was partially in reaction to the codified systems of the Roman Church's canon law that the sixteenth-century Reformers augmented their fight against church tradition by labeling canon law as legalism. With their false dichotomy between law and grace, they were able to seize upon a convenient—and false—caricature of Judaism and the Jewish people as legalists who they thought trusted in their own works of obedience to the law as their means of salvation, and they applied that caricature to the Catholic Church. For them, Jews and Catholics were works-righteousness legalists; Protestants were faith-righteousness true Christians!

Of course, this was a false premise when applied both to the Jews as well as to Catholics. Indeed, this charge has been one of the greatest prevarications and most sinister caricatures of Jews that has ever been perpetrated by the church. Judaism and the Jewish people did not and do not believe that they are saved by works of the law. To the contrary, they have consistently affirmed that their "election and salvation are by God's grace."[75] Secondly, the charge was not even a fair characterization of the Roman Church's views on salvation, for it also maintained the doctrine of salvation by grace through faith, only with interpretations and applications that differed from those of Protestantism. While Catholics did place a greater premium on works of penance and other acts of obedience to Canon Law and while they did engage in the decidedly non-biblical and legalistic practice of selling indulgences, still the Catholic understanding of salvation was that it was by grace through faith, nuanced by their own interpretations. In the end, Catholics have consistently confessed that "our justification comes from the grace of God.[76]

Jewish Grace

The greatest Christian mischaracterization of the Jewish religion has its stereotyping Judaism as a legalistic system of slavery which produces a wooden, ritualized bondage that keeps Jews from enjoying the goodness of God. Contrasting Judaism as a religion of laws with Christianity as a religion of grace is "a terrible parody of Judaism."[77] Indeed, nothing could be further from the truth. Biblical Judaism was a religion that was solidly established in grace and faith. The Jewish people of biblical times understood that their lives rested in the *chesed* of God. They also understood that God's mercies

---

[75] E. P. Sanders, *Paul, the Law, and the Jewish People* (Minneapolis, MN: Fortress Press, 1983), p. 105.
[76] *Catechism of the Catholic Church*, 3.1.3.2.2.1996).
[77] Stephen Smith, pp. 96–97.

never end, for they are new every morning![78] One Psalm even concludes each of its 26 verses with the refrain: "For his mercies endure forever."[79]

It was not until the first century that some Jews began to consider the idea that status before God was maintained by personal works of obedience to the Torah. This was particularly true of some in the Essene movement and more specifically in the Qumran Community, where "the proper observance of *Torah* maintained by the community was thought to atone for sins"[80] even though, perhaps obliquely, "this atoning work was considered to be a gracious gift of God."[81] It is likely that the teachings of these sects of Judaism elicited Paul's strong denunciations of the idea that one could be saved by the "works of the law."[82] Later, what could be misunderstood as a nuanced version of works righteousness found expression in Rabbinic Judaism's system of "doing *mitzvot* [commandments]." Some Jewish people even came to think of works of obedience to the Torah as a balancing of good deeds to outweigh sins.[83] Still, there has been no significant movement in Judaism that has not acknowledged God's grace as the sole basis of Jewish election. Even in all the extremes of doing *mitzvot*, there has always been an underlying understanding that every Jew has stood only in God's grace. As Pinchas Lapide argued, "The rabbinate has never considered the Torah as a way of salvation to God."[84] Instead, the Jewish people believe that salvation is "God's exclusive prerogative." Jews, therefore, see themselves as "advocates of 'pure grace'."[85]

The minority position in the ranks of first-century Jewish life that espoused works righteousness also invaded the church and became the target of Paul's denunciations of Galatianism. Having been trained as a Jewish rabbi, he knew better. Being a Christian apostle, however, In fact, however, he was more exercised toward Christians who had adopted this thinking, for their actions represented an affront to the gospel of Jesus: salvation by grace through faith. It was in reaction to this idea of "works righteousness" that Paul argued forcefully, "For by grace you have been saved through

---

[78] Lamentations 3:23.

[79] Psalm 136.

[80] Mark A. Seifrid, *Justification by Faith: The Origin and Development of a Central Pauline Theme* (Leiden, The Netherlands: E. J. Brill, 1992), p. 94–95, Seifrid cites the Manual of Discipline, 1QS 3:6, 8; 5:6, 7; 8:6, 10; and 9:4. Also Preston M. Sprinkle, *Paul and Judaism Revisited: A Study of Divine and Human Agency in Salvation* (Downers Grove, IL: InterVarsity Press, 2013), p. 149.

[81] Seifrid, p. 95.

[82] Romans 3:20; Galatians 2:16.

[83] Stephen M. Wylen, *Settings of Silver: An Introduction to Judaism* (Mahwah, NJ: Paulist Press, 2000), p. 147.

[84] Pinchas Lapide and Peter Stuhlmacher, *Paul: Rabbi and Apostle* (Minneapolis, MN: Augsburg Publishing House, 1984), p.38.

[85] Lapide and Stuhlmacher, p. 38.

faith . . . it is the gift of God."[86] He was merely upholding and maintaining the tradition of prophets and sages through centuries of Jewish thought, and he was defending the purpose of the life and ministry of his Lord, Jesus Christ. Paul understood that no human being has ever been or can ever be saved by works[87] and that salvation is simply and totally the free gift of God's grace.[88]

Rethinking the Dichotomy

The false law-grace dichotomy has victimized both Jews and Christians: Jews by being caricatured as dead, lifeless, mechanistic legalists and Christians by having the faith of Jesus set adrift in a virtually lawless "Gospel of the Grace of God" that has made it possible for some Christians to justify themselves in continuing in sin "that grace may abound."[89] Surely it is time to cease and desist, to stop the false caricatures of Jewish faith and grace and to stop denying the truth of the rightful existence of Christian law while excusing various Christian legalisms.[90] Christians must return to the faith of Jesus: a Jewish religion that honors the Torah, observes the commandments of Jesus, and walks unreservedly and solely by faith in the everlasting *chesed* of divine truth.

It is time to rethink the ancient and tragic law-grace bifurcation altogether. While it is true that there is law in Judaism, it is also true that there is law in Christianity. While it is true that there is grace in Christianity, it is also true that there is grace in Judaism. In fact, there is Christian law and Jewish grace! Old stereotyping, however, dies hard. Christians must follow the lead of Jesus, Paul, James, John, and Peter in recovering the balanced understanding of law and grace in Christianity, and they must cease and desist from their libelous caricatures of Jews as being legalists who are void of grace and faith.

This kind of balance can be recovered, however, only when the church fully recovers and restores the Hebraic foundations of the Christian faith so that the teachings of Jesus and the apostles are interpreted in the context of the language and culture in which they lived their lives. Neither Jesus nor the apostles can be understood unless they are repositioned in the Jewish matrix from which they came. Likewise, their teachings cannot be fairly and appropriately applied unless they are returned to the worldview and mindset of biblical

---

[86] Ephesians 2:8–9.
[87] Galatians 2:16.
[88] Titus 2:11: "For the grace of God has appeared, bringing salvation to all men."
[89] Romans 6:1.
[90] Virtually every Christian denomination has its own legalisms, which are standards of conduct, either written or tacit, that are not specifically prescribed in Holy Scripture. Legalism, therefore, is not the exclusive property of Jews and Judaism. In one way or another, virtually all Christians are in some way legalistic when they try to restrict the actions of others based on their own sensibilities and not on Holy Scripture rightly divided.

and Second Temple Judaism. Restoration is essential to renewal. Recovery of the Jewish roots of the Christian faith will bring about spiritual renewal for Christians and will help restore the loving relationship of mutuality toward the Jewish people that both Jesus and the apostle Paul espoused. Anything less will only serve to perpetuate the false and libelous caricatures that have produced so much pain for the Jewish community and have impoverished Christians as well.

Restoring the Truth

Salvation for Jews and for people of all other ethnicities who have been grafted into God's family tree of salvation[91] and thereby have become naturalized citizens of the commonwealth of Israel[92] rests entirely in the grace of God's divine mercy and in his election. As Thomas Merton points out, "The *chesed* of God is a gratuitous mercy that considers no fitness, no worthiness, and no return. It is the love by which He seeks and chooses His chosen, and binds them to Himself."[93] As David Blumenthal observes, "Faith and grace are doubly reciprocal concepts. . . . grace evokes faith and faith evokes grace."[94] This is why "faith and grace have their origin in transcendence, but they have their real existence in immanence—in the here and now."[95]

Grace, then, is not a unique idea or experience that no one had ever even considered before the advent of Christianity, an understanding that originated with Jesus himself and was carried forward into the earliest church. It is a Jewish concept through and through, one that began in time immemorial, was demonstrated powerfully in the lives of patriarchs, prophets, and sages, and was incorporated into the Christian faith as a natural product of its emergence from the matrix of biblical and Second Temple Judaism. God's grace, always manifest in loving kindness and divine favor, has been well-documented conceptually in the Hebrew Scriptures and practically in the lives of the Jewish people. Then, it has been revealed in the teachings of Apostolic Scripture and demonstrated in the lives of Christian believers from every ethnicity, culture, class, and gender for two millennia. Christian grace has a rock-solid foundation in the *chesed* tradition of the Hebrew Scriptures.

Grace: Christian Fruit—Jewish Root!

---

[91] Romans 11:17–19.
[92] Ephesians 2:12–14, 19.
[93] Thomas Merton, *A Thomas Merton Reader*, Thomas P. McDonnell, ed., (New York, Random House, 1938), p. 353.
[94] David Blumenthal, quoted in Rami Shapiro, *Amazing Chesed: Living a Grace-Filled Judaism* (Woodstock, VT: Jewish Lights Publishing, 2013), p. 89.
[95] Blumenthal in Shapiro, p. 90.

CHAPTER 10

LOVE

Christians have long considered love to be virtually exclusive to the church. As a matter of fact, through the centuries, the concept of love as *the* distinguishing mark of biblical faith has been so strongly emphasized in Christianity that its former prominence in Judaism has been depreciated to the point that many Jews have virtually lost sight of love's inherent Jewishness. Divine love—God's love for humanity and humanity's love for God—is, however, deeply rooted in Hebraic thought and experience. In fact, love is the quality of the Divine that is manifest in human beings solely because they are created in the image and likeness of God.[96] Because humankind is designed to mirror the image of God, all humans have been characterized by love and have established a significant part of their own self-identity in the love that they give and receive. Love has long been considered the noblest of human feelings or emotions[97] because love is the core value that defines the essence of God,[98] as well as the essence of the human experience of life.[99]

The lofty Hebraic perspective on divine love and the expression of love in human life, however, contrasted sharply with views of humanity in the rest of the ancient world where human life was assigned a very low value by many pagan religions. Desmond Tutu has pointed out that "the Babylonian creation narrative makes human beings have a low destiny and purpose—as those intended to be the 'scavengers of the gods.'"[100] Humans were usually wary of their gods, for they were capricious, vindictive, and generally

---

96 For a comprehensive study of the image and likeness of God in humanity, see John D. Garr, *God and Women: Woman in God's Image and Likeness* (Atlanta, GA: Golden Key Press, 2012).

97 A. N. Dhar, *Mysticism Across Cultures: Studies on Select Poets & Saints* (New Delhi, India: Atlantic Publishers, 2002), p. 44.

98 Charlie Webster, *Revitalizing Christianity* (Victoria, Canada: FriesenPress, 2011), p. 62.

99 Susan P. Halpern, *Finding the Words: Candid Conversations with Loved Ones* (Berkeley, CA: North Atlantic Books, 2010), p.13.

100 Desmond Tutu in John Witte, Jr., and Johan D. van der Vyver eds., *Religious Human Rights in Global Perspective: Religious Perspectives* (The Hague: Kluwer Law International, 1996), p. xi.

malevolent. In Judaism, as well as in Christianity, however, humanity was held in high esteem by God. Human beings were assigned a high purpose and value, that of being God's plenipotentiary over rest of the creation.[101] The God whom Jews and Christians have worshiped has always been a being of love and blessing. Unfailing love and tender mercies have always defined the God of Scripture and have given his Chosen People every reason to expect to have his beneficence lavished upon them. In return, the peoples of the Bible have reciprocated the love of God in their worship of him.

Love: The Essence of God

Richard Rice has said that "love is the essence of the divine reality, the basic source from which *all* of God's attributes arise."[102] Indeed, God has been defined and even defines himself in terms of love. Love is not, however, merely an attribute of God. It is the very essence of divine being.[103] The apostle John made the clearest and most accurate definition of the godhood of God that has ever been given when he said quite simply, "God is love."[104] Understanding God begins with recognizing the love that exists within the core of divine being, wherein the three persons of God—Father, Son, and Holy Spirit—dwell together in one being of substance in the supreme manifestation of infinite love. John Sanders says that God is "a tripersonal community in which each member of the triune being gives and receives love from the others."[105] Love, then, existed in God before all creation was spoken into existence; therefore, love that is manifest in "personhood, relationality, and community—not power, independence and control—become[s] the center for understanding the nature of God."[106] Because God is love, he delights in relating with endearment toward those whom he loves as his children.

This is why "the biblical theme of creation is not ultimately concerned with cosmogony or cosmology but with the relationship between God and God's creatures."[107] This truth becomes clear when one considers that of the 79,976 words in the Torah, less than 1,000 deal with the subject of

---

[101] Genesis 1:26.
[102] Richard Rice, "Biblical Support for a New Perspective," in *The Openness of God: A Biblical Challenge to the Traditional Understanding of God*, Clark Pinnock, Richard Rice, John Sanders, William Hasker, and David Bassinger, eds. (Downers Grove, IL: InterVarsity Press, 1994), p. 21.
[103] 1 John 4:8.
[104] 1 John 4:16.
[105] John E. Sanders, *The God Who Risks: A Theology of Divine Providence* (Downers Grove, IL: InterVarsity Press, 2007), p. 175.
[106] Sanders, p. 168.
[107] Alistair I. McFadyen, *Personhood: A Christian Theory of the Individual in Social Relationships* (Cambridge: Cambridge University Press, 1990), p. 18.

creation.[108] It is safe to say, then, that God has focused much more attention on revealing himself as the God who maintains loving relationship with his people than on being viewed as the God who is the Creator of the universe. God is understood in biblical terms more as the "covenant God" than as the "creator God," more as the "all-loving God" than as the "all-powerful God." Everything about his being, therefore, is associated with and manifest in his eternal love. The qualities of his infinitude—omnipotence, omniscience, and omnipresence—serve only to multiply the extent and impact of his love.

The Active Nature of Divine Love

In the Hebrew Scriptures, the idea of God as love is conveyed by applying to him various adjectives like חַנּוּן (channun—"gracious"),[109] רַחוּם (rachum —"compassionate"),[110] and אָרֵךְ ('arek—"patient")[111] and by describing him in terms of nouns such as חֶסֶד (chesed—"tender mercy" or "lovingkindness")[112] and חֵן (chen—"grace").[113] Additionally, a time-honored rabbinic teaching has always maintained that YHWH ("the LORD"), the personal name that God chose for himself, expresses the divine attribute of love.[114] All of these terms bespeak the active nature of divine love. God's love is not platonic, static love: it is Hebraic, active love. Indeed, in Scripture, God is not so much "love" (a substantive) as he is "loving" (a gerund or progressive verbal form). His love is not a form; it is a function of his deity. He is eternal love constantly in action, love ever being demonstrated. Jürgen Moltmann has argued that when Scripture describes God as love, it "is not concerned with defining the nature of God; rather, it tells of God's actions," making a "summation of the countless stories and experiences of God's loving action."[115]

In Hebrew thought, God's continuing blessing of the children of Israel was said to be the direct result of his love for his people: "The LORD your God turned the curse into a blessing for you because the LORD your God loves

---

108 Of the 187 chapters in the Torah (Pentateuch), only the first three deal specifically with creation. The rest deal with God's relationship with humanity, especially his Chosen People.

109 Psalm 86:15.

110 Psalm 145:8. In Scripture, term *rachum* is applied exclusively to God.

111 Numbers 14:18.

112 Psalm 42:8; Jeremiah 9:24.

113 Psalm 84:11.

114 *Sifre Deuteronomy* 27; *Piskata*, Martin Buber, ed., pp. 162a, 164a. The sages understood that God's name *Elohim* was connected with judgment while his name YHWH was connected with love. See Levi Meier, *Moses—The Prince, the Prophet: His Life, Legend, and Message for Our Lives* (Woodstock, VT: Jewish Lights Publishing, 1998) p. 147.

115 Hermann Häring, "From Divine Human to Human God," in *The Human Image of God,* Hans-Georg Ziebertz, Friedrich Schweitzer, Hermann Häring, and Don Browning, eds. (Boston, MA: Brill Publishers, 2001), p. 9.

you."[116] God even said to Israel, "I have loved you with an everlasting love; therefore I have drawn you with *chesed*."[117] Indeed, God affirmed that he chose Israel solely "because he loved [their] fathers."[118] He also promised Israel, "With everlasting love I will have compassion on you."[119] This is why Abraham Heschel has argued that God's "normal and original pathos is love or mercy."[120]

Hebraic thinking, therefore, speaks of God not from philosophical categories but from the perspective of loving relationship—his relationship with people and their relationship with him. The God of Scripture, the God who is wholly other, did not limit himself to Greek categories of transcendence and impassibility. Instead, "in the ontological freedom of God . . . [he] chose not to live alone entirely in and by himself, but to create others for fellowship with himself."[121] Sanders succinctly observes that it was in loving freedom that the "triune God decide[d] to create creatures with whom to share this agape love."[122] In so doing, as William Miller has suggested, God "remains transcendent in immanence and related in transcendence."[123] In fact, "God is the One whose transcendence becomes known in immanence and whose presence is made real in the commitment to humanization."[124] Gregory Boyd has rightly said that "God created the world for the purpose of displaying his triune love and inviting others to share in it."[125] The God of Scripture simply is the God of relationship. As Søren Kierkegaard wisely noted, "God is not an idea that one proves, but a being in relation to whom one lives."[126]

Love: The Essence of Humanity

Humanity exists as a testimony to the love of the Creator. All human beings on planet earth, without distinction as to race, ethnicity, or gender, continue to bear God's imprint—his divine image and likeness. God's human

---

[116] Deuteronomy 23:5.
[117] Jeremiah 31:3.
[118] Deuteronomy 4:37.
[119] Isaiah 54:8, ESV.
[120] Abraham Joshua Heschel, *The Prophets* (New York: HarperCollins, 1962), p. 381. Heschel maintained that even God's anger could only be described in terms of love—as *"suspended* love, as mercy withheld" (Heschel, *Prophets*, p. 378).
[121] Thomas F. Torance, *The Christian Doctrine of God, One Being Three Persons* (London, UK: T & T Clark, 1996), p. 108.
[122] Sanders, p. 176.
[123] William T. Miller, *The Book of Exodus: Question by Question* (Mahwah, NJ: Paulist Press, 2009), p. 207.
[124] James B. Nelson, *Embodiment: An Approach to Sexuality and Christian Theology* (Minneapolis, MN: Augsburg Publishing House, 1978), p. 246.
[125] Gregory A. Boyd, *Satan and the Problem of Evil: Constructing a Trinitarian Warfare Theodicy* (Downers Grove, IL: InterVarsity Press, 2002), p. 16.
[126] Søren Kierkegaard, *Kierkegaard's Concluding Unscientific Postscript,* tr. David F. Swenson (Princeton: Princeton University Press, 1941), p. 485.

creation was by intricate, delicate, and supra-intelligent design so that every individual and every aspect of human existence contribute to the overall integrity and welfare of the human race and to the reflection of the divine image in creation. Humanity, therefore, was *sui generis*, unique among all of creation. Quite simply, the first humans and all their progeny came from God, from the divine heart of pure, irrepressible love and grace. In order for God to demonstrate his very nature and essence, he created human beings in his own image so that his divine essence could also be mirrored in human love, the highest expression of humanity.

The designer and creator of humanity is the one and only God, the God of Scripture, the Designer *par excellence*. This is the God who carefully and skillfully crafted human beings so that they would reflect the image of his eternal loving nature in their own interpersonal relationships. This is why when God first spoke about his intention to create humanity, for the first time in the creation narratives, he identified himself in "the self-referential first person," thereby investing his own personal "identity in this human creature."[127] Randall Garr has rightly pointed out, therefore, that of all God's creative profundity, "only humanity is envisioned as comparable to divinity."[128] This is why Heschel defined God in terms of relationship when he said that "God means: Togetherness of all beings in holy otherness."[129] In order to mirror the image of their Creator, human beings were designed for love. From the moment that the first breath of life entered the first human being, all humans have been endowed with the capacity to love God and to love one another with the same pure love that existed first within the very being of Deity, then was extended to God's human creation, and finally was manifest in human love, albeit in almost infinitesimal dimensions when compared to infinite divine love.

In the words of John Zizioulas, even God "has no ontological content, no true being, apart from communion."[130] It is communion, therefore, that "makes being 'be': nothing exists without it, not even God."[131] As beings-in-relation, humans can fully manifest the divine image and likeness and truly demonstrate "what God is like, for God is the community of love, the eternal relational dynamic enjoyed by the three persons of the Trinity,"[132] who

---

[127] W. Randall Garr, *In His Own Image and Likeness: Humanity, Divinity, and Monotheism* (Leiden, The Netherlands: Koninklijke Brill, 2003), p. 4.

[128] Hans Walter Wolff, *Anthropology of the Old Testament*, tr. Margaret Kohl (Philadelphia: Fortress Press, 1974), p. 159.

[129] Heschel, *Prophets*, p. 109.

[130] John D. Zizioulas, *Being as Communion: Studies in Personhood and the Church* (Crestwood, NY: St. Vladimir's Seminary Press, 1985), p. 16.

[131] Zizioulas, p. 17.

[132] Grenz, Franke, p. 200.

interrelate in the divine love of perfect mutuality. While each human being individually reflects the image of God, the divine image in humanity reaches its zenith, its fullest expression, in human interpersonal relationships wherein the love that was imparted to humanity from God is lavishly expressed toward one another in the various dimensions of human relationship.

Human beings are not designed, nor were they ever intended, to "be alone."[133] Like their Creator, they function around a core of love that is the essence of their being. Just as God, within himself, is pure relationship, the perfect oneness of mutuality, the encircling and interpenetration of the three persons in the one divine Being,[134] so human beings were designed by their Creator to reflect that same divine nature by participating in the fellowship of interactive interdependence and loving mutual submission that images the one who himself is Infinite Love.

The Unity and Oneness of Love

Love, as God himself experienced it and implanted it into humanity, is an all-encompassing expression of the divine essence that pervades every dimension of human life. Like the God of Scripture who is one Lord, the love of God is one love, a divine love that is manifest in love for God, love for humanity, love for one's family, and love for one's spouse. Love for God is a reciprocation of the infinite love that God bestows upon humans. Love for humanity is a reflection of the love that God has for all his creatures. Love for one's family is a demonstration of the love that God has for his family. Love for one's mate is a manifestation of the intimacy that characterizes God's love.

For the Hebrews, this sweeping manifestation of the one love of God was seen in the language of the text of Holy Scripture. While there are many words that bespeak aspects and manifestations of love,[135] there is only one word for love itself. The Hebrew word for love is אַהֲבָה (ahavah), from the verbal root, אָהַב (ahab), meaning "to love." Simon Glustrom confirms the fact only one word "in Hebrew (ahavah) expresses all forms of love: the love of a human being for God, the love of one person for another, and the love between man and woman."[136]

---

[133] Genesis 2:18.

[134] This is a statement of the concept of perichoresis or circumincession in which the three persons of God—Father, Son, and Spirit—are said to encircle and interpenetrate one another, thereby manifesting the compound unity, the oneness of God.

[135] For example, chesed (lovingkindness, steadfast love), raya (friendship), and dod (comfort, pleasure). Each of these words, however, is merely a manifestation of ahavah, not a separate kind of love or a division of love into a descending order of goodness.

[136] Simon Glustrom, Timeless Tablets: Why the Ten Commandments Still Speak to Us (Rockville, MD: Schreiber Publishing, 2006), p. 36.

In contrast with the Hebrews, the Greeks divided love into four separate categories: ἀγάπη—*agápe* (spiritual or divine love), φιλία—*philía* (love of humankind), στοργή—*storgé* (affection), and ἔρως—*éros* (physical or sexual love). This division of love was based on the Greek dualistic worldview which maintained that the spiritual was good while the material was evil. Plato, the high priest of Greek philosophy, believed that human beings existed only because sparks of the divine (fragments of the stars and planets) had somehow become entrapped in evil matter in the form of physical bodies.[137] For him, the human body was a *soma sema*,[138] a "tomb of the soul," so that even in life, human beings were dead with their souls entombed in a material and, therefore, evil body.[139] The Gnostics took these fundamental dualistic ideas even further with their claim that both the universe and its creator were inherently evil.[140]

Because of dualistic philosophy, it was possible for the Greeks to divide love into segments, elevating *agápe* (spiritual divine love) to the highest plane and diminishing *éros* (physical human love) to the lowest plane. When the church became increasingly Gentile in its leadership and demographics, these Greek dualistic concepts produced an even greater dichotomy, connecting *agápe* with holiness and thereby producing a much stronger aversion toward *éros*. Eventually, from the time of Augustine in the early fifth century, Western Christianity came to view physical love as the "original sin" in Eden and the means by which sin was propagated from generation to generation.[141] The clear Greek linguistic dichotomy between *agápe* and *éros* further exacerbated the tendency to see even marital love as *ipso facto* evil, something to be avoided by the truly spiritual and holy ones.

The Purity and Blessing of Marital Love

The Hebrews, on the other hand, had a holistic view of love. There was only one love, God's love, and it was expressed in all aspects of life from worship of the Divine to interacting with fellow human beings to loving one's spouse. The holistic Hebrew worldview made it possible to keep every earthly manifestation of love on the high plane of the divine. Hence, the love

---

[137] McGrath, p. 28. Also John Spencer, *New Heavens, New Earth* (Lincoln, NE: iUniverse, Inc., 2002), p. 30.
[138] Plato, *Gorgias*, 492e–493a. Plato said, *"Soma estin hemin sema"* ("Our body is our tomb"). Plato also believed in reincarnation so that, as in Eastern monism, the soul seemingly could never escape the body.
[139] Marvin Pate, *From Plato to Jesus: What Does Philosophy Have to Do with Theology* (Grand Rapids, MI: Kregel Publications, 2011), p. 27.
[140] Kurt Rudolph, *The Nature and History of Gnosticism* (Edinburgh, UK: T & T Clark, Ltd.,1983), pp. 60–61.
[141] Margaret A. Farley, "Sexual Ethics," in Nelson, *Sexuality*, pp. 60–61.

that married couples had for each other, including their expressions of physical intimacy, could be seen as a godly love.[142]

There is much evidence that sexual love within the context of marriage was honored and celebrated in the prose and poetry of the Bible so that the human couple, guided by Holy Scripture, could always express the holiness of their "set-apart" relationship through intimate love. This is the why Maimonides maintained that "when a man unites with his wife in holiness—the *Shechinah* [divine presence] dwells among them."[143] Such balanced Jewish teaching elevated God-designed physical love to the level of sanctity for which God intended it. As a matter of fact, the *Zohar*[144] "perceives the act of physical love between husband and wife to be of such transcendental sanctity that the Holy Presence of God Himself joins the couple when they attain that oneness of body and soul which is the essence of marriage."[145] Sanctified (set apart) love is "holy love," one of the highest expressions of the pure love of God.

Human love and sexuality expressed thoroughly and uninhibitedly in the context of marriage is not an evil flame that somehow escaped from the pits of hell to devour the unsuspecting in a conflagration of illegitimate lust. It is, as Richard Davidson rightly describes it, "the flame of Yahweh,"[146] a fire from God that brings both warmth and light to those who rightly, carefully, and respectfully use it. "It is not just animal passion, or evolved natural attraction, but a holy love ignited by Yahweh himself!"[147] says Davidson. God's love, therefore, is the source of rightly expressed holy love in marriage.

When one, therefore, makes a comprehensive study of the love that God designed for human beings to express within the sanctity of marriage, it becomes clear that this love is a human reflection of the love of God. This is a love that empowers husband and wife to mirror the image of passionate,

---

[142] For an extensive study of the divine nature of marital love and intimacy, see John D. Garr, *Feminine by Design: The God-Fashioned Woman* (Atlanta, GA: Golden Key Press, 2013), pp. 145–284.

[143] This is Maimonides' explanation of the Talmud Tractate *Sotah* 17a.

[144] The *Zohar* is the foundational work of Jewish mysticism, a group of books that contain commentary on the mystical aspects of the Torah. It was published in Spain in the thirteenth century by Moses de Leon, who attributed it to second-century rabbi Shimon bar Yochai.

[145] Kaufman, pp. 119–120.

[146] Richard M. Davidson, *The Flame of Yahweh: Sexuality in the Old Testament* (Peabody, MA: Hendrickson Publishers, 2007), p. 630. Davidson argues that the Song of Songs 8:6 is "the climactic biblical statement on human sexuality." In this passage, the possessive nature of love is said to have "flashes of fire, the very flame of the LORD." The Hebrew word translated "the flame of the LORD" is שַׁלְהֶבֶתְיָה (*shalhebetyah*), which literally means "flame of YHWH." The "love" of the Song of Songs is active, sensuous, fiery "lovemaking," not dispassionate, platonic love. Davidson concludes, therefore, that because human sexuality within the context of marriage is described as the flame of YHWH, "human love is explicitly described as originating in God, a spark off the Holy Flame. It is, therefore, in a word, *holy* love" (p. 630). When human sexuality, expressed in the sanctity of marriage, is seen as the "fire of YHWH," intimate love can become everything that God designed it to be.

[147] Davidson, p. 630.

committed, covenantal love that God has always manifest within the context of his own being and that he has always expressed toward his people. This is the love that creates the one-flesh bond of marriage and continually renews and strengthens the supreme human interrelationship that God himself designed and instituted in the Garden of Eden.[148] Love is the cement of the oneness (*echad*) of marriage in the same way that it reinforces the oneness (*echad*) of God—Father, Son, and Spirit.[149] In fact, the pure and holy love that married partners rightly have for each other even mirrors the self-sacrificing love that Christ had for the church when he "gave himself for it."[150]

The Supreme Manifestation of Divine Love

The greatest manifestation of the divine essence was the gift of God's Son to humanity in order to redeem the fallen creation from their sins and give them the gift of eternal life. "For God so loved the world that he gave his only begotten Son that whoever believes in him should not perish but have eternal life."[151] John explained God's unfathomable love this way: "In this is love, not that we have loved God but that he loved us and sent his Son to be the atoning sacrifice for our sins."[152] When humanity did not have the capacity to love God with all their heart, soul, mind, and strength,[153] God took the initiative to infuse them with his love so that they could be drawn by his Spirit to repentance and faith. It was the most powerful love, the kind that Jesus himself demanded of others when he said, "Love your enemies."[154] Jesus could exhort his disciples to this kind of love, for he was in the process of demonstrating it himself.

Indeed, when the mind of the flesh hated God,[155] God still loved humanity so much that he freely gave what was most precious to him, his only begotten Son. Here is how Paul described the dreadful state of humanity and God's remedy for that the human condition: "We also once were foolish ourselves, disobedient, deceived, enslaved to various lusts and pleasures, spending our life in malice and envy, hateful, hating one another. But when

---

[148] Genesis 2:24; Matthew 19:5.
[149] Genesis 2:24. This text says, "A man shall leave his father and his mother, and shall be joined to his wife; and they shall become one flesh." The word translated "joined" is דָּבַק (*dabaq*), which literally means "glued." The word translated "one" is אֶחָד (*echad*) and is the same word used to describe the oneness of God in Deuteronomy 6:4.
[150] Ephesians 5:25.
[151] John 3:16.
[152] 1 John 4:10, ESV.
[153] Deuteronomy 6:5.
[154] Matthew 5:44.
[155] Romans 8:7.

the kindness and love of God our Savior appeared, he saved us, not because of righteous things we had done, but because of his mercy. He saved us through the washing of rebirth and the renewal of the Holy Spirit."[156] No wonder John first exclaimed, "See how great a love the Father has bestowed on us, that we would be called the children of God,"[157] and then continued to explain, "Hereby perceive we the love of God, because he laid down his life for us."[158] Indeed, "God demonstrates his own love toward us, in that while we were yet sinners, Christ died for us."[159]

The Capacity to Love One Another

The love of God that has been manifest for humanity to bring about redemption from sin and to impart the gift of eternal life also empowers those who believe in God to love one another. John exhorted the disciples, "If God loved us, we also ought to love one another."[160] The apostle also made this startling statement: "Beloved, let us love one another, for love is from God; and everyone who loves is born of God and knows God. He who does not love does not know God, for God is love."[161]

Love for God can be proven only by the love that humans show for one another. Again, John states the truth: "If someone says, I love God, and hates his brother, he is a liar; for the one who does not love his brother whom he has seen, cannot love God whom he has not seen."[162] This is why Jesus interconnected the two greatest commandments: "You shall love the Lord your God with all your heart, and with all your soul, and with all your mind. This is the first and greatest commandment. The second is like it, You shall love your neighbor as yourself."[163] The Master was even more graphic in his declaration of the importance of these two interconnected commandments when he said, "On these two commandments depend the whole law and the prophets."[164]

This is why the apostle Paul was able to sum up the entire corpus of God's law this way: "For the whole law is fulfilled in one word, in the statement, You shall love your neighbor as yourself."[165] In reality, Paul

---

[156] Titus 3:4-5, NASB, NIV.
[157] 1 John 3:1.
[158] 1 John 3:16, KJV.
[159] Romans 5:8.
[160] 1 John 4:11.
[161] 1 John 4:8–9.
[162] 1 John 4:20.
[163] Matthew 22:38–39.
[164] Matthew 22:40.
[165] Galatians 5:14.

could well have said, "All the law is fulfilled in one word: love," for the *Shema*, which Jesus called the first commandment, says, "Hear, O Israel, the LORD our God is one LORD. And you shall love . . ." All commandments in Holy Scripture would be fulfilled if every person simply obeyed the very first word in the *Shema* that follows the confession of monotheism: וְאָהַבְתָּ (*v'ahavtah*—"And you shall love.") Love for God and love for humanity are the core values of all biblical faith. Jesus, therefore, truly "simplified the complexity of the Mosaic law by focusing on one word,"[166] and that one word is *love*. The entire legal responsibility of believers that is outlined in the perfect law of freedom[167] is fulfilled in one word: "Love." As Hillel the Great said, "Everything else is commentary!"[168]

Finally, Jesus took the commandment of love to a higher plane when he said that both love for God and love for humanity must be unconditional. In direct contradiction to those in the Qumran community who had said that it was proper to love one's neighbor while hating one's enemy,[169] Jesus even went so far as to command his disciples to love their enemies.[170] In order to manifest the love of God fully, one must love his enemies even as Jesus did when he laid down his life for those who hated, persecuted, and finally killed him. Jesus took love, the core element of the Torah, and elevated it to the level to which it had been intended in the first place. In so doing, the yoke of the law,[171] which some had found burdensome,[172] became the easy yoke of discipleship in Messiah.[173]

Love: The Essence of Biblical Faith

The experience of divine love is the essence of biblical faith. John said, "We have come to know and have believed the love which God has for us."[174] God has always revealed himself as having loved his creation, especially humanity. In so doing, he has manifest the profound truth that

---

[166] Willem A. VanGemeren, "The Law Is the Perfection of Righteousness in Jesus Christ: A Reformed Perspective," in Greg L. Bahnsen, Walter C. Kaiser, Jr., Douglas J. Moo, Wayne G. Strickland, Willem A. VanGemeren, *Five Views on Law and Gospel* (Grand Rapids, MI: Zondervan Publishing, 1996), p. 39.
[167] James 1:25.
[168] Babylonian Talmud, *Shabbat* 31a.
[169] Dead Sea Scrolls, *Manual of Discipline* (1QS) 10:17.
[170] Matthew 5:43–48.
[171] The term *yoke of the law* was common among the Jewish people, who "spoke of the yoke of the law, the yoke of the commandments, the yoke of the kingdom and the yoke of God." They used the phrase "yoke of" to indicate entering into submission to something. For most Jews, this was a term of joy; however, for many, it was a term of restriction. See William Barclay, *The Gospel of Matthew: Chapters 11-28* (Louisville, KY: Westminster John Knox Press, 2001), p. 20.
[172] Acts 15:10.
[173] Matthew 11:28–29.
[174] 1 John 4:16.

Abraham Kuyper set forth when he maintained that for the love of his entire creation, God restrained sin and upheld the covenant order of life as the law and norm for all people.[175] The God of Scripture is a lover, not a judge! Indeed, God created the universe and humanity specifically for the manifestation of his divine love. This is why the prophet Hosea portrayed God "not as an invulnerable judge, but as a loving husband."[176] Herein is the mystery of infinite divine love, "the love of Christ which surpasses knowledge."[177]

The love of biblical faith is that of God himself. He is the God of whom Zephaniah said, "The LORD your God is in your midst, a victorious warrior. He will exult over you with joy, he will be quiet in his love, he will rejoice over you with shouts of joy."[178] The divine love is the unfathomable love that God has always had for his creation. This divine love is the source of all human love: "The love of God has been poured out within our hearts through the Holy Spirit who was given to us."[179] The love that "a person has for God is not his own but derives from God."[180] Likewise, the love that human beings have for one another is the evidence of human relationship with the Divine: "If we love one another, God abides in us, and his love is perfected in us."[181]

Christianity is a religion of love, but it is founded on the ideal of love that was well established in the Hebrew Scriptures in the love that God had for Israel, that Israel had for God, and that the Israelites had for one another. Love for God and love for humanity has one source, God. It is not a divided love of descending value from the sublime of the divine to the mundane of the human. It is one love, the *ahavah* of God, the one love that both God and humans manifest in interpersonal relationships. Love, then, is a Jewish idea that was shared with the entire world by the Jew Jesus, his disciples, and countless Christian believers around the world. Reclaiming this holistic view of love in all of its myriad manifestation establishes the divine truth on the rock-solid foundation of biblically Hebraic insight that liberates and brings fulfillment to the lives of all believers.

Love: Christian Fruit—Jewish Root!

---

[175] Abraham Kuyper, summarized in Daniel Judah Elazar and John Kincaid, eds., *The Covenant Connection: From Federal Theology to Modern Federalism* (Lanham, MD: Lexington Books, 2000), p. 85.

[176] Burton Z. Cooper, *Why God?* (Louisville, KY: Westminster John Knox Press, 1988), p. 48.

[177] Ephesians 3:19.

[178] Zephaniah 3:17.

[179] Romans 5:5.

[180] Judah Loew, *Netivot Olam* (New York: Judaica Press, 1969), vol. 2, p. 29.

[181] 1 John 4:12.

CHAPTER 11

SPIRIT

Christians have long viewed their religious experience as being directed and empowered by the Holy Spirit so that their lives continually reflect the high ideals of grace, faith, and love. Jews, on the other hand, have been stereotyped by Christians as being legalists who lack a basic understanding of the Spirit and its application in human lives because of their obsession with works of obedience to the law. Christianity has perceived itself as being spontaneous, filled with joy, and invigorated by the Spirit. At the same time, it has viewed Judaism as dull, insipid, lifeless, filled with dry ritual, and stifled by jejune legalism.

A prime example of this kind of Christian thinking was manifest by Old Testament scholar Hermann Gunkel who, though he traced early Christian perspectives on the Holy Spirit to Judaism and the Jewish people, still felt it necessary to characterize Judaism as being "spirit-impoverished" (*geistesver-lassene*).[1] Like so many scholars in the centuries before his time, Gunkel essentially set up Judaism as a straw man against which he could compare the virtues of Christianity as the epitome of spirituality. For him, historical Judaism was devoid of the spirituality that had always characterized Christianity. Indeed, though he showed signs of recovering some of the Jewish roots of Christian pneumatology, Gunkel fell into the same trap that had netted so many Christian theologians over the centuries when he said that Jesus was a "fresh sprout from the old, all-but-withered root of Old Testament prophecy"[2] and when he alleged that the time of Jesus was "so spiritually impoverished . . . that a man such as Jesus cannot come from it" but "must belong to Israel's antiquity, long past and mighty of spirit."[3] Gunkel and other scholars like him just simply could not understand how Second Temple Judaism could even remotely have been the matrix from which Jesus and the church emerged.

---

[1] Hermann Gunkel, *The Influence of the Holy Spirit: The Popular View of the Apostolic Age and the Teaching of the Apostle Paul* (Minneapolis, MN: Augsburg Fortress Press, 1979), p. 12.
[2] Gunkel, p. 12.
[3] Gunkel, p. 68.

But, the question is, where did Christianity get its ideas of Spirit and spirituality? The answer is simple: Christianity derived its understanding of the Holy Spirit and the manifestation of spirituality directly from the Jews through the lives, experiences, and writings of Hebrew prophets and sages. The Spirit is emphasized in a profound and dominant way through the entire corpus of the Hebrew Scriptures. In fact, the Holy Spirit is manifest in the second verse of Scripture, where it hovered over the "undefined matter"[4] of the newly created earth, thereby making the definitive creation possible.

It was from the matrix of the Spirit that the Word of God summoned forth the reality of material substance from the void of nothingness. "The systematic progression from chaos to cosmos unfolds in an orderly and harmonious manner,"[5] says Nahum Sarna. Though the world originated as "an indistinguished mass," it progressively developed "into an ordered cosmos by the systematic application of God's creative power,"[6] says Randall Garr. All the while the Spirit of God "fluttered" over the face of the waters like a brooding mother bird[7] so that "God's wind [spirit] foreshadows the agent and onset of the first creative act and all creative acts thereafter. It announces God and his active role in establishing a paradigmatic world from a primal environment of chaotic indistinction."[8] The Holy Spirit, therefore, was both integrally and intimately involved in the very first event in world history, the creation of the universe.

Creation Through Divine Breath

Humanity was also the product of the Holy Spirit. After God had assembled elements from the dust of the earth and then formed that humus into the first human body, what lay on the earth was still lifeless until the Lord God breathed into the nostrils of the formed earth the breath of life so that human life was created out of nothing. This is why it is the breath (*neshamah*) of the Almighty that continues to give life to human beings and continues to breathe into the human soul the inspiration of the Spirit. As Elihu said to Job, "A spirit exists in mankind, and the Almighty's breath

---

[4] Kaiser, *Toward Discovering*, p. 26.

[5] Nahum M. Sarna, *Exploring Exodus: The Origins of Biblical Israel* (New York: Schocken Books, 1986), p. 77.

[6] W. Randall Garr, *In His Own Image and Likeness: Humanity, Divinity, and Monotheism* (Leiden, The Netherlands: Koninklijke Brill, 2003), p. 183.

[7] Genesis 1:2. The feminine imagery in this text is very clear. Though God is genderless, still the principles of masculinity and femininity were created in human beings to be theomorphic—that is, to bear God's image and likeness and to reveal something about his being (Romans 1:20).

[8] W. Randall Garr, p. 181.

gives him insight."[9] The dynamics involved in both the creation story and the formula for the divine inspiration that is infused into the human heart can be understood only when the Hebrew connection between "breath," "air," "wind," and "spirit" (or "Spirit") is fully realized. The relationship between God and humanity, described in Apostolic Scripture as the infilling of the Holy Spirit, cannot be fully—and perhaps rightly—understood without being placed in the context of the Hebraic understanding of spirit, wind, and breath that the prophets of Israel experienced. One cannot even begin to understand the way in which the Holy Spirit operates within and among believers without returning to the matrix of truth from which the Christian knowledge of the Holy Spirit emerged.

Human life exists only because of breath, the intake of oxygen into the cardiopulmonary system of the body. "The most noticeable difference between sentient beings and dead things, between the living and the dead, is in the breath. Whatever lives breathes; whatever is dead does not breathe."[10] From time immemorial most civilizations, including the Hebrew community, have made a close connection between "spirit" and "wind," "air" and "breath." In most languages, breath and spirit are designated by the same term. In Hebrew, however, there are two terms that deal with spirit, רוּחַ (ruach) and נְשָׁמָה (neshamah). Ruach speaks of "wind" or "moving air" as well as "spirit." The ruach is the "vital force or power that comes from God which animates"[11] all living things such that they are all said to have נֶפֶשׁ (nefesh—"being"). This is what Job refers to as "the soul (nefesh) of every living thing."[12] In this same passage, however, Job says that the "neshamah ("breath") of all mankind" is in God's hands along with the "nefesh." The neshamah is, therefore, more than the "life force" or the "being" of humanity. Neshamah is essentially ruach in action.[13] The introduction of the neshamah ("breath of the Almighty") was the defining moment in human creation, for it was at the instant when God "breathed" his own neshamah into the human body which he had formed that humanity was literally "created"

---

9 Job 32:8, ISV.
10 Isidore Singer, et. al., eds., The Jewish Encyclopedia: A Descriptive Record of the History, Religion, Literature, and Customs of the Jewish People from the Earliest Times to the Present Day (New York: Funk & Wagnalls, 1904), p. 447.
11 Eichrodt, p. 135.
12 Job 12:10. The word nefesh is translated "creature" when it first appears in Scripture in Genesis 1:20, where it describes birds. It continues to be translated "creature" in describing other animal life (Genesis 1:24, 28, 30). When nefesh speaks of human beings, it is translated "soul" in most English versions of Scripture; however, nefesh actually indicates "life" more than it describes "soul" as the "soul" was conceived by the Greeks.
13 J. Anderson, "What Is Man?": His Origin, Life-History and Future Destiny as Revealed in the Word of God (London, UK: J. Nisbet and Co., 1888), p. 127.

out of nothing.[14] The human spirit or life was a unique creation among all of the other things that God made in the beginning.

"The life-giving breath [of humanity] cannot be of earthly origin, for nothing is found whence it may be taken. It is derived from the supernatural world, from God."[15] Indeed, it was God who blew the breath of life into Adam and continues to give breath to every human being in every generation. Isaiah confirmed this truth: "[God] gives *neshamah* to the people on [the earth], and *ruach* to those who walk in it."[16] David made it even clearer: "You send forth your *ruach*, they are created . . . you take away their *neshamah*, they expire and return to their dust."[17] Job expanded even further on this truth: "If [God] but intends it, he can call back his *ruach* (spirit) and his *neshamah* (breath). All flesh would at once expire, and mankind would return to dust."[18] While the "Spirit of God" may not be completely synonymous with the life-giving spirit or with the breath of the Almighty, it is certainly the source of the breath of life that created the spirit of humanity in humankind.

God Is Spirit

Jesus made a statement that reveals much about the nature and essence of God: "God is spirit, and those who worship him must worship in spirit and truth."[19] The absolute truth of this declaration is understood when it is clear that God is not just "*a* spirit," one among many. He is "*the* spirit," or simply "spirit," who pervades the universe and infinity beyond. He is also spirit in the fact that he is not part of any of the substance of the tri-universe of matter/energy, space, and time.[20] He is neither matter, energy, space, nor time, for he created all of these out of nothing when he spoke the universe

---

[14] God specifically emphasized that humanity was "created out of nothing" when he used the Hebrew word בָּרָא (*bara'*) three times in one sentence while describing its creation: "So God created (בָּרָא—*bara'*) humanity in his own image, in the image of God created (בָּרָא—*bara'*) he him, male and female created (בָּרָא—*bara'*) he them" (Genesis 1:27). The word *bara'* generally means "to create out of nothing," and it refers exclusively to an act of God in Scripture. It is clear that God formed the human body from the dust of the earth, from already existing material; therefore, the human body was not created "out of nothing." What was created "out of nothing" was the human spirit, the *nefesh* (life) vivified by the *neshamah* that was produced in humanity by the *neshamah* of God.

[15] Singer, *et. al.*, eds.,vol. 7, p. 407.

[16] Isaiah 42:5.

[17] Psalm 104:29–30.

[18] Job. 34:14, TNK.

[19] John 4:24. The text does not say "God is *a* Spirit," as the King James Version renders it. It says, "God is spirit."

[20] The tri-universe, which is composed entirely of energy/matter, space, and time, is a visible manifestation of the tripersonal God, who is Father, Son, and Holy Spirit. This is one of the ways in which the invisible things of God, even his eternal power and deity, are understood by the material creation (Romans 1:20).

into existence. Before any material thing existed, God simply was, and he was spirit. Spirit, therefore, is ontologically the nature of divine existence. As Paul Tillich said, the statement *God is spirit* "is the most embracing, direct, and unrestricted symbol for the divine life. It does not need to be balanced with another symbol, because it includes all the ontological elements."[21]

God has been and will eternally be manifest in three persons, Father, Son, and Holy Spirit, all three of whom are also ontologically spirit. The Father is spirit;[22] the Son (Word) is spirit;[23] and the Holy Spirit is spirit. The spirit nature of God's Godself cannot, therefore, be overemphasized. God is Spirit, and God interacts with humans on the spirit level with the human spirit that he placed in humanity when he breathed the breath of life into Adam's nostrils. The spirit of man mirrors the image of the Spirit of God; therefore, God relates to believers in the realm of the Spirit.

The Spirit of the Lord

The term *Spirit of God* was first used specifically in Scripture when speaking about Bezaleel, the craftsman who made all of the implements and appliances of the Tabernacle of Witness. God himself said of Bezaleel, "I have filled him with the Spirit of God in wisdom, in understanding, in knowledge, and in all kinds of craftsmanship."[24] It is interesting that the first reference in Scripture to someone's being "filled with the Spirit of God" speaks not of miracles or of prophecy but of craftsmanship. This is a pure testimony to the fact that the Spirit of God empowers men and women with diversities of gifts and talents and that he did so centuries before Christianity was manifest.

The term *the Spirit of the* LORD is frequently used in the Hebrew Scriptures, even though it does not appear in the Torah. It is used quite extensively in the discussion of the judges of Israel to describe events when "the spirit of the LORD came upon" men and women of faith, in some cases "mightily."[25] It was evident from these texts that the Spirit of the Lord periodically seized upon men and women so that they accomplished miraculous

---

[21] Paul Tillich, *Systematic Theology* (Chicago, IL: The University of Chicago Press, 1951), vol. 1, p.249.

[22] The "Father" is the person of God who was referenced by Jesus when he said, "God is spirit," for he continued immediately to say, "The true worshipers will worship the Father in spirit and truth; for such people the Father seeks to be his worshipers" (John 4:22–24).

[23] The Son from before all time was the divine *Memra* (*D'var, Logos*), which is spirit. This is why Jesus was able to say, "The words I speak unto you, they are spirit and they are life" (John 6:63).

[24] Exodus 31:3.

[25] The judges of Israel upon whom the "Spirit of the LORD came" included Othniel (Judges 3:10); Gideon (Judges 6:34); Jephthah (Judges 11:29); Samson (Judges 13:25; 14:6, 9; 15:4).

things beyond their natural abilities. God pours out his Spirit sovereignly "upon all whom he has chosen to execute his will" and this Spirit "imbues them with higher reason and powers, making them capable of heroic speech and action."[26] The Spirit distributes his gifts as he wills.[27] God's Spirit "comes upon" people and works in concert with the human spirit, thereby empowering them to work wonders.[28] This is what Samuel said would happen in the life of Saul: "The Spirit of the LORD will come powerfully upon you, and you will prophesy with them, and you will be changed into a different person."[29] Later, as a direct result of his disobedience, however, "The Spirit of the LORD departed from Saul."[30] Israel's next king, the "sweet psalmist of Israel,"[31] confessed near the end of his life, "The Spirit of the LORD spoke by me, and his word was on my tongue."[32] King David knew that the profound words of wisdom, praise, and worship that he had delivered to Israel in song and verse were the words of God that had been spoken through him by the Spirit of God.

Throughout the monarchy and afterward, instances in which the Holy Spirit seized upon prophets continued to be recorded in Scripture. Isaiah declared, "The Spirit of the LORD God is upon me."[33] Ezekiel confessed, "The Spirit of the LORD fell upon me, and he said to me, Say, Thus says the LORD."[34] Later, the same prophet said, "The hand of the LORD was upon me, and he brought me out by the Spirit of the LORD."[35] Micah said, "I am filled with power—with the Spirit of the LORD."[36] When "the Spirit of God came upon Zechariah," he affirmed to the people, "Thus saith God."[37] All of these prophets experienced an infilling of God's Spirit by which they spoke God's Word. Micah said, "I am filled with power, with the Spirit of the LORD."[38] It was "the Spirit of the LORD" that "took possession of Gideon."[39] "The spirit of the LORD rushed on [Samson]."[40] Ezekiel has even been called "the prophet of the Spirit" because he specifically mentions

---

[26] Singer, *et. al.,* eds., vol. 7, p. 407.
[27] 1 Corinthians 12:11.
[28] Cf. Genesis 41:38; Exodus 31:3; Numbers 24:2; Judges 3:20; 2 Samuel 23:2.
[29] 1 Samuel 10:6, NIV.
[30] 1 Samuel 16:14.
[31] 2 Samuel 23:1.
[32] 2 Samuel 23:3.
[33] Isaiah 61:1.
[34] Ezekiel 11:5.
[35] Ezekiel 37:1.
[36] Micah 3:8.
[37] 2 Chronicles 2:20, KJV.
[38] Micah 3:8.
[39] Judges 6:34.
[40] Judges 14:6.

his encounters with the Spirit forty-two times in his writings,[41] far more than any other writer in Scripture.

The Holy Spirit

The Hebrew term רוּחַ הַקּוֹדֶשׁ (*Ruach HaKodesh*—"*Holy Spirit*") does not appear in the Hebrew Scriptures. The expression that is closest to this term is וְרוּחַ קָדְשְׁךָ (*ruach kodshekhah*—"your Holy Spirit") or וְרוּחַ קָדְשׁוֹ (*ruach kodsho*—"his Holy Spirit"). *Ruach kodshekhah* was used for the first time in Psalm 51:10: "Create in me a clean heart, O God; and renew a steadfast spirit within me. Do not cast me away from your presence and do not take your Holy Spirit (*ruach kodshekhah*) from me."[42] *Ruach kodsho* was used by Isaiah describe the actions of rebellious Israel: "But they rebelled and grieved his Holy Spirit (*ruach kodsho*)," as well as to recount the Israelite remembrance of the Red Sea event when God "set"[43] his "Holy Spirit" among them: "Then his people remembered the days of old, of Moses. Where is he who brought them up out of the sea with the shepherds of his flock? Where is he who put his Holy Spirit (*ruach kodsho*) in the midst of them?"[44]

The term *Ruach ha-Kodesh* ("Holy Spirit") is equivalent to the terms *the Spirit of the* LORD and *the Spirit of God*, which are used extensively in the Hebrew Scriptures.[45] *Ruach ha-Kodesh* was also the term that the rabbis came to prefer when speaking of the Spirit because of their aversion to the use of the Tetragrammaton, the four-letter name of God, YHWH.[46] The sages and later rabbis adopted the use of such intermediary terms "as a means of avoiding anthropomorphisms in speaking of God, and thus defending a notion of his incorporeality."[47] This is why they also used the term *Shekhinah* to refer to the Holy Spirit.[48] The word *Shekhinah* literally meant "dwelling"

---

[41] Anthony C. Thiselton, *The Holy Spirit—in Biblical Teaching, Through the Centuries, and Today* (Grand Rapids, MI: Wm. B. Eerdmans Publishing Co., 2013), p. 7. Also Dale Launderville, *Spirit and Reason: The Embodied Character of Ezekiel's Symbolic Thinking* (Waco, TX: Baylor University Press, 2007), p. 44.

[42] Psalm 51:10-12.

[43] This is the NIV translation of the word that is translated "put" in most versions.

[44] Isaiah 63:10–11.

[45] Spirit of the LORD: Judges 3:10; 6:34; 11:29; 13:25; 14:6; 1 Samuel 10:6; 1 Kings 18:12; 2 Kings 2:16; Isaiah 11:2; 61:1; 63:14; Ezekiel 11:5; Micah 2:7; 3:8. Spirit of God: Genesis 1:2; 41:38; Exodus 31:3; 35:31; 1 Samuel 11:6; 19:23; 2 Chronicles 15:1; 24:20; Job 33:4.

[46] E.g., Babylonian Talmud, *Makkot* 23b.

[47] Boyarin, *Border Lines*, p. 117, referencing Robert Hayward.

[48] The *Shekhinah* was the "glory" of the Lord that rested on the mercy seat between the cherubim of glory of the Ark of the Covenant (Hebrews 9:5). Some theologians connect *Shekhinah* with the New Testament Greek word παρουσία (*parousia*), which also means "presence" and speaks of the Divine Presence. See Jean-Yves Lacoste, "The Phenomenality of Anticipation," in Neal DeRoo and John P. Manoussakis, eds., *Phenomenology and Eschatology: Not Yet in the Now* (Burlington, VT: Ashgate Publishing Co., 2009), p. 27.

or "shining" but usually indicated the "presence" of God that was in the tabernacle or temple.[49]

Alan Unterman and Rivka Horowitz point out that in Rabbinic Judaism, *Ruach ha-Kodesh* was also used to describe the inspiration of prophecy. It was employed as "a hypostatization or a metonym for God."[50] Even though Rabbinic Judaism rejected the idea that God is "tri-personal or ontologically complex,"[51] the term *Ruach ha-Kodesh* had a "certain degree of personification,"[52] and it remained "a quality belonging to God, one of his attributes,"[53] says Joshua Abelson. The *Ruach ha-Kodesh*, therefore, was understood as a manifestation of God among the people of Israel.

The Spirit of Prophecy

Throughout the Hebrew Scriptures, the terms *Spirit of God*, *Spirit of the* LORD, and *Holy Spirit* were more often than not connected with prophetic utterance. The prophets were unique characters who spoke "as they were carried along by the Holy Spirit."[54] The very Hebrew word that is translated "prophet" contains an element that is descriptive of those who had been "seized upon" or "taken over" by the Holy Spirit and who often spoke with such intensity that their manner seemed frenzied. Both the noun נָבִיא (*nabi*—prophet) and the verb נָבָא (*nabah*—"prophesy"), in their oldest forms, related to speaking in "an ecstatic state" of "religious ecstasy."[55] This idea springs from the word נָבַע (*naba*), which is cognate with *nabi* and means "to bubble up" or "to pour forth"[56] as would be the case with an artesian well. The image is that of one who is bubbling up or pouring forth words from God. This symbolism is reflected in the pseudepigraphic Testament of Job in the description of a prophetess named Hemera who "spoke ecstatically in the angelic dialect, sending up a hymn to God in accord with the hymnic style of the angels. And as she spoke ecstatically, she allow[ed] 'The Spirit' to be

---

[49] The Hebrew word מִשְׁכָּן—*mishkan* ("tabernacle") is derived from שָׁכַן (*shekin*), the same root as שְׁכִינָה —*shekhinah*. It indicates a "dwelling place" in Scripture, especially when applied to the Tabernacle of Witness, the "dwelling place" of the Lord.

[50] Alan Unterman, Howard Kreisel, and Rivka Horowitz, "Ru'ah ha-Kodesh," in Michael Berenbaum and Fred Skolnik, eds., *The Encyclopedia Judaica* (Detroit, MI: Macmillan Reference USA, 2007), vol. 17, pp. 506–509.

[51] Joshua Abelson, *The Immanence of God in Rabbinical Literature* (London, UK: Macmillan and Co., 1912), p. 207.

[52] E.g., *Peshita* 117a; Leviticus *Rabbah* 6:1; Ecclesiastes *Rabbah* 12:7.

[53] Abelson, p. 207.

[54] 2 Peter 1:21, NIV.

[55] Ludwig Koehler, Walter Baumgartner, Johann Kakob Stamm, *The Hebrew and Aramaic Lexicon of the Old Testament*, tr. M. E. Richardson (Leiden, The Netherlands: Brill Academic Publishing, 1994), p. 163.

[56] Koehler, p. 163.

inscribed on her garment."[57] In later usage, however, the word *nabi* came to be related more to religious instruction than it was to ecstatic speech, which gave rise to the definition of the word *prophet* as "a divinely appointed and gifted teacher."[58]

Stephen Cook is correct, then, when he maintains that "prophecy is consistently described in ancient Jewish literature as a major, if not the primary, function of the Holy Spirit."[59] It is important to recognize the unbroken chain of prophecy that was inspired by the Holy Spirit throughout the four thousand years that the Hebrew Scriptures chronicle. Most of the leading characters in the accounts of Scripture were "prophets." Abraham was the first person who was identified as a prophet in Scripture.[60] God himself called Abraham a prophet when he commanded Abimelech to "restore the man's wife, for *he is a prophet*, and he will pray for you, and you will live."[61] Jewish tradition also maintains that Sarah was an even greater prophet than Abraham. This contention draws support from the name *Iscah*, the alternate name given in Scripture for Sarah,[62] which means "one who looks forth." This name was thought to be indicative of Sarah's far-reaching prophetic insight as well as being evidence that she spoke intuitively by the Holy Spirit. This is why God told Abraham, "Whatever Sarah tells you, listen to her,"[63] when he was confronted with the matter of deteriorating relations between Isaac and Ishmael and Sarah and Hagar.

It is clear from Scripture that Moses was a prophet. As a matter of fact, it was said that after his time, "no prophet has raised in Israel like Moses, whom the LORD knew face to face."[64] Aaron was also said to be a prophet, actually "Moses' prophet."[65] Miriam too was called a prophetess.[66] Jewish tradition compares Miriam's other name, Puah,[67] which means "to call out," with the way in which she was prompted by the Spirit to deliver the prophetic utterance: "My Mother will give birth to a son, who will save

[57] The Testament of Job 48:1–3 quoted in James H. Charlesworth, ed., *The Old Testament Pseudepigrapha: Apocalyptic Literature and Testaments* (New York: Doubleday, 1983), vol. 1, p. 865–866.

[58] Thomas Kelly Cheyne and Paul Haupt, *The Book of the Prophet Isaiah: A New English Translation* (New York: Dodd, Mead, and Company, 1898), p. 177.

[59] L. Stephen Cook, *"On the Question of the "Cessation of Prophecy" in Ancient Judaism* (Tübingen, Germany: Mohr Siebeck, 2011) , p. 155.

[60] Genesis 20:7; Psalm 105:15.

[61] Genesis 20:7, emphasis added.

[62] Genesis 11:29.

[63] Genesis 21:12. See *Megillah* 14.1.

[64] Deuteronomy 34:10.

[65] Exodus 7:1.

[66] Exodus 15:20.

[67] Exodus 1:15.

Israel."[68] Moses, Aaron, and Miriam were sent by God as prophets to "lead" Israel[69] and to bring them out of Egypt into the Promised Land. During their wilderness experience, prophecy was so highly valued that when some decried the prophesying of other men as a diminution of Moses' image and authority, the Israelite leader exclaimed, "I wish that all the LORD's people were prophets and that the LORD would put his Spirit on them!"[70] The emphasis on the Spirit's acting through prophecy was present in Israelite history from the Exodus to the conquest of the Promised Land, for Joshua also was a prophet because the Lord transferred some of Moses' spirit to him as Moses' minister.[71]

During the time of the judges, Deborah was specifically identified as a prophetess.[72] Samuel also "was confirmed to be a prophet of the LORD,"[73] and he served with such integrity that the Lord "let none of his words fail."[74] Through Samuel's prophecy, even King Saul was empowered with by the Spirit to prophesy.[75] After Samuel, numerous prophets made ecstatic pronouncements in the courts of the kings and elsewhere during the monarchy. The prophet Nathan was of particular note, even delivering the prophetic word of God's judgment upon King David because of his sin.[76] Of considerable importance also were Elijah and Elisha, both of whom had extensive careers prophesying "the word of the LORD" and performing miracles.[77] Many prophets prophesied in word only.[78] Still others prophesied in song and with music as David had done.[79] In addition to the prophets who were named in Scripture, forty-eight other people who prophesied were unnamed. Clearly, then, prophecy in and through the agency of the Spirit was a regular, if not dominant, feature in the life of Israel throughout the time of the monarchy.

---

[68] Sotch, 2.2.

[69] Micah 6:4, NIV. The New Jerusalem Bible actually has the translation of this passage even more correct than the New International Version: "[I] sent Moses, Aaron, and Miriam to lead you," for the Hebrew word translated "lead," is פָּנֶיהָ (paneh), which means "face" or "front"—the position of leadership, which, by definition, is "standing in front and pointing the way."

[70] Numbers 11:29.

[71] Deuteronomy 34:9. Though Deuteronomy 18:15 clearly speaks of the Messiah, it also can be seen as Moses' prediction that Joshua would be a prophet when he said, "A prophet shall the LORD your God raise up to you of your brothers, like to me."

[72] Judges 4:4.

[73] 1 Samuel 3:20.

[74] 1 Samuel 3:19.

[75] 1 Samuel 10:6.

[76] 2 Samuel 7:2; 12:7–12.

[77] Elijah:1 Kings 17–21; 2 Kings 1–10; Elisha: 1 Kings 19; 2 Kings 2–13.

[78] 1 Kings 22:10–12; 2 Chronicles 18:7-11; 20:37; 25:2;

[79] 1 Chronicles 25:3.

Many of the prophets mentioned in the Hebrew Scriptures were also women, including the aforementioned Sarah and Miriam, but also including Deborah[80] and Huldah.[81] Jewish tradition adds to these four the names of Hannah, Abigail, and Esther, making a total of seven prominent prophetesses recognized in the Hebrew Scriptures.[82] Women also served as advisers to the kings, including the wise woman of Tokoa[83] and a host of other women who were unnamed. Prophecy, therefore, was not the exclusive domain of men. Indeed, when God predicted through Joel an explosion of prophecy in the "last days" when he would "pour out of [his] Spirit upon all flesh," he said that both men and women would prophesy together: "Your sons and your daughters will prophesy."[84] God did not specify any difference between the way in which the sons of Zion would prophesy and the manner in which the daughters of Zion would also prophesy. God's gift of prophecy has always been given without gender restrictions. Both men and women have prophesied before the Lord and have led the camp of God's people.

Before, during, and after the Babylonian exile and during the time of the restoration of Jerusalem and the temple, the Major and Minor Prophets of Israel were actively speaking the word of the Lord. All of the canonical prophets were inspired by the Holy Spirit. These included Jeremiah, Isaiah, Ezekiel, Daniel, Hosea, Joel, Amos, Obadiah, Jonah, Micah, Nahum, Habakkuk, Zephaniah, Haggai, Zechariah, and Malachi. The writings of these prophets are filled with numerous examples of the utterance of divine speech and of prophetic demonstrations that were enacted by those who were "carried along by the Holy Spirit."

The Cessation of Prophecy?

With the passing of Haggai, Zechariah, and Malachi, the spiritual leadership of Israel was assumed by sages and teachers, prompting the emergence of the view that prophecy had ceased in Israel. Because the Holy Spirit had been so closely associated with prophecy, it was also assumed that the Spirit had also departed or had been removed from Israel. Roger Stronstad spoke of the relative silence of Spirit-inspired activity in the post-prophetic time in

---

[80] Judges 4:4.
[81] 2 Kings 22:14; 2 Chronicles 34:22.
[82] Joseph Friedman, *The Inside Story: Biblical Personalities* (Bloomington, IN: AuthorHouse, 2013), p. 210. Hannah is thought to be a prophet because of her ecstatic prayer at the tabernacle (1 Samuel 1:9–15). Abigail's prophetic credentials include the fact that she was a key spiritual adviser to King David (1 Samuel 25:32). Esther's prophetic credentials include the Jewish belief that she was chosen to deliver Israel from her mother's womb (in the same manner in which Jeremiah was chosen [Jeremiah 1:5]).
[83] 2 Samuel 14.
[84] Joel 2:28.

Israel: "The extra-canonical literature of this period . . . witnesses to a three-fold perspective on the Spirit: 1) in Judaism the Spirit is almost always the Spirit of prophecy; 2) this prophetic gift of the Spirit has ceased with the last of the writing prophets, and 3) the revival of the activity of the Spirit is expected only in the Messianic age."[85]

Some Jews even believed that the Spirit had departed centuries earlier at the time when Solomon's temple was destroyed. As a matter of fact, as Erik Konsmo points out, the sages reported that five things were missing from the second temple which had been present in Solomon's temple: "1) the Ark, the Mercy Seat and the Cherubim; 2) the fire from heaven on the altar; 3) the *Shekinah* (visible presence of God); 4) the Holy Spirit; and 5) the *Urim* and *Thummim*."[86] Virtually all the sages agreed that, with the termination of prophecy, the "visible *'Shekinah'* had ceased to appear."[87] Still, they affirmed that "the invisible *'Shekinah'*" had not disappeared "from the hearts and minds of pure, upright Jews."[88] What the destruction of Solomon's temple had effected was the suspension of the visible and material manifestation of God.

Some post-*Tanakh* texts from the time of Second Temple Judaism, however, continued to speak about the "Spirit of Prophecy."[89] They had every right to do so, because their faith was anchored in the prophetic promise of God through Joel: "Blow the trumpet in Zion; sound the alarm on my holy hill . . . for the day of the LORD is coming. It is close at hand . . . I will pour out my spirit upon all people; your sons and your daughters shall prophesy."[90] They knew that prophecy by the Spirit would yet be manifest in Israel.

The Messiah and the Spirit

Despite the sages' lament over the cessation of prophecy and the removal of the Holy Spirit from Israel, they still had hope. While they maintained that the visible *Shekhinah* had ceased to appear, they believed that it "would return with the coming of the Messiah."[91] They also believed that the *Ruach ha-Kodesh* that had been removed with the passing of the prophets would be renewed in the Messianic Age. There was an expectation that the future Messiah would be "powerful in the Holy Spirit."[92] He would be empowered by

---

[85] Roger Stronstad, *Charismatic Theology of St. Luke* (Grand Rapids, MI: Baker Academic, 1990), p. 38.
[86] Yoma 21.2.
[87] Erik Konsmo, *The Pauline Metaphors of the Holy Spirit: The Intangible Spirit's Tangible Presence in the Life of the Christian* (New York: Peter Lang Publishing, 2010), p. 18.
[88] Konsmo, p. 18.
[89] E.g., Jubilees 25:14; 31:12.
[90] Joel 2:1, 28, NIV.
[91] Konsmo, p. 18.
[92] Psalms of Solomon 17:37.

the "glory of the Most High" and be filled with "the spirit of understanding and sanctification."[93] William Davies was correct to point out that "Rabbinic Judaism of the first century would have regarded the Messianic Age or the Age to Come as the Era of the Spirit."[94] The expectation that the operation of the Spirit would be restored to Israel in the future was a continuing theme proclaimed by the sages of Second Temple Judaism.

Due to the growing expectation of the advent of the Messianic Age during the time of the second temple, a continuing emphasis on the Spirit was present in the everyday lives of Jews even during the four hundred years of prophetic silence in Israel. This was especially true in the Qumran community, which placed special emphasis on the Spirit. The Dead Sea Scrolls affirm that "the Spirit has been given, and can still be further sought" and that while the Holy Spirit was "already active in the whole community, his work [was] continuing and progressive, not once for all."[95] The term *Holy Spirit*, in fact, occurs fifteen times in the Qumran scrolls. In this community, as well as that of apocalyptic Judaism, the work of the Holy Spirit continued to be viewed as the "spirit of prophecy."[96]

It was into the milieu of Jewish expectations regarding the Messiah and the age of the Holy Spirit that Jesus and the apostles were born. It should not have surprised anyone, therefore, when the apostle John declared that "the testimony of Jesus is the spirit of prophecy"?[97] Clearly, the emphasis of the Jesus community on the functions and operation of the Spirit were deeply rooted in the soil of biblical Judaism. David Flusser suggests that applications of "spirit" in the Dead Sea Scrolls had a profound influence on the apostolic understanding of the Holy Spirit. He noted that, for this community, the "granting of wisdom is a function of the Holy Spirit [as] the only mediator of true knowledge, which is inaccessible to carnal man."[98] In fact, the concept of "the spirit of truth" and "the spirit of error"[99] that were so strongly emphasized in apostolic teaching was found in The Community Rule of the Qumran community that predated

---

[93] Testament of Levi 18:7. See Konsmo, p. 19.

[94] William D. Davies, *Paul and Rabbinic Judaism: Some Rabbinic Elements in Pauline Theology* (Minneapolis, MN: Fortress Press, 1980), p. 216.

[95] Thiselton, p. 28. Also George J. Brooke, *The Dead Sea Scrolls and the New Testament* (London, UK: SPCK, 2005) and Géza Vermès, *The Complete Dead Sea Scrolls in English* (London, UK: Allen Lane, 1997).

[96] Robert Menzies, *Empowered for Witness* (London, UK: Continuum International Publishing Group, 2004), p. 41.

[97] Revelation 19:10.

[98] David Flusser, *Judaism and the Origins of Christianity* (Jerusalem, Israel: Magnes Press, 1988), pp. 56, 67.

[99] In John 16:13, Jesus referred to the Holy Spirit as "the spirit of truth." In 1 John 1:4–6, John said, "By this you know the Spirit of God: every spirit that confesses that Jesus Christ has come in the flesh is from God . . . By this we know the Spirit of truth and the spirit of error" (ESV).

Christianity.[100] Strong Hebrew foundations, therefore, formed the underpinning of the teachings of Jesus and the apostles regarding the Holy Spirit. Davies summarized the thought processes of all the apostles when, speaking of Paul, he declared that "the acceptance of the Gospel was not . . . the rejection of the old Judaism and the discovery of a new religion . . . but the recognition of the advent of the true and final form of Judaism, in other words, the advent of the Messianic Age of Jewish expectation."[101]

This is why the focus on the Holy Spirit was so prominent in the life and ministry of Jesus. When the Son of God began to embark upon the ministry that he had been assigned by the heavenly Father, he made the pilgrimage to the area of Qumran where his cousin John was immersing Israelites in the Jordan River. There he experienced John's immersion rite, saying to the Baptizer, "It is proper for us to do this to fulfill all righteousness."[102] Just after the baptism was complete, "the Holy Spirit descended upon [Jesus] in bodily form like a dove, and a voice came out of heaven, You are my beloved Son, in you I am well pleased."[103] Immediately, "Jesus, *full of the Holy Spirit*, left the Jordan and was *led by the Spirit* into the wilderness"[104] where he fasted and prayed for forty days and overcame every possible temptation of Satan. Then, "Jesus returned to Galilee *in the power of the Spirit*."[105]

Shortly after these experiences of the Holy Spirit, Jesus stood up in his synagogue in Nazareth on the Sabbath day to read the Torah *parashah*[106] and the *haftarah* portion[107] that had been assigned to him: "The Spirit of the LORD is upon me, because he has anointed me to proclaim good news to the poor. He has sent me to proclaim liberty to the captives and recovering of sight to the blind, to set at liberty those who are oppressed, to proclaim the year of the LORD's favor."[108] When he finished reading, Jesus rolled up the scroll, gave it back to the attendant, and sat down. Everyone in the synagogue was transfixed on Jesus, so he said to them, "Today this Scripture has been fulfilled in your hearing."[109]

---

[100] *The Community Rule* (Dead Sea Scrolls, 1 QS), 4:16. See A. R. C. Leaney, *The Rule of Qumran and Its Meaning* (London, UK: SCM, 1966, pp. 34–56.
[101] Davies, pp. 323–324.
[102] Matthew 3:15.
[103] Luke 3:22.
[104] Luke 4:1, NIV, emphasis added.
[105] Luke 4:14, emphasis added.
[106] The *parashah* is the portion of the Torah assigned for reading each week.
[107] The *haftarah* (literally, "conclusion") is the portion from the prophets that is read immediately after the final Torah section of the Torah *parashah* has been read. Harvey J. Fields, *B'chol L'vavcha: A Commentary* (New York, UAHC Press, 2001), p. 195. Also UJR Press, *Chai: Learning for Jewish Life* (Woodstock, VT: JRJ Press, 2005), p. 165.
[108] Luke 4:18–19, ESV.
[109] Luke 4:21.

Jesus continued "in the Spirit" throughout the time of his ministry, and he did so in the context of the Hebraic thought and tradition that had been outlined in the Hebrew Scriptures and in much of second-temple tradition. One prominent example of this is an often overlooked and misunderstood incident in which Jesus was accused of casting out demons by the power of Beelzebub, the prince of demons. Jesus replied to the charge, "If I cast out demons by the finger of God, then the kingdom of God has come upon you."[110] In another place, Jesus said, "I cast out demons by the Spirit of God."[111] When Jesus used the metaphor *finger of God* to refer to the Holy Spirit, his audience knew immediately that he was connecting his ministry in the Spirit with the authorship of the Ten Commandments that Scripture declared were "written with the finger of God"[112] on two stone tablets. Jesus employed this term to illustrate the fact that the same Spirit that had written the Torah in the first place was the divine agent of his ministry. He also could have been alluding to the incident when Pharaoh's magicians exclaimed, "This is the finger of God," when they realized that they did not have the power to duplicate the miracles that Moses and Aaron had performed through the agency of the Holy Spirit.[113] The idiom was a graphic illustration of the Hebraic understanding that men of God were directed by the inspiration of the Holy Spirit in the same way in which the miracles that prompted Pharaoh to release the Israelites were performed and by the same way in which the very words of God were delivered to Israel at Sinai—by "the finger of God."

Restoring the Spirit of Truth

The ministry of Jesus "in the power of the Holy Spirit" continued for three and one-half years of continuing manifestations of divine power through miracles that even included raising the dead—all in confirmation of the fact that the Age of Messiah, the Age of the Holy Spirit, that the sages had anticipated and predicted had truly come. Jesus knew that the time had come for him to "taste death for all men."[114] The Holy Spirit would lead him to Jerusalem where he would be handed over to the Romans "to be mocked and flogged and crucified."[115] In preparation for this event, however, he began to prepare his disciples so that they would be filled with the

---

[110] Luke 11:20.
[111] Matthew 12:28.
[112] Exodus 31:18; Deuteronomy 9:10.
[113] Exodus 8:29.
[114] Hebrews 2:9.
[115] Matthew 20:19, NIV.

same Holy Spirit that had driven his own ministry. "I tell you the truth, it is to your advantage that I go away; for if I do not go away, the *Paraclete* will not come to you; but if I go, I will send him to you. . . . When he, the Spirit of truth, comes, he will guide you into all the truth."[116] Then, on the evening of the day of his resurrection, in a graphic demonstration of his emphasis on the Spirit, Jesus "breathed on" his disciples and said to them, "Receive the Holy Spirit."[117] The imagery is clear: Just as God had breathed on Adam to create a "living being," so Jesus breathed upon his disciples the same breath God that would confer upon them the Holy Spirit and create the body of the Messiah.

The *Ruach ha-Kodesh* that had been powerfully manifest in the life and ministry of Jesus was to be transferred to his disciples. What had been displayed occasionally and significantly in the pre-Messianic era was to be expanded dramatically so that it would become an everyday experience for the church. Jesus had predicted this expansion when he said concerning the Holy Spirit, "He dwells with you and will be in you."[118] As four millennia of witnesses had attested, the Holy Spirit had been with the Hebrews, the Israelites, and the Jews across the sweep of election history. Now, however, the Holy Spirit that had been with the prophets and sages of Israel and with the apostles of the new community would become resident in the lives of the believers. The indwelling of the Spirit would infuse them with power for service that would impact their own lives and the lives of all of those to whom they would bear witness concerning the truth of the kingdom of God.

Jesus continued to instruct his disciples concerning the impact of this infusion of the Holy Spirit: "I am sending forth the promise of my Father upon you; but you are to stay in the city until you are clothed with power from on high. . . . you will receive power when the Holy Spirit has come upon you."[119] What Jesus promised to his disciples was only what John had predicted years before that time when he had said, "He will baptize you with the Holy Spirit and fire."[120] After ten days of concentrated prayer, the disciples did, indeed, experience what Jesus had predicted: "When the day of Pentecost had come . . . suddenly there came from heaven a noise like a violent rushing wind, and it filled the whole house where they were sitting. . . . and they were all filled with the Holy Spirit and began to speak with other tongues, as the Spirit was giving them utterance."[121] The amazing thing

---

[116] John 16:7, 13, ESV.
[117] John 20:22.
[118] John 14:17, ESV.
[119] Luke 24:49; Acts 1:8.
[120] Matthew 3:11.
[121] Acts 1:1–2, 5.

about this ecstatic experience was that the disciples of Jesus were empowered to speak languages with which they were not conversant so that Jewish believers from various nations of the world heard from them "the wonderful works of God" in their own languages![122]

Peter, the spokesman for the newly emerging community, recognized what was occurring, so he made this declaration: "Fellow Jews and all of you who live in Jerusalem, let me explain this to you . . . These people are not drunk, as you suppose. It's only nine in the morning! No, this is what was spoken by the prophet Joel: 'In the last days,' God says, 'I will pour out my Spirit on all people. Your sons and daughters will prophesy . . . even on my servants, both men and women, I will pour out my Spirit in those days, and they will prophesy.'"[123] The supposed drunkenness of those who had been "filled with the Holy Spirit" should have come as no surprise to their fellow Jews, for the Jewish people had long been viewed as a "God-intoxicated people." Indeed, as Samuel Umen says, "Jewish history is the record of a god-intoxicated, god-thirsty people."[124] The fiery presence that the earliest Christian believers experienced was characteristic of their Jewish heritage that was manifest in the prophets. Abraham Heschel underscores this fiery intensity as essential to true service of God: "A Jew should serve God with ardor. It was necessary, vital, to have fire in the soul."[125] No doubt, this is what Paul meant when he exhorted Christians to be "fervent in spirit, serving the Lord."[126]

What had been pessimistically thought to be a self-imposed banishment of the Holy Spirit had actually been a short hiatus. The *Ruach ha-Kodesh* had not abandoned Israel. God was simply searching for those who would indeed be "God thirsty," those who would seek him more intensely in the Spirit than in rationalism, more in an existential, personal experience than in a purely logical form. The general outpouring of the Holy Spirit on the first Day of Pentecost in the Christian era was further evidence that the Messiah had come. What had been experienced periodically throughout the history of God's dealings with his Chosen People from the time of Abraham was renewed and expanded when Jewish men and women were once again "filled with the Holy Spirit" and began to be exercised by the Spirit.

Because the word *ruach* is used 250 times in the Hebrew Scriptures to denote divine activity of various sorts, the use of the term *Holy Spirit* in

---

[122] Acts 2:9–11.

[123] Acts 2:14–18, NIV.

[124] Samuel Umen, *Jewish Concepts and Reflections* (New York: Philosophical Library, 1962), p. 32, cited in Wilson, *Our Father*, p. 161.

[125] Abraham Joshua Heschel, *A Passion for Truth* (New York: Farrar, Straus & Giroux, 1973), pp. 47–48.

[126] Romans 12:11. The word translated *fervent* is ζέω (zéo), which literally means "boiling" or "seething."

the Apostolic Scriptures is solidly anchored in the language and concepts of the *Tanakh*. Jesus even used an analogy based on the Hebrew word *ruach* that everyone in Israel would have understood when he declared that as "the wind blows where it wishes and you hear the sound of it, but do not know where it comes from and where it is going; so is everyone who is born of the Spirit."[127] The apostles merely took up their master's theme and expanded it by applying it to every aspect of the Christian life. Davies is correct, then, when he argues that Paul the Pharisee shared the Pharisean expectation that "the Messianic Age or the Age to Come [would be] the age of the Spirit"[128] and that the apostle fully believed that age was being fulfilled in and through Jesus. This is why Paul placed continuing emphasis on essential work of the Holy Spirit and his charisms in the lives of the earliest Christian community.

Recovering Hebraic Understanding of the Spirit

In order to understand early Christian pneumatology,[129] one must have an understanding of early Jewish thought and experience of the Holy Spirit. Likewise, in order to understand the Spirit and its application in the lives of believers today, one must recognize the foundations of pneumatological concepts in the Hebrew, Israelite, and Jewish communities of pre-Christian times and then see how Jesus and the apostles refined and expanded those concepts. Finally, the fundamental principles on which Christian pneumatology is founded must be carefully contextualized into the life of the church in every era and among every ethnicity. Failure to follow this simple, fundamental principle has produced a wide range of perspectives on the Holy Spirit that stretch from absolute cessationism[130] on the one hand to extreme mysticism and hyper-spiritualism on the other. The balanced position of theological safety is to be found only when the teachings of Apostolic Scripture are returned to the Hebraic foundations on which they were built.

Doubtless, the empowerment of the Holy Spirit for witnessing the Good News was *the* dominant theme of the earliest church. This focus was, however, merely a continuation of the centuries-old emphasis on the essential nature of the Holy Spirit. Christianity's understanding of the Holy Spirit, then, is solidly anchored on secure biblically Hebraic foundations.

Spirit: Christian Fruit—Jewish Root!

---

[127] John 3:8.

[128] Davies, p. 216.

[129] Pneumatology is "the study of the Spirit."

[130] The teaching of cessationism appeals to 1 Corinthians 13:10 ("When the perfect comes, the partial will be done away.") as meaning that when the Holy Scriptures, including the Apostolic Writings, were completed, the operation of the Spirit ceased because "the perfect thing" (Scripture) had come.

CHAPTER 12

SPIRITUALITY

Since its founding, Christianity has been recognized as a religion that is of, by, and for the Spirit. As a matter of fact, the historical event that Christians universally recognize as the birth of the church occurred on the Day of Pentecost when the 120 believers who had followed Jesus' instructions to "wait patiently in [Jerusalem] until you are clothed with power from on high"[1] received the infilling of the Holy Spirit.[2]

Even before that event, however, Jesus had predicated salvation itself upon being "born from above . . . by the Spirit."[3] In fact, he had declared that no one could even "see" or "enter the kingdom of God" unless he had been "born of the Spirit."[4] Then, before his crucifixion, resurrection, and ascension, Jesus made this profound promise to those who believed in him: "I will pray the Father, and he will give you another Helper, that he may abide with you forever, even the Spirit of truth . . . for he dwells *with you,* and will be *in you.* . . . [and] you shall receive power when the Holy Spirit has come upon you; and you shall be witnesses to me."[5] After Jesus' ascension, the Spirit that had been *with* the believers was to become resident *in* their lives.[6] The Spirit-filled and Spirit-led life, therefore, was to be the hallmark of the Christian faith from its very initiation.

The Beginning of Spirit-Filled Life

When the promise that Jesus had made was fulfilled, it occurred, interestingly enough, on one of the three pilgrimage festivals of Judaism, the Feast of *Shavuot* (Pentecost). "When the Day of Pentecost had fully come . . . they

---

[1] Luke 24:49, WNT.
[2] Acts 2:4.
[3] John 3:3.
[4] John 3:5.
[5] John 16:7; 14:16–17, emphasis added; Acts 1:8.
[6] John 14:16–17.

were all filled with the Holy Spirit and began to speak with other tongues, as the Spirit gave them utterance.'[7] Once before in recorded history such a profound event had occurred when 120 priests were officiating at the dedication of the temple in Jerusalem during the Festival of Tabernacles.[8] At that time, the Holy Spirit so filled the temple with the smoke of the divine presence that the priests were unable to perform their service before the Lord. This time, on the day of Pentecost, the Holy Spirit filled the 120 believers to such a degree that they appeared to be drunken and manifested a gift for xenoglossy by speaking languages with which they were not familiar.[9] In another parallel event, at the very first Pentecost celebration, when the law of God was given at Mt. Sinai, 3,000 people died because of idolatry in incident with the golden calf.[10] On the first Pentecost in the Christian era, however, 3,000 people received the gift of eternal life when they repented and were baptized on the day when the Holy Spirit came to indwell believers on Mt. Zion.[11]

From that day throughout the Book of Acts, the supernatural manifestations of the Spirit that had occurred periodically in the record of the Hebrew Scriptures became the hallmark of the new covenant Messianic community. The apostles went everywhere, healing the sick, exorcising demons, working miracles, and doing signs and wonders.[12] The Holy Spirit, which had been given to the children of Israel by measure, was poured out upon the Messianic community without measure when they were filled with the Holy Spirit. The Spirit that had been given to Jesus "without measure" was appropriated by him as his gift to the disciples in a degree that paralleled the level of his spiritual empowerment during his incarnation.[13] As John said, "He whom God has sent speaks the words of God; for he gives the Spirit without measure."[14] This is why Jesus made this promise to his disciples: "He who believes in me, the works that I do, he will do also; and greater works than these he will do; because I go to the Father."[15]

The Holy Spirit was experienced by these believers who had been born of the Spirit[16] so that they could live the life of the Spirit by walking in the

----

[7] Acts 2:1, 4.
[8] 2 Chronicles 5:12–14.
[9] Acts 1:15; 2:1–15.
[10] Exodus 32:28.
[11] Acts 2:41.
[12] Acts 5:12.
[13] John 3:34.
[14] John 3:14.
[15] John 14:12.
[16] John 3:16–20.

Spirit.[17] As Anthony Thiselton says, "The Spirit of God is creative; the Spirit of God is life-giving," and the work of the Spirit of God is accomplished by "the Spirit's capacity for being 'shared out' from one figure to others."[18] Clearly, "these are the most striking themes which became a practical basis for the gift of the Holy Spirit to Christians in the New Testament."[19] The shared life of the Holy Spirit became the empowering agent Christianity.

A few years later, the gift that had been experienced exclusively by the Jewish people, including the Jewish Messianic community, was extended to the Gentiles. The apostle Peter visited the house of Cornelius, the Roman centurion, at Caesarea by the Sea, where he explained the good news of salvation through Jesus Christ to those Gentiles. "While Peter was still speaking these words, the Holy Spirit fell upon all those who heard the word . . . . [and] they heard them speak with tongues."[20] At this time, the experience that had been unique to Jews and Judaism was given to Gentiles, and, from them, it was ultimately extended to the entire world.

In the decades after the Acts 2 Pentecost, Jews and Gentiles alike, by the thousands, received the same experience that the 120 believers had received on the Day of Pentecost. They were filled with the Holy Spirit and, through the operation of that Spirit, proceeded to accomplish things that were beyond their natural human abilities. Peter's shadow healed people.[21] Paul sent cloths and aprons that he had touched to those who were sick, and they were healed.[22] Agabus prophesied of a famine that became a worldwide event,[23] and he predicted the outcome of Paul's ministry wherein he would be bound and taken to Rome.[24] Paul was bitten by a venomous viper but was not harmed.[25] Philip experienced a bodily translation from the Gaza to Azotus.[26] Many other notable miracles and wonders

---

[17] Galatians 5:16–26.

[18] Thiselton, pp. 3–5.

[19] Thiselton, pp. 3-5.

[20] Acts 10:44, 46.

[21] Acts 5:15–16: "People brought the sick into the streets and laid them on beds and mats so that at least Peter's shadow might fall on some of them as he passed by. . . . and they were all being healed" (NIV).

[22] Acts 19:11–12: "God was performing extraordinary miracles by the hands of Paul, so that handkerchiefs or aprons were even carried from his body to the sick, and the diseases left them and the evil spirits went out."

[23] Acts 11:28: "Agabus stood up and began to indicate by the Spirit that there would certainly be a great famine over the world. And this took place in the reign of Claudius."

[24] Acts 21:10: "A prophet named Agabus . . . took Paul's belt and bound his own feet and hands and said, 'This is how the Jews at Jerusalem will bind the man who owns this belt and deliver him into the hands of the Gentiles.'"

[25] Acts 28:3–4.

[26] Acts 8:39: "When they came up out of the water, the Spirit of the Lord snatched Philip away. The eunuch never saw him again . . . But Philip found himself at Azotus."

were done through the power of the Holy Spirit that was operating in the lives of the apostles and other believers in the first-century community of Christian faith.[27]

Gifts and Manifestations of the Spirit

The gift of the Holy Spirit brought many other manifestations of the Spirit into the lives of believers. In 1 Corinthians 12, Paul delineated some of these, describing them as gifts (*charismata*) of the Spirit: "To one is given the word of wisdom through the Spirit, to another the word of knowledge through the same Spirit, to another faith by the same Spirit, to another gifts of healings by the same Spirit, to another the working of miracles, to another prophecy, to another discerning of spirits, to another different kinds of tongues, to another the interpretation of tongues. But one and the same Spirit works all these things, distributing to each one individually as he wills."[28]

In Romans 12, Paul also outlined still other gifts of the Holy Spirit: "Having then gifts differing according to the grace that is given to us," whether prophecy, or ministry, or teaching, or exhortation, or giving, or leadership, or mercy.[29] These gifts provided strength to the ongoing life and operation of the Christian community in its mission and witness and enabled ordinary men and women to accomplish extraordinary tasks in the overspread of the gospel and the administration of the daily life and business of the church. These "manifestations of the Spirit" were given "for the profit" of the body of believers.[30] Through them the church, both Jew and Gentile, shared the good news of Jesus with the supernatural power of the Spirit of God that convinced millions of people to believe in the Messiah of Israel and the Savior of the world. The miraculous witness that had authenticated YHWH's religion under the first covenant was multiplied many times over through the outpouring of the Holy Spirit in the new covenant.

Then, Paul also delineated the ministry gifts that Jesus as high priest had given to the church. These included the gifts of apostle, prophet, evangelist, pastor, and teacher (or pastor/teacher).[31] Paul's listing was not a delineation of ecclesiastical offices, nor was it an organizational chart. Paul did not even speak of "men" in this listing. His statement was rather an outline of gifts

---

[27] Acts 5:12.
[28] 1 Corinthians 12:8–11.
[29] Romans 12:6–8.
[30] 1 Corinthians 12:7.
[31] Ephesians 4:11.

that God had given to "humanity"[32] to empower believers for particular functions within the church. Paul also described the specific purpose for which these gifts were given: ". . . for the equipping of the saints for works of ministry to the building up of the body of Christ"[33] and "for the profit of all" the community.[34]

Ministry gifts are not ends in themselves, mere means of equipping a professional clergy to fulfill all the ministry in the church. They are gifts of service designed to empower Christian leaders to equip all believers so that they can then do the works of ministry that will build up the body of Christ.[35] Paul also made clear the duration of the time when the church would need to be empowered with these gifts: ". . . till we all come in the unity of the faith, and of the full knowledge of the Son of God, unto a complete man, to the measure of the stature of the fullness of Christ."[36] Until the church achieves the unity of the faith and comes to complete maturity, all five of these ministry gifts will continue to be essential to its proper operation. As a matter of fact, the church can never function perfectly unless each of the gifts is fully operational.

Spiritual Continuity

The profound and concentrated manifestation of the Spirit in the earliest community of Christian believers, however, did not represent anything that had never been seen in the experience of the Hebrews/Israelites who preceded the Christians. One of the most fundamental guiding principles for such understanding can be summed up in these words by Frank McGloin: "We should note carefully this similarity in the operations of the Holy Spirit, in particular men, under both Dispensations, as going to show that both Testaments, Old and New, disclose identically the same concept as to the Spirit of God."[37] There was no lurching, dramatic change in the pneumatological[38] understanding of the apostles that in any way invalidated the teachings of the

---

[32] Ephesians 4:8: "When [Jesus] ascended on high, he led captive a host of captives, and he gave gifts to men." Most versions translate this passage, ". . . he gave gifts to *men*" (emphasis added). The Greek text is clear, however, for it says, ". . . he gave gifts to *humanity*," using the Greek word ἄνθρωπος (*ánthropos*), which, though it can mean "man" in the sense of "a human being," specifically speaks of "humanity." If Paul had intended to say that God gave these gifts exclusively to males, he would have used the word ἀνήρ (*anér*), which specifically means "man" (with respect to gender).

[33] Ephesians 4:12, literal translation.

[34] 1 Corinthians 12:7.

[35] Ephesians 4:12b.

[36] Ephesians 4:13, author's translation.

[37] Frank McGloin, *The Mystery of the Holy Trinity in Oldest Judaism* (Philadelphia, PA: John Joseph McVey, 1916), p. 176.

[38] Pneumatology is the study of the Holy Spirit.

Hebrew Scriptures relating to the Holy Spirit and his operations. The apostles rather built on the solid Hebraic foundations of their faith and expanded the application of that faith to all the nations for the obedience of faith.[39]

The great infilling of the Holy Spirit that occurred on the Day of Pentecost in Acts 2, along with the subsequent manifestations of that Spirit in the lives of believers, was merely a concentrated outpouring of something that had been periodically manifest in God's religious system for more than two thousand years before that Pentecost. The supernatural had always been one of the identifying marks of the religion of YHWH, the eternal God. Before the first century, the indwelling of the Holy Spirit and the manifestation of its power to perform superhuman things through human instruments was a characteristic that was unique to biblical Judaism and the Jewish people.

In the Hebrew Scriptures, there was abundant and continuing evidence of the supernatural. As a matter of fact, all of the *charismata* of the Spirit that were detailed in the Apostolic Scriptures were manifest to one degree or another under the Abrahamic and Sinai covenants. What greater example of the word of wisdom could be considered than the sagacity of Solomon?[40] Were there greater instances when the word of knowledge was more clearly manifest in Elisha's insight into Gehazi's treachery?[41] Was there ever a more powerful manifestation of faith than what Abraham displayed throughout his life?[42] Who could forget the profound miracles worked when Moses parted the Red Sea, brought forth water from a rock, and fed some two million people with manna?[43] What greater example of healing could be advanced than the cleansing of Naaman's leprosy?[44] Could there be greater miracles than those of Elijah, who stopped and started rain at his word,[45] called down fire from heaven,[46] and raised the widow's son from the dead, or those of Elisha who made an axe head float on water[47] and raised the Shunammite's son from the dead?[48] Or who does not remember the time when King Saul was "changed into a different man" and spoke in *glossolalia* when the Spirit of God came upon him as he dwelt among the prophets?[49] Who does not recall Daniel's having the gift to interpret the unknown language written by the

---

[39] Romans 16:26.
[40] 1 Kings 4:30.
[41] 2 Kings 5:21–27.
[42] Genesis 15:6; 22:2.
[43] Exodus 14; Numbers 20; Exodus 16.
[44] 2 Kings 15:10–14.
[45] 1 Kings 17:1; 18:41–44, 17:18–23.
[46] 1 Kings 18:38.
[47] 2 Kings 6:1-7.
[48] 2 Kings 4:34–36.
[49] 1 Samuel 10:6, 10.

finger of God on the wall of the Babylonian temple?[50] Or who could forget the deliverance of the Hebrew children from the fiery furnace[51] or of Daniel from the den of lions?[52] Who would not be awed by the profound prophetic words spoken by Samuel, Jeremiah, Isaiah, and many others who faithfully proclaimed the Word of divine revelation that they had received by God. Surely the discerning of spirits was manifest when Micaiah assured Jehoshaphat that Ahab's prophets were inspired by an evil spirit, not the Holy Spirit.[53]

Aided by the supernatural Spirit of God, these Israelites foreshadowed good gifts that were to come.[54] During the time before the advent of Jesus, however, these events were at best occasional and in most times rare, for it was perhaps difficult for the Almighty to find vessels who were worthy to embody the demonstration of such power. Few men were willing to forsake the riches of Egyptian royalty to live in the desert[55] or to remain fiercely loyal to the law of God in the face of execution[56] or to suffer the rejection and ridicule of their peers and fellow countrymen. It remained for God to provide something better for the breaking forth of his kingdom through the agency of the first-century Messianic community.[57] The *charismata* that were manifest among the Hebrews and Israelites in pre-Christian times, therefore, were given bountifully to the church following the ascension of Jesus Christ and his assumption of the role of high priest for all believers and the giver of every good and perfect gift.

Western Christianity's Drift into Rationalism

As the Christian church became predominately Gentile in its leadership and demographics, it began to distance itself from its Jewish roots. When this transpired, it increasingly replaced faith and the operation of the Holy Spirit in the lives of believers with the rationalism of the Greco-Roman world.[58] Especially in Western Christianity, the works of ministry that were to be manifest in the lives of "the saints" were gradually assigned to a professional clergy and eventually reserved exclusively for them. This clergy

---

[50] Daniel 5:25.
[51] Daniel 3:20–26.
[52] Daniel 6:25–27.
[53] 1 Kings 22:18.
[54] Hebrews 10:1.
[55] Hebrews 11:27.
[56] Daniel 3:16–18.
[57] Hebrews 11:39–40.
[58] While there were continuing examples of people who exercised the gifts of the Spirit (e.g., the second-century Montanists and their reliance on ecstatic prophecy which often took them to extremes and even into heresy), most of these were largely discredited by the church leaders in their rush toward an embrace of Greek rationalism.

eventually came to see itself as possessing a higher state of holiness than the rest of the Christian believers whom increasingly described as "laity."[59] As this teaching and practice gained ascendancy in most of Christianity, the "clergy-laity gap" produced a heresy of priestly exaltation that established itself throughout the church.[60] This, too, was a further result of the emphasis on rationalism rather than on faith and on professionalism rather than on *charismata*. Ultimately, the Roman Catholic Church for all intents and purposes was dichotomized into the *ecclesia docens* ("teaching church") and the *ecclesia audiens* ("listening church"), in effect, making the teaching, governing church *the* church.[61] The laity that was the driving force of the first-century Messianic faith was essentially restricted from ministry and silenced.

When this occurred, the laity became spectators, whose function it was to observe the performance of the clergy and to be acted upon by the clergy through the sacraments of the church.[62] Ultimately, ostensibly because of the high level of illiteracy in Europe, free access to Holy Scripture was severely restricted, if not denied altogether, to the laity often upon penalty of excommunication[63] and even death.[64] In the years from 1545 to 1563, Council of Trent established the church as the rightful interpreter of Scripture and argued that church tradition was equally authoritative with Scripture.[65] One member

---

[59] The Greek word λαός—*laos* ("people") appears in Apostolic Scripture (Acts 4:25; Romans 15:11; Revelation 17:15; 21:3); however, the word λαϊκός—*laikós* ("laity") is not used in the Apostolic Scripture. The term *laity* was first used in the third century AD by Clement of Rome in his attempt to circumscribe the work of the "priesthood" (clergy) by denying it to the people (laity). From the third century AD onward, the increasing power of the clergy and the diminishing influence of the laity came to characterize most of the Christian church. See Clement, *1 Corinthians* 40:5; 41:1. Also Alexandre Faivre, *The Emergence of the Laity in the Early Church*, tr. David Smith (New York: Paulist Press, 1990), p. 15.

[60] Frank Viola and George Barna, *Pagan Christianity?: Exploring the Roots of Our Church Practices* (Carol Stream, IL: Tyndale House Publishers, 2002), p. 122. Also, Christopher Wyatt Goff, *Measuring the Clergy/Laity Gap and Its Effect on Church Health and Outreach* (Ann Arbor, MI: UMI Microfilm, 2008), pp. 30–34.

[61] Leonard Verduin, *The Reformers and Their Stepchildren* (Paris, AR: The Baptist Standard Bearer, 2001), p. 141. Also Donald K. McKim, *Major Themes in the Reformed Tradition* (Eugene, OR: Wipf and Stock Publishers, 1998), p. 113.

[62] James M. O'Toole, *The Faithful: A History of Catholics in America* (Cambridge, MA: Harvard University Press, 2008), p. 118. Also, Mark R. Kowalewski, *All Things to All People: The Catholic Church Confronts the AIDS Crisis* (Albany, NY: The State University of New York Press, 1994), p. 13.

[63] The Fourth Rule of the Index from the Council of Trent said, "Whereas, it is manifest by experience that if the Holy Bible, translated into the vulgar tongue [common vernacular], be allowed indifferently to anybody, then, on account of man's rashness, will arise from hence a greater detriment than advantage. If anyone without a license presume to read or keep by him the Bible, he shall be disqualified to receive the absolution of his sins till he 'deliver it up to the Ordinary.'" See *Evangelical Christendom*, Jan 1, 1894, vol. 43, p. 8.

[64] H. T. Spence, *The Canon of Scripture* (Dunn, NC: Forwarding the Faith Publications, 2010), pp. 21–22. English Bible translator William Tyndale was martyred primarily for translating the Bible into the language of the common people.

[65] John Lawson, *Introduction to Christian Doctrine* (Grand Rapids, MI: Zondervan Publishing House, 1980), p. 5.

of the Council of Trent maintained that "one of the parents and springs of heresies was the translation of the Holy Scriptures into the vulgar [common] languages."[66] Another prelate said, "To allow shoemakers, potters, etc., to read the Scriptures, is to give that which is holy to the dogs, and to cast pearls before swine."[67] The Roman Church insisted that it alone had the right to produce translations of Scripture, and it generally held to the Latin Vulgate until the twentieth century.[68] Since the masses were mostly illiterate and had virtually no understanding of Latin, they had no real access to Holy Scripture for themselves and were, therefore, totally dependent upon the church and its clergy for whatever understanding they had about Christian doctrine and polity. The combination of general illiteracy and restrictions on access to Scripture produced an ignorant, superstitious, and pitiful populace that could easily be manipulated both by political forces and by religious hierarchs. It also perpetuated a spiritually impoverished laity that was often devoid of God's gifts and graces.

The emphasis on professionalism and rationalism in Western Christianity produced its final and inglorious application when the church adopted the doctrine and practice of sacramentalism, wherein the sacraments of the church came to be considered to be efficacious regardless as to the spiritual condition of the priest or the communicant.[69] Sacramentalism led to a further diminution of the spiritual stature of the individual layperson and militated further against the Holy Spirit's ministering through individuals by means of his *charismata* and graces. In this environment of rationalism and professionalism, it was possible for men to know much *about* God while at the same time not *knowing* God.[70] When the focus of spirituality was on academic and intellectual achievement rather than on the empowerment of the Holy Spirit to live victorious lives of service to others through the power of the Holy Spirit, the results that were produced were, to say the least, less than

---

[66] *Evangelical Christendom*, p. 8.

[67] *Evangelical Christendom*, p. 9.

[68] Thomas Shepherd, *Friends in High Places: Tracing the Family Tree of New Thought Christianity* (Lincoln, NE: iUniverse Publishing, 2004), pp. 45–46.

[69] Roland H. Bainton, *Here I Stand: A Life of Martin Luther* (Peabody, MA: Hendrickson Publishers, 1950), p. 128. Bainton points out the nature of the medieval Catholic Church' teaching of sacramentalism: "The teaching of the Church is that the sacraments cannot be impaired by any human weakness, be it the unworthiness of the performer or the indifference of the receiver. The sacrament operates by virtue of a power within itself *ex opere operato*." *Ex opere operato* means "from the work worked."

[70] Ulrich G. Leinsle, *Introduction to Scholastic Theology* (Washington, DC: The Catholic University of America Press, 2010), p. 202. Leinsle speaks of a theology which "intends to address precisely those faculties in man that are not satisfied by purely intellectual Scholastic theology: the heart, which is supposed to come to the experiential knowledge of God through repentance." The Scholastics, the princes of Christian rationalism, focused on knowing about God. Contrast this with Jewish philosopher Zadok HaKohen's view that "knowing God [is] not a form of scholastic Aristotelianism but [is] experiential knowledge." See Alan Brill, *Thinking God: The Mysticism of Rabbi Zadok of Lublin* (Jersey City, NJ: KTAV Publishing House, 2002), p. 84.

"spiritual." Indeed, the fruit of the lives of some of the Scholastics,[71] the intellectual giants of the times, was often not Holy-Spirit led or inspired.[72] In some cases, however, Scholastics had far more spiritual insight than some of the leaders of the clerical hierarchy.

An example of this tragedy was summed up in the anecdotal words of Thomas Aquinas, who was an outstanding Scholastic and one of the greatest theologians in Roman Catholic Church history. When he visited Rome for the first time and was escorted through the splendor of the Vatican, Aquinas was jokingly told by one of the church's great prelates, "Look here, Master Thomas, now can the church no longer say, as St. Peter said—Silver and gold have I none!" To the prelate's boast, Aquinas reportedly made this ironic reply: "That is true . . . but she cannot also say, what immediately follows thereon—in the name of Jesus Christ stand up and walk!"[73]

The descent of the imperial Western church into the Dark Ages of the tenth and eleventh centuries[74] is testimony to the level of degradation[75] that is possible in religious communities when professionalism and rationalism completely replace faith and the operation of the Holy Spirit in the lives of individual believers. Cold, clinical rationalism often created more questions than answers, and hair-splitting arguments were more contentious than inspiring. It also produced the environment of such dogma and practices that eventually precipitated the Protestant Reformation and its progressively developing emphasis on faith and personal relationship with God. Through successive reformations, Christians increasingly sought God, often outside established ecclesiastical orders, in an effort to find a

---

[71] The Scholastics sought to reconcile Christian theology with classical philosophy, especially Neoplatonism and Aristotelianism. While much of their work was based in noble aims, the product of their rationalism was often inimical to true Christian faith and practice, including their own spiritual condition. See Jan Aertsen, "Aquinas' philosophy in Its Historical Setting," in *The Cambridge Comparison to Aquinas*, Norman Kretzmann and Eleonore Stump, eds. (Cambridge, UK: Cambridge University Press, 1993) and Jean Laclerq, *The Love of Learning and the Desire for God* (New York: Fordham University Press, 1970).

[72] In his *Praise of Folly,* Erasmus ridiculed the Scholastics for their "maxims, paradoxes, 'tortuous obscurities,' and ingenious subtleties spun in the schools of theology, and he scoffed at the Scholastics for seeing themselves as a new Atlas, bearing the weight of the Church 'on the props of their syllogisms'." Erasmus, quoted in C. Scott Dixon, *The Reformation and Rural Society: The Parishes of Brandenburg-Ansbach-Kulmbach 1528–1603* (Cambridge, UK: Cambridge University Press, 1996), p. 66.

[73] Thomas Aquinas, quoted in John A. Heraud, *The Life and Times of Girolamo Savonarola* (Newburyport: A. A. Call Publisher, 1851), p. 228.

[74] The term *Dark Ages*, from the Latin *speculum obscurum*, was first applied to the tenth and eleventh centuries by Caesar Baronius in 1602. It has also been applied to the period from the fall of Rome in the sixth century until the Renaissance in the thirteenth century. See John C. Dwyer, *Church History: Twenty Centuries of Catholic Christianity* (Mahwah, NJ: Paulist Press, 1985), p. 155.

[75] Lawrence Cunningham, *An Introduction to Catholicism* (Cambridge, UK: Cambridge University Press, 2009), p. 29.

personal relationship with him, and they frequently achieved their quest in the ecstatic, decidedly non-rational experiences that were well documented in the various revivals that occurred in subsequent church history.

A clear and important truth is so obvious in this historical tragedy: if the church had not denied its Judaic heritage, it would never have ceased to be a Spirit-led institution. Belief in and experience of the supernatural were essential to the biblical Judaism through which Jesus and the apostles expressed their devotion to YHWH, the God of Israel. If this belief had been perpetuated, the church would not have exalted reason over anointing and professionalism over character and *charismata*. The impact of true biblical spirituality on church history would have been astounding and would have advanced the cause of the gospel exponentially. Instead, the life-changing potential of the gospel was limited, negatively impacting the church.

Mysticism and "Spirituality"

The quest for spirituality among Christians has taken believers down many different roads and in many different directions. Christian spirituality has been so influenced by Greek dualism that the very word *spirituality* is now defined as "the state or quality of being dedicated to God, religion, or spiritual things or values, especially as contrasted with material or temporal ones."[76] It is as though Christian "spirituality" cannot be manifest in the context of physical or temporal reality; it must be divorced from the material in order to be truly "spiritual." This is why "the perennial temptation of the churches has been the fall into unworldly spiritualities (body-spirit dichotomies)."[77]

One of the very first heresies to challenge the church was Gnosticism, which was based in Greek philosophy, not Hebrew truth. The Gnostics believed that a divine spark of divinity lived in every human soul but was captivated by the evil matter of the human body, which itself was the work of an inferior god (the *demiurge* or "craftsman" who created the universe). For them, "redemption was believed to be achieved through 'revealed knowledge' (*gnosis*) that comes to the few initiated and truly spiritual people (*pneumatikoi*) and liberates them from captivity to corporeality."[78] Because it was based on Greek dualism, this highly esoteric and mystical "self-knowledge" was strongly anti-material. It stood in direct contrast to the "prophetic-apostolic worldview, which advocates

---

[76] Collins English Dictionary – Complete & Unabridged 10th Edition (New York: William Collins Sons & Co, 2009).
[77] Isaac C. Rottenberg, *Judaism, Christianity, Paganism: A Judeo-Christian Worldview and Its Cultural Implications* (Atlanta, GA: Hebraic Heritage Press, 2007), p. 108.
[78] Rottenberg, p. 96.

neither emancipation from the material world nor reabsorption into the divine All."[79]

"The flow of time," Isaac Rottenberg has noted, "is a constant reminder of the transitoriness of life." It is for this reason that "the human heart hungers to transcend history and to have a taste of eternity in the mystical-ecstatic moment (*nunc aeternum*) when time seems to stand still."[80] In Christian history, therefore, spirituality has often been related by many to the mystical. Christian mystics have sought transcendental spiritual experiences that have ranged from ecstatic visions of mystical union with God on the one extreme to simple, prayerful contemplation of Scripture, liturgy, and doctrine on the other. While there is a mystical quality to relationship with the God of Scripture, total concentration on mysticism has often been deleterious to the true work of the gospel. Finding equilibrium between extremes has been profoundly difficult through the centuries.

The idea of mysticism in Christianity was imported from the pagan Greek experience in which mysticism referred almost exclusively to secret religious rituals. In fact, the Greek word μυω (*muo*) means "to conceal" (literally "to shut the eyes or the mouth") and its derivative word μυστικός (*mystikós*) means one who is "initiated into a mystery religion." The ancient Greek practice of mysticism, however, lacked direct references to the transcendental.[81] In early Greek Christianity, the term *mystikós* referred to the biblical, the liturgical, and the contemplative, all of which were often intertwined. For the Greek Fathers, the biblical dimension pointed to allegorical interpretations of Scripture, the liturgical focused on the mystery of the Eucharist and/or the presence of Christ at or in the Eucharist, and the contemplative related to the theory and practice of the experiential knowledge of God.[82] These ideas and practices of spirituality and mysticism began to develop in the second century AD when the Hellenization of Christianity was initiated. The increasing focus on mystical rituals and allegorization of Scripture emerged in Eastern Christianity as Christian apologists turned to Greek philosophy in an effort to explain Christian ideas. This was particularly true of the profound influence that Neoplatonism had on Origen, Christianity's allegorist *extraordinaire*.[83] The penchant for allegorization was also manifest in the Western Church, as is clearly demonstrated in the writings of

---

[79] Rottenberg, p. 96.
[80] Rottenberg, p. 97.
[81] William B. Parsons, *Teaching Mysticism* (New York: Oxford University Press, 2011), p. 3.
[82] Richard King, *Orientalism and Religion: Post-Colonial Theory, India and "the Mystic East"* (New York: Routledge, 2002), p. 15.
[83] Mathew Kuefler, *The Manly Eunuch: Masculinity, Gender Ambiguity, and Christian Ideology in Late Antiquity* (Chicago, IL: The University of Chicago Press, 2001), p. 22.

Augustine.[84] Allegory enabled many Greek and Latin church fathers to turn the focus of Christian thought away from the material world that was embraced by Judaism and to focus it on other worldly spiritualities.

Monasticism and "Spirituality"

One approach to spirituality in the historical church that had strong underpinnings in Greek philosophy but very little support from Holy Scripture[85] was monasticism. The word *monasticism* is traced to the Greek word μόναρχος (*mónarchos*) which is derived from μόνος (*mónos*), meaning "alone." The focus of monasticism was the removal of the "religious" from the secular world into monasteries where, after having renounced worldly pursuits, they could focus on or devote themselves to spiritual matters, including prayer and contemplation. In this system, many of the best and brightest of the Christian world were cloistered (or cloistered themselves) in remote, sometimes virtually inaccessible sites where they could maintain splendid isolation and seek to overcome all the desires of the flesh and the material world. One reason for such isolation was the monastics' perceived need to separate themselves from the female gender in order to eliminate the possibility of sexual temptation with what was believed to be the greatest evil, even the original sin in the Garden of Eden.[86]

Monasticism was taken to a new level in the third century AD by Anthony of the Desert, an illiterate holy man who, because he had completely embraced the Greek idea that the material world was *ipso facto* evil, began to espouse and practice extreme asceticism.[87] Anthony retreated to the Egyptian desert where he adopted an eremitic lifestyle wherein he sought an elusive spirituality that he thought could be attained through acts of extreme self-abnegation, along with contemplation and meditation. Though he has been erroneously called the first monk, Anthony was, in fact, the first

---

[84] Scott A. Dunham, *The Trinity and Creation in Augustine: An Ecological Analysis* (Albany, NY: The State University of New York Press, 2008), p. 23.

[85] Church fathers like Origen, Jerome, Ignatius, John Chrysostom, and Augustine made every effort to interpret biblical texts in such a way as to support the ideas of asceticism; however, their writings were undergirded by Greek philosophical musings far more than by any legitimate interpretation of Holy Scripture. While there were some ascetics in Israel, they were the exception, not the rule.

[86] Rolf Toman, Achim Bednorz, and Ranier Warland, *Monasteries and Monastic Orders: 2000 Years of Christian Art and Culture* (Berkeley, CA: The University of California Press, 2008), p. 14. Also William Herbert Mackean, *Christian Monasticism in Egypt to the Close of the Fourth Century* (New York: The Macmillan Company, 1920), p. 46, and Charles Morris, *American Catholic: The Saints and Sinners Who Built America's Most Powerful Church* (New York: Random House, 1997), p. 357.

[87] The term *asceticism* is from the Greek word ἄσκησις (*áskesis*), which literally means "training or "exercise." The original usage of the word applied to training for Greek athletic events. It was expanded; however, to mean self-denial when used to attain a higher spirituality. See Paul A. B. Clark and Andrew Linzey, eds., *Dictionary of Ethics, Theology and Society* (Taylor & Francis, 1996), p. 58.

Christian desert ascetic[88] whose experience spawned thousands of desert hermits.[89] The principles embraced by Anthony impacted much of classical and Medieval Christianity in virtually all of its denominations. In fact, they became the most admired "spiritualities" in the church throughout the world. Most Christian churches,[90] therefore, maintained some form of monasticism in which religious orders held forth teachings of asceticism and self-abnegation as being the highest expressions of true Christian spirituality.

While both Greek and Latin church fathers made many efforts to defend the practice of monasticism, Scripture never promoted either asceticism or celibacy. The whole of Scripture is an ennoblement of interpersonal human relationships in the context of community, and it is a celebration of the sanctity of marriage and the inherent goodness of sexual congress when it is expressed within the context of marriage.[91] The Hebrew Scriptures nowhere promote isolation of individuals from the context of family and community. As a matter of fact, the least common denominator of Hebraic/Israelite culture was the family, not the individual. John Rogerson explained this fact by noting that Israel was an "aggregate of groups rather than a collection of individuals,"[92] while Robert Di-Vito affirmed the truth that in Israel, "apart from the family, the individual is scarcely a viable entity—socially, economically, or juridically."[93] The Apostolic Scriptures affirm the same Hebraic emphases that are outlined in the Hebrew Scriptures. Before the incursion of pagan ideas into the cultures of either the Hebrew or Christian communities, no hint of a higher "spirituality" of asceticism existed in either of them.

As a matter of fact, Apostolic Scripture specifically condemns required asceticism: "Let no one disqualify you, insisting on asceticism and worship of angels, going on in detail about visions, puffed up without reason by his sensuous mind."[94] Paul further argued that "the Spirit explicitly says that in later times some will fall away from the faith, paying attention to deceitful spirits and doctrines of demons, speaking lies in hypocrisy; having their

---

[88] Dag Øistein Endsjø, *Primordial Landscapes, Incorruptible Bodies* (New York: Peter Lang Publishing, 2008), p. 46.

[89] Marina Miladinov, *Margis of Solitude: Eremitism in Central Europe between East and West* (Zagreb, Croatia: Leykam International, 2008).

[90] Greek, Syrian, Ethiopian, Roman Catholic, etc.

[91] John D. Garr, *Feminine by Design: The God-Fashioned Woman* (Atlanta, GA: Golden Key Press, 2013), pp. 155–240.

[92] John W. Rogerson, "Anthropology and the Old Testament," in R. E. Clements, ed., *The World of Ancient Israel: Sociological, Anthropological and Political Perspectives* (Cambridge, UK: Cambridge University Press, 1989), p. 25, also cited in Alan Levenson, p. 163.

[93] Robert DeVito, "Old Testament Anthropology and the Construction of Personal Identity," *Catholic Biblical Quarterly* 61 (1999), pp. 226–227, also cited in Alan Levenson, p. 163.

[94] Colossians 2:18, ESV.

conscience seared with a hot iron; men who forbid marriage."[95] These Pauline declarations make it clear that the apostle did not advocate a higher "spirituality" of celibacy, monasticism, and asceticism, this despite the fact that many subsequent pagan-influenced Christian leaders attempted to wrest his writings to support their own dualistic perspectives on these subjects.

Paul's recommendation that some believers who could endure the rigors of unmarried life for the sake of the overspread of the Gospel was given, by his own admission, only "because of the *present crisis*."[96] Paul was speaking of the growing persecution of the Roman Empire against the Christians and the difficulty of maintaining the responsibilities of marriage while being heralds of the gospel under those circumstances. As a matter of fact, he specifically ordered those who were not able to contain their sexual impulses to marry,[97] and, in specific and unequivocal terms, he instructed married couples to engage regularly in sexual relations, with both male and female conjugal rights properly and biblically respected and fulfilled.[98] When Jesus spoke of those who had chosen "to live like eunuchs for the sake of the kingdom of heaven," he reached this conclusion: "He who is able to accept this, let him accept it."[99] He in no way enjoined celibacy upon his disciples. Celibacy and sexual abstinence, therefore, have never been held forth in Holy Scripture as higher spiritualities to which the finest believers should aspire. Likewise, asceticism and required regimens of self-abnegation violate the biblical premise that the entire creation is good and is to be enjoyed by human beings as celebrations of God's his provision.[100] In fact, in many Jewish circles, failure to experience what God has provided for human enjoyment is seen as disrespectful to God.

The only form of self-abnegation that Scripture required was fasting (not eating food), and that was for only one day each year on the Day of Atonement.[101] While some of the Israelite people came to consider fasting and other forms of self-abnegation important spiritual exercises, even believing that fasting resulted in the forgiveness of sins,[102] the truth is that God did not demand such degrees of self-denial. By the time of Jesus, the Pharisees fasted twice a

---

[95] 1 Timothy 4:1-3.

[96] 1 Corinthians 7:26, NIV.

[97] 1 Corinthians 7:9.

[98] 1 Corinthians 7:2–5.

[99] Matthew 19:12.

[100] John D. Garr, *Feminine by Design: The God-Fashioned Woman* (Atlanta, GA: Golden Key Press, 2013), pp. 187–188.

[101] Leviticus 23:27–32.

[102] Jacob Neusner, *Theological Dictionary of Rabbinic Judaism: Principal Theological Categories* (Lanham, MD: University Press of America, 2005), p.4. Neusner reports the belief that when the "great men of the generation fast" from Rosh Hashanah (the first day of the month Tishri) until Yom Kippur (the tenth day of Tishri), "the Holy One . . . remits a third of . . . Israel's sins."

week, on Mondays and Thursdays.[103] The followers of John the Baptizer adopted this practice.[104] Jesus and his disciples were condemned because they did not follow the Pharisean regimen of fasting.[105] Some have argued that Jesus did not completely discount the value of fasting because he associated it with prayer in Matthew 17:21 and Mark 9:29 when discussing exorcisms: "This kind comes not out except by prayer *and fasting.*" Some have suggested, however, that the preponderance of evidence from uncial Greek manuscripts indicates that the phrase *and fasting* may have been added to these texts,[106] in all likelihood because a copyist thought that "prayer alone seemed too simple."[107]

It could well be said that God's perspective on fasting and all other forms of self-abnegation is summed up in the prophetic words of Isaiah. When the Israelites complained to God, "Why have we fasted, and you have not seen it? Why have we humbled ourselves, and you have noticed?" God replied, "Even when you fast, you oppress your workers. Your fasting ends in quarreling and strife, and in striking each other with wicked fists."[108] God further described his displeasure at the approach that was then being used toward fasting during that time, in which "you bow your head like a reed and spread sackcloth and ashes under you. Is that what you call a fast?"[109] Finally, God specifically revealed what he had chosen as the proper means of self-abnegation: ". . . to loose the bonds of wickedness, to undo the straps of the yoke, to let the oppressed go free, and to break every yoke? Is it not to share your bread with the hungry and bring the homeless poor into your house; when you see the naked, to cover him, and not to hide yourself from your own flesh?"[110]

---

[103] Luke 18:12; Babylonian Talmud *b. Ta'an.* 10a, 12a). See Robert H. Stein, *Mark* (Grand Rapids, MI: Baker Academic, 2008), p. 136.

[104] Luke 18:12.

[105] Mark 2:18.

[106] Frederick Dale Bruner, *Matthew: The Churchbook* (Grand Rapids, MI: Wm. B. Eerdmans Publishing Co., 2004), p. 194. Bruner says, "Fasting makes us look at *ourselves* as at least a portion of power's source; mustard-seed faith and prayer all by itself (without even adjectives) make us look to *God* exclusively as power's source. There may be a place for fasting, but in Jesus' teaching it is not a condition for receiving God's helping power." See also Ronald J. Kernaghan, *Mark* (Downers Grove, IL: InterVarsity Press, 2007), p. 178; Arthur Wallis, *God's Chosen Fast: A Spiritual and Practical Guide to Fasting* (Ft. Washington, PA: CLC Publications, 1968), p. 142; and Donald Trump, *Knocking on Heaven's Door: A New Testament Theology of Petitionary Prayer* (Grand Rapids, MI: Baker Academic, 2006), p. 52. Trump argues that the addition of the phrase *and fasting* obviates the clear intention of Jesus' statement that such exorcisms are not the product of any human achievement but rather of the power of God through prayer.

[107] Eduard Schweizer, *The Good News According to Mark*, tr. Donald Madvig (Atlanta, GA: John Knox Press,1964), p. 189.

[108] Isaiah 58:3–4, paraphrased.

[109] Isaiah 58:5, paraphrased.

[110] Isaiah 58:6–7, paraphrased.

Divinization: The Ultimate "Spirituality"?

For many, the ultimate goal of such hyper-spirituality has been manifest in a desire and effort to become divine, to be deified or absorbed into some form of god-consciousness.[111] This system of thought has projected the idea that God is in all or that all is God or in God and that every enlightened person is, therefore, somehow divine.[112] Michael Christensen points out that this idea is at least as old as Plato, who "identified the highest aim of humanity as *eudaimonía* (to be blessed with a good internal divinity)" and who defined deification as "likeness to God so far as possible."[113] This is simply a form of *henosis*, the idea that all humans are thought to return to and be absorbed into their divine source. Such concepts have gained great ascendancy in the postmodern world where everything is focused on the individual's self-worth, self-image, and self-actualization and to the god-consciousness or even divinity that is thought to be inherent in all human beings. This is the divinization of humanity that was trumpeted by one Hollywood celebrity who stood by the ocean and shouted, "I am God, I am God, I am God."[114]

By the late second century AD, a form of ultimate mystical spirituality had come to be considered by some leaders of the Eastern Orthodox Church.[115] Finally, it became enshrined in the Orthodox doctrine of *theopoiesis* (abbreviated as *theosis*),[116] which espoused a form of deification

---

[111] This idea, which was expressed in some Greek thought that influenced the Eastern Church, had long been taken to even greater extreme by Eastern Monism. It is also a focus of modern reincarnations of ancient monism that are projected in New Age and Neo-Pagan philosophies.

[112] Even Jesus came to be viewed as the "Cosmic Christ" and, in some cases, as the "Christ Consciousness" that everyone can achieve so that, in effect, everyone is "Christ," even if he is not "Christian."

[113] Michael J. Christensen, "The Problem, Promise, and Process of *Theosis*," in *Partakers of the Divine Nature: The History and Development of Deification in the Christian Traditions*, Michael J. Christensen and Jeffery A. Wittung, eds.(Grand Rapids, MI: Baker Academic, 2007), p. 25. See Plato *Theaetetus*, 176b in Edith Hamilton and Huntington Cairns, eds., *The Collected Dialogues of Plato* (New York: Pantheon Books, 1961), p. 881.

[114] Shirley MacClaine quoted in David John Tracey, *Jung and the New Age* (Philadelphia, PA: Brunner-Routledge, 2001), p. 77.

[115] Irenaeus (AD 130-200) first projected a foundation for *theosis* by saying, "The Word of God, our Lord Jesus Christ, who did, through His transcendent love, become what we are, that He might bring us to be even what He is Himself" (Irenaeus, *Against Heresies*, 5, preface). Theophilus of Antioch (AD 120-215) also said, "For if He had made him immortal from the beginning, He would have made him God. . . . so that if he should incline to the things of immortality, keeping the commandment of God,he should receive as reward from Him immortality, and should become God" (Theophilus, *To Autolycus*, II, 27).

[116] Gregory Nazianzus coined the neologism θέοωσις (*théosis*) from the Greek verb θεόν (*théon*). See Gavin Flood, Orthodox Christianity and World Religions," in Augustine Cassiday, ed., *The Orthodox Christian World* (New York: Routledge, 2012), p. 577. The noun *theopoiesis* literally means "making divine" or "making God" and describes the ancient mystical thought of "human ascent to the unknowable, immutable infinite." For more detail, see Catherine Keller, "Theopoiesis and the Pluriverse: Notes on a Process," in *Theopoetic Folds: Philosophizing Multifariousness*, Roland Faber and Jeremy Fackenthal, eds. (Bronx, NY: Fordham University Press, 2013), pp. 181-183.

or divinization. While the thinking of the Christian leaders who developed this concept and endeavored to live by it was noble and well-intended, the concept itself became a doctrine of the church only because a significant number of the Greek Fathers and theologians of the Eastern Church were heavily influenced by Greek philosophy. Dionysius, one of the major proponents of mystical divinization in the sixth century, was strongly influenced by the Neoplatonists Proclus and Damascius.[117] Maximus the Confessor, another of the doctrine's strongest promoters in the seventh century, based his thought largely on the Neoplatonism of Stephanus from whom he appropriated the idea of the eternity of the world and the pre-existence of souls.[118]

The early precursors of the *theosis* doctrine simply sought to imitate God by fulfilling his will in their lives, as best they could discern it. This approach to spirituality was in some ways parallel with the aspirations of Methodism in its approach to the doctrine of sanctification that emerged some fifteen centuries later.[119] Eventually, the concept developed into a view that ascetic spirituality would enable one to reacquire the likeness of God that some thought had been lost because of the sin of Adam and Eve. Finally, the concept was refined into a form of divinization in which the believer was thought to have acquired some degree of divinity. Basil the Great described it this way: "Through the Spirit we acquire likeness to God; indeed we attain what is beyond our most sublime aspirations—we become God."[120] Athanasius of Alexandria also said, "We are not made gods from the beginning; first we are mere humans, then we become gods,"[121] and he ascribed the agency of deification to the Holy Spirit: "By the participation of the Holy Spirit, we are knit into the Godhead."[122] Divinization, then, eventually became the goal or the highest aspiration of Orthodox spirituality. In fact, *theosis* has been viewed in Orthodox teaching as the very purpose for the existence of human life. Some Greek theologians have even declared that Jesus would have become human solely for the purpose of making *theosis*

---

[117] See Sarah Coakley and Charles M. Stang, *Re-thinking Dionysius the Areopagite* (John Wiley and Sons, 2009), and Andrew Louth, *Denys the Areopagite* (New York: Continuum Books, 1989), pp. 20–21. Also, Lossky, p. 29.

[118] Edward Moore, *Origen of Alexandria and St. Maximus the Confessor* (Boca Raton, FL: Universal Publishers, 2004), p. 135. Also, Edwin Hatch, *The Influence of Greek Ideas on Christianity* (New York: Harper and Row, 1957), pp. 238ff, and Brian Duignan, *Ancient Philosophy: From 600 BCE to 500 CE* (New York: Britannica Educational Publishing, 2011), pp. 157–159.

[119] Christensen and Wittung, eds., p. 221.

[120] Basil, *Holy Spirit,* quoted in Milton Walsh, *Witness of the Saints: Patristic Readings in the Liturgy of the Hours* (San Francisco, CA: St. Ignatius Press, 2012), p. 326.

[121] Irenaeus, *Against Heresies*, III. IV.38.4.

[122] Athanasius, *Four Discourses Against The Arians*, 3.24–25.

possible even if Adam and Eve had not sinned and there was no need for the redemption of fallen humanity.[123]

Origen had argued that the "human and divine began to be woven together, so that by prolonged fellowship with divinity, human nature might become divine."[124] Maximus even took the matter much further, asserting that *theosis* is actually a form of perichoresis, an "interpenetration" of God and humanity. In doing so, he used the term *perichoresis* that had been developed three centuries earlier by the Cappadocian Fathers to describe the intimate interaction of the three persons of the Trinity within and among themselves in the very essence of deity.[125] Such ideas were further refined by various branches of Orthodoxy such as those of the Russian Orthodox Church. Boris Jakim explains some of these nuances: "It is the fusion of the Creator and creation, a fusion that is simultaneously the *kenosis* of the Divinity and the *theosis* of the humanity, and that concludes with the perfect glorification of the God-Man."[126] Nicholas of Cusa went even further, promoting the divinization of the intellect rather than the salvation of the soul as God's highest will for human beings.[127]

Orthodox *theosis* came to project ultimate spirituality as being a process that was designed to eventuate in the achievement of *likeness to* or *union with* God.[128] This process included *katharsis*, which bespeaks the purification of both the mind and body,[129] and *theoria*, which is contemplation.[130] The Orthodox have believed that this level of spirituality is gained through revelation by means of ascetic pursuits, not by academic achievement as with the academicians and the Scholastics of Western Christianity.[131] It is for this reason that Orthodox ascetic theology is defined as "a way of life rather than the pursuit

---

[123] Vladimir Lossky, "Theology and Mysticism in the Tradition of the Eastern Church" in Vladimir Lossky, *The Mystical Theology of the Eastern Church* (St. Vladimir's Seminary Press, 1997), pp. 29–33.

[124] Origen, *Hymns on Faith*, 18.2. See Sebastian Brock, *The Luminous Eye: The Spiritual World Vision of Saint Ephrem the Syrian* (Kalamazoo, MI: Cistercian Publications, 1991), p. 79.

[125] Perichoresis is the mutual encircling and interpenetration of the three modes (persons) of divine existence in one being of divine spirit substance (God).

[126] Boris Jakim, quoted in Christensen and Wittung, eds., p. 28. In this instance, the *kenosis* of Jesus ("self-emptying" of his equality with God when he became fully human—as taught by Paul in Philippians 2:7) is held forth as a converse parallel of the *theosis* of humanity, with the final result of the emergence of a "God-Man," a divine human.

[127] Nancy J. Hudson, *Becoming God: The Doctrine of Theosis in Nicholas of Cusa* (Washington D.C.: Catholic University of America Press, 2007), p. 183.

[128] See Emil Bartos, *Deification in Eastern Orthodox Theology: An Evaluation and Critique of the Theology of Dumitru Staniloae* (Bloomington, IN: Indiana University Press, 1999), p. 187.

[129] Alfred Kentigern Siewers, *Re-Imagining Nature: Environmental Humanities and Ecosemiotics* (Lanham MD: Rowman & Littlefield, 2014), p. 61.

[130] The Greek word *theoria* means "contemplation." It is the source of the English word *theory*. In the case of its connection with *theosis*, *theoria* is contemplation of the divine Trinity through prayer in an effort to "know" God.

[131] Lossky, p. 128. Also Alexander Chow, *Theosis, Sino-Christian Theology and the Second Chinese* (New York: Palgrave Macmillan, 2013), p. 150.

of knowledge *about* God."[132] For the Orthodox, becoming divine is "the purification of the self, seeing the grace of God operating in the hearts of all beings."[133] In the tenth century, Symeon expressed the reason for maintaining this lifestyle: "He who is God by nature converses with those whom he has made gods by grace, as a friend converses with his friends, face to face."[134]

A second key to the Orthodox concept of ultimate spirituality as being the process of becoming divine was the experience of *theoria*, which first was contemplation of the created universe and then of the "higher and endless contemplation of the mystery of the Trinity,"[135] the three-person manifestation of God. Through self-abnegation and meditation, the Orthodox believed that one could achieve a level of holiness that is the same as God's holiness.[136] *Theosis* through *theoria* could be achieved, however, only through impeccable Christian living combined with continuous, faithful, and ultimately *silent* prayer.[137] In fact, the ascetic prayer called *Hesychasm* focuses specifically on *theosis*.[138] This process was facilitated by acts of self-abnegation which were designed to overcome the flesh and focus the heart on higher spiritualities. This idea was what led Nicodemos the Hagiorite to say, "Know that if your mind is not deified by the Holy Spirit, it is impossible for you to be saved."[139] Purification of the heart was also connected simultaneously with the perception and apprehension of wisdom.[140] For the Orthodox, therefore, the life of God was given to the believer through the Holy Spirit in three stages: struggles in life, experience of the knowledge of God, and resurrection.[141]

This kind of thinking also impacted Western Christianity to some degree as well.[142] Robert Imperato points out that "just as the Second Vatican Council's

---

[132] Cornelia A. Tsakiridou, *Icons in Time, Persons in Eternity: Orthodox Theology and the Aesthetics of the Christian Image* (Burlington, VT: Ashgate Publishing Co., 2013).

[133] Augustine Casiday, ed., *The Orthodox Christian World* (New York: Routledge, 2012), p. 576.

[134] Symeon, quoted in Alan Richardson and John Bowden, eds., *The Westminster Dictionary of Christian Theology* (Philadelphia, PA: The Westminster Press, 1983), p. 148.

[135] Bernard McGinn, ed., *The Essential Writings of Christian Mysticism* (New York: Random House, 2006), pp. 56, 277, 309, 519.

[136] John Witte and Frank S. Alexander, eds., *The Teachings of Modern Orthodox Christianity on Law, Politics, & Human Nature* (New York: Columbia University Press, 2007), p. 7.

[137] John K. Katsonsis, *"An Orthodox Christian Study on Unceasing Prayer,"* posted at the website: http://www.saintandrewgoc.org/blog/2012/7/12/an-orthodox-christian-study-on-unceasing-prayer.html.

[138] Christopher D. L. Johnson, *The Globalization of Hesychasm and the Jesus Prayer: Contesting Contemplation* (New York: Continuum International Publishing Group, 2010), p. 35.

[139] Chrysostomos, *Orthodox and Roman Catholic Relations from the Fourth Crusade to the Hesychastic Controversy* (Etna, CA: Center for Traditionalist Orthodox Studies, 2001), pp. 292–230.

[140] Pavel Florensky, *The Pillar and Ground of the Truth: An Essay in Orthodox Theodicy in Twelve Letters* (Princeton, NJ: Princeton University Press, 2004), p. 254.

[141] Lossky, pp. 8–9, 39, 133, 196.

[142] Myk Habets, *Theosis in the Theology of Thomas Torrance* (Burlington, VT: Ashgate Publishing, 2009), p. 14;

affirmation that the Eucharistic liturgy is the source and summit of Christian life has brought about deeper appreciation of the centrality of the Eucharist in Christian life and spirituality, so too there has been a deeper recognition that the central Christian mystery, the Trinity, with its far-reaching practical implications, constitutes the heart and soul of Christian spirituality."[143] Some postmodern Christians, however, have taken the ideas of *theosis* to clearly heretical extremes. A few charismatic Christian Universalists even believe that the only way Christ will return to earth will be in "Manifested Sons of God" who will reign on earth and lead other humans to perfection. This kind of thought flows in the same vein as that of M. Scott Peck, who said, "All of us who postulate a loving God . . . eventually come to a single terrifying idea: God wants us to become Himself (or Herself or Itself). We are growing toward godhood."[144]

Human Divinity in Scripture?

When seeking scriptural support for their theory of *theosis*, the Greek fathers appealed to 2 Peter 1:1-4. This passage is accurately translated—as virtually all versions render it—in the following manner: "His divine power has granted to us all things that pertain to life and godliness, through the knowledge of him who called us to his own glory and excellence, by which he has granted to use his precious and very great promises, so that through them *you may become partakers of the divine nature*, having escaped the corruption that is in the world because of sinful desire."[145] Many of those who today espouse *theosis* prefer to use the Revised English Bible's rendering of penultimate clause of this passage: "[you] may come to share in the very being of God."[146] There is a profound difference, however, between a believer's sharing in the "very being" of God and partaking of the divine nature.

---

[143] Michael Downey, *Understanding Christian Spirituality* (Mahwah, New Jersey: Paulist Press, 1997), p. 44.

[144] M. Scott Peck, *The Road Less Traveled* (New York: Simon and Schuster, 1978), pp. 269-270.

[145] 2 Peter 1:3-4, ESV, emphasis added.

[146] 2 Peter 1:4b, REB. Johan Leemans, "God Became Human in Order that Humans Might Become God: A Reflection on the Soteriological Doctrine of Divinization," in *The Myriad Christ: Plurality and the Quest for Unity in Contemporary Christology*, Terrence Merrigan and Jacques Haers, eds. (Leuven, Belgium: Leuven University Press, 2000), p. 209; John Main, *The Way of Unknowing: Expanding Spiritual Horizons through Meditation* (Eugene, OR: Wipf and Stock Publishers, 1990), p. 31; Michael Barber, *Should Christianity Abandon the Doctrine of the Trinity?* (Boca Raton, FL: Universal Publishers, 2006), p. 84; et al. This "interpretation" (certainly not "translation") of 2 Peter 1:4b and the Orthodox *theosis* doctrine are used to form a basis for the erroneous assertion that all the major world religions, Hinduism, Judaism, Christianity, Islam, Sikhism, and Buddhism, share the idea of the divinization of human beings. See W. Owen Cole, *Six World Faiths* (New York: Continuum Publishing Group, 1996). Virtually all other translations render the text: "partake of the divine nature" (ABPE, NIV, ESV, NASB, KJV, ISV, D-RB, WEB, YLT, WBT, et. al.). Darby (DBT) translates it even more accurately: ". . . ye may become partakers of [the] divine nature," because no definite article is associated with the phrase *divine nature* in the Greek text.

The principles of the divine nature should be manifest in believers' lives; however, that does not imply "sharing in the very being of God."

Rather than speaking of a divination that only a few elite specialists in self-abnegation, meditation, and mystical spirituality can achieve, Peter addressed all believers as participants in the divine nature by using a plural subject and a plural verb in this declaration. Then, the apostle noted that such participation is not potential but actual. It is something that has already been done. It is not something that believers strive for: it is something that has already been accomplished by God on their behalf. Rather than promoting the divinization of human beings, Peter's declaration speaks of the calling of God and the impartation of divine grace that empowers believers to partake of the divine nature by becoming children of God through the spiritual rebirth that will empower them to partake further of divine nature through sanctification and, ultimately, through the resurrection when one finally totally "escapes the corruption of the world." James Starr observes that "participation in the divine nature follows from knowing Christ as salvific sovereign." It is a participation that "has a *present* component in the readers' progressive assimilation to Christ's virtue or moral excellence or righteousness," and it is a participation that "has a *future* component in the reader's entry into the incorruption of Christ's eternity."[147] Lewis Smedes summarized this process succinctly: "Christ communicates Himself in a way that changes us without diminishing us, transforms us without deifying us, Christianizes us without making us Christs."[148]

Paul confirmed this thesis in his discourse in Romans 8: "The anxious longing of the creation waits eagerly for the revealing of the sons of God. For the creation was subjected to futility, not willing, but because of him who subjected it, in hope that the creation itself will be set free from its slavery to corruption into the freedom of the glory of the children of God. . . . even we ourselves groan within ourselves, waiting eagerly for our adoption as sons, the redemption of our body."[149] Though many sects have promoted a "Manifested Sons of God" doctrine in which they maintain that such an experience can be obtained in this present human life,[150] the apostle made it clear that the full manifestation of divine sonship will occur only in the resurrection: "For indeed in this house [body] we groan, longing to be clothed with our dwelling

---

[147] James Starr, "Does 2 Peter 1:4 Speak of Deification?" in Christensen and Jeffery Wittung, eds., pp. 84–85, author's emphasis.

[148] Lewis Smedes, *All Things Made New* (Eugene, OR: Wipf & Stock Publishers, 1998), p. 188.

[149] Romans 8:19–23.

[150] Ian Curtis, *Jesus: Myth or Reality?* (Lincoln, NE: iUniverse, 2006), p. 195. Also Russell Sharrock, *Covenant Theology: A Critical Analysis of Current Pentecostal Covenant Theology* (Morrisville, NC: Lulu Press, 2006), p. 172, and Gary DeMar, Dave Hunt, and Gary North, *The Debate over Christian Reconstruction* (Waterbury Center, VT: Dominion Press, 1988), p. 177.

from heaven . . . Now he who has prepared us for this very purpose is God, who has given us the Spirit as a deposit, guaranteeing what is to come."[151] Paul repeatedly speaks of being "children of God," not "gods," a process that began with adoption as "children of God" and is completed in the resurrection.

This was also the apostle John's belief: "Beloved, now we are children of God, and it is not appeared as yet what we will be. We know that when he appears, we will be like him, because we will see him just as he is."[152] Peter, then, was not talking about the divinization of redeemed human beings in the present life. He was speaking of the reception of the divine nature in salvation that is further developed in sanctification and is finally completed in the resurrection. This was what Paul described: "[He] will transform the body of our humble state into conformity with the body of his glory, by the exertion of the power that he has even to subject all things to himself."[153] The purpose of God is not to deify human beings; instead, it is to make them fully human as he intended them to be in the beginning and as they would have been if Adam and Eve had partaken of the Tree of Life rather than the Tree of the Knowledge of Good and Evil. When this occurs, believers will be clothed with an immortal body like the resurrected body of Jesus; however, they will still be human, not divine. As in Jewish thought, they will be restored to *Gan Eden*,[154] to the perfect human state in which their primordial ancestors were created with one exception: they will be clothed upon with immortality because they will have experienced the one thing that Adam and Eve did not experience: eating of the Tree of Life.[155]

The second passage used to support the doctrine of *theosis* is Psalm 82:6, which says, "You are gods [*elohim*]; and all of you are children of the most High." Despite Orthodox interpretation, this passage does not ascribe deity or divinity to human beings. The context, which assures the right interpretation of the text, begins with this statement: "God presides in the great assembly; he renders judgment among the 'gods.'"[156] This statement is connected directly with the account of Job 1:6: "Now there was a day when the sons of God came to present themselves before the LORD,

---

[151] 2 Corinthians 2:3–5.
[152] 1 John 3:2.
[153] Philippians 3:11.
[154] Alan Avery-Peck, Jacob Neusner, *The Routledge Dictionary of Judaism* (New York: Routledge, 2004), pp. 41–42.
[155] Revelation 2:7.
[156] Psalm 82:1, NIV. The New American Standard Version renders the text as "God takes his stand in his own congregation; he judges in the midst of the rulers." This translation is parallel with that of the Jewish Publication Society: "God standeth in the congregation of God; in the midst of the judges he judgeth." Jewish tradition recognizes the term "gods" in this text to mean the judges of Israel.

and Satan also came among them." These "sons of God" were angels who made up the heavenly court not a pantheon of "gods." The use of the term *son of God* to describe both angels and men was not uncommon in Scripture.

The account of Psalm 82 continues with God's enjoining upon his people the practice of social justice for the poor and needy, after which the Eternal said, "I have said, you are gods; and all of you are children of the most High." The faithful Israelites were "gods" in the same sense as the "gods" among whom God rendered judgment (an earthly court as it were), not in the sense that they shared God's own divinity. They were "gods" in the sense that they were children of the living God. Finally, in the next verse, God concludes, "Nevertheless you will die like men and fall like any one of the princes."[157] Accordingly, Asaph cries out, "Arise, O God, judge the earth! For it is you who possesses all the nations."[158] In John 10:34, Jesus alluded to this passage in his debate with the Pharisees over the question of his own divinity, saying that if God called "gods" the mere men to whom the Word of God came, then why would anyone accuse him of blasphemy when he said "I am God's Son"? As a matter of fact, before Jesus' day, the term *Son of God* had been applied to the kings of Israel[159] as well as to others.[160]

Bearing Nothing Earthly

Orthodox *theosis* differs from teaching of Apostolic Scripture in that it projects ultimate spirituality as being manifest in self-abnegation and contemplation (particularly contemplation of the mysteries of the Trinity). The apostles, however, maintained that true spirituality was manifest in living the life of the Spirit so that one would fulfill the commandments of

---

[157] Psalm 82:7.

[158] Psalm 82:8.

[159] Boyarin, *The Jewish Gospels*, pp. 26–28.

[160] Adam is called the "son of God" in Luke 3:38. Additionally, men were called the "sons of God" in the time of Noah in Genesis 6:1-8. These men were probably nobles, aristocrats, and kings who "married" the "daughters of men" when, overcome with lust, they initiated the practice of polygamy and the abuse of women. See Meredith G. Kline, "Divine Kingship and Genesis 6:1-4," *Westminster Theological Journal* 24 (1962), pp. 187-204. Also Walter C. Kaiser, Jr., Peter H. Davids, F. Bruce, and Manfred Brauch, *Hard Sayings of the Bible* (Downers Grove, IL: InterVarsity Press, 1996), pp. 106–108. Their greatest evil was the corruption of the genealogy of the righteous. This is clear first from the fact that Noah found grace in God's eyes because he was perfect in his pedigree ("generations," *pl.*). It is also clear that these "sons of God" were not angels, because these they *married* the daughters of men and by doing so engaged in relationships that angels do not—and cannot—experience. Jesus emphatically said in Matthew 22:30 that in the resurrection humans "neither marry nor are given in marriage" because they will be "like the angels in heaven." The specific reason for an absence of marriage in the resurrection is the fact that the resurrected will be immortal and, like the angels, will, therefore, have no reason for procreation. The "giants" who were born to the unions of the "sons of God" and the "daughters of men" in Noah's day were simply "men of renown."

God contained in the Hebrew Scriptures and in the teachings of Jesus.[161] For them, sanctification was not self-mortification, self-flagellation, or self-abnegation. It was the process of being submitted to the truth of God's Word. Jesus had established this fact when he prayed to his Father, "Sanctify them [the disciples] through your truth; your word is truth."[162] Paul refined the concept further established by Jesus' words: "Sanctify them by the washing of water by the Word."[163] Sanctification, therefore, is not attained by acts of self-abnegation. It is obtained by faith—the manifestation of the faith necessary to live the Word of God and keep God's commandments through the empowerment of the Holy Spirit.

Even though Orthodox Christianity admitted that human beings cannot become God in his transcendent essence (*ousía*), thereby experiencing the kind of *henosis* or absorption into God that pagan Greek philosophy envisioned, still it argued, as in the case of Maximus, "A sure warrant for looking forward with hope to deification of human nature is provided by the incarnation of God, which makes man god to the same degree as God himself became man."[164] In order to avoid the charge that *theosis* was actually a form of *henosis*, later scholars, particularly Gregory Palamas, posited a differentiation between the essence (οὐσία—*ousía*) and the energies (ἐνέργεια—*enérgeia*) of God, arguing that humans can be divinized by experiencing the energies of God but not the divine essence. Virtually all patristic texts maintain that humans remain human by nature; however, the mixing of terms of humanity and divinity remains problematic. David Hart may have been right to have wondered "if a kind of reverse Prometheanism does not lurk somewhere within such a theology, a refusal on the part of the theologian to be a creature, a desire rather to be dissolved into the infinite fiery flood of God's solitary and arbitrary act of will."[165]

Maximus' prescription for achieving *theosis* was this: "A sure warrant for looking forward with hope to deification of human nature is provided by the incarnation of God which makes man God to the same degree as God Himself became man. . . . Let us become the image of the one whole God, bearing nothing earthly in ourselves, so that we may consort with God and become gods, receiving from God our existence as gods."[166] In Orthodox thought regarding

---

[161] 1 Corinthians 7:19; 1 John 5:3; 2 Peter 2:21.
[162] John 17:17.
[163] Ephesians 5:26.
[164] Maximus, *Philokalia*, vol. II, p. 178.
[165] David Bentley Hart, *The Doors of the Sea: Where Was God in the Tsunami?* (Grand Rapids, MI: Wm. B. Eerdmans Publishing Co., 2005), pp. 90–91.
[166] Maximus, *Philokalia, Vol. 2: The Complete Text*, G. E. H. Palmer, Philip Sherrard, and Kallistos Ware, trs. and eds. (New York: Macmillan, 1982), p. 178.

the deification of man, therefore, the key is in the phrase *bearing nothing earthly in ourselves,* which is an expression of dualism that sees the material as inherently evil while the spirit alone is good. The self-abnegation and the contemplative life that came to characterize Eastern Orthodox spirituality also impacted the Roman Catholic Church and, in many ways, the communities that the Reformation produced.

Commitment to vows of chastity, celibacy, poverty, and even silence became characteristic of the best and brightest of Western Christians. Just as in the Eastern Church, self-denial—the "overcoming" of the world by withdrawal from the earthy—became the order of the day for centuries. Leaders thought that forms of self-abnegation and even self-flagellation brought one to a higher plane of spirituality. To see the extent to which this idea impacted the church, one need only to consider the case of Francis of Assisi, who was so committed to denying himself any form of pleasure that he would actually sprinkle ashes on his food so that when he ate it, he would not "enjoy" it. Likewise, if the occasion ever arose when he experienced any sexual desire, he would also throw himself into a ditch full of ice.[167] The desperate effort to avoid experiencing the earthy in order to transform oneself into the sublime world of a heavenly spirituality caused thousands to deny the inherent goodness of God's creation and to inflict upon themselves stringencies that Scripture never demanded of them. No wonder Paul observed that "self-imposed piety, humiliation, and severe treatment of the body . . . are of no value in checking self-indulgence."[168]

While seeking to "know God," rather than to "know about God," is commendable and, indeed, is a very Hebraic idea, there is no evidence from Holy Scripture that any human being can ever become divine. Being "like Christ" or possessing the "image and likeness of God" cannot be equated with becoming God or even having some derivative divinity. Becoming a "partaker of the divine nature" occurs simultaneously with being "born from above"[169] or being "begotten by the Word of God."[170] At salvation, however, human beings are not transformed into demigods or super-humans. They continue to be fully human but with the indwelling of the Holy Spirit that makes them the children of God. It also empowers them to receive the fullness of the life of the new creation in Christ: "Beloved, now we are children of God, and it has not appeared as yet what we will be. We know that when he appears, we

---

[167] Jaroslav Pelikan, *Jesus Through the Centuries: His Place in the History of Culture* (New Haven, CT: Yale University Press, 1985), p. 138.
[168] Colossians 3:20, NIV.
[169] John 3:3.
[170] James 1:18.

will be like him, because we will see him just as he is."[171] In life on earth, humans will continue to be humans, not divine or semi-divine creatures. And even in the resurrection, humans will still be humans—glorified to be sure—but still humans. Because of faith in God's Word—the truth and the person of the Word—they will have received the divine gift of being fully human (as Jesus was in his incarnation) as God designed them to be in the beginning, but they will still be human, not God or gods. In the resurrection, believers will be clothed upon with bodies that are like the glorified body in which Jesus rose from the dead, as Paul specifically said, "[He] will transform the body of our humble state into conformity with the body of his glory by the exertion of the power that he has even to subject all things to himself."[172]

More "Spiritual" than God?

The problem with many of the efforts toward divinization, hyper-spirituality, and extreme perfectionism is that while motives for such efforts seem worthy of applause, their actual implementation tends to proceed from the premise that one can achieve a higher spirituality through his own efforts either in doing "spiritual" things or in self-abnegation. This condition often manifests itself in forms of self-righteousness in which one thinks that being closer to God—and, therefore, more spiritual—is augmented or achieved by what one does or does not do. Very often this leads to withdrawal from real-life fellowship in the context of community. Sometimes it can be manifest in detachment from reality when the individual's idea of spirituality becomes supreme and dominates activities without respect to relationship. In these cases, a legalism develops that is immediately revealed in the judgmentalism that excludes other believers who do not share the individual's theory or "vision." The truly dangerous aspect of this kind of approach to spirituality is that it elevates self and human action above faith and hinges self-worth on personal achievement rather than on obedience to divine imperatives out-lined in Holy Scripture.

"Shall mortal man be more just than God? shall a man be more pure than his maker?" Eliphaz, asked Job, perhaps rhetorically.[173] The answer is, Yes, and especially so if it makes him think that his status is self-generated. There is something inherent in human nature that promotes autonomy, self-assertion, self-reliance, and self-sufficiency and encourages the belief that people can achieve or maintain status before God on the basis of their own actions or

---

[171] 1 John 3:2.
[172] Philippians 3:21.
[173] Job 4:17; 25:4.

demeanor. This "self-righteousness" syndrome, which plagued some parts of both Judaism and earliest Christianity, was vitriolically denounced by the apostle Paul.[174] It represented the assumption and imposition of a "righteousness" or "spirituality" that God neither desired nor required.[175]

Solomon offered this word of wisdom that should be considered by all believers: "Do not be excessively righteous, and do not be overly wise."[176] Christians should learn to manifest the level of justice and righteousness for which God designed them by achieving the balance of biblical spirituality rather than drifting to one side into an emotionless Stoic existence or to the other side into unbridled Epicurean hedonism. They should learn to achieve the balanced Hebraic Christian life that does not romanticize unnecessary and non-obligatory self-abnegation but also does not glorify self-indulgence and self-gratification. It should find the middle ground of biblical safety between the extremes of mysticism and rationalism.

A Hebraic "This-Worldly" Spirituality

From a biblical perspective, being a "spiritual" human being entails engagement with life in the "here and now," not in visions about life in a dimension far, far away. This is because biblical spirituality does not bifurcate life into "spiritual" and "carnal" realms or into "spiritual" and "material" polarities, as was the case with Greek philosophy. This is why as Amanda Porterfield rightly says, "the underlying Jewish foundation of early Christianity worked against dualistic tendencies to separate spirituality from material life. . . . a strong Judaean tradition of commitment to the God of creation, history, and this-worldly law limited the influence of philosophical idealism."[177] It is for this reason that the Hebraic teaching that was advocated by prophets and apostles "tended to desacralize and undemonize the world."[178] As Rottenberg has noted, "there is a this-worldliness to biblical faith that Christianity has often had a harder time holding on to than has Judaism, especially when the witness of Moses and the prophets—the only Bible known to the earliest Christians—was somehow seen as inferior to the allegedly much more spiritual nature of the gospels and the apostolic writings."[179]

---

[174] Galatians 2:16; 3:11

[175] Nicholas T. Wright, *Justification: God's Plan and Paul's Vision* (Downers Grove, IL: InterVarsity Press, 2009), p. 116.

[176] Ecclesiastes 7:16.

[177] Amanda Porterfield, *Healing the History of Christianity* (New York: Oxford University Press, 2005), p. 46.

[178] Rottenberg, p. 96.

[179] Rottenberg, p. 130.

Jewish spirituality was based in public worship, in reading and interpreting Scripture, and in corporate prayers. Private spirituality was strongly molded by public spirituality. Jews believed that *da'at* (knowledge) and *hokmah* (wisdom) came from "meditating in the Torah of God," by repeating over and over the words of Scripture so that they were ingested and inculcated into the very fiber of human being. This is the lesson that was so memorably stated in opening words of the Book of Psalms: "Blessed is the one who does not walk in step with the wicked or stand in the way that sinners take or sit in the company of mockers, but whose delight is in the law of the LORD, and who meditates on his law day and night."[180] The Psalmist then offered this vivid simile to describe a person who lives by the maxim of delight and meditation in God's Word: "That person is like a tree planted by streams of water, which yields its fruit in season and whose leaf does not wither—whatever they do prospers."[181]

The key declaration in this text that ensures the success and prosperity of such a righteous and "spiritual" person is this: "[He] meditates on [God's] Torah day and night." The Hebrew word translated "meditate" is הָגָה (*hagah*), which means to "moan," "mutter," or "growl."[182] Fundamentally, the word means to soliloquize by repeating over and over again to one's self the words of the Torah (Scripture) so that those words actually become a part of one's essence. The image that establishes the repetitive nature of soliloquizing the words of Scripture is that of a ruminating cow which chews its cud, swallows, regurgitates, chews again, swallows, regurgitates, and chews yet again.

Mark Futato contrasts this kind of "meditation" with biblical meditation wherein the Hebrew word *hagah* "is used for low animal sounds like the cooing of a dove[183] or the growl of a lion[184]" and is also used "for human speech, whether articulate[185] or not.[186]"[187] In the text of Psalm 1, the word *hagah*, therefore, "does not describe a silent activity but means to 'read in an undertone' or to 'mutter while meditating.'"[188] It is clear, therefore, that biblical meditation engages both the voice and the mind in the act of ruminating over the words of Scripture by soliloquizing them verbally to oneself. This is

---

[180] Psalm 1:1–2, NIV.
[181] Psalm 1:3, NIV.
[182] The meaning of "growling" or "rumbling" is often associated with the metaphor of thunder that erupts as the voice of God issues forth from the divine mouth (as in Job 37:2 and John 12:29).
[183] Isaiah 38:14.
[184] Isaiah 31:4.
[185] Psalm 35:28.
[186] Isaiah 16:7.
[187] Mark David Futato, *Interpreting the Psalms: An Exegetical Handbook* (Grand Rapids, MI: Kregel Academic, 2007), p. 68.
[188] Futato, p. 68.

confirmed by the fact that the Hebrew word *hagah* is parallel with other cognitive Hebrew terms[189] such as זָכַר—*zakar* ("remember")[190] and שִׂיחַ—*shiyach* ("reflect on" or "consider").[191]

This is the opposite of the idea of "meditation" as set forth in current postmodern culture which is based on the ideas and practices of Eastern Monism. In Eastern religions and philosophies, meditation begins with the inane chanting of a mantra in order to drive out all conscious thought in an effort to contact the wisdom eye (*prajana-chakshu*), the "third eye," which is believed to be centered in the area around the pituitary gland in the middle of the forehead. In contacting the wisdom eye, one is thereby thought to gain insight.[192] In modern adaptations of this system, meditation is often characterized by silence, wherein both speech and thought are suppressed.

Jewish tradition also teaches that the *Shekhinah* (Divine Presence) was present in daily lives and was of inestimable value to the community and the individual. The transcendence of God prompted the spiritual Jew always to seek the revelation of God's glory through study of the Torah.[193] Because the Torah was seen as the ultimate revelation of God's will, it was worthy of con-templation, meditation, and obedience. "Basic categories of Israel's faith, such as election, covenant, liberation from slavery, prophecy, and the promise of a future reign of *shalom*, all point to the fundamental belief that YHVH is the sovereign Lord of history."[194] This contrasts with the soteriological conse-quence of non-Semitic religions which propose that "humanity's ultimate ful-fillment or salvation is conceived in terms of . . . an escape from this historical life."[195] Rottenberg has rightly noted that "in the Hebrew Scriptures, the search for salvation is never resolved by an escape from history, either through metaphysical speculation or through a mystical absorption into an eternal Now."[196] First and foremost, the biblical focus on spirituality is, therefore, on the history of the Jewish people, "but is reinforced in the Christian view that the covenant is renewed and extended through the life and ministry Jesus of

---

[189] Futato, p. 68.

[190] Psalm 63:6 says, "When I *remember* you on my bed, I *meditate* on you in the night watches" (emphasis added).

[191] Psalm 77:12 says, "I will *consider* [*reflect on*] all your works and *meditate* on all your mighty deeds" (emphasis added).

[192] Raimundo Panikkar *Dwelling Place for Wisdom* (Louisville, KY: Westminster/John Knox Press, 1993), p. 64. Also David Frawley, *MantraYoga and the Primal Sound: Secrets of Seed (Bija) Mantras* (Twin Lakes, WI: Lotus Press, 2010), p. 22.

[193] In Psalm 119:70, 174 David declared, "I delight to do your will, O my God; your Torah is within my heart. . . . I long for your salvation, O LORD, and your Torah is my delight."

[194] Rottenberg, p. 97.

[195] Murray A. Rae, "Creation and Promise" in *Behind the Text: History and Biblical Interpretation*, Craig Bartholomew and C. Stephen Evans, eds. (Grand Rapids, MI: Zondervan Publishing, 2003), vol. 4, p. 289.

[196] Rottenberg, p. 97.

Nazareth, who is confessed as the Messianic Mediator of redemption for all people."[197]

Biblical spirituality, then, is inherently connected with study and application of Scripture. As Rottenberg has said, reading the Bible "is bound to bring about a rude awakening from dreamy thoughts and heart's desires, because the God of Israel is proclaimed as entering the realm of time, as dwelling among his people, and using history as an avenue of revelation and a channel of redemption."[198] This is why "biblical revelation calls to *faith* over against the kind of religious thought that emphasizes discovery of the divine within one's own being."[199] This living faith that is connected inexorably to the history of a God who has acted and continues to act in the present offers ever-expanding new dimensions and new futures based in real time among real people. In doing so, it constantly moves the believer into new horizons and delivers him from "the mythos of the All" that is both ahistorical and "leads to a *status quo* view of things as they are."[200]

Privatizing Mysteries

The Scriptures speak extensively about the movement of the Spirit upon the inner man; however, inner experiential spiritual manifestations of faith must always be lived out within the context of community, particularly the dominion of God. "Both Judaism and Christianity affirm that life in the presence of the God of Israel is life in covenant relationship and partnership."[201] When Christians have been severed from solid grounding in the Hebrew Scriptures, they have often been "precariously perched to go doctrinally airborne and take a spiritual flight from this world to the heavenly world above."[202] Without the dynamics of divine social justice in the kingdom of God, religious experiences over-focus on the mystical and an isolation from the this-worldly spirituality of the Scriptures into a purely subjective and self-centered spirituality that is little more than self-divinization. In this case, many Christians of virtually all denominations have abandoned the community of believers for the sect or cult, leaving the "apostolate to the world" in favor of lingering alone "endlessly in the Garden" with "sweet Jesus.[203] This hyper-personalization of faith

---

[197] Rottenberg, p. 98.
[198] Rottenberg, p. 97.
[199] Rottenberg, p. 97.
[200] Rottenberg, p. 97.
[201] Rottenberg, p. 102.
[202] Wilson, *Exploring*, p. 37.
[203] Rottenberg, p. 99.

has often produced the arrogance of subjectivity expressed in the Tom T. Hall refrain that was popularized by Kris Kristofferson: "Me and Jesus got our own thing going; we don't need anybody to tell us what it's all about."[204]

Some Christians of this sort are like spiritual hummingbirds, flitting from one nectar stem to another, pausing just long enough to imbibe the elixir of one more sweet-tasting delight and then darting away. Here today, gone tomorrow, they are like the Israelites of whom the prophet said, "They go to the east, west, north and south, seeking the word of the LORD but never finding it"[205] because they are looking for the wrong thing. They are searching for a titillating emotional experience, a momentary existential delight that satisfies only their own ego inflation, self-indulgence, and self-fulfillment. While they may gain some evanescent scintillation from the sparkling flashes of ephemeral self-gratification, they have little interest in bonding with others in a mutually supportive and enduring community of faith and working within the context of that community to bring forth social justice and blessing to others. Because their motives are skewed, they are a far cry from experiencing the kind of spirituality that God commends in Scripture. Daniel Migliore is correct when he concludes that "freedom in Christ is utterly different from the self-indulgence that characterizes consumer culture." This is the kind of spirituality that has "a heightened readiness to be servants in God's work of reconciliation in Christ," a spirituality that struggles "against hostility, injustice, and other evils at work within us and around us."[206]

Much of the idea of religious experience or spirituality, therefore, has drifted into what Richard King calls "the privatisation of mysticism," which simply locates "the mystical in the psychological realm of personal experiences,"[207] the feelings and emotions unleashed in an existential moment. When this occurs, mysticism and spirituality come to be seen "as a personal matter of cultivating inner states of tranquility and equanimity" which removes the Christian focus from the biblical mandate "to transform the world" and places it on alleviation "of anxiety and stress"[208] of the individual. Richard Mouw and Sander Griffoen have described this kind of highly personalized "spirituality" and its results: "Popular spiritual monisms, of which the recent 'New Age' phenomenon is one (but only one) prominent

---

204 Tom T. Hall, "Me and Jesus," (Nashville, TN: Sony/ATV Acuff Rose Music, 1972).
205 Amos 8:12.
206 Daniel L. Migliore, *Faith Seeking Understanding: An Introduction to Christian Theology* (Grand Rapids, MI: Wm. B. Eerdmans Publishing Co., 2004), p. 243.
207 King, p. 21.
208 King, p. 21.

example, have flourished in Western societies in recent years because dislocated modern individuals—people operating without strong familial, ecclesial and national bonds—become convinced that their only alternative to an "atomistic" selfism is absorption into an undifferentiated cosmic All.'"[209] This is why "shallowness, superficiality, and emotional mush have . . . become apt descriptors for many current expressions of Christianity."[210] Because of the multiplicity of accretions that have been added to the biblical ideal of spirituality, "it may require considerable time to scrape away the layers built up over time . . . if the Hebraic features of the church's original face are to be uncovered and warmly embraced,"[211] says Marvin Wilson.

Recovering the Balance of Biblically Hebraic Spirituality

David Perrin observes that "spirituality is considered a fluid thing, something that relates directly to the concrete circumstances of everyday life in all its complexities. The commitment to diversity and the unexpected is the key to spirituality, because spirituality is embodied in the activities of everyday life that have these same characteristics."[212] For this reason, "spirituality, in practice, does not tend to look for indicators of official religiosity. Rather, it seeks an expression of the intuitive/embodied/felt presence of God in one's life. In this way Christian spiritualities, and their expression in lived experience, are, to a large degree, bound together through *praxis* (practice), and not exclusively through beliefs dictated by religious systems."[213] True Spirituality is informed and governed by Scripture, but it is not straightjacketed by bureaucratic restrictions.

Marvin Wilson expounds a profound biblical truth when he notes that "to the Hebrew mind, everything is theological. That is, the Hebrews make no distinction between the sacred and the secular areas of life. They see all of life as a unity."[214] Everything in life, therefore, is spiritual. It is in this context that the truly spiritual person is able to see the miracles in everyday life just as Abraham Heschel did when he announced to a stunned audience that he had just experienced a miracle. Then, the philosopher/rabbi confessed that he had just witnessed the setting of the sun.[215] For Heschel, "religious reality does not begin with the essence of God but with His presence, not with

---

[209] Richard J. Mouw and Sander Griffioen, *Pluralisms and Horizons: An Essay in Christian Public Philosophy* (Grand Rapids, MI: Wm. B. Eerdmans Publishing Co., 1993), p. 121.

[210] Wilson, *Exploring*, p. 69.

[211] Wilson, *Exploring*, p. 69.

[212] David B. Perrin, *Studying Christian Spirituality* (New York: Routledge, 2007), p. 45.

[213] Perrin, p. 46.

[214] Marvin Wilson, *Our Father*, p. 156.

[215] Abraham Joshua Heschel, noted in Rifat Sonsino, *The Many Faces of God: A Reader of Modern Jewish Theologies* (New York: URJ Press, 2004), p. 161.

dogma or metaphysics but with that sense of wonder and the ineffable which is experienced by every man."[216] With this mindset of spirituality, it is possible to focus on deed more than creed, to dwell on justice and mercy rather than on contemplating the mysteries of the divine essence. It is also possible to learn to be fully human like the only person who ever was fully human: Jesus Christ. In truth, the quest of biblical faith and spirituality is to become fully human by replicating in human existence the life of Jesus Christ. The ideal is to become completely Christian by becoming entirely "like Christ." Indeed, "Christian living is the Spirit-assisted response to the Incarnate Word of God, Jesus Christ, who reveals the face of the invisible God."[217]

Christian spirituality, therefore, has little to do with what people do for God. "We will never be able to love, pray, think, feel, work, meditate, fast or even die our way into a deeper spiritual life if we rely on human effort or clever schemes alone. There is nothing we can do—nothing we have to do—to find a way to God, because in Jesus Christ God has already made his way to us,"[218] says Gerald Sittser. True spirituality is experiencing the God "who is [present]," the YHWH of Scripture. "The 'I AM' of biblical revelation does not invite us to . . . philosophize about the divine *being*, but rather to recognize God as *being there*, present as the Holy One in our midst, involved in historical existence. . . . God's true being is known through God's saving acts."[219] As Martin Buber so aptly noted, biblical revelation means that "the human substance is melted by the spiritual fire which visits it, and there now breaks forth from it a Word, a statement which is human in its meaning and form, human conception and human speech, and yet witness to Him who stimulated it and to His will."[220] Biblical revelation of God's purposes for humanity destroys the philosophical bifurcation between the spiritual ideas and the material body. As Bert Blans has poignantly and rightly observed, "the discovery of the Hebrew foundations of the Bible, that hardly coincide with ecclesiastical teachings, allowed for a reconciliation of body and spirit in the paean to erotic divine love."[221]

---

[216] Heschel, *God in Search of Man*, p. 3, noted in Fred Sklonik, et. al, eds, *Encyclopaedia Judaica* (Jerusalem, Israel: Keter Publishing House, 2007), vol. 6, p. 612.

[217] Downey, p. 45.

[218] Gerald L. Sittser, *Water from a Deep Well: Christian Spirituality from Early Martyrs to Modern Missionaries* (Downers Grove, IL: InterVarsity Press, 2007), p. 48.

[219] Rottenberg, p. 160.

[220] Martin Buber, *The Eclipse of God: Studies in the Relation Between Religion and Philosophy* (New York: Harper Brothers, 1952), p. 173.

[221] Bert Blans and Marcel Poorthuis, "The Return of the Gods: The Clash Between Monotheism and Polytheism in German Romanticism," in *The Boundaries of Monotheism: Interdisciplinary Explorations Into the Foundations of Western Monotheism, Anne-Marie Korte and Maaike De Haardt, eds.* (Leiden, The Netherlands: Koninklijke Brill NV, 2009), p. 104.

The truly "spiritual" are those who are Spirit-filled and Spirit-led believers, those who dare to walk in the Spirit. These are not escapists who seek a mystical flight from the reality of the world. They understand the implications of Jesus' prayer when he said, "Father, I pray not that you should take them from the world but that you should protect them from the evil one."[222] They are, therefore, fully engaged in life, making holy every aspect of human existence, experiencing the divine in everything. Those who understand the true nature of biblical spirituality are not "God-seekers." They have not had to look for God because God has already found them. They bask in the presence of the God who has always been searching for them, not vice versa.[223] They are not "God-chasers," because God is not trying to escape from them or hide from them. They are God-engagers, God-experiencers, even God-wrestlers (as Jacob of old).[224] They contend for the blessing while accepting the divine calling to walk daily with God in his presence.

The True Measure of Spirituality

While a far too significant portion of Christianity thinks of spirituality in terms of supernatural manifestations of the Spirit or in terms of charisma, the Scriptures are clear as to the measure of spirituality. "By their fruit, you shall know them," Jesus said plainly and simply.[225] "Every good tree brings forth good fruit," the Master declared. Paul outlined the distinguishing marks of Christian spirituality when he catalogued the "Fruit of the Spirit." Here is the apostle's list: "love, joy, peace, patience, kindness, goodness, faithfulness, gentleness, and self-control."[226] The fruit of the Spirit, not the gifts of the Spirit, comprise the true yardstick of biblically Hebraic spirituality!

Paul had already made it clear that it was not charisma but this kind of fruit that was the evidence of the indwelling Spirit and the life of a truly spiritual person. When he concluded an extended discourse on the "gifts" of the Spirit and urged all believers to desire the "greater gifts," the apostle said, "Yet I will show you the most excellent way."[227] Immediately, he entered into a discussion of the very first fruit of the Spirit, comparing love and its results to what many people would consider to be the most powerful evidence of spirituality. "If I speak in tongues of men or of angels

---

[222] John 17:15, NIV.
[223] John 4:23.
[224] The name *Israel* means "God-wrestler." See John D. Garr, *Life from the Dead*, pp. 225–226.
[225] Matthew 7:16.
[226] Galatians 5:22–23.
[227] 1 Corinthians 12:31.

. . . If I have the gift of prophecy and can fathom all mysteries and all knowledge, and if I have faith that can move mountains . . . If I give all my possessions to feed the poor, and if I surrender my body to burned, but do not have love, it profits me nothing."[228] Finally, Paul concluded, "Love never fails; but if there are gifts of prophecy, they will pass away; if there are tongues, they will cease; if there is knowledge, it will pass away."[229]

Here is the truth: "What we know is incomplete, and what we prophesy is incomplete."[230] The lesson is simple. All the manifestations of the Spirit in the world will fail to accomplish God's purposes in one way or another. The only thing that will never fail to fulfill God's designs and purposes for all people is love! Abraham Heschel said it well: "When faith is completely replaced by creed, worship by discipline, love by habit; when the crisis of today is ignored because of the splendor of the past; when faith becomes an heirloom rather than a living fountain; when religion speaks only in the name of authority rather than with the voice of compassion—its message becomes meaningless."[231]

It is no mistake, then, to understand that "the themes of love and repentance derive from Hebrew Scripture and carry through all of Christian spirituality."[232] The experience of the Spirit in the lives of men and women in the Hebrew Scriptures is the foundation for a balanced spirituality for believers today. God is looking for one thing that is far more important than charisma or charismata. He is looking for character. True spirituality manifests itself in godly character. Even though it is evident that Satan and the charlatans he commissions can duplicate gifts, spiritual manifestations,[233] and existential experiences the one thing that neither he nor they can ever do is to live a godly life, continually manifesting godly character. Such victorious living is possible only by the empowerment of the Spirit wherein one can "walk with God in the Spirit" and do so without condemnation.[234]

A Spiritual Restoration

Through the centuries, various renewal movements have been manifest in the fires of revival. The Methodist awakening of the eighteenth century and the holiness revival of the nineteenth century brought spiritual renewal both

---

[228] 1 Corinthians 13:1-3.
[229] 1 Corinthians 13:8, ESV.
[230] 1 Corinthians 13:9, ISV.
[231] Heschel, *God in Search*, p. 3.
[232] Robert Imperato, *Early and Medieval Christian Spirituality* (Lanham, MD: The University Press of America, 2002), p. 5.
[233] 2 Thessalonians 2:9; 2 Timothy 3:8; Acts 17:11; Matthew 7:15.
[234] Galatians 5:16; Romans 8:4–5.

to England and the United States. At the turn of the twentieth century, a great spiritual revival was ignited from the embers of those renewal movements. Despite the fact that much of the church at that time posited a cessationist theology by maintaining that all the supernatural manifestations of the Holy Spirit had ceased with the death of the apostles and the canonization of the New Testament Scriptures, still many believers began to seek what most had thought unobtainable. They began to pray for the infilling of the Spirit and its accompanying manifestations that had characterized the first-century faith of the apostles. And, in various ways at about the same time, believers began to experience those manifestations again.

The operations of the Spirit which once had been unique to the Israelites, then to the first-century church, began to be manifest again, generally among mostly humble, semiliterate people. While enthusiasm over the restoration of clearly biblical experiences of the Spirit brought forth excesses and abuses, the obvious truth was that something had happened that could not be explained away. The Holy Spirit was at work. As the twentieth century unfolded, what had been projected by all the pundits to be a century of the decline and demise of Christian faith became one of the finest eras of explosive growth in the breaking forth of the kingdom of God. This was but another demonstration of the truth contained in the statement of Paul that "where sin increased, grace increased all the more"[235] and his contention that people "can do nothing against the truth, but for it."[236]

In more recent times, people of virtually every denomination have received the Holy Spirit and manifestations of the *charismata*. The numbers have increased rapidly until they have come to reach into the millions with the largest identifiable demographic in Christianity today being those who profess to be Spirit-filled.[237] Again, enthusiasm over the restoration of a New Testament experience has brought forth excesses and abuses; however, it is a simple fact that millions of people have experienced the infilling of the Holy Spirit and have witnessed manifestations of the Spirit that have changed lives and matured believers. Various renewal movements have produced a restoration of the first-century operations of a uniquely Jewish experience in which ordinary people are moved by the Spirit of the God of Israel to do extraordinary, even supernatural things. The gifts of the Spirit

---

[235] Romans 5:20, NIV.
[236] 2 Corinthians 13:8.
[237] Vinson Synan, *In the Latter Days: The Outpouring of the Holy Spirit in the Twentieth Century* (Fairfax, VA: Xulon Press, 2001), p. 20. Also James T. Flynn, Wie Liang Tjiong, and Russell W. West, *A Well-Furnished Heart: Restoring the Spirit's Place in the Leadership Classroom* (Fairfax, VA: Xulon Press, 2002), p. 153.

that were first manifest in Judaism and then perfected in the first-century church have been renewed and restored in varying degrees in various faith communities.

While significant parts of Christianity still consider spirituality to be the product of self-abnegation, isolation, or contemplation, some are awakening to a new this-worldly spirituality, one which mirrors the original Hebraic heritage of the Christian faith. While many Christians mistake being spirited—vivacious, animated, and emotional—for being spiritual,[238] others have come to the realization that biblically Hebraic spirituality is a deep, abiding passion for truth and for justice in the earth that is best advanced with the empowerment of the Holy Spirit. Without a doubt, all of Christianity "needs a strong dose of the 'earthiness, the holistic 'this-worldliness' that has marked the Judaic tradition."[239] In fact, "Hebraic thought . . . serves as a needed corrective" in that it "anchors Christianity to this earthly world."[240] Such a "biblical materialism" is central to the worldview that has been advanced "via the people of Israel and Judaism."[241] It was central to the worldview and mindset of the apostles, and it must be fully restored to the Christian community for its own health and for the advancement of the kingdom of God.

Can it be that someday soon the centuries-old argument that "Christianity is essentially a spiritualistic, unworldly kind of faith" will at long last be "laid to rest as a myth, a fiction, even a lie"?[242] Only the God of the present and of the future knows the answer to that question. One thing that is certain is that if and when the church fully recovers the Hebraic foundations inherent in its faith, it will return to the faith of the fathers, a living faith that is of, for, and by the Holy Spirit. When believers have a clear understanding of their Hebraic heritage, they can "maintain balance and avoid temptation to escape the struggles and painful realities below for contemplated pleasures above."[243] When Christian spirituality is finally restored to its biblical foundations, Christians will be fully engaged in the here and now, advancing the kingdom of God through Spirit-inspired and Spirit-anointed acts of justice and divine mercy, powerfully demonstrated through the diverse *charismata* of the Holy Spirit.

Spirituality: Christian Fruit—Jewish Root!

---

[238] The contrast between "spirited" and "spiritual" can be seen in a horse that may well be "spirited" but certainly is not "spiritual"!

[239] Rottenberg, p. 131.

[240] Wilson, *Exploring*, p. 37.

[241] Rottenberg, p. 31.

[242] Rottenberg, p. 131.

[243] Wilson, *Exploring*, p. 37.

CHAPTER 13

DISCIPLESHIP

Near the conclusion of his earthly ministry, Jesus gave the Great Commission to his apostles: "Go therefore and *make disciples* of all the nations."[1] Clearly, the community that Jesus designed was to be engaged continually in the dynamics of discipleship. The church of Jesus was to be comprised of disciples who would make other disciples who, in turn, would make still other disciples until the entire world would be confronted with the good news: "Christ has died, Christ is risen, Christ will come again."[2] From its inception, therefore, Christianity has always been fundamentally a discipleship-based faith tradition. Tragically, however, far too many Christians today know far too little about the true nature of discipleship in the way in which Jesus taught it and his apostles practiced it in the earliest Christian community.

Christian discipleship was not created in Hellas or in Plato's academy, nor did it emerge from the traditions of eastern mystery religions. And it was certainly not an innovation that Jesus created out of whole cloth. Christian discipleship was birthed from the matrix of biblical and Second Temple Judaism, the system of praise, worship, and service in which Jesus and his disciples expressed their devotion to God. From the time that the synagogal system emerged in Israel immediately after the Babylonian captivity, the importance of instruction in the Hebrew Scriptures became more and more formalized in teacher-disciple relationships. Since during his incarnation, Jesus was in every way a proper Jew living in the context of the Torah, he

---

[1] Matthew 28:19, emphasis added.
[2] These are the words from the "Memorial Acclamation" that originated in the liturgies of the Syrian Orthodox Church and the Maronite Church. It was later adopted by the Anglican, Lutheran, and Methodist churches and was restored to the Roman Catholic Church in Vatican II. See Berard L. Marthaler, *The Creed: The Apostolic Faith in Contemporary Theology* (New London, CT: Twenty-Third Publications, 1987), p. 201. Also Don S. Mermentrout and Robert Boak Slocum, eds., *An Episcopal Dictionary of the Church* (Norwich, UK: Church House Publishing, 2005), p. 328.

maintained complete continuity with his people and their faith as well as with their recognized system for the transfer of knowledge, belief, and practice. He was acclaimed by his community as a "rabbi" (master or teacher),[3] and those who followed him were referred to as "disciples"[4] no less than 205 times in the Gospels alone.

In order to begin to understand the true nature of discipleship, it is vital to recognize the fact that Jesus never once commanded his followers "make Christians." As a matter of fact, the term *Christian* appears only four times in Apostolic Scripture. The earliest followers of Jesus did not call themselves "Christians." Instead, they preferred to be known as *"Notzrim,"*[5] and they preferred to describe their movement as "The Way."[6] Over time, the essential identity of the believing community with the Messiah became established in the Greek term Χριστιανός (*Christianós*— "Christians"). Antiochian gainsayers[7] first derisively called the community of believers in Jesus "Christians" some seventeen years after the Acts 2 Pentecost, in effect disparaging them for being "like Christ,"[8] whom they despised as a fraud and a charlatan. Even though, as time passed, the followers of Jesus came to be identified as "Christians" and, then, to identify themselves as "Christians," the word *Christian* was unknown to Jesus.

Similarly, Jesus did not command his apostles to make "believers." The term *believer* is used only twice in Apostolic Scripture. While it is obvious that those who were followers of Jesus were believers in the Messiah, it is also true that they were not universally called "believers" in the first century. In similar fashion, Jesus did not commission his apostles to "make converts."

---

[3] In John 3:32, Nicodemus said of Jesus, "Rabbi, we know that you are a teacher who has come from God." In Mark 12:14, Jesus' fellow Jews said, "Rabbi, we know that you are true . . . for you are not swayed by appearances but truly teach the way of God." Though the formal title of *rabbi* was not established until after the emergence of Rabbinic Judaism at the end of the first century AD, spiritual leaders were called *moreh* ("teacher") and *rabbi* ("my master") before and during the time of Jesus.

[4] Matthew 10:1.

[5] The term *Notzrim* was self-adopted by the earliest community of believers in Jesus. It means the followers of the *Netzer*, the Hebrew word that Isaiah used to describe the anticipated Messiah: "Then a shoot will spring from the stem of Jesse, and a *netzer* (branch) from his roots will bear fruit" (Isaiah 11:1). The earliest Jewish community that recognized Jesus as Messiah drew from the "Branch of David" imagery for the identity of their community.

[6] The term *The Way* was an adaptation of the Jewish emphasis on *halakhah* (the way in which one should walk). *Halakhah* was the accepted, normative standard for conduct within Jewish communities of faith, including the Jewish followers of Jesus.

[7] Acts 11:26. See John MacArthur, *Acts 1-12 MacArthur New Testament Commentary* (Chicago, IL: Moody Press, 1994), p. 315. Also Lyman Abbott, *The Acts of the Apostles* (New York: A. S. Barnes & Co., 1876), p. 136. Abbott says that the inhabitants of Antioch were "notorious for employing names of derision."

[8] The Greek word *Christos* (Christ) is a direct translation of the Hebrew word *Mashiach* (Messiah). The term *Christian*, then, is an Anglicized Greek translation of the word *Messianic*.

The term *convert* is not used in all of Scripture but is a later invention used to describe those who "turn in a different direction," which was the meaning of the English word that was derived from the Old French word *convertir* and ultimately from the Latin word *convertere* (*con-* ["altogether"] and *vertere* ["turn"]).[9]

What, then, was the divine commission that came from the lips of Jesus? It was to make "disciples," a term and practice that ubiquitously appears in Apostolic Scripture 270 times. The implication of making disciples was making followers, a term that is also mentioned 12 times in Scripture and is the essence of the activity of discipleship. Just from the weight of textual use of the word *disciple* to describe the followers of Jesus, it is evident that the foremost ambition of the earliest believers was to "make disciples." In reality, however, when Jesus called his apostles, required them to "follow" him,[10] and then instructed them to "make disciples" of the nations, he was not introducing a completely new idea that had never been considered before. He was merely redirecting the traditional Jewish activity that had been enshrined in the opening words of the Mishnah,[11] the foundation of the Talmud and other later Jewish commentaries on the Torah.

In *Pirkei Avot*[12] 1:1, the Mishnah says, "Be deliberate in judgment,[13] raise up many disciples, and make a fence around the Torah." When it came to interpreting these words of the Mishnah during the time of Jesus, the School of Shammai argued that one should teach only "those who were intelligent, cultured, from a good religious family, and wealthy."[14] At the same time, however, the School of Hillel said, "Teach all men, because many sinners in Israel were attracted to the study of the Torah and became good people and some even came to be counted among the righteous and the chasidim."[15] Hillel also "challenged his fellow scholars to interact and align with the rest of the community: 'Do not keep yourself aloof from the community.'"[16] The concept for making disciples of all

---

[9] The term *convert* may not have been used in earliest Christianity because the Jews who came to believe in the Messiah were not changing religions or "turning altogether." Instead, they were simply accepting Jesus as the fulfillment of their Messianic expectation.

[10] Matthew 4:19; 16:24; Luke 9:23, 57–62; John 21:19.

[11] The word *mishnah* means "repetition."

[12] *Pirkei Avot* means the "Ethics of the Fathers."

[13] Jacob Neusner says the statement means, "Be patient when you judge—when you make up your mind." Jacob Neusner, *Learn Mishnah* (Springfield, NJ: Behrman House, 1978), p. 10.

[14] Michael D. Palmer and Stanley M. Burgess, eds., *The Wiley-Blackwell Companion to Religion and Social Justice* (Malden, MA: John Wiley & Sons, 2012), p. 297.

[15] *Avot d'Rabbi Natan* A 3; B 4. See Palmer and Burgess, p. 297.

[16] Mishnah, *Avot* 2:5; *Tosefta, Berakhot* 2:21. See Palmer and Burgess, p. 297.

nations was not, therefore, a new idea that Jesus and his disciples created. It was, instead, prefaced in the sages at least a decade and as much as a century before the time of Jesus' ministry, especially in the teachings of Hillel.

What Does the Word *Disciple* Mean?

The English word *disciple* comes directly from the Latin *discipulus*, which means "scholar" or "learner." The word *discipulus* was derived from the infinitive *discere* which means "to discern" or "to learn." Essentially, then, the word *disciple* means "a learner." The Greek word in the Apostolic Scriptures that is translated "disciple" is μαθητής (*mathetés*), which also means "learner" or "pupil." Since the word *mathetés* is the source of the English word *mathematics*, it is easy to see that disciplined study is strongly associated with the Greek term for disciple.

A much more definitive understanding of the meaning of the word *disciple* is established, however, when the Hebrew word that is translated *mathetés* in Greek is examined. Since it is clear that when Jesus called his followers "disciples," he was speaking Hebrew or Aramaic, not Greek or Latin, the Hebrew text and language must be examined if an accurate understanding of discipleship is to be established. The Hebrew word for "disciple" is תַּלְמִיד (*talmid*).[17] This word means "taught" and "accustomed to" or "used to (the yoke)." The word *talmid* is a scriptural *hapax legomenon* because it is used only in 1 Chronicles 25:8 where it describes students. The word *talmid*, however, eventually became the most common term for students or learners in the Jewish world. When Jesus spoke of his followers, he called them *talmidim*.

Originally the word *talmid* was applied to students of music. This, of course, confirms that a true disciple is not merely a repository for knowledge, for music is enjoyed only when it is performed, when the theory is translated into enjoyable sound as a result of the vigorous discipline of practice. Biblical disciples, then, were both learners *and* doers, those who applied themselves to the rigors of studying in order to do and constantly engaged in the discipline of practicing the fulfillment of God's instructions for life in the ancient world.

Further examination of the word *talmid* produces even greater clarity, for *talmid* comes from the verbal stem לָמַד (*lamad*), which means "to

---

[17] The word *talmid* appears in 1 Chronicles 25:8, where it is translated "scholar" (KJV, JPS), "pupil" (NASB, NJB, ESV), "student" (NIV, NKJ, NRS), "learner" (BBE), "apprentice" (TNK). *Talmid* is masculine singular. Other forms are of *talmid* are *talmidim* (masculine plural), *talmidah* (feminine singular), and *talmidot* (feminine plural).

learn."[18] In the ancient world, the *lamad* was a "goad," a sharp, pointed stick that was used to train oxen. In Hebrew the goad is a מַלְמַד (*malmad*),[19] literally "the thing that teaches." From this visual imagery, it is clear that being a disciple means being trained by the goad of spiritual and Scriptural discipline in much the same way in which oxen were trained by means of a goad.

Also important to the etymological study of *lamad* is the fact that this word is seen in the eleventh letter of the Hebrew *aleph-bet*, the ל (*lamed*). In ancient Hebrew, this letter was simply a pictograph of an ox goad.[20] The *lamed* is positioned at the very center of the Hebrew *aleph-bet*, towering over all the other Hebrew characters. It is the only Hebrew letter that ascends above the top line. For this reason alone, it stands out and is instantly discernible in all Hebrew texts. The *lamed* has, therefore, been the object of much reflection by Israel's sages through the millennia. Since God has done nothing by happenstance, they reason, there must be significance in the fact that the *lamed* is so tall. From this fact, the sages understood that learning is man's highest endowment.[21] As Marvin Wilson has said, the Jews understood that "life is for learning, and learning is for life."[22]

Hebrew's highest letter brings life's greatest rewards and in the end is the strength of salvation and eternal life. Isaiah well said, "[The LORD] will be the stability of your times: a wealth of salvation, wisdom, and knowledge."[23] The goad of learning, the rigor of study, inculcates understanding that leads to wisdom. The letter *lamed* is a visual picture of the success that comes to those who yield to the unrelenting pressure of its prodding to move ever onward and upward. It produces and maintains a mindset of instruction that

---

[18] Interestingly, the word *lamad* does not appear in the Hebrew Scriptures until Deuteronomy 4:1. This is because Deuteronomy is a teaching book, the summation of the first four books of the Torah. In a sense, Deuteronomy is Torah repeated. This is indicated by the name Deuteronomy, which literally means "second law." It is fitting, therefore, that the word *lamad* is first used in Deuteronomy, for this book is Torah taught and explicated.

[19] The term that is used in Judges 3:31 is מַלְמַד (*malmad*), where it is translated "ox-goad."

[20] In ancient times, each of the 22 letters of the Hebrew alphabet was a pictograph (in a manner similar to hieroglyphic and cuneiform writing). For example, the aleph (א) originally represented the picture of an ox head, the beth (ב), a house, and the gimel (ג), a camel. The lamed (ל) was originally a pictograph of a goad, the principal instrument for training and directing oxen in the ancient agrarian society. If *lamed* is viewed (and perhaps turned on its side), the visual image of a goad becomes clear The ascending stroke of the lamed is a yud (י), which is the pictograph of a hand. If this part of the *lamed* is visualized as being taken in hand, it is easy to see that the pointed end of the image is a perfect instrument for prodding an ox first for training and then for directing its work.

[21] Michael L. Munk, עולם האותיות *The Sacred Letters as a Guide to Jewish Deed and Thought* (Brooklyn, NY: Mesorah Publications, 1983), p. 139.

[22] Marvin R. Wilson, quoted in Bethany Bray, "Gordon College Professor Begins 50th Year of Teaching," Salem, MA, *News*, September 4, 2012. See Wilson, *Our Father*, pp. 307ff.

[23] Isaiah 33:6.

ever enriches and blesses. And as wisdom grows, learning continues to increase: "A wise man will hear and will increase learning."[24]

True Christian disciples are *talmidim*, yielded to the flexible and easy *lamad* with which Jesus gently prods those who are yoked together with him. With biblical discipline, they are assured that their lives will be filled with happiness. They experience the exercise of receiving the divine wisdom and insight that bring abundant life. It is no wonder that Solomon, after all his musings about the futility of life, drew this conclusion: "The words of the wise are like goads, their collected sayings like firmly embedded nails . . . When all is said and done, this is the conclusion of the matter: Revere God and observe his commandments! For this applies to all mankind."[25] No wonder Jesus said that God's command "is eternal life."[26]

When the *lamad* imagery is considered as a background, Jesus' invitation in Matthew 11:29 becomes much more clear and understandable: "Take my yoke upon you, and learn of me, for I am gentle and lowly in heart, and you will find rest for your souls." The metaphor is the same: being yoked together with Jesus means learning—learning the teachings of Jesus, which are, after all, "easy." And, one could just as readily say that Jesus' *lamad* (goad) is not cruel, for it does not inflict unnecessary and excessive pain. It generates just enough discomfort to move the heart in the right direction of closer relationship with God and with one's fellow man. Profound insight can be gained into a significant part of the Hebraic heritage that has been obscured from Christian view for centuries when the meaning and significance of the Hebrew letter *lamed* and the Hebrew word *lamad* in both biblical and post-biblical contexts are analyzed. Through this simple *lamad* model, the deep well of understanding that has enriched the lives of countless Jewish people through history can be restored to Christians who reconnect with the Jewish roots of their faith, including the language of Scripture itself.

Learning and Teaching

The verb *lamad* means "to teach"[27]; however, it also means "to learn."[28] It is interesting that in Hebrew thought, teaching and learning are intertwined

---

[24] Proverbs 1:5.
[25] Ecclesiastes 12:11, NIV; 13, TNK.
[26] John 12:50.
[27] Passages of Scripture where *lamad* means "to teach" include Deuteronomy 4:10; Psalm 119:71; Isaiah 1:17; Jeremiah 10:2; Micah 4:3.
[28] Passages of Scripture where *lamad* means "to learn" include Deuteronomy 4:1, 10; Judges 3:2; Psalm 25:5; Jeremiah 31:34; Daniel 1:4.

as meanings of the same word.[29] Laird Harris points out that "while Greek uses two different words for 'to learn' (*manthano*) and 'to teach' (*didasko*), each having its own content, goal, and methods, Hebrew uses the same root for both words because all learning and teaching is ultimately to be found in the fear of the LORD."[30] A teacher, then, is a learner, and a learner is a teacher. As a matter of fact, in Bible days, the only reason for learning the Torah was so that one could then teach the Torah. Yaacov Emden[31] writes that "learning in order to teach others is the most basic intention one should have while learning and that anyone who does not do so will have no reward."[32] Dan Roth observes that the profound importance of this assertion is proven in Scripture: "In *Devarim* [Deuteronomy] 6:7, the Torah places the command to teach Torah before the command to learn it. The *Ksav Sofer*[33] writes that this order seems illogical because one has to learn before one can teach. He answers that the Torah is teaching us that one's own learning must be done with the motivation of teaching others later."[34] One source for this idea is *Pirkei Avot* 6:6 which lists "learning with the intent of teaching" as one of the forty-eight tools that are essential for acquiring Torah. This is a great lesson that teaching and learning go hand in hand and that each individual should be both a learner and a teacher for life. When learning ceases, teaching ends. This is the reason that society's most learned teachers are also called scholars, from the Latin word *scola*, which means "school." *Scola* (scholar), then, fundamentally means "student." And the true scholar is one who is ever learning, expanding the range of his erudition as a student.

From the moment of birth (and perhaps before), learning begins as the newly created life exercises every aspect of sensory perception to gather information that is then analyzed and acted upon. Infants learn at a prodigious rate from their parents and siblings and then from extended family and others. At the same time, however, even infants are giving lessons to those around them. Indeed, it is often difficult to discern who is reacting to whom! Parents learn amazing lessons from their infant children (even as their own parents predicted!). Toddlers become teachers of their younger—and older—siblings. Everyone, then, is both

---

[29] The *piel* form of the verb *lamad* means "to teach," while the *qal* form means "to learn." P. I. Sabbathi, *Soulzer: Be a Soldier to Save Your Soul* (Bloomington, IN: WestBowPress, 2014), p. 221.

[30] R. Laird Harris, Gleason L. Archer Jr., and Bruce K. Waltke, eds., *Theological Wordbook of the Old Testament* (Chicago, IL: Moody Publishers, 2003), p. 212.

[31] Yaacov Emden, *Sefer Lechem Shamayim* (Baltimore, MD: Shaftek Enterprises, 2007).

[32] Dan Roth, *Relevance: Pirkei Avos for the Twenty-first Century* (Jerusalem, Israel: Feldheim Publishers, 2007), p. 116, note 22.

[33] *Ksav Sofer* was written by Rabbi Abraham Shmuel Binyamin Sofer (Samuel Wolf Schreiber), one of the foremost Hungarian rabbis of the nineteenth century.

[34] Roth, p. 116, n. 22.

learning and teaching even from infancy. As life advances, it is easy for people to plateau in the learning process, thinking that they have acquired all the knowledge necessary for their lives or careers. Stagnation can result, at which point life descends into monotony and boredom. The wise, however, are always curious, always sensitive to new stimuli and new insight. Their lives are enriched because they see themselves as learners for life. They also maintain a passion for passing on to others what they have learned.

The *lamad*, therefore, is intrinsically involved in both learning and teaching. Indeed, learning is the irritating process of being goaded into proper and productive action by the rigors of discipline. It is the process of being trained so that one becomes accustomed to and comfortable with knowledge and understanding. It is the pain that brings the gain of a richer, fuller life in which one is positioned to act rather than constantly being acted upon. It is the bleeding that precedes the blessing, the drill that produces the thrill. The *lamad* of training, then, is the essence of discipleship.

Studying To Do; Doing To Teach

Another term that is cognate with the words *lamad* and *talmid* is *limud* ("learning"). This is the word that is translated "disciple" in Isaiah 8:16.[35] Learning and discipleship, therefore, are interconnected. Perhaps this is why learning has always been sacred to the Hebrew people. The progression from knowledge to understanding to wisdom[36] has been the quest of prophets and sages, of apostles and teachers, of men and women of God from time immemorial. The passion for knowing, with a view toward doing and understanding, is central to both individual and corporate Jewish identity.[37] Literacy and education have long been the hallmark of those people whom the God of the universe has uniquely identified as his chosen.[38]

In the seventh generation from the Edenic family, Enoch was said not to have experienced death because of his determination to walk with God and to please God.[39] In Hebrew, Enoch's very name חֲנוֹךְ (*Hanokh*) means

---

[35] Isaiah 8:16 says, "Bind up the testimony, seal the law among my disciples (*limudai*)."

[36] The "knowledge-to-understanding-to-wisdom" progression is set forth by Solomon as the educational process in Proverbs 2:5–9. See Michael R. Mitchell, *Leading, Teaching, and Making Disciples* (Bloomington, IN: LifeWay Publishing, 2010), p. 187.

[37] Louis Jacobs, *The Book of Jewish Practice* (Springfield, NJ: Behrman House, 1987), p. 5.

[38] Adele Berlin, ed., *The Oxford Dictionary of the Jewish Religion* (New York: Oxford University Press, 2011), p. 127. Also Anita Diamant and Howard Cooper, *Living a Jewish Life: A Guide for Starting, Learning, Celebrating, and Parenting* (New York: HarperPerennial, 1991), p. 79, and Geoffrey Wigoder, *The Encyclopedia of Judaism* (New York: Macmillian Publishing, 1989), p. 82.

[39] Genesis 5:24; Hebrews 11:5.

"dedicated" or "educated."[40] For this reason, he is believed by the Jewish people to have been the first human who was wholly dedicated to the process of learning and was, therefore, the first educated man, the first educator, and the first scientist. The generations subsequent to Enoch also featured men and women who were passionate about knowledge and understanding of God and the world that God had created for their sustenance and pleasure. They individually and corporately heard God's voice as it communicated profound insight to them. Together they recorded the greatest document of knowledge, understanding, and wisdom ever produced, the Holy Scriptures.

As has been demonstrated throughout Scripture, the first and foremost purpose of every disciple must be to study God's Word. Study, however, must be with a view to doing God's Word. Studying to do and doing to teach might even be defined as the Ezra Methodology. In the post-exilic rebuilding of Jerusalem, Ezra became the shining example of this strong Hebraic concept. "For Ezra had set his heart to study the law of the LORD, and to do it, and to teach his statutes and ordinances in Israel."[41] The progression is simple: study, do, teach. In actuality, study produces doing, and doing becomes teaching—a perfect example of dynamic modeling, the most powerful form of teaching.

Bypassing doing after studying and proceeding immediately to teaching is a huge mistake. Studying in order to teach is a Gentile idea that has come to pervade much of the Christian church. Indeed, the only reason some leaders study is so that they can teach or preach. This tragic mistake in leadership is reinforced by the generally held Christian view that the best ministers, preachers, or teachers are those who are the greatest pulpiteers;[42] however, this is not the case.[43] This philosophy leads to lackluster performance of the Word

---

[40] The Hebrew name חֲנוֹךְ (Hanokh) is from the root חָנַךְ (hanakh), which means "to dedicate," "to narrow (the usage of)," "to train," "to educate," and "to become wise." See Alan Segal, Life After Death: A History of the Afterlife in Western Religion (New York: Doubleday, 2004), p. 154. Hanakh is also the root of the word Hanukkah, the Festival of the Dedication (mentioned in John 10:22) which celebrates the rededication of the temple after it was polluted by Antiochus Epiphanes.

[41] Ezra 7:10, NRSV.

[42] A pulpiteer is one who is considered to be an eloquent preacher.

[43] In reality, as Craig Evans has observed, "the contemporary pulpit sermon is not the equivalent of the preaching and teaching that is found in the Scriptures." Craig A. Evans, "Preacher and Preaching: Some Lexical Observations," Journal of the Evangelical Theological Society, vol. 24, no. 4 (December 1981), pp. 315–322. As a matter of fact, as David Norrington declares, contemporary pulpit preaching "cannot be found in the Judaism of the Old Testament, the ministry of Jesus, or the life of the primitive church." Ultimately, he says, "The sermon was conceived in the womb of Greek rhetoric. It was born into the Christian community when pagans-turned-Christians began to bring their oratorical styles of speaking into the church. By the third century, it became common for Christian leaders to deliver a sermon. By the fourth century it became the norm." David C. Norrington, To Preach or Not: The Church's Urgent Question (Omaha, NE: Ekklesia Press, 2013), p. 69. For a discussion of the Greek origins of pulpiteers, see Frank Viola and George Barna, Pagan Christianity?: Exploring the Roots of Our Church Practices (Carol Stream, IL: Tyndale House Publishers, 2002), p. 101.

and will of God in the lives of too many Christians because many pulpiteers fail to "practice what they preach." The church must return to the Hebraic method that Jesus employed, the Ezra Methodology—that of studying in order to do and then doing in order to teach. This mindset was the focus of the holy men and women of God with whom God dealt in ancient times and through whom he conveyed the understanding encapsulated in Holy Scripture.[44] They not only *received* God's instructions; they also *acted* upon them. As they studied what God had already communicated to his servants, they received additional insights into God's will and purposes for their own time and were thereby empowered to accomplish his designs first for their own lives and then for their communities.

Learning without doing is tantamount to sin, for James made it clear that anyone who knows to do good and fails to do it is a sinner.[45] It is akin to believing without decision and action. Theory without praxis is meaningless and even deceptive.[46] Anything that is not practical and practicable is not spiritual, despite the elevated emotion or euphoria that it may invoke. The evidence of belief is action based on understanding and belief.[47] True communication, including the communication of the gospel, is not completed, therefore, unless it leads to decision and to action based on that decision. This is why Thomas Aquinas (following Augustine's thinking) gave the Christian preacher three tasks: to instruct the intellect, to kindle the emotions, and to form the will.[48] As Charles Gardner has said, "The emotion is valuable only as it results in intelligent decision. It is through voluntary action that the real man functions, and the preaching that does not secure this is useless or worse than useless."[49] Without the evidence of action upon learning, true discipleship is never manifest; therefore, believers can never be "disciples" unless they act on their knowledge.

Study: Humanity's Highest Endowment

The word *lamad* also means "to study." Study for learning is vital to life. It equips human beings with the knowledge that is necessary for exercising the power of reason. The capacity for learning, therefore, is one of the elements that separate humans from the rest of creation. It is God's precious

---

44 2 Peter 1:21.

45 James 4:17.

46 James L. Marsh, *Critique, Action, and Liberation* (Albany, NY: The State University of New York Press, 1995), p. 57.

47 Kelly James Clark, *Return to Reason* (Grand Rapids, MI: Wm. B. Eerdmans Publishing Co., 1990), p. 99.

48 Thomas Aquinas, quoted in George Edgar Sweazey, *Preaching the Good News* (New York, Prentice-Hall, 1976), p. 22.

49 Charles S. Gardner, *Psychology and Preaching* (New York: The MacMillan Company, 1918), p. 207.

gift to humankind, the endowment of bearing the divine image and likeness. The image and likeness of God are manifest, among other things,[50] in the power of reason and the free will to act on what is reasoned.[51] Intellectual capacity and conscience (the connection between the brain and the heart) enable human beings to develop a consciousness of the Divine, to learn of his Word, and by grace through faith to experience redemption and then to express spirituality by doing God's Word.

Learned people who have attained wisdom stand head and shoulders above the rest of the crowd of humanity, like the *lamed* does in the midst of the Hebrew letters of the biblical text. They have subjected themselves willingly to the discipline of study, analysis, and reflection. They, therefore, enjoy enriched lives of success and fulfillment and of service to their fellowman. Their learning becomes teaching both through the dynamic modeling of their actions and through their words of wisdom and challenge. In effect, their "doing" becomes "teaching," or as Francis of Assisi reportedly said, "Preach the gospel always; if necessary use words."[52]

Learning is the core of *education* and the foundation of discipleship. This English word is derived from the Latin *ex ducere*, which means to "lead" (*ducere*) "out" (*ex*). It is a simple fact that learning leads people out of ignorance, out of darkness, out of superstition, out of misery, out of suffering.[53] The Gentile world throughout history has suffered from illiteracy and ignorance, and it has been dominated by superstitions founded in false religions featuring pantheons of gods. At the same time, the Jews have enjoyed a high level of literacy—specially biblical literacy—which has been fostered by the freedom and fulfillment they have had from worshipping the one and only God, the God who can be personally approached as *Avinu, Malkeinu* (our Father, our King).[54] A prime example of this differentiation was manifest in 1346-52 AD when as much at 60% of the population of Europe died as a result of the

---

[50] The "image and likeness of God" is manifest in the power of reason, free will, conscience, speech, creativity, dominion, and personhood, but most powerfully in relationality. See John D. Garr, *God and Women*, pp. 149–241.

[51] John Garr, *God and Women,* pp. 170–173.

[52] This quotation has never been authenticated. The closest statement from Francis that is authentic is, "All the Friars . . . should preach by their deeds" (*Orthodox Order of Friars Minor*, Rule XII).

[53] Sara B. Kiesler and Charles F. Turn, eds., *Fundamental Research and the Process of Education: Final Report of the Committee on Fundamental Research Relevant to Education* (Washington, DC: National Academy of Sciences, 1977), p. 2.

[54] The *Avinu Malkeinu* is the prayer that is central to the liturgy of the High Holy Days of *Rosh Hashanah* (the Festival of Trumpets and the Jewish civil New Year) and *Yom Kippur* (the Day of Atonement). It was first used by Rabbi Akivah during a special intercession for rain. The prayer is important because it underscores the fact that God is first "our Father" (*Avinu*) and then "our King"(*Malkeinu*), which, in itself, is a testament to the personhood of God and to the fact that he is not impassable but can be reached by and responds to the prayers of his children.

Black Death. Jews, however, did not die from the bubonic plague in such large numbers because they had the scriptural knowledge to "be clean, and change your garments"[55] and to keep their homes free of rodents[56] and the attendant fleas that were the means of spreading the plague.[57]

Studying God's Instruction

A disciple of Christ must be a student of God's instruction before he can then do what God has said. God is, therefore, the first and foremost teacher. He has taught his people through prophets, sages, and apostles who were the authors of the entire corpus of the Hebrew Scriptures, including the *Tanakh* and the Apostolic Writings. The very first compilation of the knowledge of God was the Torah, the first five books of the Bible.[58] It is unfortunate that the ancient and honorable Hebrew word תּוֹרָה (*Torah*) has been translated "law" in virtually all English versions of Scripture.[59] Its true meaning is "instruction," the words of insight from a wise Father to his children. The word *torah* comes from the root יָרָה (*yarah*), which, as an archery term, means "to aim at a mark and hit it." The best way to ensure that Christians "hit the mark" by doing what God has instructed them to do is for them to study the Bible of Jesus, the Torah, elucidated and expanded by the Prophets and the Sacred Writings and completed by the Apostolic Scriptures. When Christians are not knowledgeable of the Scriptures, they often "miss the mark"[60] and find themselves succumbing to temptation and sin. Obviously, believers need the Torah (instruction) of God so they can "hit the mark."

Is it any wonder then that King David exclaimed, "I desire to do your will, O my God; your Torah is within my heart. . . . I have longed for your

---

[55] Genesis 35:2.

[56] Leviticus 7:21. The Israelites were commanded not to touch unclean animals; therefore, the Jews kept their homes free of rodents. Because the Jews observed this commandment, not as many of them contracted bubonic plague as did the non-Jewish population of Europe. Because no one understood the cause of the plague, those Jews who did not contract the disease were charged with poisoning the wells of the cities and thereby causing the widespread suffering and death. This indictment became an excuse for the persecution and murder of countless Jews.

[57] John D. Garr, *Life from the Dead,* pp. 290–292.

[58] The word *Torah* can be applied to the Ten Commandments, to the Pentateuch (the five books of Moses), and to the entire corpus of the Hebrew Scriptures; however, it generally connotes the Pentateuch.

[59] The Hebrew word תּוֹרָה (Torah) was translated in the Septuagint version with the Greek word νόμος (*nómos*), which actually means "the study of" (as in the word *astronomy*, the "study of the stars"). When *nómos* was translated into Latin, the word *lex*, which means "law," was used. The genitive form of *lex, legis,* is the basis for the English word *legislation.* Because of the enormous influence of the Latin Vulgate on English translations, the Hebrew word *torah* was rendered "law," thereby obscuring the actual meaning of the original Hebrew text. Unfortunately for the English-speaking world and the other nations whose languages are Latin based, "instruction" in Scripture (Torah) became "law."

[60] The Greek word for "sin" in the Apostolic Scriptures is ἁμαρτία (*harmartía*), which means "missing the mark" or "failure." *Harmartía* translates the Hebrew חָטָא (*chata*) which also means "miss the way."

salvation, O LORD; and your Torah is my delight."[61] History's wisest king observed, "The command is a lamp; and the Torah is light; and reproofs of instruction are the way of life."[62] Indeed, the incarnate Torah himself declared, "If you love me, you will obey what I command. . . . If you keep my commandments, you will abide in my love; just as I have kept my Father's commandments, and abide in his love."[63] If Jesus demonstrated his submission to the will of his Father by obedience to God's instructions, how much more should Christian disciples submit to the Lordship of Jesus by keeping his commandments![64]

The importance of studying the Word of God is seen in Paul's instructions to Timothy: "Do your best to present yourself to God as an approved worker who does not need to be ashamed, handling the word of truth with precision."[65] Intense study is necessary to avoid the shame of inaccurately interpreting God's Word.[66] This is the vision that keeps God's people from casting off restraint and lapsing into hedonism: "He who keeps the law, happy is he."[67] With the understanding of rightly divided Holy Scripture, believers can be taught, corrected, and instructed in righteousness, thereby becoming mature (perfect or complete) and fully equipped unto all good works.[68] It is then that the light of God's Word can shine through them so that others may see their *good works* and glorify the Father in heaven.[69]

Christians who desire to be true disciples of Christ must learn to honor and study God's instruction manual for successful human living. They must become students of Scripture, permitting the *lamad* of God's instruction to prod them toward right conduct and proper posture in their relationship with God and with man. Love for God and love for mankind will be fulfilled in their lives because they will learn from the entire corpus of Holy Scripture how to do so.[70]

Study as Worship

Many, if not most, Christians would agree with Solomon's assessment: "Be warned: the writing of many books is endless, and much study wearies

---

61 Psalm 40:8; 119:174.
62 Proverbs 6:23, ESV.
63 John 14:15; 15:10.
64 John 15:10.
65 2 Timothy 2:15, ISV paraphrased.
66 2 Corinthians 4:2.
67 Proverbs 29:18.
68 2 Timothy 3:17.
69 Matthew 5:16.
70 It is the *Tanakh* that gives the instructions that enable believers to fulfill every "good work" in their lives to the glory of God (2 Timothy 3:17).

the body."[71] Study is, indeed, hard work, part of the discipline of discipleship; however, its assets far outweigh the liabilities involved in its acquisition. Intensive study of the Holy Scriptures is an act of submission to God and is the most reliable way in which God can speak to his people and cause them to understand his will and his ways. Even the most intense and profound subjective spiritual experiences must be judged by the written Word of God.[72] Study of the Word of God with a view to doing the Word, therefore, is an act of submission to the divine will, the essence of true worship. When believers pray, they speak with God; when they study, God speaks to them.[73]

Unlike most Christians, the Jewish people ultimately developed a common understanding that the study dynamic of discipleship, rather than being wearisome, is actually one of the highest forms of worship. When Christians think of worship, images of the Sunday morning "worship service" come to view, with singing, praying, giving, preaching, and sharing Communion. Study is perhaps something that is done in preparation for worship, but could Christians ever conceive of study, itself, as an act of worship, even perhaps one of the highest forms of worship?

Studying in order to do what God has said is the ultimate form of submission to God; therefore, it is a high form of worship, which is biblically defined as prostrating oneself in the presence of the Deity. The words for worship both in Hebrew (שָׁחָה—*shachah*) and Greek (προσκυνήω—*proskunéo*) mean to "prostrate oneself in the presence of the Deity." The meaning of *proskunéo* is even more graphic because it means to kiss, as in the case of "a dog licking its master's hand." The Aramaic word for worship, סְגִד (*segid*),[74] also means to "bow down or do obeisance to," with the connotation of total submission to a superior (as the king).

The Jewish sages understood that humbly submitting oneself to the wisdom of God revealed in the Hebrew Scriptures was worship in the truest sense of the word because it was the ultimate act of prostrating oneself before God. True prostration before God—submission to his will—is demonstrated in the study of the Scriptures with a view to doing what God has said. Study of God's Word in order to mold one's lifestyle to that Word is worship in the truest sense of the old English antecedent of the word *worship* which

---

[71] Ecclesiastes 12:12.

[72] 2 Peter 1:16–20. See John W. Wyckoff, Wave E. Nunnally, Edgar R. Lee, Randy Hurst, and Charles T. Crabtree eds., *The Bible, the Word of God* (Springfield, MO: Gospel Publishing House, 2003), p. 37.

[73] Ray Vander Laan, *Faith Lessons on the Promised Land* (Grand Rapids, MI: Zondervan Publishing House, 1999), p. 6.

[74] The word *segid* is employed in Daniel 2:46; 3:6, 10, 12, 14, 15, 18, 28.

was *worthship*, meaning "to ascribe worth to." Abraham Joshua Heschel encapsulated this Jewish approach to study by saying that while the Greeks study in order to comprehend, the Hebrews study "in order to revere" or worship.[75] God's Word and ways are ineffable: only by doing them does one understand them.[76] When believers fully submit their lives to God's Word, when they study what he has said with complete devotion and intensity so that they may revere him by carrying out his instructions, they do, indeed, ascribe worth to him: they worship him.

Improvement: the Spirit of Perfection

Continual improvement in the earth is the goal of Judaism. This philosophy is encapsulated in the concept of *Tikkun Olam* (restoring or repairing the world), in which it is believed that people can work in partnership with God to restore what was lost in the lapse of the first humans into rebellion against God and the subsequent human abuse of the earth and its peoples.[77] Human beings are to work toward the restoration of the terrestrial environment—ecologically, socially, economically, politically, and spiritually. This is, no doubt, the reason that so many Jews have chosen professions that involve health and welfare. Those who understand this holistic approach to life cannot have one set of ethics for the "spiritual realm" and another for the "secular realm." They cannot abuse their environment, their society, their government, or their religion. As a matter of fact, as Michelle Abraham has wisely said, one whose "inner world is in moral balance is ready and able to practice *tikkun olam.*"[78] Jewish emphasis on education, then, is based on the philosophy of continual self-improvement and the improvement of the world. And, that emphasis has produced some of the greatest accomplishments in virtually all fields of learning, as Jews have led the way in the betterment of the human race.

Dedication to improvement of the human lot is in the context of God's command to Adam and Eve to "subdue the earth."[79] This is an ongoing

---

[75] Heschel, *God in Search of Man*, p. 34.

[76] This is why when God offered the Torah to Israel, they replied, "Whatever you have said, we will do and we will hear (understand)." This dynamic confirms the idea that many, if not most, of the things that God requires of believers are ineffable. They cannot be understood unless they are done, for it is in the doing that the understanding comes.

[77] David Shatz, Chaim Waxman, and Nathan J. Diament, eds., *Tikkun Olam: Social Responsibility in Jewish Thought and Law* (New York: Rowman & Littlefield Publishers, 1997); Eliot N. Dorff, *The Jewish Approach to Repairing the World (Tikkun Olam): A Brief Introduction for Christians* (Woodstock, VT: Jewish Lights Publishing, 2008).

[78] Michelle Shapiro Abraham, *Repairing Our World from the Inside Out: A Three-Session Adult Education Program on Jewish Ethics* (New York: UAHC Press, 2002), p. 7.

[79] Genesis 1:28.

work that is transgenerational and universal.[80] Working in concert with God is such a massive job that no one person or no one generation can ever accomplish his plan. Indeed, one should never expect to see all of the fruits of his labors manifest in his lifetime. Working continually to improve oneself and one's environment is the essence of the spirit of perfection which was enjoined upon all believers by Jesus himself when he said simply and unequivocally, "Be perfect, therefore, as your heavenly Father is perfect."[81] The perfection that Jesus required, however, is not the achievement of the apex of excellence; it is continually walking with God to improve every aspect of one's life. This requires the rigors of study, the essence of discipleship. David Lutz and Paul Mimbi describe it this way: "The goal of reflection, sociality, creativity, moral responsibility and individuality is self-improvement or perfection. . . . That human beings are perfectible means that they have the capacity of being 'continually made better and receiving perpetual improvement.'"[82]

The spirit of improvement is the factor that has contributed to the value which Judaism has traditionally placed on education. It is reflected in the Jewish view that the role of humanity in the earth is to be the same as it was at the beginning of creation: to be the keeper of the garden. If continual improvement is to be made by each succeeding generation, the knowledge acquired in each generation must be passed on to the next. This was one of the primary reasons for which God chose Abraham in the beginning: "For I know [Abraham], that he will command his children and his household after him, and they shall keep the way of the LORD, to do justice and judgment."[83] Jewish perspectives on learning, therefore, involve both the acquisition and the transmission of knowledge, the combination of which produces the true dynamics of discipleship.

"Come, Walk the Road with Me."

Returning Christian discipleship to the matrix from which it was birthed certainly brings greater understanding to both the concept and

---

[80] Geoffrey Wainwright Cushman, *Lesslie Newbigin: A Theological Life* (New York: Oxford University Press, 2000), p. 324.

[81] Matthew 5:48. The word for "perfect" in Hebrew is תָּמִים (*tameem*) which means "complete." It does not mean "moral perfection" as much as it means "thoroughly made," or being "brought to completion."

[82] David Lutz and Paul Mimbi, eds., *Shareholder Value & the Common Good* (Nairobi, Kenya: Strathmore University Press, 2005), p. 135, quoted in William Godwin, *Enquiry Concerning Political Justice* (New York: Oxford University Press, 1971), p. 58. Though writing on the theme of business management, Lutz and Mimbi have the concept of perfection right when they say, "Absolute perfection is impossible for human beings, because their potential is unbounded."

[83] Genesis 18:19.

praxis of discipleship as it was manifest in the time of Christ. The Hebraic *rabbi-talmidim* relationship empowered a dynamic exchange of knowledge, understanding, and wisdom that was and remains the essence of discipleship. The learning process was carried out in relationship, even apprenticeship as it were, featuring a "come-walk-the-road-with-me" dynamic in which *talmidim* followed their *rabbi* from place to place and were thereby engaged in the great practical lessons of life in the course of everyday living. This teacher-student relationship was one of continuing engagement, and the learning process was more the imitation of praxis than the exchange of philosophical ideas. It was an exercise of following and thereby learning from example.

Classic examples that demonstrate the proper teacher-student dynamic can be seen in the Moses-Joshua, Elijah-Elisha, and Paul-Timothy relationships. Joshua served as Moses' personal attendant and servant for decades before he was appointed to lead Israel. In that relationship, he learned by observing the actions and instructions of his mentor.[84] Elijah's most important work may well have taken place near the end of his career when for ten years he discipled Elisha and equipped him with the skills the young prophet would need for a "double-portion" ministry.[85] All of the apostles of Jesus followed him throughout the land of Israel for more than three years as he instructed them in the things concerning the kingdom of God. The apostle Paul discipled many *talmidim*, but the most memorable among them was Timothy, whom he instructed in God's Word so that he could replicate the apostle's vision, passion, and commitment in his own ministry.[86] All of these disciples—Joshua, Elisha, the apostles, and Timothy—learned the lessons of life and ministry as they carefully followed and imitated the faith and practice of their instructors. They walked with their teachers on the divine path of discipleship that equipped them for success as servant leaders for God's people.

In Jewish life and culture in biblical times, teaching by example was the most common vehicle for the transfer of knowledge. The sages employed the "come-walk-the-road-with-me"[87] method with their disciples. A sage's disciples followed as he taught them both by example and by word. They learned these lessons as they sat in the rabbi's home, as they walked with him

---

[84] Exodus 24:13; Numbers 11:28; Joshua 1:1.

[85] Allan C. Tuffs, *And You Shall Teach Them to Your Sons: Biblical Tales for Fathers and Sons* (New York: URJ Books and Music,1997), p. 59.

[86] 2 Timothy 1:6.

[87] The Jewish sages were not disconnected from their disciples, appearing with them only briefly to deliver lectures and then returning to their ivory towers. They were engaged with them in the affairs of life. The disciples literally followed their rabbis and were taught lessons from what occurred in the course of unfolding daily life.

on the road, and as they worshiped and studied with him in the synagogue. They learned to stay very close to the rabbi, to hang on his every word, and to observe what he did as well as what he said. One of the greatest honors in first-century Israel, therefore, was to be "covered in the dust" of one's rabbi.

In the Mishnah, Jose ben Yo'ezer encapsulated this idea and practice well when he said, "Let your house be a meeting place for the wise; you shall become dusty in the dust of their feet; and you shall drink in their words thirstily."[88] The setting of the first clause of this statement is obviously in a house; therefore the second clause could be interpreted to indicate that *talmidim* should sit on the floor at the feet of their rabbi (as the custom was), thereby becoming covered with the dust of his feet.[89] Of course, in this instance, the "dust-of-his-feet" statement could have been entirely metaphorical because when a rabbi was in his house, neither the stone floor nor his feet would likely have been dusty enough to have "covered" his *talmidim* "with dust of his feet." This would certainly have been true if the study was being done in a Beit Midrash, which always had even the highest value in the Jewish community.[90]

A second application, therefore, may have been more likely in the first-century milieu. Being covered in the dust of the rabbi's feet would have been graphically demonstrated when *talmidim* followed so closely in the footsteps of their peripatetic sages that they thereby literally became covered with the dust of their feet. The dusty roads of the Middle East would certainly have lent themselves more to one's becoming "dusty in the dust of their feet" than the floor of a rabbi's home or a *Beit Midrash*. Whether sitting or walking, however, the idea of the text was that "the disciple should always remain within the ambit of his master's 'dust' or influence."[91] Whatever the case, the expression *dust of your feet* was certainly used by Jesus in connection with the teaching and hearing of his disciples: "If anyone will not welcome you or listen to your words, leave that home or town and shake the dust off your feet."[92]

---

[88] Mishnah, *Pirkei Avot* 1:4.

[89] Marcus van Loopik, ed., *The Ways of the Sages and the Way of the World* (Tübingen, Germany: Mohr Siebeck: 1991), pp. 178–181.

[90] A *Beit Midrash* (literally, "House of Study") was a significant part of the synagogue (assembly or meeting) of the Jewish people in the time of Jesus. This became even more obvious when, centuries later, newly emerging Jewish communities anywhere in the world usually built a *Beit Midrash* before they constructed a *Beit Tefillah* ("House of Prayer"). This action confirmed the priority that Jews placed on teaching and learning God's Word. Before one can pray and worship properly, one must learn the Holy Scriptures "which are able to make [one] wise unto salvation" (2 Timothy 3:15).

[91] Martin Sicker, *The Moral Maxims of the Sages of Israel: Pirkei Avot* (Bloomington, IN: iUniverse, 2004), p. 29.

[92] Matthew 10:14; Mark 6:11; Luke 9:5.

And so it was with the disciples of Jesus. Those who had followed the Master on the dusty roads of Israel were covered with dust, but not just the sandy granules of the Judean byways. They were covered with the dust of his teaching. Indeed, they glowed with golden "Jesus dust"! Others could tell "that they had been with Jesus," not because of what they said, but because of what they did.[93] In following the Master, they had so conformed their lives to his lifestyle that, for all intents and purposes, the Messiah lived in and through them.[94] This is how Paul was able to say, "I have been crucified with Christ and I no longer live, but Christ lives in me. The life that I now live in the body, I live by faith in the Son of God."[95] It was also the basis for the apostle's declaration that the mystery of the gospel was quite simply, "Christ in you."[96]

When Jesus said to his disciples, "Follow me," he was speaking of more than a mere physical activity. Walking the road with Jesus was following the Master in the sense of imitating his lifestyle. This is clear from the Greek words that are translated "follow" or "followers." The word μιμέομαι (miméomai), translated "follow,"[97] means "to imitate." The word μιμετής (mimetés), translated "follower,"[98] actually means "an imitator." Herein is the essence of the Christian life and of Christian discipleship manifest. To be "Christ-like" (Christian) is to imitate the life of Jesus by doing the things that Jesus did and by keeping his commandments. When Jesus instructed his disciples to "follow me," he was asking them to commit themselves to a life of imitation in which they would even emulate their Master's actions.[99] Then, those who had followed Rabbi Yeshua were able to extend their Lord's instructions to others, saying to them, "Follow me as I follow Christ."[100] Their actions so imitated the life of Christ that they had become living epistles "known and read of all men."[101] They had become dynamic models of the biblically Hebraic lifestyle. For a true disciple, there is no greater pleasure or fulfillment than replicating the knowledge and actions of one's teacher. This is the reward of intense observation, of insightful analysis, of unending rumination, and of practical demonstration.

---

[93] Acts 4:13.

[94] In John 14:23, Jesus said, "If anyone loves me, he will keep my word; and my Father will love him, and we will come to him and make our abode with him." In Colossians 1:27, Paul declared, "This is the secret: Christ lives in you."

[95] Galatians 2:20, NIV.

[96] Colossians 1:27.

[97] 2 Thessalonians 3:7, 9.

[98] 1 Corinthians 4:16; 1 Corinthians 11:1; Ephesians 5:1; Philippians 3:17; 1 Thessalonians 1:6; Hebrews 6:12; 1 Peter 3:13.

[99] The use of the word emulate is proper in this instance because Jesus said that his disciples would not only replicate the works that he had done but that they would do "greater works" (1 John 4:12).

[100] 1 Corinthians 11:1.

[101] 2 Corinthians 3:2.

Christian disciples faithfully replicate the life of the Messiah, their Master, as they follow in his footsteps and do the things that he has commanded them.[102]

Sitting at the Feet of Jesus

Jesus was not, as some Christian scholars have argued, a poor, unkempt, itinerant Cynic philosopher who employed pithy aphorisms in blatant attacks upon the social order of his day.[103] He was not, as others have maintained, a Buddhist monk.[104] Jesus was a Jew, and his religion was Judaism. Though it was said of him that he taught with a level of authority that the other sages of his time did not seem to possess,[105] Jesus lived in complete continuity with the faith of his ancestors.[106] Neither he nor his disciples had any intention of starting a new religion called Christianity that would replace Judaism, and they were certainly not followers of a religion or philosophy that was foreign to the faith of their fathers.

Because Jesus was very much a Torah-observant Jew, he had great respect for the traditions of his family and his people. It was only natural, therefore, that when he embarked upon his mission and ministry to his people, he employed the teaching methodologies that were widely used throughout the land of Israel in that time. Jesus was a rabbi, a teacher of the Torah. All the Gospels portray Jesus as employing the same teaching techniques that the rabbis of his time used.[107] He taught his disciples by sitting among them while they sat at his feet. The phrase *sitting at the feet of* was actually a common description of the disciple-rabbi relationship. Paul employed this form when he spoke of the fact that he had been educated in the Torah while he "sat at the feet of Gamaliel," who was the most prominent disciple of Hillel the Great, one of Israel's most outstanding sages.[108]

It should have come as no surprise, then, when the Scriptures confirmed that both men and women were disciples of Jesus, including the famous example of Mary, the sister of Lazarus. Because she "sat at the feet of Jesus," this woman was clearly a disciple even in a time when most women

---

102 Matthew 28:20.

103 F. Gerald Downing, Burton Mack, and John Dominic Crossan have argued that Jesus was a Cynic philosopher. For an excellent discussion and refutation of this argument, see Ben Witherington III, *The Jesus Quest: The Third Search for the Jew of Nazareth* (Downers Grove, IL: InterVarsity Press, 1997), pp. 58–92.

104 Charles Francis Aiken, *The Dhamma of Totama the Buddha and the Gospel of Jesus Christ* (Boston, MA: Marlier and Company, 1900).

105 Matthew 7:29; Mark 1:22.

106 Matthew 5:17-18; John 15:10.

107 Keener, p. 188. Also Craig A. Evans, *The Routledge Encyclopedia of the Historical Jesus* (New York: Routledge, 2010), p. 476.

108 Acts 22:3.

were excluded from being among the *talmidim* of the sages.[109] Jesus recovered and restored the historical teaching of Scripture that women should learn the Word of God, a teaching that had been abandoned by most of the sages due to the influence of Hellenism.[110] Then later, Paul specifically commanded that both Jewish and Greek women in the church should learn God's Word.[111]

Jesus also taught in parables.[112] As a matter of fact, more than one-third of all his teaching was done by means of parables. This methodology was not, however, unique to Jesus, as some Christian teachers have assumed. In the ancient Jewish world, the use of parables was a very popular method for transferring knowledge from teacher to disciple. Simple material objects and everyday activities were used to present eternal truths in such a way that the common people could understand and relate to them. Sometimes, Jesus' use of parable was unique in that he was able to conceal his meaning from skeptics while at the same time revealing his meaning to his disciples.[113] Jesus, therefore, was a master of the art of the parable.

Jesus did employ one practice that seemed to be a departure from the traditional approach of the sages of his time. He chose his disciples,[114] whereas the disciples of other sages usually chose their teacher.[115] Like the other sages, however, he taught his disciples directly,[116] spending virtually all

---

[109] Luke 10:39.

[110] Because women were teachers, prophets, and leaders in ancient Israel, there should have been no reason for their exclusion from the ranks of the *talmidim*. It may well have been the influence of Hellenism and its insistence that women, except for the *hetaera* (prostitutes or "companions"), be restricted from learning philosophy and, in general terms, remain illiterate and under the protection of their husband or guardian.

[111] 1 Timothy 2:11–12. Paul said, "Let the women learn in quietness and submission." This was precisely the same requirement that was placed upon the *talmidim* of the Jewish rabbis of that time. The primary (if not the only) reason for learning the Torah was so that one could teach the Torah, so it was evident that even though Paul was at that time now allowing the illiterate women who had come to Christianity from the Hellenistic world to teach, his restrictions were temporal, not permanent. As a rabbi himself, the apostle would not have instructed the women to learn the Word of God if he were not expecting them to teach.

[112] Brad Young has thoroughly documented the parallels between Jesus' use of parables and that of the rabbis and sages of Israel. See Brad H. Young, *The Parables: Jewish Tradition and Christian Interpretation* (Grand Rapids, MI: Baker Academic, 2008). See also Richard Gribble, *The Parables of Jesus: Cycle A* (Lima, OH: CSS Publishing Co., 1998), p. 14.

[113] Mark 4:10–12. For a discussion of this phenomenon, see Robert H. Stein, *An Introduction to the Parables of Jesus* (Philadelphia, PA: The Westminster Press, 1981), p. 34.

[114] Matthew 4:19, 21; 9:9; John 1:43-51. Dave Earley and Ben Gutierrez, *Ministry Is . . . How to Serve Jesus with Passion and Confidence* (Nashville, TN: B & H Publishing Group, 2010), p. 43. Also Roger E. Van Hern, *The Gospels: The Third Readings* (Grand Rapids, MI: Wm. B. Eerdmans Publishing Co., 2001), p. 158.

[115] Haim Hillel Ben-Sasson, ed., *A History of the Jewish People* (Tel Aviv, Israel: HDvir Publishing House, 1969), p. 329.

[116] Richard Peace, *Conversion in the New Testament: Paul and the Twelve* (Grand Rapids, MI: Wm. B. Eerdmans Publishing Co., 1999), p. 197.

of his time instructing them in the things pertaining to the Kingdom of God.[117] His relationship with his disciples was that of Master to pupils.[118] Indeed, the general public often called Jesus "Master,"[119] and he declared to them that he was, indeed, their only Master.[120]

One of the most powerful dynamics of Jesus' rabbinic teaching style was the fact that his communication was done in the context of community.[121] This was an intimate setting where Jesus was *with* his disciples and engaged with them one-on-one. It is in the context of a learning community such as the one which Jesus maintained that knowledge is best transferred from teacher to student. This is why rabbinic education has always been so effective in conveying the truths of Jewish faith. The enduring impact of Jesus' teaching in the midst of his Messianic community was confirmed by the fact that what he taught his disciples concerning the Kingdom of God was so deeply embedded in their hearts that they remained faithful to his message in the face of massive persecution until virtually all of them died of martyrdom.

Sitting at Jesus' Feet Today

Many Christians today take a romantic view of the life and ministry of Jesus, wishing that somehow they, too, could experience the same joy that the disciples shared when they "sat at the feet of Jesus." The truth is, however, that this can still be done today. In a very real way, Jesus is with his people now. As a matter of fact, he promised that he would be with believers even to the end of the age.[122] And, so he is. He has sent all his disciples another teacher, the Holy Spirit, who can be in the hearts of all the believers on the earth simultaneously, teaching all of them the Word and will of God.[123] Unlike the incarnate Jesus, who was localized in one place at a time, the Holy Spirit is everywhere. He is both with the believers and also in them, and his job description is to "guide into all truth."

Everyone who is a believer, therefore, can still sit at the feet of Jesus in humble and quiet submission to his words as they listen to the still small voice of the Spirit that instructs them in the will and ways of God.[124] All that

---

[117] Matthew 4:23 says, "Jesus went about all Galilee, teaching in their synagogues, and preaching the gospel of the kingdom." Even after his resurrection, Jesus spent 40 days teaching his disciples "the things concerning the kingdom of God" (Acts 1:3). Even after the resurrection, Jesus was still a rabbi!

[118] Dean L. Overman, *A Case for the Divinity of Jesus: Examining the Earliest Evidence* (Lanham, MD: Roman and Littlefield Publishers, 2010).

[119] John 13:13; Luke 17:13. The word *rabbi* actually means "my master."

[120] Matthew 23:10.

[121] Green, *et. al.*, p. 708.

[122] Matthew 28:20.

[123] John 14:16.

[124] 1 Kings 19:11–13.

is required is to make time to hear from the Master. He will never ignore or cast out those who approach him in faith with a sincere heart focused on divine truth and righteousness.[125] And, through the Holy Spirit, he will lead and guide them into divine and eternal truth.[126]

Those who come to sit at the feet of Jesus today, therefore, should not be surprised when they discover that they begin to learn Hebraic truth. After all, Jesus was a Jew, and what he taught his disciples was confirmed by the Torah, the Prophets, and the Writings of the Hebrew Scriptures. Those who want to be among the *talmidim* of Jesus should prepare themselves to hear something different from conventional Christian thought. The living Jesus will challenge every paradigm, encouraging all believers to return to the faith of the Jewish fathers. The result, however, is an invigorating, life-changing exercise of walking with God in the light of divine truth that is inspired and directed by the Holy Spirit.

Restoring Biblically Hebraic Discipleship

The very idea of discipleship, then, cannot be understood unless it is returned to the biblical matrix from which it emerged some 2,000 years ago. The word *disciple* has profound connotations that are more distinct and clear when examined in the light of the dynamic teacher-student relationship that was common in the time of Jesus and his apostles. It is, therefore, virtually impossible for one to understand the core issues of discipleship—much less the nuances of its finer details—unless they are returned to the worldview and lifestyle of the Master himself.

When the etymological and conceptual foundations of discipleship are considered, amazing truths emerge, most of which serve to expand and enrich understanding of this important subject and some of which expose the errors and misunderstandings that have been added to the biblical truth through the Hellenization and Latinization of Christian faith. Anyone who has a genuine desire to *be* a disciple should want to *understand* discipleship as it was practiced in the time of Jesus. Only then can the level of discipleship that turned the world upside down reemerge to effect a similar universal result in the postmodern world today.[127]

The ultimate function of Christian ministry, then, is to make disciples, which, in essence, is to make learners or students. Discipleship is not a case of the warm fuzzies, the emotional crescendo of an existential moment. It is

---

[125] John 6:37.
[126] John 16:13.
[127] Acts 17:6.

the discipline of learning about God's Word and will and then doing it. Discipleship is not just feeling or believing: it is learning and doing. A disciple is one who is taught, one who has been subjected to the discipline of learning. In effect, there is no discipleship without discipline.[128] It is the discipline of study that produces the disciple, the learner, the scholar. This is why those who through sloth or indifference shun discipline will never be disciples! Jesus himself even emphasized the fact that the discipline of Christian discipleship is demanding and rigorous: "Whosoever does not bear his cross cannot be my disciple . . . whosoever that forsakes not all he has cannot be my disciple."[129] God's *lamad* of discipline may well place demands of self-sacrifice upon the disciple that will be painful; however, the rewards of yielding to the goad of discipleship produce the benefits of partnership with God and the blessings that accrue thereby.

This is the core message of Christianity's *Mega-Mitzvah* (Great Commission). The foundation of Christian discipleship is learning and teaching, and the foundation of the learning and teaching is the Word of God and the commandments of Jesus. Converts are made to the faith of Jesus so that they may become *talmidim* through the discipline of obedience to divine instructions. The fundamental meaning of the term that Jesus used to describe his followers, therefore, sheds an entirely different light on the true nature of Christian discipleship. Christian discipleship is an exercise of learning through the discipline of instruction in Christ's teaching. It is yielding one's self to the goad of training, permitting the pointed *lamad* to prick one's heart and marshal one's actions in the right and proper direction and to the God-determined end.

This lifestyle of learning opens one to God's profound promise: "See, God is mighty . . . in strength and in mind. . . . He opens their understanding by discipline . . . If they will serve obediently, they shall spend their days in happiness, their years in delight."[130] O that believers everywhere would seek the Lord and worship before him in the beauty of his holiness, studying his Word and his ways and then dynamically modeling his instructions, thereby conveying by example the teaching of the living God and the good news of his grace!

Discipleship: Christian Fruit—Jewish Root!

---

128 Donald P. McNeill, Douglas A. Morrison, and Henri J. M. Nouwen, *Compassion: A Reflection on the Christian Life* (New York: Random House, 1982), p. 86. McNeill, Morrison, and Nouwen maintain that "without discipline discipleship is little more than hero worship or fadism: without discipleship discipline easily becomes a form of emulation or self-assertion. Discipline and discipleship belong together."
129 Luke 4:27; 14:23.
130 Job 36:5, 10–11, TNK.

CHAPTER 14

SERVANTHOOD

A debilitating leadership vacuum plagues and paralyzes postmodern societies in today's world.[1] The abdication of responsibility is obvious in nearly every field of endeavor—from politics, to medicine, to law, to business, and, sad to say, to ministry. Where are the statesmen for whom principle and the general welfare are of greater value than electability or political expediency? Where are the medical and legal giants for whom ethical conduct is of greater value than popularity among amoral pressure groups or ill-gotten financial gains? Where are the businessmen for whom commitment to the work ethic and to fairness and honesty is more important than the bottom line? And, by all means, where are the spiritual leaders to whom the salvation and development of the souls of men are more important than position, power, influence, success, or financial gain? With such a profound dearth of leadership in modern society, it is the responsibility of the church to lead the way in providing intellectual, moral, and emotional challenge to a society that is adrift in the rising tide of postmodernity, Neo-Paganism, and amoral secular humanism.[2] Tragically, the church has largely failed to execute this responsibility because it has chosen to follow Gentile leadership paradigms and measures of success rather than the Hebraic model that Jesus practiced and espoused.

Unfortunately, the traditional leadership style that has pervaded both society and the church has long been autocratic control and domination of the lives and actions of others. This perspective on leadership has been practiced throughout history and throughout the world in virtually every culture.

---

[1] Deborah Rigling Gallagher, *Environmental Leadership: A Reference Handbook* (Thousand Oaks, CA: SAGE Publications, 2012), p. 42. Wheatley says that "there is almost a consensus that there is a leadership crisis in today's world—a crisis of 'leadership vacuum' and of leadership that 'has failed us'" in Margaret J. Wheatley, *Finding Our Way: Leadership for an Uncertain Time* (San Francisco, CA: Berrett-Koehler Publishes, 2005), pp. 164–166.

[2] Wolfgang Amann, Michael Pirson, Claus Dierksmeier, Ernst von Kimakowit, and Heiko Spitzeck, *Business Schools Under Fire: Humanistic Management* (Basingstoke, UK: Palgrave Macmillian, 2011), p. 281.

Often both followers and leaders have preferred autocratic leadership styles because they relieve followers of the necessity of thinking for themselves and of taking responsibility for their own actions, and they give leaders virtually unlimited power which they often relish and generally maintain with murderous efficiency.

For most of its existence, the Christian church has also been plagued by abusive, ineffective leadership because it has drawn its leadership models from Gentile cultures that have been dominated by power-mad autocrats whose egocentricity and even megalomania have driven them to exercise absolute power. Even in the modern and postmodern secular worlds, old patterns of abusive domination have continued, with new tyrants rising daily, ruling with terror, torturing and slaughtering their own subjects in order to eradicate dissent. The church, likewise, has continued to be victimized by leaders who have demanded absolute authority, have ruled with iron fists, and have smashed any dissent. Beginning with the monarchical bishops of ancient Eastern Christianity,[3] continuing with the papacy of Western Christianity,[4] and remaining consistent in much of Protestantism,[5] Christian leadership has been patterned after imperial empires and the perquisites that secular potentates have arrogated to themselves. Jesus hit the nail on the head when he said that autocratic domination has always been the hallmark of Gentile cultures and societies.[6]

The Jesus Model of Servanthood

In direct contrast with the rest of the world, Jesus described the type of leadership that was to be exercised within the community of believers that he had established when he made this bold and unequivocal declaration: "Whosoever will be great among you, let him be your servant: even as the Son of man came not to be ministered unto, but to minister, and to give his life a ransom for many."[7] The Master's statement was made in reaction to no small amount of jockeying for position and power in the ranks of his

---

[3] The emergence of monarchical bishops in the Eastern Church simply appropriated the leadership paradigm of civil and secular leadership in the Greek city-state. See John D. Garr, *The Church Dynamic: Hebraic Foundations for Christian Community* (Atlanta, GA: Golden Key Press, 2014).

[4] The papacy was simply patterned after the civil government of Rome wherein a Caesar or emperor ruled autocratically. See John D. Garr, *Church Dynamic*.

[5] Protestantism made efforts to distance itself from the autocratic forms of government that characterized both Eastern and Western Christianity before the sixteenth-century reformation movements. Though some movements tried to adopt either republican or democratic forms of government, most of the denominations that distilled from the reform movements gravitated toward traditional autocratic forms of government.

[6] Mark 10:46.

[7] Matthew 20:26–28.

own disciples, particularly in their expectation of eminence and privilege in the eschatological dominion to come.[8] In fact, "a dispute" had arisen among them "as to which one of them was to be regarded as the greatest" in the kingdom of God.[9] The reaction of Jesus was swift, univocal, and unequivocal: "You know that the rulers of the Gentiles lord it over them, and their great men exercise authority over them. That is not the way it should be among you. Instead, whoever wants to be great among you must be your servant and whoever wants to be first among you must be your slave."[10]

The Master's intent was unmistakable. When he held up as an example the dominance of Gentile rulers over their subjects, Jesus exposed the extremes to which an unbridled quest for power and recognition would inevitably and logically develop. The lesson was unambiguous, for the disciples knew that "Gentile dominion was the expression of autocracy in all its aspects."[11] As Samuel Greenwood observed, "The belief that might is right, and that this might is physical, had held the thoughts of mortals from the most primitive times"[12] among all the non-Israelite nations. Of a truth, "the phrase 'Gentile dominion' was truly and terribly earned and maintained. Brute force was the god to whom the Gentile world burned incense."[13] In citing this example, Jesus powerfully exposed the kind of spirit that had manifest itself even among the disciples whom he had ordained as apostles.

In requiring that his disciples lead by serving, Jesus made two important declarations. First, in the typical rabbinic style of leading by example, he said, ". . . the Son of Man did not come to be served, but to serve, and to give his life a ransom for many."[14] Jesus set himself forth as the example *par excellence* of the leadership style that his disciples should imitate and follow. Second, Jesus said that political jockeying was characteristic of the Gentile nations and by implication that it had never been God's design for such attitudes and conduct to be present in the Jewish community. When God chose Abraham and his descendants after him, he was not looking for a military machine that would conquer the world. He was looking for a

---

8 Ben Witherington III, *The Gospel of Mark: A Socio-Rhetorical Commentary* (Grand Rapids, MI: Wm. B. Eerdmans Publishing Co., 2001), p. 269.

9 Luke 22:24, ESV.

10 Matthew 20:26–27, ISV.

11 Samuel Greenwood, *Footsteps of Israel: From Eden to the City of God* (Boston, MA: A. A. Beauchamp, 1922), p. 182.

12 Greenwood, p. 182.

13 Greenwood, p. 182.

14 Matthew 20:28.

kingdom of priests[15] that would bring his justice and peace to all the nations.[16] This is why Jesus told his disciples, "The kings of the Gentiles dominate them, and those who have authority over them are called 'Benefactors.'"[17] Then, later in the context of the same subject, Jesus further warned his disciples about the dangers of heaping to themselves grandiloquent titles: "You are not to be called rabbi, because you have one teacher, and you are all brothers. And call no man your father on earth, for you have one Father, who is in heaven. Neither be called instructors, for you have one instructor, the Christ."[18]

In further developing the background of his teaching on leadership, Jesus pointed out the Gentile quest for public recognition invaded Israel and had come to characterize some of the Pharisees and scribes in Israel: "Everything they do is done for people to see: They make their phylacteries wide[19] and their tassels on their garments long;[20] they love the place of honor at banquets and the most important seats in the synagogues; they love to be greeted with respect in the marketplaces and to be called 'Rabbi' by others."[21] There are three key elements in this instruction: 1) titles can be tools for

---

[15] Exodus 19:6.

[16] Genesis 18:19.

[17] Luke 22:25, HCSB. This was an allusion to the common practice wherein the autocrats and even bureaucrats in Roman and other Gentile societies exercised cruel dominion over the people, all the while styling themselves "Patrons" or "Benefactors" of the same dominated people because of the grand, munificent gestures they made in providing public facilities and services and minimal provisions of food for the poor at less than subsistence levels. The social welfare systems of Rome and other Gentile empires, such as they were, were motivated entirely from a desire to dominate and control the common people and not from a perceived responsibility to serve and meet human need.

[18] Matthew 23:8–10, ESV.

[19] The word *phylactery* is a transliteration of the Greek word φυλακτήριον (*phulaktērion*), which described amulets, charms, or safeguards used in the Hellenic world. This Greek word translated the Hebrew word תְּפִילִין (*tefillin*). Tefillin were not considered by Judaism to be amulets. They were worn in order to fulfill the instruction that God gave to Israel, "Tie [the commandments] on your hands and bind them on your foreheads" (Deuteronomy 6:8). The Israelites took the commandment literally and constructed leather boxes into which they inserted scrolls inscribed with the Hebrew text of the *Shema* and of this commandment. Then, they tied those boxes to their right hands (and arms) and to their foreheads. During the time of Jesus, some of the people had become ostentatious in demonstrating their obedience to the commandment by making their *tefillin* very large. Their pretentious actions prompted Jesus to call them hypocrites in Matthew 23:13. While *tefillin* were likely worn continually in the most ancient of times, they came to be used only during the synagogue prayers, perhaps because the word תְּפִילִין (*tefillin*) is related to תְּפִלָּה (*tefillah*), the word for prayer.

[20] One of the wealthy men in first-century Israel was called *Ben Tzitzit HaKeset* (the Son of the Fringed Pillow) because he had fashioned the *tzitziyot* (fringes) that the Torah required to be attached to the four corners of the Israelite's *tallit* (outer garment or mantle) in such an ostentatious manner that they were long enough to touch the ground. It is said, however, that this man was so rich that his extra-long *tzitziyot* were never allowed to touch the ground because he had his servants place pillows on the ground in front of him so that his delicate feet would not touch the dirt or the stone streets. Because of this, he was the "Son of the Fringed Pillow." See Burton L. Visotzky, *Sage Tales: Wisdom and Wonder from the Rabbis of the Talmud* (Woodstock, VT: Jewish Lights Publishing, 2011), p. 109

[21] Matthew 23:6–8, NIV.

imposing or reinforcing divisions among the children of God in which those who have either gained or arrogated to themselves the titles are exalted (or exalt themselves) above the rest of the community; 2) divine instructions regarding grooming and dress can be taken to extremes in which they promote class distinctions or the arrogant display of being "more spiritual"—and, therefore, more powerful—than others; and 3) in order to avoid this class distinction based on ecclesiastical or political office or even on charismatic gift, the members of the Jesus community were to recognize one another simply as "brothers" and "sisters."[22] In other words, they were to be true extended family wherein all the siblings were equal, and no one was considered to be better, more spiritual, or more powerful than any other member of the community.

Jesus also used another similar incident to underscore the importance of servanthood and the ability to endure the rigors and demands of servant leadership. When the mother of the apostles James and John approached Jesus with this personal request, "Grant that one of these two sons of mine may sit at your right and the other at your left in your kingdom," Jesus replied to her, "You don't know what you are asking." Then he turned to the apostles and asked, "Can you drink of the cup I am going to drink?" When they replied, "We can," then Jesus made this prediction: "You will indeed drink from my cup." Finally, he concluded by saying that "to sit at my right or left is not for me to grant. These places belong to those for whom they have been prepared by my Father."[23] In this incident, the Son of God underscored the fact that leadership in the community of faith is not attained by human bargaining, political manipulation, sovereign largesse, or nepotism but only through divine appointment, and he underscored the fact that administrative positions in the eschatological kingdom will be made on the basis of the degree of service that leaders have provided to the community of faith and not on the basis of the power that they may have wielded therein.

The simple lesson of leadership that Jesus modeled in his own life and taught to the community of faith was that it should be demonstrated through a mindset of servanthood. The only people who would be qualified

---

[22] Matthew 23:8; John 13:35. When Ananias prayed for Saul following the incident when he was blinded during his encounter with the living Jesus on the Damascus Road, he said, "Brother Saul, the Lord Jesus who appeared unto you . . . has sent me, that you might receive your sight and be filled with the Holy Spirit" (Acts 9:17). When Paul related this story, he said that Ananias "stood beside me and said, 'Brother Saul, receive your sight!'" (Acts 22:13). Obviously Ananias and Saul did not even know one another; however, when Saul became a believer, he was immediately a "brother" to Ananias.

[23] John R. Lohlenberger, ed., *The Evangelical Parallel New Testament* (New York: Oxford University Press, 2003), p. 143.

to lead in the Christian church would be the ones who were gifted to serve. It would never be the ones who were the most Machiavellian manipulators of people and circumstances. It would never be the ones who could seize power and viciously maintain it. It would never be the ones who would become self-appointed "lords over God's heritage."[24] The greatest leaders in the church would be the ones who would be the greatest servants.

The exhortation that Jesus gave to his disciples to be servants of God's people, then, clearly established the ground rules and gave a true and proper paradigm for Christian leadership in every generation. Spiritual leadership as ministry is never to be fulfilled by giving orders: it is to be manifest in nurturing people. Believers in today's world, therefore, are not looking to be dominated; they are looking for help in realizing their God-given potential. The truly God-anointed and appointed leader "helps give birth to ideas and dreams, developing and nurturing people to realize their God-given potential,"[25] says Jeanne Porter. Christians are not looking for membership; they are looking for relationship.

What Jesus said when he gave his servant leadership exhortation[26] was very telling, but it has been obscured for most Christians. "The rulers of the Gentiles dominate . . . but you are not to be like that."[27] The Master's response to the question, "who is greatest among you," was not a commandment that going forward his disciples should never be concerned with politico-religious domination. Instead, it was a declaration that the issue of who would be the greatest among them should never have arisen among them in the first place. The reason for this was the fact that with the influence of the divine instructions in the Hebrew Scriptures and without the influence of the philosophies and traditions of Gentile cultures, questions of dominance or class distinctions would never have arisen in the Hebrew/Israelite/Jewish community.[28] God had designed the nation of Israel in such a way as to preclude any such development among them. All that was necessary was for his Chosen People to follow his instructions that placed

---

[24] 1 Peter 5:3.

[25] Jeanne L. Porter, *Leading Ladies: Transformative Biblical Imagers for Women's Leadership* (Philadelphia, PA: Innisfree Press, 2000), p. 14.

[26] The term *servant leadership* was coined by Robert Greenleaf. Robert K. Greenleaf, noted in Larry C. Spears and Michele Lawrence, *Focus on Leadership: Servant-Leadership for the Twenty-First Century* (New York: John Wiley & Sons, 2002), pp. 3, 18. The note is from Robert K. Greenleaf, *The Servant as Leader: A Journey into the Nature of Legitimate Power and Greatness* (Mahwah, NJ: Paulist Press, 1997).

[27] Luke 22:26, NIV.

[28] Michael Terry, *Reader's Guide to Judaism* (New York: Fitzroy Dearborn Publishers, 2000), p. 198. Terry maintains that "the ideal that Jesus preached so steadfastly—the democratization of Jewish society—was the ideal championed by the Pharisees [who were] unmistakably Jesus' teachers."

restrictions on leaders and underscored their responsibility for maintaining the self-determination of the people. By following God's prescription for national and community governance and social interaction, the Israelites would live in peace and prosperity — and in complete equality before their God.

Lessons from Ancient Israel

Long before the time of Christ, God had begun a grand experiment in leadership that defied the norms of the ancient world. Israel itself was never designed by God to be dominated by autocrats or hierarchs. YHWH was king, the only king, and Israel was his servant-bride.[29] The entire nation was liberated from Egyptian bondage for one specific purpose: so that they could come to God's mountain and enter into a love-slave relationship with their God to be the servant nation through whom his salvation could be extended to the entire world.[30] The Israelites were to serve the service that served the needs of humanity. They were to be a servant kingdom of priests who would hold forth God's truth to the nations.

From that most ancient of times when the family of Abraham was incorporated as a nation, God gave clear instructions regarding its spiritual, social, and civil interaction, and his instructions represented as much a departure from the strategies employed in the rest of human societies as was his requirement that his chosen nation should be fiercely monotheistic. The overriding characteristics of God's community were to be the principles of unity and equality.[31] Like their God, the people of Israel were to be one, and their interrelationships with one another were to image the divine unity.[32] The political equality of the people, with neither nobles nor peasants, was a fundamental principle of the Torah. The Sinai covenant provided for a commonwealth, not a monarchy, plutocracy, oligarchy, or autocracy, and the

---

[29] George A. F. Knight, *Servant Theology: A Commentary on the Book of Isaiah 40–55* (Grand Rapids, MI: Wm. B. Eerdmans Publishing Co., 1984), p. 162.

[30] Exodus 9:1: "Then the LORD said to Moses, Go to Pharaoh and say to him, This is what the LORD, the God of the Hebrews, says, Let my people go, so that they may worship me." The reason for Israel's deliverance was so that they could worship or serve their God (Exodus 7:16; 8:1). See Christoph Barth, *God with Us: A Theological Introduction to the Old Testament* (Grand Rapids, MI: Wm. B. Eerdmans Publishing Co., 1991), p. 60.

[31] Wolfhart Pannenberg, *Systematic Theology, Volume 1* (Grand Rapids, MI: Wm. B. Eerdmans Publishing Co., 1991), p. 150. Pannenberg rightly says that "The unity of humanity in the sense of a principal equality of all members of the race as such, no matter to what culture, people, or specific race they might belong, is an idea which itself has presuppositions in the history of religion. It is closely related to the emergence of monotheistic views. . . . The idea of the unity of humanity is grounded in the concept of the one God." Equality and mutuality among the believing community, therefore, are entirely dependent upon commitment to monotheist faith.

[32] Psalm 133:1.

form of the Hebraic government was to be that of a republic.[33] All of the people were to be represented and involved in the organization and operation of the civil government that God established for their protection and well-being. All the people were to share in the dominion over the earth that had God promised to Adam and Eve.[34] God would guide and protect them by appointing and anointing prophets and sages; however God himself would be King.

Moses was never an autocrat. As a matter of fact, the Scriptures say that he was the most humble man on the face of the earth.[35] He never attempted to establish a hierarchy to support an autocracy. Instead, he followed God's instructions for charging the people to choose from among themselves leaders whom he then appointed and installed in offices of oversight, not domination, offices which were designed for service, not control. Moses then followed God's instructions through the advice of his father-in-law and instructed the community of Israel, "Choose wise and discerning and experienced men from your tribes, and I will appoint them as your heads."[36] When this plan was set forth, the people responded, "The thing which you have said to do is good."[37] This strategy for involvement of "all the people" through leaders whom they elected and submitted for appointment by the prophet became a continuing exercise in Israel. Joshua followed Moses' example: "Appoint three men from each tribe. I will send them out to make a survey of the land and to write a description of it, according to the inheritance of each. Then they will return to me."[38]

The people were clearly involved in the ongoing leadership of Israel during the time of the judges: "Then Jephthah went with the elders of Gilead, and the people made him head and chief over them; and Jephthah spoke all his words before the LORD at Mizpah."[39] The same strategy was employed by King David, who "said to all the assembly of Israel, If it seems good to you, and if it is from the LORD our God, let us send everywhere to our kinsmen who remain in all the land of Israel, also to the priests and Levites who are with them in their cities with pasture lands, that they may meet with us; and let us bring back the ark of our God to us . . . then all the

---

[33] A republic is a representative democracy in which the people choose leaders to represent them in the affairs of government.
[34] Genesis 1:26.
[35] Numbers 12:3.
[36] Deuteronomy 1:13.
[37] Deuteronomy 1:14.
[38] Joshua 18:4.
[39] Judges 11:11.

assembly said that they would do so, for the thing was right in the eyes of all the people."[40] Centuries later, this same convention was still being employed in the earliest Christian community: "Select from among you, brethren, seven men of good reputation, full of the Spirit of wisdom, whom we may put in charge of this task."[41] These consistent approaches to establishing spiritual leadership in the community of faith confirm the fact that servant leadership was the paradigm in Hebraic understanding and that the people were always to be involved in the recognition of their leaders.

From the very beginning of the nationhood of Israel, the leaders were called heads of houses, heads of thousands, and sometimes simply heads, but all of them were servant leaders.[42] These heads took the form of two classes of officers: phylarchs (governors of tribes) and patriarchs (governors of families). From the time of Hebrew life in Egypt throughout Israelite history, both of these classes of leaders were called "elders."[43] The term *elder* came to be the dominant and most common appellative for leaders in Israel,[44] so much so that it was a term of choice in the earliest church.[45] Both in ancient Israel and in the first-century church, however, it was clear that the leaders were to be selected or affirmed by the people and that the authority that they were given was derived from those over whom it was to be exercised, not from a hierarchy. Biblical leadership was never to be imposed upon the people autocratically; it was to be established by a track record of service that prompted the people to recognize God's gift for their oversight and protection and to confirm and support that divine gift.

Enoch Wines maintained that "every tribe formed its own commonwealth, having its own particular interests; while all united became a great republic, with a common weal."[46] Each tribe essentially functioned as a separate state, with its own system of justice. Collectively they formed a national identity that brought them into a divine unity that was maintained in the cohesion in their diversity, not by uniformity of either their social or religious distinctives. This was a unity that respected the personhood of each individual member of the collective community

---

[40] 1 Chronicles 13:3–4.

[41] Acts 6:3.

[42] Numbers 17:3, 25:15; Joshua 22:14; 23:2.

[43] Enoch C. Wines, *The Hebrew Republic*, originally published in 1861 as *Commentary on the Laws of the Ancient Hebrews, Book II* (Uxbridge, Mass.: American Presbyterian Press, 1980), p. 100.

[44] Exodus 3:16; Deuteronomy 32:7; Judges 8:14; 11:5; 1 Kings 12:6–8; Ezra 10:14; Ezekiel 8:1; 14:1; 20:1; Lamentations 5:12; 1 Timothy 5:17.

[45] Acts 14:23; 16:4; 11:30; 1 Timothy 5:17–19; Titus 1:5; James 5:15; 1 Peter 5:1-5; Revelation 19:4.

[46] Wines, p. 101.

without creating an environment where rugged individuality ruled at the expense of the community.[47] By basing unity on equality of person,[48] the collective community could be mutually reinforcing and relational to each of the individuals without becoming controlling and manipulative. The common weal was the supreme goal, and the equality of every individual reinforced the commitment to the family of Israel, the collective social unit of nationhood.

Moses' principle for the foundation of the Israelite nation was in direct contradistinction to the land from which he and the Israelites had been extracted by the divine hand. There, the Egyptian priesthood believed in a form of dualism and practiced a duality of governance. "In the political system framed by this philosophical dogma," the higher spiritual essence of the universe was manifest in the "sacerdotal aristocracy" while the lower material essence was manifest in the common people.[49] The nobility and the common people were separated by an impassable genetic hereditary gulf.[50] The superior hierocracy acted upon the inferior and passive commonalty (the plebeians, the proletariat, or *hoi polloi*). Moses clearly rejected this concept of dualism and replaced it with a philosophy of unity in Israelite life and governance. Nowhere in the Torah is there any hint of an establishment of caste,[51] an appropriation of perquisites and privileges to one class and hereditary inferiority to others.[52] There was to be no nepotism in Israel, as was demonstrated clearly when Gideon refused to become the permanent leader of the Israelites or to allow his descendants to rule after him.[53] Leaders were to be appointed by God as needed.

---

[47] Peter J. Gentry and Stephen J. Wellum, *Kingdom Through Covenant: A Biblical Theological Understanding of the Covenants* (Wheaton, IL: Crossway Publishing, 2012), p. 580. Gentry and Wellum note that "ancient Israel valued the community over the individual. The interests of the group were more important than those of a single individual, no matter how clever or skilled and talented the entrepreneur."

[48] Paul D. Hanson, *The People Called: The Growth of Community in the Bible* (New York: Harper & Row Publishers, 1986), p. 469. Hanson says, "The early Yahwistic community was committed to the equality of its members, and indeed we can recognize a persistent egalitarian impulse influencing the laws and institutions of early Israel. Both in terms of the benefits enjoyed by the members of the community and the responsibilities they bore toward others, the emphasis placed on equality and inclusiveness stands out within the ancient world."

[49] Wines, p. 397.

[50] Wines, p. 397.

[51] The prime example of the transgenerational domination of a society by a caste system birthed in polytheism is India, where the priestly Brahmin caste controlled the other castes, the Kshatriyas, Vaishyas, and Shudras while excluding others, the Dalit, from the caste system altogether as "untouchables."

[52] Wines, p. 397. Wines argued that the unity which Moses established "was not that species of unity . . . in which vast multitudes of human beings are delivered up to the arbitrary will of one man. It was a unity, effected by the abolition of caste; a unity, founded on the principle of equal rights; a unity, in which the whole people formed the state."

[53] Judges 8:22–23.

The unity of God was reflected in the unity of Israel. All Israelites were created equal, and all were gifted for specific functions in the commonwealth. There were no lords and serfs, no aristocracy and peasants. There were leaders, to be sure, but leaders were servants of the populace, not vice versa. Leaders were respected and revered because they comported themselves as servants of God and of the people, using God, the Shepherd of Israel, as their role model,[54] not the despots of the nations around them. The principles of equality and mutuality were established in the Torah and were demonstrated in the ongoing life of the believing community.

Though God had instituted an official priesthood among the Israelites to carry out the service and ritual that he had prescribed in the Torah, it was never his intention to remove the responsibility for spiritual, social, and educational development from the context of the individual family and repose it in a hierarchical priesthood. The priests were to serve God by serving those who would worship him.[55] The Hebrew Scriptures even describe those who ministered in Israel's tabernacle as being "servants who serve the services that serve."[56] In this text, the Hebrew word עֲבֹדָה—*abodah* ("service") is used three times in sequence to emphasize[57] the fact that the priestly order was designed by God to be servants who served the services of the tabernacle which, in turn, served the people.[58] In this case, the word *abodah* in reference to the word *abadim* ("servants") essentially makes a four-fold repetition of the idea of servant leadership in Israel's sanctuary. While this multiple use of the same word may seem like a coincidence, it could well serve the midrashic purpose of underscoring the importance of a servant mentality in those who are leaders of God's people and the worship

---

[54] Scott Hahn, *Kingdom of God as Liturgical Empire: A Theological Commentary on 1–2 Chronicles* (Grand Rapids, MI: Baker Academic, 2012), p. 49. Hahn notes that "Moses [was] the archetypal leader of Israel, who was a shepherd in the image of God and is called 'the shepherd of Israel' (Moses in Exodus 3:1; Psalm 77:20; Isaiah 63:11; God in Genesis 49:24; Psalm 80:1)."

[55] Michael Goldberg, *Why Should Jews Survive? Looking Past the Holocaust toward a Jewish Future* (New York: Oxford University Press, 1995), p. 167.

[56] Numbers 4:47.

[57] The repetition of words in the Hebrew text is the way of emphasizing the importance of the statement that is being made or of creating a superlative. Repetition is a signal that something important is being declared in the context.

[58] The Hebrew text says, עֲבֹדַת עֲבֹדָה וַעֲבֹדַת (*abodat abodah v'abodat*). Perhaps the best of the usual translations of this text is this: "Everyone who could come to do the service of ministry and the service of bearing burdens in the tent of meeting" (ESV). In reality, these Levites were the servants (עֲבָדִים—*abadim*) who served (עֲבֹדַת—*abodat*), and they served the services (עֲבֹדָה—*abodah*) that served (עֲבֹדַת—*abodat*) the work of the tabernacle (or the "oracle" of the tabernacle, as the Hebrew word מַשָּׂא—*massa*, which is rendered "work," can also be translated). This text stresses the fact that the importance of "service" cannot be overemphasized whenever ministry or leadership is discussed.

of God. Service was, therefore, central to leadership and ministry in every aspect of the established order for liturgical ministration in ancient Israel from the time that God instituted the priesthood.

Lessons from Second Temple Judaism

This principle was expanded and became even more apparent when the temple and its attendant infrastructure were destroyed in the Babylonian invasion of Nebuchadnezzar. At that time, when the people began to search for means that would perpetuate their knowledge and worship of God, the most embryonic form of what was to become the synagogal movement emerged. A grand experiment in the democratization of religion was born.[59] The synagogue represented the reassumption of the biblical roles that God had given to Israel in the first place when he made them "a kingdom of priests."[60] In this setting, every person could rightly approach the *bema*[61] of the synagogue to read the Torah and the Prophets and expound upon them. Every man essentially became a priest in his home, and the home became the locus for spiritual, social, and educational development. Religious exercise came to be manifest in the context of community. This synagogal community functioned with a plurality of leaders, with various functions fulfilled by men of different gifting and training. When teaching elders (first called sages, then rabbis) emerged in the communities, they were considered to be the first among equals in the community[62] and saw themselves as facilitators of the spiritual development of all its members, not as autocratic rulers.

Serving services that serve is a rigorous task today as it was during the Israelite wilderness journey. Those who are called by God to lead the community of faith are charged with serving the diverse ministry dynamics that serve the needs of God's people. This service requires a pure heart that is not puffed up with the narcissism of over-exaggerated self-worth. Serving services requires a humble heart, a willingness to work with people even when those people are their own worst enemies. These are the people about whom Paul instructed Timothy in the techniques of true servant leadership: "The Lord's servant must not be quarrelsome, but must be kind to everyone, able to teach, not resentful. With gentleness correcting those who are in

---

[59] Oliver Leaman, *Judaism: An Introduction* (New York: I. B. Tauris & Co., 2011), p. 173.

[60] Exodus 19:6.

[61] The *bema* is an elevated platform from which the services of the synagogue are conducted.

[62] The "first-among-equals" principle was formalized in Rabbi Judah ha-Nasi who was formally recognized as the *nasi* ("prince"), but not king. See Leo Trepp, *A History of the Jewish Experience* (Springfield, NJ: Behrman House Publishing, 2006), p. 92.

opposition, if perhaps God may grant them repentance leading to the knowledge of the truth."[63]

Servanthood: The Mind of Christ

With a Hebraic perspective in mind, it was, therefore, to be expected that service would also be inherent in Messiahship. Servanthood was perfectly fulfilled in the mindset that drove the ministry of Jesus: "Christ Jesus, who, though he was in the form of God, did not regard equality with God as something to be exploited, but made himself nothing, taking the very nature of a servant . . . and humbled himself and became obedient to death."[64] The text that is translated "made himself nothing" literally says that Jesus "emptied himself." Some have suggested that in becoming human, Jesus emptied himself of his deity so that when he was on earth he was not fully divine; however, this theory is impossible, for Paul declared that "all the fullness of deity lived in [Jesus] bodily."[65] As the context of this passage demonstrates, the kenosis (emptying) of the Son of God which Paul described was clearly the laying aside of his equality with the Father when he became less than the Father by also becoming human.

It was in this "emptied" state that Jesus could, in fact, say, "My Father is greater than I."[66] The mystery of Deity is that Jesus was both equal with and less than God at the same time: "equal with" in his ever-inherent, eternally preexistent deity, "less than" in his absolute humanity. This form of divine contraction,[67] then, is the supreme example of biblically Hebraic servant ministry and leadership that was demonstrated by true men and women of God throughout the Hebrew Scriptures and was sealed in the life of Jesus and subsequently in the lives of his apostles.[68] It is the giving up of "rights" in order to serve God and community. True service becomes possible only when one chooses to enter the plane of vulnerability. This truth was clearly demonstrated in the life of Jesus who, when he was became incarnate,[69] made himself vulnerable to temptation[70] and to death so

---

[63] 2 Timothy 2:24–25.

[64] Philippians 2:5–7.

[65] Colossians 3:9.

[66] John 14:28.

[67] The self-limitation of God that was manifest when the Word of God (God's only begotten Son) became human was first demonstrated in the *tzimtzum* that occurred when God contracted himself from a portion of infinity in order to have a space where nothing existed wherein he could create the universe and everything in it out of nothing. Self-limitation and contraction have always characterized God from the moment of creation to the present day. See John D. Garr, *Life from the Dead*, pp. 41–43.

[68] The *tzimtzum* of God and the kenosis of Christ set the example for self-limitation in servant leadership.

[69] Hebrews 2:14.

[70] Hebrews 4:15.

that he could overcome sin in the flesh[71] and destroy the devil who had the power of death.[72] Had Jesus considered his equality with the Father something to grasped at and exploited, he could never have become Isaiah's suffering servant, take upon himself all of humanity's sin, and bring healing to humankind through his wounds.[73]

In his kenosis discourse, Paul's use of Jesus as the example *par excellence* of servant ministry was addressed to all believers: "Your attitude should be the same as that of Christ Jesus." Those who have the mind of Christ are not always grasping at "rights" and privileges, demanding the best, in the manner of a *prima donna* of the performing arts. They are ready to empty themselves of what is rightfully theirs in order to accomplish the greater good for their fellowman and for God's cause in the earth. Henry Budd explains this servant mentality: "Our contemporary mind-set, conditioned by our culture, tells us to insist on our rights. But Jesus tells us that we must consider ourselves unprofitable servants . . . the servant mind embraces responsibility and is prepared to lay aside rights for the cause of Christ."[74] Leadership, then, is not a position of glamor and privilege, of entitlement and prestige. It is not a position of power. Leadership is an opportunity for service.

This psychology of service must be ingrained into the consciousness of Christian leaders if they are to be effective. Before leaders can lead competently, they must first have been servants. Dietrich Bonhoeffer said of Christian leadership's servanthood role: "The church does not need brilliant personalities but faithful servants of Jesus and the brethren. The question of trust, which is so closely related to that of authority, is determined by the faithfulness with which a man serves Jesus Christ, never by extraordinary talent which he possesses. Authority can only be attained by the servant of Jesus Christ who seeks no power of his own, who himself is a brother among brothers submitted to the authority of the Word."[75] Simply stated, God always prefers character over charisma, and he always prefers service over adroit cleverness.

Christian leadership involves taking the yoke of Christ's servanthood. It is not, therefore, so much a natural talent that is produced from personality as it is a learned trait. The natural human tendency is to gravitate toward

---

[71] Romans 8:3.
[72] Hebrews 2:14–16.
[73] Isaiah 53:3-11.
[74] Henry Budd, quoted in Kenneth O. Gangel, *Feeding and Leading: A Practical Handbook on Administration in Churches and Christian Organizations* (Grand Rapids, MI: Baker Books, 1989) p. 31.
[75] Dietrich Bonhoeffer, *Life Together: The Classic Exploration of Faith in Community* (New York: HarperCollins Publishers, 2009), p. 109.

self-interest, self-assertion, and self-aggrandizement. Servanthood is learned as one takes up his cross and follows the Servant of God, the Lord Jesus. The model is Christ, and the handbook is Holy Scripture. Ultimately, the greatest Christian leaders are those who are "devoted to the service of the saints,"[76] those who follow in the footsteps of Jesus by laying down their lives for the sheep. The examples and lessons are clear and unequivocal. All that is needed are those who are humble enough to walk in the light of the Word and be the servant shepherds for whom God and his people are looking.

First-Century Servanthood

These Hebraic ideals of religious and social equality[77] and pluriformity[78] prompted Paul to declare, "There is neither Jew nor Greek, there is neither slave nor free man, there is neither male nor female; for you are all one in Christ Jesus."[79] With the teaching of the apostles, class distinctions had been limited by the equality of earliest Christianity, and, as in the Jewish matrix from which it emerged, the nascent Christian community enjoyed the egalitarian blessing of pluriformity of belief and practice without the imposition of a rigid orthodoxy.[80] It was in this philosophical and spiritual milieu that truly biblical servant leadership could flourish. The question of who was "in charge" was answered in the demand that Jesus made for Christian leaders to be "servants" of God[81] and the community.[82] "The absence of normal social distinctions within Christian congregations (status, class, education, age, wealth, etc.), though at variance with pagan social

---

[76] 1 Corinthians 16:15.

[77] Carl Joachim Friedrich, *The Philosophy of Law in Historical Perspective* (Chicago, IL: University of Chicago Press, 1958), p. 10. Friedrich says, "The markedly egalitarian spiritual attitude toward the law that one finds in ancient Judaism stands out in sharp contrast to the legal thought of the Greeks, at least as expressed in the legal philosophy of Plato and Aristotle, which is markedly that of a spiritual elite. The egalitarian attitude was taken over by Christianity from Judaism in spite of Christianity's sharp objection to the pharisaical legalistic ethics."

[78] Magnus Zetterholm, *Approaches to Paul: A Student's Guide to Recent Scholarship* (Minneapolis, MN: Fortress Press, 2009), p. 213. Zetterholm says that "the Hebrew Bible pleads for theological pluriformity, which is why we find this realized in rabbinic literature." See also Stephen Westerholm, *The Blackwell Companion to Paul* (Chichester, UK: Blackwell Publishing, 2011), p. 164. Westerholm points out that there was even "textual pluriformity of the Scriptures in the first century." Also Delio DelRio, *Paul and the Synagogue: Romans and the Isaiah Targum* (Eugene, OR: Wipf and Stock Publishers, 2013), p. xx. DelRio maintains that "the state, and even acceptance, of the Scriptures in the first century can be described as one of pluriformity."

[79] Galatians 3:28.

[80] Peter R. Ackroyd, *Continuity: A Contribution to the Study of the Old Testament Religious Tradition* (Oxford, England: Basil Blackwell, 1962), p. 14. Ackroyd argues that "uniformity of religious life appears as the less natural form; pluriformity, complexity in the interrelationship of differing groups as the normal. . . . One of the best arguments . . . in favour of belief in God is this very diversity in human thought."

[81] Romans 1:1; Titus 1:1.

[82] Colossians 1:24; 2 Corinthians 8:18.

groups, nevertheless served to reinforce the religious beliefs of Christians that were also at variance with those of their pagan neighbors," says David Aune.[83]

It was this perspective that obviated any perceived need for a rigidly defined and tightly controlled hierarchical power structure in the early church. Indeed, it was this "low level of internal structure [that] also fostered the ideal that all men were brothers."[84] Jacob Neusner points out that in this approach to community and leadership, because "members are completely equal with each other, no matter how much status distinction the 'world' might assign," a community is developed in which "all the societal barriers fall, economic, class, birth, age, and sex. Peasant is equal to landowner, slave to master, woman to man, youth to age."[85] Then, consistent with this egalitarian ideal, there is an "absence of a hierarchical structure of organization."[86]

When Jesus and the apostles established the church as a reformed Judaism[87] among the many Judaisms of their day, they appropriated the model for community life and worship that they had inherited from their forefathers: the synagogue.[88] They did not look to Gentile models for leadership in order to establish a pyramidal hierarchy. They continued to function under a plurality of eldership in which decisions were made collectively for business,[89] theology,[90] and recognition of divine appointment.[91] There was no attempt at self-exaltation or the autocratic imposition of personal agendas.

The greatest of apostolic leaders viewed themselves not as "lords over God's heritage," but as "slaves of the Lord Jesus Christ"[92] and "servants" of

---

[83] David E. Aune, *Prophecy in Early Christianity and the Ancient Mediterranean World* (Grand Rapids, MI: Wm. B. Eerdmans Publishing Co., 1983), p. 216.

[84] Aune, p. 216.

[85] Jacob Neusner, *Christianity, Judaism and Other Greco-Roman Cults, Part 2: Early Christianity* (Eugene, OR: Wipf and Stock Publishers, 1975), p. 5.

[86] Neusner, *Christianity*, p. 5.

[87] The Judaism of Jesus was a reformation of restoration in which he sought to return his Jewish community to the original foundations of the Hebraic and Jewish faith (Hebrews 9:10). This is why Jesus sought to strengthen the commandments of the Torah that had been diminished through attempts at circumventing the central intentions of commandments by means of circumlocution and exegetical gymnastics (Matthew 5;17–48).

[88] This is evident because even decades after the ascension of Jesus, James still referred to Jewish Christian congregations as being synagogues (James 2:2). This truth is obscured by most translations which render the Greek word συναγωγή (*sunagogé*) as "assembly" or "meeting" rather than "synagogue" as it clearly should be translated.

[89] Acts 6:1–4.

[90] Acts 15:6.

[91] Galatians 2:9.

[92] The use of the title *slave* was ubiquitous among the apostles. This was the case with Peter: 2 Peter 1:1; with James: James 1:1; with John: Revelation 1:1; with Paul: Romans 1:1; Titus 1:1; and with Jude: Jude 1:1. In each case, the apostles used the Greek term δοῦλος (*doulos*) which, though it is generally translated "servant," literally means "slave." The use of this term by so many of the early Christian leaders to introduce themselves in their writings could have been be a coincidence.

the people.[93] As a matter of fact, the title of choice among the apostles was not "apostle" or "bishop" but "slave." All the gifts of the Spirit that operated powerfully through them were given "to the profit of everyone"[94] and to "build up the body of Messiah until all come to maturity and the full knowledge of the Son of God."[95] No Caesars or Hitlers, these apostles! No politico-religious potentates, these overseers! No personal kingdom builders, these shepherds! In fact, the apostles understood that in the final analysis, there is only one Lord, and he simply does not need "lords over God's heritage"[96] who follow the models of the abusive world order rather than the examples set by God the Father and by Jesus Christ himself. God is not desperately searching for self-ordained autocrats to control and dominate his people. He is seeking for facilitators who will lovingly work with his people to help them mature and develop in the most holy faith and exercise the gifts and callings of God in their lives.

The earliest church knew nothing of leadership styles adopted in its later Gentile counterpart. Because it followed the biblically Hebraic model of servant leadership, it had avoided the tyranny of the dictatorial bureaucrats who later came to dominate Gentile Christendom. When the church succumbed to the imposition of hierarchical dominance instead of servant leadership, it paid a great price for abandoning its Hebraic foundations in favor of Greek philosophy and Roman organizational structure. The low point of this pattern for leadership was achieved in the Dark Ages of the tenth and eleventh centuries when Christendom sank into spiritual bankruptcy, moral debauchery, and intellectual stagnation. The tragedy of such dramatic departures from biblical models was the believers who languished in superstition and ignorance and who could not possibly have fulfilled any gift of service that God may have had for their lives.

The earliest church escaped this tragedy because its leaders knew that the entire church was commissioned to preach the gospel, to facilitate the breaking forth of the kingdom of God, and to join in corporate worship of the King of kings. All the members of the community were encouraged to develop their own spiritual gifts and to bring them to full flower. Everyone in the community was to be submitted to one another "out of respect for God."[97] Each believer was to assume responsibility for his own spiritual growth by engaging the Eternal God in a very personal relationship

---

[93] 2 Corinthians 4:5.
[94] 1 Corinthians 12:7.
[95] Ephesians 4:11–13.
[96] 1 Peter 5:3.
[97] Ephesians 5:21.

in which he could receive divine guidance for himself. He assumed control of his life, took responsibility for his own growth, and thereby came to maturity in Christ. This was why the earliest church was a powerhouse that turned the world upside down.[98]

Facilitators and Equippers

Jesus' exhortation to servanthood clearly establishes the ground rules and gives a true and proper paradigm for Christian leadership. Truly effective leadership in the church today will return to the model which Jesus and the apostles appropriated from their Hebraic tradition. It is that which is revealed throughout the Word of God: people with a service mentality whose goal is to be facilitators or equippers and servants of other believers so that *those believers* may fulfill *their* callings and ambitions for God. Kenneth Gangel says that "spiritual leadership as ministry is not giving orders but nurturing the people of God."[99] Church growth researcher George Barna notes that "the leaders of successful churches unanimously concurred that one of their most important roles was that of being a ministry cheerleader." Gangel maintains that the true Christian leader "understands that he functions in order to facilitate the ministry of others."[100] One such leader said, "My role is to equip [believers] to minister, then to support them as they are doing it. The paperwork just has to pile up. My primary responsibility is to spend time with the people, either equipping them or encouraging them as they use those gifts."[101] When leaders have their priorities placed on service rather than on being served, they are in a position to be truly effective.

The responsibility for making people winners rests on the shoulders of the leaders. This process requires a lot of hard work. Andrew Carnegie wisely observed, "When you work with people, it is a lot like mining for gold . . . you must literally move tons of dirt to find a single ounce of gold. However, you do not look for the dirt—you look for the gold!"[102] Kenneth Blanchard argues that "everyone is a potential winner. Some people are disguised as losers. Don't let their appearance fool you."[103] Ralph Waldo Emerson

---

[98] Acts 17:6.
[99] Gangel, p. 39.
[100] Gangel, p. 41.
[101] George Barna, *User-Friendly Churches: What Christians Need to Know About the Churches People Love to Go To* (Ventura, CA: Regal Books, 1991), p. 47.
[102] Andrew Carnegie, quoted in John Blaydes, *The Educator's Book of Quotes* (Thousand Oaks, CA: Corwin Press, 2003), p. 94.
[103] Kenneth H. Blanchard and Spencer Johnson, *The One Minute Manager* (Ann Arbor, MI: University of Michigan Press, 1981), p. 71.

reported, "Our chief want is someone who will inspire us to be what we know we could be."[104] Every person is looking for leaders who are so burdened with the servant mentality of wanting to equip others for success that they are willing to spend the time necessary to qualify themselves for that role and then to do it.

The Jesus model, therefore, demands that leadership be motivated by love and be manifest through the vehicle of service. Leaders must develop personal power by gaining the confidence, trust, and commitment of followers, and this can be accomplished only through true service that has no ulterior motive or hidden agenda. Any other motive will be quickly exposed. Servanthood is the mark, then, of true Christian leaders who always serve the people and never abuse or exploit them. They are like the Lord himself, the Good Shepherd, who laid down his life for the sheep.[105] Laying down one's life means giving up ambitions and personal rights more than it means becoming a martyr. And, as Isaiah so poignantly confessed, "All we like sheep have gone astray."[106] Every person, saint or sinner, needs the gentle hand of a shepherd whose sole desire is to serve and to enhance the spiritual welfare of God's sheep.

The psychology of truly effective leadership in the church is that which is revealed throughout the Word of God: people with a service mentality whose goal is to be facilitators, equippers, and servants of others so that others may fulfill their callings in God. This philosophy of service must be ingrained into the consciousness of a Christian leader if he is to be effective. Robert Greenleaf argued that servanthood is the first qualification for leadership. He suggests that leaders should be servants before they become leaders,[107] for without having served, they do not truly know how to lead others, and they will inevitably fail to realize the full potential of a true servant-leader.

Need-Driven Servanthood

Just as the priests and Levites served the needs of the tabernacle and temple, so true servant leaders serve the needs of God's people. Leadership, then, is needs driven, not power driven. True leadership, especially that which is exercised in the community of faith, must be driven by personal

---

104 Ralph Waldo Emerson, *The Conduct of Life: The Collected Works of Ralph Waldo Emerson*, Barbara L. Packer and Joseph Slater, eds. (Cambridge, MA: Harvard University Press, 2003), p. 145.
105 John 10:11.
106 Isaiah 53:6.
107 Robert K. Greenleaf, quoted in Don M. Frick, *Robert K. Greenleaf: A Life of Servant Leadership* (San Francisco, CA: Berrett-Koehler Publishers, 2004), p. 5.

power,[108] not position power.[109] Personal power is developed from the bottom up, with the people giving consent to being led because they discern that the leader has their own self-interest at heart. Position power is ordered from the top down, with leaders exercising calculated domination of their subjects in order to maintain their position and power. Personal power is given freely to leaders by those who are being led. Position power is delegated and imposed from hierarchs. Personal power is driven by divine gifts and the inspiration of the Holy Spirit. Position power operates through learned skill sets. In the personal-power model, leadership is exercised out of love; the position-power model operates out of fear.[110] The personal-power model encourages people to think for themselves and to develop their own gifts. The position-power model restricts freedom and thought, forcing subjects into tightly controlled orthodoxies of belief and practice.

Until recently, most Christian institutions have functioned largely under the assumption that people do not want to think for themselves; therefore stringent rules and standards of conduct have been established so that organizations and leaders essentially have become the consciences of the people. Ministers have been threatened, coerced, and forced to conform to organizational standards with the threat of punishment, demotion, or removal of status. Very little room has been allowed for creative thought. Leaders have exercised rigid, autocratic control over people in their charge. This style of leadership has produced resentment, splintering, and fragmentation of organizations, communities, and personnel. Such is the inevitable long-range ineffectiveness of the position-power model.[111] Although there are many people

---

[108] Personal power is defined as "influence over others, the source of which resides in the person instead of being vested by the position he or she holds." Personal power flows from the personal charisma, talents, and communication skills of the leader. See Ricky Griffin and Gregory Moorhead, *Organizational Behavior: Managing People and Organizations* (Mason, OH: South-Western Cengage Learning, 2010), p. 361.

[109] Position power is defined as "authority and influence bestowed by a position or office on whoever is filling or occupying it." For millennia, it has been the dominant form of leadership and the exercise of power in virtually all societies and, sadly, in most churches.

[110] Niccolò Machiavelli, the sixteenth-century Italian philosopher and politician argued that fear was the best motivation for the exercise of power: "It is much safer to be feared than loved because . . . love is preserved by the link of obligation which, owing to the baseness of men, is broken at every opportunity for their advantage; but fear preserves you by a dread of punishment which never fails." He also argued for "the employment of cunning and duplicity in statecraft or in general conduct." Political manipulation through scheming duplicity came to be termed *Machiavellian*. See Niccolò Machiavelli, *The Prince*, tr. Luigi Ricci (London, England: Grant Richards, 1903), p. 66. See also Daniel N. Jones and Delroy L. Paulhus, "Machiavellianism" in Mark R. Leary and Rick H. Hoyle, *Handbook of Individual Differences in Social Behavior* (New York: The Guilford Press, 2009), p. 257–273.

[111] Position power is effective in the short term because it can eliminate confusion and provide more intense focus on organizational objectives. In the long term, however, position power is inefficient because those who are being led feel powerless to effect changes that they deem necessary to their own lives.

who really are lazy and do not want to think for themselves, most want to assume responsibility for their own actions and are just waiting for their gifts to be discovered, facilitated, and nurtured by true servant leaders. They are waiting for servant leaders who have truly learned how to bless others by bowing the knee of mutual submission[112] in order to equip the saints for works of ministry.[113]

Solomon gave the paradigm for ministry that is needs driven: "In addition to being a wise man, the Preacher also taught the people knowledge; and he pondered, searched out and arranged many proverbs. The Preacher sought to find just the right words and to write words of truth correctly. The words of wise men are like goads, and masters of these collections are like well-driven nails; they are given by one Shepherd."[114] Solomon's approach to servant leadership was to ensure that he was teaching the people the knowledge and wisdom that would be securely anchored in their hearts and would goad them into proper action. He did this, as Ezra did, first by studying every resource that was at his disposal. Then, he proceeded, not by pontificating, but by "listening,"[115] which is the meaning of the word אָזַן—azen ("give ear," "listen to," "hear") that is usually translated "pondered," "weighed," or "searched out." Part of the "listening" involved considering various apothegms, aphorisms, dicta, and maxims; however, another significant part of Solomon's listening was hearing the hearts of the people and thereby discerning their needs (and not just musing and postulating from an ivory tower). The truly effective servant leader is one who is with the people, listening and responding to their needs.

Next, Solomon "sought to find just the right words" so that he could "write words of truth correctly." The Wise Man was diligent to speak the truth and to speak it in terms that it could be understood and practiced. Then, he used those "right words" not just to impress his hearers with his intellectual prowess but to "goad" them into doing what God wanted them to do. These words were like "firmly embedded nails" that could not be easily extracted and would keep his subjects anchored in divine truth so that they could fulfill his father David's prayer: "One thing I have asked of the LORD, that will I seek after: that I may dwell in the house of the LORD all the days of my life, to gaze upon the beauty of the

---

112 Ephesians 5:21.
113 The principle of bowing the knee in order to bless is powerfully demonstrated in the Hebrew word for "bless," בָּרַךְ —barak, which means both "to kneel" and "to bless." Bowing the knee (בֶּרֶךְ—berek) is the posture and key to blessing (בְּרָכָה—berakah).
114 Ecclesiastes 12:9.
115 This is the translation of the TNK.

LORD and to seek him in his temple."[116] Solomon learned from his father that "those who are planted in the house of the LORD will flourish in the courts of our God."[117] He knew that "goodness and mercy would follow" them all the days of their lives, and that they would "dwell in the house of the LORD forever."[118] The words of wisdom that Solomon established were those that had been given to him by the Shepherd of Israel himself,[119] words which prompted him to reach this conclusion: "Fear God and keep his commandments, for this is what it means to be human."[120]

Time for Restoration

Millions in the church today are certain that something is missing, and they are searching for it. Membership in traditional systems-based institutions dominated by self-serving bureaucracies is declining daily, as thousands become disillusioned and leave organized religion. The people are voting with their feet! The challenge for the believer, however, is not simply to react to perceived evils but to be proactive and apperceptive by returning to the biblical models that were the foundation of the church. Believers must reclaim the Jewish roots of their Christian faith both for doctrine and polity in the body of Messiah. They must restore the "Jesus model" for servant leadership so that once again the church may flourish in true spirituality and godly lifestyles. They must look "unto the rock whence we are hewn,"[121] to the biblical Judaism through which Jesus and the apostles manifest their faith and devotion to God. It is in Hebraic truth that insight will be found that will establish the hearts of believers and open profound vistas for service and blessing to humankind.

While ministers and congregations are searching everywhere for success, often adopting ideas from pop psychology and postmodern philosophy in desperate attempts to find self-actualization, an infallible standard is outlined in the pages of Holy Scripture. This is the Hebraic servant leadership model that Jesus employed and enjoined upon his disciples. This model worked in the first century. No doubt it will work in today's world when the church rediscovers, restores, and reemploys it.

Servanthood: Christian Fruit—Jewish Root!

---

116 Psalm 27:4, NIV.
117 Psalm 92:13, NIV.
118 Psalm 23:6.
119 Psalm 80:1.
120 Ecclesiastes 12:13, ESV.
121 Isaiah 51:1.

CHAPTER 15

WITNESS

As Jesus was preparing to ascend into heaven, he gave his disciples clear and specific instructions: "I am sending the promise of my Father upon you; but you are to stay in the city until you are clothed with power from on high. . . . You will receive power when the Holy Spirit has come upon you; and you shall be my witnesses both in Jerusalem, and in all Judea and Samaria, and even to the remotest part of the earth. . . . Go therefore and make disciples of all the nations, baptizing them in the name of the Father and the Son and the Holy Spirit, teaching them to observe all that I have commanded you."[1]

All believers in Jesus, therefore, have been commissioned by their Lord to be witnesses unto him wherever they may be, even in the most remote corner of the earth. The command to be witnesses to Christ is Christianity's *Mega-Mitzvah*[2] (Great Commission). The community that Jesus established, therefore, was and continues to be a witnessing community. Indeed, bearing witness through the agency of the Holy Spirit to the good news of the atoning death and glorious resurrection of Jesus[3] is the *sine qua non* of the Christian experience. Joe Jones argues masterfully that "the Gospel-called church is, through the Holy Spirit, given a *defining mission of witness in word and deed to the living triune God.* All that is intrinsic to the church being truly the church of Jesus Christ can be understood as implied in this comprehensive mission of witness."[4]

Inherent in the call to Christian discipleship was the dynamic of assuming the easy yoke of the gospel and learning from Jesus[5] with one goal in

---

[1] Luke 24:49; Acts 1:8; Matthew 28:19.
[2] The Hebrew word *mitzvah* means "commandment." The Great Commission, therefore, is Christianity's *Mega-Mitzvah* (Great Commandment).
[3] 1 Corinthians 15:1–4 declares that the gospel is the message of the death and resurrection of Jesus for the sins of the world.
[4] Joe R. Jones, *A Grammar of Christian Faith: Systematic Explorations in Christian Life and Doctrine* (Lanham, MD: Rowman & Littlefield Publishers, 2002), p. 28 (Jones' emphasis).
[5] Matthew 11:29.

mind, that of being witnesses unto him and teaching people in all nations what the Messiah did and what he commanded.[6] Being engaged in spreading the good news of Jesus, therefore, became the creative and uniting force in Christianity. Franz Rosenzweig observed, "Christian faith . . . the bearing witness of the eternal way, is creative in the world; it unites those who bear witness into a union in the world."[7] Shirley Guthrie rightly says that "the confessions of the church . . . have united the Christian community in its one task of bearing witness to the one Christian confession that Jesus is Lord."[8]

From the very beginning of the ministry of Jesus, witness was an essential dynamic of the emerging community and its faith. John the Baptizer set the example of being a witness to Christ and encapsulating the gospel message when he declared, "Behold the Lamb of God who removes the sin of the world."[9] God himself also bore witness to Jesus on two different occasions, on the second of which he commanded the disciples to hear and obey Jesus: "This is my beloved Son with whom I am well-pleased; listen to him!"[10] Additionally, the works that Jesus did in the Father's name also continually bore witness of the fact that he was the Messiah of Israel and the Savior of the world.[11] Jesus ordained twelve apostles to bear witness to the Israelite nation that he was Lord.[12] Then, he commissioned seventy-two others to go before him proclaiming, "The kingdom of God has come near."[13] Later the apostle Paul summarized the bold and unabashed nature of the continuing witness that the disciples of Jesus gave to others concerning the Master when he said, "I am not ashamed of the gospel of Christ, for it is the power of God unto salvation."[14] Witness to God's good news for the nations, then, was a defining part of the *raison d'être* of the Christian faith.

Foundations of Christian Witness

The witness of the gospel was not, however, a totally new dynamic that had never before been seen in the world. Witness was also an intrinsic part

---

[6] Matthew 28:20.

[7] Franz Rosenzweig, *The Star of Redemption* (Madison, WI: The University of Wisconsin Press, 2005), pp. 363–364. Rosenzweig, a non-observant Jew, considered becoming a Christian; however, he determined that before he did, he should become an observant Jew as Jesus and the apostles were. In the process of doing so, he became a *"baal teshuva"* (master of repentance), fully observant of Judaism, and he never followed through with his intention to convert to Christianity.

[8] Shirley G. Guthrie, *Christian Doctrine* (Louisville, KY: Westminster John Knox Press, 1994), p. 24.

[9] John 1:29.

[10] Matthew 3:17; 17:5.

[11] John 5:36; 10:25.

[12] Mark 3:34.

[13] Luke 10:1, 11.

[14] Romans 1:16.

of the faith that God had delivered to the patriarchs and people of Israel. Hayim Perelmuter maintains that "mission is central to Judaism and to its development, and [that] evangelization, in one form or another, has been its technique."[15] Witnessing to the truth and grace of God dates to the time of Noah when God had viewed the human scene and had determined that it was irremediable. When he proposed to destroy all humanity and begin a new creation, however, a profound fact emerged: "Noah found grace in the eyes of the LORD."[16] It seems that tucked away in virtual isolation and anonymity amidst all the evil and debauchery that had overwhelmed the descendants of Adam in that day, one man stood out as a *tzadik*, a righteous perpetuator of the relationship that God had originally designed for humanity. This righteous one had not, however, chosen to practice his faithfulness to God and his Word totally in the privacy of his own family. He was a preacher or herald of righteousness who confronted his age with the inconvenient truth that divine imperatives are not optional but must be obeyed.[17] Despite the preponderance of evil that had come to characterize the inhabitants of planet Earth, Noah was the one consistent voice who stood for the truth as God had delineated it, and he was a witness of that truth to the inhabitants of the earth. This patriarch of biblical faith warned his generation of the impending doom, and he followed God's instruction to build the ark that saved his household and terrestrial animal life.

Generations later, some of the strongest principles of witness were laid down in the life of Abraham. In fact, Jewish tradition recognizes Abraham "not only as the first Jew but as the first missionary" in that "he proclaimed one God (Genesis 13:4) and he brought in converts (Genesis *Rabbah* to Genesis 12:5)."[18] James K. Aitken points out that "all the Palestinian targumic translations of the Pentateuch on Genesis 21:33 present Abraham informing strangers about the God of Israel."[19] Robert Hayward notes that Targum Pseudo-Jonathan is a "reminder to Jewish audiences that Abraham was historically active as a preacher of the universal God."[20] It is said that when Abraham

---

[15] Hayim Goren Perelmuter, "Judaism's Missionary Tradition," in *Introduction to Judaism: Instructor's Guide and Curriculum*, Stephen J. Einstein, Lydia Kukoff, and Hara Person, eds. (Emeryville, CA: UAHC Press, 1999), p. 106.

[16] Genesis 6:8, KJV.

[17] 2 Peter 2:5. The word that Peter used to describe Noah was the Greek κῆρυξ (*kerux*), which means a herald who had been appointed by a sovereign to bear the news and make official announcements.

[18] Perelmuter, p. 106. Also Solomon Schechter, *Aspects of Rabbinic Theology* (New York: Schocken Books, 1961), p. 84.

[19] James K. Aitken, "Jewish Tradition and Culture," in *The Early Christian World*, Philip E. Esler, ed. (New York: Routledge, 2000), p. 93.

[20] Robert Hayward, *Targums and the Transmission of Scripture into Judaism and Christianity* (Leiden, The Netherlands: Koninklijke Brill, 2010), p. 34.

established his tent complex under the oak of Mamre[21] near Hebron, he did so in order to be strategically positioned at a center of travel and commerce and in an area where polytheists often engaged in pagan rites[22] so that he could be a clear and obvious witness to the one God who had revealed himself to him. Abraham and Sarah also kept their tent open on all four sides so that they could welcome any passersby into their family temple where they could receive the Abrahamic witness to monotheism and to the grace, mercy, and blessing of God.[23]

When God engaged Abraham in covenant and blessing, he specifically made the Patriarch this promise: "In you shall all the families of the earth be blessed." What God said was so unequivocal and inviolable that he repeated it twice.[24] The blessing was not just something that would take place centuries or millennia afterward. It was a dynamic that was already in place in Abraham and Sarah's life through the profound example of hospitality that they had established in their archetypal home. Abraham's hospitality and his generosity in sharing both his resources and his divine wisdom and understanding with those who were not included in the covenant became the foundation of what the sages called *hakhnasat orchim* (literally "bringing in of strangers"), the *mitzvah* of showing *gemilut hasadim* ("giving of lovingkindness")[25] by providing hospitality to guests and even to strangers.[26] According to George Peters, the call of Abraham "is the beginning of a divine counterculture designed both to arrest evil and unfold the gracious plan, salvation and purpose of God."[27] It was the amazing spirit of deference that Abraham possessed that empowered him to extend hospitality to everyone who interacted with him and his family. Abraham and Sarah were witnesses to God's grace two millennia before the coming of the Messiah.

Centuries later, God summoned the Israelite descendants of Abraham to Mt. Sinai so that they could be transformed from a family into a nation, a

---

[21] Abraham's tent was actually in a grove of terebinth trees in which the famous "Oak of Abraham" was situated. The "Oak of Abraham" was still known to exist as late as the time of Constantine in the fourth century AD. Henry Warrum, *Some Religious Weft and Warp* (Indianapolis, IN: The Hollenbeck Press, 1915), p. 153.

[22] In the fourth century AD, Constantine's mother discovered that pagan rites were still being celebrated at Mamre. See Charles Odahl, *Constantine and the Christian Empire* (New York: Routledge, 2004), p. 193.

[23] Nancy Fuchs and Nancy H. Wiener, *Judaism for Two: A Spiritual Guide for Strengthening and Celebrating Your Loving Relationship* (Woodstock, VT: Jewish Lights Publishing, 2005), p. 55-56.

[24] Genesis 12:3; 28:14.

[25] Byron L. Sherwin, *Jewish Ethics for the Twenty-First Century: Living in the Image of God* (Syracuse, NY: Syracuse University Press, 2000), p. 135.

[26] Eisenberg, p. 539.

[27] George W. Peters, *A Biblical Theology of Missions* (Chicago, IL: Moody Press, 1972), p. 23.

kingdom of priests.[28] God's nation was not to be an all-conquering military juggernaut. It was to be a servant nation, a kingdom of intercessors who would teach the other nations of the world God's ways.[29] A significant part of God's design was for this servant nation to be a witness to all the other nations of the divine truth that God had revealed to Moses on the mountain.[30] Israel's function was to be "the priesthood of God among the nations to mediate God's revelation, salvation and purpose."[31] Like father Abraham, who was a prophetic intercessor for the blessing of all the families of the earth,[32] they were to be heralds of the divine truth of God's Torah to the nations.

The ideal, then, was for Israel to be God's servant, "who by the power of the Spirit will bring justice to the nations awaiting Torah."[33] Some forty years after God had given the Israelites his Torah at Sinai, he made their responsibility to be his witnessing servant nation very clear to them. Immediately before the people passed through the Jordan River and entered the Promised Land after their sojourn in the wilderness, God renewed the covenant that he had made with their fathers at Sinai. In the process, however, he commanded them to construct a physical demonstration of his intention to bring his Torah to the nations through the Chosen People. "When you have crossed the Jordan into the land the LORD your God is giving you, set up some large stones and coat them with plaster. . . . you shall write on the stones all the words of this very law most distinctly."[34] Joshua fulfilled these divine instructions by erecting pillars at Gilgal, less than a mile from Jericho, on which the words of the Torah were inscribed.[35] A second part of the injunction—that of building a massive altar of uncut stones[36]—was accomplished on Mt.

---

[28] Exodus 19:6.

[29] Mitch Glaser and Zhava Glaser, *The Fall Feasts of Israel* (Chicago, IL: Moody Press, 1987), p. 210.

[30] Walter C. Kaiser, Jr., *Mission in the Old Testament: Israel as a Light to the Nations* (Grand Rapids, MI: Baker Academic, 2000), p. 58. Kaiser notes: "The nation of Israel, as 'servant,' is called to be that light to the nations. This is practically a replication of the promise made through Abraham that 'in you all the families of the earth shall be blessed.'"

[31] Peters, p. 23. Also George R. Hunsberger, *Bearing the Witness of the Spirit: Lesslie Newbigin's Theology of Cultural Plurality* (Grand Rapids, MI: Wm. B. Eerdmans Publishing Co., 1998), p. 97.

[32] A part of Abraham's divine commission was that through him "all the families of the earth" would be blessed (Genesis 12:3). Abraham demonstrated the extent of his prophetic calling to bless *all* the families and nations of the world when he interceded on behalf of Sodom and Gomorrah after God had announced his plans to destroy those evil cities (Genesis 18:23-32).

[33] Waldemar Janzen, "Suffering Servants," quoted in Braden P. Anderson, *Chosen Nation: Scripture, Theopolitics, and the Project of National Identity* (Eugene, OR: Wipf and Stock Publishers, 2012), p. 124.

[34] Deuteronomy 27:2, NIV; 8, NASB.

[35] Michael David Coogan, Marc Zvi Brettler, Carol Ann Newsom, and Pheme Perkins, eds., *The New Oxford Annotated Bible* (New York: Oxford University Press, 2007), p. 228.

[36] Deuteronomy 27:5–7.

Ebal, the tallest mountain in the area near Shechem.[37] It was there that "Joshua wrote on stones a copy of the law of Moses."[38] This, too, was done in order to bear witness to the nations around them of the truth of God's Torah and his system of atonement and blessing.[39]

In having Israel to erect pillars and write upon them "most distinctly" the words of the Torah, God "intended for all the surrounding nations to benefit from the instructions that were given to the Israelites, too. This radically advanced law was to be Israel's wisdom in the sight of the nations that surrounded them."[40] God's requirement that the Israelites erect pillars and inscribe his Torah upon them was not, however, a unique practice in the ancient world. Hammurabi, who was the king of Babylon around the time of Abraham, had his 300 laws, the Code of Hammurabi, inscribed in 3,500 lines of cuneiform characters on a seven-foot-tall basalt stele as a witness to the nations of Babylon's legal system[41] so that all non-Babylonians would know and understand what was required of them in that kingdom.

What was unusual about God's pillars and the Torah inscribed upon them, however, was that the words were written "most distinctly." The sages of Israel—particularly Rashi—have suggested that the term *most distinctly* means that the words of the Torah were written in large letters in the seventy languages[42] of the world's seventy nations.[43] This was done, said the sages, in order to spread Torah among the nations, thereby fulfilling the ultimate purpose for Israel's existence: to be God's "light to the nations," the spiritual center of the world.[44] This was but another demonstration of the time when

---

[37] Joshua 8:30–31.

[38] Joshua 8:32. Some have suggested that a second pillar with the Torah inscribed upon it may have been erected on Mt. Ebal because Shechem thereafter was called "the plain of the pillar," as in Judges 9:6 (KJV). If this were the case, God's intention for his Chosen People to proclaim his law in the sight of the nations in order to establish a witness to them of divine truth could not have been more clear. The Torah was written on pillars in both Gilgal and Shechem. See Samuel M. Jackson, ed., *The New Schaff-Herzog Encyclopedia of Religious Knowledge* (New York: Funk and Wagnalls Co., 1910), p. 295.

[39] Coogan, p. 228. Also Ovadiah Bertinoro, ed., *The Mishnah* (Brooklyn, NY: Mesorah Publications, 1979), p. 117.

[40] Gary Strunk, *As He Is* (Ringgold, GA: Teach Services Publishing, 2012), p. 130.

[41] The stele of Hammurabi is now displayed in the Louvre in Paris. Fred Kleiner, *Gardner's Art through the Ages: The Western Perspective* (Independence, KY: Cengage Learning, 2008), vol. 1, p. 44.

[42] In Jewish tradition, the nations have been numbered at seventy because Genesis 10 lists exactly seventy descendants of Noah's sons Shem, Ham, and Japheth. In the case of each of these three, the Scripture reports that "these are the sons of Japheth [v. 5] . . . of Ham [v. 20] . . . of Shem [v. 31] . . . in their lands, each with his own *language*, by their families, in their *nations*" (emphasis added).

[43] Louis Ginzburg, *The Legends of the Jews*, Henrietta Szold, tr. (Charleston, SD: BiblioBazaar, 2007), vol. 1, p. 108.

[44] Eliezer Schweid, *The Land of Israel: National Home or Land of Destiny* (Cranbury, NJ: Associated University Presses, 1985), p. 56. Many have suggested that when a flat map of the world is drawn, Jerusalem can clearly be seen as the center of the world.

all the nations heard the Ten Commandments in their own languages when God thundered the Torah from Sinai.[45]

And so it was that Israel became God's witness nation. Repeatedly—indeed, incessantly—the Israelites recited the greatest of the Torah Commandments, the *Shema*: "Hear, O Israel, the LORD our God, the LORD is one," and every time those words of Scripture erupted from their hearts and lips, they underscored and bore witness to the bedrock foundation of all biblical faith: the oneness and unity of God. Since that time, millions of Jews around the world have continued the tradition of proclaiming this declaration of monotheistic faith, and countless ones among them have not ceased to lift up these words even when experiencing martyrdom for their faith.

God's continuing plan for Israel to be his nation to bear witness to him as the one and only God was encapsulated in the declaration that he made through the prophet Isaiah, "You are my witnesses . . . my servant whom I have chosen, so that you may know and trust me and understand that I am the One. Before me no God was formed, nor will there be one after me. I, yes I, am the LORD, and apart from me there is no savior. . . . 'You are my witnesses,' says the LORD, 'that I am God.'"[46] According to Isaiah, the heart of Israel's witness to the nations was to be the same as it was in the days of Abraham, the testimony to the divine truth of monotheism: the Lord God is the one and only God. The same prophet was exercised by the Spirit to speak God's commission for Israel to be his witnessing nation: "I, the LORD . . . will make you to be a covenant for the people and a light for the Gentiles."[47]

In fact, whether Israel was faithful or wayward, still that nation was—and remains—*the* witness in the world that YHWH is God alone. In fact, God himself declared this truth to the prophet Malachi, "I am YHWH, I change not; therefore, you children of Jacob are not consumed."[48] Despite multiple and continuing efforts by Gentile despots to effect their genocide, the Jewish people, whether they were righteous or disobedient, have proven and continue to affirm the immutability of God's covenant promises by their very continued existence. The living proof that the God of Scripture is trustworthy is demonstrated by his faithfulness to the covenantal promises

---

[45] The sages taught that when the Ten Commandments were delivered at Sinai, God's words to Israel were divided into seventy languages so that all the nations heard the words of the Torah. Sejin Park, *Pentecost and Sinai: The Festival of Weeks as a Celebration of the Sinai Event* (New York: T & T Clark International, 2008), p. 213. Paul seems to confirm this in Romans 10:18. King David also said that the heavens themselves "declare the glory of God" because "their voice goes out into all the earth" (Psalm 19:1–4).

[46] Isaiah 43:10, 12, ISV, NIV.

[47] Isaiah 42:6, NIV.

[48] Malachi 3:6.

that he made to Israel. Indeed, the continued existence of the Chosen People is the greatest living proof that God exists!

Shortly before the time of Jesus, the Jewish people began to pursue very seriously and in a systematic manner the Isianic commission to be God's witnesses and his means of enlightening the Gentiles. During the time of the sages, the men of the Great Assembly directed their followers to "raise up many disciples."[49] From this instruction, a new mission emerged in Second Temple Judaism: the work of proselytization. Peripatetic Jewish sages traveled far and wide in the known world, expending enormous energy and expense in the effort to convert Gentile idolaters to the faith of Abraham and the teachings of the Torah. This movement began as early as the second century BC and continued well into the fifth century AD.[50] The extreme fervor for proselytization that some of the Jews manifest in the time of Jesus even prompted him to observe, "You travel over land and sea to win a single convert."[51] Though some of their motives and methods may have been questionable, the Pharisees and others who were engaging in the mission of proselytizing were fulfilling the biblical mandate to be witnesses to God and to illuminate the dark Gentile world. As Paul noted, motives and methods for proclamation of the good news may not always be good; however, the important thing is that the gospel is proclaimed.[52]

The Witness of Jesus and the Apostles

It was certainly not an innovative methodology, therefore, when Jesus sent out the twelve apostles and then commissioned seventy-two additional emissaries to bear witness of the breaking forth of God's kingdom among the people of Israel. And when the time came for the Abrahamic and Sinaitic covenants to be expanded and extended to the nations, it was not strange that Jesus gave virtually the same instructions to his disciples that the 120 scribes and sages of the Great Assembly had given to their disciples: "Go and make disciples of the nations."[53] Jesus had laid claim to Isaiah's prophecy as much more than a revelation that Israel was to be God's light to the

---

[49] Mishnah, *Pirkei Avot* 1.1.

[50] Irina Levinskaya, *The Book of Acts in Its First-Century Setting, Vol. 5: Diaspora Setting, Bruce W. Winter,* ed. (Grand Rapids, MI: Wm. B. Eerdmans Publishing Co., 1996), vol. 5, p. 21. Also, Martin Goodman, *Judaism in the Roman World: Collected Essays* (Leiden, The Netherlands: Koninklijke Brill, 2007), pp. 94-96.

[51] Matthew 23:15. This declaration was part of the ongoing intramural debate between Jesus and some of his contemporaries over their misguided actions and their penchant for circumventing Torah teachings to accommodate their own traditions.

[52] Philippians 1:15.

[53] Matthew 28:19.

nations. He said—and it was said of him—that the prophet's words confirmed his Messiahship and his mission in the world.[54] Even at his birth, Zechariah the priest at the temple had predicted that Jesus would be "a light to lighten the Gentiles and the glory of Israel."[55] It should have surprised no one, therefore, when Jesus said to his disciples, "I am the light of the world."[56] In this case, however, as Waldemar Janzen has noted, the task to be God's light to the nations "is not transferred away from Israel to [the Suffering Servant], but rather Israel is *incarnated* in this person who will fulfill its divine mandate. This person will simultaneously restore Israel and accomplish Israel's mission of being a light of the nations."[57] It is clear then that Jesus did not set about to negate God's commission for Israel to be the light of the nations. Instead, he actually personified that mission. Incontrovertibly, Jesus was the light of the world—the glory of Israel and the light of the Gentiles.

In the Sermon on the Mount, Jesus said this to his disciples: "You are the light of the world," thereby assigning to them the responsibility for bringing the light of God's Word, his own Gospel of the Kingdom, to the nations. Later, he instructed them, saying, "You will be my witnesses in Jerusalem, and in all Judea and Samaria, and to the ends of the earth."[58] Finally, when persecution scattered the earliest Jewish followers of Jesus beyond the confines of Jerusalem, the disciples carried the message of the good news with them. Employing the same missionary techniques that their counterparts in traditional Judaism had used, they figuratively—but in some ways quite literally—"turned the world upside down."[59]

It should have come as no surprise, therefore, when Paul claimed Isaiah's prophecy as a validation of his own ministry as the apostle to the nations: "This is what the Lord has commanded us, 'I have placed you as a light for the Gentiles, that you may bring salvation to the end of the earth.'"[60] Jesus had transferred his anointing as the personification of God's light for the world to his disciples so that his reformed and restored Jewish community was gifted to bring Israel's light to the nations. Indeed, the Christian movement succeeded far beyond the capacity of the Jewish nation in taking the faith of Abraham and the truth of the Torah to the nations of the world. This became especially true in the second century AD, when Hadrian crushed the Bar Kokhba revolt and then forbade Jews upon the penalty of death from

---

[54] Luke 4:18.
[55] Luke 2:32.
[56] John 8:12.
[57] Janzen in Anderson, p. 124.
[58] Acts 1:8.
[59] Acts 17:6.
[60] Acts 13:47.

engaging in proselytizing Gentiles to their faith.[61] When the Roman emperor's imperial edict and its ensuing persecution silenced the Jewish witness, the Jews "were forced to forget—our world mission," says Shlomo Riskin. "Thankfully, Christians took up this mission,"[62] he adds.

The Romans forcibly removed the Jewish witness from the stage of history; however, because the church had followed in the footsteps of its other siblings from Second Temple Judaism, the proclamation of the message of monotheism and God's instructions in Torah continued. In fact, it was expanded exponentially and swept across the earth. The genius of Christianity was its inclusiveness, the philosophy in which it could welcome people of all ethnicities into its ranks without many of the restrictive requirements of historical Judaism. Following the ethos of Paul, who maintained that in Christ "there is neither Jew nor Gentile, slave nor free, male nor female,"[63] the church was able to move beyond the exclusivity—and a degree of elitism—that had restricted the Jewish witness. Through the reformed Judaism that Jesus had established, the sound of God's Word went into all the earth,[64] borne by the lips of ever-increasing numbers of Christian witnesses.

Dynamics of Christian Witness

Being Witnesses: The witnessing of early Christianity was focused on witness as a state of being more than as an activity. This was in keeping with what God had said to Israel: "You *are* my witnesses," and on what Jesus had told his disciples, "You *shall be* witnesses unto me." Living faithful and faith-filled lives by following God's instructions in Holy Scripture and by imitating the life of Christ was, in and of itself, a profound witness to the world. When those who came into contact with the newly emerging Christian community observed the believers, they "recognized that they had been with Jesus."[65] These believers were called Christians first at Antioch, not only because they were aggressively bearing witness of their faith but because they also were simply living their lives "like Christ."[66]

Personal Testimony: Because the Jesus community was established on the principle of love for God and love for humanity and on the supreme sacrificial

---

[61] Peter J. Leithart, *Defending Constantine: The Twilight of an Empire and the Dawn of Christendom* (Downers Grove, IL: InterVarsity Press, 2010), p. 132.

[62] Shlomo Riskin, "In Defense of Religious Pluralism and Ethical Absolutism," in *Covenant and Hope: Christian and Jewish Reflections*, Robert W. Jenson and Eugene B. Korn, eds. (Grand Rapids, MI: Wm. B. Eerdmans Publishing Co., 2012), p. 127.

[63] Galatians 3:28. This declaration has been called the Magna Carta of Christian faith.

[64] Psalm 19:4.

[65] Acts 4:13, ESV.

[66] Acts 11:26.

love of Jesus in giving his life for the salvation of the world, Christian faith was most effectively communicated to others by means of personal testimony. This was the case even with Paul, who, when he was asked to answer for his faith, simply reverted to his "Damascus Road" testimony.[67] Instead of giving an in-depth discourse on soteriology, he related the event in which the living Jesus dramatically appeared to him and gave him this commission: "I have appeared to you to appoint you as a servant and as a witness of what you have seen and will see of me."[68] And the apostle repeated this same personal testimony over and over again.

Person-to-Person Witness: Face-to-face, person-to-person interaction has always been the most effective way of communicating the love for God and man that both Judaism and Christianity demonstrate. Perhaps this is why Rosenzweig identified the essential nature of Christian witness as being an action of individual to individual, noting that the witness of Christian faith "unites [believers] as individuals; for bearing witness is always a matter of individuals. And besides the individual here is supposed to bear witness about his position in relation to an individual; for the testimony refers to Christ; Christ is the mutual content of all the testimonies of faith."[69] Jesus called all of his disciples personally, and he dealt with them as individuals before he related to them as a newly united faith community. The followers of Jesus continued to employ the same strategy and techniques that Jesus used. Because Christianity became a community where the salvation of the individual was emphasized along with the corporate salvation of the community, it was able to break out from ethnically defined and constrained faith and to appeal to all races and ethnicities, incorporating them readily into its ranks.[70] This, too, facilitated the rapid expansion of the faith of Abraham into circles into which it had not extensively penetrated for some two millennia.

The Power of the Holy Spirit: Christian witness has always been most effective when it has been exercised through the power of the Holy Spirit. This is the power that Jesus said would come upon the 120 believers in the Upper Room "when the Holy Spirit has come upon you."[71] It was the indwelling Holy Spirit that transformed the mercurial and undependable Simon Bar-Jonah, a reed blowing in the wind, into Peter, the rock-solid anchor of stability for the earliest

---

[67] Acts 22:6–16; 26:12–18.
[68] Acts 26:16, NIV.
[69] Rosenzweig, p. 363.
[70] Christianity's emphasis on individual salvation over corporate salvation often had a downside when it was taken to extremes that minimized the importance of the family and community nature of the faith. This approach often resulted in a fragmented, even fratricidal Christianity that was unable to provide the strength and protection that Hebraic societies maintained.
[71] Acts 1:8.

community of faith.[72] The Holy Spirit empowers ordinary people to do extraordinary things, including making a powerful witness to the gospel. Bearing witness through the power of the Spirit was the methodology that Paul employed. "I did not come with eloquence or human wisdom as I proclaimed to you the testimony about God. . . . My message and my preaching were not with wise and persuasive words, but with a demonstration of the Spirit's power,"[73] the apostle said. Paul's sole motivation for using this strategy in his witnessing efforts was "so that your faith might not rest on human wisdom, but on God's power."[74] When the gospel is witnessed by the dynamic Spirit, it penetrates the hearts of the hearers and not just their minds. It is not anchored in philosophical ideas; it rests securely on the spiritual experience of God's power.

Two Witnessing Communities

Witness to the God of Scripture has continued through the centuries by two witnessing communities, Rabbinic Judaism and Christianity, the faith siblings born from the matrix of biblical and Second Temple Judaism. Jacques Doukhan describes this unique relationship between Israel and the church in this manner: "[B]oth peoples, the church and Israel, were needed as God's people, but not in the sense that God contracted two different and parallel covenants. . . . And also not in the sense that God contracted two successive covenants . . . For God's initial plan was, indeed, to have only 'one people' to witness to Him."[75] Christianity has never replaced Judaism as a viable part of God's testimony to the world. It has simply come alongside the Jewish community as naturalized spiritual citizens of the commonwealth of Israel to share in the task of taking the light of the written and living Torah to the nations of the world. In doing so, it has aggressively fulfilled the mission that God assigned to Israel, a mission that was taken up by Jesus as Messiah and Savior of the world and then assigned to his disciples as "the light of the world."

By its very continued existence and viability, Israel remains a witness to God's sovereignty and covenant faithfulness.[76] Paul Van Buren said it well:

---

[72] Randy McKean and Kay S. McKean, *The Mission: Powerful Readings Focused on the Mission Jesus Christ Has Given to Every Disciple* (Billerica, MA: Discipleship Publications International, 1994), p. 76.

[73] 1 Corinthians 2:1, 4.

[74] 1 Corinthians 2:5.

[75] Jacques B. Doukhan, *The Mystery of Israel* (Hagerstown, MD: Review and Herald Publishing Association, 2004), p. 75. For a superb extended discussion of the unique relationship between Israel and the church, see also Jacques B. Doukhan, *Israel and the Church: Two Voices for the Same God* (Peabody, MA: Hendrickson Publishers, 2002)

[76] K. Hannah Holtschneider, *German Protestants Remember the Holocaust: Theology and the Construction* (Münster, Germany: Lit Verlag, 2001), p. 119. Holtschneider says, "The attempt to wipe out Jewish life on earth meant an attempt to deny the reality of G-d, because Jews are the prime witnesses to G-d's reality. Assaulting G-d's witnesses ultimately means denying the possibility of Christian faith."

"Israel serves the world primarily by being itself, that is, by being faithful to its own particular calling to live according to God's Torah and not according to the ways of the world."[77] Israel's witness to the nations, therefore, has been more a state of being than an activity. Indeed, the affirmation of the God of Scripture is inseparable from the Jewish soul. The witness of the *Shema*, "Hear, O Israel, the LORD our God, the LORD is one," has been liturgically exclaimed daily in Jewish life for more than three millennia. It is also a living witness that is demonstrated through faithfulness to the instructions that God gave his people in the Torah. It is the witness of a walk of faith that is fulfilled in obedience to divine imperatives.[78] The testimony of the *Shema* has also echoed in final words of countless Jews as they sanctified God's name in martyrdom rather than renounce their faith.

The followers of the Jewish Jesus continued in this same dynamic of witness. They were directed to proclaim the good news of God's dominion, the Gospel of God.[79] In continuity with their co-religionists, the Jews, they were instructed to make many disciples of all nations. What Israel had been instructed in the renewal of the covenant at the time of their entrance into the Promised Land—to write the words of the Torah *most distinctly*—the followers of Jesus accomplished by proclaiming the truth of the living Torah *most distinctly* to the nations.[80] Christians were instructed by Jesus to witness to their faith and its authenticity by a lifestyle of discipleship. They were responsible for responding to those who asked of them reasons for their hope by sharing their faith with "gentleness and reverence."[81] They were to stand alongside the Jewish people as living witnesses to the world about the sovereignty of God and about his blessing for all humanity.[82] This witness was a demonstration of what human beings can be and what they can do when they are called and empowered by God to be instruments of his *shalom* in the earth.

Witnessing Until the End

The witness of both the Jewish and Christian communities will continue until the end of the age, at which time it will be fully vindicated and validated

---

77 Paul M. Van Buren, *A Theology of the Jewish-Christian Reality: Part 2, A Christian Theology of the People of Israel* (Lanham, MD: The University Press of America, 1995), p. 206.
78 James 2:2–24.
79 1 Thessalonians 2:2. The Gospel of Jesus Christ is inherently the Gospel of God, for it is the good news that God's dominion has come and is breaking forth in the lives of individuals and in the life of the world through faith in the death and resurrection of Jesus and by the power of the Holy Spirit.
80 Deuteronomy 27:8.
81 1 Peter 3:15.
82 Van Buren, p. 206. Van Buren says, "[T]he church has been called to serve the world alongside of Israel in its service to the world."

by the coming of the Messiah. Though scoffers have always been present to question the legitimacy of the witness,[83] in the end, the Messiah will come.[84] To the shock and dismay of the entire world, a new dominion will be established that will rule over all the earth.[85] The Messiah will then fulfill God's oath to David that of the fruit of his loins according to the flesh, he would raise up the Messiah to sit on his throne.[86] God himself will be sovereign on Planet Earth. The throne that will be set in place will be that of the Ancient of Days[87] and of the Lamb.[88] The gospel of God will have been fulfilled. The witness to divine truth will have been vindicated. The kingdom will be given to the saints of the Most High God.[89] Everlasting peace will ensue on the planet where universal conflict and bloodshed have reigned since time immemorial.

Ultimately, all witness to the God of Scripture, therefore, is eschatological in nature: it points to the great denouement of the ages when the Prince of Peace will establish the universal dominion of God and will bring to completion the ongoing proclamation of the good news that was inaugurated in Abraham, expanded at Sinai, and completed at Calvary. Christian witness was and is, in the words of Henning Reventlow, a "consequence, unrenounceable and biblical, of Jewish and early Christian hope in the final establishment of God's power. In early Christian faith, this hope was chiefly founded in and kindled by the witnessing of Christ's resurrection by the experience of the living and beneficial presence of the exalted one."[90] The witness of both Jew and Christian to the one God and to the everlasting truth of his Word will be fulfilled in that day when the "LORD . . . will stand on the Mount of Olives" and "the LORD will be king over the whole earth." Of a truth, "on that day there will be one LORD, and his name the only name."[91] The righteous of all generations and nations will stand with the Messiah on Mount Zion, and "all the nations . . . will go up year after year to worship the King, the LORD Almighty, and to celebrate the Festival of Tabernacles."[92] The witness of Israel and the church will have been completed, and the Messiah of both will reign over all!

Witness: Christian Fruit—Jewish Root.

---

83 2 Peter 3:3.
84 Revelation 22:12.
85 Revelation 22:5.
86 Acts 2:30.
87 Daniel 7:9.
88 Revelation 22:3.
89 Daniel 7:18, 27.
90 Henning Graf Reventlow, *Eschatology in the Bible and in Jewish and Christian Tradition* (Sheffield, UK: Sheffield Academic Press, 1997), pp. 39–40.
91 Zechariah 14:4, 9, 16.
92 Zechariah 14:16.

CHAPTER 16

ELECTION

Is God a universalist or a particularist? Does the Eternal relate in some way to every human being, or does he relate only to a particular people? Does God's universal sovereignty preclude the possibility of his participation in a particularist engagement? Indeed, has there ever been such a thing as a "Chosen People"? The answer to these questions is quite simple: God is both a universalist and a particularist.[1] God does relate universally to every human being; however, he is also related uniquely to a particular people, and that particular people has been chosen by God to be the agent of his universal plans to bring his dominion of justice and *shalom* to the entire human race. Brian McClaren has succinctly summarized this truth thus: "[T]he way God brings salvation to others is by giving it to some, recruiting them as agents of salvation to others. So he blesses the whole world by blessing one nation" when that nation becomes his emissary in the world.[2]

---

[1] This kind of answer is completely in context with Hebraic thinking, which is able to hold in dynamic tension seemingly polarized issues so that both can be seen as truth. See Marvin R. Wilson, *Exploring*, p. 5. In contrast, Aristotelian logic forced Greek thinking—and Christian theologies developed in the context of Greek thought—to postulate that there can only be one truth and that all other ideas that appear to be opposed to or in contradiction to that "one truth" must be destroyed. Richard Lim notes that the acceptance of controlled dissensus in the earliest church was gradually replaced by the Greek and Roman notion of simplicity which insisted that there could be only one truth and that dissensus had to be controlled through *homonoia*—a social idea that insisted on agreement with an utter lack of disputation. See Richard Lim, *Public Disputation, Power, and Social Order in Late Antiquity* (Berkeley, CA: The University of California Press, 1994), p. 20. Lim also observes that at the time at which the church crystallized into hierarchical structures, it sought to "domesticate the perceived threat of dissensus" by mobilizing "hierarchical forms of authority against a culture that validated individualistic claims and rational argumentation." At that same time, says Daniel Boyarin, rabbinic Judaism was moving away from the amoraic dialectic that led to conclusions on normative law as demonstrated in the Jerusalem Talmud to the rejection of the desire for "certain knowledge" which characterized the Babylonian Talmud. See Boyarin, *Border Lines*, pp. 151–153. Much later, Thomas Aquinas even maintained that philosophy (scientific inquiry) and theology had to be reconciled into "one truth" on the basis of this same argument that "there can be only one truth." See Ted Byfield, *The Christians: Their First Two Thousand Years; A Glorious Disaster: A.D. 1100 to 1300: The Crusades: Blood, Valor, Iniquity, Reason, Faith* (Edmonton, Canada: Society to Explore and Record Christian History, 2003), vol. 7, p. 199.

[2] Brian D. McLaren, *A New Kind of Christian: A Tale of Two Friends on a Spiritual Journey* (San Francisco, CA: John Wiley & Sons, 2001), p. 230.

When Jesus, therefore, said to his Jewish disciples, "You did not *choose* me, but I chose you, and appointed you that you should go and bear fruit,"[3] he was not introducing a completely new concept of divine election that had never been considered before. Likewise, Paul was not creating a new theology when he declared, "But we should always give thanks to God for you, brethren beloved by the Lord, because God has *chosen* you from the beginning for salvation through sanctification by the Spirit and faith in the truth."[4] Similarly, Peter did not invent a novel religious idea when he said of the Gentiles who had come to faith in Jesus, "But you are a *chosen* race, a royal priesthood, a holy nation, God's own special people, so that you may proclaim the excellencies of him who has called you out of darkness into his marvelous light."[5]

Indeed, the concept of election—of being particularly chosen by God from among the diverse peoples of the world to be ordained unto a life of faith and obedience to divine imperatives—was nothing new when it was used by Jesus and the apostles to describe the work that God was doing in calling out a remnant from among the Israelites and later from among the Gentiles to be uniquely his people, ordained to fulfill his purposes in the earth. In fact, the idea of being chosen by God predated Christian thought by at least two millennia.

The Universality of God

It is an undeniable fact that God is connected to all human beings. Paul reported this truth succinctly and unequivocally: "We are [all] God's offspring."[6] The apostle was merely speaking in context with the Psalmist's declaration: "The earth is the LORD's and all it contains; the world and those who dwell in it."[7] Since God is the creator of everything that exists in the universe, he is the Lord of creation, and everything in the universe belongs to him. This is especially true of humanity, for the human race was specifically

---

[3] John 15:16, emphasis added.

[4] 2 Thessalonians 2:13, emphasis added.

[5] 1 Peter 2:9, NASB, NKJV, emphasis added. The New King James Version captures the essence of the Greek phrase, λαὸς εἰς περιποίησιν (*laos eis peripoiesin*), "a people of his own possession."

[6] Acts 17:28. Paul said, "For in him we live and move and exist, as even some of your own poets have said, 'For we also are his children.' Therefore since we are God's offspring, we should not think that the divine being is like gold or silver or stone—an image made by human design and skill." It is interesting that Paul was broadminded enough to be able to quote from the Greek poet Aratus to add support for his contention that human beings are God's offspring. The apostle commended truth wherever he found it! See Donald Campbell, Wendell Johnston, John F. Walvoord, and John A. Witmer, *Theological Wordbook: The 200 Most Important Theological Terms and Their Relevance for Today* (Nashville, TN: Thomas Nelson, 2000), p. 54.

[7] Psalm 24:1. This psalm is quoted in 1 Corinthians 10:26: "The earth is the LORD's, and all it contains."

created for the purpose of bearing the image and likeness of God. In this sense, human beings—all of them—are theomorphic, that is, they image the God who created them, and they reveal something about him.[8] In fact, Paul declared that "the invisible attributes of God, namely, his eternal power and divine nature, have been clearly perceived . . . in the things that have been made."[9] And there is nothing in the creation that could reveal truth about God's nature more clearly than the humans whom he said were created in his image and likeness.

Perhaps this is why Paul asserted the universal impact of the Torah upon all human beings when he declared that the "Gentiles who do not have the Torah do instinctively the things in the Torah" because they "are a law to themselves" and "they demonstrate that the requirements of the Torah are written on their hearts, a fact to which their own consciences testify, while their reasoning rebukes or defends them."[10] The question is, When was the Torah written on the hearts of all nations? The answer is simple: it occurred when God breathed his divine breath into the nostrils of the first human that he had formed from the dust of the earth and in that process vivified humanity.[11] Whenever God breathes, inherent in the divine breath is the impartation of the Word of God, for all Scripture is God-breathed.[12] Hence, all human beings have a deposit of God's Word inherent in the very breath of life that they continually breathe. The foundational declarations of divine instructions have always been impressed by God upon the very fiber of human existence. This is why "God is now declaring to all people everywhere to repent,"[13] for "the grace of God has appeared that offers salvation to all people."[14] God's eternal plan has always been to provide the means for the reconciliation of the entire human race to himself, thereby fulfilling his universality.

The Particularity of God

The universality of God was the reason for which God sovereignly engaged in particularity, choosing one man, one family, and one nation to serve the interest of bringing divine revelation to the whole of humanity. Richard Bauckham rightfully concludes that "Jewish monotheism is characterized by

---

[8] The manifestation of the image and likeness of God in all human beings of all time is clearly established in the words of this divine command that was given in the time of Noah: "Whoever sheds human blood, by humans shall their blood be shed; for in the image of God has God made mankind" (Genesis 9:6, NIV).
[9] Romans 1:20, ESV.
[10] Romans 2:14–15, author's translation based on ESV, NASB, NIV, ISV, AND ABPE.
[11] Genesis 3:7.
[12] 2 Timothy 3:16, NIV.
[13] Acts 17:30.
[14] Titus 2:11.

its way of relating YHWH's particularity as Israel's God to his universality as Creator and sovereign Lord of all."[15] Gabriel Fackre is right when he says that "the particular bonding with Israel does not preclude the covenant of the Creator with all humankind before and concurrent with the Abrahamic-Mosaic stream."[16] The dynamics of the way in which divine particularity serves divine universality was very well encapsulated by Fackre when he concluded that "the gift to and claim upon Israel are related to Israel's role as that of a 'light to the Gentiles,' a particularity within the universality of the divine working."[17] G. C. Berkhower has summarized this understanding by demonstrating that divine revelation in Scripture serves the purpose of illuminating "the relations between the universality and particularity of the divine activity" so that *"its taking place is historically limited"* and "cannot, and may not, be *generalized.*"[18] Though postmodern philosophers and theologians may question the particularity of God with questions like "How could God even dare choose only one?" or with acerbic epigrams like British journalist William Ewer's "How odd of God/To choose the Jews!"[19]), the fact remains that God did uniquely and exclusively choose one man, one family, one nation.

The biblical concept of election is founded in the sovereignty of God; however, as Reuen Thomas has wisely observed, "election . . . does not refer to personal salvation. . . . It refers to a service, to a purpose, to a mission."[20] It is God who has always sought a collective people who would accomplish his purposes and for individuals with whom he could have relationship. Jesus, himself, established this truth: "But the hour is coming, and now is, when the true worshipers will worship the Father in spirit and truth; for the

---

[15] Richard Bauckham, *Jesus and the God of Israel: God Crucified and Other Essays on the New Testament's Christology of Divine Identity* (Crownhill, UK: Authentic Media, 2008), p. 84.

[16] Gabriel Fackre, *The Christian Story: Authority: Scripture in the Church for the World* (Grand Rapids, MI: Wm. B. Eerdmans Publishing Co., 1987), p. 202.

[17] Fackre, p. 202.

[18] G. C. Berkhower, *General Revelation: Studies in Dogmatics* (Grand Rapids, MI: Wm. B. Eerdmans Publishing Co., 1955), p. 310, Berkhower's emphasis.

[19] This epigram was likely a witty expression of British gentility's covert Antisemitism. Perhaps the most appropriate reply to Ewer's epigram was that made by Ogden Nash, "It wasn't odd; the Jews chose God!"

[20] Reuen Thomas, *Divine Sovereignty* (Boston, MA: D. Lothrop & Company, 1885), p. 174. Paul made this clear in Romans 8:29 when he said that "the *ones* [God] foreknew, he also did predestinate to be conformed to the image of his Son" (emphasis added). The word which is translated "predestinate," προορίζω (*proorízo*), is found only twice in Scripture (Romans 8:29; Ephesians 1:5). In both cases, the emphasis is on the collective ("the *ones,*" [pl.]), not the individual. It is the plans, purposes, programs, and works of God that are predetermined, foreordained, or predestinated. Individuals choose of their own free will which role they will fulfill in God's predestined plans. This understanding is settled in Hebraic thought wherein it is understood that human beings were granted individual sovereignty of the power of choice simply by God's decision to limit his own universal sovereignty in order to accommodate for human free will. This follows from the fact that if God is sovereign over all, he is also sovereign over his own sovereignty and can limit his sovereignty when and to whatever degree he sovereignly wills.

Father is *seeking such* to worship him,"[21] but he anchored it on the declaration of Ezekiel: "[God] searched for a man among them who would build up the wall and stand in the gap before me for the land."[22] The God of Scripture, therefore, is a relational being who constantly searches for human beings whom he can engage to fulfill his purposes and share his love by worshiping him in spiritual truth. As Abraham Heschel has said, history is not a record of man's search for God but of God's search for man.[23] Unfortunately, historical Christian thought has largely replaced the idea of God's search for man with man's search for God. William Hordern had it right when he argued that such thought distorted the clear purposes of God in salvation history: "Thus the uniqueness of the biblical religion, with God's search for man, was lost, and the Bible was seen as an interesting page in the ongoing search of man for God."[24] Heschel drew the only reasonable conclusion about Israel's divine election when he said, "There is no concept of a chosen God but there is the idea of a chosen people. . . . We have not chosen God; He has chosen us."[25] It was in the context of this principle that Jesus said to his disciples, "You did not choose me, but I chose you and appointed you."[26]

This fundamental truth establishes the fact that history is linear and covenantal.[27] Salvation history started somewhere (with creation) and has proceeded rectilinearly toward an end (with the Messianic Age),[28] and it is based on God's sovereign covenantal election of a people to be uniquely his. God's particularity, therefore, is established in the covenant that he initiated in electing a Chosen People. The first time that YHWH, the Eternal God, entered into a covenant with anyone occurred when he chose Abraham because of the patriarch's implicit faith in his Word. And when God chose Abraham, the covenant that he made with him was unilateral, unconditional,

---

21 John 4:23.

22 Ezekiel 22:30.

23 Heschel, *God in Search*, p. 425.

24 William Hordern, *The Case for a New Reformation Theology* (London, UK: Westminster Press, 1959), quoted in Barry L. Callen, *Discerning the Divine: God in Christian Theology* (Louisville, KY: Westminster John Knox Press, 2004), p. 39.

25 Heschel, *God in Search*, p. 425.

26 John 15:16.

27 In contrast, Greek philosophy and various monist religions view history as being cyclical (endlessly repeating itself) and causal (with one event precipitating another *ad infinitum*).

28 Hans Ucko, *The People and the People of God: Minjung and Dalit Theology in Interaction* (Hamburg, Germany: Lit Verlag Münster, 2002), p. 18. Ucko says, "Salvation history is linear and begins in the dawn of creation and ends with the end of history. A particular geography is chosen for God's action in history that seems to eclipse God's dealings with people throughout time and places. For salvation history the people Israel is called to be the very people of salvation history." Jacob Neusner says, "Cyclical thinking is . . . alien to sages . . . because it presupposes an eternal return, an endless recapitulation of the pattern." Jacob Neusner, *Rabbinic Judaism: The Theological System* (Boston, MA: Brill Academic Publishers, 2002), p. 247.

and eternal, initiated entirely by God and based solely on God's faithfulness, not Abraham's performance.[29] Mal Couch encapsulates this truth well: "The Abrahamic covenant is a unilateral covenant, a divine covenant in which God alone pledges Himself to a course of action through Abraham and his seed, which cannot be reversed (else God would prove untrue) and cannot be annulled by the failure either of Abraham or his seed, for the existence and continuance of the covenant depends not upon the fidelity of Abraham or his seed, but on God alone."[30]

When Abraham inquired of God, "How shall I know that I will inherit [*this* land]?"[31] God instructed him to make a sacrifice, after which he spoke to him in this manner: "To your descendants have I given this land, from the river of Egypt to the great river, the River Euphrates . . ."[32] Then, the narrative continued: "On the same day the LORD made a covenant with Abram." Abraham, therefore, was the first man with whom God entered into a covenant in which he promised that he would forever maintain a special relationship with him and his descendants. "The LORD appeared to Abram and said to him . . . 'I will establish my covenant between me and you and your descendants after you in their generations, for an *everlasting* covenant, to be God to you and your descendants after you. Also, I give to you and your descendants after you the land in which you are a stranger, all the land of Canaan, as an everlasting possession; and I will be their God.'"[33]

The land contract that was an intrinsic part of the Abrahamic covenant focused God's particular attention and focus upon one geographical space. The land from the Wadi of Egypt to the River Euphrates was singled out specifically as the physical place that God would assign to Abraham and his descendants—again, "forever." It was as though God were choosing a set-apart land mass in which to establish his capital city, the place where he would place his name.[34] This real estate would be the canvas on which

---

[29] Genesis 15:17. The unilateral nature of the Abrahamic covenant was demonstrated in the fact that when God instructed Abraham to take the animals that would confirm the covenant, cut them in half, and lay them out in two rows on the ground, only God passed between the pieces of the sacrifice (Genesis 15:17, 20). The fact that Abraham did not pass between the pieces of the sacrifice meant that the covenant and its continuance were dependent solely upon God's faithfulness and not on Abraham's performance.

[30] Mal Couch, ed., *Dictionary of Premillennial Theology: A Practical Guide to the People, Viewpoints, and History of Prophetic Studies* (Grand Rapids, MI: Kregel Publications, 1996), p. 27. Also, Terence E. Fretheim, *Abraham: Trials of Family and Faith* (Columbia, SC: The University of South Carolina Press, 2007), p. 38.

[31] Genesis 15:8.

[32] Genesis 15:18.

[33] Genesis 17:1, 7–8.

[34] 1 Kings 11:36; Ezra 6:12. Some have suggested that God literally stamped his name in the topography of the city of Jerusalem because the three valleys (Kidron, Hinnom, and Tyropoeon) that circumscribe and intersect the city between its three mountains (Ophel, Zion, and Moriah) form the Hebrew letter ש (*shin*), which is the first letter of God's name *Shaddai* and the universally recognized Jewish symbol for that name.

he would paint the mural of his dealings with humanity from Abraham's day until the day of the Messiah. According to the land conveyance in the Abrahamic covenant, God is also as much a particularist when it comes to geography as he is when it comes to people. Just as he uses one people to bless all people, so he uses one land to demonstrate his plans for the entire earth.

The divine agreement between God and Abraham brought about a startling transformation. Abraham, who was a Babylonian by birth and a Syrian by nationality,[35] became the father of another nation, the nation of faith in the Eternal God. As far as God was concerned, Abraham was transformed from a Gentile into a chosen vessel to father a holy nation that would bear his name among the Gentiles. From the time that Abraham had crossed over the river Euphrates, he had been called a "Hebrew."[36] His leaving the land of Ur of the Chaldees and later departing from his father's house in Haran of Syria constituted the acts of faith that prompted God to extend his promise and covenant to Abraham. So, after the making of the covenant, Abraham became more than a Hebrew—he became the father of all the faithful who would ever live.[37]

Just as God had promised Abraham, it was over four centuries before the benefits of his covenant became reality.[38] Through those ensuing years, Abraham's progeny through his promised son Isaac were God's Chosen People because of the Abrahamic covenant. While seventy souls entered into the land of Egypt during the time of the famine,[39] over four centuries later six hundred thousand men, together with women and children,[40] were ready to be delivered from the slavery into which they had been forced by Pharaoh.

The Purpose for Divine Election

God's particularity in electing Abraham and his linear descendants to be his "Chosen People" was designed to achieve a greater purpose than restricting

---

[35] Genesis 11:31. Interestingly, Abraham's descendants continued to be known as Syrians long after the time of his grandson Jacob and his great-grandson Joseph. God even instructed the post-Sinai Israelites to give this account of their patrimony: "My father was a Syrian, about to perish, and he went down to Egypt and sojourned there, few in number; and there he became a nation, great, mighty, and populous" (Deuteronomy 26:5).

[36] In Hebrew, the word עִבְרִי—ivri ("Hebrew") is from עֵבֶר (eber), which means "beyond" or "across" and hence, "from the other side," but it is more particularly from the verbal stem עָבַר (avar), which means "to pass over." The term eber can also be traced to Eber, one of the descendants of Shem (Genesis 10:21). Since Abraham was the first "chosen" vessel of God, he was in a sense the "first Jew."

[37] Romans 4:16 says, "The promise comes by faith, so that it may be by grace and may be guaranteed to all Abraham's offspring—not only to those who are of the law but all those who have the faith of Abraham, who is the father of us all" (NIV, ESV).

[38] Genesis 15:13.

[39] Genesis 46:27.

[40] Exodus 12:37.

himself to being a mere tribal deity. The Almighty did not choose Abraham in order to establish a super race of human beings or demigods who would have exclusive access to him to the exclusion of all other people. In fact, God chose Abraham in order to produce through him a servant nation which he could use in order to effect his greater design, the work of bringing salvation and redemption to the entire human race and fully restoring what had been lost in the rebellion of Adam and Eve, the corporate heads of the human race, in the Garden Eden. The plan of God had been devised before all creation, and God was merely enlisting agents to fulfill that plan by redeeming unto himself a people for his name.[41]

God made this clear when he issued this profound promise to Abraham: "I will bless those who bless you, and the one who curses you I will curse. And in you all the families of the earth will be blessed."[42] In another instance of promise, God covenanted with Abraham that "through your offspring all nations on earth will be blessed, because you have obeyed me."[43] God's act of choosing Abraham and his descendants after him, therefore, had much larger implications than the divine election of one family: it was designed to impact all of humanity with the blessing that God would pour upon the patriarch's descendants. In the progeny of Abraham, God would create a servant nation that would extend the insight and understanding of his divine Word and the blessing of his eternal purposes to all the "families of the earth."[44]

Divine particularity, therefore, was designed to serve the purpose of divine universality. Aaron Hughes wisely and succinctly maintains that "Judaism is universally relevant precisely on account of its particularity," for "in its singularity, the universal is both encountered and sustained."[45] Emmanuel Levinas is correct when he argues that "Jewish universalism has always revealed itself in its particularism," so that "Jews—because of and not despite of their religious particularity—provide a lesson for all."[46] The vision of God's universality would never have been fulfilled in the earth if it were not for his particularity, his sovereign choice of a particular people

---

[41] Revelation 13:8; 1 Peter 1:20; Ephesians 1:4.

[42] Genesis 12:3.

[43] Genesis 22:18, NIV.

[44] Norbert Lohfink, *The God of Israel and the Nations: Studies in Isaiah and the Psalms* (Collegeville, MN: Liturgical Press, 2000), p. 49. Also, H. Wayne House, *Israel: The Land and the People–An Evangelical Affirmation of God's Promises* (Grand Rapids, MI: Kregel Academic, 1998), p. 270.

[45] Aaron W. Hughes, *Rethinking Jewish Philosophy: Beyond Particularism and Universalism* (New York: Oxford University Press, 2014), p. 46.

[46] Emmanuel Levinas, "Jewish Thought Today," in *Difficult Freedom: Essays on Judaism*, tr. Seán Hand (Baltimore, MD: Johns Hopkins University Press, 1997), p. 164, quoted in Hughes, p. 46.

to facilitate his plan for all humanity. Consequently, "it is Judaism's particularity that 'conditions universality.'"[47]

Israel, a Covenant Nation

A profound miracle was effected by God's intervention through the hand of his servant Moses to deliver Abraham's descendants from Egyptian bondage. Events were set in motion that would further reify God's particularity and serve the unfolding of his universal vision for humanity. The children of Abraham through Isaac and Jacob passed through the Red Sea and gathered before the great mountain of the Lord called Sinai to make a covenant with God that would transform them into his holy nation,[48] a people chosen above all the rest of earth's inhabitants.[49] When this covenant was made, however, it merely supplemented and expanded the covenant that God had made with Abraham more than four centuries earlier, for it could never replace or abrogate that covenant: "The law, which was four hundred and thirty years later, cannot annul the [Abrahamic] covenant that was confirmed before by God in Christ, that it should make the promise of no effect."[50]

Speaking expressly and shockingly in thunderous tones, God delivered the Ten Commandments to the Israelites as they stood in fear and awe before Sinai.[51] Both Israel and the entire world heard the proclamation of God's commandments that day.[52] Israel, however, responded affirmatively to God's invitation, saying, "All that you have said we will do, and we will hear."[53] Israel had such faith in God's Word that they agreed to do his commandments before they understood (heard) them! So, God chose all of Israel as his nation and established his covenant with them; however, the Word of God declares that at precisely that same time he made further

---

[47] Hughes, p. 46, referencing Emmanuel Levinas, *In the Time of the Nations*, tr. Michael B. Smith (Bloomington, IN: The Indiana University Press, 1994), pp. 3–4.

[48] Deuteronomy 10:15. Sol Scharfstein, *The Five Books of Moses* (Jersey City, NJ: KTAV Publishing House, 2005), p. 172.

[49] Charles Leslie, *A Short and Easy Method with the Jews, Wherein the Certainty of the Christian Religion Is Demonstrated* (Spitalfields, England: 1812), p. 123. Leslie said, "Thus a nation or people taken into federal covenant with God, more peculiarly than any other nation upon the earth, may be called blessed above all the nations of the earth: and an holy people, in respect of the holiness of their laws, covenant, promises, &c. given to them by God."

[50] Galatians 3:17.

[51] Exodus 19:16.

[52] Exodus 19:18–19; Psalm 68:8; Hebrews 12:26.

[53] Exodus 24:7. This passage is translated, "We will do everything the LORD has said; we will obey"; however, the text actually says, "We will do everything the LORD has said; and we will hear (וְנִשְׁמָע— *v'nishma*')." Since the Hebrew word שְׁמַע (*shema*), which usually means "to hear" can also mean "to understand," the sages have interpreted this text to mean that the Israelites agreed to observe God's instructions even before they understood them. God's Word is often ineffable: in order to *understand* it, one must *do* it.

selection and designated a part of Israel to have an even more particularist relationship with him. "[God] rejected the clan of Joseph; and the tribe of Ephraim he did not choose. But he chose the tribe of Judah, the mountain of Zion, which he loves."[54] For this reason, "when Israel went out of Egypt, the house of Jacob from a people of strange language, Judah became his sanctuary, and Israel his dominion."[55] The tribe of Judah, then, became a uniquely chosen people unto God—a nation within a nation, as it were. Judah was not exalted above the other tribes; however, its people were given a specific calling and assignment. It was Judah to whom God entrusted his sayings.[56] And, it was Judah, more than all of the other tribes of Israel, that was zealous for the law and the Word of God.[57]

When the Hebrew Israelites Became "Jews"

As time progressed, particularly following the reigns of David and Solomon, the tribe of Judah, with Benjamin and much of Levi, became even more separated from the rest of Israel in the divided kingdom. The northern tribes followed Jeroboam while Judah, Benjamin, and Levi followed Rehoboam, Solomon's son. Additionally, "numbers of all the tribes joined the kingdom of Judah on account of the idolatry introduced by the kings of Israel."[58] Scripture confirms this enlargement of Judah by the addition of the righteous from the ten northern tribes: "Out of all the tribes of Israel such as set their hearts to seek the LORD God of Israel came to Jerusalem, to sacrifice unto the LORD God of their fathers. So they strengthened the kingdom of Judah."[59] God's wisdom in having chosen Judah above the others at the time of the Exodus was validated in the fact that Judah continued to maintain God's religious system while the majority

---

[54] Psalm 78:67–68.

[55] Psalm 114:1–2.

[56] 2 Chronicles 30:12; Romans 3:1–2.

[57] Singer et. al., eds., vol. 7, p. 328. This text notes the declaration in Exodus *Rabbah* 24:1 that at the time of the Red Sea crossing, the other tribes refused to enter the slimy bed of the sea until the tribe of Judah set them the example by plunging in." It also reports that "the people of Judah are said to have been versed in the Law."

[58] Ethelbert W. Bullinger, *Number in Scripture: Its Supernatural Design and Spiritual Significance* (Grand Rapids, MI: Kregel Publications, 1967), p. 80.

[59] 2 Chronicles 11:16–17. This passage of Scripture disproves the argument that the Ten Tribes of Israel were "lost." While it is true that large numbers of Northern Kingdom were carried into the Syrian captivity, it is also true that significant numbers joined Judah in the Southern Kingdom. Later, following the Babylonian conquest of Judah, significant numbers of the tribe of Judah were also dispersed among the nations. The diasporas, therefore, were not restricted to the ten tribes, and those tribes were never "lost." As a matter of fact, some three decades after Jesus ascended, his brother James addressed his epistle to "the *twelve* tribes scattered abroad" (James 1:1). It is obvious, then, that the ten tribes were not "lost" either in the time of Jesus or afterward. They came to be included among "the Jews" in Judea whom they joined, and they continued to be included among all "the Jews" in the Diaspora.

of the northern tribes lapsed into idolatry and, as a result, experienced the first Israelite Diaspora when God sent the Assyrian armies against them to carry them into captivity. Judah remained faithful to God and continued in the land.

It was during this time that the members of the tribe of Judah came to be known by the appellation יְהוּדִים (*yehudim*— "Jews"), which was derived from the word יְהוּדָה (*Yehudah*—"Judah"). The first scriptural record of the use of this term is found in 2 Kings 16:6. By the time that the Babylonian captivity had ended, however, the term *Yehudi (Jew)*[60] had come to be the commonly accepted name for the people of Judah and as well as for the members of the other eleven tribes who had aligned themselves with Judah. Finally, the word *Jew* came to be synonymous with all of God's Chosen People, with members of the other tribes of Israel proudly calling themselves Jews.[61] All the Hebrews and all the Israelites, therefore, were eventually included under the title *Jew*. The term came to connote a nationality or an ethnicity. In fact, while the term *race* has sometimes been applied to the Jewish people, the terms *nationality* and *ethnicity* are particularly apropos for describing the Jews since, in the strictest sense of the meaning of this word, the Jews are not a race within themselves.[62] As lineal descendants of the Hebrews or Israelites, they are an ethnic group, though they are understood primarily in religious terms.[63] This is what has empowered the Jewish people to maintain their distinctiveness despite centuries of being involuntarily dispersed among the nations of the world.

How Did One Become a Jew?

Since there were no Jews prior to Abraham, how, then, could any Gentile ever become a Jew?[64] In the ancient Israelite world, there were two ways

---

[60] The English word *Jew* is derived from the Old French *juiu* from the Greek *Ioudaios*. It is, in effect, an Anglicized contraction of *Yehudi*.

[61] In Acts 19:14, one of the temple priests (of the tribe of Levi) was called a Jew. In Acts 19:34, as well as in Acts 21:39, Paul, who was clearly from the tribe of Benjamin (Romans 11:1), was called a Jew.

[62] Michael B. Hart, "Jews and Race: An Introductory Essay," in *Jews and Race: Writings on Identity and Difference, 1880-1940*, Mitchell Bryan Hart, ed. (Boston, MA: Brandeis University Press, 2011), p. xiii. Hart quotes the well-known Israeli writer A. B. Yehoshua: "Jews are not a race and never viewed themselves as such." See A. B. Yehoshua, "Who Is a Jew?," in *Contemplate* 3 (2005–2006), p. 73. Also Christopher Hutton, *Race and the Third Reich: Linguistics, Racial Anthropology, and Genetics in the Dialectic of Volk* (Cambridge, UK: Polity Press, 2005), p. 54. Hutton notes, "The Jews are not a race in the sense of anthropological race *(Systemrasse)*."

[63] Daniel J. Elazar, "Jewish Religious, Ethnic, and National Identities," in *National Variations in Jewish Identity: Implications for Jewish Education*, Steven M. Cohen and Gabriel Horenczyk, eds. (Albany, NY: State University of New York Press, 1999), p. 43. Elazar notes that "Jews are an ethnic group" that is sustained in some parts of the world by their religion and in other parts by family, language, other aspects of culture, concern for the Jewish state, and, in some cases, by Antisemitism.

[64] It could be said that in some way, every Gentile who has ever become a Jew has followed the example of Abraham, the Assyrio-Babylonian who became the "first Jew" by accepting monotheism and believing in the "One God" to the degree that he did precisely what God instructed him to do.

in which one could become a Jew. First, those who were born of Israelite parents automatically were Jews genetically and genealogically through God's covenant with Abraham and his descendants. Secondly, provision was made for those who wished to accept the Torah through faith to become fellow citizens with those Jews of fleshly lineage. From the very outset of the Exodus, the Lord said, "And when a stranger . . . wants to keep the Passover to the LORD, let all his males be circumcised, and then let him come near and keep it; and he shall be as a native of the land."[65] Later God reconfirmed this position: "The stranger who dwells among you shall be to you as one born among you, and you shall love him as yourself."[66] Certain initiation requirements—circumcision (for men), sacrifice, and learning and accepting the Torah—were placed upon Gentiles to be included in Israel; however, once those qualifications were met, the Gentiles legally became Israelites.

Is it possible that Gentiles in the flesh actually became Israelites or Jews? As far as God was concerned their acceptance of the terms of the covenant between himself and the children of Israel transformed them into Jews just as it had transformed Abraham, the Assyrio-Babylonian, into a Jew.[67] Though at first they were called *gerim* (aliens) or later proselytes and were often considered second-class citizens by some elitist Jews, those who accepted the covenant of God eventually came to recognized as Jews even it if was generations later through their progeny. The exclusivity of some Jews could never obviate the impartiality of God. In fact, according to the prophet Isaiah, those Gentiles who accepted God's covenant and "laid hold on his Sabbath" were to have a place in God's house "*better than* that of sons and daughters."[68]

Since God has no respect of persons,[69] the criteria that made Abraham the chosen of God (and, in that sense, the first Jew) can make anyone a Jew in the eyes of God. Abraham discovered and embraced monotheism,[70] and he had the faith that was necessary to believe God by carrying out his instructions. As Abraham's selection was totally predicated upon his faith in God, so becoming chosen of God has always been by faith in God to accept his will. This faith transformed a Babylonian into a Hebrew, and, through the centuries, it has transformed many strangers of various ethnicities into

---

[65] Exodus 12:48.

[66] Leviticus 19:34.

[67] In this case, the term *Jew* is used to connote being "chosen of God."

[68] Isaiah 56:3–7.

[69] Acts 10:34; Romans 2:11; James 2:1–13.

[70] Lori Hope Lefkovitz, *In Scripture: The First Stories of Jewish Sexual Identities* (Lanham, MD: Rowman & Littlefield Publishers, 2010), p. 145. Lefkovitz notes that Abraham is "credited with being the first monotheist and by extension the first Jew." Though Abraham was a Hebrew and his descendants were Israelites, he was, in effect, the first Jew because he was the father of faith and of the covenant.

Jews. "Thus 'through his faith' Abraham became the father of both Jew and Gentile who have faith comparable to Abraham's."[71]

Such was the case in the days of Esther. When the Jews were given permission to defend themselves on the day on which Haman had planned their genocide, "many of the people of the land *became Jews*, because fear of the Jews fell upon them."[72] Apparently, many of the people of the Persian Empire so believed in God's protection of the Jews that they were willing to abandon their Persian religions and ethnicity and become Jews. Whether their instinct was one of faith or of self-preservation, the simple fact is that Scripture specifically declares that they "*became Jews*," not that they "wanted to become Jews" or that they "pretended to be Jews" or that "they disguised themselves as Jews."

The conversion of Gentiles to Judaism became more common especially during and after the second century BC. During this time, non-Jews became Jews in a variety of ways, "whether by political enfranchisement, religious conversion, veneration of the Jewish God, observance of Jewish rituals, association with the Jews, or other means."[73] By the time of the first century of the Common Era, Jews and Judaism had become actively and intensely involved in encouraging Gentiles to convert to Judaism. This period provided "the first secure attestation of the notion of conversion to Judaism, the idea that a gentile can deny his . . . polytheism and accept the one true God."[74] Building on the older conversion prerequisites of circumcision (for men), sacrifice, and accepting and learning Torah, the sages added a new requirement, which was immersion in water, specifically immersion in the waters of the *mikveh*.[75] Ultimately, immersion became the final step in Gentile conversion to Judaism.[76] The moment that a proselyte broke the plane of the water after having totally immersing himself in the waters of the *mikveh*, a forensic change occurred. Before that moment, even if he had been circumcised, had offered a sacrifice, and had learned Torah, he had continued to be a Gentile. As the Mishnah said, "So long as a Gentile has not been

---

[71] Gordon D. Fee, "Who Are Abraham's True Children?" in *Perspectives on Our Father Abraham: Essays in Honor of Marvin R. Wilson*, Steven A. Hunt, ed. (Grand Rapids, MI: Wm. B. Eerdmans Publishing Co., 2010), p. 133.

[72] Esther 8:17.

[73] Shaye J. D. Cohen, *The Beginnings of Jewishness: Boundaries, Varieties, Uncertainties* (Berkeley, CA: The University of California Press, 1999), p. 342.

[74] Cohen, p. 342.

[75] Each of these four requirements was to be performed publicly, that is, in the presence of witnesses.

[76] Cohen, p. 342. Cohen notes that "the rabbis in the second century C.E. standardized the conversion process by demanding that all converts accept the commandments of the Torah, that men be circumcised, that all converts immerse properly, and that these steps be taken publicly and thus be verifiable. When a gentile has complied with all the rabbinic requirements and performed the prescribed ceremony, the rabbis declare him (or her) to be 'like an Israelite in all respects.' The gentile has become a Jew."

immersed, he is still a Gentile."[77] At the moment when immersion was complete, however, and the Gentile emerged from the waters, he was instantly transformed into a Jew.[78] Emergence from the *mikveh* was believed to constitute the elevation into a new life.[79] It signified the Gentile's symbolic passing through the Red Sea, "the sea that makes an end,"[80] and his crossing over to join the Jewish people on the other side. It was like having been buried in the grave and then being resurrected.[81] It was like reentering the womb and being born again.[82] Proselytes were reborn—this time, into the family of Abraham, Isaac, and Jacob. They were no longer Gentiles: they were Jews!

Universalizing the Exclusive Covenant

Throughout the Hebrew Scriptures, the Eternal God continued to recognize those who accepted his covenants as being his Chosen People. It was in his divine plan, however, to make the way easier for all people to be included among them. In the fullness of time, it was the covenant that he had made with Abraham that prompted the Father to send his Son, made of woman under the Torah to redeem them who were under the Torah and bring them to the adoption of sons.[83] Zachariah, the father of John the Baptizer, prophesied: "Blessed is the Lord God of Israel; for he has visited and redeemed his people, and has raised up a horn of salvation for us in the house of his servant David . . . to perform the mercy promised to our fathers and *to remember his holy covenant*, the oath which he swore to our ancestor Abraham."[84] Jesus was the fulfillment of the promise that God had made to Abraham two millennia before that time when he said, "In Isaac your *seed* shall be called."[85]

---

[77] Mishnah, *Berakhot* 288; *Pesachim* 8.8.

[78] This was similar to the practice of immersing in the waters of the *mikveh* any dishes or utensils that had been crafted by Gentiles so that the "impurity of the Gentiles" could be removed. Before the immersion, such items could not be used by Jews; after immersion they were permitted to them. See Numbers 31:21–23. Also Babylonian Talmud, *Abodah Zarah* 75b.

[79] Lawrence H. Shiffman, *Who Was a Jew? Rabbinic and Halakhic Perspectives on the Jewish–Christian Schism* (Jersey City, NJ: KTAV Publishing, 1985), pp. 35–37.

[80] Paul L. Dunteman, *The Christian Life and the History of Israel: Discovering How Israel's Journey Parallels the Christian's Spiritual Walk Today* (Maitland, FL: Xulon Press, 2009), p. 207. Dunteman notes that "according to its root in Hebrew, the Sea of Reeds [the proper name for the Red Sea] is the 'sea that makes an end.'"

[81] Elyse Goldstein, *ReVisions: Seeing Torah Through a Feminist Lens* (Woodstock, VT: Jewish Lights Publications, 2001), p. 94.

[82] Michael Lerner, *Tikkun Reader* (Lanham, MD: Rowman & Littlefield Publishers, 2007), p. 160.

[83] Galatians 4:4–5.

[84] Luke 1:68–69, 72–73.

[85] Genesis 21:12; Romans 9:7; Hebrews 11:18. In Galatians 3:16, Paul interpreted the fact that because the word *seed* in the Genesis text was singular rather than plural, the text indicated that God was promising the Messiah to Abraham.

From the very beginning of his ministry, Jesus practiced the covenantal religious system under which he had been born. He staunchly maintained that the Jews alone (including those Gentiles who had fully embraced the terms of God's covenant with Israel) were God's Chosen People. Jesus well knew that God's law was to "go forth from Zion and the word of the LORD from Jerusalem."[86] He knew that to the Israelites alone belonged "the adoption, the glory, the covenants, the giving of the law, the service of God, and the promises."[87] Indeed, it was the Israelites "from whom, according to the flesh, Christ came."[88] Even when Jesus addressed one of the lost sheep of Israel (a Samaritan woman), he boldly and unreservedly declared: "Salvation is from the Jews."[89]

During his conversation with the Samaritan woman at the well of Jacob, however, Jesus predicted that a time would soon come when a change would take place in the practice of God's religion, which also implied a modified approach to the manner in which God would include others among his Chosen People. He declared that the true worshipers of the Eternal God would begin to worship him in spiritual truth.[90] Until that time, the people had worshiped YHWH in a system that had been given by God and was a revelation of divine truth; however, the ritual through which the worshippers had obeyed the commandments had often become routine and jejune. Isaiah had reported God's distaste for ritualistic worship: "Bring your worthless offerings no longer . . . I hate your new moon festivals and your appointed feasts. . . . I am weary of bearing them."[91] God's system, including his festivals, was not deficient; the pretentious ritualism of the people was.

The time was coming, however, when those who would offer acceptable worship to God would have to do so through the motivation of the Holy Spirit with the solid focus of *kavanah* that the sages also later emphasized. God would be worshiped in spiritual truth. The Messiah declared that since God is Spirit, they who worship him must do so in the

---

86 Isaiah 2:3.
87 Romans 9:4.
88 Romans 9:5.
89 John 4:22.
90 Raymond Thomas Stamm, *Search the Scriptures: New Testament Studies in Honor of Raymond T. Stamm* (Leiden, Netherlands: E. J. Brill, 1969), p. 41, and Ethelbert W. Bullinger, *Word Studies on the Holy Spirit* (Grand Rapids, MI: Kregel Academic, 1979), p. 75. The phrase in John 4:24, "*in spirit and truth,*" is the Greek figure of speech hendiadys in which two elements designate the same reality. The text can, therefore, be rendered as "in the Spirit which is the truth." This is confirmed by Jesus' declaration that "the words I speak unto you are Spirit and they are life" (John 6:63). The hendiadys can also be translated "in the Spirit of truth," or "in spiritual truth."
91 Isaiah 1:13–14.

Spirit as well as in the truth that he had given.[92] This is why Paul, himself a Pharisee, declared, that "the letter [*of the law*] kills, but the Spirit gives life."[93] Mere ritualistic obedience would not suffice: the worshippers would be required to worship in Spirit as well as in truth.

Since the covenants of God until that time had pertained only to the lineal descendants of Abraham, Jesus could not direct his earthly ministry outside that sphere because he had been born within the boundaries of the Abrahamic covenant amended and expanded at Sinai. He declared that he was sent only to the lost sheep of the house of Israel;[94] therefore, he instructed his apostles not to go in the way of the Gentiles.[95] When the time would come, however, for the renewal and expansion of the Abrahamic covenant and its Sinaitic emendation, the Word of God had predicted that others besides the fleshly Jews would have access to that covenant. Isaiah had foretold this great event: "I, the LORD, have called you in righteousness . . . I will keep you and *give you as a covenant to the people, as a light to the Gentiles.*"[96] Simeon, the priest who dedicated the infant Jesus at the temple, reiterated this prophetic promise,[97] and Jesus claimed it for himself as he embarked upon his ministry.[98]

Jesus set the stage for expanding the covenant to the Gentiles on the basis of the spiritual fulfillment of God's Word in addition to the physical fulfillment thereof when he declared, "I have other sheep, which are not of this fold; I must bring them also, and they will hear my voice; and *they will become one flock with one shepherd.*"[99] The Son of God predicted that there would be a time when there would be one religion for all humanity, one fold in which all of God's sheep would be gathered together. There would, indeed, be "one Lord, one faith, and one baptism, one God and Father of all" who would be "in you all."[100] What had been required physically of the Israelites would now be required spiritually of the Gentiles.[101] Believers from among the nations would be included in God's covenant people through the impartation of the Holy Spirit into their lives.

---

92 John 4:24.
93 2 Corinthians 3:6.
94 Matthew 15:24.
95 Matthew 10:5–6.
96 Isaiah 42:6.
97 Luke 2:32.
98 Luke 4:18.
99 John 10:16, emphasis added.
100 Ephesians 4:5.
101 A good example of this principle is circumcision. Under the first covenant, circumcision was a physical requirement; under the renewed covenant, it became a spiritual requirement.

Prior to the time when the renewed covenant[102] in the blood of Jesus was sealed through the testator's death,[103] the message of the Messiah had been directed only to the fleshly children of the covenant. After the death and resurrection of the Son of God, however, these were the words of the commission that Jesus gave to his disciples: "Go and make disciples of the nations,"[104] and, "You shall be witnesses to me in Jerusalem, and in all Judea and Samaria, and to the end of the earth."[105] As the door of salvation was opened to the Gentiles, the immutable principle for inclusion among God's Chosen People remained constant. Only those who had made a covenant with God were qualified to inherit with Christ,[106] and this principle has remained constant across the annals of time. The new covenant that YHWH made with Israel and the rest of the world through the death of his Son was this: "I will put my laws into their minds and I will write them on their heart; and I will be their God, and they shall be my people."[107]

The renewal of God's covenant and its expansion were extended to the entire world, including the Gentiles, and were predicated upon one thing and one thing only—faith.[108] This was the covenant that God made with the world: "That whoever believes in him shall not perish, but have everlasting life."[109] The criteria for inclusion among God's Chosen People were expanded to include accepting Messiah Jesus by faith as the everlasting atonement for sin.[110] Just as Abraham was justified by faith, so when the Abrahamic covenant was renewed to include all believing humanity, "the just shall live by faith."[111]

Confession of faith in the atoning death and glorious resurrection of the Jewish Messiah effected the rebirth and the spiritual circumcision of the heart that Moses[112] and Jeremiah[113] had predicted would come. The subsequent baptism of believers in water was an outward demonstration of their

---

[102] The "New Testament" or "New Covenant" was, in reality, a "renewed" covenant. As Jeremiah 31:31-34 and Hebrews 8:6-13 made very clear, the first covenant was not destroyed but was, instead, written in the hearts of the believers. The newness of the "new covenant" was not its substance but where and how it was written—this time on the hearts and in the minds of the believers, not on tablets of stone or on parchment. God's instructions remained the same. The place where they were written changed.
[103] Hebrews 9:15–17.
[104] Matthew 28:19.
[105] Acts 1:8.
[106] Psalm 50:5.
[107] Hebrews 8:10.
[108] Romans 3:28.
[109] John 3:16.
[110] 1 John 2:2.
[111] Romans 5:1; Galatians 3:11.
[112] Deuteronomy 10:16.
[113] Jeremiah 4:4.

death to sin, their burial into Christ,[114] and their resurrection to newness of life.[115] Christian baptism, therefore, became a fulfillment of Second Temple Judaism's requirement that converts to YHWH's religion immerse themselves in the *mikveh*.[116] Those who were baptized then became catechumens and, as such, were taught the Word of God in a manner similar to the way in which proselytes to Judaism were taught the same Torah. They also participated in the one sacrifice for sin under the new covenant —Jesus, himself—and they shared in the new sacrificial system of praise, prayer, and worship of God in the Spirit.[117] While previously God's covenants had applied exclusively to the *fleshly* lineage and had been sealed with the *fleshly* sign of circumcision, the Messiah renewed the covenant as a *spiritual* covenant which by a *spiritual* birth translated the believer into the *spiritual* dimensions of the kingdom where they functioned alongside natural Israel in God's election. The principle of becoming chosen of God by making a covenant with him, however, remained constant.

The Covenant of Faith

The great similarity between the covenant of Abraham and that of Christ is very obvious. Both were given because of faith, and both promised an inheritance. Paul notes this similarity: "Just as Abraham believed God, and it was accounted to him for righteousness. Therefore know that only those who are of faith are sons of Abraham. And the Scripture, foreseeing that God would justify the nations by faith, preached the gospel to Abraham beforehand, saying, 'In you all the nations shall be blessed' . . . Christ has redeemed us from the curse of the law . . . that the blessing of Abraham might come upon the Gentiles in Christ Jesus, that we might receive the promise of the Spirit through faith. . . . For you are all sons of God through faith in Christ Jesus. . . . And if you are Christ's, then are you Abraham's seed, and heirs according to the promise."[118] The new covenant, therefore merely renewed both the Abrahamic and the Sinaitic covenants and extended them to all peoples "for the obedience of faith."[119]

---

[114] Colossians 2:12.
[115] Romans 6:3–4.
[116] The fact that the *mikveh* was used in earliest Christian baptism is seen in the baptism of 3,000 believers on the day of Pentecost in Jerusalem where there is neither a lake nor a river. (Only the Brook Kidron trickles between Jerusalem and the Mount of Olives). The immersion of the 3,000 was accomplished in the many *mikva'ot* that were scattered around the temple complex and beyond.
[117] Hebrews 13:15–16; Revelation 5:8; 8:3; Philippians 4:18.
[118] Galatians 3:6–8; 13–14, 26, 29.
[119] Romans 16:26.

The Abrahamic covenant, then, was not abolished in Christ, but was rather extended by him to all men, both Jew and Gentile. All believers in Jesus, Jew and Gentile, become the spiritual children of Abraham by virtue of their faith. Paul further explained this concept by saying, "For they are not all Israel who are of Israel, nor are they all children because they are the seed of Abraham; but, 'in Isaac shall your seed be called.' That is, those who are the children of the flesh, these are not the children of God; but the children of the promise are counted as the seed."[120] Faith and faithfulness are requisites for those who are counted among the children of Abraham. Indeed, as Jesus said, those who are Abraham's children will do the *works* of Abraham as well as manifest the faith of the Patriarch.[121]

The Renewal of Covenantal Torah

The covenant of the Torah given at Sinai was a system of praise, worship, and service that, by the first century AD, had come to be called "Judaism."[122] This Judaism was never obviated or superseded by the ministry of Jesus. Since Jesus, himself, confessed that he had not come to destroy the Torah but to complete it,[123] the new covenant was not a totally unexpected religion but a renewal of the first covenant on the basis of a better and eternal sacrifice.[124] It was another step in God's unfolding plan for the ages and the religion that he had given and would perfect forever through the death, burial, resurrection, and ascension of his only begotten Son, Jesus the Messiah.

It was not that the first covenant was bad and the second good. It was not that the first covenant was "old," antiquated, and passé, and the second covenant was "new" in the sense that it was something never seen before and just then newly invented. In Paul's estimation, the first covenant was always good.[125] According to the author of Hebrews, the second covenant was better.[126] In reality, the new, renewed covenant expanded and amended the

---

120 Romans 9:6-8, 23–26.

121 John 8:39.

122 The term *Judaism* was used by Paul to describe his own experience: "I was advancing in Judaism beyond many of my contemporaries among my countrymen, being more extremely zealous for my ancestral traditions" (Galatians 1:14). The translation of the Greek text is accurate, for the word rendered "Judaism" is Ἰουδαισμός (*Ioudaismós*), of which "Judaism" is but a transliteration. The word *Ioudaismós* was commonly used in the first-century AD Greek world to describe the religion and culture of the Jewish people. The Hebrew word from which the Greek *Ioudaismós* was translated, יַהֲדוּת (*Yahadut*), was used as early as 120 BC in 2 Maccabees 2:21; 8:1.

123 Matthew 5;17.

124 Hebrews 9:23. Because of the sacrifice of Jesus, the covenant could be renewed by being written in the hearts of the believers (Hebrews 8:10).

125 Romans 7:12.

126 Hebrews 7:19–22.

Sinai covenant in the same way in which the Sinai Covenant had expanded and amended the Abrahamic covenant. The Abrahamic covenant was of grace and faith.[127] The new covenant brought an expansion of the grace and truth that the Sinai covenant had manifested.[128] "The new covenant written on the heart, heralded by Jeremiah, is not different from the 'old' covenant in content, only in medium."[129] Indeed, "it is a covenant of perfection, giving a consummation to the successive covenants renewed with Noah, with Abraham, and with the Hebrews."[130] The Sinai covenant did not need to be abrogated and superseded; it only needed to be renewed and completed, and it received both in and through Jesus. The term *new covenant*, then, "suggests a 'refreshing, 'renewing,' or 'recent updating' of the original (older) covenant of grace that became enlarged anew and to its fullest expression of grace in the coming of Jesus."[131]

In the person of Jesus, the Messiah himself became God's renewed covenant to both Jew and Gentile, fulfilling the divine promise to Isaiah: "Behold my servant, whom I uphold, my chosen, in whom my soul delights; I have put my Spirit upon him; he will bring forth justice to the nations. . . . I will give you as a covenant for the people, a light for the nations, to open the eyes that are blind, to bring out the prisoners from the dungeon, from the prison those who sit in darkness."[132] When Jesus was queried by John's disciples as to whether or not he was the promised Messiah, he reiterated the words of Isaiah to validate his Messiahship: "The blind receive sight, the lame walk, the lepers are cleansed and the deaf hear, the dead are raised up, and the poor have the gospel preached to them."[133] God, indeed, did establish the Messiah as a covenant for the people of Israel and as a light for the Gentiles. The renewed covenant opened the door of faith to the nations so that "whosoever believes upon [the Messiah] will . . . have everlasting life."[134]

God's Promise of Gentile Inclusion

While during his incarnation and ministry in Israel, Jesus maintained the continuity of the divine covenant with the fleshly descendants of Abraham. He instructed his disciples, "Do not go in the way of the Gentiles, and do

---

[127] Hebrews 11:8–19.
[128] John 1:14.
[129] Austin Stone, "Speaking of the Law," *First Things*, Issues 159-163 (Institute on Religion and Public Life, 2006), p. 4.
[130] John Sutcliffe, *A Commentary on the Old and New Testament* (London, England: John Mason: 1839), vol. 2, p. 607.
[131] Wilson, *Exploring*, p. 71.
[132] Isaiah 42:1, 6–7, ESV.
[133] Matthew 11:5.
[134] John 3:16.

not enter any city of the Samaritans, but rather go to the lost sheep of the house of Israel."[135] As he neared the time for the completion of his divine assignment, however, he was heard to say, "I have other sheep, which are not of this fold; I must bring them also."[136] Finally, after his resurrection, Jesus gave the Great Commission: "Go therefore and make disciples of all the nations."[137] The instructions of Jesus, however, were not entirely original to them, for the Hebrew prophets had made startling predictions about Gentile inclusion in God's blessings. Paul's "revelation" concerning Gentile inclusion in Abraham's promise by the means of faith alone was not merely a rabbinic *midrash* or gloss on his part. It was based in the infallible words of Hebrew prophets, some of them stretching beyond the time of Abraham.

One of the most ancient prophetic indications of Gentile inclusion is found in the story of Noah's blessing (and curse) upon his descendants. At this time, the patriarch identified the God whom he blessed[138] as being "the God of Shem,"[139] indicating that the God of Scripture would be identified with Noah's first son, the father of the Semites, including the Hebrews/Israelites/ Jews. Then, in a somewhat cryptic statement, Noah extended this blessing to include the descendants of Japheth, saying, "May God extend Japheth's territory, and let him dwell in the tents of Shem."[140] In effect, Noah predicted that the descendants of Japheth would worship the God of Shem and share in his blessing. It is apparent from this prophecy that the nations that descended from Japheth would "live in the tents of Shem" and worship the God of Shem. The Aramaic *Targum Pseudo-Jonathan* interprets this to mean that "the Lord shall beautify the borders of Japheth, and his sons shall be proselytized, and dwell in the schools of Shem." Based on the blessing of Japheth as included in the blessing of Shem, Talmudic scholars continued to teach Gentile inclusion in Israel. The sages said that this passage means that "the words of Japheth shall be in the tents of Shem,"[141] and from this, the rabbis found approval for the translation of the Torah into Gentile languages, particularly Greek.[142]

Eugen Pentiuc observes that "these ancient Jewish interpretations are close to the christological approach that sees Japheth dwelling in Shem's tent

---

[135] Matthew 10:5–6.

[136] John 10:16.

[137] Matthew 28:19.

[138] Noah blessed "the God of Shem," not Shem himself; however, this action indicated that Shem was to be blessed of God. This principle was reiterated in the Melchizedek blessing wherein the priest-king of Salem blessed both Abraham and God (Genesis 14:19–20).

[139] Genesis 9:26.

[140] Genesis 9:27a, NIV; b, JPS.

[141] Babylonian Talmud, *Megillah* 9b. The sages reasoned from this passage that the message of the Torah would be heralded to the nations of the world and would elicit Gentile conversion to Judaism.

[142] *Deuteronomy Rabbah* 1:1.

as a hint at the Gentiles joining the Christian church, which originally consisted only of Jewish (Semite) faithful."[143] Derek Kidner agrees, noting that "the fulfillment of the words leaps to the eye of the New Testament in the ingathering of the Gentiles."[144] Marvin Wilson expands upon this theme: "All Christians are spiritual Semites, for they share in the inheritance of Abraham's family. . . . Shem's tent of blessing through Abraham is large enough to include every Christian." Then, expresses his hope that "every Christian is large-minded and wise enough to enter that tent to explore and appropriate the richness and depth of that blessing."[145] Ernst Hengstenberg has noted that "the real home of piety and salvation will be with Shem, to whom Japheth in the felt need of salvation shall come near. . . . The kingdom of God shall be established in Shem, and Japheth shall be received into its community" so that "by the posterity of the Patriarchs all the nations of the earth shall be blessed."[146]

Isaiah, in particular, had no hesitation in predicting that Gentiles would be included in the Israel of God when he said in God's name: "Arise, shine, for your light has come, and the glory of the LORD has risen upon you. . . . the nations [Gentiles] will come to your light."[147] Then, the prophet used even more explicit language: "All the flocks of Kedar will be gathered together to you. The rams of Nebaioth will serve you. They will be accepted as offerings on my altar."[148] In this case, God used the two oldest grandsons of Abraham (through Ishmael) to confirm that the Abrahamic blessing would be to all the nations of the earth as he had promised the Patriarch.[149] Ishmael would, indeed, be the "wild ass of a man"[150] who perfectly exemplified the "wild olive tree" to which Paul alluded in his analogy of God's family tree.[151] The prophet had already predicted, however, that "the foreigners who bind themselves to the LORD to minister to him, to love the name of the LORD, and to be his servants . . . these I will bring to my holy mountain and give them joy in my house of prayer . . . for my house will be called a house of prayer for all nations."[152]

[143] Eugen J. Pentiuc, *Jesus the Messiah in the Hebrew Bible* (Mahwah, NJ: Paulist Press, 2006), p. 127.

[144] Derek Kidner, *Genesis* in *Tyndale Old Testament Commentary* (Downers Grove, IL: InterVarsity Press, 1967), p. 104, quoted in Wilson, *Exploring*, p. 65.

[145] Wilson, *Exploring*, p. 65. Wilson gives an excellent overview of Noah's prophecy on pages 64–65.

[146] Ernst Wilhelm Hengstenberg, *Christology of the Old Testament and Commentary on the Messianic Predictions*, tr. Theodore Meyer (Edinburgh, UK: T. & T. Clark, 1858), vol. 1, pp. 32-35.

[147] Isaiah 60:1, 3.

[148] Isaiah 60:7.

[149] Genesis 18:18.

[150] Genesis 16:12, NRS.

[151] Romans 11:17–24.

[152] Isaiah 56:6–7, NIV.

Amos also predicted Gentile inclusion: "In that day I will raise up David's fallen *sukkah* . . . I will raise up its ruins and rebuild it as in the days of old . . . that they may possess the remnant of Edom and all the nations who are called by my name, declares the LORD who does this."[153] This straightforward prophecy affirms that all the peoples of the nations that were called by the name of the Lord were to be included in God's possession in the time when the house of David was being restored. As surely as God's promises were secure to Israel, they were also certain for the Gentiles, for those who had been no people were to be included in the people of God, a part of the kingdom of priests and the holy nation of the Israel of God.[154]

Children of Faith *Counted as* Fleshly Children

Paul expanded on the thought of Gentile inclusion in this manner: "Therefore remember that you, once Gentiles in the flesh . . . were without Christ, being aliens from the commonwealth of Israel and strangers from the *covenants of promise,* having no hope and without God in the world. But now in Christ Jesus you who once were far off have been made near by the blood of Christ."[155] Those who were formerly nothing more than "Gentiles in the flesh" and aliens from Israel and its covenants, were translated into the kingdom of God,[156] and became a part of God's Chosen People (in effect, becoming naturalized citizens of Israel.) Joshua Garroway discusses the complexities of this phenomenon: "[I]f 'Christianity' truly did begin within Judaism so that the Jews who became 'Christians' *remained* Jews, why is it outrageous to suppose that Gentiles who became 'Christians' . . . also *became* Jews? If 'Christianity' composed a species within the genus of Judaism, then why should we not understand baptism into Christ as a means by which Gentiles converted to Judaism? . . . Gentiles did become Jews . . . They became Gentile-Jews."[157]

Paul declared that the divine mystery that the Gentiles would be accepted before God on equal terms with the Jews—a mystery which had been concealed from previous generations—had been revealed to the apostles and prophets by the Spirit: "I, Paul, the prisoner of Christ Jesus for the sake of you Gentiles—assuming that you have heard of the stewardship of God's grace that was given to me for you, how the mystery was made known to me

---

[153] Amos 9:11–12.
[154] 1 Peter 2:9.
[155] Ephesians 2:11–13.
[156] Colossians 1:13.
[157] Joshua D. Garroway, *Paul's Gentile-Jews: Neither Jew nor Gentile, but Both* (New York: Palgrave Macmillan, 2012), p. 148.

by revelation . . . which was not made known to people in other generations as it has now been revealed by the Spirit to God's holy apostles and prophets. The mystery is that the Gentiles are fellow heirs, members of the same body, and partakers of the promise in Christ Jesus through the gospel."[158] Two of the seven mysteries[159] of the Apostolic Scriptures involved the interrelationship of the Jews and the Gentiles: 1) the mystery that Israel was hardened in part so that the Gentiles could be grafted into God's family tree[160] and 2) that the Gentiles would be fellow heirs, members of the same body politic, naturalized citizens of the nation of Israel, and partakers of God's promises to Abraham in Messiah Jesus through the gospel.[161]

The Abrahamic covenant and its more far-reaching implications, therefore, were applicable not only to Abraham's fleshly progeny but also to his faith descendants. Paul affirmed: "For the promise to Abraham or to his descendants that he would be the heir of the world was not through the Law, but through the righteousness of faith. . . . For this reason it is by faith, in order that it may be in accordance with grace, so that the promise will be guaranteed to all the descendants, not only to those who are of the Law, but also to those who are of the faith of Abraham, who is the father of us all."[162] The apostle to the Gentiles concluded that God's promises to Abraham were guaranteed to both his lineal descendants through the Torah and to his spiritual descendants through faith. Paul's argument, therefore, was for full Gentile inclusion, not for Jewish exclusion! Indeed, after all of his analysis, he reached this conclusion: "If you belong to the Messiah, then you are Abraham's descendants, heirs according to the promises."[163] The faith of Abraham—and, in effect, the Patriarch himself—continues in all those who are "Abraham's children" by faith. As Abraham Heschel said, "The life of him who joins the covenant of Abraham continues the life of Abraham. . . . We are Abraham."[164] Divine election is continually perpetuated by those "who are of the faith of Abraham, who is the father of us all."[165]

---

[158] Ephesians 3:1, 2–3 (ESV), 5 (NIV), 6, (ESV).

[159] The seven "mysteries" mentioned in Apostolic Scripture are 1) the mystery of the incarnation of God (1 Timothy 3:16); 2) the mystery of Christ's indwelling believers (Colossians 1:27); 3) the mystery of Christ's covenant relationship with the church (Ephesians 5:31–32); 4) the mystery of iniquity (2 Thessalonians 2:7); 5) the mystery of Babylon (Revelation 17:5); 6) the mystery of Israel's partial hardening (Romans 11:25); and 7) the mystery of the resurrection and change (1 Corinthians 15:51–53).

[160] Romans 11:25: "I do not want you, brethren, to be uninformed of this mystery . . . that a partial hardening has happened to Israel until the fullness of the Gentiles has come in."

[161] Ephesians 3:6: "The mystery is that through the gospel the Gentiles are heirs together with Israel, members together of one body, and sharers together in the promise in Christ Jesus" (NIV).

[162] Romans 4: 13, 16.

[163] Galatians 3:29.

[164] Abraham Joshua Heschel, *God in Search of Man* (New York: Farrar, Straus & Giroux, 1955), p. 201.

[165] See the excellent discussion of Abraham and his faith in Wilson, *Exploring*, pp. 81-93.

Then, Paul further explained the principles of faith and obedience to God through which the Gentiles could be accepted before God on equal terms with the Jews. "For indeed circumcision is of value if you practice the Law . . . so if the uncircumcised man keeps the requirements of the Law, will not his uncircumcision be regarded as circumcision? . . . For he is not a Jew who is one outwardly, nor is circumcision that which is outward in the flesh. But a Jew is one inwardly, and circumcision is a matter of the heart, by the Spirit, not by the letter."[166] Circumcision, the fleshly sign in which the lineal descendants of Abraham had come to trust, was, therefore, totally secondary to the faith that Abraham had demonstrated when he was chosen by God.

When Gentiles, therefore, receive the righteousness of God through faith, their faith is counted as circumcision so that they, in effect, become spiritual descendants of Abraham, and, therefore, essentially become Jewish in the same manner in which the Gentile Abraham became the first Jew. They are included within the particularist covenant of Hebrews/Israelites/Jews. Since the fullest manifestation of the righteousness of God is in the person of Jesus Christ,[167] Gentiles receive righteousness through faith in Jesus. This faith righteousness, then, is, as Paul noted, *counted as* circumcision of the flesh so that for them circumcision becomes a spiritual experience rather than a fleshly rite.[168] The Greek word translated "counted as" in Romans 2:26 is λογίζομαι (*logizomai*). It is the same word used in Romans 4:3: "Abraham believed God, and it was *accounted to* [credited to] him for righteousness," and in Romans 9:8: "The children of the promise are *counted as* Abraham's offspring" (NIV). Just as Abraham's faith was *counted as* righteousness, so the substitutionary righteousness of Christ in the heart of the uncircumcised believer is *counted as* circumcision and the reborn child of the promise of God is *counted as* (included among) the fleshly children.

This is the principle upon which a Gentile by circumcision of the heart (rebirth) can be spiritually converted to The Way, the "Jesus Judaism," and become a Jew.[169] A "spiritual Jew" is a spiritual child of Father Abraham through faith. The inclusion of the Gentiles in the family of God through faith, however, does not obviate God's covenant with the natural Jews, for

---

[166] Romans 2:25–29.
[167] Romans 10:4; 1 Corinthians 1:30.
[168] Colossians 2:11–12: In [Christ] you were also circumcised with a circumcision made without hands . . . having been buried with him in baptism, in which you were also raised up with him through faith in the working of God, who raised him from the dead."
[169] The emphasis on Gentiles "becoming" Jews is entirely on the spiritual. Gentiles can no more physically become Jews than they can change their gender "by faith." Instead, they are adopted into God's family of covenant salvation in much the same way as Ruth, the Gentile woman, was (Ruth 4:13).

the gifts and callings of God, both natural and spiritual, are irrevocable.[170] The promises of God to the lineal descendants of Abraham, Isaac, and Jacob can never be suspended or abrogated any more than the promises of God to the spiritual descendants of Abraham through the Messiah can be invalidated![171]

Some have suggested that only fleshly Jews who believe in Jesus can become "spiritual Jews" and that Gentiles who believe in the Messiah can only become "spiritual Gentiles." This argument falls short on two points: 1) The term *spiritual* does not always denote spirituality or a higher plane of maturity in the Spirit of God. It is used to reveal something of the spirit, or the intangible or immaterial, as opposed to something of the flesh, or the tangible or material. Such is the case in 1 Corinthians 15:44, which speaks of a *natural* body and a *spiritual* body; in Ephesians 5:19, which admonishes believers to sing *spiritual* songs; in Ephesians 6:12, where the nature of Christian warfare is described as being against *spiritual* wickedness in high places; and in Revelation 11:8, where Jerusalem is *spiritually* called Sodom and Egypt. While *spiritual* can be an adjective that denotes spirituality, it is also used as a substitute for the prepositional phrase *in spirit.* 2) By the time of Jesus, the term *Jew* had come to identify all of God's Chosen People, regardless as to their tribal identity. If the Gentiles were "fellow heirs, of the same body, and partakers of his promise."[172] and were no more strangers "from the covenants of promise,"[173] then they most surely could be recognized as "Jewish" or chosen of God. At the same time, their religion was still biblical Judaism, the faith on which Jesus had renewed and expanded the "new covenant." And, indeed, this was what prompted Peter, the apostle to the Jews, to make this declaration regarding the Gentiles: "To the pilgrims of the dispersion . . . you also, as living stones, are being built up a spiritual house . . . You are a chosen generation, a royal priesthood, a holy nation, his own special people . . . who once were not a people but are now the people of God."[174] Peter's specific quotation of Hosea 1:6, 9 demonstrates that Gentiles who have experienced the rebirth are considered spiritually and prophetically—but never physically or genealogically—to be "Israelites" or "Jews."

---

[170] Romans 11:29.

[171] Some have suggested that the spiritual seed utterly replaced the natural Jews and that Christianity superseded Judaism. This position is based on an arrogant ignorance of hundreds of prophecies of both the Hebrew and Apostolic Scriptures. Anyone who honestly studies the New Testament in the context of its first-century culture, history, and grammar instantly recognizes that biblical faith has continuity and is not subject to being capriciously destroyed and replaced by another religion.

[172] Ephesians 3:6.

[173] Ephesians 2:12.

[174] 1 Peter 1:1; 2:5, 9–10.

By accepting the Lord Jesus Christ and his righteousness, the Gentiles became a part of God's holy nation, his Chosen People. They came to be included spiritually among the children of Abraham, and the basis for their inclusion was the same as the basis of Abraham's election: faith. As such, they also became heirs of the world, as God had promised to Abraham.[175] Those who believed in Jesus became "spiritual Jews," included among the children of the promise, the seed of Abraham through faith. They came alongside natural Israel as spiritual partners in the promises and covenants of God. In fact, even to this day, Gentiles who come to faith in Jesus also become naturalized citizens of Israel: "You [Gentiles] are no longer strangers and aliens, but you are fellow citizens with the saints [Jews], and are of God's household."[176] In effect, they are converted from the world of paganism, the worship of false gods, and captivity to evil and are born again into the Israelite kingdom of faith in the one and only true God. They are grafted into God's family tree of covenant salvation, where they have partaken of the rich sap of divine truth by being connected with the holy root system of biblical Judaism, God's faith for all humanity.[177] In reality, all Christians who come to faith in Jesus engage in the same practices that have always transformed Gentiles into Jews: 1) Circumcision (in this case, the original circumcision that God desired, the circumcision of the heart),[178] 2) Sacrifice (in this case, rather than making a sacrifice in the temple, they receive God's only sacrifice for sin, the person of Jesus Christ,[179] 3) Learning Torah (in this case, their rabbi is Jesus, and their instructor is the Holy Spirit,[180] and 4) Immersion (in this case, baptism in water into Christ.[181]

Irrevocable Covenants and the Jewish People

God's plan for Gentile inclusion did not demand or even suggest Jewish exclusion. Natural Israel, the Jews according to the flesh, continue in covenantal relationship with God. Paul made this truth crystal clear: "God's gifts and his call are irrevocable."[182] For this reason and for this reason alone, the benefits of the covenant that God made with Abraham and his lineage according to the flesh still pertain to the Jews. Paul affirmed this truth by quoting the

---

175 Romans 4:13.
176 Ephesians 2:19. See Gotthard Victor Lechler and Karl Gerok, Johann Peter Lange, eds., *Theological and Homiletical Commentary on the Acts of the Apostles* (Edinburgh, Scotland: T. and T. Clark, 1864), p. 10.
177 Romans 11:17–18. See Garroway, p. 151: "Although such Gentiles have no physiological relationship whatsoever to the patriarchs, God is nonetheless grafting them into the family tree of Israel."
178 Deuteronomy 10:61, Jeremiah 4:4; Romans 2:29.
179 Romans 3:25; Hebrews 10:12; 1 John 2:2.
180 Matthew 5:17–48; John 16:13.
181 Romans 6:4; Colossians 2:12.
182 Romans 11:29, NIV.

prophet Isaiah in saying that except the Lord of *Sabaoth* had left Israel a seed, they would have been as Sodom and Gomorrah[183] and by declaring that God's Word had always promised that a remnant of Israel would be saved.[184] Indeed, the continuing blessing of God upon the Jews is the proof that God used to confirm his own immutability: "For I am the LORD, I do not change; therefore you are not consumed, O sons of Jacob."[185] Because God never changes or abandons his covenant commitments, his personal promises to the descendants of Abraham continue to be fulfilled, and they will never be abrogated.

Despite the fact that generation after generation of Christian theologians has argued that "ethnic Israel, the Jewish particularity . . . were supposed to come to an end"[186] and that "Jewish particularity no longer had any reason to continue, since all of God's children were now to be brought into the universal church,"[187] the truth remains that God's relationship with Israel has never been destroyed, and it will never be destroyed. Though Christian theologians have continued to posit the arrogant triumphalist heresy of supersessionism in which they have argued that Christianity has replaced Judaism and that Christians have replaced Jews in the economy of salvation, the truth is that Israel, the Jewish people, remains God's Chosen People and will continue to remain his Chosen People forever. God's particularity in relationship to the Jewish people, therefore, has not been replaced or obviated by God's universality because he "wants all people to be saved and to come to a knowledge of the truth"[188] by his command for all people everywhere to repent[189] and by his making the provision of atonement for the sins of all humanity through the death and resurrection of his Son.[190]

Paul revealed a profound truth when he declared that the Torah was a "guardian to bring us to Messiah."[191] While his statement was universal, directed to "us" (both the Galatian Gentiles to whom he was writing and the Israelites who were his fleshly kinsmen), the apostle's specific subject was the Jewish people. The Greek word that Paul used to describe the "guardian" of Israel was παιδαγωγός (*paidagogós*). This word has often been translated "schoolmaster" (KJV), "tutor" (NKJV, NASB), "disciplinarian" (NRSV), "slave" (NJB), "custodian" (CJB), or "servant" (ESV). Each of these translations,

---

[183] Romans 9:29, quoting Isaiah 1:9.
[184] Romans 9:27, referencing Isaiah 10:22.
[185] Malachi 3:6.
[186] Shaye J. D. Cohen, *Why Aren't Jewish Women Circumcised? Gender and Covenant in Judaism* (Berkeley, CA: The University of California Press, 2005), p. 83.
[187] Cohen, p. 83.
[188] 1 Timothy 2:4, NIV.
[189] Acts 17:30.
[190] Romans 3:25.
[191] Galatians 3:24.

however, is clearly deficient in the light of the Greek word that Paul used to describe the relationship of the Torah to Israel. *Paidagogós* is most accurately translated, as it is in the NIV and ESV, as "guardian."

In the Hellenic world, a *paidagogós* was a family servant who was designated as a guardian or protector of the children in a household. He was responsible for training the children in etiquette, deportment, and social graces and for escorting them to their teachers. The *paidagogós* was not, however, the ultimate teacher, tutor, or schoolmaster for the children. The children of wealthy families remained under the supervision of the pedagogue and were not permitted so much as to step out of the house without his company until the time of puberty.[192] The *paidagogós* tradition was precisely what Paul had in mind when he said, "But before faith came, under law we were guarded, being shut up to the faith about to be revealed."[193] The Greek word translated "guarded" ("kept" in the KJV) is ἐφρουρούεθα (*ephrourouetha*). This word means "to keep in a state of security" as "under military guard." It does not have any indication of being incarcerated for crimes or as a material witness. Instead, it connotes the idea of having one's safety ensured.[194] The Torah, therefore, was a guardian, not a curse to Israel; it was a means of protection, not of enslavement. It was for this reason that David could say with millions of Jews before and after him, "Your Torah is my delight."[195]

The Torah, then, was designed by God to be a means of protecting Israel and keeping them from the evils of the Gentile world until they could be brought to Messiah, who would be their ultimate teacher.[196] The Torah, therefore, is a blessing, not a curse.[197] It is the "perfect law that gives freedom."[198]

---

[192] Hans-Dieter Betz, *Galatians* (Philadelphia, PA: Fortress Press, 1979), p. 177.
[193] Galatians 3:23, author's translation.
[194] *The Analytical Greek Lexicon* (London, UK: Samuel Bagster & Sons, 1967), p. 432.
[195] Psalm 119:74.
[196] In Romans 2:14, Paul demonstrated his understanding that the core and fundamental principles of the Torah were even "written on the hearts" of the Gentiles who did not formally have the Torah in their possession: "The Gentiles who do not have the Law do instinctively the things of the Law . . . in that they show the work of the Law written in their hearts, their conscience bearing witness and their thoughts alternately accusing or else defending them." So in a very real sense, God had written the Torah on the hearts of all human beings—Jew and Gentile alike—so that the fundamental instructions of the Law, the Ten Commandments, were in some way inscribed in the very essence of their humanity and were manifest in the action of the human conscience (Romans 2:15). This, in turn, was God's way of using the Torah to bring Gentiles to the Messiah, along with the Jewish people, and to include them in the covenant of promise to Abraham so that they, too, could be "justified by faith" (Galatians 3:24).
[197] When Paul declared that "Christ redeemed us from the curse of the Law" (Galatians 3:13), he was not saying, "Christ has redeemed us from the Law," nor was he saying that the law was a curse. He was underscoring the fact that the curses that were directed against those who disobeyed the divine commandments of the Torah (Deuteronomy 28:15–45) had been removed by the Messiah when he became a curse by taking on himself the sins of all humanity. The Torah did, indeed, contain curses; however, it was not *en se* a curse.
[198] James 1:25, NIV.

Consequently, faith in the validity of God's Word and works of obedience to the commandments in that word, then, are two complementing parts of one continuum, with the latter serving as evidence of the existence of the former.[199] This is the "reacting nomism" that Richard Longenecker described as he viewed Jewish tradition at the time of Paul, the "molding [of] one's life in all its varying relations according to the Law in response to the love and grace of God."[200] Though some have abused the Torah, its function as a guardian is still the same—to bring Israel to Messiah, that they may all be justified by faith. The Torah and its covenant with Israel remain God's means of maintaining the corporate identity of his Chosen People, of keeping them in check against infidelity, of maintaining their faith in him until the time of his salvation history is completed when the Messiah comes.

The purpose of the Torah in its relationship with Israel has never changed. Through the centuries and even to this day, it has continued to be a guardian of the Jewish people, ensuring the continuity of their faith in the one and only God. Despite every attempt by the tyrants of history to effect the genocide of the Jewish people, the Torah has preserved them as a distinct and recognizable entity in the world. Rita Brownstein has very poignantly and accurately reported that "while the Jews have kept the Torah in even the most hostile conditions, perhaps it is more correct to say that it is the Torah, with its infinite wisdom and goodness, that has kept the Jews."[201] If the Torah were ever a guardian to bring Israel to Messiah, it remains such and will continue to remain such until the time that the Messiah comes to renew, restore, fulfill, complete, and teach the Torah to Israel and to the nations,[202] revealing perfectly all of his ways[203] and bringing everlasting peace on earth.

---

[199] James 2:17–18.

[200] Richard N. Longenecker, *Paul, the Apostle of Liberty* (Carol Stream, IL: Tyndale House, 1966), p. 76.

[201] Rita Milos Brownstein, *Jewish Holiday Style* (New York: Simon & Schuster, 1999), p. 43.

[202] Jewish tradition has long expected that the coming of the Messiah will bring about a change in the Torah. See Joseph Klausner, *The Messianic Idea in Israel from Its Beginning to the Completion of the Mishnah*, tr. W. F. Stinespring (New York: Ulan Press, 2012), pp. 445–450; Gershom Gerhard Scholem, *On Kabbalah and Its Symbolism (Mysticism and Kaballah)* (New York: Schocken Books, 1965), pp. 66–68; and Gershom Scholem, *Messianic Idea in Judaism, and Other Essays on Jewish Spirituality* (New York: Schocken Books, 1971), pp. 19–24, 53–58, 65–67. In Midrash *Qohelet* 2.1 (a commentary on Ecclesiastes 2:1), the midrashist declared that "all the Torah which you learn in this world is 'vanity' in comparison with Torah [which will be learnt] in the world to come." Feemi Adeyemi says "This seems to indicate that the Torah to be learned in the world to come will probably not be the one that is learned in this age." Femi Adeyemi, *The New Covenant Torah in Jeremiah and the Law of Christ in Paul* (New York: Peter Lang Publishing, 2006), p. 81. Many rabbis have commented that it is not so much the Torah that will be changed in the Messianic Age as it is the heart and comprehension of the people so that it will be differently and more satisfactorily studied" (Adeyemi, p. 82).

[203] David Sears, *Compassion for Humanity in the Jewish Tradition* (Northvale, NJ: Jason Aronson, 1998), p. 152. Sears quotes David Kimchi, noting that "'Torah shall go forth from Zion' to all nations. The teacher will be the Messianic King, concerning whom it states, 'And he shall judge the nations.'"

A Prophetic Restoration

God's plan for the Jewish people and the nation of Israel is to be unfolded in a threefold restoration: the land of Israel is to be restored to the people of Israel; the people of Israel are to be restored to the land of Israel; and the people of Israel are to be restored to their God. The Zionist movement that began in the late nineteenth century has brought millions of Jewish people back to the land of Israel from the dispersion among the nations and has brought about the reestablishment of the nation of Israel in a part of the land which God promised to Abraham has been a direct result of the faith which those Jews who have made *aliyah* have had in God's promise to Abraham. Their faith in God's covenant has brought the benefits of that covenant to them. Through this means, the land has been restored to the people, and the people have been restored to the land.

The next stage of restoration is for the people of Israel to be restored to God. A significant percentage of the Jewish world population is either non-observant, secular, agnostic, or atheistic. The prophets predict a move of God that will turn the hearts of the Jewish people and the nation of Israel back to God and to his Word. At that time, they will experience what Isaiah prophesied: "Israel will be saved by the LORD with an everlasting salvation."[204] The apostle Paul alluded to this very same prophetic promise when he declared unequivocally that "all Israel will be saved."[205] Paul did not invent this scenario, however. He was relying on another of Isaiah's prophecies: "Your people, *all of them righteous*, shall possess the land for all time."[206] Then the apostle quoted directly from Isaiah's further prediction that "the Redeemer will come to Zion and to those who turn from transgression in Jacob,"[207] saying that his vision of the salvation of "all Israel" would occur when "the deliverer will come from Zion and banish ungodliness from Jacob."[208] Paul realized that it was not a part of his job description to determine who would be saved. Though he understood that "all who are descended from Israel are not Israel,"[209] still he

---

[204] Isaiah 45:17.

[205] Romans 11:26.

[206] Isaiah 60:21, TNK, emphasis added. Even the sages recognized three exceptions for Jews who would not inherit life in the resurrection of the dead: "These are the ones who do not have a share in the World-to-Come: He who says that the resurrection of the dead is not in the Torah, and the Torah is not from Heaven; and an Epicurean" (Mishnah, *Sanhedrin* 11:1-2). Paul chose to leave the divine judgment of who would be saved in the hands of the only Person qualified to make that judgment: YHWH, the righteous judge.

[207] Isaiah 59:20.

[208] Romans 11:26, ESV.

[209] Romans 9:6, NIV.

had the calm assurance that "the Lord knows those who are his."[210] And, he was fully convinced that "the gifts and the calling of God are irrevocable."[211] For Paul, then, the spiritual restoration of all Israel was to be of the same nature as both the restoration of the nation of Israel and the resurrection of the righteous dead at the end of the age, for he described that renewal in these terms: "What will their acceptance be but life from the dead?"[212]

Whatever the case may be, the people and nation of Israel will come to the light of the Messiah. This is why the kingdom of God will be established in the nation of Israel rather than in some other nation of the world. Jerusalem will be God's capital city when his kingdom physically comes on earth. The camp of the saints of the Most High God will be in the Holy City for the thousand years of the Messiah's reign.[213] The inheritance of the land from the Euphrates to the river of Egypt that has been promised to the children of Abraham will be inherited by both the natural and spiritual Jews, who will reign with the Messiah over the entire earth from his capital city, Jerusalem, Israel, and from his capitol in the restored temple. The Messiah will reign in the place where God has chosen from time immemorial to place his name, and יְרוּשָׁלַם (Yerushalayim) will finally be the "foundation of world peace."

God's great purpose in returning the land of Israel to the people of Israel, in bringing the Jews again from the Diaspora, and in turning their hearts again to God is designed to set the stage for Israel's national day of salvation[214] and the subsequent coming of Messiah. When that day comes, God's four-thousand-year-old covenant with Abraham will have been made sure to all his children, both the natural and the spiritual.[215] The Messiah will reign over all the earth in a kingdom that will manifest the nature of the unchanging God by perfectly implementing the principles of biblical Judaism. When this great prophetic event occurs, those who are of the faith of Abraham, God's Chosen People of every generation—both Jew and Gentile—will inherit the earth just as God promised Israel in the *Tanakh*[216] and as Jesus promised the church in the Apostolic Scriptures.[217]

Election: Christian Fruit—Jewish Root.

---

210 2 Timothy 2:19.
211 Romans 11:29.
212 Romans 11:15.
213 Revelation 20:6–9.
214 Zechariah 12:10; 13:1; Romans 9:27.
215 Romans 4:16.
216 Psalm 37:11.
217 Matthew 5:5; 25:34.

CHAPTER 17

CHURCH

When Jesus asked his disciples who they understood him to be, Peter's effusive answer encapsulated one of the most profound truths in all of Holy Scripture: "You are he, the Messiah, Son of the living God."[1] Realizing that his heavenly Father had revealed the ultimate truth about his very nature, Jesus immediately replied, "On this rock I will build my church; and the gates of hell shall not prevail against it."[2] Jesus assured his disciples that he was ready to initiate an effort that was destined to succeed even in the face of even the vilest opposition. Did the church that Jesus planned to build, however, represent a totally new reality that had never been considered in the history of humanity? Was Jesus the ultimate innovator, or was he merely taking another step in the unfolding drama of salvation history?

Many scholars have taken Jesus' "I-will-build-my-church" declaration to mean that his divine mission on earth was to clean the religious slate of what God had been doing for four thousand years and start totally fresh again. For them, the "church" was an amazing innovation that was truly *sui generis*,[3] a wonderful institution that no one had ever conceived before. Some have even argued that God had finally decided to abolish the jejune and failed religion of the "Old Testament" that was called Judaism and was announcing was announcing the birth of the vibrant and efficacious new faith of the "New Testament" that would be called Christianity. As late as the twentieth century, this theme had become so pervasive in Germany that some scholars called for the complete dejudaization of Christian faith[4] and musical giants contrasted Jesus with the "pervasive metaphor of Judaism as

---

[1] Matthew 16:16.
[2] Matthew 16:18, ESV.
[3] Tim S. Perry, *Radical Difference: A Defence of Hendrik Kraemer's Theology of Religions* (Waterloo, Canada: The Wilfrid Laurier University Press, 2001), p. 98.
[4] Many Christian theologians and Christian academic organizations had agendas similar to the 1939 German Institute for the Study and Eradication of Jewish Influence on German Church Life, which announced its task as "The Dejudaization of the Religious Life as the Task of German Theology and Church." Susannah Heschel, *The Aryan Jesus: Christian Theologians and the Bible in Nazi Germany* (Princeton, NJ; Princeton University Press, 2008), p. 2.

the very stuff of egoism, that Judaism which Jesus came to destroy."[5] Over time, the argument has continually been made that God had finally concluded that after centuries of working with the Jewish people through the Law, his only viable course of action was to terminate the old covenant that he had made with the Israelites and, finally, to establish a new covenant with a new Chosen People, the church. Whereas Israel and the Law had failed miserably, the church and its new faith would surely be poised to accomplish all of God's purposes in the earth.

But was this what God intended? Was this the work that Jesus came to do? In order to find answers to these and other questions about what Jesus said and did, it is essential to place his words and his actions into the context from which they came. Serious students of the life and ministry of Jesus must return to Second Temple Judaism, to the life and practices of first-century Jewry. "The key concepts of Jesus' teaching, therefore, cannot be understood apart from the Jewish heritage."[6] What Jesus said and did can never be fully understood if it is transplanted into Gentile soil, no matter in what part of the non-Israelite world one may choose to locate them. His words were spoken by a Jew in the land of the Jews to no one but Jews.[7] Only when Christians return to this place, this people, and this time can they truly comprehend the meaning and function of the church and then contextualize them for application in their own societies and cultures.

Supersessionism and Ecclesiology

To this very day, however, the majority of Christian theologians still echo the traditional and historical Christian party line, championing some of the views that one of the church's earliest and most devastating heretics created. In the early second century, Marcion of Sinope argued for a Christianized Gnosticism in which he maintained that Jesus was the good God from heaven who replaced and destroyed the evil God of the Jews, who Marcion believed had created the evil material world and the false religion of Judaism. Through the efforts of such heretics as Marcion, Christianity

---

[5] Richard Wagner, *Jesus of Nazareth and Other* Writings, tr. William Ashton Ellis (Lincoln, NE: The University of Nebraska Press, 1995), noted in Paul Lawrence Rose, *Wagner: Race and Revolution* (New Haven, CT: Yale University Press, 1992), p. 56. Rose points out that Wagner did not attempt to state the role of Judaism since there was "no need for him to do so, since . . . Christianity has abrogated the old law, that is, the Jewish law."

[6] *Within Context: Guidelines for the Catechetical Presentation of Jews and Judaism in the New Testament* (Secretariat for Catholic-Jewish Relations of the National Conference of Catholic Bishops, the Education Department of the United States Catholic Conference, and Interfaith Affairs Department of the Anti-Defamation League of B'nai B'rith, 1986), p. 59.

[7] Matthew 15:24.

came to recognize Judaism as "null and void" and to consider itself not only "the self-appointed heir to Judaism" but also the religion that replaced "the parent faith altogether."[8] It was in this situation that "contempt [for the Jews] became a 'virtue'" among Christians, says Paul O'Shea.[9] By the time of the Middle Ages, this ancient Gnostic heresy had clothed itself in the ostentatious garments of Christian triumphalism *vis-à-vis* the Jews wherein it was continually argued that God had replaced Judaism with Christianity and Jews with Christians in the economy of salvation. In century after century, supersessionism, in various guises, has continued to characterize much, if not most, of the Christian church. Sadly, a virtual neo-Marcionism, as it were, continues to survive in the teaching and practice of Christian replacement and displacement doctrines. And to this day, an astounding number of scholars and church leaders continue to promote the insidious heresy that is often called "replacement theology" and is thought to be an outworking of "covenant theology,"[10] as well as other Christians traditions.

The Criterion of Dissimilarity

Over the past two centuries, a many Christian scholars have come to maintain that anything in the Apostolic Scriptures which suggests even a remote connection between Jesus and the Jewish people or between the nascent church and Second Temple Judaism must be an editorial gloss made by a redactor to suit his own preconceived theological agenda. No possible continuity could exist between the Old Testament and the words of Jesus, they say. This idea has been enshrined in the "Criterion of Discontinuity,"[11] which defies both reason and the most foundational principles of biblical hermeneutics

---

[8] Paul O'Shea, *A Cross Too Heavy: Pope Pius XII and the Jews of Europe* (New York: Palgrave Macmillan, 2011), p. 35.

[9] O'Shea, p. 35.

[10] Paul P. Enns, *The Moody Handbook of Theology* (Chicago, IL: Moody Publishers, 1989), p. 15. Enns notes that the replacement theology which maintains that the church has replaced Israel in God's program is a distinctive of Reformed Theology, which is a development from Calvinistic theology.

[11] The Criterion of Dissimilarity is a development in the historical-critical method of interpretation of Scripture which includes form criticism, redaction criticism, literary analysis, and historical analysis. This theory has often led to the rejection of most, if not all, of the declarations of Jesus as they are reported in the Gospels. Indeed, the Jesus Seminar, which has taken these forms of criticism to their "logical" extremes, has concluded that the only saying attributed to Jesus Gospels which is almost certain to have actually come from his mouth is, "Render unto Caesar the things that belong to Caesar" (Mark 12:17). Every other saying is suspected of being invented out of whole cloth by subsequent Christian leaders or of being redacted to fit emerging theological concepts. See Craig A. Evans, *Fabricating Jesus: How Modern Scholars Distort the Gospels* (Downers Grove, IL: InterVarsity Press, 2006, and Ben Witherington III, *The Jesus Quest: The Third Search for the Jew of Nazareth* (Downers Grove, IL: InterVarsity Press, 1995).

and exegesis.[12] This criterion maintains the absurd proposition that, in order to be accepted as having been authentic, any saying or action that is attributed to Jesus must be dissimilar to both Jewish sayings before and during his time and also to teachings of the church after his time. John P. Meier is entirely correct when he concludes that "the criterion of discontinuity, instead of giving us an assured minimum about Jesus, winds up giving us a caricature by divorcing Jesus from the Judaism that influenced him and from the Church that he influenced."[13]

Christian theology has finally arrived full circle to a biblically untenable position which, in effect, maintains that true religion must be "anything but the God of the Jews."[14] In so doing, the church has embraced the position held by virtually all heathen religions, by monistic New Age philosophy, and by the emerging Neo-Paganism that now threatens not only biblical religion but also the very fabric of civilization itself. When the church and Christianity are divorced from their Jewish context and their Hebrew foundations, they become aberrant forms of religion that neither Jesus nor his apostles would recognize.

Nowhere has this supersessionist view been more devastating to Christian theology and polity than in its ecclesiology, its very self-definition—the way in which the church views itself. The neo-Marcionite heresy of supersessionism argues for a Christian church that has been wrenched from its moorings in the safe harbor of biblically Hebraic truth and set adrift in a maelstrom of ominous abstractions, in the pernicious winds of doctrine that have blown in from the musings of philosophers and mystics, whose views lack foundations in biblical truth, and in teachings and practices that Jesus and apostles would have found ridiculous and heretical. Because it has been divorced from its historical context, the church has come to define itself in diverse and often non-biblical terms. Both the church and its constituent membership, therefore, are suffering from classical symptoms of identity crisis. It has long lost its biblical identity, and it no longer knows who or what it is or where it is going. This endemic and debilitating condition demands a healing balm, a recovery of self-identity. The church must

---

[12] The Criterion of Dissimilarity divorces the sayings and actions of Jesus reported in the Gospels from their context, thereby defying two of the fundamental rules of biblical hermeneutics: 1) Scripture interprets Scripture and 2) context interprets text. No text can be rightly interpreted unless it is placed in its grammatical, historical, and cultural context. Not allowing Scripture to interpret itself is utterly absurd. At the same time, taking the sayings of Jesus out of their context creates the environment where the old dictum, "A text without a context is a pretext," is readily applied. In fact, this dictum should probably be modified to say, "A text without a context is a pretext for proof texts!"

[13] John P. Meier, "Basic Methodology," in *Handbook for the Study of the Historical Jesus*, Tom Holmén and Stanley E. Porter, eds. (Leiden, The Netherlands: Koninklijke Brill, 2011), p. 316.

[14] Rottenberg, *Christianity*, pp. 93–103.

find its way back home, back to the matrix from which it emerged—the Hebraic faith of Jesus and the apostles.

The Great Parenthesis?

Many Christians, particularly those in the dispensationalist wing of evangelicalism, believe that the church has been a great parenthesis to which God was forced to resort because the majority of the first-century Jewish community did not receive Jesus as Messiah and Lord. Charles Ryrie says that "the church did not exist in Old Testament times but was constituted on the Day of Pentecost."[15] Others have argued that "since the church is the body of Christ . . . it could not have begun until Pentecost."[16] They have concluded, therefore, that "the church is . . . totally unforeseen in the Old Testament."[17] Stephen O'Leary describes this absurdity more colorfully: "The epoch of the church was a new dispensation of grace, which occupied a 'mysterious, prophetic time warp,' a 'great parenthesis,' which had no place in God's original plans."[18] Analyzing the projections of Plymouth Brethren dispensationalist J. N. Darby, Ernest Sandeen summarized the "Great-Parenthesis" position this way: "After the rejection of Jesus by the Jews, 'God had broken the continuity of history, stopped the prophetic clock, and instituted the church.'"[19]

But was God caught off guard when the majority of the Israelite nation failed to accept his Son Jesus as the Messiah? Was the omniscient God totally in the dark on this development? Was he utterly surprised? Was he so angered that his plans had been stymied that he destroyed what he had been working to achieve for four millennia and started all over again? Such ideas are patently absurd! In reality, God had already predicted Israel's unbelief: "Go and tell this people: 'Keep on listening, and do not perceive . . . Render the hearts of this people insensitive, their ears dull, and their eyes dim."[20] Additionally, Isaiah's prophecy was made in the context of the awesome vision in which he saw "the LORD high and lifted up."[21]

---

[15] Charles C. Ryrie, *Basic Theology: A Popular Systematic Guide to Understanding Biblical Truth* (Chicago, IL: Moody Press, 1986), p. 463.

[16] See the report of Millard J. Erickson, *A Basic Guide to Eschatology: Making Sense of the Millennium* (Grand Rapids, MI: Baker Books, 1998), p. 117.

[17] Erickson, *Basic Guide*, p. 117.

[18] Stephen D. O'Leary, *Arguing the Apocalypse: A Theory of Millennial Rhetoric* (New York: Oxford University Press, 1994). p. 138.

[19] Ernest Sandeen, *The Roots of Fundamentalism: British and American Millenarianism 1800–1930* (Chicago, IL: The University of Chicago Press, 2008). See also Ovid Need, Jr., *Death of the Church Victorious: Tracing the Roots and Implications of Modern Dispensationalism* (Mulberry, IN: Sovereign Grace Publishers, 2002), pp. 212–224.

[20] Isaiah 6:9–10.

[21] Isaiah 1:6–4.

What Isaiah actually witnessed, however, was a Christophany,[22] a fact that was clearly pointed out by the apostle John when he declared: "He has blinded their eyes and hardened their hearts, so they can neither see with their eyes, nor understand with their hearts . . . Isaiah said this because he saw Jesus' glory and spoke about him."[23] There was, moreover, a divine strategy involved in this phenomenon: "Did they stumble so as to fall beyond recovery?" Paul asked. Before he responded to his own rhetorical question, the apostle thundered: "May it never be!"[24] Then he explained that because Israel had transgressed, "salvation has come to the Gentiles to make them jealous."[25] God was neither surprised nor angry when the leaders of Israel did not receive his Son. As a matter of fact, he had orchestrated and planned it that way! As Peter definitively said, "[Jesus] was delivered up according to the predetermined plan and foreknowledge of God."[26] There was nothing accidental or unexpected in Israel's partial hardness or the rejection of Jesus by the temple leaders. It was part of a mystery that had been concealed in Scripture for centuries, a mystery that was unfolding according to God's plan of salvation for all humanity.[27]

The church, then, was not, as John Phillips has mistakenly argued, "a new piece of cloth altogether" in which "Jews and Gentiles who converted to Christ became members of the church, a new entity entirely in God's dealings with men."[28] The church was not a new and unprecedented thing that had been inserted, unexpectedly and parenthetically, into God's plan for the ages. It was, instead, a continuation of the unfolding plan of salvation. The church of Jesus was formed in complete continuity with the workings of God that had begun with Abraham and had continued to develop progressively through the centuries of life in the Israelite nation. Indeed, as Richard Cooke has rightly said, "the Christian Church is not a creation, but a development, a continuation under more vitalizing influences, of the Church

---

[22] Christophanies (manifestations of Christ) were pre-incarnational appearances of the divine *Logos* (which became incarnate in Jesus) either as a man or as an angel (Genesis 22:14; 31:11, 13; Exodus 14:19; Isaiah 63:9; Malachi 3:1). In this case in Isaiah 6, the *Logos* appeared as himself in the pre-incarnational glory that he reassumed post-incarnationally (Revelation 1:10-17). These appearances of God as either man or angel are also called theophanies (manifestations or appearances of God). Reimund Bieringer, *The New Testament and Rabbinic Literature* (Leiden, The Netherlands, Koninklijke Brill NV, 2010), p. 458.

[23] John 12:40–41 (NIV). King David also confirmed this truth: "May their eyes be darkened that they cannot see" (Romans 11:10).

[24] The language of the King James Version translation is more picturesque: "God forbid!"

[25] Romans 11:11, NIV, NASB.

[26] Acts 2:23.

[27] Romans 11:25.

[28] John Phillips, *Exploring Romans: An Expository Commentary* (Grand Rapids, MI: Kregel Academic, 1969), p. 246.

originally founded in the family of Abraham."[29] It should not, therefore, surprise anyone who understands this cardinal truth that "unless the Old Testament is known, the church cannot even know who it is."[30] This observation by Elizabeth Achtemeier is congruent with Ronald Heine's declaration that "the Old Testament is intertwined in the church's gospel in such a way that it cannot be extricated without destroying the gospel."[31] No wonder Sidney Greidanus said, "Without the Old Testament we cannot know what the church is, for the New Testament describes the church in images from the Old Testament."[32] The Hebrew Scriptures are the foundation of the Apostolic Scriptures and, therefore, are the means of giving Christian faith and experience a context in which they can be understood.

Peter projected a prime example of this parallel imagery when he used Isaiah's definition of Israel as "the people whom I formed for myself so that they might declare my praise"[33] to describe the church as "a chosen race, a royal priesthood, a holy nation, God's own people, in order that you may proclaim the mighty acts of him who called you out of darkness into his marvelous light."[34] How would the church know what it means to be "the temple of the living God"[35] without understanding the temple of the Hebrew Scriptures? How would it comprehend that in some dimension, it participates in "the Israel of God"[36] if it had never had any connection with Israel and the Jewish people? How can it understand the "bride of Christ" if it cannot understand Israel as the bride of YHWH?[37]

The Apostolic Scriptures, says John Bright, depict the church as "God's covenant and servant people, called to exhibit the righteousness of his Kingdom before the world, charged with proclaiming that Kingdom in the world and summoning men to its covenant fellowship."[38] This identity, this calling, and this charge, however, were directed by God to the Israelite nation

---

[29] Richard Joseph Cooke, *Christianity and Childhood: or, The Relation of Children to the Church* (Cincinnati, OH: Cranston and Stowe, 1891), p. 141.

[30] Elizabeth Achtemeier, "The Canon as the Voice of the Living God," in *Reclaiming the Bible for the Church*, Carl E. Braaten and Robert W. Jenson, eds. (Grand Rapids, MI: Wm. B. Eerdmans Publishing Co., 1995), p. 126.

[31] Ronald E. Heine, *Reading the Old Testament with the Ancient Church: Exploring the Formation of Early Christian Thought* (Grand Rapids, MI: Baker Academic, 2007), p. 193.

[32] Sidney Greidanus, *Preaching Christ from the Old Testament: A Contemporary Hermeneutical Method* (Grand Rapids, MI: Wm. B. Eerdmans Publishing Co., 1999), p. 29.

[33] Isaiah 43:21.

[34] 1 Peter 2:9.

[35] 2 Corinthians 6:16.

[36] Galatians 6:16.

[37] Ephesians 5:25; Jeremiah 3:14. Jewish tradition says that God was married to Israel under the *chuppah* (canopy) of the cloud of glory at Mt. Sinai.

[38] John Bright, *The Kingdom of God* (Nashville, TN: Abingdon Press, 1980), p. 259.

before there was such a thing as the Christian church! Binyamin Elon confirms the identity of Israel in this manner: "The historical continuity of God's people, Israel, with God's covenant has been unbroken since patriarchal times."[39] John Durham demonstrates the calling, declaring that God chose Israel to be "a display-people, a showcase to the world how being in covenant with Yahweh changes a people."[40] William Dumbrell explains the charge: "Israel's task within the Promised Land to exhibit trust in God's covenantal directions is intended to summon the nations to share its experience."[41] It is undeniably true, therefore, that "the Churches of the Old Testament and of the New are identical. Both are called by the same terms of endearment in addition to their technical designations."[42] No doubt, Richard Cooke was right when he said that "whatever we find in [the New Testament] Church, the same may be seen in the Church of the patriarchs. Nothing has been, or can be added to what constituted the Church at Pentecost. And nothing is in that Church that is not a development of everything essential to human salvation in the ancient commonwealth of Israel."[43]

The church, then, was not an innovation that was introduced for the very first time by Jesus and his disciples. It was rather the continuation of God's dealing with his covenant people, Israel. In fact, it was, quite simply, the continuation of God's covenant community. The dynamics of the church of the "New Testament" were nothing more than continuations of the dynamics that were manifest in the church of the "Old Testament." Once that simple truth is understood, it is much easier to proceed with the task of unraveling the true nature and work of the church.

Ecclesiology

The term *church* is both very familiar and very misunderstood, and generally at the same time. What is the church? Who is a part of it? When did it

---

[39]Binyamin Elon, *God's Covenant with Israel: Establishing Biblical Boundaries in Today's World* (Toronto, Canada: New Leaf Publishing Group, Balfour Books, 2005), p. 17.

[40] John I. Durham, *Exodus* (Waco, TX: Word Books, 1987), p. 263.

[41] William J. Dumbrell, *Covenant and Creation: An Old Testament Covenant Theology* (Crown Hill, UK: Paternoster/Authentic Media, 2013), p. 76.

[42] Richard Joseph Cooke, *Christianity and Childhood: or, The Relation of Children to the Church* (Cincinnati, OH: Cranston and Stowe, 1891), p. 141. Interestingly, the Hebrew Scriptures use the terms *bride* (Isaiah 62:5; Jeremiah 32:2), *kingdom of priests* (Exodus 19:6), *holy nation* (Exodus 19:6), and *chosen people* (1 Chronicles 16:13; Psalm 33:12) to describe Israel while the Apostolic Scriptures use the terms *bride* (Revelation 19:7), *kingdom of priests* (1 Peter 2:9), *holy nation* (1 Peter 2:9), and *chosen people* (1 Peter 2:9) to describe the church. Perhaps the most important appellative that is applied to both Israel and the church is the term *bride*. God is married to both Israel and the church; however, since God is not a bigamist, both Israel and the church must somehow participate in one bride. Any ecclesiology that does not in some way include Israel is clearly deficient.

[43] Cooke, p. 141.

320

begin? Where does it exist? What is its structure? How does it operate? Why does it exist? What is its ultimate end? Does the church make Christians, or do Christians make it the church? Is the church merely a local congregation of believers? Is it a denomination? Is it a network of denominations? Is it the entire Christian community? Is the church congregational, presbyterial, or episcopal? These are the questions of ecclesiology, the branch of systematic theology that studies the nature and mission of the church. Anyone who has interacted to any degree with believers of various Christian communions knows that the answers to these questions are many, and they are widely divergent.

Much of the misunderstanding of the term *church* comes from the fact that it has been used indiscriminately to describe so many different things. In modern parlance, the word *church* can be applied to an architectural structure ("We went to church today."), to the worship that is practiced in a building ("Church was wonderful today!"), to the Christian church in general (the "invisible church"), to a denomination in particular, to a local congregation, to a "cell church," and to a "house church." Adding to this dilemma of definition is the basic lack of understanding of the very nature and essence of the church that is common to virtually all Christians, regardless as to the nature of their denominational affiliation or lack thereof.

Sadly, throughout the history of the Christian church, none of the massive and exhaustive efforts of research, analysis, and debate that have gone into theology, Christology, and other matters of doctrine and polity has been devoted to ecclesiology. In the early centuries of ecclesiastical history, exhaustive study and extensive debate were devoted to matters of theology and Christology.[44] In the high Middle Ages, study was given to soteriology, the atonement of Christ.[45] In the sixteenth and later centuries, the focus of theological development was on the doctrine of salvation by grace through faith.[46] In the twentieth century, pneumatology, the study of the Holy Spirit, received extensive study.[47] If such exhaustive efforts had also been devoted to the study and discussion of ecclesiology, perhaps a far more scripturally-accurate definition of the church would have been forthcoming. If so, the church may well have been spared the excesses that have threatened the very fabric of its existence, challenging even the promise of Jesus that the "gates of hell" would not prevail against it. The sad truth is that so little effort has been given to the study of

---

44 McGrath, p. 11.
45 Ronald K. Rittgers, *The Reformation of Suffering: Pastoral Theology and Lay Piety in Late Medieval and Early Modern Germany* (New York: Oxford University Press, 2012), p. 70.
46 Kenan B. Osborne, *A Theology of the Church for the Third Millennium: A Franciscan Approach* (Leiden, The Netherlands: Koninklijke Brill NV, 2009), p. 203.
47 Veli-Matti Kärkkäinen, *The Holy Spirit: A Guide to Christian Theology* (Louisville, KY: Westminster John Knox Press, 2012), p. 85.

the church that ecclesiology is hardly even mentioned in many texts on systematic theology.[48] As Georges Florovsky has said, the development of the doctrine of the church has hardly passed its "pretheological phase."[49]

To analyze the subject of ecclesiology, however, is to touch the very foundation of Christian self-identity. Christians' understanding of themselves, of who they are and what they are doing, is determined to a large degree by ecclesiological considerations. The converse is also true, for ecclesiology is determined essentially by who Christians envision themselves to be and what they do in response to their perceived self-identity. The fragmented nature of the Christian church, therefore, is largely the result of an inadequate understanding of ecclesiology. Far too many Christians have no idea what the church really is, and they certainly do not understand how it should function in continuity with the first-century community of Jesus and the apostles.

In a church that is supposed to be seeking the "unity of the faith" and the "full knowledge of the Son of God,"[50] how can different groups of Christians arrive at such widely diverse and divergent ecclesiologies? The answer is quite simple when the truth is acknowledged. Most—if not all—ecclesiologies were developed and are sustained within different social, political, and economic milieus. Ecclesiological perspectives are profoundly affected by tradition. One needs only to make a cursory survey of ecclesiastical history to see that the church has been viewed in many diverse ways. It should be obvious that all of these interpretations cannot be wholly correct, and it should perhaps be suggested that none of them is necessarily totally wrong. No doubt, the truth can be found in the middle ground between polarized extremes or in an amalgamation of ideas into one balanced position that is both biblical and practical.

Etymologically Speaking

The etymological trail that produced the modern English word *church* traces from the Middle English word *kirke* to the Old English *kyrike,* to the Old Norse *kirkja,* to the German *kirika,* to the late Greek *kyrike,* to the older Greek *kuriakón* (κυριακόν) which literally meant "belonging to the Lord,"[51] (from the Greek words κύριος [*kúrios*—"owner," "lord," "ruler"] and κύρος [*kyros*—"leader," "master," "supreme power"]). *Kuriakón,* in turn, was

---

[48] Donald Goergen, Ann Garrido, and Benedict M. Ashley, *The Theology of Priesthood* (Collegeville, MN: The Liturgical Press, 2000), p. 84.

[49] Georges Florovsky, quoted in Colin W. Williams, William Hordern, Carl E. Braaten, John Macquarrie, Paul Hessert, and Roger L. Shinn, *The Church, New Directions in Theology Today* (Philadelphia, PA: Westminster Publishing House, 1969), vol. 4, p. 11.

[50] Ephesians 4:12.

[51] Hans Küng, *The Church* (New York: Sheed and Ward Publishers, 1967), pp. 82–83.

derived from the Indo-European word *kewe* ("hero"). "Belonging to the Lord," however, is such a nebulous definition that it lacks specific meaning and application. Of course, the "church" belongs to the Lord, but what does that mean for understanding the nature, purpose, and function of the church.

For theological and ecclesiological purposes, the word *church* must be evaluated in the light of the New Testament Greek term which is translated "church" in virtually all English versions of Scripture, and that term is ἐκκλεσία (*ekklesía*)[52]. In classical Greek,[53] the word *ekklesía* meant an assembly of the citizens of a πόλις (*pólis*[54] — "city-state"), with the understanding that those who were of this assembly had the right to vote on civic issues, including the election of magistrates, the confirmation of political decisions, and the adjudication of appeals regarding judicial decisions.[55] From this background, it is clear that the Greek term used to denominate the community of believers in Jesus in the Apostolic Scriptures referred specifically to an assembly or a gathering of people.

Because it is derived from the Greek verbal form ἐκκαλέω (*ekkaléo*), meaning "to summon forth," the word *ekklesía* essentially means "those who are called out." The *ekklesía* in ancient Greece was the convocation or assembly of those who, as citizens of a city-state, were "summoned forth" in a collective assembly to decide upon or affirm legislative, judicial, and executive matters of importance to their communities. This background of the word *ekklesía* has prompted scholars to describe the church as "the called out," those who have been called out of the world and into the service of God through their faith in Jesus as Messiah and Lord.[56] From the further development of the background of the word, it is obvious that this definition is deficient in its ability to define the word *church* properly.

What is meant by "the called out" or "those summoned forth"? Who are called, and to what are they summoned? To gain the full import of this

---

[52] Karl L. Schmidt, "ἐκκλεσία," in *Theological Dictionary of the New Testament*, Gerhard Kittel and Gerhard Friedrich, eds., tr. Geoffrey W. Bromiley, 10 vols. (Grand Rapids, MI: Wm. B. Eerdmans Publishing Co., 1964–1976), vol. 3, p. 504.

[53] The Greek word *ekklesia* can be found from the fifth century BC onward in the writings of Herodotus, Thucidides, Zenophon, Plato, and Euripides.

[54] The Greek word *pólis* is the root of the English word *metropolis*.

[55] Eric G. Jay, *The Church: Its Changing Image Through Twenty Centuries, Vol. 1: the First Seventeen Centuries, Volume 2: 1700–the Present Day.* (London, UK: SPCK Publishing, 1977), p. 6. *Ekklesia*, however, can also be a generic term to designate an unorganized group of people, such as the mob that threatened Paul at Ephesus (Acts 18:32).

[56] J. Rodman Williams, *Renewal Theology: Systematic Theology from a Charismatic Perspective* (Grand Rapids, MI: Zondervan Publishing, 1992), p. 17. Also, Donald S. Armentrout and Robert Boak Slocum, *An Episcopal Dictionary of the Church: A User-Friendly Reference for Episcopalians* (New York: Church Publishing, 2000), p. 160.

meaning of the word *ekklesía* and its translation as *church*, it is necessary to go behind the Greek text of the Apostolic Scriptures and return to the Hebrew in which the words of Jesus and the apostles were originally either thought, spoken, or written. In essence, it is essential to return to the Hebrew foundations of Christian faith in order to arrive at a proper definition of the one English word that most often denominates the community of believers in Jesus. And this is true not only of those who use the English word *church* but also of those who use various transliterations of the Greek word *ekklesía*.[57]

The spiritual application of the secular Greek word ἐκκλεσία that was used to describe the Jesus movement as it extended itself into the Gentile world becomes clear when consideration is given to the Hebrew word that was rendered ἐκκλεσία by the translators of the Septuagint Version of the Hebrew Scriptures, the text which the Greek-speaking fathers of the church employed.[58] This version was developed in the third century BC when, at the behest of Alexander the Great, seventy scholars in Alexandria translated the Hebrew Scriptures into Greek to make it possible for the Hellenized Jews of the Diaspora to read the Scriptures in Greek, the *lingua franca* of the Mediterranean Basin.[59]

Seventy-seven times the Septuagint translators used the Greek word ἐκκλεσία to translate the Hebrew word קָהָל (*kahal*), which means "community" or "congregation." Just like *ekkaléo*, the verbal root of *ekklesía*, means to call or summon, so the verbal root of *kahal*, קָהַל, means to "call together" or to "assemble people" when used in the *hiphil*.[60] Both Hebrew words are derived from קוֹל (*kol*), the word for voice, and because of this connection, they ultimately refer to the verbal summoning of an assembly or to the act of assembling. Like its Greek counterpart, *ekklesía*, the Hebrew *kahal* can also

---

[57] Interestingly, *ekklesía* was transliterated, rather than translated, into Latin as *ecclesia*. Because of this, the Romance languages that are derived from Latin avoided the confusion of having *ekklesía* translated as "church" by rendering it as *iglesia* (Spanish), *eglise* (French), *chiesa* (Italian), and *igreja* (Portuguese). In these languages, the term is rightly understood to mean "congregation" and is often translated with the equivalent of "congregation."

[58] Albrecht Dihle, *Greek and Latin Literature of the Roman Empire: From Augustus to Justinian* (New York: Routledge, 1989), pp. 335–338. Also Ronald E. Heine, *Reading the Old Testament with the Ancient Church* (Grand Rapids, MI: Baker Academic, 2007), p. 38. Heine says, "The Septuagint was to the early church what the King James Version of the Bible was to the English-speaking Protestant church from the middle of the seventeenth century to well into the second half of the twentieth century. It was the version read in the services of the church . . . and it was the version on which the studies and debates of the church's scholars were based." It should be noted that the usage of the Septuagint in worship exercises in the ancient churches had considerable impact upon discussions about the canon of Scripture.

[59] Frank W. Walbank, *The Hellenistic World* (Cambridge, MA: Harvard University Press, 1981), p. 224. Also, Antonia Tripolitis, *Religions of the Hellenistic-Roman Age* (Grand Rapids, MI: Wm. B. Eerdmans Publishing Co., 2002), p. 68.

[60] William Gesenius, *Gesenius' Hebrew and Chaldee Lexicon* (Grand Rapids, MI: Baker Book House, 1992), p. 726.

be used to describe a gathering crowd.[61] *Kahal* generally refers to the "congregation" or, more specifically, to the "community" of the people of Israel (e.g., קְהַל יִשְׂרָאֵל [*kahal Yisrael*—congregation of Israel]; קְהַל יהוה [*kahal YHWH*—congregation of Yahweh]; and קְהַל הָאֱלֹהִים [*kahal haElohim*—congregation of God]). It often denotes the general assembly of the people of Israel, including men, women, and children. Yil Kang says *kahal* means "a community gathered for a discussion"[62] as well as a people of covenant, God's community. Robert Bonfil also maintains that *kahal* means "the public, the population as a whole, the people."[63]

In addition to *kahal,* a second Hebrew word that is often translated "congregation" is עֵדָה (*'edah*), which appears 149 times in the Hebrew Scriptures. This word refers to the collective people when they were gathered, particularly at the Tent of Meeting. *'Edah* means "to gather at a designated place."[64] It originally meant "the gathering of people who were called to listen to the laws of God and to worship God."[65] Some have suggested that the fact that this term first appeared in Exodus 12:3 indicates that the "congregation" or the "church" of Israel actually came into being with the issuance of God's command (call) that the Israelites celebrate Passover and leave Egypt.[66] The word *'edah* points to the congregation as centered in the cult of the Torah, especially in corporate worship. Lothar Coenen has suggested, therefore, that *'edah* is "the unambiguous and permanent term for the ceremonial community as a whole."[67][68] He maintains that *kahal,* on the other hand, is the "ceremonial expression for the assembly that results from the covenant, for the Sinai community and, in the deuteronomistic sense, for the community in its present form."[69]

In Greek, ἐκκλεσία (*ekklesía*) is almost always used to translate קְהַל (*kahal*);[70] however, it is never used to translate עֵדָה (*'edah*), which is always

---

[61] Numbers 14:5; 17:12.

[62] Yil Gyoung Kang, *Enhancing Understanding the Church Through Preaching on Ecclesiology in the Korean American Immigrant Church* (Ann Arbor, MI: ProQuest, 2008), p. 33.

[63] Robert Bonfil, *Jewish Life in Renaissance Italy* (Berkeley, CA: The University of California Press, 1994), p. 190.

[64] Kang, p. 33.

[65] Kang, p. 33.

[66] Lothar Coenen, "Church" in Colin Brown, ed., vol. 1, p. 291.

[67] Coenen, "Church" in Colin Brown, ed., p. 291.

[68] Lothar Coenen, "Elect, Choose," in Colin Brown, ed., vol. 1, pp. 336–543.

[69] Coenen, "Church" in Colin Brown, ed., p. 291.

[70] *Kahal* is occasionally rendered as *sunagogé* in the Septuagint; however, out of the 82 times that *kahal* is used in the Hebrew Scriptures, it is translated *ekklesia* 72 times in the Septuagint. In Proverbs 5:14, both *kahal* and *'edah* are used in the same passage of Scripture to describe Israel: "I was almost in utter ruin in the midst of the *kahal* and the *'edah*."

rendered by the term συναγωγή (*sunagogé*—"synagogue").[71] Originally, the word *sunagogé* was not used to designate a Jewish house of worship. It simply meant a "meeting," "gathering," or "assembly."[72] It was only later that it was appropriated as a description for a fixed place where Jews assembled for fellowship, study, and prayer. The translation of *'edah* with *sunagogé* underscores the fact that the *'edah*, unlike the *kahal*, was a meeting or assembly.[73] In fact, the *'edah* (congregation) was essentially an assembly of the *kahal* (community).

Campegius Vitringa declared that "the term קָהָל, *Kahal*, is used in a narrower, more restricted sense than the term עֵדָה, *Edah*. *Kahal* strictly denotes *the whole of any multitude of people* united in the bonds of one society, and constituting some kind of republic or city; while the term עֵדָה, *Edah*, simply signifies any gathering or assembly of men, whether it be great or small, but especially one which is fixed and appointed."[74] In this context, Cooke has observed that "we are not surprised that *Edah* never occurs in Genesis, while *Kahal* is found there four times. In three of these, it is used in connection with Abraham, in whose family . . . the Church, the *called out*, began its formal existence."[75]

Since the term *kahal* was first used to describe the Abrahamic family and the term *'edah* was first used to describe the "congregation" of Israel assembled at Sinai, it is clear that the "church in the wilderness" about which Stephen spoke was comprised of those who had received a corporate summons from YHWH to enter into covenant with him. The implication of the term *kahal*, therefore, is "those who have been summoned" to covenantal relationship with God as his *ekklesía*. The *'edah* is the *sunagogé* of God,[76]

---

[71] Millard J. Erickson, *Christian Theology* (Grand Rapids, MI: Baker Academic, 1983), p. 955. The Hebrew word *'edah* is translated by the Greek word *sunagogé* 131 times out of the 141 times that it is used in the Hebrew text. It is never translated *ekklesía*, however.

[72] This is clear from other uses of *sunagogé* in the Septuagint, as in Genesis 1:9: "Let the waters below the heavens be gathered [*sunagogen*]. . ." and in Exodus 23:6: " . . . when you gather [*sunagogé*] in the work from your field."

[73] The distinction between *'edah* and *kahal* can be seen in the fact that some members of the *'edah* could not partake in the *kahal*. These included *mamzers* (illegitimate children), as well as their descendants to the tenth generation, and men who had been emasculated. See Deuteronomy 23:2–4.

[74] Campegius Vitringa, *De Synagoge Vetere Libri Tres* (Weissenfels, Germany: Wehrmann, 1726), vol. 3, p. 80.

[75] Cooke, p. 144. It is undeniable that the foundation of the "church in the wilderness," the *kahal* of Israel, was laid in the family and tent of Abraham. The Tabernacle of Witness and the Temple of Solomon were patterned after Sarah and Abraham's tent.

[76] In the Apostolic Scriptures, the word *sunagogé* is used twice to describe the meetings of the *ekklesía*. In James 2:2, the apostle specifically says, "If someone comes into your *sunagogé* [synagogue, meeting, or assembly] . . ." Hebrews 10:25 says, "Not neglecting the *episunagogé* [assembling together], as is the habit of some." In both cases, the word *sunagogé* (synagogue) is used to describe Christian gatherings. Interestingly, scholars have had no trouble translating *sunagogé* as "*synagogue* of the Jews" (Acts 14:1; 17:1) and "*synagogue* of Satan" (Revelation 2:9; 3:9); however, they simply could not bring themselves to translate precisely the same Greek word as "synagogue" when it spoke of Christian assemblies! Apparently they thought that everyone knows that Christians go to church, not synagogue.

the congregation of those who have responded to God's summons and have assembled in his presence. In biblical language, then, wherever the term *church* appears, it connotes the community of those who have been summoned to be in covenant with God and to meet in fellowship, study, and worship.

The term *church*, therefore, is not exclusive to the New Testament, for the word which the apostles chose to use as an expression of their corporate identity was the same as that which had been used by the Jewish people since the time of Abraham, and more definitively since the time of the Exodus. This is why Stephen called Israel "the church [ἐκκλεσία] in the wilderness."[77] This is also why the Book of Hebrews uses the terms *assembly* and *church of firstborn ones* practically in apposition to one another.[78] The New Testament writers understood that the word *ekklesía* translated their Hebrew word *kahal*, and they understood that it meant the community as the congregation of God. There was absolute continuity in the minds of Jesus and the apostles between the congregation under the first covenant and the congregation under the renewed covenant, the church described in the Hebrew Scriptures and the church discussed in the Apostolic Scriptures. Jesus did nothing new, therefore, when he called unto him whom he would and ordained twelve apostles to be the foundational pillars of his reformed congregation (church).[79] He was merely restoring David's fallen *sukkah* (tabernacle)[80] to its original purpose[81] and reforming it by introducing the new covenant sealed in his own blood.[82] English translations, therefore, should always have rendered the Greek term *ekklesía* as "community" or "congregation," not "church."

The ongoing popularity of the word *church*, rather than *community* or *congregation*, in English Scriptures can be traced directly to *Bishop Bancroft's Rules to Be Observed in the Translation of the Bible*, the fifteen instructions of King James through the Archbishop of Canterbury to those who produced the Authorized (King James) Version of the Bible (which was actually an interpretation of the earlier translation called the Bishops'

---

[77] Acts 7:38. This is why Hebrews 2:12 quotes Psalm 22:22 ("I will declare your name among my brethren: in the midst of the congregation [*kahal*] will I praise you.") as: "I will declare your name unto my brethren, in the midst of the church [*ekklesía*] will I sing praise unto you." It is clear that the *kahal* in the Hebrew Scriptures is the same as the *ekklesía* in the Apostolic Scriptures.

[78] Hebrews 12:23.

[79] Mark 3:13–14; 1 Corinthians 12:28; Ephesians 2:20.

[80] Amos 9:11.

[81] Amos 9:11; Acts 15:16.

[82] Hebrews 9:10, 12, 15.

Bible).[83] Rule 3 specifically states: "*The old Ecclesiastical Words* [are] *to be kept*, viz. the word *Church* [is] not to be translated *Congregation* &c."[84] If these rules had not forbidden the use of the word *congregation* in deference to the old ecclesiastical term *church*, generations of Christians in English-speaking nations would have readily recognized the church of Jesus Christ to be the *congregation of God*, a continuation in complete continuity with the congregation of Israel, not a totally new innovation introduced to replace Israel in the economy of salvation. No one would ever have thought of the *congregation* as a building, and no one would have ever thought that *congregation* was something done in the building. "Church" would always have been "community" or "congregation," a corporate body of believers, not an institution or an architectural facility. Then, the English-speaking Christian community might more readily have understood Paul's olive-tree metaphor in Romans 11 to reveal the fact that Israel had come to include Gentile branches who were grafted into God's family tree, the "commonwealth of Israel,"[85] to share with the Jewish people in the spiritual root and fatness of biblical Judaism.[86] It could also have recognized the church as part of the continuation, not the replacement, of Israel and the new covenant as a re-newed covenant, not a complete innovation.

Who Are the Community?

The question that begs to be asked is this: Who are the people who comprise the congregation of God, the assembly of those who are called out to be in covenant with God? The answer was clear under the First Testament: it was the entire assembly of the descendants of Abraham through Isaac and Jacob who made the exodus from Egypt and appeared before the Lord at Sinai, and it was all of their subsequent posterity.[87] While all of Israel was

---

[83] W. H. Stevenson, *King James's Bible: A Selection* (New York: Routledge, 2013), p. 517–518. Also, Gordon Campbell, *Bible: The Story of the King James Version 1611-2011* (New York: Oxford University Press, 2010), p. 35. Campbell points out that Bishop Bancroft had opposed King James' plan for a new translation of the Bible; however, when the royal decree was made, he moved to control the "new" translation by selecting the translators and formulating the rules that would guide their work so that the end result would be more in line with the older Bishop's Bible.

[84] Stevenson, p. 517. *Ekklesia* was to be translated "church" in the New Testament; however, precisely the same Greek word was translated "congregation" in the Old Testament in the King James Version.

[85] Ephesians 2:12.

[86] Romans 11:17.

[87] God said to the Israelites at Sinai, "Nor is it with you only that I make this sworn covenant, but with him who is not here with us this day" (Deuteronomy 29:14–15). The sages believed that in some mystical way "all the souls [of all the Jews] were present then, although their bodies were not yet created" (Solomon Buber, *Midrash Tanhuma, Nizza Im*, 8:25b). "Every Jew to this day is therefore to consider him- or herself as having stood before Sinai and as having responded, 'We will do.'" The covenant at Sinai was effective, therefore, to all the descendants of the Israelites. See Van Buren, p. 154.

denominated tribally and was arranged accordingly around the Tent of Meeting in the Sinai desert, they were collectively considered *kahal*, the "community of God." While there were various elections in Israel, including those described by Jacob[88] and David,[89] the whole of Israel was the *kahal*, the ones called out to enter into covenant with YHWH. All of Israel, therefore, was the *church* in the wilderness.

The answer is equally clear under the Renewed Covenant. Just as the "church in the wilderness" was baptized into one body unto Moses in the cloud and in the sea at their exodus from Egypt,[90] so all believers have been baptized by one Spirit into one body[91] by being buried with Christ in baptism[92] at their exodus from sin and their translation into the kingdom of God.[93] This includes every person who has been "called out," for "there is *one* body, and one Spirit, even as you are *called* in *one* hope of your calling."[94] This calling is a summons into covenant with God: "Therefore, my brethren, you were also made to die to the law by the body of Christ; so that you might be married to another, to him who was raised from the dead."[95] All believers in Messiah Jesus are the children of God who have been "betrothed to one husband" with a view toward being presented as "a pure virgin" to Christ[96] when the marriage of the Lamb has come and his wife has made herself ready.[97]

The church is not merely the sum of all the local entities comprised of Christian believers. In virtually every instance of the use of the word *ekklesía* in the New Testament, it referred to a local body of believers. The title *ekklesía* was generally applied to a body comprised of all believers in a city;[98] however, it also denoted house churches or congregations meeting in homes.[99] In two cases, it was used to refer to all believers in a larger geographical area.[100] In every case, however, a single group of believers is never considered as a mere part of the whole church, branches of a larger entity, or "franchises" of the church. The fullness of the universal church is found in

---

[88] Genesis 49:1–28 details Jacob's blessings of all twelve of his sons.
[89] Psalm 78:67–69; 114:1–2.
[90] 1 Corinthians 10:2.
[91] 1 Corinthians 12;13.
[92] Colossians 2:12.
[93] Colossians 1:13.
[94] Ephesians 4:4, emphasis added.
[95] Romans 7:4, NASB, KJV.
[96] 2 Corinthians 11:2.
[97] Revelation 19:7.
[98] Acts 5:11; 8:1; 11:22; 12:1, 5; 13:1.
[99] Romans 16:5; Colossians 4:15.
[100] Acts 9:31; 1 Corinthians 16:19.

each of its localized manifestations. As Erickson says, "Each community, however small, represents the total community, the church."[101]

Every believer and every community, therefore, is rightly included in the "church" just as much as every Jew was included in Israel. Corporate bodies of believers that have arrogated to themselves exclusive rights to the term *church* have been guilty of shattering the unity of the church. The Roman Catholic Church started the trend by exalting its bishop to primacy as a politico-ecclesiastical potentate and declaring, "*Extra ecclesiam nulla salus*" ("outside the church there is no salvation"). Subsequently, denomination after denomination and movement after movement has asserted that those who were not members of their denomination or subscribers to their dogma were not part of the redeemed community of Christ, the church. Others have *magnanimously* recognized that those who are outside their denomination are "saved," but, in their own elitism, they have relegated them to the status of second-class citizens of the kingdom of God. These arrogant positions are nothing more than spiritual egocentricity and narcissism, and they are an affront both to God and to the unity and equality of the church.

The Church and Pentecost

Despite popular opinion to the contrary, the church is not a "new" thing. Most Christian scholars conclude that the church began on the Day of Pentecost. And, they are absolutely right, but they are simply in the wrong century! The church did not begin on Pentecost in Acts 2. It began on Pentecost in Exodus 20. The church was born on the very first Pentecost (*Shavuot*) at Mt. Sinai.[102] In fact, Pentecost was the only festival that God could have had in mind when he instructed Moses to tell Pharaoh, "Let my people go so that they can celebrate a festival in the desert to honor me."[103] The church, therefore, was born on the Day of Pentecost at Sinai when the nation of Israel was "born in a day."[104] God's nation was the same thing as his church. In

---

[101] Erickson, p. 956.

[102] Deuteronomy 29:1. See Albert Gerhards and Clemens Leonhard, *Jewish and Christian Liturgy and Worship: New Insights* (Leiden, The Netherlands: Koninklijke Brill, 2007), p. 282. Also, Jacob Neusner, *A Life of Rabban Yohanan Ben Zakkai: Ca. 1-80 C.E.* (Leiden, The Netherlands: Koninklijke Brill, 1962), p. 82.

[103] Exodus 5:1, CJB. The chronicle of the events that occurred after the Exodus from Egypt on the Day of Unleavened Bread after Passover offers strong evidence that the Israelites heard the voice of God from Mt. Sinai on the day of *Shavuot* (Pentecost). The event was certainly not at the time of *Sukkot* (Tabernacles), for not enough time had passed. The Israelites were liberated on Passover. They left Rameses in Egypt on what would become the first day of Festival of Unleavened Bread (Numbers 33:3). It is likely that they passed through the Red Sea on the day that would become the Festival of Firstfruits (the Sunday after Passover—Leviticus 23:15). And it is likely, if not certain, that they received the Torah on the day of Pentecost.

[104] Isaiah 66:8.

reality, when the apostles celebrated Pentecost (*Shavuot*) in Acts 2, "they did so as part of an existing worshipping community that had been born 2,000 years earlier with the Abrahamic promise,"[105] one that was constituted as God's *kahal* 1,500 years before that time at Mt. Sinai. Then, fifteen centuries later, the church was "born again" at Mt. Zion when the 120 believers in Jesus received the gift of the Holy Spirit that he had promised them.[106] The earliest church, therefore, merely continued in continuity with the ancient community of Israel, and it continued in the synagogal model in which Jesus and the apostles had been reared.[107] The *ekklesía* of Apostolic Scripture was still the *kahal* of the Hebrew Scriptures. The church was—and it always will be—a Jewish entity. In fact, Christianity is the "other Judaism," the Jesus-reformed faith community.

Even if scholars were in the correct century when asserting that the church "began" on the day of Pentecost in Acts 2, it would still be necessary to conclude that the church must have existed before Pentecost, for Jesus said, "*I* will build my church."[108] If Jesus, himself, did the building, even if it were only laying the foundation, it must have begun before his death, resurrection, and ascension. And, indeed, he did lay the foundation of the restored congregation when he "set some in the church, first apostles"[109] by ordaining the twelve disciples and calling them apostles.[110] The apostles and other disciples of Jesus were the foundations of the restored community of those who had faith in God and in Jesus as Messiah and Lord.

The Church Modeled in Temple and Synagogue

The church of Jesus Christ was developed according to the pattern of the temple and the synagogue, both of which were intrinsically involved in the lives of first-century Jews. The church even came to be thought of as the spiritual temple, the new habitation of God through the Spirit.[111] Expanding upon the theme that had been mentioned before by prophets and sages in Israel,[112] the apostles declared that God's presence was resident, not on a mountain or in a building,[113] but in the congregation of his chosen. While the earliest Christians continued to worship at the temple, they proclaimed

---

[105] Robert W. Bleakney, personal communication.
[106] Acts 2:1–4.
[107] James Gall, *The Synagogue, Not the Temple, the Germ and Model of the Christian Church* (London, England: Simpkin, Marshall, Hamilton, Kent & Co., 1890), p. 28. Also Lyman Coleman, *The Antiquities of the Christian Church* (Andover, MA: Gould, Newman & Saxton, 1841), p. 332.
[108] Matthew 16:18.
[109] 1 Corinthians 12:28.
[110] Mark 3:13–14.
[111] Ephesians 2:21–22.
[112] 2 Chronicles 2:6; Isaiah 66:1–2.
[113] Hebrews 12:18, 22.

that God lived in and was manifest through the collective body of his people. Stephen encapsulated this teaching in his famous apology: "The Most High does not dwell in houses made with human hands; as the prophet says: 'Heaven is my throne, and the earth is my footstool. What kind of house will you build for me, says the LORD, or what is the place of my rest?'"[114]

The Holy Spirit had proven his residency in the church both corporately and individually on the Day of Pentecost immediately following Christ's ascension. The community that was being built "on the foundation of the apostles and prophets with Jesus Christ himself being the chief corner stone" was "growing into a holy temple in the Lord . . . also being built together into a dwelling of God in the Spirit."[115] Later, even Gentiles were found to be "living stones" who were also "built up a spiritual house,"[116] for "the Holy Spirit fell on all those who were listening to the message" at the household of Cornelius, the "God-fearing" Roman centurion. The apostles were assured that God had added these Gentiles to their faith community when they heard them "speaking with tongues and exalting God"[117] just as they had done in Acts 2.

The earliest church was, therefore, altogether a Jewish entity, a sect of Judaism. Until the event at the house of Cornelius, they were all Jews. The apostles of Jesus made no effort to separate themselves from biblical Judaism, the faith of their ancestors, nor did they seek to sever their relationship with their "kinsmen according to the flesh."[118] They were Israelites "to whom [*belonged*] the adoption as sons, the glory, the covenants, the giving of the Law, the temple worship, and the promises."[119] Jesus, himself, had affirmed to them that he had not come to abrogate the *Torah* or to destroy the prophets but rather to complete and perfect them.[120] Even Paul, the apostle who championed the cause of Gentile inclusion in the church, continually testified that he remained a Pharisee[121] and that he was faithful to observe God's ancient religion.[122] In fact, Paul saw his divine appointment as one of tailoring Judaism for Gentiles,[123] not as the author of a new theology and polity for Gentiles. Thirty years after the resurrection

---

[114] Acts 7:48–49.
[115] Ephesians 2:20–22.
[116] 1 Peter 2:5.
[117] Acts 10:44–46.
[118] Romans 9:3.
[119] Romans 9:4, ESV, edited.
[120] Matthew 5:17; Hebrews 12:2.
[121] Acts 23:6.
[122] Acts 20:21–24; 24:14.
[123] Wilson, *Exploring*, p. 100.

of Jesus, the multiplied thousands of Jews who believed in Jesus as Messiah and Lord were "all . . . zealous of the law."[124]

First-century Judaism was not monolithic; there were many Judaisms, varied expressions, interpretations, and manifestations of the biblical religion which God had given to Moses at Sinai. There were, therefore, many different synagogues—synagogues of the Pharisees, synagogues of the Essenes, synagogues of the Herodians, and synagogues of the Qumran community. Even the "synagogue of Satan" described in Revelation 2:9 was likely a synagogue that was trying to syncretize Hellenism with Jewish tradition. And, there were also synagogues of the Jesus Movement which were called the Way, the *ekklesía*, and eventually Christianity. From the time of Ezra, the Jewish people had formed corporate communities of believers who shared a common understanding of *halakhah*, the way one should walk in obedience to God's commandments. All that was required for the synagogue to exercise corporate public worship was a *minyan* (quorum[125]) of ten people.[126] When this corporate body was solidified, it formed the core of a synagogue.

It is only reasonable, then, that while the first-century church was considered corporately to be "the temple of God,"[127] local assemblies of the church were still termed synagogues.[128] From its earliest days, then, the Christian congregations were denominated in worshipping communities that were called synagogues. This practice continued for at least thirty years after

---

[124] Acts 20:20. The Greek text uses the term *myriads*, which means "tens of thousands," to describe the numbers of Torah-observant Jews who were part of the earliest church.

[125] The Jewish idea for ten as a quorum is based in the fact that when the ten spies whom Moses commissioned to scout the Promised Land returned with an "evil report," God said, "How long will this evil 'assembly' complain against me." From this, the sages said that the "ten men" constituted the "assembly." The *minyan* was also thought to have been revealed in the ten members of Noah's family whom God spared from the flood. Likewise, it was revealed in Abraham's negotiation with God over Sodom and Gomorrah when God finally said that would spare the cities for ten righteous men.

[126] The word *minyan* means "count," or "number." At first the *minyan* was ten people over the age of thirteen (men and women); however, after Hellenism began to influence Judaism, the *minyan* was restricted to ten men, as it remains in a significant percentage of Jewish communities today. See Korina Zamfir, *Men and Women in the Household of God: A Contextual Approach to Roles and Ministries in the Pastoral Epistles* (Göttingen, Germany: Vandenhoeck & Ruprecht, 2013), p. 385, n. 218, referencing *Megillah* 4.11; 23a, discussed in Bernadette J. Brooten, *Women Leaders in the Ancient Synagogue: Inspirational Evidence and Background Issues* (Saarbrücken, Germany: OmniScriptum GmbH & Co., 1982), pp. 94–95. In an interview with the *Jewish Chronicle*, the Rev. Dr. Hockman said, "The exclusion of women from religious life was a concession on the part of the Rabbinic law to the spirit of that age," which was the "Hellenistic civilization, when no woman of moral character could take part in public life." See Hockman, "Why I Resigned," in *The Reform Advocate*, Chicago, IL, September 4, 1915, vol. XLX, p. 118.

[127] 1 Corinthians 3:16; Ephesians 2:21.

[128] In the first century, the Greek term *sunagogé* (synagogue) simply meant a "meeting" or "assembly." It did not connote a building.

the resurrection of Jesus and probably well beyond that time. James, the leader of the Jerusalem church, called the gatherings of the Jewish Christians "synagogues" in his letter to the twelve tribes in the Diaspora when he said, "If a man comes into your *synagogue* with a gold ring and dressed in fine clothes . . . and you pay special attention to him . . . have you not discriminated among yourselves?"[129] Translators of most English versions of the Scriptures have concealed the truth of this simple statement by choosing to render the Greek word συναγογή (*sunagogé*) in this passage as "assembly," "meeting," or "gathering." Each of these renderings of the Greek word *sunagogé* is accurate; however, the lack of consistency in rendering the same word as "synagogue" throughout the Apostolic Scriptures is problematic.[130] Whether the reason for such inconsistency has been Judaeophobia, anti-Judaism, or perhaps even Antisemitism or whether it has simply been an effort to maintain continuity with historical church tradition, the lack of consistency in translation has concealed an obvious truth from those who have read the Scriptures in English translations. That truth is that the congregations of the earliest church, particularly among the Jews, were still called synagogues at least three decades after the Acts 2 Pentecost.

Since the earliest congregations of Christians were still called synagogues, it should surprise no one that the nascent church continued the synagogue tradition in which all of its earliest communicants had been reared and with which they were totally comfortable. Initially, believers in Jesus continued to participate in the synagogues of the Pharisees and other sects of Judaism. When their presence was barred by existing authorities or when they could no longer recite the central synagogue prayer, the *Amidah,* because it had been modified to include a malediction against heretics, specifically against the *Notzrim,* the followers of Jesus, the *Netzer* or Branch of David, they were forced to form their own congregations. They did not, however, abandon the synagogal model in favor of a "church" model. Indeed, there was no such thing as a "church model" for them to follow. They simply maintained both the liturgy and the structure of the synagogues with which they had always been familiar, applying only the principles and motives of the Jesus reformation that had brought the fullest degree of completion to their sect of Judaism that could be realized short of the *eschaton.*[131]

---

[129] James 2:2–4, NASB, NIV, edited.

[130] E.g., translators had no problem rendering *sunagogé* as "*synagogue* of the Jews" in Acts 17:10 and elsewhere and as "*synagogue* of Satan" in Revelation 2:9; 3:9.

[131] Hebrews 9:10. In Acts 24:14, Paul confessed that in being a Christian, he belonged to a sect of Judaism: "According to the Way which they call a sect I do serve the God of our fathers, believing everything that is in accordance with the Law and that is written in the Prophets."

Today, the term *synagogue* creates many of the same problems that the term *church* does. Most Christians think of a synagogue as a building where Jews worship, when in truth, the synagogue, like the church, is not actually a building but a gathering of people. In and before the first century, synagogues were collectives of believers who were gathered in homes or in multipurpose public buildings for fellowship, study, and prayer. Most evidence suggests that synagogues as architectural structures designated exclusively as places of corporate worship among Jews were not prevalent until the third century AD.[132] Likewise, Christianity apparently had no single-purpose church buildings until after Constantine the Great assumed *de facto* leadership of Christianity in 325 AD.[133] As the emperor of Rome and the *Pontifex Maximus* of Roman polytheism, Constantine was comfortable with the traditional worship of the Greco-Roman pantheon of deities that demanded the erection of soaring temples with spectacular images of the gods that were designed to impress the largely illiterate masses. After his "conversion" to Christianity in 312 AD, Constantine gave Christianity favored status. Then, his mother Helena embarked on an extensive effort to construct basilicas[134] and cathedrals[135] as shrines to mark sites of significant events in Christian history in the Holy Land and elsewhere. When Emperor Theodosius I (379-395 AD) made Christianity the official religion of the state of Rome, the concept of housing what was by then Gentilized Christianity in basilicas and cathedrals became well entrenched.

Synagogal Functions: Church Dynamics

The functions of the first-century synagogue were first and fundamentally manifest in the home. The synagogal model which was fulfilled in every observant Jewish home became essential to the survival of Judaism after the destruction of the temple in 70 AD and the subsequent passage of its cultus into virtual oblivion. It was then that the rabbis ruled that prayer, study of Torah, and *tzedakah* (social justice) in home and synagogue had replaced and fulfilled the temple ritual. Though the transition from the Israelite focus

---

[132] Peter W. van der Horst, "Was the Synagogue a Place of Sabbath Worship before 70 CE?" in Steven Fine, ed., *Jews, Christians and Polytheists in the Ancient Synagogue* (London, UK: Routledge, 1999), p. 16. Also James L. Papandrea, *A Pilgrim's Guide to the Eternal City* (Eugene, OR: Wipf and Stock Publishers, 2012), p. 5, and Pieter Willem van der Horst, *Japeth in the Tents of Shem: Studies on Jewish Hellenism in Antiquity* (Leuven, Belgium: Peeters Publishers, 2002), p. 62.

[133] Constantine established himself as both a civil and religious authority when he summoned the bishops of the church for the Council of Nicaea and served as its moderator.

[134] A basilica was a civic structure, much like the modern city hall.

[135] Cathedrals were similar to temples. They came to be called "cathedrals" because they contained a *cathedra*, a "seat" or throne of a bishop. The Greek word καθέδρα (*kathédra*) means "seat."

on the temple and its cultus to its focus on family and synagogue was in many ways traumatic, it was, nonetheless, possible because the foundation for that transition had already been laid some six hundred years earlier during and immediately after the Babylonian captivity when the synagogue emerged as a forum for fellowship, study, and worship. In reality, however, the synagogue that was manifest after the destruction of Solomon's temple was merely an extension of the worshipping Jewish home.

The functions of the synagogue eventually became titles that Jews applied to it. Since the term *synagogue* is a Greek-based word, it came to be applied to these corporate meetings of the Jews only after Judaism began to be influenced by Hellenism when the conquests of Alexander the Great were extended to the Aramaic world that included Israel. Before and after that time, the synagogue was described by the Israelites with Hebrew terms that indicated its functions, not its form. The synagogue, therefore, came to be called a *Beit Knesset* (House of Meeting), a *Beit Midrash* (House of Study), and a *Beit Tefillah* (House of Prayer).[136] While, for the sake of convenience, the meetings of the Jewish people for fellowship, study, and prayer were called by the Greek term *synagogue*, they continued to be identified by the three Hebrew names that described and specified their functions. These three functions were of enormous importance to each family, to each corporate worshipping community, and to the entire nation of Israel. In like manner, they were profoundly important to the success and growth of corporate Christian congregations that emerged from and were patterned after the synagogue in the first century of the Christian era.

Beit Knesset

The synagogue was first a *Beit Knesset*, a "House of Meeting." This nomenclature was doubtless derived from the designation of the first sanctuary in Israel, the Tabernacle in the Wilderness as the "Tent of Meeting."[137] The *Beit Knesset* was a gathering of the people where they met with God and with one another. The *Beit Knesset* fulfilled the people's need for corporate social interaction, fellowship, and the transaction of community affairs, including the judicial functions of the community. This function of the corporate meeting made the social intercourse possible that bound the community together as an extended family. This was the community as a house for both spiritual and social fellowship. It reinforced the concept in Judaism that salvation—and

---

[136] Jack Finegan, *Discovering Israel: An Archaeological Guide to the Holy Land* (Grand Rapids, MI: Wm. B. Eerdmans Publishing Co., 1981), p. 41.
[137] Exodus 33:7–11.

relationship with God—was a corporate and community affair, not just a matter of rugged individualism. It encouraged all the individual Jews to look upon themselves as integral parts of a corporate whole. Jewish men and women did not live and die to themselves. They were not islands lost in the sea of humanity. They were essential elements in a family, a community, and a corporate nation. What they were and what they did affect the welfare of the whole.

The *Beit Knesset* also included the dynamics of the *Beit Din*, the "House of Judgment,"[138] where legal matters were settled by a court of the rabbis.[139] Among the Jews, legal matters governing individual and corporate lives were not settled by autocrats or secret tribunals. They were resolved in the context of community. Such affairs were also considered to be theological, spiritual matters, for all of life was sacred to God. When members of the community had conflicts, they brought them to the *Beit Din* of the *Beit Knesset* for resolution. They realized that their Scriptures guaranteed safety "in the multitude of counselors"[140] and in the presence of two or three witnesses,[141] not in some executive fiat exercised by an autocrat. The *Beit Knesset* guaranteed corporate deliberation and resolution of community interpersonal affairs.

The importance of maintaining the *Beit Din* function of the *Beit Knesset* in the earliest Christian church is readily apparent in the instruction that Jesus gave regarding injured parties in the community of faith.[142] One who was offended should first go to the offender to seek resolution. If this action was unsuccessful, he was to take witnesses with him and again seek resolution. If both approaches failed, he was to bring the matter "before the church," that is, before the *Beit Din* of his *Beit Knesset* for resolution that could even have included the excommunication of the offending party from the community: "If he refuses to listen even to the church, let him be unto you as a Gentile and a tax collector."[143]

The *Beit Knesset* also served the need for spiritual fellowship in the Jewish community. This was the *koinonía* ("sharing") for which the earliest Christian community was famous and which is essential to the very essence

---

[138] Joel Lurie Grishaver and Stuart Kelman, eds., *Learn Torah With . . . 5756 Torah Annual: A Collection of the Year's Best Torah* (Los Angeles, CA: Alef Design Group, 1999), p. 151.

[139] In ancient times, the *Beit Din* was comprised of three rabbis, one chosen by both parties in a conflict and a third impartial judge. In this way, justice was served to both of the conflicting parties. Joyce Eisenberg and Ellen Scolnic, *Dictionary of Jewish Words: A JPS Guide* (Philadelphia, PA: The Jewish Publication Society, 2001), p. 16.

[140] Proverbs 11:14; 15:22; 24:6.

[141] Matthew 18:16.

[142] Matthew 18:15–16.

[143] Matthew 18:17.

of the church as a fellowshipping community.[144] This function of the *Beit Knesset* provided for the continual face-to-face personal interaction of the members of the community in which they could share spiritual relationship both with one another and with God and in which they could engage with each other socially in the context of the extended family of the congregation.

Beit Midrash

The second function of the synagogue was that of a *Beit Midrash*, "House of Study." This was the ancient form and true pattern for the modern Bible study, where the congregation met together for interactive study of Torah, the Word of God, with every member of the assembly fully participating. This function was also manifest even in the collective worship of the synagogal liturgy, during which every Jew had the opportunity to come to the *bema*,[145] read the Torah and the *Haftarah* portions,[146] and explicate and expound upon them. While the position of teacher (which ultimately became "rabbi") was present, the teacher was not looked upon in ancient times as the sole authority or repository of the understanding of Torah. All the people were expected to be students of the Word of God, and they were equally afforded the opportunity to address the community with their understanding and wisdom.[147]

Eventually, the concept of the *Beit Midrash* became so important in Judaism that it became a separate facility built alongside the synagogue as a part of its spatial complex. Indeed, when a new community emerged, it generally built a *Beit Midrash* before it built a synagogue as a house of worship. This underscored the importance that the Jewish people attached to study and learning. In parts of Europe, the *Beit Midrash* also came to be called in Yiddish the *schul*,[148] the place where both children and adults were educated in Torah and other matters. To this day, many Ashkenazi Jews still refer to their synagogue as the *schul*.

---

[144] Lorelei F. Fuchs, *Koinonia and the Quest for an Ecumenical Ecclesiology: From Foundations through Dialogue to Symbolic Competence for Communionality* (Grand Rapids, MI: Wm. B. Eerdmans Publishing Co., 2008), p. 6

[145] The *bema* was a raised platform where speakers read from the Torah and addressed the community.

[146] The *Haftarah* portions are selections from the prophets of the Hebrew Scriptures. Jesus was reading the *Haftarah* in Luke 4:17–21.

[147] As Hellenism influenced Second Temple Judaism, this right was restricted to men, and women were even excluded from study of Torah, much less explicating it.

[148] The High German word *scuola* and the Yiddish word *schul* are derived from the Latin word *schola* (which meant "intermission of work" or "place of instruction") and the Greek word *skhole* (which meant "spare time" or "learned discussion"), hence a place for lectures and "school." The English word *school* is also derived from this same source.

From the time of Ezra when the synagogal model was fully recognized and institutionalized, study of the Torah has been considered invaluable and incumbent upon every individual, every home, and every worshipping community. Ultimately, the value of Torah study became so important in the Jewish community that it came to be recognized as one of the highest forms of worship.[149] Study is also the other element of communication with the Divine that accompanies prayer. It is the part of the conversation in which God gives direction to his people's lives and speaks to them through his Word.

The earliest Christian community maintained continuity with their Jewish forbears in underscoring the importance of study and learning the Word of God. This is why Jesus commended his fellow Jews for "searching the Scriptures."[150] The disciples of Jesus were enjoined to give themselves to study and to learning the Word of God.[151] The earliest church, like the rest of the Jewish community, was to be a learned—and a learning—body of believers.

Beit Tefillah

The third function of the synagogue was that of the *Beit Tefillah*, "House of Prayer." Even the temple in Jerusalem was called by the prophet a house of prayer, not a house of sacrifice.[152] This statement alone was a basis for the sages' determination that prayers held a position of higher importance in God's economy than sacrifice.[153] Prayer is the outcry of the human heart that offers praise and petition to God. Though it is looked upon in Christian circles more as petition, it is considered by the Jewish people as praise. As Abraham Heschel noted, "[I]n Jewish liturgy praise rather than petition ranks foremost. It is the more profound form, for it involves not so much the sense of one's own dependence and privation as the sense of God's majesty and glory."[154] Most of the synagogue prayers, therefore, are acts of praise, and even the petitions that are in the *Siddur*, the Jewish prayer book, are introduced and concluded with praise. Through the functions of the *Beit*

[149] Stephen M. Brown, *Higher and Higher: Making Jewish Prayer Part of Us* (New York: United Synagogue of America, 1980), p. 3.

[150] John 5:39.

[151] In 2 Timothy 2:15, Paul instructed all believers to "study to show yourself approved before God." In 1 Timothy 2:11, he instructed the women of the church to "learn."

[152] Isaiah 56:7.

[153] Jonathan Klawans, *Purity, Sacrifice, and the Temple: Symbolism and Supersessionism in the Study of Ancient Judaism* (New York: Oxford University Press, 2006), p. 207.

[154] Abraham Joshua Heschel, *Moral Grandeur and Spiritual Audacity,* Susannah Heschel, ed. (New York: Farrar, Straus and Giroux, 1996), p. 111.

Tefillah, prayer even "becomes something more than petition, something beyond praise; it becomes a harmony between the human and the divine," said Israel Abrahams.[155] It also becomes the corporate outcry of praise and petition that further binds the community together.

The synagogue offers each Jewish person the opportunity for intimacy with the Divine, for his very sanctuary is called *Beit Tefillah*, a House of Prayer. Prayer is considered so vital to Jewish life that one must fully concentrate on the prayer with the manifestation of *kavanah* for it to be considered of any value.[156] Mindless repetition of words and phrases (*a la* the mantras chanted by Eastern monists) is entirely worthless in approaching God. This is why Jesus, himself, noted that "vain repetitions" in prayer were meaningless.[157] As Paul Gooch has noted, "The phenomenology of prayer discloses not a mindless repetition into obliteration, but a *relationship*."[158] Relationship, in which one both addresses God and hears from him, is the key to biblically Hebraic prayer.

The Jewish approach to prayer is that of entering the presence of a king who is also one's father. The title of one of the synagogues most important prayers, *Avinu Malkeinu*[159] ("our Father, our King"), is very telling. When one prepares to pray the *Amidah*, (*Ha-Tefillah*—"*The* Prayer"), the most ancient and most important prayer in the synagogal liturgy, he must stand (for he is in the presence of the King of the universe). Then, to ensure focus and concentration on his forthcoming act, he takes three small steps backward, followed by three small steps forward to demonstrate to himself that he is entering God's presence, and then he bows as an act of fealty to God. This entire process is an aid to the attitude of intense concentration in which everything else is set aside, and one focuses wholly on the Eternal. "Know before whom you stand" is the dictum that defines the importance of focus or *kavanah* in approaching God in prayer.

Hebraic prayer is not an exercise in trying to bend God to human will and desire, trying to incite God to do what the individual wants. Instead, it is an effort to conform one's self to the divine will, an exercise in cooperating with God to bring about his plan in one's life. It is not a means of wrangling with God, hoping to get him to change his mind. Instead, it is a dynamic for

---

155 Israel Abrahams, "Some Rabbinic Ideas on Prayer," in Israel Abrahams and Claude G. Montefiore, eds., *The Jewish Quarterly Review*, January, 1908, vol. XX, No. 78, p. 288.
156 *Kavanah* is "focus" or "concentration."
157 Matthew 6:7.
158 Paul W. Gooch, *Reflections on Jesus and Socrates: Word and Silence* (New Haven, CT: Yale University Press, 1996), p. 155.
159 The *Avinu Malkeinu* is actually a prayer that is recited during *Rosh Hashanah* and *Yom Kippur* and during the Ten Days of Awe between these two holy days.

changing the believer's heart. In fact, as Joseph Soloveitchik noted, "prayer is always the harbinger of moral reformation."[160] True prayer, then, is as much listening as it is talking—listening for divine conversation that directs the heart, convicts of sin, leads to repentance, and conforms to God's Word. This is one reason for the Jewish experience of corporate liturgical prayer in which most of the *Siddur* is devoted to praying the words of Holy Scripture.[161] Christians would do well to learn this important lesson from the Jewish tradition on which the earliest liturgy of the church was founded, for it is impossible to "ask wrongly" when one prays the "alive and powerful"[162] words of Scripture.[163]

It is clear that the earliest church maintained continuity with the Jewish community from which it emerged, especially in prayer. As a matter of fact, it was said of the believers that they were faithfully devoted to "the prayers," which in all likelihood referred to the collective prayers that were being prayed in all of the synagogues. The text of Acts 2:42 does not say that the believers were devoted to "prayer" even though most texts translate the passage that way. It literally says that they were devoted to "*the* prayers." As Ulf Ekman has said, "It was entirely natural for the Apostles to pray the prayers that were used in the synagogue and Temple."[164] This can be clearly understood when it is demonstrated that the Disciples' Prayer (the so-called "Lord's Prayer") is but a synopsis of synagogue prayers that preceded the Christian era. When Christians pray together or individually the "Lord's Prayer," they are engaging in praying the prayer rooted in *the* prayers of the ancient synagogue.

Synagogal Dynamics in the First-Century Church

Each of the three synagogal dynamics, the *Beit Knesset*, the *Beit Midrash*, and the *Beit Tefillah*, was clearly and specifically manifested in the lives of the earliest believers in Jesus. As a matter of fact, the clearest delineation of the experience of first-century Christianity makes this explicit: "They were continually devoting themselves to the apostles' teaching and to fellowship, to the breaking of bread, and to the prayers."[165] The connection between the dynamics of the pre-Christian synagogue and the earliest Christian community could not be clearer. The believers in Jesus as Messiah and Lord continually

---

[160] Joseph B. Soloveitchik, *The Lonely Man of Faith* (New York: Doubleday, 1965), p. 65.
[161] The *Siddur* is the Jewish prayerbook which contains the prayers that the people pray corporately.
[162] Hebrews 4:12.
[163] James 4:3.
[164] Ekman, p. 3.
[165] Acts 2:42, NASB, NIV.

devoted themselves to three activities: teaching, fellowship, and prayers. They had meetings that were either *Beit Midrash*, *Beit Knesset*, or *Beit Tefillah*, respectively—or all three at the same time! The Jesus community "continued steadfastly" in the apostles' teaching (*Midrash*), fellowship—including the "table fellowship" of breaking bread—(*Knesset*), and the prayers (*Tefillah*).

It is clear, then, that the earliest believers in Jesus had no intention of breaking away from the faith of their fathers and embracing a new religion that was completely foreign to all that they had known and experienced throughout their lives. In both the self-definition of the community's identity and in the dynamics of its faith and practice, the early "church" maintained continuity with the faith of Abraham and the dynamic system of praise, worship, and service of biblical and Second Temple Judaism. The "church" was a *kahal*, a community of faith, and it assembled as an *'edah*, a congregation of the righteous to exercise the roles of *Beit Knesset*, *Beit Midrash*, and *Beit Tefillah*.

Time for Restoration

Can there be any doubt, then, that the foundations of the church were laid in Abraham's family sanctuary and that the church was formally organized when God summoned the "called-out" Israelites from Egypt and brought them to Sinai so that they could enter into a covenant with him to be his Chosen People, his nation, his bride, his community, his congregation, his church? Charles Hodge said it well: "God has ever had but one Church in the world. The Jehovah of the Old Testament is our Lord; the God of Abraham, Isaac, and Jacob, is our covenant God and Father; our Saviour was the Saviour of the saints who lived before his advent in the flesh. . . . The faith which saved Abraham was, both as to its nature and as to its object, that which is the condition of salvation under the Gospel."[166]

The continuity of the church between the "Old" and "New" Testaments is further confirmed by the fact that the church even today still rests on the same promises and covenant. The covenant made with Abraham "is the covenant of grace under which we now live, and upon which the Church is now founded."[167] Paul strongly affirms that the "blessing of Abraham" has come upon the Gentiles "through Jesus Christ" so that "we might receive the promise of the Spirit through faith."[168] If the promise is the same to the

---

[166] Hodge, pp. 551–552.
[167] Hodge, p. 550.
[168] Galatians 3:14.

church, including the Gentiles, as it was to Abraham, then the condition is the same: believers are now justified by faith, because Abraham was so justified. As Hodge observed, "This doctrine, that the Church now rests on the Abrahamic covenant, in other words, that the plan of salvation revealed in the Gospel was revealed to Abraham and to the other Old Testament saints, and that they were saved just as men since the advent of Christ are saved, by faith in the promised seed, is not a matter incidentally revealed."[169] The Hebrew heritage of Christianity "is wrought into the very substance of the Gospel. It is involved in all the teachings of our Lord, who said that he came not to destroy, but to fulfill; and who commanded inquirers to search the Old Testament Scriptures if they would learn what he taught."[170]

Lewis Chafer, therefore, was clearly mistaken when he declared that "God is pursuing two distinct purposes: one related to the earth with earthly people and earthly objectives involved, which is Judaism; while the other is related to heaven with heavenly people and heavenly objectives involved, which is Christianity . . . Israel is an eternal nation, heir to an eternal land, with an eternal kingdom, on which David rules from an eternal throne, so that in eternity . . . never the twain, Israel and the church, shall meet."[171] Israel and the church will not only meet in the one future kingdom of God, they have also already met, for the church was and is but an extension and further development of Israel, the church in the wilderness.

The purposes of God involving Israel and the church are integrally and delicately intertwined, and both speak of a people that is both earthly and heavenly. Abraham was a truly earth-bound believer; however, the vision that drove his faithfulness was the heavenly city whose architect and builder is God.[172] The faith of Israel has been in the resurrection of the dead and the reign of the Olam ha-Ba. Any Christian ecclesiology that does not in some dimension include Israel and the Jewish community, therefore, is fundamentally flawed. Christians should be very careful to keep their ecclesiology more inclusive than exclusive. The church should never be deceived into thinking, as it has in the past, that Gentile Christian inclusion requires Jewish exclusion.

The command that God gave to Moses is still good advice for Christians today: "See that you make all things according to the patterns shown you in the mountain."[173] The community in heaven is the primeval archetype, ancient

---

[169] Hodge, p. 551.
[170] Hodge, p. 551.
[171] Lewis Sperry Chafer, quoted in Jonas E. Alexis, *Christianity and Rabbinic Judaism: Surprising Differences, Conflicting Visions and Worldview Implications—From the Early Church to our Modern Time* (Bloomington, IN: Thomas Nelson, 2012), p. 388.
[172] Hebrews 11:9–10.
[173] Exodus 25:40; Hebrews 8:5.

Israel is the prototype, and the Mount Zion community of the first century is the pattern from which believers can contextualize the faith of the apostles in today's multicultural world. When they do, they will find themselves building on the Rock, not on the sands of human tradition, and the lives that they build and bring to maturity will survive the raging storms of time and will stand for eternity.[174] Indeed, the very gates of hell will never prevail against the *kahal*, the *ekklesía*, the community of faith which Jesus restored, renewed, and filled with his Holy Spirit.

The continuity of the God's community from the pattern in heaven to the demonstration in Abraham, to the manifestation in Israel, to the fulfillment in the apostolic congregation provides a solid foundation for understanding the church and its purpose in the world today. Embracing the Hebraic foundations of the church of Jesus Christ will help believers maintain balance in a changing world and avoid another of the terrible revolutionary expeditions over the precipice of heresy that has devastated the church again and again. The siren song of postmodernity's multiculturalism and syncretism lures those toward the rocks of destruction who are ignorant of the church's true foundations. God, however, will have none of it, for he will continue to apply his "Israel strategy" to the church, saying, "Your sins have been your downfall! . . . Return to the LORD your God,"[175] for the Lord is married to the church as he is to "backsliding Israel,"[176] and he will never give up on either of them.

In the end, God will be victorious over all the malapropisms of his people, whether Jew or Gentile. Divine fidelity has never been constrained by human infidelity, and it never will be. God will eventually have a *kahal/ekklesía* that will be without spot and wrinkle, prepared as a bride adorned for her husband, and that bride will be as Jewish in appearance and demeanor as the one that was joined to the Lord at Sinai. No matter how many times and how dreadfully the church may have fallen and may yet fall into aberrations from its original design and intent, God will yet bring it forth even from the very jaws of hell itself and establish it as the Holy City that is set on a hill whose light will shine into all the world. As G. K. Chesterton said, "Christendom has had a series of revolutions and in each one of them Christianity has died. Christianity has died many times and risen again; for it had a God who knew the way out of the grave."[177]

Church: Christian Fruit—Jewish Root!

---

174 Matthew 7:24–27.
175 Hosea 14:1–2.
176 Jeremiah 3:14.
177 G. K. Chesterton, *The Collected Works of G. K. Chesterton, Volume 2* (San Francisco, CA: Ignatius Press, 1986), p. 382.

CHAPTER 18

RESURRECTION

"Your brother will rise again," Jesus said reassuringly to Martha, the bereaved and grieving sister of his very close friend Lazarus. Martha's response was very telling: "I know that he will rise again in the resurrection on the last day."[1] As a Jewish woman of faith, she was confessing what most of the Jewish people in her day believed and what they affirmed three times daily in their synagogues[2] as the cardinal principle of faith: that in the great denouement at the end of the age, all the righteous who have died in faith will be resurrected bodily to stand before their Lord.

Jesus, however, had a new and profound word of insight and promise for Martha: "I am the resurrection and the life. Whoever believes in me, though he die, yet shall he live."[3] Upon hearing these words, Martha made precisely the same foundational confession of faith that the apostle Peter had made when Jesus had asked him who he believed him, the son of man, to be. "I believe that you are the Messiah, the Son of God," she said. Immediately, she ran to her sister Mary and told her, "The Master is here and is calling for you," whereupon Mary rushed out to meet Jesus, pouring out her heart's grief before him. Then, in the shortest verse in the Bible, the Scripture says simply, "Jesus wept." Clearly, the Master understood and commiserated with the sorrow of bereavement that this faithful family was experiencing. He, however, had a definitive answer to their grief, as he commanded, "Lazarus, come forth!" Immediately life came into the decaying body of Lazarus, and he exited the tomb.

This amazing demonstration of divine power proved that Jesus had the power of life and death, something that Scripture had long said was solely

---

[1] John 11:23–24.
[2] Since before the time of Jesus, Jews have affirmed their faith in the resurrection three times each day in the *Amidah*, the synagogue prayer *par excellence*. In the second of the eighteen benedictions of the *Amidah*, called the *Gevurot* ("Powers"), the Jewish people affirm in four separate statements their belief that God will "keep faith with those in the dust of the earth" to bring them forth in the resurrection. They conclude their affirmation with these words: "Blessed are you, O God, who gives life to the dead."
[3] John 11:25, ESV.

in the province of God himself.[4] Though the dead had been resuscitated by the faith-filled prayers of prophets[5] and though Jesus himself had raised Jairus' daughter[6] from the dead as well as the widow's son at Nain[7], he had just raised a man who was had been dead for four days, which was well past the time for legally defined death in the ancient world.[8] When he called forth Lazarus from the dead, Jesus proved that he was the personification of the resurrection!

By far, the most important resurrection that Jesus performed, however, took place when through the power of the Holy Spirit, he brought himself forth from the dead.[9] "For just as the Father has life in himself, even so he gave the Son also to have life in himself," Jesus said. The Eternal Father "who alone has immortality"[10] gave the same eternal life to his Son, so that "in him was life, and the life was the light of men."[11] Therefore, after being subjected to mock trials by both the Roman authorities and the Roman-appointed rulers of the temple and after being brutally beaten by Roman soldiers, crucified on a Roman cross, killed by a spear in the hand of a Roman executioner, and placed in a sealed tomb guarded by Roman authority,[12] Jesus arose triumphantly from the dead, demonstrating for all time that he had the keys to death and the grave.[13]

---

[4] 1 Samuel 2:6; Job 1:1; Romans 4:17.

[5] 1 Kings 17:21–22; 2 Kings 4:35.

[6] Matthew 8:28–43.

[7] Luke 7:11–17.

[8] According to rabbinic tradition, death was not confirmed until three days after the cessation of breath and heartbeat (Genesis *Rabbah* 100.7; Leviticus *Rabbah* 18:1; Ecclesiastes *Rabbah* 12:6; and Talmud, *Mo'ed Katan* 3:5). "During that time, according to the classical Rabbis, the soul hovers over the grave, hoping to be restored to the body." Bernard S. Jackson, ed., *The Jewish Law* (Amsterdam, The Netherlands: Amsteldijk, 1997), p. 101. In the ancient Jewish world, therefore, "the tomb . . . was not immediately closed over the dead. During the first three days it was customary for the relatives to visit the grave to see whether the dead had come to life again." Singer, et. al., vol. 3, p. 434.

[9] The bodily resurrection of Jesus was an act of the triune God—Father, Son, and Spirit. Scripture specifically says the Father resurrected Jesus: "God raised him up again, putting an end to the agony of death, since it was impossible for him to be held in its power"(Acts 2:24; cf. Romans 4:24; Romans 19:9; 1 Peter 1:21). Scripture also says that Jesus resurrected himself: "Destroy this temple, and in three days I will raise it up" (John 2:19). Additionally, Scripture says that the Holy Spirit resurrected Jesus: "If the Spirit of him who raised Jesus from the dead is living in you . . . he will give life to your mortal bodies through his Spirit who dwells in you" (Romans 8:11). Sergius Bulgakov describes this dynamic: "There is no contradiction here; on the contrary, one can and must harmonize His resurrection of Himself and His being raised by God. . . . we have the very *fact* of the resurrection . . . and here it is indicated that the resurrection is the work of Christ Himself. . . . However, in His state of humiliation, the Son of God does not raise Himself . . . the Father raises Him by the Holy Spirit." Sergius Bulgakov, *The Lamb of God* (Grand Rapids, MI: Wm. B. Eerdmans Publishing Co., 2009), p. 382.

[10] 1 Timothy 6:16.

[11] John 1:4.

[12] Markus Bockmuehl, *Jewish Law in Gentile Churches: Halakah and the Beginning of Christian Public Ethics* (Edinburgh, UK: T & T Clark, 2000), pp. 23–48.

[13] Revelation 1:18.

It was very early in the morning of the third day of his entombment, long before sunrise, when some of the women who were among his disciples made their way to the tomb in order to see that the body of their Master was being properly interred.[14] When they arrived at the tomb and discovered that the stone which was covering its entrance had been rolled away and that the tomb empty, they were crestfallen because they thought that someone had stolen the body and deprived them of their right to show their last respects to their Lord, Jesus. Then, one of the women, Mary Magdalene, came face to face with the Master and with the reality that his body was, indeed, missing from the tomb, but only because he had risen from the dead.[15]

The resurrection of Jesus was not a ruse or a plot concocted by his disciples in order to deceive their fellow countrymen and cover up the ignominy of his crucifixion. It met all the criteria necessary for being recognized as an established historical fact.[16] The resurrected Jesus was personally seen in a wide variety of different circumstances[17]—and even by total skeptics,[18] including those who recognized his post-resurrection corporeality and confirmed that what they had seen was not an apparition, a spirit, or a figment of their imagination.[19] His post-resurrection appearances were not limited to one or two instances during a very short span of time. In fact, they took place continually for forty days after the resurrection, including one appearance to 500 people.[20] His ascension into heaven was witnessed by at least 120 people. The large number of eyewitnesses, coupled with the fact that all of those who saw the resurrected Jesus were willing to die as martyrs[21] rather than recant their testimony, offers solid proof that Jesus was, indeed, resurrected from the dead.[22] These truths prompted Orthodox Jewish scholar Pinchas Lapide to conclude that the resurrection was a historical event that God used

---

[14] Mark 16:1. Bockmuehl, pp. 23–48.

[15] John 20:12–16.

[16] The historicity of Jesus' resurrection is concrete despite the best arguments of skeptics such as those recorded in John W. Loftus, *The Christian Delusion: Why Faith Fails* (Amherst, NY: Prometheus Books, 2010), p. 307.

[17] Matthew 28:10; Luke 24:13–22; John 20–21; Acts 1:3–9

[18] John 2:25. The classic example of incredulity regarding Jesus' resurrection was manifest in the skepticism of Thomas, one of the twelve apostles. When he was told of Jesus' resurrection, Thomas exclaimed in utter exasperation, "Unless I shall see in his hands the print of the nails and put my finger into the print of the nails and thrust my hand into his side, I will not believe."

[19] Luke 24:42–43. The story related in this passage confirms that Jesus was "flesh and bone" and that he "ate food."

[20] 1 Corinthians 15:6.

[21] It is of no insignificant consequence that the Greek word for "witness," μάρτυς—*martus*, is the same as the word for "martyr."

[22] These were among the people about whom John spoke when he declared, "I saw the souls of them that were beheaded for the *witness* of Jesus" (Revelation 20:4, emphasis added).

to open the door of faith to the Gentiles. Lapide said, "I accept the resurrection of Jesus not as an invention of the community of disciples, but as an historical event. . . . I believe that the Christ event leads to a way of salvation which God has opened up in order to bring the Gentile world into the community of God's Israel."[23]

The Pivot Point of Faith

The resurrection of Jesus was the pivotal event in all of human history.[24] Had Jesus not resurrected from the dead, there would have been no proof that he was, indeed, the Messiah, the Son of God. Thomas Miller maintains that "the resurrection validates for all time that [Jesus] is indeed God in the flesh."[25] Karl Barth said, "If Jesus Christ is not risen—bodily, visibly, audibly, perceptibly, in the same concrete sense in which He died . . . if He is not also risen, then our preaching and our faith are vain and futile; we are still in our sins."[26] While the death of Jesus provided the once-for-all atonement for sins, his death would have been meaningless had he not resurrected from the dead. Paul made this clear when he declared that while Jesus was "delivered over to death for our sins," he was "raised again for our justification."[27] If Jesus had not been resurrected, no human being could ever fully achieve right relationship with God[28] by being fully justified by divine grace and faith in Jesus' atoning death[29] and having the righteousness of Christ imputed to them.[30]

Christian faith, then, hinges on the resurrection of Jesus. Again, Paul confirmed this cardinal truth: "If Christ has not been raised, your faith is futile; you are still in your sins."[31] He continued even more graphically by saying, "If only for this life we have hope in Christ, we are of all people most to be pitied."[32] Then the apostle gave the clincher: "But in fact Christ has

---

[23] Lapide and Moltmann, p. 59. Lapide maintained that Christianity would never have expanded beyond Jerusalem if the resurrection of Jesus had not been a historical fact. See Pinchas Lapide, *The Resurrection of Jesus: A Jewish Perspective* (Eugene, OR: Wipf & Stock Publishers, 2002). Also Shahan, ed., p. 33.

[24] John H. Leith, *Basic Christian Doctrine* (Louisville, KY: Westminster/John Knox Press, 1993), p. 140. Leith says, "The pivotal event in human history is God's raising Jesus Christ from the dead, vindicating the life and ministry and declaring him to be Lord."

[25] Thomas Allen Miller, *Did Jesus Really Rise from the Dead?: A Surgeon-Scientist Examines the Evidence* (Wheaton, IL: Crossway, 2013), p. 145.

[26] Karl Barth, *Church Dogmatics IV.1: The Doctrine of Reconciliation* (New York: T & T Clark International, 1956), p. 351

[27] Romans 4:25.

[28] Romans 3:22; 9:30; 2 Corinthians 5:21.

[29] Romans 3:24.

[30] Romans 4:11.

[31] 1 Corinthians 15:17, NIV.

[32] 1 Corinthians 15:19, NIV.

been raised from the dead," and he guaranteed the purpose of Christ's resurrection, "[He is] the firstfruits of those who have fallen asleep."[33] Jesus is the firstfruits of the resurrection, for "in Christ all will be made alive. But each in his own order: Christ the firstfruits, after that those who are Christ's at his coming."[34] The firstfruits are the solid evidence that a bountiful harvest is forthcoming! The resurrection of Jesus is proof positive that all the "dead in Christ" will rise from the dead.[35] Indeed, the resurrection from the dead at the end of time "is the necessary sequel to Jesus' resurrection."[36]

A Strong Pre-Christian Tradition

The expectation of the divine gifts of life, health, and healing is encapsulated in various benedictions and prayers that the Jewish people have prayed daily for centuries, some of them even before the time of Jesus. As a part of the early morning prayers that precede the fourteen morning blessings which individuals say when they rise from sleep, the Jewish people thank God for the renewed energy and consciousness that they feel upon waking up by reciting this blessing: "Blessed are you, O LORD our God, King of the universe, who restores souls to dead corpses (*hamachizir n'shamot lifgarim metim*)."[37] The daily use of the metaphor of resurrection to describe simple awakening from sleep ingrains into the Jewish mind the understanding that God is, indeed, the one who is faithful not only to awaken sleeping souls each day but also to awaken those who sleep in the dust of the earth by the power of resurrection in the *Olam haBa* (the "World to Come").

Well before the time of Jesus, what came to be called "The Prayer" in the synagogue extolled God's *gevurot*, his "powers" as the one who faithfully brings life and resurrection to his Chosen People. The second blessing of this prayer poignantly sums up the confidence that every Jewish believer since before the time of Jesus has had in God's power to heal the living and to revive the dead:

> You are mighty forever, O LORD. You give life to the dead. You are great to save.

---

[33] 1 Corinthians 15:21.

[34] 1 Corinthians 15:23.

[35] 1 Thessalonians 4:16.

[36] Joost Holleman, *Resurrection and Parousia* (Leiden, The Netherlands: Koninklijke Brill Publishers, 1996), p. 704.

[37] Lawrence A. Hoffman, *My People's Prayer Book: Vol. 2: The Amidah* (Woodstock, VT: Jewish Lights Publishing, 1998), p. 75.

You sustain life with lovingkindness. You give life to the dead with great mercy. You support the falling, and heal the sick, freeing the prisoners and keeping faith with those who sleep in the dust.

Who is like you, master of powers, and who resembles you, king of death and of life,[38] and the one who causes salvation to spring up!

You are reliable and faithful to give life to the dead. Blessed are you, O LORD, giving life to the dead.[39]

With this profound declaration of faith, the Jewish people have daily affirmed their resolute faith that the God whom they worship and serve has the power over life and death and that he will "keep faith with those who sleep in the dust" by bringing them forth unto life through the resurrection of the righteous dead. It is by no means incidental that Jesus himself prayed some form of this prayer, the *Amidah*, as he participated in the synagogue services of his day.

Since before the first century, then, biblical Judaism has maintained as one of its most fundamental tenets the expectation that the righteous dead will be resurrected at the end of the age. Indeed, there were hints throughout the Hebrew Scriptures that the resurrection of the righteous is inevitable. Those allusions were made very explicit in Daniel's recapitulation of the resurrection expectation.[40] Finally, during the centuries before and after the advent of the Common Era, fierce debates arose in the Jewish community about the prospects for a resurrection. The Sadducees were famous for their utter denial of any possibility of resurrection. They were entirely this-worldly in their worldview and mindset. The Pharisees, on the other hand, were adamant in their understanding that all biblical faith pointed to an ultimate teleological end—a goal that would be fulfilled in the dramatic resurrection of all the righteous dead from the dust of the earth so that they might live forever in the presence of God. This event would represent the ultimate imposition of divine justice upon the earth wherein the righteous would be rewarded for their faithfulness to God, and the unrighteous would be judged for their infidelity.

Continuing Faith

It should have come as no surprise, then, that the earliest Jewish disciples of Jesus would have been strong believers in the resurrection. Jesus

---

[38] The *Gevurot* declaration that God is the "King of death and life" is based on the specific statement that is made in two passages of Scripture: Deuteronomy 32:39, "I [the LORD] deal death and give life; I wounded and I will heal: None can deliver from my hand" (TNK), and 1 Samuel 2:6, "The LORD deals death and gives life, casts down into *Sheol* and raises up" (TNK).

[39] Author's translation.

[40] Daniel 12:3–9.

himself constantly sided with the Pharisees against the Sadducees on the issue of resurrection. When he addressed their questions about the resurrection, he even said, "You are in error because you do not know the Scriptures or the power of God."[41] Jesus maintained that because the Lord said, "I am the God of Abraham, the God of Isaac, and the God of Jacob,"[42] he is and will ever be the God of resurrection. God did not say, "I was the God of Abraham"; he said, "I am the God of Abraham." Since God is not the God of the dead, Jesus said, he must be the God of resurrection who will bring the Patriarchs forth from the dead so that he will be their God in the future as well as in the past. In order for God to be able to say to Moses, "I am the God of Abraham, the God of Isaac, and the God of Jacob" in some dimension, "Abraham, Isaac, and Jacob must still have had life, even though they have died, because God speaks of himself as being their God, as if they are still alive,"[43] and they await only the resurrection to complete the full bodily restoration of life. Jesus and Rabbi Simai[44] agreed that the only way that God could fulfill Exodus 3:6, "I am the God of Abraham," was by resurrecting the patriarchs. As Kevin Madigan notes, "Jesus' belief in the resurrection to come, then, is grounded theologically in faith in the God of creation to bring life out of death, in the power of God as the creator of the cosmos."[45]

Jesus, however, took the resurrection one step further. He said, "I am the resurrection and the life. He who believes in me will live even if he dies,"[46] and he continued by saying, "Everyone who lives and believes in me will never die."[47] He told the woman at the well of Samaria, "Whoever drinks the water I give them will never thirst. Indeed, the water I give them will become in them a spring of water welling up to eternal life."[48] Since Jesus was the resurrection and the life, he could give *mayim chayim* ("living water") to those who believed in him. In effect, Jesus promised that those who believed that he was the Messiah and Savior would never really die because, for them, their physical death would only be a simple transition

---

[41] Matthew 22:29, NIV.

[42] Exodus 3:6.

[43] George Martin, *The Gospel According to Mark: Meaning and Message* (Chicago, IL: Loyola Press, 2005), p. 323.

[44] *Sifre Deuteronomy, Ha'azinu* 306. See Stephen M. Wylen, *The Seventy Faces of Torah: The Jewish Way of Reading the Sacred Scriptures* (Mahway, NJ: Paulist Press, 2005), p. 52.

[45] Madigan and Levenson, p. 16.

[46] John 11:25.

[47] John 11:26 ESV. Because the dead in Christ will be resurrected, it will be as though they have never died.

[48] John 4:14, NIV.

into eternal life in the resurrection at the end of the age. In the meantime, they would merely "sleep" in Jesus.[49]

The apostles of Jesus made the resurrection theme a central device in their proclamation of the good news of God's kingdom. Their specific "emphasis was on the resurrection from the dead to which Jesus' own resurrection gave witness."[50] Paul was especially adamant about the importance of the resurrection for Christian believers: "If the dead are not raised, not even Christ has been raised . . . and if Christ has not been raised, your faith is worthless."[51] Christian faith, therefore, is meaningless without the resurrection, for while the Christian believer is saved from his sins by the crucifixion of Christ, the only way in which he can be justified is by the resurrection of the Messiah.[52] Indeed, it is only through "the resurrection of Jesus from the dead" that Christians are "begotten again unto the hope of life."[53] Christianity, therefore, has no basis for existence without the historical event of the resurrection of Jesus and without the future event of the general resurrection of the righteous dead. Christianity is a resurrection religion which owes the core of its identity to the Jewish concept of the resurrection of the dead.

A Bodily Event

Both traditional Jews and Christians have consistently understood that the resurrection is bodily and not merely a spiritual exercise. Though some elements in both faiths have tried to syncretize biblical resurrection theology with the Greek concept of the immortality of the soul or with the view that resurrection is symbolic of living a good life so that one lives on in the memory of others, the truth is that biblical resurrection is bodily resurrection. Thomas Torrance concludes wisely, "If there is no resurrection, human nature is no longer genuinely human. Since man is the concrete reality he is, resurrection of man in the nature of the case can be only *bodily resurrection*—any 'resurrection' that is not bodily is surely a contradiction in terms."[54] While some scholars have occupied themselves with trying to figure out how God could possibly reassemble the scattered atoms or DNA of disintegrated human bodies,[55] like those whose

---

[49] 1 Thessalonians 4:14.

[50] Dieter Zeller, et.al., *Resurrection in the New Testament: Festschrift to J. Lambrecht* (Leuven, Belgium: Leuven University Press, 2002), p. 245.

[51] 1 Corinthians 15:16–17.

[52] Romans 4:25.

[53] 1 Peter 1:3.

[54] Thomas F. Torrance, *Space, Time and Resurrection* (Edinburgh, Scotland: T & T Clark, Ltd., 1976), p. 87.

[55] If God has the very hairs of the head of every human being numbered (Luke 12:7), he certainly has catalogued every aspect of human DNA!

flesh has been vaporized by the explosive devices of modern warfare, the truth is that the resurrected body will not simply be the reconstituted body of present human existence. The resurrected life will be far more than mere resuscitated human life as it is presently known. In fact, there is significant evidence in Scripture to support the view that the "spiritual body,"[56] which Paul believed would be similar to, if not the same as, the glorified body in which Jesus was resurrected,[57] will be a body that will be "from heaven," not from the earth.[58]

The Resurrection to Come

Eventually, according to God's plan, the time that Hosea called the "last days" and that Daniel called "the end" will come when the universal kingdom of God, the reign of peace and justice, will be established over all the earth.[59] This eventuality will be initiated by the promised act of God that has always been the overarching theme of biblical eschatology,[60] the long-anticipated resurrection of the dead, wherein all believers in the God of Israel, both the living and the dead, will experience a corporeal change from mortality into immortality.[61] The prophet Daniel described this event in this manner: "Multitudes who sleep in the dust of the earth will awake . . . Go your way, Daniel, because the words are rolled up and sealed until the time of the end. . . . You will rest, and then at the end of the days you will rise to receive your allotted inheritance."[62] Isaiah expressed it this way: "Your dead shall live; their bodies shall rise. You who dwell in the dust, awake and sing for joy! For your dew is a dew of light, and the earth will give birth to the dead."[63] Hosea portrayed it this manner: "I will deliver this

---

[56] 1 Corinthians 15:44–45. Paul said of death and resurrection, "It is sown a natural body, it is raised a spiritual body. . . . So it is written: 'The first man Adam became a living being'; the last Adam, a life-giving spirit."

[57] Philippians 3:21. Paul taught that Jesus "will transform our lowly bodies so that they will be like his glorious body." (NIV).

[58] 2 Corinthians 5:1–2. Paul says that believers groan within themselves seeking to be "clothed with our house which is *from heaven*," with the "building of God" that is "not made with hands, eternal in the heavens" (KJV, emphasis added). This bespeaks the resurrection assumption of a heavenly body similar to the glorified body of Jesus and suggests that the resurrection takes place in heaven, not in the earth. Further confirmation of this premise is seen in 1 Thessalonians 4:14 where Paul maintains that "those who sleep in Jesus will God *bring with* him" (emphasis added).

[59] Daniel 12:13; 7:22.

[60] Eschatology is the study of the last things which deals with the coming of the Messiah, the resurrection of the dead, and the establishment of the kingdom of God on earth.

[61] 1 Corinthians 15:54.

[62] Daniel 12:2, 9, 13.

[63] Isaiah 26:19, ESV.

people from the power of the grave; I will redeem them from death. Where, O death, are your plagues? Where, O grave, is your destruction?"[64] Paul summed it up this way: "Behold, I tell you a mystery; we will not all sleep [in death], but we will all be changed, in a moment, in the twinkling of an eye, at the last trumpet; for the trumpet will sound, and the dead will be raised imperishable, and we will be changed."[65] Then the apostle concluded by quoting the Hosea's words directly, "Where, O death, is your victory? Where, O death, is your sting?" Then the apostle exulted, "Thanks be to God! He gives us the victory through our Lord Jesus Christ."[66] The final chapter in the saga of salvation history, then, speaks entirely of life from the dead in the resurrection—the dynamic physical and spiritual change wherein both the living and the dead will inherit eternal life in the everlasting kingdom of YHWH and his Messiah.

This is the event of which Jesus spoke when he said, "Truly, truly I say to you, he who hears my word, and believes him who sent me, has eternal life, and does not come into judgment, but has passed out of death into life. Truly, truly, I say to you, an hour is coming and now is, when the dead will hear the voice of the Son of God, and those who hear will live. . . . Do not marvel at this; for an hour is coming, in which all who are in the tombs shall hear his voice, and will come forth; those who did the good deeds to a resurrection of life, those who committed the evil deeds to a resurrection of judgment."[67] Jesus was merely repeating and giving context to the words that the prophet Daniel had spoken centuries before his time: "Many of those who sleep in the dust of the ground will awake, these to everlasting life, but the others to disgrace and everlasting contempt."[68] Daniel's angelic visitor assured him that the vision and promise that had been given him would be "rolled up and sealed until the time of the end. . . . You will enter into rest and rise again for your allotted portion at the end of the age."[69]

Restoration at the End: Recapitulating the Beginning

If one is hoping to understand the end, the best place to look is in the beginning. This is what God specifically said to Isaiah, "Remember the former things long past, for I am God, and there is no other; I am God, and there is no one like me, declaring the end from the beginning . . . saying,

---

[64] Hosea 13:14, NIV.
[65] 1 Corinthians 15:51–52.
[66] 1 Corinthians 15:55, 57, NIV.
[67] John 5:24-29.
[68] Daniel 12:2.
[69] Daniel 12:9, 13.

'My purpose will be established, and I will accomplish all my good plea-sure.'"[70] God's final action toward humankind is wrapped up in his first action toward humanity. The same God who, in the beginning, gathered together the dust of the earth, formed it into a human body, and then breathed his breath into that body so that it became a living being, will, in the end, resurrect the righteous dead in a far better state than that of his original creation and imbue them with eternal life. Jon Levenson gives a powerful description of this action: "Like creation, resurrection is a preem-inently *super*natural act, a miraculous reversal of the course of nature. Through it, God thus transforms death, nature's last word, into a prelude to his own new act of creation, the re-creation of human beings in a form that is bodily yet immune to the vulnerabilities and ravages of biological life. So conceived, resurrection thus recapitulates but also transcends the creation of humanity. The miracle of the end-time restores the miracle of the beginning."[71]

Just as God created human life in the beginning out of nothing when he breathed his *neshamah* into humanity, depositing there the *nishmat chayyim* ("breath of life"), so will he deposit eternal life into resurrected bodies in the end. This is what Tertullian taught so eloquently: "If God produced all things whatever out of nothing, He will be able to . . . call forth the flesh too from . . . whatever *abyss* it may have been engulphed. And surely He is most competent to re-create who created, inasmuch as it is a far greater work to have produced than to have reproduced. . . . On this principle, you may be quite sure that the restoration of the flesh is easier than its first formation."[72] This insight also prompted Irenaeus to draw a similar conclusion: "Surely it is much more difficult . . . to make man an animated and rational creature, than to reintegrate again that which had been created and then afterwards decomposed into earth. . . . God's power is sufficient for the resurrection given that he had formed human being in the beginning."[73]

The end is perfectly revealed from the beginning. In the beginning, God created life in a universe where there was no life. In the end, he will create life again—this time out of death—when "he enlivens those who, without his saving breath, would have lain forever inert."[74] Levenson describes how this

---

[70] Isaiah 46:9–10.

[71] Jon D. Levenson, *The Death and Resurrection of the Beloved Son: The Transformation of Child Sacrifice in Judaism and Christianity* (New Haven, CT: Yale University Press, 1995), p. 6.

[72] Tertullian, *On the Resurrection of the Flesh*, XI, in Alexander Roberts, *The Ante-Nicene Fathers, Volume 3: Latin Christianity: Its Founder, Tertullian,* James Donaldson, Arthur Cleveland Coxe, eds. (New York: Charles Scribner's Sons, 1885), p. 553.

[73] Irenaeus, *Against Heresies*, 5.3.2, partially quoted in Madigan and Levenson, p. 230.

[74] Madigan and Levenson, p. 229.

eschatological work of God recapitulates the beginning work of God: "[T]he God who created will also re-create, and the miraculous potentials he activated at the beginning will again be seen at the end, when he restores the flesh-and-blood people Israel to their land and station, renders justice to Jew and Gentile alike, reverses the very real tragedy of death, and ushers in a better world without it."[75] Resurrection, therefore, is *the* eschatological unit, the event that will occur at the end point of history which will "transform and redeem history" and will "open onto a barely imaginable world beyond anything that preceded it."[76]

As life and resurrection personified,[77] Jesus is the *Aleph* and the *Tav*, the *Alpha* and the *Omega*, the beginning and the end.[78] He is the "first and the last, the living one."[79] As the *Aleph*, Jesus is creation personified. He is the *re'shiyth*, the *arche*, "the beginning" personified. "In the beginning was the *Logos/Memra*," the Word who "was God."[80] His is the "first" of everything that exists, "the beginning of the creation of God,"[81] the "firstborn (or the source) of the creation" in that "by means of him all things were created in the heavens and upon the earth."[82] In truth, Jesus is the Word of God through whom all things were created in the beginning.[83] The Jesus who is resurrection and life is the *Logos/Memra* who created human life in the beginning. By the same token, Jesus is the *Tav*, "the last," and as such he is the eschaton personified. This is how he announced himself to John: "I am the first and the *éschatos*."[84] He is the other extreme of creation: he is eschatology consummated, the "coming one." If Jesus was the author of all creation, including human life, he will certainly be the author of all recreation. The creator of life in the beginning will be the re-creator of life in the end. Beginning with the resurrection of the righteous dead and continuing to the creation of new heavens and a new earth wherein the righteous will dwell,[85] he will effect the consummation of all things. What he has in store for the righteous

---

[75] Jon Levenson, p. 22.

[76] Jon Levenson, pp. 22–23.

[77] Jesus himself declared that he was life and resurrection personified: "I am the resurrection and the life" (John 11:25).

[78] Revelation 22:13.

[79] Revelation 1:17.

[80] John 1:1.

[81] Revelation 3:14.

[82] Colossians 1:15 says that Jesus is "the firstborn of all creation"; however, this does not mean that he was the first thing created by God, for the statement continues, "for by him all things were created, both in the heavens and on earth . . . all things have been created through him and for him." If Jesus were a created being and not God, then he created himself, which is impossible.

[83] Hebrews 11:3.

[84] Gerhard Sauter, "Protestant Theology," in *The Oxford Handbook of Eschatology*, Jerry L. Walls, ed. (New York: Oxford University Press, 2008), p. 258.

[85] Isaiah 65:17; 66:22; 2 Peter 3:13.

in the resurrection is unimaginable. "No eye has seen, no ear has heard and no one's heart has imagined all the things that God has prepared for those who love him."[86] Through the eye of the Spirit, however, believers in the God of Scripture can discern the promises of God for the future when death is swallowed up in life, the life of the Son of God.

Eternal Life

Resurrection in both the Hebrew and Apostolic Scriptures is resurrection to "eternal life." Daniel was the first to use the term *eternal life* in Scripture;[87] however, his use of the phrase certainly summed up all the expectations of the prophets and sages of Israel, as well as those of the apostles of Jesus. This eternal life, however, is not a purely spiritual existence, the survival of human consciousness, or a perpetuation of the immortal soul. Job said, "In my *flesh* I will see God."[88] Physical embodiment is inherent in resurrection. It would be a mistake, however, "to imagine that the 'eternal life' that the deserving receive is simply a restoration of their old quotidian reality, only without the pain and injustice."[89] For those who are resurrected, the body will be different "from the kind they knew in their mortal life, for now they have become immune to death and the bodily infirmities associated with it. . . . Their new life is thus not a mere continuation of the old but rather a radical transformation of it."[90] Resurrection life will be a new form of existence that humanity has never experienced before except in the resurrection of Jesus himself. Believers will live in a "glorious body" like the one that Jesus had when he was resurrected from the grave.

Paul made this truth very clear: "We know that if the earthly tent which is our house is torn down, we have a building from God, a house not made with hands, eternal in the heavens. Meanwhile we groan, longing to be clothed with our heavenly dwelling . . . so that what is mortal may be swallowed up by life."[91] The resurrection body, then, will have no direct connection with the mortal body in which life was lived on earth. The resurrection body will not be the old mortal body reassembled, reconstituted, and revitalized so that it can then live forever in the same state in which it had previously lived. This would not be the kind of eternal life that Scripture envisions. Instead, eternal life will be lived in a

---

[86] 1 Corinthians 2:9.
[87] Daniel 12:2.
[88] Job 19:26.
[89] Jon Levenson, p. 189.
[90] Jon Levenson, pp. 106–107.
[91] 2 Corinthians 5:1–2, 4, NASB, NIV, NASB.

spiritual body that will clothe the revived human spirit in a totally new physical reality which will reconstitute "living being"[92] in a new and better form. This time, in contrast with the human body that was received in the Genesis creation, the new spiritual body will be imbued with eternal life from the moment of resurrection for in the act of being raised from the dead, it will have partaken of the fruit of the Tree of Life that Adam and Eve never tasted.[93]

It is clear, then, that, over the centuries, Rabbinic Judaism and Christianity have stood alongside each other in one powerful witness to the undeniable belief in the eschatological resurrection of the righteous dead. From their first-century emergence from Second Temple Judaism, both sibling faiths have striven "to uphold faith in a God who transcends nature and can overcome it, even bringing back the whole person, body and soul, as God who acts in history, fulfilling his amazing promises to his people."[94] And, by the grace of God, both religions still believe in and await the advent of the last day when those who sleep in the dust of the earth[95] will hear the sound of the shofar[96] and the voice of God[97] and will come forth in the resurrection.

Resurrection from the dead is a cardinal tenet of Christian faith. In fact, without the doctrine of the resurrection, there would be no Christian faith. The profound belief of millions of Christians through the centuries in the resurrection of Jesus and in the promise of their own personal resurrection from the dead, however, is anchored in the pre-Christian belief of prophets and sages in the powers of God to keep faith with those who are in the dust of the earth and to bring them forth unto eternal life at the end of the days.

Resurrection: Christian Fruit—Jewish Root!

---

92 The term *living being* was used to describe the final product in God's creation of humanity. "God breathed into his nostrils the breath of life, and he became a living being." The phrase *living being* has generally been translated "living soul," employing the Greek term ψυχή—*pseuché* ("soul"). In Hebrew thought, however, the "soul" (actually "being") is a combination of body and spirit, not something that is added to body and spirit as in Greek thought.

93 It is clear that Adam and Eve did not eat of the Tree of Life, for if they had done so, they would have lived forever. This is the explicit reason for which God expelled them from the Garden of Eden: "Now, lest he reach out his hand and take also of the tree of life and eat, and live forever" (Genesis 3:22, ESV). God's action was one of mercy, not judgment, for he knew that if Adam and Eve had eaten of the Tree of Life in their fallen state, they would have become immortal and, therefore, irredeemable sinners. Even in judgment, therefore, God is always a God of mercy and blessing.

94 Madigan and Levenson, p. 237.

95 Daniel 12:2; John 5:25.

96 1 Corinthians 15:52; 1 Thessalonians 4:16.

97 John 5:25.

CHAPTER 19

ETERNITY

The Holy Scriptures unequivocally declare that "God lives forever and ever."[1] As a matter of fact, God is the "high and lofty one who inhabits eternity."[2] He "alone is immortal," and he lives in light that is so unapproachable that no human being "has ever seen him" or, for that matter, "can see him."[3] Because God is infinite, his limitless expanse far transcends the universe, the energy-space-time continuum that he created "in the beginning" out of nothing.[4] Because he exceeds the components of this tri-universe,[5] he both exists outside time and at the same time can operate within the time constraints that he established for the universe when he created time.[6] If he were constrained by time, he would also be constrained to the limits of the universe, for time is one of the three elements of which the universe consists. If the universe were coterminous with God, God could not have been its creator, and either the universe would be God (as in pantheism) or there would be two gods, and, therefore no God. If God existed in time, even endless time, then time would be everlastingly coexistent with him. He could not, therefore, have been its Creator,[7] and there would, also, in effect, be two Gods. God is timeless only in the sense

---

[1] Psalm 90:1-17.

[2] Isaiah 57:15.

[3] In John 6:46, Jesus said, "No one has seen the Father." In John 1:18, the apostle said "No one has ever seen God." In 1 Timothy 6:16, Paul declares that "no one has seen or can see [the Father]."

[4] Genesis 1:1.

[5] The "universe" is actually a "tri-universe" comprised of space, energy, and time. It is not part space, part energy, and part time. It is all space, all energy, and all time. (Energy is interchangeable with matter according to Einstein's Theory of Relativity.) According to Romans 1:20, the created tri-universe is a revelation of the Creator himself. In the same manner in which the tri-universe is space, energy, and time, God is the tri-unity of Father, Son, and Spirit in one divine being of spirit substance.

[6] This is all part of the self-limitation of God which he sovereignly imposed upon himself when he chose to create the universe. This was the divine contraction (*tzimtzum*) or kenosis that was first manifest in the beginning of creation and then again in the dynamic of "emptying" which the divine *Logos* undertook in order to become human and thereby make the redemption of fallen humanity possible.

[7] Norman L. Geisler and H. Wayne House, *The Battle for God: Responding to the Challenge of Neotheism* (Grand Rapids, MI: Kregel Academic, 2001), p. 86.

that he is beyond time and sequence.[8] "Being beyond time" means "existing eternal-now" or "existing unending-now," says Kent Lin.[9]

God is the only being who exists "from everlasting to everlasting."[10] Everything else exists in time because it was formed from the elements of the original explosion of divine creativity that produced the energy/space/time tri-universe. The eternal truth about God is set forth in these words: "In the beginning you laid the foundations of the earth, and the heavens are the works of your hands. They will perish, but you remain . . . you are the same, and your years will not come to an end."[11] It is confirmed by this declaration: "Your word, LORD, is eternal . . . Your faithfulness extends to every generation."[12] It is firmly established in this statement: "You, LORD, reign forever; your throne endures from generation to generation."[13]

Since human beings are part of the "works of God's hands,"[14] they are time-bound creatures. Eternity is, therefore, ultimately incomprehensible to them. "What is your life?" James asks. "You are a mist that appears for a little time and then vanishes."[15] Hughes Old describes the dilemma of humanity as "the precariousness of human existence, the transience of our happiness, the fallibility of our very nature."[16] How can those to whom such an infinitesimal amount of time is allotted[17] begin to comprehend the infinite? Human beings surely cannot employ the empirical method to discover the mysteries of eternity. Zophar the Naamathite asked the same enigmatic question millennia ago when he challenged Job, saying, "Can you discover the mysteries of God? Can you probe the limits of the Almighty?"[18] What can be known about eternity is, therefore, the product of divine self-disclosure—the

---

[8] Clark H. Pinnock, Richard Rice, John Sanders, William Hasker and David Basinger, *The Openness of God: A Biblical Challenge to the Traditional Understanding of God* (Downers Grove, IL: InterVarsity Press, 1994), p. 120.

[9] Kent C. Lin, *The Rationality of Christian Doctrines* (Maitland, FL: Xulon Press, 2009), p. 88.

[10] Psalm 90:2. In this passage, the phrase *from everlasting* is defined by the Psalmist himself as "before the mountains were born or you gave birth to the earth and the world."

[11] Psalm 102:25–26, NIV; 27, NASB.

[12] Psalm 119:89–90.

[13] Lamentations 5:19.

[14] Psalm 138:8; 139:13–15.

[15] James 4:14, ESV.

[16] Hughes Oliphant Old, *The Reading and Preaching of the Scriptures in the Worship of the Christian Church* (Grand Rapids, MI: Wm. B. Eerdmans Publishing Co., 2004), vol. 5, p. 276.

[17] Scripture says that God has allotted 70 years to human beings (Psalm 90:10). Since a "single day is like a thousand years with the Lord" (2 Peter 3:8), the seventy years of human lifespan is equivalent to 25 million years for God. Of course, this comparison is theoretical, not actual, for God is eternal, living outside time. The Psalmist and the apostle Peter advance the "thousand years as one day" statement to underscore the infinite eternity of God and the infinitesimal duration of human life, and they do so in order to emphasize the faithfulness of God (2 Peter 3:8).

[18] Job 11:7.

revelation that God has made of himself. Fortunately for humankind, the "eternal God wills to communicate Himself to His creatures and glorify Himself in them."[19] The God of the Bible is the God "who moves towards the world, lays claim to it, and gives Himself to it."[20] Humanity can, therefore, understand those aspects of the divine mysteries that God has chosen to reveal in his Word and through his creation.[21] This "understanding" is achieved, however, by means of faith and faith alone. As the author of Hebrews declared, "By faith we understand that the universe was formed at God's command, so that what is seen was not made out of what was visible."[22] Faith brings understanding that cannot be achieved empirically.

What Is Eternity?

Emil Brunner provided a point of departure for considering what God has chosen to reveal about eternity. "We must not start with the concept of eternity as human thought itself naturally construes it, understanding eternity as timelessness or as infinite duration." Instead, he said, "We must start with the Biblical conception of God. God alone is eternal because He is the Lord of time, which He has created."[23] Antje Jackelén developed this same theme: "The eternity of God should not be understood as timelessness, but rather as the fullness of time and power over time."[24] Clearly, God's absolute sovereignty includes his sovereignty over time. He created raw time in the beginning, and then he set the cosmic clock in motion when he said, "Let there be lights in the expanse of the heavens to separate the day and the night, and let them be for signs and for seasons and for days and years."[25] Finally, God sealed his authorship and control of time by creating the Sabbath: "So God blessed the seventh day and hallowed it." God's sovereignty over time is also confirmed in the words of Jesus: "The Son of man is Lord of the Sabbath."[26] As Jackelén has observed, "The climax of the first biblical creation story is therefore the creation of holy time with social and cosmic dimensions."[27] Every aspect of time—including its weekly recapitulation in

---

[19] Emil Brunner, *Dogmatics III: Christian Doctrine of the Church, Faith & the Consummation* (London, UK: James Clark & Co., 2002), p. 376.

[20] Brunner, p. 376.

[21] Romans 1:20.

[22] Hebrews 11:3.

[23] Brunner, p. 376.

[24] Antje Jackelén, *Time & Eternity: The Question of Time in Church, Science and Theology*, tr. Barbara Harshaw (West Conshohocken, PA: Templeton Foundation Press, 2005), p. 62.

[25] Genesis 1:14.

[26] Matthew 12:8.

[27] Jackelén, p. 65.

divine and human rest—was created and controlled by God, the Lord of time and eternity.

The eternity of God is manifest from and is parallel with his aseity.[28] Ron Highfield has explained this important principle in this manner: "God's eternity is closely associated with his being the source of his own life and hence the source of all other existence and life."[29] The Scriptures leave no doubt that God has always existed and that he will never cease to exist.[30] There was never a time when he was not, and there will never be a time when he will not be. Only God can say, "Before me no God was formed, nor shall there be any after me."[31] This can be true only because God simply is. Unlike human beings, God is the source of his own being. The aseity of God, revealed in his self-chosen name *YHWH* ("I am because I am"), is the foundation of his eternity ("I will be there").

The eternity which only God possesses *in se* is "a perpetual Now, the still point of past and future,"[32] says Nancy Clasby. God dwells in the eternal present. For him, there is no past to forget and no future about which to dream. He is the now God. In actuality, "God experiences the time of past, present, and future simultaneously."[33] Thomas Aquinas argued, therefore, that "there is a crucial difference between the 'now' of time and the 'now' of eternity."[34] Norman Geisler and Wayne House explain Aquinas' argument this way: "God's *now* has no past or future; time's *now* does."[35] This is why God never refers to himself (or is referred to by others) as the God who *was*. "I am the God of Abraham, the God of Isaac, and the God of Jacob," the Almighty said.[36] Jesus affirmed this same truth when he declared, "Before Abraham was, I am."[37] Though Jesus was time bound because of his incarnation in human flesh, entering time and being limited by it as the incarnate Son of God the *Logos* who inhabited that human flesh was, is, and ever shall be timeless, existing outside time eternally with the Father.

---

[28] The term *aseity* is from the Latin *ab* ("from") and *se* ("self"). It describes God as being the self-existent one, the source of his own existence. It also connotes absolute independence.

[29] Ron Highfield, *Great is the Lord: Theology for the Praise of God* (Grand Rapids, MI: Wm. B. Eerdmans Publishing Co., 2008), p. 294.

[30] Isaiah 40:28.

[31] Isaiah 43:10, ESV.

[32] Nancy T. Clasby, *God, the Bible, and Human Consciousness* (New York: Palgrave Macmillan, 2008), p. 225.

[33] Lin, p. 120.

[34] Aquinas, 1a.10.4, ad.2.

[35] Geisler and House, p. 81.

[36] Exodus 3:6. Interestingly, God did not say, "I am the God of Abraham, Isaac, and Jacob." Jesus argued that God's saying, "I am the God of Abraham, the God of Isaac, and the God of Jacob" proved that he was the God of the living, not the dead.

[37] John 8:58. When Jesus made this statement, he was asserting that he was (is) God.

God is always the I AM. In truth, God simply *is*, for God is not bound by time or any other dimension. When God determined to disclose something about his person by means of his own divine name, he said, "I am that I am." God, therefore, is the only being who can truly say, "I am," and he can say so eternally. God is YHWH, the "I AM," or, perhaps more accurately, the "I WILL BE."[38] His very identity is connected with his eternity. As Dennis Danielson says, "God dwells in an eternal present that transcends our categories of time and tense."[39]

Because of his infinity and eternity, God is present in the past, he is present in the present, and he is present in the future—all at the same time. Indeed, God dwells (present tense) contemporaneously in eternity past, in the present, and in eternity future. James Arieti and Patric Wilson well sum up God's eternal presence this way: "God dwells in this eternity, gazing on all time as a simultaneous present."[40] Karl Barth described this phenomenon analytically as the pretemporality, supratemporality, and posttemporality of God.[41] He understood eternity to refer to the life of God that was antecedent to time and history, that accompanies and completes time and history, and that succeeds time and history.[42] This concept is confirmed by another possible meaning of the divine name YHWH: "I will be there." It is not, however, that God will be in the future when the future arrives. He is already there now and has eternally been there. This is why the writer of Hebrews could say, "Jesus Christ [is] the same yesterday and today and forever."[43] This prompted Augustine to observe that "God, in eternity, knows all things simultaneously . . . the intelligence's knowing . . . is not partial, not in an enigma, not through a glass, but complete total openness, face to face . . . concurrent, without any temporal successiveness."[44]

The term *eternity*, like all other theological terms, therefore, must begin with God. Thomas Aquinas said, "Eternity has no relation to time in the

---

[38] Exodus 3:14. In fact, the ineffable name that God chose for himself is a statement of both his aseity and his eternity. יהוה (YHWH) is a summation of אֶהְיֶה אֲשֶׁר אֶהְיֶה (ehyeh asher ehyeh—"I am what I am" or "I will be what I will be"). God named—and, therefore, identified—himself in terms of both his aseity and his eternity. Being the source of his own existence is the basis for God's eternity. He is eternally because he produces his own existence. Only God can make this statement: "I am because I am."

[39] Dennis Danielson, *The Cambridge Companion to Milton* (Cambridge, UK: Cambridge University Press, 1989), p. 151.

[40] Arieti and Wilson, p. 131.

[41] Karl Barth, *Church Dogmatics*, II,1, Geoffrey W. Bromiley and Thomas F. Torrance, eds. (London, UK: T & T Clark International, 1957), pp. 191–193.

[42] Adrian Langdon, *God the Eternal Contemporary: Trinity, Eternity, and Time in Karl Barth* (Eugene, OR: Wipf & Stock Publishers, 2012), pp. 74–75.

[43] Hebrews 13:8.

[44] Augustine, *Confessions* 12.13,16. See Paula Frederickson, *Augustine and the Jews: A Christian Defense of Jews and Judaism* (New Haven, CT: Yale University Press, 2010), p. 206.

sense of endless time, but stands for a definition of quality with respect to God's being."[45] Aquinas, therefore, made a distinction between eternity and endless time.[46] As Geisler and House note, Aquinas believed that "endless time is not eternity: it is just more time . . . only an elongation of time."[47] Barth also maintained that "eternity is not . . . an infinite extension of time both backwards and forwards." For Barth, time could have nothing to do with God.[48] In essence, eternity is the life of God, eternal life, the immortality that Paul argued is the exclusive property of the Father.[49] Since Jesus himself was declared by the apostle to be "eternal life [personified],"[50] it is only reasonable that God can also be said to be eternity. He is, in fact, called "The Eternal."[51] In his being, God is eternity. Indeed, Barth convincingly argued that "according to the Bible it is not being as such, but that which endures, duration itself, which is the divine."[52]

Jackelén points out that "humans wish to understand temporality and transitoriness in light of the antithesis of eternity."[53] Eternity, however, said Brunner, is "not merely *negation* of time . . . it is *fulfillment* of time, the fulfillment of that element of duration as eternal life."[54] Ron Highfield maintained that "time is not approached as a container in which life becomes possible but as a mode of life."[55] He argued, therefore, that "a theology faithful to Scripture will understand God's eternity as everlastingness rather than timelessness"[56] because "Scripture is interested in everlasting life, not everlasting time."[57] Boethius also connected eternity with everlasting life, terming it "the simultaneous possession, altogether, of endless life."[58] As Aquinas observed, "Eternity is the measure of a

[45] Torben Christensen, *The Divine Order: A Study in F. D. Maurice's Theology* (Skjern, Denmark: Guillanders Bogtrykkeri, 1973), p. 273.
[46] Thomas Aquinas, *Summa Theologica* 1a.10.1.
[47] Geisler and House, p. 81.
[48] Barth, pp. 621–625.
[49] 1 Timothy 6:12.
[50] 1 John 5:20 says, "We know that the Son of God has come . . . This [person] is the true God and *eternal life*" (emphasis added). The word translated "this" in the Greek is ὅυτος (*houtos*)
[51] God is called "The Eternal" because of his self-designation as the "I AM."
[52] Barth, pp. 608–610.
[53] Jackelén, p. 65.
[54] Brunner, p. 379.
[55] Highfield, p. 294. Also John Frame, *The Doctrine of God* (Phillipsburg, NJ: Presbyterian and Reformed Publishing, 2002), pp. 554–556. Frame notes that God is free from limiting characteristics of temporal creatures: "the limitation of beginning and end," "the limitation of change," "the limitation of ignorance," and "the limitation of temporal frustration."
[56] Highfield, p. 301.
[57] Highfield, p. 294.
[58] Boethius, *Philosophiae Consolationis*, V.VI.10.

permanent being."[59] Everlastingness, therefore, has more to do with life than it does with time, and that life is eternal life personified in the Messiah.

A Hebraic View of Time and Eternity

The Hebrew word that most often designates eternity or "everlasting" is עוֹלָם (*'olam*),[60] which means "of long duration," "antiquity," "futurity," "forever,"[61] "everlasting,"[62] "perpetual,"[63] "permanent,"[64] "ancient,"[65] and "world."[66] Essentially, the word *'olam* means "for an unlimited amount of time" or time for which there is no specific end. Thus, in antiquity, a bondservant who had become a love-slave to his master could be said to have committed himself to serving him "forever" (*le'olam*).[67] In similar fashion, subjects could say of their king, "O king, live forever,"[68] or "May my lord live forever (*le'olam*)."[69] Sometimes *'olam* is used with the term וָעֶד—*va'ed* ("as far as" or "forever") to mean "forever and ever."[70] In other instances, *'olam* is connected with the word עַד—*'ad* ("for all time"), as in the phrase מֵהָעוֹלָם וְעַד הָעוֹלָם (*m'ha'olam v'ad ha'olam*)[71] to mean "from the everlasting to the everlasting," or simply "from everlasting to everlasting."[72] The phrase *m'olam 'ad 'olam* demonstrates that time stretches backward into the past as well as forward into the future. It also designates the concept of eternity past and eternity future. Thorlief Boman points out, therefore, that "in the term *'olam* is contained a designation of time extending so far that it is lost to our sight and comprehension in darkness and invisibility. It is characteristic of the nature of this term that it

[59] Thomas Aquinas, *Summa Theologica* (New York: Cosimo, Inc., 2007), vol. 1, p. 42.

[60] The word *'olam* appears in Scripture 205 times.

[61] Genesis 3:22.

[62] Genesis 9:16.

[63] In 37 instances, NASB translates *'olam* as "perpetual." In 19 instances KJV translates *'olam* as "perpetual."

[64] In eleven instances, NASB translates *'olam* as "permanent."

[65] In sixteen instances, NASB translates *'olam* as "ancient." In 7 instances, KJV translates *'olam* as "ancient."

[66] Psalm 73:12. When *'olam* is translated "world," it means "in this present age" or during this "lifetime."

[67] Exodus 21:6 says, "His master shall bore his ear through with an awl, and he shall be his slave forever [*le'olam*]" (ESV). The NIV captures the essence of the implied meaning of this statement with its rendering: "Then he will be his servant for life."

[68] Daniel 3:9; 6:6, 21. When he addressed the kings of the realm, Daniel used the Aramaic word עָלַם (*'alam*) in "O king, live forever (*'alam*)." In Daniel 7:18; 12:3, 7, the text uses the Hebrew עוֹלָם (*'olam*).

[69] 1 Kings 1:31.

[70] Exodus 15:18 declares that God is king "for ever and ever (*'olam va'ed*)."

[71] The phrase *m'ha'olam v'ad ha'olam* is usually contracted to *m'olam ad 'olam*, eliminating the definite article, *ha*.

[72] Psalm 90:2; 103:17; Jeremiah 7:1; 25:56.

can be used of hoary antiquity as well as of the unbounded future."[73] This fact, in itself, establishes the unique Hebrew connection between the past and the future and the Hebraic understanding that the future can be understood, discerned, or predicted only in the context of the past.

Because of the uses of *'olam* in connection with situations in which time is clearly limited, some have suggested that the Hebrew Scriptures do not speak of endless time. To this assertion, Conrad von Orelli responds: "When Hebrew antiquity's ability to form the concept of boundless time is disputed, it is the result of a prejudice."[74] This prejudice, and, therefore, misunderstanding flows from the effort to impose a Greek "either-or" mindset on the Hebrew "both-and" mindset.[75] The truth is that, when applied to God, such phrases as *m'olam 'ad 'olam* cannot be considered to speak of limited existence of God or of God totally constrained by time. The Lord is God *"from everlasting to everlasting,"*[76] both in the sense that he exists from unlimited time in the past to unlimited time in the future and in the sense that he preexists and postexists time itself. In the context of this Hebraic understanding of time, eternity, therefore, transcends time.

Discerning the Future from the Past

As Brunner so has so eloquently observed, the concept of eternity "is from the outset bound up with history. For it is in history that this self-communication and apprehension takes place. God's coming to us is the theme of revelation history and saving history. Only within this history can the eternity be known which God communicates."[77] Jackelén rightly says, "Yahweh is the God of Israel's history who becomes the God of world history."[78] The prophets and sages of Israel, therefore, "had the task of telling the people the meaning of the particular time in which they lived in view of a

---

[73] Thorlief Boman, *Hebrew Thought Compared with Greek*, tr. Jules L. Moreau (New York: W. W. Norton & Co., 1960), p. 151.

[74] Conrad von Orelli, *Die hebräischen Synonyma der Zeit und Ewigkeit genetisch und sprachvergleichend dargestellt* (Leipzig, Germany: 1871; republished Ithaca, NY: Cornell University Library, 2009), p. 72, quoted in Boman, p. 151.

[75] Whereas Greek philosophy posits the idea that there can be only one truth, Hebrew recognizes the fact that truth is often found in polar opposites and it, therefore, holds both positions in dynamic tension. This is true for the word *'olam*, which means both "in the distant past" and "in the far-reaching future" as well as "eternity past" and "eternity future." The Hebraic understanding, therefore, is that the future can be predicted by observing the past. Eternity future will reflect the principles of eternity past.

[76] Psalm 90:2. By applying the phrase *from everlasting to everlasting* to the existence of God, the Psalmist understood that God existed before the universe was created and that he will continue to exist after its end or when "the elements will be destroyed with intense heat, and the earth and its works will be burned up" (2 Peter 3:10).

[77] Brunner, p. 376.

[78] Jackelén, p. 66.

new divine act which was about to take place,"[79] and they did so by reviewing the acts of God in the past. "The nature of the present time was felt to be determined either by the saving acts of God in the past . . . or by the saving fact of God in the future."[80]

This is why both the God of revelation and the revelation of God are essential to human beings. Without God and divine revelation, as Isaac Rottenberg has observed, "One may find divine power in the spirits that inhabit the universe . . . one may believe in a nameless numinous power, a nebulous *mysterium tremendum* . . . or . . . find God in one's own ego as part of the divine 'All.'" The God of Scripture, however, "does not invite us to . . . philosophize about divine being, but rather to recognize God as *being there*, present as the Holy One in our midst, involved in historical existence."[81] Jürgen Moltmann wisely concluded that "the more the covenant is taken seriously as the revelation of God, the more profoundly one can understand the historicity of God and the history in God."[82] Without a clear and accurate perception of the past, understanding the present or the future is impossible. "For the Jews the one and only basis for the continuity of events was God. It was God who ordained the times . . . the events of history were acts of God, and their sequence depended upon the free will of God."[83]

While most cultures occupied their time with trying to discern the future, the Hebraic culture was content to observe the past for lessons about how to live in the present while trusting the future to the God who says, "I will be there."[84] The only reliable information that is available to anyone is obtained by observing the past as one moves through the present into the future. As Winston Churchill aptly said, "The longer you can look back, the farther you can look forward."[85] Indeed, without the past, there is no future. This understanding is confirmed by Solomon's dictum, "There is nothing new under the sun,"[86] which was based on his observation that "whatever is has already been, and what will be has been done before; for God will seek to do again what has occurred in the past."[87]

---

[79] Albert Nolan, *Jesus Before Christianity* (Maryknoll, NY: Orbis Books, 1978), p. 91.

[80] Nolan, p. 91.

[81] Rottenberg, p. 160.

[82] Jürgen Moltmann, *The Crucified God,* tr. R. A. Wilson and John Bowden (New York: Harper & Row, 1974), p. 271.

[83] Nolan, p. 76.

[84] "I will be there" is one of the possible translations of *"ehyeh asher ehyeh,"* though it is usually rendered in most translations of Exodus 3:14 as "I AM THAT I AM" or "I AM WHO I AM."

[85] Winston Churchill, quoted in Richard Langworth, *Churchill by Himself: The Definitive Collection of Quotations* (London, UK: Ebury Press, 2008), p. 576.

[86] Ecclesiastes 1:9.

[87] Ecclesiastes 3:15, NET.

This is why it was always important to the Israelite nation to have leaders and seers who "understood the time, with knowledge of what Israel should do."[88] God saw to it that he always had such servants at his disposal, for the axiom of revealed truth maintains, "Surely the LORD God does nothing unless he reveals his secret counsel to his servants the prophets."[89] And the means for understanding God's design for the present and the future was this: "Please inquire of past generations, and consider the things searched out by their fathers. (For we are only of yesterday) . . . Will they not teach you and tell you, and bring forth words from their minds?"[90]

True biblical understanding of humanity's destiny, therefore, "has its origin in paradise," and from that origin—and only in the context of that origin—"flows into the fullness of the *plêrôma* of the Kingdom, into the mystery of the final *apocatastasis*, the recapitulation of all things in heaven and earth in Christ."[91] James Barlow confirmed and expanded upon this important truth in this manner: "Without the concept of God as the Lord of history, the Jews would have had no sense of history at all and no inkling of a great and glorious destiny. Conversely, without this concept of history the God of the Jews would have been no different from the gods of other nations."[92]

Eternal Life

Faith in the God who inhabits eternity empowers humans to "take hold of the eternal life" to which they have been called,[93] to taste of eternity even in mortal life.[94] "Eternal life is our present possession," says John MacArthur. "Though the body is dying, the spirit is already endowed with incorruptibility."[95] The eternal kingdom of God that is to come is already present in the lives of believers through faith. "One does not need to wait for death. One can experience eternity now."[96] Though eternal life can be fully realized only in the future, it has already been "inaugurated in the present."[97]

---

[88] 1 Chronicles 12:32.

[89] Amos 3:7.

[90] Job 8:8–10.

[91] Evdokimov, p. 38.

[92] James C. Barlow, *God and Eternity* (Indianapolis, IN: Dog Ear Publishing, 2008), p. 37.

[93] 1 Timothy 6:12.

[94] Eternal life is not something that believers will be given at a time in the future. It is already being lived by those who have believed. The Spirit that the believer receives at the new birth is the "guarantee [earnest or down payment] of our inheritance until we acquire possession of it" (Ephesians 1:13–14, ESV).

[95] John MacArthur, *The Vanishing Conscience and Hard to Believe* (Nashville, TN: Thomas Nelson, 2003), p. 153.

[96] Green, *et. al.*, p. 471.

[97] Green, *et. al.*, p. 471.

As Brunner has said, "Faith is the reception of that which by its nature can have no ending, and it originates through the self-communication of the God who is above time, of Him who is Himself immutable."[98] The biblical concept of eternity is, therefore, diametrically opposed to the views of monism and of Greek philosophy which insist that eternity is somehow inherent to humanity's own being and that man shares in the eternal through knowledge of what truly is, the *ontos on*.[99] It also contradicts the ideas of the Vedic Upanishads who taught that humans participate in the eternal through mystical experiences.[100] The Bible "does not speak of an eternity which man essentially possesses in himself and which he can recognize as his own true being. It speaks rather of the eternity that comes *to* man, which lays hold of him, which is bestowed upon him."[101]

What God has planned for faithful humanity is "everlasting life." The promises of God are "everlasting," with no limit on their duration. In similar fashion, "everlasting life" is life without time limitations, not just life for a long time that may or may not come to an end. If "eternal life" were for a limited time, it would be no different from ordinary life that inevitably ends, as Scripture clearly affirms: "It is appointed unto man once to die."[102] If there were any doubt about the intent of the Hebrew Scriptures to speak of eternity as "everlasting" and having no end, Jesus made Hebraic understanding clear: "I am the living bread that came down out of heaven; if anyone eats of this bread will live forever."[103] Eternity is "life forever." In this case, in order to express the idea of "forever," the Greek translation of the Master's Hebrew declaration used the word αἰών (*aión*), which originally and fundamentally meant "life" or "being," but was later extrapolated to mean "forever," "eternity," or "perpetuity of time." It could well be said, therefore, that eternity for human beings is the endless life that is conveyed to the faithful from the essence of God himself: "In him was life, and the life was the light of men."[104] The gift of God to the believer is eternal life,[105] an impartation of the

---

[98] Brunner, p. 379.

[99] Helmut Wautischer, *Tribal Epistemologies: Essays in the Philosophy of Anthropology* (Farnham, UK: Ashgate Publishing, 1998), p. 216. Plato's neologism *ontos on* was a combination of the adverb made from the participle in order to intensify its meaning. This term literally meant "the beingly being"; however, it is usually rendered as "the really real."

[100] The *Vedanta* declares, "Brahman (the ultimate Reality behind the phenomenal universe) . . . is consciousness. Brahman . . . is existence. Brahman is the . . . Eternal Nature of every human being, creature, and object." See Irvine Robertson, *What the Cults Believe* (Chicago, IL: Moody Press, 1966), p. 118.

[101] Brunner, p. 375.

[102] Hebrews 9:27.

[103] John 6:51.

[104] John 1:4.

[105] Romans 6:23.

essence of God's everlastingness.[106] In the words of Boethius, "Eternity is the complete possession all at once of illimitable life."[107] The promise of Jesus is secure, therefore, for "whoever believes on [Christ] shall have everlasting life."[108] As the Psalmist declared, "the lovingkindness of the LORD is from everlasting to everlasting on those who fear him."[109]

Everlasting Victory

While the word *'olam* is the predominant Hebrew term for "eternity," there is another Hebrew word for "eternity" which, although used less frequently in Scripture, is, nevertheless, powerful in its implications, a fact that has been widely understood in mystical Judaism.[110] This word is נֶצַח (*netzach*), which means "perpetuity," "everlastingness," "forever," "strength," and "victory."[111] *Netzach* was certainly the Hebrew word that the apostle Paul was thinking when he declared, "Death is swallowed up in victory,"[112] for he was quoting directly from the prophecy of Isaiah, which says, "The LORD God . . . will swallow up death לָנֶצַח—*la'netzach*."[113] Virtually all Bible translations[114] render *la'netzach* in this Isaian passage as "forever"; however, Paul rendered it "in victory," using the Greek word νῖκος—*nikos* ("victory" or "utterly vanquish") to translate the Hebrew.[115] So, the translation of Isaiah's prophetic utterance that is Holy-Spirit inspired is: "The LORD . . . will swallow up death *into victory*." The connection that *netzach* makes between eternity and victory establishes the Hebrew prospect on the final destiny of the last enemy of humanity. Death will be utterly vanquished, swallowed up into the eternity of

---

[106] 1 John 3:2 declares that "we know that when Christ appears, we shall be like him." The likeness of the believer to Christ was explained by Paul in Philippians 3:21 as the state which will be achieved when God "will transform the body of our humble condition into the likeness of [Christ's] glorious body."

[107] Boethius, *Confessions* IV.11.17.

[108] John 3:16, KJV.

[109] Psalm 103:17.

[110] In mystical Judaism, *netzach* is one of the ten *sefirot* (literally, "counting," figuratively "emanations" of or from God). It is "endurance," "fortitude," or "patience." It also involves the idea of "leadership," the power to inspire to action. See Rabbi Jonathan, *Pesikta Rabbati* 32b, noted in *A Rabbinic Anthology*, Claude G. Montefiore and H. M. J. Loewe, eds. (Cambridge, UK: Cambridge University Press, 2012), p. 40.

[111] *Netzach* is translated in Job 4:20; 14:20; 20:7; 23:7; 36:7; Psalm 9:18; 44:23; 49:9; 52:5; Jeremiah 3:5; Lamentations 5:20; and Amos 8;7 as "forever." It is translated in Jeremiah 15:18 as "unending" in NIV and "perpetual" in KJV and NASB. It is translated in Job 34:36 as "to the limit" in NASB, TNK, and NKJV and as "to the utmost" in NIV and NRSV.

[112] 1 Corinthians 15:54.

[113] Isaiah 25:8.

[114] *La'netzach* in Isaiah 25:8 is translated "victory" in the KJV to parallel its translation of 1 Corinthians 15:54.

[115] It is clear that Paul was translating his Greek directly from the Hebrew, for the Septuagint Greek version that was customarily used by Greek-speaking Jews and Christians rendered this text as κατέπιεν θάνατος ἰσχύσας (*katépien ho thánatos ischúsas*), "Death has prevailed and swallowed up [men]."

God's being.[116] Mortality will be "swallowed up by life."[117] YHWH, the Eternal, will destroy death once and for all in the victory of his eternal life.

The word *netzach* is also connected in Hebrew thought with the virtue of endurance, patience, or longsuffering. This is probably the Hebrew word that Paul was thinking when he was writing about the fruit of the Spirit and listed "endurance"[118] or "patience"[119] as one of those fruit. It could well be the word that Jesus was thinking when he declared, "The one who *endures* to the end will be saved."[120] The salvation of the believer is connected with patiently enduring until the end when death, the last enemy of humanity,[121] will be forever vanquished by being swallowed up into eternal life. This is the truth that prompted Paul's powerful answer to his own rhetorical question, "O death, where is your victory?" when he said, "Thanks be to God, who gives us the victory through our Lord Jesus Christ."[122] Perhaps this is why Paul also exulted, "For I am convinced that neither death, nor life . . . will be able to separate us from the love of God, which is in Christ Jesus our Lord."[123]

Relationship with God through Christ is eternity defined. It is *netzach* — forever, eternal victory! "The wages of sin is death; but the free gift of God is eternal life in Christ Jesus our Lord."[124] Once and for all, Jesus Christ has "abolished death and brought life and immortality to light through the gospel."[125] Those who have received Jesus have already received eternal life and are living it. Eternity has already broken in on time. Death has been swallowed up into eternity. Everlasting life is a present reality and a coming finality[126] because as Jesus himself said, "I am the living one; and I was dead, and behold, I am alive forevermore, and I have the keys of death and of hades."[127] Nothing could have prevented God's total victory over the sting of death at Calvary,[128] and nothing can restrain the inevitability of his triumph over death itself.

---

[116] The Greek text says that "death will be swallowed up *into* victory," not that death will be swallowed up *in* victory as most English translations render it. The Greek word is εἰς (*eis*) specifically means "into," "unto," "to," or "among." Death, therefore, is swallowed up *into* the victory of eternity or *into* eternal life.

[117] 2 Corinthians 5:4. The Greek word translated "swallowed up" here, καταπίνω (*katapino*), is the same word that Paul used in 1 Corinthians 15:54: "Death will be swallowed up into victory."

[118] Galatians 5:22.

[119] Romans 5:3.

[120] Matthew 10:22, NRSV, emphasis added.

[121] 1 Corinthians 15:26.

[122] 1 Corinthians 15:56–57.

[123] Romans 8:39.

[124] Romans 6:23.

[125] 2 Timothy 1:10.

[126] Jürgen Moltmann, *The Coming of God: Christian Eschatology*, tr. Margaret Kohl (London, UK: SCM Press, 1996), pp. 70–71. Moltmann speaks of eternal life as the finality, the "healing of this life into the completed wholeness for which it is destined."

[127] Revelation 1:17–18.

[128] 1 Corinthians 15:56.

Jesus will lead all the righteous out of death and into eternal life because he is the one who knows the way out of the grave.

Everlasting Dominion

There is one thing about the future that is certain: "The LORD will rule as king forever and ever."[129] And, at the same time, the Ruling One says of his Son Jesus, "Your throne, O God, is for ever and ever."[130] Not only will the Lord of heaven and his Son reign in the infinite expanses of eternity; this inevitable and irrevocable promise has also been given to all believers in God and his Messiah: "The throne of God and of the Lamb will be in it, and his servants will . . . see his face, and his name will be in their foreheads. . . . they will have no need of the light of a lamp nor the light of the sun, because the Lord God will illumine them; and they will reign for ever and ever."[131] Immanuel, the Son of the Most High, who is the Wonderful Counsellor, the Prince of Peace, and the Mighty "God with us," will establish the reign of God wherein it can be said, "of the increase of his government and peace there shall be no end."[132] God will have the final word in world history, and the word that will forever be spoken by him will be *shalom!*[133] The *shalom* that God brings, however, is not just peace in the sense of the absence of war. It is peace as security and wholeness. "To enjoy *shalom* is to enjoy health, satisfaction, success, safety, well-being, and prosperity."[134] This is, indeed, the "peace of God," the peace that "surpasses all understanding."[135]

As the eternity of God's peace unfolds, therefore, may Jew and Gentile join together in singing the Song of Moses and the Song of the Lamb, saying, "The LORD reigns for ever and ever"[136] and "Great and marvelous are your works, O Lord God, the Almighty; righteous and true are your ways, King of the nations!"[137] May they exult in the God of Israel and in his Son, *Yeshua HaMashiach*, singing the refrain: "To him who sits on the throne, and to the Lamb, be blessing and honor and glory and dominion, forever and ever!"[138]

Eternity: Christian Fruit—Jewish Root!

---

[129] Exodus 15:18, ESV.
[130] Hebrews 1:8.
[131] Revelation 22:3.
[132] Isaiah 9:7.
[133] The word *shalom* was the final word of the Aaronic Benediction that God dictated to Moses and commanded to be placed upon the children of Israel (Numbers 6:24–26). *Shalom* will be God's last word!
[134] Ann Spangler, ed., *The Names of God Bible* (Grand Rapids, MI: Baker Publishing Group, 2011), p. 45.
[135] Philippians 4:7.
[136] Exodus 15:18.
[137] Revelation 15:3.
[138] Revelation 5:13.

EPILOGUE

From an overview of selective Christian doctrines and practices, it is quite obvious that everything in Christian faith that is authentic has a Jewish background. Sadly, there are beliefs and activities in Christianity that are departures from, if not downright perversions of, the original faith of Jesus and the apostles. Severed from its Jewish roots and transplanted into the compromised soil of philosophies that are foreign to the revelation of the God of Scripture, Christianity has produced fruit that has often been deformed and sometimes downright dangerous. One needs only to look at the heresy of supersessionism to see the profoundly perverted and evil fruit that Christian triumphalism vis-à-vis the Jewish people has produced in its contempt for the Jews and for Judaism, the religion of Jesus and his first disciples.[1] The church itself has suffered dramatically from this aberrant, even anti-social behavior wherein Christianity, the child, has risen up in an almost psychotic impulse of antipathy against its parent (biblical Judaism) and against its sibling (Rabbinic Judaism) and has wreaked havoc on both. What Jules Isaac called "The Teaching of Contempt" has scarred the church and has violated the Jewish people.[2] The church has suffered lost self-identity and lost credibility, but the Jewish people have suffered exponentially more. The indictment of history stands unimpeachable. The verdict is "Guilty"!

A History of Contempt

Anyone who dares to take an honest look at the history of the Christian church and the self-destructive effects of its attitudes and actions toward the Jewish people is left with no alternative but to recognize the cruel suffering that Judaeophobia, anti-Judaism, and Antisemitism have inflicted upon the Jewish people for over nearly two thousand years and, even more intensely, in the past

---

[1] James F. Moore, *Christian Theology After the Shoah: A Re-Interpretation of the Passion Narratives* (Lanham, MD: University Press of America, 1993), p. 28. Moore argues that "all of Christian theology of the past has been riddled with an integral teaching of contempt for the Jews" which was "at least as viral among the early church fathers . . . as in later centuries."

[2] Jules Isaac, *The Teaching of Contempt: Christian Roots of Anti-Semitism* (Atlanta, GA: Anti-Defamation League of B'nai B'rith, 1964).

CHRISTIAN FRUIT—JEWISH ROOT

thousand years. The church's systematic and unrelenting efforts to isolate the Jews and to heap upon them contempt, violence, and mayhem is legendary and can never be erased from the pages of history.[3] Every Christian in the world today should be required to read the systematically reported and succinctly stated chronicles of Christian violence against the Jews in Máttis Kantor's *Codex Judaica: Chronological Index of Jewish History, Covering 5,764 Years* so that they can see for themselves the exhaustive list of suffering and loss of life that Jews have experienced through history, most of it at the hands of Christians.[4]

In perpetrating this great evil against the Jews, the church has violated two divine imperatives, one from the lips of Jesus, the other from the pen of the apostle Paul. It has disgraced the memory of its Lord and Savior by insisting that, despite his own protestations to the contrary, Jesus destroyed Judaism and replaced it with Christianity. Never mind the fact that Jesus himself said, *"Think not* that I have come to destroy the Torah or the Prophets."[5] Christianity knew better! Its leaders knew that God really did destroy Judaism, and the only thing that was needed was an adequate sarcophagus in which to entomb that failed and lifeless religion forever.

At the same time, Christianity has also besmirched the memory of Paul, who insisted that believers should not be arrogant toward the Jews. Never mind that the apostle addressed the Christians with this memorable command: *"Boast not* against the natural branches of God's family tree.[6] So what if he unequivocally declared that "all Israel shall be saved"[7] and then enjoined acts of mercy upon Gentile Christians toward the Jewish people.[8] Christianity knew better! Its leaders knew that to be Jewish was to be damned. They

---

[3] Zev Garber, *Academic Approaches to Teaching Jewish Studies* (Lanham, MD: University Press of America, 2000), p. 225. Garber says that "the teachings of the Fathers of the Church," have forced scholars of reconciliation to go all the way back "to the New Testament, especially St. Paul's reflections in Romans 9–11 . . . to retrieve the rather more positive theological appreciation of Jews and Judaism that Paul actually embedded therein." They have been compelled to do so because they can find little, if any philo-Semitic statements about the Jews or Judaism in the writings of either the Eastern or Western church fathers.

[4] Máttis Kantor, *Codex Judaica: Chronological Index of Jewish History* (New York: Zichron Press, 2005), pp. 185–274. Kantor's list of cases of violence against the Jews from the beginning of the eleventh century through the Holocaust of the twentieth century covers 89 pages of condensed, straightforward, and shocking historical text that should be read by every Christian in the world.

[5] Matthew 5:17. One has to wonder how any Christian theologian or spiritual leader in his right mind could pervert the specific and unequivocal words of Jesus, "Think not that I have come to destroy the Torah or the Prophets," into an argument that Jesus destroyed Judaism.

[6] Romans 11:18. How could any Christian theologian or spiritual leader even suggest that Christians should hate Jews and direct acts of violence against them and then appeal to Paul's teachings of justification by grace through faith in the shed blood of Jesus? The record of ecclesiastical history, however, speaks for itself.

[7] Romans 11:26.

[8] Romans 11:31.

argued that Jews had to be targeted for contempt because they rejected Jesus as the Messiah and that they had to be persecuted and even murdered because they were truly the "Christ-killers," guilty of the crime of deicide.[9]

There they are, however, two clear and unequivocal divine imperatives that all manners of exegetical gymnastics and diabolical sermonizing can never delete or modify: *"Think not!"* and *"Boast not!"* One would think that even the most simple-minded person—the proverbial wayfaring man though a fool[10]—much less the intellectual giants of the church, could not possibly have erred therein and would have understood and obeyed such lucid divine imperatives. But the record of history is clear. Christian leaders, blinded by their contempt for the Jews, have led the blind, prejudiced, and superstitious masses, and both have rushed headlong over the precipice of heresy and have fallen into the pit of perversion.[11] Christians have been the Jews' worst enemy,[12] and, in the process, they have been their own worst enemy.[13] Contempt for and violence against the Jewish people has been contempt for and violence against the church itself. Apparently the church has never learned the wisdom of Sigmund Freud's famous and accurate dictum, "Hatred of the Judaism is at bottom hatred for Christianity."[14]

Time for Repentance

Can anyone doubt, therefore, that a profound and massive work of repentance and renewal must take place in the Christian church, a work that will reconnect it with its Jewish roots. Christianity must do its first works over.[15] It must return to the faith once delivered to the saints.[16] For centuries, Christianity has been going the wrong way, dashing headlong down a destructive path. It is time to make *teshuvah*[17] by making an 180-degree turn and going in

---

[9] Arnold James Rudin, *Christians & Jews Faith to Faith: Tragic History, Promising Present, Fragile Future* (Woodstock, VT: Jewish Lights Publishing, 2011), p. 97. Rudin says, "Deicide, literally the killing of God, proclaimed that Jews collectively had willfully murdered Jesus of Nazareth. As punishment for this infamous act, the Jewish people then, now, and forever are guilty of the heinous crime of murdering divinity."

[10] Isaiah 35:8.

[11] Matthew 15:14. If Paul had been present during the Middle Ages he might have said something like this: "Blindness in part is happened to the *church*" rather than to Israel (Romans 11:25, NKJV).

[12] Morris Paul, *Jewish Themes in the New Testament: Am Yisrael Chai!* (Crown Hill, UK: Paternoster, Authentic Media Limited, 2013), p. 126.

[13] Michael L. Brown, *60 Questions Christians Ask About Jewish Beliefs and Practices* (Grand Rapids, MI: Baker Books, 2007), p. 200.

[14] Sigmund Freud, *Moses and Monotheism* (New York: Random House, 1939), p. 145.

[15] Revelation 2:5.

[16] Jude 1:3.

[17] The Hebrew word *teshuvah* ("repentance") means "to turn" or "to turn around." True repentance is never complete until one overcomes the same temptation that produced sin in the first place. The proof of true Christian repentance will be manifest when temptation arises again and is overcome.

the opposite direction. Far too many Christians have been pricked by their consciences, but they have made 360-degree turns and continued on in their folly! Enough of the Judaeophobia, anti-Judaism, and Antisemitism! Enough of cloaking hatred for the Jews in the guise of defending the gospel of Jesus Christ! The church must be filled with Godly sorrow over its past actions toward the Jews and Judaism and make this resolution: "Never again!" Then, it must work carefully, assiduously, and systematically at restoring what it has lost—its first love, the pure love of Jesus, the absence of which has made its great sins against the Jewish people possible but even more reprehensible. This means reattaching Christian faith and practice to the Jewish roots which the church severed centuries ago and which still remain largely unattached. It means restoring the Hebraic foundations on which Jesus and the apostles built the church in the first place. It means restoring a posture of respect and loving support for the Jewish family of Jesus.

This work must be an unrelenting effort of unequivocal commitment to recovering truth and then living by it. Mushy sentimentality will only endure for a moment. True godly love for the Jewish people and for the legacy that their ancestors bequeathed to the Christian church will stand forever. Only those Christians who have fully come to understand that their faith is inherently Jewish will be able to transcend the "fair-weather-friend" syndrome and maintain commitment to the Jewishness of their own faith while standing unreservedly with the Jewish people in the face of every obstacle and every fiery dart of the enemy. Since Christians in history were primarily responsible for the divisions that occurred within God's family, Christians must take the initiative to recover what has been lost by committing themselves to the task of restoration and renewal. "If your brother has something against you, go . . . and be reconciled," Jesus said in the Sermon on the Mount.[18] "If post-Holocaust Christianity is to have anything worthwhile and credible to say, it must honestly confront Christianity's complicity in the Holocaust and also return repentantly to Christianity's Jewish roots."[19]

Restoring Christianity's Jewish Roots

Christianity must experience a rebirth of freedom to recover the Jewish roots of the faith of Jesus and the apostles. Old carnal attitudes of doubt, suspicion, and even hatred toward the Jewish people must be recognized and

---

[18] Matthew 5:24.
[19] Zev Carber, Foreword to Henry F. Knight, *Confessing Christ in a Post-Holocaust World: A Midrashic Experiment* (Westport, CT: Greenwood Publishing Group, 2000), p. xii.

removed. The cancer of contempt for the Jews must be excised. The church must recover the absolute truth of its own Jewishness, and it must do so wholeheartedly and unreservedly. It can no longer afford to reject the Jewishness of its Lord and of the reformed faith community that he established. It must restore its Jewish connection. As Amy-Jill Levine said in simple but profoundly true terms, "If you get the [Jewish] context wrong, you will certainly get Jesus wrong."[20] Carlo Martini summed it up well, "In its origins Christianity is deeply rooted in Judaism. Without a sincere feeling for the Jewish world, therefore, and a direct experience of it, one cannot understand Christianity."[21] As Edward Flannery so wisely declared, "An over-Hellenized, over-Latinized Christianity needs a re-Judaizing process to restore it to its inherent ideal."[22]

"Today's church is in need of renewing," says Marvin Wilson. "If it is to reflect its biblical origins, the church must have an understanding and appreciation of its Hebraic heritage and the Jewish people to whom Christians are indebted for bequeathing so much of their spiritual heritage."[23] Kevin Madigan and Jon Levenson have rightly said that one cannot "adequately understand the New Testament apart from the Jewish literature of its own time . . . And when Christians read the New Testament and other early Christian literature in this context, they become keenly aware that the familiar claims of the radical distinctiveness of Christianity over against Judaism are at least overdrawn and often downright wrong."[24] Christianity's woeful ignorance and benign neglect for the Jewish roots of its teaching and polity must be corrected. The church can never be nursed back to health until it is reattached to its roots, and it will never achieve unity until it resolves the proto-schism in which it separated itself from Jews and Judaism.

Christianity must also come to a new appreciation of the Hebrew language, the language that Jesus read and spoke. Like the sixteenth-century Christian scholar Johann Reuchlin, Christians need "to delve into a linguistic domain that [has] long been considered at best obsolete,"[25] just like the

---

[20] Amy-Jill Levine, quoted in David Ban Biema, "Re-Judaizing Jesus," *Time* magazine, vol. 171, no. 12, March 24, 2008, p. 17.

[21] Carlo Martini, quoted in John T. Pawlikowski, "Judaism and Catholic Morality: The View of the Encyclical," in *Veritatis Splendor: American Responses*, Michael E. Allsopp and John J. O'Keefe, eds. (Kansas City, MO: Sheed and Ward, 1995), p. 177.

[22] Edward Flannery, quoted George Cornell, "The Church after Jesus Loses Is Jewish Context," Fredericksburg, VA *Free Lance-Star*, Friday, March 28, 1975, p. 16.

[23] Wilson, *Exploring*, p. 63.

[24] Kevin J. Madigan and Jon Douglas Levenson, *Resurrection: The Power of God for Christians and Jews* (New Haven, CT: Yale University Press, 2008), p. 236.

[25] Peter Wortsman in Johann Reuhlin, *Recommendation Whether to Confiscate, Destroy, and Burn All Jewish Books*, Peter Wortsman, ed. and tr. (Mahwah, NJ: Paulist Press, 2000), p. 3. Originally published as *Doctor Johannsen Reuchlins Augenspiegel* (Tübingen, Germany: Thomas Anshelm, 1511).

Jewish people who have spoken that language for at least four millennia. In the same way in which Reuchlin became "an enthusiastic student of [Jewish] sacred literature," because he saw in it "the spiritual foundation of Christianity,"[26] Christians should commit themselves to the study of the Hebrew language and Jewish literature, for "just as the Jews themselves were reviled as . . . an alien body that had long since outlived its usefulness, so too was their language and literary heritage . . . held in ill repute"[27] in historical Christianity. The church, therefore, should repent of its disdain for and ignorance of Hebrew, for the study of Hebrew is vital for recovering the Hebraic—and, therefore, biblical— roots of the Christian faith. One cannot possibly understand the message of the Scriptures fully without a working knowledge of the language of Scripture,[28] for, as Peter Wortsman has said, "It was with Hebrew words that the Judeo-Christian God quite literally *called* the world into being. . . . The Hebrew language as such is a bridge, a lasting link between God and man."[29]

William Campbell points to Paul's Romans 11 analogy of roots and branches, noting that "the branches do not constitute the living tree," for it is "the holiness of the roots [that] determines the sanctity of all the branches." All of this analogy, he says, points "decisively to the Jewish roots of Christianity" and to "the links with Jerusalem."[30] The Gentile Christian branches that were grafted "contrary to nature" into the olive tree of Israel owe their status to the rich sap from the roots of the tree.[31] The roots bear the branches that bear the fruit, not vice versa. The prophets, sages, Messiah, and apostles of Israel and the holy Word that they brought forth comprise the solid root system that supports the tree of salvation and keeps it standing tall despite the raging storms of life and the hellish heat of draught. Recovery of a healthy respect for all the Jewish roots of Christianity—especially of the Jewish Jesus, the tap root—will revitalize the church and refocus its mission in the earth.

Experiencing the fulness of the faith of Jesus and the apostles is not, however, something that can be obtained by osmosis along with salvation or Christian baptism. It demands active, even aggressive, pursuit. Jesus said it well, "The kingdom of heaven is breaking forth, and impassioned

---

26 Wortsman, p. 3.

27 Wortsman, p. 3.

28 With the exception of a few passages that were written in Aramaic, the Hebrew Scriptures were composed entirely in Hebrew. Likewise, the Apostolic Scriptures were either originally written in Hebrew (as is quite likely for the four Gospels) or were thought in Hebrew and then translated into Greek.

29 Wortsman, p. 4, author's emphasis.

30 William Campbell, quoted in *Reading Paul in Context: Explorations in Identity Formation: Essays in Honour of William S. Campbell*, Kathy Ehrensperger and J. Brian Tucker, eds. (New York: T & T Clark International, 2010), p. 89.

31 Romans 11:17.

people lay hold of it."[32] In Wilson's words, "This priceless heritage is not genetically acquired; it must be personally owned. It is not a gift to be *passively* received but a legacy that must be *actively* seized."[33] Truth will make anyone who acquires it free, but it is never free.[34] It comes with a price.

Accompanying the unfolding discovery, restoration, and implementation of Hebraic truth is a return to the spirit of deference that characterized Abraham and the great leaders of the Israelite community and the earliest Christian church. The Abrahamic spirit of welcoming hospitality, the open-arms embracing of other believers who may not have yet come to the understanding that their Christian faith is inherently Jewish, is also being revived. Hebraic Christian communities are learning to implement the Jewish concept of holding seemingly contradictory concepts in dynamic tension. They are also recognizing the importance of loving neighbor as self by lowering their defenses and accepting others with warm mutuality. They are coming to understand that legalism of any sort—Christian or Jewish—is offensive to God and to other people; therefore, they are seeking to banish the spirit of judgmentalism from their hearts and their communities. These actions are very important to the emergence of a genuine Christian Hebraist mentality that makes the praxis of love far more important than rigid creedalism and elitist, exclusivist attitudes and conduct.

The good news is that the work of restoration and renewal of the Jewish roots of the Christian faith is well underway. Amazing biblical truths are being rescued from the dust of centuries of ecclesiastical neglect for Christianity's Hebrew foundations, and Christians are achieving greater maturity, balance, and stability in their lives as a result. What was initiated in the sixteenth century by the Christian Hebraists[35] and the *veritas Hebraica*[36] ("Hebrew truth") that they promoted has been greatly accelerated. Much work remains to be accomplished—more prayer, more study, more thinking, more discussion,

---

[32] Matthew 11:12, author's translation.

[33] Wilson, *Exploring*, p. 67, author's emphasis.

[34] John 8:32.

[35] The term *Christian Hebraist* has been given to scholars who believed that the study of Hebrew was necessary for proper exegesis of Holy Scripture. Though it can be applied to scholars who lived from 450 to 1800 AD, it generally described those from the sixteenth century forward.

[36] The term *veritas Hebraica* was probably coined in the early fifth century by Jerome as description of his desire to go *ad fontes* ("[back] to the sources") for accurate translation of Holy Scripture. Jerome espoused studying both Hebrew and Greek in order to render more accurate translations of Scripture. The result was his Latin Vulgate. By the turn of the sixteenth century, Christian Hebraists seized upon Jerome's argument to maintain that even the Latin Vulgate could no longer be fully trusted as it had been for a thousand years in the Western Church. They called for a return to the Hebrew texts and to rabbinic sources for exegesis of Scripture that was not clouded by church tradition.

more interaction. The church has not yet arrived, but it is on the way, and the pace is increasing.

A long and arduous task lies ahead, much like the one that faced the people of Judah when they mustered the faith needed to undertake what must have seemed like an impossible task: rebuilding Jerusalem and the temple after the Babylonian captivity. The Christian Hebraists of this day may have the same shortage of manpower and *matériel* that Ezra and Nehemiah faced. They may well be ridiculed by those who observe their efforts with great skepticism.[37] If they can maintain their dignity and aplomb when challenged with the question, "Who in the world dare you, and what on earth do you think you're doing," they will doubtless be able to give the same answer that the restorationists of that day did: "We are the servants of the God of heaven and earth, and we are rebuilding the temple that a great king in Israel established many years ago."[38]

As Marvin Wilson has said, however, "If today's church is to uncover more of the depth and breadth of the Christian faith, concern about accessing the very foundational teachings of Christianity, our Hebraic heritage, is not an option, but a necessity."[39] The primary task, therefore, for one who seeks to be a "biblical" Christian involves "a commitment to try to recover and restore as much as is possible of the original face of Christianity" by "peeling off some of the masks or layers, which hide, paint over, or make obscure the rich first-century Jewish context of the early church."[40] The work of restoration is a noble task that requires faith and endurance, but when it is finally completed, it will be worth every ounce of strength exerted. May the noble rebuilders of this day be encouraged by the words of consolation that Amos gave to the bold restorationists of his day: "The glory of this latter house will be greater than that of the former house, and in this place will I give peace, says the LORD of hosts."[41]

In reality, rediscovering Christianity's Jewish roots is like uncovering a golden key that unlocks the treasures of Holy Scripture which inevitably enrich the lives of those who embrace God's Word with uncompromising faith. What has long been obscured by the Hellenization, Latinization, and even paganization of the Christian faith is becoming apparent again. Christians by the thousands are rediscovering that every authentic expression of Christian faith has a Jewish root, and they are committing themselves to restoring the fullness of their faith in *Yeshua HaMashiach*, Jesus Christ the Lord.

Christian Fruit—Jewish Root!

---

[37] Nehemiah 4:3.
[38] Ezra 5:11.
[39] Wilson, *Exploring*, p. 21.
[40] Wilson, *Exploring*, p. 69.
[41] Haggai 2:9.

BIBLIOGRAPHY

Abbott, Lyman, and Thomas Jefferson Conant. *A Dictionary of Religions Knowledge: For Popular and.* New York: Harper & Brothers, Publishers, 1875.

_____*The Acts of the Apostles.* New York: A. S. Barnes & Co., 1876.

Abelson, Joshua. *The Immanence of God in Rabbinical Literature.* London, UK: Macmillan and Co., 1912.

Abraham, Michelle Shapiro. *Repairing Our World from the Inside Out: A Three-Session Adult Education Program on Jewish Ethics.* New York: UAHC Press, 2002.

Abrahams, Israel, and Claude G. Montefiore, eds. *The Jewish Quarterly Review,* January, 1908, vol. XX, No. 78.

Adams, Nicholas, George Pattison, and Graham Ward, eds. *The Oxford Handbook of Theology and Modern European Thought.* Oxford, UK: Oxford University Press, 2013.

Adeyẹmi, Fẹmi. *The New Covenant Torah in Jeremiah and the Law of Christ in Paul.* New York: Peter Lang Publishing, 2006.

Aiken, Charles Francis. *The Dhamma of Totama the Buddha and the Gospel of Jesus Christ.* Boston, MA: Marlier and Company, 1900.

Alexis, Jonas E. *Christianity and Rabbinic Judaism: A History of Conflict Between.* Bloomington, IN: WestBow Press, 2013.

Algazi, Gadi, Valentin Groebner, and Bernhard Jussen, eds. *Negotiating the Gift: Pre-modern Figurations of Exchange.* Göttingen, Germany: Vandenhoeck & Ruprecht, 2003.

Allen, Grant. *Evolution of the Idea of God.* London, UK: Grant Richards, 1897.

Allsopp, Michael E. and John J. O'Keefe, eds. *Veritatis Splendor: American Responses.* Kansas City, MO: Sheed and Ward, 1995.

Amann, Wolfgang, Michael Pirson, Claus Dierksmeier, Ernst von Kimakowit, and Heiko Spitzeck. *Business Schools Under Fire: Humanistic Management.* Basingstoke, UK: Palgrave Macmillian, 2011.

Anders, Max. *What You Need to Know About the Bible in 12 Lessons.* Nashville, TN: Thomas Nelson, 1995.

Anderson, J. *"What Is Man?": His Origin, Life-History and Future Destiny as Revealed in the Word of God.* London, UK: J. Nisbet and Co., 1888.

Anderson, William P. *A Journey Through Christian Theology.* Minneapolis, MN: Augsburg Fortress, 2010.

Angus, Samuel. *The Mystery Religions and Christianity.* New York: Citadel Press, 1989.

Aquinas, Thomas. *Summa Theologica* 1a.10.1.

Arieti, James A., and Patrick A. Wilson. *The Scientific & the Divine: Conflict and Reconciliation from Ancient Greece to the Present.* Oxford, UK: Rowman & Littlefield Publishers, 2003.

Armentrout, Donald S., and Robert Boak Slocum. *An Episcopal Dictionary of the Church: A User-Friendly.* New York: Church Publishing, 2000.

Armstrong, Karen. *In the Beginning: A New Interpretation of Genesis.* New York: The Ballantine Publishing Group, 1996

Ashton, John. *The Religion of Paul the Apostle.* New Haven, CT: Yale University Press, 2000.

Athanasius, *Four Discourses Against The Arians.* 3. 24–25.

Aune, David E. *Prophecy in Early Christianity and the Ancient Mediterranean World.* Grand Rapids, MI: Wm. B. Eerdmans Publishing Co., 1983.

Augustine, *Confessions* 12.13,16.

Avery-Peck, Alan, and Jacob Neusner. *The Routledge Dictionary of Judaism.* New York: Routledge, 2004.

Babylonian Talmud, *Makkot* 23b; *Sanhedrin* 98b; *Sukkah* 52a; *Ta'an* 10a, 12a. *Yeban* 2; *Yevamot* 46a.

Bainton, Roland H. *Here I Stand: A Life of Martin Luther.* Peabody, MA: Hendrickson Publishers, 1950.

Barber, Michael. *Should Christianity Abandon the Doctrine of the Trinity?.* Boca Raton, FL: Universal Publishers, 2006.

Barclay, William. *The Gospel of Matthew: Chapters 11-28.* Louisville, KY: Westminster John Knox Press, 2001.

Baring-Gould, Sabine. *The Origin and Development of Religious Belief: Polytheism and Monotheism.* London, UK: Rivingtons, 1884.

Barlow, James C. *God and Eternity.* Indianapolis, IN: Dog Ear Publishing, 2008.

Barna, George. *User-Friendly Churches: What Christians Need to Know About the Churches People Love to Go To.* Ventura, CA: Regal Books, 1991.

Barth, Christoph. *God with Us: A Theological Introduction to the Old Testament.* Grand Rapids, MI: Wm. B. Eerdmans Publishing Co., 1991.

Barth, Karl. *Church Dogmatics IV.1: The Doctrine of Reconciliation.* New York: T & T Clark International, 1956.

_____*Church Dogmatics*, II,1 Geoffrey W. Bromiley and Thomas F. Torrance, eds. (London, UK: T & T Clark International, 1957), pp. 191-193.

Bartholomew, Craig, and C. Stephen Evans, eds. *Behind the Text: History and Biblical Interpretation.* Grand Rapids, MI: Zondervan Publishing, 2003.

Bartos, Emil. *Deification in Eastern Orthodox Theology: An Evaluation and Critique of the Theology of Dumitru Staniloae.* Bloomington, IN: Indiana University Press, 1999.

Bauckham, Richard. *Jesus and the God of Israel: God Crucified and Other Essays on the New Testament's Christology of Divine Identity.* Crownhill, UK: Authentic Media, 2008.

Bauer, Walter, Frederick W. Danker, William F. Arndt, and Felix W. Gingrich, eds. *Greek-English Lexicon of the New Testament and Other Early Christian Literature.* Chicago: The University of Chicago Press, 1999.

Baxter, J. Sidlow. *Awake, My Heart: Daily Devotional Studies for the Year.* Grand Rapids, MI: Kregel Publications, 1960.

Beaulieu, Peter D. *Beyond Secularism and Jihad?: A Triangular Inquiry into the Mosque, the Manger, and Modernity.* Lanham Md: The University Press of America, 2012.

Ben-Sasson, Haim Hillel, ed. *A History of the Jewish People.* Tel Aviv, Israel: HDvir Publishing House, 1969.

Benedict XVI, Biuliano Vigni, and Vincenzo Santarcangelo. *Learning to Believe.* London, UK: St. Paul's Publishing, 2012.

Berenbaum, Michael, and Fred Skolnik, eds. *The Encyclopedia Judaica.* Detroit, MI: Macmillan Reference USA, 2007.

Berkhof, Hendrikus. *Christian Faith: An Introduction to the Study of Faith.* Grand Rapids, MI: Wm. B. Eerdmans Publishing, 1979.

Berkhower, G. C. *General Revelation: Studies in Dogmatics.* Grand Rapids, MI: Wm. B. Eerdmans Publishing Co., 1955.

_____*The Person of Christ.* Grand Rapids, MI: Wm. B. Eerdmans Publishing Co., 1954.

Berlin, Adele, ed. *The Oxford Dictionary of the Jewish Religion.* New York: Oxford University Press, 2011.

Bertinoro, Ovadiah. *The Mishnah: A New Translation.* New York: Mesorah Publications, Ltd., 1979.

Betz, Hans-Dieter. *Galatians.* Philadelphia, PA: Fortress Press, 1979.

Biale, David. *Eros and the Jews: From Biblical Israel to Contemporary America.* Berkeley, CA: The University of California Press, 1997.

Biema, David Ban "Re-Judaizing Jesus," *Time* magazine, vol. 171, no. 12, March 24, 2008, p. 17.

Blackaby, Henry. *Discovering God's Daily Agenda.* Nashville, TN: Thomas Nelson, Inc., 2007.

Blanchard, Kenneth H., and Spencer Johnson. *The One Minute Manager.* Ann Arbor, MI: The University of Michigan Press, 1981.

Blaydes, John. *The Educator's Book of Quotes.* Thousand Oaks, CA: Corwin Press, 2003.

Blumfield, Wendy. *Life After Birth: Every Woman's Guide to the First Year of Motherhood.* Shaftesbury, UK: Element Books, Ltd., 1992.

Bockmuehl, Markus. *Jewish Law in Gentile Churches: Halakah and the Beginning of Christian Public Ethics.* Edinburgh, UK: T & T Clark, 2000.

Boethius. *Philosophiae Consolationis.* V.VI.10.

Bokedal, Tomas. *The Formation and Significance of the Christian Biblical Canon: A Study in Text, Ritual, and Interpretation.* London, UK: Bloomsbury T. & T Clark, 2014.

Boman, Thorlief. *Hebrew Thought Compared with Greek*, tr. Jules L. Moreau. New York: W. W. Norton & Co., 1960.

Bonfil, Robert. *Jewish Life in Renaissance Italy.* Berkeley, CA: The University of California Press, 1994.

Bonhoeffer, Dietrich. *Life Together: The Classic Exploration of Faith in Community.* New York: HarperCollins Publishers, 2009.

_____*Witness to Jesus Christ.* John de Gruchy, ed. Minneapolis, MN: Augsburg Press, 1991.

Boyarin, Daniel. *Border Lines: The Partition of Judaeo-Christianity.* Philadelphia, PA: The University of Pennsylvania Press, 2004.

_____*The Jewish Gospels: The Story of the Jewish Christ.* New York: The New Press, 2012.

Boyd, Gregory A. *Satan and the Problem of Evil: Constructing a Trinitarian Warfare Theodicy.* Downers Grove, IL: InterVarsity Press, 2002.

Bozeman, Theodore Dwight. *The Precisianist Strain: Disciplinary Religion and Antinomian Backlash in Puritanism to 1638.* Chapel Hill, NC: The University of North Carolina Press, 2004.

Braaten, Carl E., and Robert W. Jenson, eds. *Reclaiming the Bible for the Church.* Grand Rapids, MI: Wm. B. Eerdmans Publishing Co., 1995.

Bradshaw, Paul F. *The Search for the Origins of Christian Worship: Sources and Methods for the Study of Early Liturgy.* Charlottesville, VA: The University of Virginia Press, 2002.

Bray, Bethany. "Gordon College Professor Begins 50th Year of Teaching," Salem, MA, *News,* September 4, 2012.

Bright, John. *The Kingdom of God.* Nashville, TN: Abingdon Press, 1980.

Brill, Alan. *Thinking God: The Mysticism of Rabbi Zadok of Lublin.* Jersey City, NJ: KTAV Publishing House, 2002.

Brock, Sebastian. *The Luminous Eye: The Spiritual World Vision of Saint Ephrem the Syrian.* Kalamazoo, MI: Cistercian Publications, 1991.

Brooke, George J. *The Dead Sea Scrolls and the New Testament.* London, UK: SPCK, 2005.

Brooten, Bernadette J. *Women Leaders in the Ancient Synagogue: Inspirational Evidence and Background Issues.* Saarbrücken, Germany: OmniScriptum GmbH & Co., 1982.

Brown, Colin, ed. *The New International Dictionary of New Testament Theology.* Grand Rapids, MI: Zondervan Publishing House, 1975.

Brown, Michael L. *Answering Jewish Objections to Jesus: Volume 4: New Testament Objections.* Grand Rapids, MI: Baker Book House, 2007.

_____*60 Questions Christians Ask About Jewish Beliefs and Practices.* Grand Rapids, MI: Baker Books, 2007.

Brown, Stephen M. *Higher and Higher: Making Jewish Prayer Part of Us.* New York: United Synagogue of America, 1980.

Brownstein, Rita Milos. *Jewish Holiday Style.* New York: Simon & Schuster, 1999.

Bruner, Emil. *The Mediator: A Study of the Central Doctrine of the Christian Faith.* Cambridge, UK: The Lutterworth Press, 1934.

_____*Dogmatics III: Christian Doctrine of the Church, Faith & the Consummation.* London, UK: James Clark & Co., 2002.

Bruner, Frederick Dale. *Matthew: The Churchbook.* Grand Rapids, MI: Wm. B. Eerdmans Publishing Co., 2004.

Buber, Martin, ed. *Piskata.*

Buber, Martin. *I and Thou.* tr. Ronald Gregor Smith. New York: Charles Scribner's Sons, 1958.

_____*Israel and the World: Essays in a Time of Crisis.* New York: Schocken Books, 1948.

_____*The Eclipse of God: Studies in the Relation Between Religion and Philosophy.* New York: Harper Brothers, 1952.

_____*Types of Faith.* London, UK: Routledge & Kegan Paul, 1951

Buber, Solomon. *Midrash Tanhuma, Nizzabim,* 8:25b.

Bullinger, Ethelbert W. *Number in Scripture: Its Supernatural Design and Spiritual Significance.* Grand Rapids, MI: Kregel Publications, 1967.

_____*Word Studies on the Holy Spirit.* Grand Rapids, MI: Kregel Academic, 1979.

Bulgakov, Sergius. *The Lamb of God.* Grand Rapids, MI: Wm. B. Eerdmans Publishing Co., 2009.

Buxbaum, Yitzhak. *Jewish Spiritual Practices.* Northvale, NJ: Jason Aronson, Inc., 1994.

Byfield, Ted. *The Christians: Their First Two Thousand Years; A Glorious Disaster: A.D. 1100 to 1300: The Crusades: Blood, Valor, Iniquity, Reason, Faith.* Edmonton, Canada: Society to Explore and Record Christian History, 2003.

Callen, Barry L. *Discerning the Divine: God in Christian Theology.* Louisville, KY: Westminster John Knox Press, 2004.

Campbell, Donald, Wendell Johnston, John F. Walvoord, and John A. Witmer. *Theological Wordbook: The 200 Most Important Theological Terms and Their Relevance for Today*. Nashville, TN: Thomas Nelson, 2000.

Campbell, Gordon. *Bible: The Story of the King James Version 1611-2011*. New York: Oxford University Press, 2010.

Campbell, Heidi. *Exploring Religious Community Online: We Are One in the Network*. New York: Peter Lang Publishing, 2005.

Carole, Susan B. *Called Into Communion: A Paradigm Shift in Holiness Theology*. Eugene, OR: Wipf and Stock Publishers, 2013.

Casiday, Augustine ed. *The Orthodox Christian World*. New York: Routledge, 2012.

Charlesworth, James H., ed. *The Old Testament Pseudepigrapha: Apocalyptic Literature and Testaments*. New York: Doubleday, 1983.

_____*Jesus and Archaeology*. Grand Rapids, MI: Wm. B. Eerdmans Publishing Co., 2006.

Chesterton, G.K. *The Collected Works of G. K. Chesterton, Volume 2*. San Francisco, CA: Ignatius Press, 1986.

Cheyne, Thomas Kelly, and Paul Haupt. *The Book of the Prophet Isaiah: A New English Translation*. New York: Dodd, Mead, and Company, 1898.

Chilton, Bruce D., and Jacob Neusner, *Classical Christianity and Rabbinic Judaism: Comparing Theologies*. Grand Rapids, MI: Baker Academic, 2004.

Chow, Alexander. *Theosis, Sino-Christian Theology and the Second Chinese*. New York: Palgrave Macmillan, 2013.

Christensen, Michael J. *Partakers of the Divine Nature: The History and Development of Deification in the Christian Traditions*. Michael J. Christensen and Jeffery A. Wittung, eds. Grand Rapids, MI: Baker Academic, 2007.

Christensen, Torben. *The Divine Order: A study in F. D. Maurice's Theology*. Skjern, Denmark: Guillanders Bogtrykkeri, 1973

Chrysostomos. *Orthodox and Roman Catholic Relations from the Fourth Crusade to the Hesychastic Controversy*. Etna, CA: Center for Traditionalist Orthodox Studies, 2001.

Clark, Kelly James. *Return to Reason*. Grand Rapids, MI: Wm. B. Eerdmans Publishing Co., 1990.

Clasby, Nancy T. *God, the Bible, and Human Consciousness*. New York: Palgrave Macmillan, 2008.

Clements, R. E., ed. *The World of Ancient Israel: Sociological, Anthropological and Political Perspectives*. Cambridge, UK: Cambridge University Press, 1989.

Coakley, Sarah, and Charles M. Stang. *Re-thinking Dionysius the Areopagite*. John Wiley and Sons, 2009.

Cocker, Benjamin Franklin. *Christianity and Greek Philosophy; or The Relation Between the Spontaneous and Reflective Thought in Greece and the Positive Teaching of Christ and the Apostles*. New York: Harper & Brothers, Publishers, 1872.

Cohen, Shaye J. D. *The Beginnings of Jewishness: Boundaries, Varieties, Uncertainties*. Berkeley, CA: The University of California Press, 1999.

_____*Why Aren't Jewish Women Circumcised? Gender and Covenant in Judaism*. Berkeley, CA: The University of California Press, 2005.

Cole, W. Owen. *Six World Faiths*. New York: Continuum Publishing Group, 1996.

Coleman, Lyman. *The Antiquities of the Christian Church*. Andover, MA: Gould, Newman & Saxton, 1841.

Collins English Dictionary - Complete & Unabridged 10th Edition. New York: William Collins Sons & Co, 2009.

Constitutions of the Apostles, III, X.

Cook, Stephen. *On the Question of the "Cessation of Prophecy" in Ancient Judaism*. Tübingen, Germany: Mohr Siebeck, 2011.

Cooke, Richard Joseph. *Christianity and Childhood: or, The Relation of Children to the Church*. Cincinnati, OH: Cranston and Stowe, 1891.

Cooper, Burton Z. *Why God?* Louisville, KY: Westminster John Knox Press, 1988.

Couch, Mal, ed. *Dictionary of Premillennial Theology: A Practical Guide to the People, Viewpoints, and History of Prophetic Studies*. Grand Rapids, MI: Kregel Publications, 1996.

Crichton, James D. *Christian Celebration: The Mass*. New York: Cassell Publishers, Ltd., 1971.

Cross, F. L., and E. A. Livingstone, eds. *Oxford Dictionary of the Christian Church*. New York: Oxford University Press, 1974.

Curtis, Ian. *Jesus: Myth or Reality?* Lincoln, NE: iUniverse, 2006.

Cushman, Geoffrey Wainwright. *Lesslie Newbigin: A Theological Life.* New York: Oxford University Press, 2000.

Dahl, Nils. *Jesus in the Memory of the Early Church.* Minneapolis, MN: Augsburg Press, 1976.

Danielson, Dennis. *The Cambridge Companion to Milton.* Cambridge, UK: Cambridge University Press, 1989.

Davidson, Ivor J., and Murray A. Rae, eds.. *God of Salvation: Soteriology in Theological Perspective.* Burlington, VT: Ashgate Publishing Co., 2011.

Davidson, Richard M. *The Flame of Yahweh: Sexuality in the Old Testament.* Peabody, MA: Hendrickson Publishers, 2007.

Davies, William D. *Paul and Rabbinic Judaism: Some Rabbinic Elements in Pauline Theology.* Minneapolis, MN: Fortress Press, 1980.

Davis, Jerome. *Christianity and Social Adventuring.* New York: Century Company, 1927.

DelRio, Delio. *Paul and the Synagogue: Romans and the Isaiah Targum.* Eugene, OR: Wipf and Stock Publishers, 2013.

DeMar, Gary, Dave Hunt, and Gary North. *The Debate over Christian Reconstruction.* Waterbury Center, VT: Dominion Press, 1988.

DeRoo, Neal, and John P. Manoussakis, eds. *Phenomenology and Eschatology: Not Yet in the Now.* Burlington, VT: Ashgate Publishing Co., 2009.

DeVito, Robert. "Old Testament Anthropology and the Construction of Personal Identity." *Catholic Biblical Quarterly* 61. 1999.

Dhar, A. N. *Mysticism Across Cultures: Studies on Select Poets & Saints.* New Delhi, India: Atlantic Publishers, 2002.

Diamant, Anita, and Howard Cooper. *Living a Jewish Life: A Guide for Starting, Learning, Celebrating, and Parenting.* New York: HarperPerennial, 1991.

Dihle, Albrecht. *Greek and Latin Literature of the Roman Empire: From Augustus to Justinian.* New York: Routledge, 1989.

Dilling, David R. *Martin Buber on Meaning in Education.* Ann Arbor, MI: University Microfilms.

Dixon, C. Scott. *The Reformation and Rural Society: The Parishes of Brandenburg-Ansbach-Kulmbach 1528–1603.* Cambridge, UK: Cambridge University Press, 1996.

Dockery, David S., and Gregory Alan Thornbury. *Shaping A Christian Worldview: The Foundations of Christian.* Nashville, TN: B & H Publishing Group, 2002.

Donin, Hayim, and Hayim Halevy Donin. *To Pray as a Jew: A Guide to the Prayer Book and the Synagogue Service.* New York: Basic Books, 1980.

Dorff, Eliot N. *The Jewish Approach to Repairing the World (Tikkun Olam): A Brief Introduction for Christians.* Woodstock, VT: Jewish Lights Publishing, 2008.

_____ and Louise E. Newman, eds. *Contemporary Jewish Theology.* New York: Oxford University Press, 1999.

Dorsette, Catherine. *The Worth of a Man.* Bloomington, IN: AuthorHouse, 2014.

Downey, Michael. *Understanding Christian Spirituality.* Mahwah, New Jersey: Paulist Press, 1997.

Duignan, Brian. *Ancient Philosophy: From 600 BCE to 500 CE.* New York: Britannica Educational Publishing, 2011.

Dumbrell, William J. *Covenant and Creation: An Old Testament Covenant Theology.* Crown Hill, UK: Paternoster/Authentic Media, 2013.

Dunham, Scott A. *The Trinity and Creation in Augustine: An Ecological Analysis.* Albany, NY: State University of New York Press, 2008.

Dunn, James D. G. *Jesus, Paul, and the Law: Studies in Mark and Galatians.* Louisville, KY: Westminster John Knox Press, 1990.

Dunteman, Paul L. *The Christian Life and the History of Israel: Discovering How Israel's Journey Parallels the Christian's Spiritual Walk Today.* Maitland, FL: Xulon Press, 2009.

Durham, John I. *Exodus.* Waco, TX: Word Books, 1987.

Dwyer, John C. *Church History: Twenty Centuries of Catholic Christianity.* Mahwah, NJ: Paulist Press, 1998.

Earley, Dave, and Ben Gutierrez. *Ministry Is . . . How to Serve Jesus with Passion and Confidence.* Nashville, TN: B & H Publishing Group, 2010.

Ebeling, Gerhard. *The Truth of the Gospel: An Exposition of Galatians*, tr. David Green. Minneapolis, MN: Fortress Press, 1985.

Ecclesiastes *Rabbah* 12:6; 12:7.

Edersheim, Alfred. *The Temple: Its Ministry and Services*. Grand Rapids, MI: Kregel Publications, 1997.

Edwards, James R. *The Gospel According to Mark*. Grand Rapids, MI: Wm. B. Eerdmans Publishing Co., 2002.

Edwards, Richard M. *Scriptural Perspicuity in the Early English Reformation*. New York: Peter Lang Publishing, 2009.

Einstein, Stephen J., Lydia Kukoff, and Hara Person, eds. *Introduction to Judaism: Instructor's Guide and Curriculum*. Emeryville, CA UAHC Press, 1999.

Eisenberg, Joyce, and Ellen Scolnic. *Dictionary of Jewish Words: A JPS Guide*. Philadelphia, PA: The Jewish Publication Society, 2001.

Eisenberg, Ronald L. *Jewish Traditions: A JPS Guide*. Philadelphia, PA: Jewish Publication Society, 2004.

Ekman, Ulf. *Take, Eat: A Book on Holy Communion*. Uppsala, Sweden: Livets Ords Förlag, 2012.

Elazar, Daniel Judah, and John Kincaid, eds. *The Covenant Connection: From Federal Theology to Modern Federalism*. Lanham, MD: Lexington Books, 2000.

Ellis, Marc H. *Ending Auschwitz: The Future of Jewish and Christian Life*. Louisville, KY: Westminster/ John Knox Press, 1994.

Ellwood, Robert S. *The Encyclopedia of World Religions*. New York: Infobase Publishing, 2007.

Elon, Binyamin. *God's Covenant with Israel: Establishing Biblical Boundaries in Today's World*. Toronto, Canada: New Leaf Publishing Group, Balfour Books, 2005.

Elswit, Sharon Barcan. *The Jewish Story Finder: A Guide to 668 Tales Listing Subjects and Sources*. Jefferson, NC: McFarland & Company, Inc., Publishers, 2012.

Elwell, Walter A. *Evangelical Dictionary of Theology*. Grand Rapids, MI: Baker Publishing Group, 1984.

Emden, Yaacov. *Sefer Lechem Shamayim*. Baltimore, MD: Shaftek Enterprises, 2007.

Emerson, Ralph Waldo. *The Conduct of Life: The Collected Works of Ralph Waldo Emerson*, Barbara L. Packer and Joseph Slater, eds. Cambridge, MA: Harvard University Press, 2003.

Endsjø, Dag Øistein. *Primordial Landscapes, Incorruptible Bodies*. New York: Peter Land Publishing, 2008.

Enns, Paul P. *The Moody Handbook of Theology*. Chicago, IL: Moody Publishers, 1989.

Enos, Richard Leo, and Lois Peters Agnew, eds. *Landmark Essays on Aristotelian Rhetoric Vol. 14*. Abingdon, UK: Routledge, 1998.

Erickson, Millard J. *A Basic Guide to Eschatology: Making Sense of the Millennium*. Grand Rapids, MI: Baker Books, 1998.

_____*Christian Theology*. Grand Rapids, MI: Baker Academic, 1983.

Esler, ed., Philip E. *The Early Christian World*. New York: Routledge, 2000.

Evans, Craig A. *Fabricating Jesus: How Modern Scholars Distort the Gospels*. Downers Grove, IL: InterVarsity Press, 2006.

Evans, Craig S. *The Routledge Encyclopedia of the Historical Jesus*. New York: Routledge, 2010.

Evdokimov, Paul. *Woman and the Salvation of the World*. tr. Anthony P. Gythiel. Crestwood, NY: St. Vladimir's Seminary Press, 1994.

Faber, Roland, and Jeremy Fackenthal. *Theopoetic Folds: Philosophizing Multifariousness*. Bronx, NY: Fordham University Press, 2013.

Fackre, Gabriel. *The Christian Story: Authority: Scripture in the Church for the World*. Grand Rapids, MI: Wm. B. Eerdmans Publishing Co., 1987.

Feinberg, John S. *No One Like Him: The Doctrine of God*. Wheaton, IL: Crossway Books, 2001.

Ferguson, Duncan S. *Bible Basics: Mastering the Content of the Bible*. Louisville, KY: Westminster John Knox Press, 1995.

Ferguson, Everett, ed. *Encyclopedia of Early Christianity, Second Edition*. New York: Routledge, 1999.

Fields, Harvey J. *B'chol L'vavcha: A Commentary*. New York, UAHC Press, 2001.

Fine, Steven, ed. *Jews, Christians and Polytheists in the Ancient Synagogue*. London, UK: Routledge, 1999.

Finegan, Jack. *Discovering Israel: An Archaeological Guide to the Holy Land*. Grand Rapids, MI: Wm. B. Eerdmans Publishing Co., 1981.

Finn, Thomas Macy. *From Death to Rebirth: Ritual and Conversion in Antiquity*. Mahwah, NJ: Paulist Press, 1997.

Flannery, Edward, in George Cornell. "The Church after Jesus Loses Is Jewish Context," Fredericksburg, VA *Free Lance-Star*, Friday, March 28, 1975, p. 16.

Florensky, Pavel. *The Pillar and Ground of the Truth: An Essay in Orthodox Theodicy in Twelve Letters.* Princeton, NJ: Princeton University Press, 2004.

Flusser, David. *Judaism and the Origins of Christianity.* Jerusalem, Israel: Magnes Press, 1988.

_____*The Sage from Galilee: Rediscovering Jesus' Genius, Stephen Notley, ed..* Grand Rapids, MI: Wm. B. Eerdmans Publishing Co., 2007.

Flynn, James T., Wie Liang Tjiong, and Russell W. West. *A Well-Furnished Heart: Restoring the Spirit's Place in the Leadership Classroom.* Fairfax, VA: Xulon Press, 2002.

Frame, John. *The Doctrine of God.* Phillipsburg, NJ: Presbyterian and Reformed Publishing, 2002.

Frawley, David. *Mantra Yoga and the Primal Sound: Secrets of Seed (Bija) Mantras.* Twin Lakes, WI: Lotus Press, 2010.

Frederickson, Paula. *Augustine and the Jews: A Christian Defense of Jews and Judaism.* New Haven, CT: Yale University Press, 2010.

Freeman, Samuel. *The Case of Mixt Communion.* London, England: T. Basset, 1683.

Fretheim, Terence E. *Abraham: Trials of Family and Faith.* Columbia, SC: The University of South Carolina Press, 2007.

_____Terrence. *The Suffering God: An Old Testament Perspective.* Philadelphia: Fortress Press, 1984.

Freud, Sigmund. *Moses and Monotheism.* New York: Random House, 1939.

Frick, Don M. *Robert K. Greenleaf: A Life of Servant Leadership.* San Francisco, CA: Berrett-Koehler Publishers, 2004.

Friedman, Joseph. *The Inside Story: Biblical Personalities.* Bloomington, IN: AuthorHouse, 2013.

Friedrich, Carl Joachim. *The Philosophy of Law in Historical Perspective.* Chicago, IL: The University of Chicago Press, 1958.

Fuchs, Lorelei F. *Koinonia and the Quest for an Ecumenical Ecclesiology: From Foundations through Dialogue to Symbolic Competence for Communionality.* Grand Rapids, MI: Wm. B. Eerdmans Publishing Co., 2008.

Fuchs, Nancy, and Nancy H. Wiener. *Judaism for Two: A Spiritual Guide for Strengthening and Celebrating Your Loving Relationship.* Woodstock, VT: Jewish Lights Publishing, 2005.

Futato, Mark David. *Interpreting the Psalms: An Exegetical Handbook.* Grand Rapids, MI: Kregel Academic, 2007.

Gabriel, Richard A. *Gods of Our Fathers: The Memory of Egypt in Judaism and Christianity.* Westport, CT: Greenwood Press, 2002.

Gall, James. *The Synagogue, not the Temple, the Germ and Model of the Christian Church.* London, England: Simpkin, Marshall, Hamilton, Kent & Co., 1890.

Gallagher, Deborah Rigling. *Environmental Leadership: A Reference Handbook.* Thousand Oaks, CA: SAGE Publications, 2012.

Gangel, Kenneth O. *Feeding and Leading: A Practical Handbook on Administration in Churches and Christian Organizations.* Grand Rapids, MI: Baker Books, 1989.

Garber, Zev. *Academic Approaches to Teaching Jewish Studies.* Lanham, MD: University Press of America, 2000.

Gardner, Charles S. *Psychology and Preaching.* New York: The MacMillan Company, 1918.

Garr, John D. *Feminine by Design: The God-Fashioned Woman.* Atlanta, GA: Golden Key Press, 2013.

_____*God and Women: Woman in God's Image and Likeness.* Atlanta, GA: Golden Key Press, 2012.

_____*Life from the Dead: The Dynamic Saga of the Chosen People.* Atlanta, GA: Golden Key Press, 2014.

_____*Passover the Festival of Redemption.* Atlanta, GA: Golden Key Press, 2002.

_____*Rediscovering the God of Scripture.* Atlanta, GA: Golden Key Press, 2014.

_____*The Church Dynamic: Hebraic Foundations for Christian Community.* Atlanta, GA: Golden Key Press, 2014.

Garr, W. Randall. *In His Own Image and Likeness: Humanity, Divinity, and Monotheism.* Leiden, The Netherlands: Koninklijke Brill, 2003.

Garroway, Joshua D. *Paul's Gentile-Jews: Neither Jew nor Gentile, but Both.* New York: Palgrave Macmillan, 2012.

Geisler, Norman L., and H. Wayne House, *The Battle for God: Responding to the Challenge of Neotheism.* Grand Rapids, MI: Kregel Academic, 2001.

Genesis *Rabbah* 100.7

Gentry, Peter J., and Stephen J. Wellum, *Kingdom Through Covenant: A Biblical Theological Understanding of the Covenants.* Wheaton, IL: Crossway Publishing, 2012.

Gerhards, Albert, and Clemens Leonhard. *Jewish and Christian Liturgy and Worship: New Insights.* Leiden, The Netherlands: Koninklijke Brill, 2007.

Gesenius, William. *Gesenius' Hebrew and Chaldee Lexicon.* Grand Rapids, MI: Baker Book House, 1992.

Girdlestone, Robert B. *Synonyms of the Old Testament.* Peabody, MA: Hendrickson Publishers, 2000.

Glaser, Mitch, and Zhava Glaser. *The Fall Feasts of Israel.* Chicago, IL: Moody Press, 1987.

Glueck, Nelson. *Hesed in the Bible,* tr. Alfred Gottschalk. Eugene, OR: Wipf & Stock Publishers, 2011.

Glustrom, Simon. *The Language of Judaism* (Lanham, MD: Rowman & Littlefield Publishing, 2004.

————*Timeless Tablets: Why the Ten Commandments Still Speak to Us.* Rockville, MD: Schreiber Publishing, 2006.

Gnuse, Robert. *Heilgeschicte as a Model for Biblical Theology: The Debate Concerning the Uniqueness and Significance of Israel's Worldview.* Lanham, MD: The University Press of America, 1989.

Godwin, William. *Enquiry Concerning Political Justice.* New York: Oxford University Press, 1971.

Goergen, Donald, Ann Garrido, and Benedict M. Ashley. *The Theology of Priesthood.* Collegeville, MN: The Liturgical Press, 2000.

Goff, Christopher Wyatt. *Measuring the Clergy/Laity Gap and Its Effect on Church Health and Outreach.* Ann Arbor, MI: UMI Microfilm, 2008.

Goff, Philip, and Paul Harvey. *Themes in Religion and American Culture.* Chapel Hill, NC: The University of North Carolina Press, 2004.

Goldberg, Michael. *Why Should Jews Survive?: Looking Past the Holocaust toward a Jewish Future.* New York: Oxford University Press, 1995.

Goldingay, John. *Approaches to Old Testament Interpretation.* Leicester, UK: InterVarsity Press, 1981.

Goldstein, Elyse. *ReVisions: Seeing Torah Through a Feminist Lens.* Woodstock, VT: Jewish Lights Publications, 2001.

Gooch, Paul W. *Reflections on Jesus and Socrates: Word and Silence.* New Haven, CT: Yale University Press, 1996.

Gowan, Donald E. *The Westminster Theological Wordbook of the Bible.* Louisville, KY: Westminster John Knox Press, 2003.

Grant, F. C. *Ancient Roman Religion.* Huntsville, AL: Liberal Arts Press, 1957.

Green, Arthur. *Radical Judaism: Rethinking God and Tradition.* New Haven, CT: Yale University Press, 2010.

Green, Joel B., Scot McKnight, and I. Howard Marshall, eds. *Dictionary of Jesus and the Gospels: A Compendium of Contemporary Biblical.* Downers Grove, IL: InterVarsity Press, 1992.

Greenacre, Roger, and Jeremy Haselock. *The Sacrament of Easter.* Leominster, UK: Fowler Wright Books, 1995.

Greenleaf, Robert K. *The Servant as Leader: A Journey into the Nature of Legitimate Power and Greatness.* Mahwah, NJ: Paulist Press, 1997.

Greenwood, Samuel. *Footsteps of Israel: From Eden to the City of God.* Boston, MA: A. A. Beauchamp, 1922.

Greidanus, Sidney. *Preaching Christ from the Old Testament: A Contemporary Hermeneutical Method.* Grand Rapids, MI: Wm. B. Eerdmans Publishing Co., 1999.

Gribble, Richard. *The Parables of Jesus: Cycle A.* Lima, OH: CSS Publishing Co., 1998).

Griffin, Ricky, and Gregory Moorhead. *Organizational Behavior: Managing People and Organizations.* Mason, OH: South-Western Cengage Learning, 2010.

Grishaver, Joel Lurie, and Stuart Kelman, eds. *Learn Torah With . . . 5756 Torah Annual: A Collection of the Year's Best Torah.* Los Angeles, CA: Alef Design Group, 1999.

Grudem, Wayne. *Systematic Theology: An Introduction to Biblical Doctrine.* Grand Rapids, MI: Zondervan Publishing, 1994.

Gunkel, Hermann. *The Influence of the Holy Spirit: The Popular View of the Apostolic Age and the Teaching of the Apostle Paul.* Minneapolis, MN: Augsburg Fortress Press, 1979.

Hahn, Scott. *Kingdom of God as Liturgical Empire: A Theological Commentary on 1–2 Chronicles.* Grand Rapids, MI: Baker Academic, 2012.

Hall, Archibald. *A Treatise on the Faith and Influence of the Gospel*. Glasgow, Scotland: William Collins, 1831.

Hall, Christopher A. *Reading Scripture with the Church Fathers*. Downers Grove, IL: InterVarsity Press, 1998.

Halpern, Susan P. *Finding the Words: Candid Conversations with Loved Ones*. Berkeley, CA: North Atlantic Books, 2010.

Hals, Ronald. *Grace and Faith in the Old Testament*. Minneapolis: Augsburg Press, 1980.

Hamblin, William James, and David Roth Seely, *Solomon's Temple: Myth and History*. London, UK: Thames & Hudson, Ltd., 2007.

Hamilton, Edith, and Huntington Cairns, eds. *The Collected Dialogues of Plato*. New York: Pantheon Books, 1961

Hamilton, Victor P. *The Book of Genesis: Chapters 1-17*. Grand Rapids, MI: William B. Eerdmans Publishing Co., 1990.

Hardon, John, ed. *Modern Catholic Dictionary*. Bardstown, KY: Eternal Life Publications, 2000.

Häring, Hermann. *The Human Image of God,* Hans-Georg Ziebertz, Friedrich Schweitzer, Hermann Häring, and Don Browning, eds. Boston, MA: Brill Publishers, 2001.

Harman, David. *Illiteracy: A National Dilemma*. Cambridge, UK: Cambridge University Press, 1987.

Harmening, William M. *Mystery at Corinth: Seeking a Jewish Answer to a Christian Mystery*. Lincoln, NE: iUniverse Publishing, 2006.

Harpur, Tom. *For Christ's Sake*. New York: Oxford University Press, 1986.

Harrington, Daniel J. and Christopher R. Matthews, eds. *Encountering Jesus in the Scriptures*. Mahwah, NJ: Paulist Press, 2012.

Harris, Laird, Gleason L. Archer Jr., and Bruce K. Waltke, eds. *Theological Wordbook of the Old Testament*. Chicago, IL: Moody Publishers, 2003.

Hart, David Bentley. *The Doors of the Sea: Where Was God in the Tsunami?* Grand Rapids, MI: Wm. B. Eerdmans Publishing Co., 2005.

Hart, Mitchell Bryan, ed. *Jews and Race: Writings on Identity and Difference, 1880-1940*. Boston, MA: Brandeis University Press, 2011.

Hatch, Edwin. *The Influence of Greek Ideas on Christianity*. New York: Harper and Row, 1957.

Hayes, John H., and James M. Miller, eds. *Israelite and Judaean History*. London, UK: SCM, 1977.

Hayward, Robert. *Targums and the Transmission of Scripture into Judaism and Christianity*. Leiden, The Netherlands: Koninklijke Brill, 2010.

Heine, Ronald E. *Reading the Old Testament with the Ancient Church: Exploring the Formation of Early Christian Thought*. Grand Rapids, MI: Baker Academic, 2007.

Helyer, Larry R. *Exploring Jewish Literature of the Second Temple Period: A Guide for New Testament Students*. Downers Grove, IL: InterVarsity Press, 2002.

Henry, Carl F. H. *God, Revelation and Authority*. Wheaton, IL: Crossway Books, 1999.

Hengstenberg, E. W. *Christology of the Old Testament and Commentary on the Messianic Predictions*, tr. Theodore Meyer. Edinburgh, Scotland: T. & T. Clark, 1858.

Heschel, Abraham Joshua. *A Passion for Truth*. New York: Farrar, Straus & Giroux, 1973.

_____*God in Search of Man: A Philosophy of Judaism*. New York: Farrar, Straus and Giroux, 1955.

_____*Heavenly Torah: As Refracted Through the Generations,* Gordon Tucker, ed. and tr. New York: Continuum International Publishing Group, 2006.

_____*Man Is Not Alone: A Philosophy of Religion*. New York: Farrar, Straus and Giroux, 1951.

_____*Moral Grandeur and Spiritual Audacity*. Susannah Heschel, ed. New York: Farrar, Straus and Giroux, 1996.

_____*The Prophets*. New York: HarperCollins, 1962.

Highfield, Ron. *Great is the Lord: Theology for the Praise of God*. Grand Rapids, MI: Wm. B. Eerdmans Publishing Co., 2008.

Hilbun, John C. *The Disciple's Life in Christ Jesus*. Maitland, FL: Xulon Press, 2010.

Hockman, "Why I Resigned," in *The Reform Advocate,* Chicago, IL, September 4, 1915, vol. XLX, p. 118

Hodge, Charles. *Systematic Theology, Vol. 3*. Grand Rapids, MI: Wm. B. Eerdmans Publishing Co., 1973.

Hodge, Charles. *Systematic Theology*. London, UK: Thomas Nelson and Sons, 1872.

Hoffman, Lawrence A. *My People's Prayer Book: Vol. 2: The Amidah*. Woodstock, VT: Jewish Lights Publishing, 1998.

_____ and David Barrow, eds., *My People's Passover Haggadah: Traditional Texts, Modern Commentaries*. Woodstock, VT: Jewish Lights Publishing, 2008.

Holcomb, Justin S. *On the Grace of God*. Wheaton, IL: Crossway, 2013.

Holleman, Joost *Resurrection and Parousia*. Leiden, The Netherlands: Koninklijke Brill NV, 1996.

Holmén, Tom, and Stanley E. Porter, eds. *Handbook for the Study of the Historical Jesus*. Leiden, The Netherlands: Koninklijke Brill, 2011.

Holtschneider, K. Hannah. *German Protestants Remember the Holocaust: Theology and the Construction*. Münster, Germany: Lit Verlag, 2001.

Hopkins, Richard R. *How Greek Philosophy Corrupted the Christian Concept of God*. Springville, UT: Horizon Publishers, 1998.

Hordern, William. *The Case for a New Reformation Theology*. London, UK: Westminster Press, 1959.

Horton, Michael. *The Gospel-Driven Life: Being Good News People in A Bad News World*. Grand Rapids, MI: Baker Books, 2009.

House, E. *Treatise on Infant Church Membership*. Rochester, NY: Wm. Alling & Co: 1835.

House, H. Wayne. *Israel: The Land and the People–An Evangelical Affirmation of God's Promises*. Grand Rapids, MI: Kregel Academic, 1998.

Hudson, Nancy J. *Becoming God: The Doctrine of Theosis in Nicholas of Cusa*. Washington D.C.: The Catholic University of America Press, 2007.

Hughes, Aaron W. *Rethinking Jewish Philosophy: Beyond Particularism and Universalism*. New York: Oxford University Press, 2014.

Hunt, Steven A. *Perspectives on Our Father Abraham: Essays in Honor of Marvin R. Wilson*. Grand Rapids, MI: Wm. B. Eerdmans Publishing Co., 2010.

Hurtado, Larry. *Lord Jesus Christ: Devotion to Jesus in Earliest Christianity*. Grand Rapids, MI: Wm. B. Eerdmans Publishing Co., 2003.

Hutton, Christopher. *Race and the Third Reich: Linguistics, Racial Anthropology, and Genetics in the Dialectic of Volk*. Cambridge, UK: Polity Press, 2005.

Imperato, Robert. *Early and Medieval Christian Spirituality*. Lanham, MD: The University Press of America, 2002.

Ingham, Richard. *A Handbook on Christian Baptism: Christian Baptism, Its Subjects*. London, England: E. Stock Publishers, 1871.

Intrater, Keith, and Dan Juster, *Israel, the Church, and the Last Days*. Shippensburg, PA: Destiny Image Publishers, 2003.

Irenaeus, *Against Heresies*, 5, preface.; 5.1; 5.3.3; III. IV.38.4.

Irwin, Kevin W. *Models of the Eucharist*. Mahwah, NJ: Paulist Press, 2005.

Jackson, Bernard S., ed. *The Jewish Law*. Amsterdam, The Netherlands: Amsteldijk, 1997.

Jacobs, Louis. *The Book of Jewish Practice*. Springfield, NJ: Behrman House, 1987.

Jackelén, Antje. *Time & Eternity: The Question of Time in Church, Science and Theology*, tr. Barbara Harshaw. West Conshohocken, PA: Templeton Foundation Press, 2005.

Jansen, Henry. *Relationality and the Concept of God*. Amsterdam-Atlanta, GA: Rodopi B.V., 1994.

Jay, Eric G. *The Church: Its Changing Image Through Twenty Centuries, Vol. 1: the First Seventeen Centuries, Volume 2: 1700–the Present Day*. London, UK: SPCK Publishing, 1977.

Jefferies, James J. *Wake-up Call*. Maitland, FL: Xulon Press, 2005.

Jerome. *Questiones Hebraicae in Genesim*.

Johnson, Christopher D. L. *The Globalization of Hesychasm and the Jesus Prayer: Contesting Contemplation*. New York: Continuum International Publishing Group, 2010.

Johnson, Elizabeth. *She Who Is: The Mystery of God in Feminist Theological Discourse*. New York: Crossroad Publishing Company, 1998.

Johnson, Maxwell E., and John Francis Baldovin. *Between Memory and Hope: Readings on the Liturgical Year*. Collegeville, MN: The Liturgical Press, 2000.

Johnson, Wayne G. *Morality: Does "God" Make a Difference?* Lanham, MD: The University Press of America, 2005.

Jonathan, Rabbi. *Pesikta Rabbati* 32b.

Kaiser, Jr., Walter C. *Toward Rediscovering the Old Testament*. Grand Rapids, MI: Zondervan Publishing Co., 1991.

_____ *Mission in the Old Testament: Israel as a Light to the Nations*. Grand Rapids, MI: Baker Academic, 2000.

_____, Peter H. Davids, F. Bruce, and Manfred Brauch. *Hard Sayings of the Bible*. Downers Grove, IL: InterVarsity Press, 1996.

Kantor, Máttis. *Codex Judaica: Chronological Index of Jewish History*. New York: Zichron Press, 2005.

Kang, Yil Gyoung. *Enhancing Understanding the Church Through Preaching on Ecclesiology in the Korean American Immigrant Church*. Ann Arbor, MI: ProQuest, 2008.

Kärkkäinen, Veli-Matti. *The Holy Spirit: A Guide to Christian Theology*. Louisville, KY: Westminster John Knox Press, 2012.

Kaufman, Gordon D. *Theological Imagination: Constructing the Concept of God*. Louisville, KY: Westminster John Knox Press, 1981.

Kaufman, Michael. *Love, Marriage, and Family in Jewish Law and Tradition*. Northvale, NJ: Jason Aronson, 1996.

Keener, Craig S. *The Historical Jesus of the Gospels*. Grand Rapids, MI: Wm. B. Eerdmans Publishing Co., 2009.

Kernaghan, Ronald J. *Mark*. Downers Grove, IL: InterVarsity Press, 2007.

Kessler, Edward, and Neil Wenborn, eds. *The Dictionary of Jewish-Christian Relations*. Cambridge, UK: Cambridge University Press, 2005.

Kidner, Derek. *Genesis* in *Tyndale Old Testament Commentary*. Downers Grove, IL: InterVarsity Press, 1967.

Kierkegaard, Søren. *Kierkegaard's Concluding Unscientific Postscript,* tr. David F. Swenson. Princeton: Princeton University Press, 1941.

Kiesler, Sara B., and Charles F. Turn, eds. *Fundamental Research and the Process of Education: Final Report of the Committee on Fundamental Research Relevant to Education*. Washington, DC: National Academy of Sciences, 1977.

King, David. "Ignorance of Our Own Spirit: or, Practical Reflections on Luke ix. 55, 56 in *Evangelical Christendom.*

King, Richard. *Orientalism and Religion: Post-Colonial Theory, India and "the Mystic East."* New York: Routledge, 2002.

Kittel, Gerhard, and Gerhard Friedrich, eds. *Theological Dictionary of the New Testament*, vol. 3 of 10 vols., tr. Geoffrey W. Bromiley, Grand Rapids, MI: Wm. B. Eerdmans Publishing Co., 1964-1976.

Klausner, Joseph. *The Messianic Idea in Israel from Its Beginning to the Completion of the Mishnah*, tr. W. F. Stinespring. New York: Ulan Press, 2012.

Klawans, Jonathan. *Purity, Sacrifice, and the Temple: Symbolism and Supersessionism in the Study of Ancient Judaism*. New York: Oxford University Press, 2006.

Kline, Meredith G. "Divine Kingship and Genesis 6:1-4." *Westminster Theological Journal* 24 (1962), pp. 187-204.

Knierim, Rolf P. *The Task of Old Testament Theology: Method and Cases*. Grand Rapids, MI: Wm. B. Eerdmans Publishing Co., 1995.

Knight, George A. F. *Servant Theology: A Commentary on the Book of Isaiah 40-55*. Grand Rapids, MI: Wm. B. Eerdmans Publishing Co., 1984.

Knight, Henry F. *Confessing Christ in a Post-Holocaust World: A Midrashic Experiment*. Westport, CT: Greenwood Publishing Group, 2000.

Koehler, Ludwig, Walter Baumgartner, and Johann Jakob Stamm. *The Hebrew and Aramaic Lexicon of the Old Testament*. tr. M. E. Richardson. Leiden, The Netherlands: Brill Academic Publishing, 1994.

Koenig, Bernie. *Natural Law, Science, and the Social Construction of Reality*. Lanham, MD: The University Press of America, 2004.

Kogan, Michael S. *Opening the Covenant: A Jewish Theology of Christianity*. New York: Oxford University Press, 2007.

Kolb, Robert, and Charles P. Arand. *The Genius of Luther's Theology: A Wittenberg Way of Thinking for the Contemporary Church*. Grand Rapids, MI: Baker Academic, 2008.

Konsmo, Erik. *The Pauline Metaphors of the Holy Spirit: The Intangible Spirit's Tangible*. New York: Peter Land Publishing, 2010.

Korte, Anne-Marie, and Maaike De Haardt, eds. *The Boundaries of Monotheism: Interdisciplinary Explorations Into the Foundations of Western Monotheism*. Leiden, The Netherlands: Koninklijke Brill NV, 2009.

Köstenberger, Andreas J., and Peter T. O'Brien. *Salvation to the Ends of the Earth: A Biblical Theology of Mission*. Downers Grove, IL: InterVarsity Press, 2001.

_____and Richard Duane Patterson, eds. *Invitation to Biblical Interpretation: Exploring the Hermeneutical Triad of History, Literature, and Theology*. Grand Rapids, MI: Kregel Academic, 2011.

Kowalewski, Mark R. *All Things to All People: The Catholic Church Confronts*. Albany, NY: State University of New York Press, 1994.

Kretzmann, Norman, and Eleonore Stump, eds. *The Cambridge Comparison to Aquinas*. Cambridge, UK: Cambridge University Press, 1993.

Kuefler, Mathew. *The Manly Eunuch: Masculinity, Gender Ambiguity, and Christian Ideology in Late Antiquity*. Chicago, IL: The University of Chicago Press, 2001.

Küng, Hans. *The Church*. New York: Sheed and Ward Publishers, 1967.

Kuntaraf, Jonathan O., and Kathleen Kiem Hoa Kuntaraf. *God's Book of Wisdom*. Hagerstown, MD: Review and Herald Publishing Association, 2007.

Laclerq, Jean. *The Love of Learning and the Desire for God*. New York: Fordham University Press, 1970.

Lakeland, Paul. *Postmodernity: Christian Identity in a Fragmented Age*. Minneapolis, MN: Fortress Press, 1997.

Langdon, Adrian. *God the Eternal Contemporary: Trinity, Eternity, and Time in Karl Barth*. Eugene, OR: Wipf & Stock Publishers, 2012.

Langford, Thomas A. *Reflections on Grace*. Philip A. Rolnick and Jonathan R. Wilson, eds. Eugene, OR: Wipf & Stock, 2007.

Langworth, Richard. *Churchill by Himself: The Definitive Collection of Quotations*. London, UK: Ebury Press, 2008.

Lapide, Pinchas, and Jürgen Moltmann. *Jewish Monotheism and Christian Trinitarian Doctrine: A Dialogue by Pinchas Lapide and Jürgen Moltmann*. Philadelphia, PA: Fortress Press, 1981.

_____, and Peter Stuhlmacher. *Paul: Rabbi and Apostle*. Minneapolis, MN: Augsburg Publishing House, 1984.

_____*The Resurrection of Jesus: A Jewish Perspective*. Eugene, OR: Wipf & Stock Publishers, 2002.

Lardner, Nathaniel. *The Works of Nathaniel Lardner*. Whitefish, MT: Kessinger Publishing, 2010.

Launderville, Dale. *Spirit and Reason: The Embodied Character of Ezekiel's Symbolic Thinking*. Waco, TX: Baylor University Press, 2007.

Lawson, John. *Introduction to Christian Doctrine*. Grand Rapids, MI: Zondervan Publishing House, 1980.

Lazareth, William Henry, ed. *Reading the Bible in Faith: Theological Voices from the Pastorate*. Grand Rapids, MI: Wm. B. Eerdmans Publishing Co., 2001.

Leadingham, Everett. *I Believe, Now Tell Me Why*. Beacon Hill Press, 1994.

Leaman, Oliver. *Judaism: An Introduction*. New York: I. B. Tauris & Co., 2011.

Leaney, A. R. C. *The Rule of Qumran and Its Meaning*. London, UK: SCM, 1966.

Leary, Mark R., and Rick H. Hoyle. *Handbook of Individual Differences in Social Behavior*. New York: The Guilford Press, 2009.

Leviticus *Rabbah* 18:1.

Lechler, Gotthard Victor, and Karl Gerok, Johann Peter Lange, eds. *Theological and Homiletical Commentary on the Acts of the Apostles*. Edinburgh, Scotland: T. and T. Clark, 1864.

Lee, Witness. *Christ in His Excellency*. Goshen, IN: Living Stream Ministry, 2000.

_____*Life-Study of Exodus*. Anaheim, CA: Living Stream Ministry, 2011.

Lefkovitz, Lori Hope. *In Scripture: The First Stories of Jewish Sexual Identities*. Lanham, MD: Rowman & Littlefield Publishers, 2010.

Leinsle, Ulrich G. *Introduction to Scholastic Theology*. Washington, DC: The Catholic University of America Press, 2010.

Leith, John H. *Basic Christian Doctrine*. Louisville, KY: Westminster/John Knox Press, 1993.

Lemche, Herbert Karl. *The Old Testament Between Theology and History: A Critical Survey*. Louisville, KY: Westminster John Knox Press, 2008.

Lemche, Niels Peter. *The Old Testament Between Theology and History: A Critical Survey*. Louisville, KY: Westminster John Knox Press, 2008.

Lerner, Michael. *Tikkun Reader*. Lanham, MD: Rowman & Littlefield Publishers, 2007.

Leslie, Charles. *A Short and Easy Method with the Jews, Wherein the Certainty of the Christian Religion Is Demonstrated*. Spitalfields, England: 1812.

Leupold, Herbert Karl. *Exposition of Genesis*, vol. 1. Chillicothe, OH: DeWard Publishing Co., 2010.

Levene, Osher Chaim. *Set in Stone: The Meaning of Mitzvah Observance*. Jerusalem, Israel: Targum Press, 2004.

Levenson, Alan T. *The Wiley-Blackwell History of Jews and Judaism*. Chichester, UK: Blackwell Publishing, 2012.

Levenson, Jon D. *The Death and Resurrection of the Beloved Son: The Transformation of Child Sacrifice in Judaism and Christianity*. New Haven, CT: Yale University Press, 1995.

Levinas, Emmanuel. *Difficult Freedom: Essays on Judaism*, tr. Seán Hand. Baltimore, MD: Johns Hopkins University Press, 1997.

_____*In the Time of the Nations*, tr. Michael B. Smith. Bloomington, IN: Indiana University Press, 1994.

Leviticus *Rabbah* 6:1.

Lewis, Warren. and Hans Rollmann, eds. *Restoring the First-Century Church in the Twenty-First Century: Essays on*. Eugene, OR: Wipf and Stock Publishers, 2005.

Lin, Kent C. *The Rationality of Christian Doctrines*. Maitland, FL: Xulon Press, 2009.

Lim, Richard. *Public Disputation, Power, and Social Order in Late Antiquity*. Berkeley, CA: The University of California Press.

Lister, Rob. *God is Impassible and Impassioned: Toward a Theology of Divine Emotion*. Wheaton, IL: Crossway, 2013.

Loew, Judah. *Netivot Olam*. New York: Judaica Press, 1969.

Loftus, John W. *The Christian Delusion: Why Faith Fails*. Amherst, NY: Prometheus Books, 2010.

Lohfink, Norbert. *The God of Israel and the Nations: Studies in Isaiah and the Psalms*. Collegeville, MN: Liturgical Press, 2000.

Lohlenberger, John R., ed. *The Evangelical Parallel New Testament*. New York: Oxford University Press, 2003.

Longenecker, Richard N. *Paul, the Apostle of Liberty*. Carol Stream, IL: Tyndale House, 1966.

_____*New Testament Social Ethics for Today*. Grand Rapids, MI: Wm. B. Eerdmans Publishing Co., 1984.

Longmann III, Tremper. *Old Testament Essentials: Creation, Conquest, Exile and Return*. Downers Grove, IL: InterVarsity Press, 2014.

Lossky, Vladimir. *The Mystical Theology of the Eastern Church*. Yonkers, NY: St. Vladimir's Seminary Press, 1976.

Louth, Andrew. *Denys the Areopagite*. New York: Continuum Books, 1989).

Lutz, David, and Paul Mimbi, eds. *Shareholder Value & the Common Good*. Nairobi, Kenya: Strathmore University Press, 2005.

MacArthur, John. *Acts 1-12 MacArthur New Testament Commentary*. Chicago, IL: Moody Press, 1994.

_____*The Vanishing Conscience and Hard to Believe*. Nashville, TN: Thomas Nelson, 2003.

Maccoby, Hyam. *Antisemitism and Modernity: Innovation and Continuity*. Abingdon, UK: Routledge Press, 2006.

_____*The Mythmaker: Paul and the Invention of Christianity*. San Francisco, CA: HarperSanFrancisco Publishers, 1986.

Machiavelli, Niccolò. *The Prince*, tr. Luigi Ricci. London, England: Grant Richards, 1903.

Mackean, William Herbert. *Christian Monasticism in Egypt to the Close of the Fourth Century*. New York: The Macmillan Company, 1920.

MacKnight, James. *The Harmony of the Four Gospels*. London, UK: Longman, Hurst, Rees , and Orme, 1809.

Macquarrie, John. *Principles of Christian Theology*. New York: Charles Scribner & Sons, 1966.

Madigan, Kevin, and Jon D. Levenson. *Resurrection: The Power of God for Christians and Jews*. New Haven, CT: Yale University Press, 2008.

Main, John. *The Way of Unknowing: Expanding Spiritual Horizons through Meditation*. Eugene, OR: Wipf and Stock Publishers, 1990.

Makkreel, Rudolph A., and Sebastian Luft, eds. *Neo-Kantianism in Contemporary Philosophy*. Bloomington, IN: The Indiana University Press, 2010.

Manning, Brennan. *The Signature of Jesus: The Call to a Life Marked by Holy Passion and Relentless Faith*. Colorado Springs, CO: Multnomah Books, 1988.

Manual of Discipline (Dead Sea Scrolls,), 1QS 3:6, 8; 4:16; 5:6, 7; 8:6, 10; 9:4; 10:17.

Marsh, James L. *Critique, Action, and Liberation*. Albany, NY: State University of New York Press, 1995.

Marten-Finnis, Susanne. *Vilna as a Centre of the Modern Jewish Press, 1840–1928*. Bern, Switzerland: Peter Lang AG, European Academic Publishers, 2004.

Marthaler, Berard L. *The Creed: The Apostolic Faith in Contemporary Theology*. New London, CT: Twenty-Third Publications, 1987.

Martin, George. *The Gospel According to Mark: Meaning and Message*. Chicago, IL: Loyola Press, 2005.

Matera, Frank J. *Romans*. Grand Rapids, MI: Baker Academic, 2010.

Mattes, Mark, ed. *Twentieth-Century Lutheran Theologians*. Göttingen, Germany: Vandenhoeck & Ruprecht, 2013.

Maximus, *Exposito in Psalmum* 43.

_____*Philokalia*, vol. II, p. 178.

McClure, Jim B. *Grace Revisited*. Geelong, Australia: Trailblazer Ministries, 2010.

McCormack, Bruce L., and Joseph White. *Thomas Aquinas and Karl Barth: An Unofficial Catholic-Protestant Dialogue*. Grand Rapids, MI: Wm. B. Eerdmans Publishing Co., 2013.

McDonald, David. *Lent: Giving Up Guild for Forty Days*. Littleton, CO: Samizdat Creative, 2011.

McDonald, Lee Martin, and James A. Sanders, eds. *The Canon Debate*. Grand Rapids, MI: Baker Publishing Group, 2002.

McDonald, Lee Martin. *The Origin of the Bible: A Guide for the Perplexed*. New York: T & T Clark, 2011.

McFadyen, Alistair I. *Personhood: A Christian Theory of the Individual in Social Relationships*. Cambridge: Cambridge University Press, 1990.

McGinn, Bernard, ed. *The Essential Writings of Christian Mysticism*. New York: Random House, 2006.

McGloin, Frank. *The Mystery of the Holy Trinity in Oldest Judaism*. Philadelphia, PA: John Joseph McVey, 1916.

McGrath, Alister E. *Christian History: An Introduction*. Chichester, UK: John Wiley & Sons, Ltd., 2013.

_____*Christian Theology: An Introduction*. Malden, MA: Blackwell Publishing, 1993.

McKim, Donald K. *Major Themes in the Reformed Tradition*. Eugene, OR: Wipf and Stock Publishers, 1998.

_____*Westminster Dictionary of Theological Terms*. Louisville, KY: Westminster John Knox Press, 1996.

McMichael, Ralph N. *Eucharist: A Guide for the Perplexed*. New York: T & T Clark International, 2010.

McNeill, Donald P., Douglas A. Morrison, and Henri J. M. Nouwen. *Compassion: A Reflection on the Christian Life*. New York: Random House, 1982.

Megillah 4.11; 23a.

Meier, Levi. *Moses—The Prince, the Prophet: His Life, Legend, and Message for Our Lives*. Woodstock, VT: Jewish Lights Publishing, 1998.

Menzies, Robert. *Empowered for Witness*. London, UK: Continuum International Publishing Group, 2004.

Mermentrout, Don S., and Robert Boak Slocum, eds. *An Episcopal Dictionary of the Church*. Norwich, UK: Church House Publishing, 2005.

Merrigan, Terrence, and Jacques Haers, eds. *The Myriad Christ: Plurality and the Quest for Unity in Contemporary Christology*. Leuven, Belgium: Leuven University Press, 2000.

Merrill, Eugene H. *Everlasting Dominion: A Theology of the Old Testament*. Nashville, TN: Broadman & Holman Publishing, 2006.

Merton, Thomas. *A Thomas Merton Reader*, Thomas P. McDonnell, ed. New York, Random House, 1938.

Meszler, Joseph B. *A Man's Responsibility: A Jewish Guide to Being a Son, a Partner in Marriage, a Father, and a Community Leader*. Woodstock, VT: Jewish Lights Publishing, 2008.

Metzger, Bruce M. "Considerations of Methodology in the Study of Mystery Religions," *Harvard Theological Review* 48 (1955).

Meyers, Carol. *Women in Scripture: A Dictionary of Named and Unnamed Women in the Hebrew Bible, the Apocryphal/Deuterocanonical Books, and the New Testament*. Grand Rapids, MI: Wm. B. Eerdmans Publishing, 2001.

Midrash *Qohelet* 2.1

Migliore, Daniel L. *Faith Seeking Understanding: An Introduction to Christian Theology*. Grand Rapids, MI: Wm. B. Eerdmans Publishing Co., 2004.

Migne, Jacques–Paul *Patrologiae cursus completus [Series Graeca]* 91:641B.

Miladinov, Marina. *Margis of Solitude: Eremitism in Central Europe between East and West*. Zagreb, Croatia: Leykam International, 2008.

Miller, Thomas Allen *Did Jesus Really Rise from the Dead?: A Surgeon-Scientist Examines the Evidence*. Wheaton, IL: Crossway, 2013.

Miller, William T. *The Book of Exodus: Question by Question*. Mahwah, NJ: Paulist Press, 2009.

Mimpriss, Robert. *The Gospel History of Our Lord's Life & Ministry*. London, England: Thomas Varty Educational Depository, 1842.

Mishnah *Avot* 2:5, 5.21; *Berakhot* 5:5, 288; *Pesachim* 8.8; *Ta'anit* 3:8.

Mitchell, Michael R. *Leading, Teaching, and Making Disciples*. Bloomington, IN: LifeWay Publishing, 2010.

Moffett, Samuel H. *A History of Christianity in Asia: Beginnings to 1500*. San Francisco: HarperSanFrancisco, 1992.

Moll, Sebastian. *The Arch-Heretic Marcion*. Tübingen, Germany: Mohr Siebeck, 2010.

Molnar, Paul. *Divine Freedom and the Doctrine of the Immanent Trinity*. London, UK: T & T Clark, Ltd., 2002.

Moloney, Francis J. *A Body Broken for a Broken People: Eucharist in the New Testament*. Peabody, MA: Hendrickson Publishers, 1997.

Moltmann, Jürgen. *The Crucified God*. tr. R. A. Wilson and John Bowden. New York: Harper & Row, 1974.

_____*The Coming of God: Christian Eschatology*, tr. Margaret Kohl. London, UK: SCM Press, 1996.

Montefiore, Claude G. *The Bible for Home Reading*. Oxford, UK: Horace Hart, 1896.

_____and H. M. J. Loewe, eds. *A Rabbinic Anthology*. Cambridge, UK: Cambridge University Press, 2012.

Moore, Daniel F. *Jesus, an Emerging Jewish Mosaic: Jewish Perspectives, Post-Holocaust*. New York: T. & T. Clark International, 2008.

Moore, Edward. *Origen of Alexandria and St. Maximus the Confessor*. Boca Raton, FL: Universal Publishers, 2004.

Moore, James F. *Christian Theology After the Shoah: A Re-Interpretation of the Passion Narratives*. Lanham, MD: University Press of America, 1993.

Morris, Charles. *American Catholic: The Saints and Sinners Who Built America's Most Powerful Church*. New York: Random House, 1997.

Mouw, Richard J., and Sander Griffioen. *Pluralisms and Horizons: An Essay in Christian Public Philosophy*. Grand Rapids, MI: Wm. B. Eerdmans Publishing Co., 1993.

Mozley, J. K. *The Impassibility of God*. Cambridge, UK: Cambridge University Press, 1926.

Mulder, Anne-Claire. *Divine Flesh, Embodied Word: Incarnation as a Hermeneutical Key to a Feminist Theologian's Reading of Luce Irigaray's Work*. Amsterdam, The Netherlands: Amsterdam University Press, 2006.

Munk, Michael L. *The Sacred Letters as a Guide to Jewish Deed and Thought*. Brooklyn, NY: Mesorah Publications, 1983.

Nabarz, Payam. *The Mysteries of Mithra: The Pagan Belief that Shaped the Christian World*. Rochester, VT: Inner Traditions Publishing, 2005.

Nash, John F. *Christianity: The One, the Many: What Christianity Might Have Been and Could Still Become*. Bloomington, IN: Xlibris Corporation, 2007.

Nassi, Tzvi. (Hirsch Prinz), *The Great Mystery or How Can Three Be One?* London: William Macintosh, 1863.

Nazianzus. Gregory. *Nicene and Post-Nicene Fathers*, tr. Philip Schaff and Henry Wace. Grand Rapids, MI: Wm. B. Eerdmans Publishing Co., 1974.

Need, Jr., Ovid. *Death of the Church Victorious: Tracing the Roots and Implications of Modern Dispensationalism*. Mulberry, IN: Sovereign Grace Publishers, 2002.

Nelson, James B. *Embodiment: An Approach to Sexuality and Christian Theology*. Minneapolis, MN: Augsburg Publishing House, 1978.

_____*Sexuality and the Sacred: Resources for Theological Reflection.* Louisville, KY: Westminster/ John Knox Press, 1994.

Ner-David, Haviva. *Life on the Fringes: A Feminist Journey Toward Traditional.* Elmwood Park, NJ: JFL Publishing, 2000.

Neusner, Jacob. *A Life of Rabban Yohanan Ben Zakkai: Ca. 1-80 C.E.* Leiden, The Netherlands: Koninklijke Brill, 1962.

_____*Christianity, Judaism and Other Greco-Roman Cults, Part 2: Early Christianity.* Eugene, OR: Wipf and Stock Publishers, 1975.

_____*Learn Mishnah.* Springfield, NJ: Behrman House, 1978.

_____*Judaism: The Evidence of Mishnah.* Chicago, IL: The University of Chicago Press, 1981.

_____*Rabbinic Judaism: The Theological System.* Boston, MA: Brill Academic Publishers, 2002.

_____*Theological Dictionary of Rabbinic Judaism: Principal Theological Categories.* Lanham, MD: The University Press of America, 2005.

Neville, Robert C. *A Theology Primer.* New York: State University of New York Press, 1991.

Newell, J. Philip. *Echo of the Soul: The Sacredness of the Human Body.* Norwich, UK: Canterbury Press Norwich, 2000.

Niebuhr, H. Richard. *The Meaning of Revelation.* Louisville, KY: Westminster John Knox Press, 1941.

Nissen, Johannes. *The Gospel of John and the Religious Quest: Historical and Contemporary.* Eugene, OR: Wipf and Stock Publishers, 2013.

Nolan, Albert. *Jesus Before Christianity.* Maryknoll, NY: Orbis Books, 1978.

Nussbaum, Otto. *Die Aufbewahrung der Eucharistie.* Bonn, Germany: Hanstein Publishing, 1979.

Ockenga, Harold John. *The Word of the Lord: The Campbell Morgan Bible Lectureship, July, 1951.* Glasgow, UK: Pickering and Inglis, 1951.

O'Leary, Stephen D. *Arguing the Apocalypse: A Theory of Millennial Rhetoric.* New York: Oxford University Press, 1994.

O'Meara, Thomas. *The Encyclopedia of Religion.* New York: Macmillan,1987.

O'Neil, Daniel. *Heaven's Eagle.* Nashville, TN: Thomas Nelson Publishing, 2013.

O'Shea, Paul. *A Cross Too Heavy: Pope Pius XII and the Jews of Europe.* New York: Palgrave Macmillan, 2011.

O'Toole, James M. *The Faithful: A History of Catholics in America.* Cambridge, MA: Harvard University Press, 2008.

Odeyemi, Oluwole J. *Where God Was on 9/11: The Unravelling of the Many Mysteries of the Bible.* Central Milton Keynes, UK: AuthorHouse UK, 2005.

Olasky, Marvin. *The Religions Next Door: What We Need to Know About Judaism.* Nashville, TN: Broadman & Holman Publishers, 2004.

Old, Hughes Oliphant, *The Reading and Preaching of the Scriptures in the Worship of the Christian Church*, Vol. 5. Grand Rapids, MI: Wm. B. Eerdmans Publishing Co., 2004.

_____*Worship: Reformed According to Scripture.* Louisville, KY: Westminster John Knox Press, 2002.

Origen, *Hymns on Faith,* 18.2.

Osborne, Kenan B. *A Theology of the Church for the Third Millennium: A Franciscan Approach.* Leiden, The Netherlands: Koninklijke Brill NV, 2009.

Oswalt, John N. *The Bible among the Myths: Unique Revelation of Just Ancient Literature.* Grand Rapids, MI: Zondervan Publishing, 2009.

Overman, Dean L. *A Case for the Divinity of Jesus: Examining the Earliest Evidence.* Lanham, MD: Roman and Littlefield Publishers, 2010.

Paddock, Fred, and Mado Spiegler. *Judaism and Anthroposophy.* Great Barrington, MA: SteinerBooks, 2003.

Palmer, Michael D., and Stanley M. Burgess, eds. *The Wiley-Blackwell Companion to Religion and Social Justice.* Malden, MA: John Wiley & Sons, 2012.

Panikkar, Raimundo. *Dwelling Place for Wisdom.* Louisville, KY: Westminster/John Knox Press, 1993.

Pannenberg, Wolfhart. *Systematic Theology, Volume 1.* Grand Rapids, MI: Wm. B. Eerdmans Publishing Co., 1991.

Papandrea, James L. *A Pilgrim's Guide to the Eternal City.* Eugene, OR: Wipf and Stock Publishers, 2012.

Park, Sejin. *Pentecost and Sinai: The Festival of Weeks as a Celebration of the Sinai Event.* New York: T & T Clark International, 2008.

Parsons, William B. *Teaching Mysticism.* New York: Oxford University Press, 2011.

Pate, Marvin. *From Plato to Jesus: What Does Philosophy Have to Do with Theology*. Grand Rapids, MI: Kregel Publications, 2011.

Paul, Morris. *Jewish Themes in the New Testament: Am Yisrael Chai!*. Crown Hill, UK: Paternoster, Authentic Media Limited, 2013.

Peace, Richard. *Conversion in the New Testament: Paul and the Twelve*. Grand Rapids, MI: Wm. B. Eerdmans Publishing Co., 1999.

Peck, M. Scott *The Road Less Traveled*. New York: Simon and Schuster, 1978.

Pelikan, Jaroslav. *Jesus Through the Centuries: His Place in the History of Culture*. New Haven, CT: Yale University Press, 1985.

Pentiuc, Eugen J. *Jesus the Messiah in the Hebrew Bible*. Mahwah, NJ: Paulist Press, 2006.

Perrin, David B. *Studying Christian Spirituality*. New York: Routledge, 2007.

Perry, Tim S. *Radical Difference: A Defence of Hendrik Kraemer's Theology of Religions*. Waterloo, Canada: The Wilfrid Laurier University Press, 2001.

Peshita 117a.

Phillips, John. *Exploring Romans: An Expository Commentary*. Grand Rapids, MI: Kregel Academic, 1969.

Phillips, John. *Exploring the Old Testament Book by Book: An Expository Survey*. Grand Rapids, MI: Kregel Publications, 2009.

Pinnock, Clark, Richard Rice, John Sanders, William Hasker, and David Bassinger. *The Openness of God: A Biblical Challenge to the Traditional Understanding of God*. Downers Grove, IL: InterVarsity Press, 1994.

Plato, *Gorgias*, 492e-493a.

_____*Phaedrus* 70b.

_____*Theaetetus* 176b.

Plaut, W. Gunther, and David E. S. Stein. *The Torah: A Modern Commentary*. New York: UJR Press, 2005.

Porter, Jeanne L. *Leading Ladies: Transformative Biblical Imagers for Women's Leadership*. Philadelphia, PA: Innisfree Press, 2000.

Porterfield, Amanda. *Healing the History of Christianity*. New York: Oxford University Press, 2005.

Prager, Denis, and Joseph Telushkin, *Nine Questions People Ask About Judaism*. New York: Simon & Schuster, Inc., 1975.

Price, Joseph, and Donald W. Musser, eds. *New and Enlarged Handbook of Christian Theology*. Nashville, TN: Abingdon Press, 1993.

Prophet, Elizabeth Clare. *Inner Faces of God, Kabalah*. Livingston, MT: Summit University Press, 1992.

Ramsay, William M. *The Layman's Guide to the New Testament*. Louisville, KY: John Knox Press, 1981.

Reuchlin, Johann. *Recommendation Whether to Confiscate, Destroy, and Burn All Jewish Books*. Mahwah, NJ: Paulist Press, 2000. Originally published: Tubingen, Germany: Thomas Anshelm, 1511.

Reventlow, Henning Graf. *Eschatology in the Bible and in Jewish and Christian Tradition*. Sheffield, UK: Sheffield Academic Press, 1997.

Richardson, Alan, and John Bowden, eds. *The Westminster Dictionary of Christian Theology*. Philadelphia, PA: The Westminster Press, 1983.

Rieger, Joerg. *Christ and Empire: From Paul to Postcolonial Times*. Minneapolis, MN: Fortress Press, 2007.

Rittgers, Ronald K. *The Reformation of Suffering: Pastoral Theology and Lay Piety in Late Medieval and Early Modern Germany*. New York: Oxford University Press, 2012.

Roberts, Alexander. *The Ante-Nicene Fathers, Volume 3: Latin Christianity: Its Founder, Tertullian*, James Donaldson, Arthur Cleveland Coxe, eds. New York: Charles Scribner's Sons, 1885.

Robertson, Irvine. *What the Cults Believe*. Chicago, IL: Moody Press, 1966.

Roetzel, Calvin J., ed. *The HarperCollins Bible Dictionary*. New York: HarperCollins,1996.

Rosenberg, Shelley Kapnek. *Raising a Mensch*. Philadelphia, PA: Jewish Publication Society, 2003.

Roth, Dan. *Relevance: Pirkei Avos for the Twenty-first Century*. Jerusalem, Israel: Feldheim Publishers, 2007.

Fritz A. Rothschild, ed. *Between God and Man: An Interpretation of Judaism from the Writings of Abraham J. Heschel*. New York: The Free Press, 1959.

Rose, Paul Lawrence. *Wagner: Race and Revolution*. New Haven, CT: Yale University Press, 1992.

Rottenberg, Isaac C. *Judaism, Christianity, Paganism: A Judeo-Christian Worldview and Its Cultural Implications*. Atlanta, GA: Hebraic Heritage Press, 2007.

Rousseau, John J. *Jesus and His Word: An Archaeological and Cultural Dictionary*. Minneapolis, MN: Augsburg Fortress Press, 1995.

Rudin, Arnold James. *Christians & Jews Faith to Faith: Tragic History, Promising Present, Fragile Future*. Woodstock, VT: Jewish Lights Publishing, 2011.

Rudolph, Kurt. *The Nature and History of Gnosticism*. Edinburgh, UK: T & T Clark, Ltd.,1983.

Ruether, Rosemary Radford. *Faith and Fratricide: The Theological Roots of Anti-Semitism*. New York: Seabury Press, 1974.

Russell, Bertrand. *History of Western Philosophy*. London, UK: Routledge Classics, 2004.

Russell, Letty M. *Household of Freedom: Authority in Feminist Theology*. Philadelphia: The Westminster Press, 1987.

Ryken, Leland, James C. Wilhoit, and Trember Longman III, eds. *Dictionary of Biblical Imagery*. Downers Grove, IL: InterVarsity Press, 1998.

Ryrie, Charles C. *Basic Theology: A Popular Systematic Guide to Understanding Biblical Truth*. Chicago, IL: Moody Press, 1986.

Sabbathi, P. I. *Soulzer: Be a Soldier to Save Your Soul*. Bloomington, IN: WestBowPress, 2014.

Sanders, E. P. *Paul, the Law, and the Jewish People*. Minneapolis, MN: Fortress Press, 1983.

Sanders, John Ernest. *The God Who Risks: A Theology of Divine Providence*. Downers Grove, IL: InterVarsity Press, 2007.

Sandmel, Samuel. *Judaism and Christian Beginnings*. New York: Oxford University Press, 1978.

Sarna, Nahum M. *Exploring Exodus: The Origins of Biblical Israel*. New York: Schocken Books, 1986.

Scharfstein, Sol. *The Five Books of Moses*. Jersey City, NJ: KTAV Publishing House, 2005.

Schechter, Solomon. *Aspects of Rabbinic Theology*. New York: Schocken Books, 1961.

Scholem, Gershom Gerhard. *Messianic Idea in Judaism, and Other Essays on Jewish Spirituality*. New York: Schocken Books, 1971.

_____*On Kabbalah and Its Symbolism (Mysticism and Kabbalah)*. New York: Schocken Books, 1965.

_____*Origins of the Kabbalah*. Princeton, NJ: The Princeton University Press, 1962.

Schönborn, Christoph. *Living the Catechism of the Catholic Church: Volume 2, The Sacraments*. San Francisco, CA: Ignatius Press, 2000.

Schwartz, Howard. *Reimagining the Bible: The Storytelling of the Rabbis*. New York: Oxford University Press, 1998.

_____*Tree of Souls: The Mythology of Judaism*. Oxford: Oxford University Press, 2004.

Schweizer, Eduard. *The Good News According to Mark* tr. Donald Madvig. Atlanta, GA: John Knox Press,1964.

Segal, Alan. *Life After Death: A History of the Afterlife in Western Religion*. New York: Doubleday, 2004.

Seifrid, Mark A. *Justification by Faith: The Origin and Development of a Central Pauline Theme*. Leiden, The Netherlands: E. J. Brill, 1992.

Shahan, Michael, ed. *A Report from the Front Lines: Conversations on Public Theology: A Festschrift in Honor of Robert Benne*. Grand Rapids, MI: Wm. B. Eerdmans Publishing, 2009.

Shapiro, Rami. *Amazing Chesed: Living a Grace-Filled Judaism*. Woodstock, VT: Jewish Lights Publishing, 2013.

Sharrock, Russell. *Covenant Theology: A Critical Analysis of Current Pentecostal Covenant Theology*. Morrisville, NC: Lulu Press, 2006.

Shatz, David, Chaim Waxman, and Nathan J. Diament, eds. *Tikkun Olam: Social Responsibility in Jewish Thought and Law*. New York: Rowman & Littlefield Publishers, 1997.

Shepherd, Thomas. *Friends in High Places: Tracing the Family Tree of New Thought Christianity*. Lincoln, NE: iUniverse Publishing, 2004.

Sherwin, Byron L. *Jewish Ethics for the Twenty-First Century: Living in the Image of God*. Syracuse, NY: Syracuse University Press, 2000.

Shiffman, Lawrence H. *Who Was a Jew? Rabbinic and Halakhic Perspectives on the Jewish–Christian Schism*. Jersey City, NJ: KTAV Publishing, 1985.

Shillington, George. *Jesus and Paul Before Christianity: Their World and Work in Retrospect*. Eugene, OR: Wipf and Stock Publishers, 2011.

Sicker, Martin. *The Moral Maxims of the Sages of Israel: Pirkei Avot*. Bloomington, IN: iUniverse, 2004.

Siewers, Alfred Kentigern, *et.al. Re-Imagining Nature: Environmental Humanities and Ecosemiotics*. Lanham MD: Rowman & Littlefield, 2014.

Sifre *Deuteronomy* 27.

Sifre Deuteronomy, Ha'azinu 306.

Simon-Peter, Rebekah. *The Jew Named Jesus: Discover the Man and His Message*. Nashville, TN: Abingdon Press, 2013.

Singer, Isidore, et. all., eds. *The Jewish Encyclopedia: A Descriptive Record of the History, Religion, Literature, and Customs of the Jewish People from the Earliest Times to the Present Day*. New York: Funk & Wagnalls, 1904.

Sittler, Joseph. *Evocations of Grace: The Writings of Joseph Sittler on Ecology, Theology, and Ethics*, Steven Bouma-Prediger and Peter W. Bakken, eds. Grand Rapids, MI: Wm. B. Eerdmans Publishing Co., 2000.

Sittser, Gerald L. *Water from a Deep Well: Christian Spirituality from Early Martyrs to Modern Missionaries*. Downers Grove, IL: InterVarsity Press, 2007.

Sklonik, Fred, et. al, eds. *Encyclopaedia Judaica*, vol. 6. Jerusalem, Israel: Keter Publishing House, 2007.

Smedes, Lewis. *All Things Made New*. Eugene, OR: Wipf & Stock Publishers, 1998.

Smith, Harmon L. *Where Two or Three Are Gathered: Liturgy and the Moral Life*. Eugene, OR: Wipf & Stock Publishers, 1989.

Smith, Stephen. *Saving Salvation*. Harrisburg, PA: Morehouse Publishing, 2005.

Snyder, Christopher A. *An Age of Tyrants: Britain and the Britons A.D. 400-600*. University Park, Pa: Pennsylvania State University Press, 1998.

Snyder, Graydon F. *First Corinthians: A Faith Community Commentary*. Macon, GA: Mercer University Press, 1992.

Soloveitchik, Joseph B. *The Lonely Man of Faith*. New York: Doubleday, 1965.

Sonsino, Rifat. *The Many Faces of God: A Reader of Modern Jewish Theologies*. New York: URJ Press, 2004.

Spangler, Ann, ed. *The Names of God Bible*. Grand Rapids, MI: Baker Publishing Group, 2011.

Spears, Larry C., and Michele Lawrence. *Focus on Leadership: Servant-Leadership for the Twenty-First Century*. New York: John Wiley & Sons, 2002.

Spence, H. T. *The Canon of Scripture*. Dunn, NC: Forwarding the Faith Publications, 2010.

Spencer, John. *New Heavens, New Earth*. Lincoln, NE: iUniverse, Inc., 2002.

Sprinkle, Preston M. *Paul and Judaism Revisited: A Study of Divine and Human Agency in Salvation*. Downers Grove, IL: InterVarsity Press, 2013.

Sproul, Robert C. *God's Love: How the Infinite God Cares for His Children*. Colorado Springs, CO: David C. Cook Publishing, 2001.

Stamm, Raymond Thomas. *Search the Scriptures New Testament Studies in Honor of Raymond T. Stamm*. Leiden, Netherlands: E. J. Brill, 1969.

Starr, Lee Anna. *The Bible Status of Woman*. Zarephath, NJ: Pillar of Fire Press, 1955.

Stein, Robert H. *An Introduction to the Parables of Jesus*. Philadelphia, PA: The Westminster Press, 1981.

Stein, Robert H. *Mark*. Grand Rapids, MI: Baker Academic, 2008.

Stevenson, W. H. *King James's Bible: A Selection*. New York: Routledge, 2013.

Stigers, Harold G. *A Commentary on Genesis*. Grand Rapids, MI: Zondervan Publishing, 1976.

Stinson, Jerald M. "A Love Story." *Harvard Divinity Bulletin*, vol. 35–36, p. 107.

Stronstad, Roger. *Charismatic Theology of St. Luke*. Grand Rapids, MI: Baker Academic, 1990.

Sumney, Jerry L. *Reading Paul's Letter to the Romans*. Atlanta, GA: Society of Biblical Literature, 2012.

Sutcliffe, John *A. Commentary on the Old and New Testament*. London, England: John Mason: 1839.

Sweazey, George Edgar. *Preaching the Good News*. New York, Prentice-Hall, 1976.

Swidler, Leonard, and Arlene Swidler, eds. *Women Priests: A Catholic Commentary on the Vatican Declaration*. Mahwah, NJ: Paulist Press, 1977.

Swindoll, Charles. *Insights on James, 1 & 2 Peter*. Carol Stream, IL: Tyndale House, 2010.

Synan, Vinson. *In the Latter Days: The Outpouring of the Holy Spirit in the Twentieth Century*. Fairfax, VA: Xulon Press, 2001.

Taliaferro, Charles, Victoria S. Harrison, and Stewart Goetz, eds. *The Routledge Companion to Theism*. New York, Routledge, 2013.

Talmage, Frank. *Disputation and Dialogue: Readings in the Jewish-Christian Encounter.* Jersey City, NJ: KTAV Publishing House, 1975.

Talmud, *Mo'ed Katan* 3:5.

Tchividjian, Tullian. *One Way Love: Inexhaustible Grace for an Exhausted World.* Colorado Springs, CO: David C. Cook, 2013.

Terry, Michael. *Reader's Guide to Judaism.* New York: Fitzroy Dearborn Publishers, 2000.

Tertullian, *On the Resurrection of the Flesh,* XI.

Theophilus, *To Autolycus,* II, 27.

Thielman, Frank. *Paul & the Law: A Contextual Approach.* Downers Grove, IL: InterVarsity Press, 1994.

Thiselton, Anthony C. *The First Epistle to the Corinthians: A Commentary on the Greek Text.* Grand Rapids, MI: Wm. B. Eerdmans Publishing Co., 2000.

_____*The Holy Spirit—in Biblical Teaching, Through the Centuries, and Today.* Grand Rapids, MI: Wm. B. Eerdmans Publishing Co., 2013.

Tignor, Robert L. *Egypt: A Short History.* Princeton, NJ: The Princeton University Press, 2010.

Tillich, Paul. *Systematic Theology, Vol. 1.* Chicago, IL: The University of Chicago Press, 1951.

Toman, Rolf, Achim Bednorz, and Ranier Warland. *Monasteries and Monastic Orders: 2000 Years of Christian Art and Culture.* Berkeley, CA: The University of California Press, 2008.

Torrance, Thomas F. *Space, Time and Resurrection.* Edinburgh, Scotland: T & T Clark, Ltd., 1976.

_____*The Christian Doctrine of God, One Being Three Persons.* London, UK: T & T Clark, 1996.

Tosefta *Berakhot* 2:21

Tracey, David John. *Jung and the New Age.* Philadelphia, PA: Brunner-Routledge, 2001.

Trepp, Leo. *A History of the Jewish Experience.* Springfield, NJ: Behrman House Publishing, 2006.

Tripolitis, Antonia. *Religions of the Hellenistic-Roman Age.* Grand Rapids, MI: Wm. B. Eerdmans Publishing Co., 2002.

Troeltsch, Ernst. *The Christian Faith.* Minneapolis, MN: Augsburg Fortress Press, 1991.

Trump, Donald. *Knocking on Heaven's Door: A New Testament Theology of Petitionary Prayer.* Grand Rapids, MI: Baker Academic, 2006.

Tsakiridou, Cornelia A. *Icons in Time, Persons in Eternity: Orthodox Theology and the Aesthetics of the Christian Image.* Burlington, VT: Ashgate Publishing Co., 2013.

Tuffs, Allan C. *And You Shall Teach Them to Your Sons: Biblical Tales for Fathers and Sons .* New York: URJ Books and Music,1997).

Turnbull, Neil. *Get a Grip on Philosophy.* East Sussex, UK: The Ivy Press, 1999.

Ucko, Hans. *The People and the People of God: Minjung and Dalit Theology in Interaction.* Hamburg, Germany: Lit Verlag Münster, 2002.

Umen, Samuel. *Jewish Concepts and Reflections.* New York: Philosophical Library, 1962.

Underwood, Ralph L. *Pastoral Care and the Means of Grace.* Minneapolis, MN: Augsburg Fortress Press, 1993.

Unknown, *Chai: Learning for Jewish Life.* Woodstock, VT: URJ Press, 2005.

Unknown, *The Analytical Greek Lexicon.* London, UK: Samuel Bagster & Sons, 1967.

Unknown, *Within Context: Guidelines for the Catechetical Presentation of Jews and Judaism in the New Testament.* Secretariat for Catholic-Jewish Relations of the National Conference of Catholic Bishops, the Education Department of the United States Catholic Conference, and Interfaith Affairs Department of the Anti-Defamation League of B'nai B'rith, 1986.

Van Buren, Paul Matthews. *A Theology of the Jewish-Christian Reality: A Christian Theology of the People Israel.* Lanham, MD: The University Press of America, 1995.

Van der Borght, Eduardus. *The Unity of the Church: A Theological State of the Art of and Beyond.* Leiden, The Netherlands: Koninklijke Brill, 2010.

van der Horst, Pieter Willem. *Japeth in the Tents of Shem: Studies on Jewish Hellenism in Antiquity.* Leuven, Belgium: Peeters Publishers, 2002.

Vander Laan, Ray. *Faith Lessons on the Promised Land.* Grand Rapids, MI: Zondervan Publishing House, 1999.

Van Gemeren, Willem A., Greg L. Bahnsen, Walter C. Kaiser, Jr., Douglas J. Moo, Wayne G. Strickland. *Five Views on Law and Gospel.* Grand Rapids, MI: Zondervan Publishing, 1996.

Van Hern, Roger E. *The Gospels: The Third Readings.* Grand Rapids, MI: Wm. B. Eerdmans Publishing Co., 2001.

van Loopik, Marcus ed. *The Ways of the Sages and the Way of the World*. Tübingen, Germany: Mohr Siebeck: 1991.

Van Wijk-Bos, Johanna W. H. *Making Wise the Simple: The Torah in Christian Faith and Practice*. Grand Rapids, MI: Wm. B. Eerdmans Publishing Co., 2005.

Verduin, Leonard. *The Reformers and Their Stepchildren*. Paris, AR: The Baptist Standard Bearer, 2001.

Vermès, Géza. *The Complete Dead Sea Scrolls in English*. London, UK: Allen Lane, 1997.

Vernant, Jean-Pierre. *Mythe et pensée chez les Grècs: Études de psychologie historique*. Paris, France: La Découverte, 1966.

Viola, Frank, and George Barna. *Pagan Christianity?: Exploring the Roots of Our Church Practices*. Carol Stream, IL: Tyndale House Publishers, 2002.

Visotzky, Burton L. *Sage Tales: Wisdom and Wonder from the Rabbis of the Talmud*. Woodstock, VT: Jewish Lights Publishing, 2011.

Vitringa, Campegius. *De Synagoge Vetere Libri Tres*. Weissenfels, Germany: Wehrmann, 1726.

Von Allmen, Jean-Jacques. *The Lord's Supper*. Cambridge, UK: James Clarke & Co., 2002.

von Harnack, Adolf. *Marcion: Das Evangelium vom Fremden Gott*. Darmstadt, Germany: Wissenschaftliche Buchgesellschaft, 1960.

_____*Zeitschrift fur die Neutestamentiche Wissenschaft und die Kunde der aelteren Kirche*, vol. 1. Berlin: Forschungen und Fortschritte, 1900.

von Orelli, Conrad. *Die hebräischen Synonyma der Zeit und Ewigkeit genetisch und sprachvergleichend dargestellt*. Leipzig, Germany: 1871. republished Ithaca, NY: Cornell University Library, 2009.

von Rad, Gerhard. *Old Testament Theology: The Theology of Israel's Prophetic Traditions*, vol. I. Louisville, KY: Westminster John Knox Press, 1962.

Vorspan, Albert, and David Saperstein, *Jewish Dimensions of Social Justice: Tough Moral Choices of Our Time*. New York: UAHC Press, 1998.

Wagner, Richard. *Jesus of Nazareth and Other* Writings, tr. William Ashton Ellis. Lincoln, NE: The University of Nebraska Press, 1995.

Wakefield, Gordon S. *The Westminster Dictionary of Spirituality*. Louisville, KY: Westminster Press, 1983.

Walbank, Frank W. *The Hellenistic World*. Cambridge, MA: Harvard University Press, 1981.

Wallace, Robin Knowles. *The Christian Year: A Guide for Worship and Preaching*. Nashville, TN: Abingdon Press, 2011.

Walle, Alf H. *Pagans and Practitioners: Expanding Biblical Scholarship*. New York: Peter Lang Publishing, 2010.

Wallis, Arthur. *God's Chosen Fast: A Spiritual and Practical Guide to Fasting*. Ft. Washington, PA: CLC Publications, 1968.

Jerry L. Walls, ed. *The Oxford Handbook of Eschatology*. New York: Oxford University Press, 2008.

Walsh, Milton. *Witness of the Saints: Patristic Readings in the Liturgy of the Hours*. San Francisco, CA: St. Ignatius Press, 2012.

Watson, Francis. *Text and Truth: Redefining Biblical Theology*. Edinburgh, UK: T. & T. Clark, 1997.

Watson, Richard. *An Exposition of the Gospels of St. Matthew and St. Mark and Some Other Detached Parts of Holy Scripture*. London, UK: John Mason, 1833.

Wautischer, Helmut. *Tribal Epistemologies: Essays in the Philosophy of Anthropology*. Farnham, UK: Ashgate Publishing, 1998.

Webster, Charlie. *Revitalizing Christianity*. Victoria, Canada: FriesenPress, 2011.

Wedgwood, R., and William Whiston. *Essay on the Constitutions or Decrees of the Holy Apostles*. London, England: Simpkin, Marshall, and Co., 1851.

Wegman, Herman. "De 'komaf' van het liturgisch gedenken. Anamnesegespiegeld aan menselijk ervaren," in *Tijdschrift voor Theologie*, vol. 25, 2 (1985).

Welker, Michael. *What Happens in Holy Communion?* Grand Rapids, MI: Wm. B. Eerdmans Publishing Co., 2000.

Westerholm, Stephen. *The Blackwell Companion to Paul*. Chichester, UK: Blackwell Publishing, 2011.

Westley, Dick. *A Theology of Presence: The Search for Meaning in the American Catholic Experience*. Evanston, IL: Northwestern University Press, 1988.

Wheatley, Margaret J. *Finding Our Way: Leadership for an Uncertain Time*. San Francisco, CA: Berrett-Koehler Publishes, 2005.

Wiersbe, Warren W. *Wiersbe's Expository Outlines on the New Testament*. Colorado Springs, CO: Cook Communications, 1992.

Wigoder, Geoffrey. *The Encyclopedia of Judaism*. New York: Macmillian Publishing, 1989.

Williams, Colin W., William Hordern, Carl E. Braaten, John Macquarrie, Paul Hessert, and Roger L. Shinn, eds. *The Church, New Directions in Theology Today, Vol. 4*. Philadelphia, PA: Westminster Publishing House, 1969.

Williams, J. Rodman. *Renewal Theology: Systematic Theology from a Charismatic Perspective*. Grand Rapids, MI: Zondervan Publishing, 1992.

Wilson, Barrie. *How Jesus Became Christian*. New York: Macmillan Publishing, 2008.

Wilson, Marvin R. *Exploring Our Hebraic Heritage: A Christian Theology of Roots and Renewal*. Grand Rapids, MI: Wm. B. Eerdmans Publishing Co., 2014.

_____*Our Father Abraham: Jewish Roots of the Christian Faith*. Grand Rapids, MI: Wm. B. Eerdmans Publishing Co., 1989.

Wines, Enoch C. *The Hebrew Republic*, originally published in 1861 as *Commentary on the Laws of the Ancient Hebrews, Book II*. Uxbridge, Mass.: American Presbyterian Press, 1980.

Wingren, Gustaf. *Creation and Gospel: The New Situation in European Theology*. New York: Edwin Mellen Publishing, 1979.

_____*Creation and Law*, tr. Ross Mackenzie. Philadelphia, PA: Muhlenberg Press, 1961.

Witherington III, Ben. *The Gospel of Mark: A Socio-Rhetorical Commentary*. Grand Rapids, MI: Wm. B. Eerdmans Publishing Co., 2001.

_____*The Jesus Quest: The Third Search for the Jew of Nazareth*. Carol Steam, IL: InterVarsity Press, 1997.

Witte, John. and Frank S. Alexander, eds. *The Teachings of Modern Orthodox Christianity on Law, Politics, & Human Nature*. New York: Columbia University Press, 2007.

Witte, Jr., John, and Johan D. van der Vyver eds. *Religious Human Rights in Global Perspective: Religious Perspectives*. The Hague: Kluwer Law International, 1996.

Wolff, Hans Walter. *Anthropology of the Old Testament*. tr. Margaret Kohl. Philadelphia: Fortress Press, 1974.

Wright, Charles Henry, and Charles Neil, eds. *A Protestant Dictionary*. London, England: Hodder and Stoughton, 1904.

Wright, Nicholas T. *Justification: God's Plan and Paul's Vision*. Downers Grove, IL: InterVarsity Press, 2009.

Wyckoff, John W., Wave E. Nunnally, Edgar R. Lee, Randy Hurst, and Charles T. Crabtree, eds. *The Bible, the Word of God*. Springfield, MO: Gospel Publishing House, 2003.

Wylen, Stephen M. *Settings of Silver: An Introduction to Judaism*. Mahwah, NJ: Paulist Press, 2000.

_____*The Seventy Faces of Torah: The Jewish Way of Reading the Sacred Scriptures*. Mahway, NJ: Paulist Press, 2005.

_____*The Jews in the Time of Jesus*. Mahwah, NJ: Paulist Press, 1996.

Yancey, Philip. *The Bible Jesus Read*. Grand Rapids, MI: Zondervan Publishing, 2002.

Young, Brad H. *The Parables: Jewish Tradition and Christian Interpretation*. Grand Rapids, MI: Baker Academic, 2008.

Zahl, Paul F. M. *Grace in Practice: A Theology of Everyday Life*. Grand Rapids, MI: Wm. B. Eerdmans Publishing Co., 2007.

Zamfir, Korina. *Men and Women in the Household of God: A Contextual Approach to Roles and Ministries in the Pastoral Epistles*. Göttingen, Germany: Vandenhoeck & Ruprecht, 2013.

Zeller, Dieter, et.al. *Resurrection in the New Testament: Festschrift to J. Lambrecht*. Leuven, Belgium: Leuven University Press, 2002.

Zetterholm, Magnus. *Approaches to Paul: A Student's Guide to Recent Scholarship*. Minneapolis, MN: Fortress Press, 2009.

Zirkind, Naomi. *Strength and Dignity: Torah Wisdom for Women on their Multitude of Vital Roles*. Seattle, WA: CreateSpace Publishing, 2013.

Zizioulas, John D. *Being as Communion*. Crestwood, NY: St. Vladimir's Seminary Press, 1985.

GENERAL INDEX

GOLDEN key PRESS

Featuring the Informative, Inspiring Books of
Dr. John D. Garr

Our Lost Legacy: Restoring Christianity's Hebrew Foundations is a provocative, inspiring primer on the Jewish roots of the Christian faith. This volume presents selected essays in which Dr. Garr urges the church to recover its Hebrew heritage. These pages call Christians back to the Bible, to the roots of faith and understanding of their Hebrew Lord.

240 pages, ISBN 0-96782797-2-2.

God and Women: Woman in God's Image and Likeness is a comprehensive, scholarly examination of the way in which God created woman in the beginning in order to mirror the divine image and likeness. These pages will take you back to the beginning when God created male and female coequal and consubstantial.

320 pages, ISBN 978-0-9794514-4-7.

Coequal and Counterbalanced: God's Blueprint for Women and Men is an in-depth analysis of God's creation of humanity with a focus on the coequality of male and female that makes it possible for men and women to live counterbalanced and complementary lives of loving mutuality and respect.

368 pages, ISBN 978-0-9794514-9-2.

Feminine by Design: The God-Fashioned Woman is an exhaustive study of the manner in which God designed woman in the beginning of time with all the unique qualities, characteristics, preferences, and predilections that made the woman uniquely feminine and provided the means by which every woman can achieve self-fulfillment.

368 pages, ISBN 978-0-9794514-5-4.

Blessings for Family and Friends provides you with solid information about God's blessing system and with demonstrations and examples of blessings that you can pronounce over your family and friends for all occasions. This is a spectacular gift book that you will want to keep for yourself. Amazing blessings await you in this inspiring book.

160 pages, ISBN 978-0-9794514-3-0.

The Hem of His Garment: Touching the Power in God's Word discusses the context of the woman who was healed when she touched the hem of Jesus' garment. You will simply be amazed at the great impact that the ancient Jewish tradition of attaching fringes to the four corners of their mantles had upon the lives of biblical people, including this woman.

160 pages, ISBN 0-96782797-0-6.

Living Emblems: Ancient Symbols of Faith will help you understand the biblical symbols that were designed by God and by his people Israel. Each emblem is full of rich insight that points to the person and work of the Messiah, Jesus. Recognizing these spiritual truths is a profound means of underscoring the truth of Christianity's Jewish connection.

160 pages, ISBN 096782797-1-4.

God's Lamp, Man's Light is a masterful analysis of the menorah, the only biblical symbol that has the distinction of being designed by God himself. As you read this book, you will be amazed at the wealth of insight that has been hidden from the historical church because of its separation from Judaism and things Jewish.

160 pages, ISBN 0-9678279-4-9.

Family Worship is a provocative look at the modern home that offers clear answers for families in crisis and for those who want to restore their families to biblical foundations. Reading this book will be a life-changing experience for you and for your family as you learn to begin to adopt a biblical family lifestyle by putting into operation the things that the Bible teaches about family.

240 pages, ISBN 978-0-9794514-7-8.

Bless You! is a systematic, comprehensive study of the biblically Hebraic concept of blessing and the impact that it has had in the lives of believers from ancient times until today. This powerful dynamic of biblical faith can now be experienced in every Christian home. As you read this, you will recover a key part of the faith of Jesus and the apostles.

160 pages, ISBN 096782797-7-3.

Passover: The Festival of Redemption helps Christians understand the biblical festival that is part of their heritage, celebrating the Exodus and Calvary. With this exciting resource, you can celebrate Passover just as Jesus and the disciples did. And you can remember the Lord's death as he commanded at the time when he died.

160 pages, ISBN 978-0-9794514-6-1.

Life from the Dead: The Dynamic Saga of the Chosen People examines the sweep of history to discover the amazing divine protection that has been upon the children of Abraham in order to preserve them through constant threat of extinction and to establish them as the people of God.

380 pages, ISBN 978-1-940685-20-5.

Generosity: The Righteous Path to Divine Blessing is a study of the Hebraic foundations of biblical giving with a view to understanding why believers should tithe and give of their means. It is only through the Hebraic model of generosity that people can find the amazing blessings that God has promised to those who obey him.

380 pages, ISBN 978-1-940685-20-5

Order from:
Hebraic Christian Global Community
P.O. Box 421218
Atlanta, Georgia 30342, U.S.A.
www.HebraicCommunity.org

HEBRAIC CHRISTIAN
GLOBAL COMMUNITY™

Understanding the Jewish roots of our faith is a golden key that unlocks the treasures of Holy Scripture and enriches Christian lives. This fundamental concept is the focus of Hebraic Christian Global Community, an international, transdenominational publishing and educational resource for the Christian church.

Hebraic Christian Global Community features individuals and congregations who share the vision for restoring Christianity's Hebraic foundations, for networking together in true community, and for returning the church to a biblical relationship of loving support for the international Jewish community and the nation of Israel.

We publish *Restore!* magazine, a high-quality journal featuring theological balance and scholarly documentation that helps Christians recover their Hebraic heritage while strengthening their faith in Jesus.

We also distribute books from Golden Key Press in order to disseminate high-quality teaching about Christianity's Hebraic foundations that is non-threatening and non-judgmental and helps believers grow in Christian understanding.

We also provide various media resources through *New Treasures* media productions. Many of these can be accessed on our website.

The ministry of Hebraic Christian Global Community is made possible by our many partners around the world who share in our *Golden Key Partnership* program. We invite you to join us in sharing the satisfaction of knowing that you are a partner in an organization that is making a difference in the world by restoring Christians to their biblically Hebraic heritage, by eradicating Judaeophobia and anti-Semitism, by supporting Israel and the international Jewish community, and by encouraging collaborative efforts among those who share this vision.

For information about Hebraic Christian Global Community and all our resources and services, contact us at:

Hebraic Christian Global Community
P.O. Box 421218
Atlanta, Georgia 30342, U.S.A.
www.HebraicCommunity.org

HEBRAIC HERITAGE
CHRISTIAN CENTER

Hebraic Heritage Christian Center is an institution of higher education that is dedicated to the vision of restoring a Hebraic model for Christian education. A consortium of scholars, spiritual leaders, and business persons, the Center features a continually developing curriculum in which each course of study is firmly anchored in the Hebrew foundations of the Christian faith.

The vision for Hebraic Heritage Christian Center combines both the ancient and the most modern in an educational program that conveys knowledge, understanding, and wisdom to a worldwide student population. The Center seeks to restore the foundations of original Christianity in order to equip its students with historically accurate, theologically sound understanding of the biblical faith that Jesus and the apostles instituted and practiced. At the same time the Center endeavors to implement the finest in innovative, cutting-edge technology in a distance-learning program that delivers its user-friendly courses by the Internet.

Among the wide range of services and products that Hebraic Heritage Christian Center offers are the publications of Hebraic Heritage Press. These are delivered both in traditional print media as well as in electronic media to serve both the Center's student population and the general public with inspiring and challenging materials that have been developed by the Center's team of scholars.

Those who are interested in sharing in the development of Hebraic Heritage Christian Center and its commitment to restoring the Jewish roots of the Christian faith are invited to join the Founders' Club, people who support this team of scholars and leaders by becoming co-founders of this institution. Many opportunities for endowments are also available to those who wish to create a lasting memorial to the cause of Christian renewal and Christian-Jewish rapprochement.

Contact us at:

Hebraic Heritage Christian Center
P.O. Box 421218
Atlanta, Georgia 30342
www.HebraicCenter.org